The Big Questions
A Short Introduction to Philosophy

Ninth Edition

ROBERT C. SOLOMON
University of Texas at Austin

KATHLEEN M. HIGGINS
University of Texas at Austin

WADSWORTH
CENGAGE Learning·

Australia • Brazil • Japan • TPPUB • Mexico • Singapore • Spain • United Kingdom • United States

WADSWORTH
CENGAGE Learning·

The Big Questions: A Short Introduction to Philosophy, Ninth Edition
Robert C. Solomon and Kathleen M. Higgins

Publisher/Executive Editor: Clark Baxter

Senior Sponsoring Editor: Joann Kozyrev

Senior Media Editor: Phil Lanza

Assistant Editor: Joshua Duncan

Editorial Assistant: Marri Straton

Market Development Manager: Joshua I. Adams

Brand Manager: Jennifer Levanduski

Marketing Communications Manager: Linda Yip

Senior Content Project Manager: Josh Allen

Art Director: Riezebos Holzbaur/Andrei Pasternak

Print Buyer: Sandee Milewski

Senior Rights Acquisitions Specialist: Mandy Groszko

Production Service: S4 Carlisle Publishing Services

Text Designer: Riezebos Holzbaur/Tim Heraldo

Copy Editor: S4Carlisle Publishing Services

Cover Designer: Riezebos Holzbaur/Tae Hatayama

Cover Image: paper background © shutterstock/R Studio, Brush stroke circle texture © shutterstock/optimarc

Compositor: S4Carlisle Publishing Services

For product information and technology assistance, contact us at **Cengage Learning Academic Resource Center, 1-800-423-0563**

For permission to use material from this text or product, submit all requests online at **www.cengage.com/permissions.** Further permissions questions can be emailed to **permissionrequest@cengage.com**

Library of Congress Control Number: 2012950399

ISBN-13: 978-1-133-61064-9

ISBN-10: 1-133-61064-1

Wadsworth, Cengage Learning
10 Davis Drive
Belmont, CA 94002-3098
USA

Cengage Learning products are represented in Canada by Nelson Education, Ltd.

For your course and learning solutions, visit **academic.cengage.com**

Purchase any of our products at your local college store or at our preferred online store **www.ichapters.com**

Printed in the United States of America
1 2 3 4 5 6 7 17 16 15 14 13

For our nieces and nephews,

Jem, Jesi, Danyal, Rachel, and Carrie Solomon,
Caitlin Higgins, Jeffrey and Matthew Cook,
Allison, Rachel, Daniel, Brett, and Marcus Felten,
Kevin and Emily Daily

Contents

Preface

It was the fall of 1806, in the college town of Jena, in what we now call Germany. Most students and professors would have been getting ready for their classes, with mixed annoyance and anticipation. The professors would have been finishing up their summer research; the students would have been doing what students usually do at the end of the summer.

But this year school would not begin as usual.

Napoleon's troops were already approaching the city, and you could hear the cannon from the steps of the university library. French scouts were already in the town, walking around the university, stopping for a glass of wine in the student bars, and chatting casually with the local residents, many of whom were in sympathy with the new French ideals of "liberty, equality, and fraternity."

As the battle was about to begin, a young philosophy instructor named **Georg Wilhelm Friedrich Hegel** was hastily finishing the book he was writing—a very difficult philosophy book with the forbidding title *The Phenomenology of Spirit*. But "spirited" is what the book was, and it perfectly captured the tension, excitement, and anxiety of those perilous days. It was the end of an old way of life and the beginning of a new one. The book was a vision of consciousness caught in the midst of gigantic forces and looking for direction in a new and terrifyingly human world. It was an appeal for hope and thoughtful effort toward universal understanding and a belief in what was then innocently called the "perfectibility of humanity."

Transfer the situation to our own times—it was as if life in our society were about to change completely, with all our old habits and landmarks, our ideas about ourselves and the ways we live, replaced by something entirely new and largely unknown. We talk about "game changers" and "tipping points," but, in fact, most of what we consider drastic changes are mere shifts of emphasis, sometimes inconvenient advantages that accompany new and improved technologies and techniques. If so many of us can get so melodramatic about computers, smart phones, and the Internet, how would we react to a *real* change in our lives? Hegel and his students felt confident, even cheerful. Why? Because they had a *philosophy*. They had a vision of themselves and the future that allowed them to face the loss of their jobs, even the destruction of their society and the considerable chaos that would follow. Their ideas inspired them and made even the most threatening circumstances meaningful.

A class of our students who had been reading Hegel's philosophy were asked to characterize their own views of themselves and their times. The answers were not inspiring. For many of them, the word *dull* seemed to summarize the world; others spoke of "crisis" and "despair." One said that life was "absurd" and another that it was "meaningless." When asked why, they answered that gasoline was expensive, that most of them weren't getting the job interviews they really wanted, and that television programs were bad. We agreed that these events were less than tragic, hardly "absurd," and didn't make life "meaningless." Everyone agreed that the specters of nuclear war and terrorism had put a damper on our optimism, but we also agreed that the likelihood of such catastrophes was debatable and that, in any case, we all had to live as best we could, even if under a shadow. But why, then, in these times of relative affluence and peace (compared to most of the world throughout most of history) were our answers so sour? What were we missing that Hegel and his students, confronting the most terrible battles ever known, seem to have had—something that made them so optimistic and fulfilled? Again, the answer is a philosophy.

Georg Wilhelm Friedrich Hegel was born in Stuttgart in 1770. While he was a college student, he was enthusiastic about the French Revolution (1789–1795) and an admirer of Napoleon. Hegel was teaching at the University of Jena in 1806 when Napoleon marched in and took over the town, ending the 800-year-old Holy Roman Empire and initiating widespread reforms throughout the German states. It was in this atmosphere of international war and liberal hopes that Hegel formulated his philosophy, which centered on the notion of Spirit, by which he meant the unity of the world through human consciousness. His method was **dialectic**—that is, he tried to demonstrate how contradictory views can be reconciled and shown to be, in fact, different aspects of one underlying phenomenon—ultimately, of Spirit. Hegel is still considered one of the great synthesizers of human knowledge and values; his *Encyclopedia* (first published in 1817) is a short synthesis of the whole of human life, including logic, science, and psychology as well as philosophy, art, religion, metaphysics, and ethics. He died in 1831.

Philosophy, religion, and science have always been closely related. The emphasis shifts, but the point of these endeavors is the same: the importance of ideas and understanding, of making sense out of our world and seeing our lives in some larger, even cosmic, perspective. *Ideas* define our place in the universe and our relations with other people; ideas determine what is important and what is not important, what is fair and what is not fair, what is worth believing and what is not worth believing. Ideas give life meaning. Our minds need ideas the way our bodies need food. We are starved for visions, hungry for understanding. We are caught up in the routines of life, distracted occasionally by those activities we call "recreation" and "entertainment." What we have lost is the joy of thinking, the challenge of understanding, the inspirations as well as the consolations of philosophy.

Philosophy is simply *thinking hard* about life, about what we have learned, about our place in the world. Philosophy is, literally, the *love of wisdom*. It is the search for the larger picture, and this involves the demand for *knowledge*—the kind of knowledge that allows us to understand our lives and the world around us. It is, accordingly, the insistence on the importance of *values*, a refusal to get totally caught up in the details of life and simply go along with the crowd. Philosophy and wisdom define our place in the universe and give our lives meaning.

When undergraduates ask questions about the meaning of life and the nature of the universe, it is philosophy that ought to answer the questions. But thousands of students, not trained in hard thinking but starved for ideas and understanding, will retreat to the easier alternatives—pop philosophies of self-help, exotic religious practices, extremist politics. If the hard thinking of philosophy does not address the big questions, then perhaps these alternatives will. The difference between philosophy and the popular alternatives is ultimately one of quality—the quality of ideas, the thoroughness of understanding. Because we all live by our ideas anyway, the choice becomes not whether to do philosophy or not do philosophy, but whether to accept cheap and unchallenging substitutes or to try the real thing. The aim of this book is to give you an introduction—to the real thing.

The Subject of Philosophy

Philosophy is sometimes treated as an extremely esoteric, abstract, and specialized subject that has little to do with any other subjects of study—or with the rest of our lives. This is simply untrue. Philosophy is nothing less than the attempt to understand who we are and what we think of ourselves. And that is just what the great philosophers of history, whom we study in philosophy courses, were doing: trying to understand themselves, their times, and their place in the world. They did this so brilliantly, in fact, that their attempts remain models for us. They help us formulate our own ideas and develop our own ways of clarifying what we believe.

Throughout this book, we have tried to introduce at least briefly many of the great philosophers throughout history. (Brief biographies are included in the chapters.) But philosophy is not primarily the study of *other* people's ideas. Philosophy is first of all the attempt to state clearly, and as convincingly and interestingly as possible, *your own* views. That is *doing* philosophy, not just reading about how someone else has done it.

This book is an attempt to help you do just that—to *do* philosophy, to state what you believe, using the great philosophers and the great ideas of the past as inspiration, as a guide to ways of putting together your own views, and to provoke the present alternatives that you may not have thought of on your own. The aim of the book—and at least one aim of the course you are taking—is to force you to think through your ideas, connect them, confront alternative views, and understand what you prefer and why you prefer it. Some students inevitably think that once they are speaking abstractly, it doesn't matter what they say. So they talk utter nonsense, they express ideas they have never thought about, or they recite mere words—for example, the popular word *value*—without having any sense of what they as individuals believe to be true. A very bright student one year claimed that he did not exist. (He received a grade anyway.) Some students even feel that it doesn't matter if they contradict themselves—after all, "It's only ideas." But if we see the world through ideas, if they determine how we feel about ourselves and live our lives, then our ideas make all the difference. So it is urgent— as well as intellectually necessary—that you ask, at every turn, "Do I really believe that?" and, "Is that compatible with other things I believe?" Good philosophy, and *great* philosophy, depends on the seriousness and rigor with which such questions are asked. The aim of this book to help you ask them, to help you build for yourself a philosophical presentation of your own view of the world.

The task of summarizing your views about the meaning of life and the nature of the universe in a single course may sound overwhelming. But no matter how crude your first efforts, this kind of integrative critical thinking—putting it all together—is essential to what you will be doing all through your life: trying to keep your priorities straight, to know who you are, and to be sure of what you believe. The purpose of this course, which may be your first introduction to philosophy, is to get you started. Once you begin to think about the *big questions*, you may well find, as many students and almost all professional philosophers have found, that it is one of the most rewarding and most accessible activities you will ever learn—you can do it almost anywhere, at any time, with anyone, and even alone. And if it seems difficult to begin (as it always does), that is because you are not used to thinking as a philosopher, because our ideas are inevitably more complex than we originally think they are, and because, once you begin thinking, there is no end to the number of things there are to think about. So consider this as a first attempt, an exploratory essay, a first difficult effort to express yourself and your positions—not just your views on this issue or that one, but your entire view of the world. Engaging in the activity of *doing* philosophy, even if it is only for the first time, is what makes philosophy so exciting and challenging.

The first chapter of the book consists of a set of preliminary questions to get you to state your opinions on some of the issues that make up virtually every philosophical viewpoint. Some of the questions you will find amusing; some of them are deadly serious. But between the two, the outlines of what you believe and don't believe should begin to become clear. Each succeeding chapter also begins with a set of preliminary questions. And again the point is to encourage you to reflect on and state your views on these subjects before we begin to develop the views that philosophers have argued. Each chapter includes a discussion of various alternative viewpoints, with brief passages from some of the great philosophers. Special terms, which probably are new to you but have become established in philosophy, are introduced as they are needed, as a way of helping you make distinctions and clarify your positions more precisely than our ordinary language allows. (A glossary containing most of these terms—which are boldface in the text— appears at the back of the book.) Each chapter ends with a set of concluding questions that will help you locate your own views among the alternatives of traditional philosophy. There is a bibliography at the end of each chapter containing suggestions for further reading; you can explore those topics that interest or challenge you, because no textbook can substitute for original works.

For the Instructor

This ninth edition is flexible for teaching a variety of individually structured courses in introductory philosophy at both the college and advanced high school levels. In this edition I have summarized the general layout of each chapter toward the beginning (usually within the first few paragraphs or at the end of the first section). There are three categories of boxed text: *Quotations/Excerpts* offer a wide variety of excerpts from key philosophical writings, as well as relevant popular sources. *Biographical* boxes provides a glimpse into the lives of many of the philosophers covered in the main text. *Informational* boxes set forth the beliefs of individuals and philosophical movements and point out links between philosophical theory and its application to societies worldwide. As in the eighth edition, my intention is for these to make such material available to those instructors who choose to use it but dispensable for those who do not.

In this edition I have split up the previous Chapter 10, "Philosophy, Sex, Race, and Culture." Chapter 10 is now exclusively about non-Western philosophy, and the coverage of African-American philosophy and feminist philosophy has mostly been shifted to Chapter 9 (the chapter on justice), except for the discussion of feminist ethics, which is now in Chapter 8 (the chapter on the good life). I have expanded discussion on a number of topics through the book, including Berkeley's arguments against material substance (Chapter 4); Descartes's argument for the existence of God and the external world (Chapter 5); feminist ethics (Chapter 8); and (to some extent) artistic censorship (Chapter 11). I have also included consideration of some topics that were not or were barely discussed in the previous edition: the nontraditional conceptions of God of Karl Rahner and Marcus Borg (Chapter 3); string theory (Chapter 4); Descartes's wax argument (Chapter 5); two of Derek Parfit's teleporter cases (Chapter 6); eliminative materialism (Chapter 6); Bejamin Libet's empirical basis for denying free will (Chapter 7); Harry Frankfurt's critique of the Principle of Alternative Possibilities as a basis for moral responsibility (Chapter 7); the trolley problem (Chapter 8); Plato's account of the Ring of Gyges and the question of piety in the *Euthyphro* (Chapter 8); the morality of patriotism and partiality more generally (Chapter 9); just war theory (Chapter 9); cosmopolitanism (Chapter 9); and contemporary art and debates over what makes something art (Chapter 11).

The discussion in each chapter is more or less self-contained, and the chapters can be used in just about any order. Some instructors prefer to start with the "God" chapter, for example, others with the more epistemological chapters on "Knowledge," "Truth," "Self," and "Freedom." The opening chapters, with their broad collection of both playful and serious philosophical questions and varied discussions of the "Meaning of Life," may be helpful in loosening up and relaxing nervous first-time students of philosophy and getting them to talk in a more free-wheeling way than they do if they are immediately confronted with the great thinkers or the most intractable problems of philosophy. So, too, the opening questions can help get students to think about the issues on their own before diving into the text. To motivate students to write and think about philosophical questions, to get them used to *interacting* with the text and arguments, we would encourage students to write their own responses and comments directly in the margins of book. The closing questions of each chapter, by the way, also serve as potential exam questions or questions to prompt classroom discussion.

Kathleen M. Higgins

Acknowledgments

I thank all those readers, both students and colleagues, who responded kindly and critically to my earlier text, *Introducing Philosophy* (Harcourt Brace Jovanovich, 1977; Seventh Edition, 2000). The present text is a fresh attempt to reach an audience not as well addressed by that book, and I am indebted to all who pointed out the need for the new book and helped me develop and refine it.

I especially thank all those people who taught me the joys and skills of philosophy, and how to teach it. First of all, there is my father, Charles M. Solomon, who always encouraged me. There is Robert Hanson, who first thrilled me with Parmenides and Heraclitus at Cheltenham High School, and Doris Yocum, who taught my first philosophy course. I learned so much about teaching philosophy from Elizabeth Flower, James Ross, Peter Hempel, and Frithjof Bergmann, and I continue to learn from great colleagues like Bob Kane, Stephen Phillips, and Paul Woodruff. I also thank Donette Moss, the late Winkie Conlon, and Shirley Hull for their much-needed care and attention. Thanks to Jon Solomon for his advice on exotic matters in the book. Thanks, too, to Stephen Waters, Mark Gilbertson, Victor Guarino, Michael Thomas, Thomas E. Moody, Stanley M. Browne, Ronald Duska, Albert B. Randall, Emrys Westacott, Gary Prince, Janet McCracken, Timothy Davis, Charlie Huenemann, George Matejka, Christopher Trogan, Butian Zhang, Mathias Bildhauer, Clancy Martin, Karen Mottola, Cleavis Headley, Dave Hilditch, George Matejka, and Erin Frank. Thanks also to David Tatom, Bill McLane, Steve Wainwright, and Worth Hawes.

Robert C. Solomon

In addition to the individuals mentioned above, I would like to thank the reviewers who assisted with the preparation of this edition: Mark Alfano, Michael Anker, Ryan Emerick, Chenyang Li, Kevin Maxwell, Susan Peterson, Michael Rooney, Corine Sutherland, and Chris Weigel. I would also like to thank Sarah Canright, Markus Weidler, and Alex Neill for their help. In particular, thanks to Joann Kosyrev, DaisukeYasutake, Howard Voeks, Mohanarengan Dilli, Joshua Duncan, Mandy Groszko, Kristine Janssens, Patricia Steele, and Marri Straton for their help in the preparation of this edition. Special thanks to Vivekananthan Sekar for doing the index and to Jill Hernandez for preparing the eBank Instructor's Manual.

Kathleen M. Higgins

About the Authors
〜〜

Robert C. Solomon (1942–2007) was internationally renowned as a teacher and lecturer in philosophy. He was Quincy Lee Centennial Professor and Distinguished Teaching Professor at the University of Texas at Austin. He received his Ph.D. from the University of Michigan and over the course of his career taught at numerous institutions, including Princeton University, the University of Pittsburgh, the University of Auckland, and the University of California, in addition to the University of Texas. He authored over forty books, including *Introducing Philosophy, A Short History of Philosophy* (with Kathleen M. Higgins); *The Passions; In the Spirit of Hegel; About Love; Above the Bottom Line* (4th ed., with Clancy Martin); *Ethics and Excellence; The Joy of Philosophy; True to Our Feelings;* and was coeditor of *Twenty Questions* (5th ed., with Lee Bowie and Meredith Michaels) and *Since Socrates* (with Clancy Martin).

Kathleen M. Higgins is professor of philosophy at the University of Texas at Austin. She received her Ph.D. from Yale University, and has taught at the University of Auckland and the University of California, Riverside, in addition to the University of Texas. She is author of several books, including *Nietzsche's "Zarathustra"; The Music of Our Lives; What Nietzsche Really Said* (with Robert C. Solomon); *Comic Relief; A Short History of Philosophy* (with Robert C. Solomon); *A Passion for Wisdom* (with Robert C. Solomon); and *The Music between Us: Is Music the Universal Language?* She has edited or coedited numerous books, including *Aesthetics in Perspective,* and *Thirteen Questions in Ethics and Social Philosophy* (2nd ed., with Lee Bowie and Meredith Michaels).

Zhuangzi (Chuang Tzu) (369?-286?, fl. 350-300 BCE)

Mencius (Mengzi) (371-289)

Jesus Christ (ca. 5 BCE-30 CE)

Aristotle (384-322)

St. Paul (ca. 10 CE-ca. 65 CE)

Plato (427-347)

St. Augustine (354-430)

Socrates (ca. 469 or 470-399)

Muhammad (ca. 570-632)

Mozi (Mo Tzu) (ca. 470-ca. 391)

St. Anselm (ca. 1033-1109)

Heraclitus (536-480)

Thomas Aquinas (1225-1274)

Sunzi (Sun Tzu) (544-496)

Martin Luther (1483-1546)

Confucius (551-479)

Thomas Hobbes (1588-1679)

Buddha (Siddhartha Gautama) (563-483)

René Descartes (1596-1650)

Laozi (Lao-Tzu) (570-490)

Blaise Pascal (1623-1662)

Pythagoras (ca. 570-490)

Baruch Spinoza (1632-1677)

Thales (ca. 624-546)

John Locke (1632-1704)

Homer (ca. 750-700 (dates uncertain))

Isaac Newton (1642-1727)

Zoroaster (628?-551?)

Gottfried Wilhelm von Leibniz (1646-1716)

Moses (fl.* 1220-1200? (Jewish trad. 1393-1273))

Bishop Joseph Butler (1692-1752)

Hindu Vedas (ca. 1500)

David Hume (1711-1776)

Abraham (ca. 1900 BCE)

Jean-Jacques Rousseau (1712-1778)

Immanuel Kant (1724-1804)

Mary Wollstonecraft (1759-1797)

Georg Wilhelm Friedrich Hegel (1770-1831)

Arthur Schopenhauer (1788-1860)

John Stuart Mill (1806-1873)

Harriet Taylor (1807-1858)

Charles Darwin (1809-1882)

Søren Kierkegaard (1813-1855)

Henry David Thoreau (1817-1862)

Frederick Douglass (1817-1895)

Karl Marx (1818-1883)

William James (1842-1910)

Friedrich Nietzsche (1844-1900)

John Dewey (1859-1952)

Mahatma Gandhi (1869-1948)

Bertrand Russell (1872-1970)

Albert Einstein (1879-1955)

Paul Tillich (1886-1965)

Ludwig Wittgenstein (1889-1951)

Martin Heidegger (1889-1976)

Charles Hartshorne (1897-2000)

Karl Rahner (1904-1984)

Ayn Rand (1905-1982)

Jean-Paul Sartre (1905-1980)

Nelson Goodman (1906-1998)

Simone de Beauvoir (1908-1986)

Albert Camus (1913-1960)

Benjamin Libet (1916-2007)

John Rawls (1921-2002)

Malcolm X (1925-1965)

Martin Luther King Jr. (1929-1968)

Sara Ruddick (1935-2011)

Robert Nozick (1938-2002)

Steve (Stephen Bantu) Biko (1946-1977)

*The abbreviation "fl." means "flourished." From the Latin *floruit*, "he (or she) flourished," indicating the central period of a person's career.

Raphael Sanzio, *The School of Athens,* fresco, detail 1509–1511.
Stanza della Segnatura, Vatican Palace, Rome.
© Scala/Art Resource, New York.

Introduction
Doing Philosophy

The unexamined life is not worth living.
— Socrates, fifth century BCE

Know thyself!
— Oracle at Delphi (Socrates' motto)

～❦～

Philosophy is all about our beliefs and attitudes about ourselves and the world. Doing philosophy, therefore, is first of all the activity of stating, as clearly and as convincingly as possible, what we believe and what we believe in. This does not mean, however, that announcing one's allegiance to some grand-sounding ideas or, perhaps, some impressive word or "ism" is all that there is to philosophy. Philosophy is the development of these ideas, the attempt to work them out with all their implications and complications. It is the attempt to see their connections and compare them with other people's views—including the classic statements of the great philosophers of the past. It is the effort to appreciate the differences between one's own views and others' views, to be able to argue with someone who disagrees and resolve the difficulties that they may throw in your path. One of our students once suggested that she found it easy to list her main ideas on a single sheet of paper; what she found difficult was showing how they related to one another and how she might defend them against someone who disagreed with her. In effect, what she was saying was something like this: she would really enjoy playing quarterback with the football team, as long as she didn't have to co-operate with the other players—and then only until the other team came onto the field. But playing football is cooperating with your team and running against the team that is out to stop you; philosophy is the attempt to coordinate a number of different ideas into a single viewpoint and defending what you believe against those who are out to **refute** you. Indeed, a belief that can't be tied in with a great many other beliefs and that can't withstand criticism may not be worth believing at all.

Socrates was one of the greatest philosophers of all times, though he never recorded his philosophy in writing. (All that we know of him comes down to us from his student Plato and other philosophers.) Socrates was born in approximately 469 or 470 BCE and lived his whole long life in Athens. He had a spectacular gift for rhetoric and debating. He had a much-gossiped-about marriage, had several children, and lived in poverty most of his life. He based his philosophy on the need to "know yourself" and on living the "examined life," even though the height of wisdom, according to Socrates, was to know how thoroughly ignorant we are. Much of his work was dedicated to defining and living the ideals of wisdom, justice, and the good life. In 399 BCE he was placed on trial by the Athenians for "corrupting the youth" with his ideas. He was condemned to death, refused all opportunities to escape or have his sentence repealed, and accepted the cruel and unfair verdict with complete dignity and several brilliant speeches, dying as well as living for the ideas he defended.

Beyond Buzzwords

To defend your ideas is quite different from insisting, no matter how self-righteously, on the mere sound of a word. To say that you believe in freedom, for instance, may make you feel proud and righteous, but this has nothing to do with philosophy or, for that matter, with freedom, unless you are willing to spell out exactly what it is you stand for, what it is that you believe, and why it is that this *freedom*, as you call it, is so desirable. But most students, as well as many professional philosophers, get caught up in such attractive, admirable words, which we can call "buzzwords." These sound as if they refer to something quite specific and concrete (like the word *dog*), but in fact they are among the most difficult words to understand, and they provide us with the hardest problems in philosophy. *Freedom* sounds as if it means breaking out of prison or being able to speak one's mind against a bad government policy; but when we try to say what it is that ties these two examples together, and many more besides, it soon becomes clear that we don't know exactly what we're talking about. Indeed, virtually everyone believes in freedom, but the question is *what* it is that they believe in. Similarly, many people use such words as *truth, reality, morality, love,* and even *God* as buzzwords, words that make us feel good just because we say them. But to express the beliefs these words supposedly represent is to do something more than merely say the words; it is also to say what they mean and what it is in the world (or out of it) to which we are referring. Buzzwords are like badges; we use them to identify ourselves. But it is equally important to know what the badges stand for.

The words *science* and *art* are examples of buzzwords that seem to be ways of identifying ourselves. How many dubious suggestions and simpleminded advertisements cash in on the respectability of the word *scientific*? What outrageous behavior is sometimes condoned on the grounds that it is *artistic*? And in politics, what actions have not been justified in the name of *national security* or *self-determination*? Such buzzwords not only block our understanding of the true nature of our behavior, but they also can be an obstacle—rather than an aid—in philosophy. Philosophers are always making up new words, often by way of making critical distinctions. For example, the words *subjective* and *objective,* once useful philosophical terms, now have so many meanings and are so commonly abused that the words by themselves hardly mean anything at all. Would-be philosophers, including some of the more verbally fluent philosophy students, may think that they are doing philosophy when they merely string together long noodle chains of such impressive terms. But philosophical terms are useful only insofar as they stay tied down to the problems they are introduced to solve, and they retain the carefully defined meanings they carry. Buzzwords become not aids for thinking but rather *substitutes* for thinking, and long noodle chains of such terms, despite their complexity, are intellectually without nutritional value.

The abuse of buzzwords explains the importance of that overused introductory philosophical demand, "Define your terms." In fact, it is very difficult to define your terms, and most of the time, the definition emerges at the *end* of the thought process rather than at the beginning. You think you know quite well what you mean. But when certain philosophical terms enter our discussion, it is clear why this incessant demand has always been so important; many students seem to think that they have learned some philosophy just because they have learned a new and impressive word or two. But that's like believing that you have learned how to ski just because you have tried on the boots. The truth, however, is to be found in what you go on to do with them.

Articulation and Argument: Two Crucial Features of Philosophy

Philosophy is, first of all, **reflection**. It is stepping back, listening to yourself and other people (including the great philosophers), and trying to understand and evaluate what it is that you hear, and what it is that you believe. To formulate your own philosophy is to say what it is that you believe as clearly and as thoroughly as possible. Often we believe that we believe something, but as soon as we try to write it down or explain it to a friend we find that what seemed so clear a moment ago has disappeared, as if it evaporated just as we were about to express it. Sometimes, too, we think we don't have any particular views on a subject, but once we begin to discuss the topic with a friend it turns out that we have very definite views, as soon as they are articulated. Articulation—spelling out our ideas in words and sentences—is the primary process of philosophy. Sitting down to write out your ideas is an excellent way to articulate them, but most people find that an even better way, and sometimes far more relaxed and enjoyable, is simply to discuss these ideas with other people—classmates, good friends, family—or even, on occasion, a stranger with whom you happen to strike up a conversation. Indeed, talking with another person not only forces you to be clear and concrete in your articulation of your beliefs; it allows you—or forces you—to engage in a second essential feature of doing philosophy: arguing for your views. Articulating your opinions still leaves open the question whether they are worth believing, whether they are well thought out and can stand up to criticism from someone who disagrees with you. Arguments serve the purpose of testing our views; they are to philosophy what practice games are to sports—ways of seeing just how well you are prepared, how skilled you are, and, in philosophy, just how convincing your views really are.

Primary Features of Philosophy

Articulation: putting your ideas in clear, concise, readily understandable language.

Argument: supporting your ideas with reasons from other ideas, principles, and observations to establish your conclusions and overcome objections.

Analysis: understanding an idea by distinguishing and clarifying its various components. For example, the idea of "murder" involves three component ideas: killing, wrongfulness, and intention.

Synthesis: gathering together different ideas into a single, unified vision. For example, the Pythagorean notion of the "harmony of the spheres" synthesizes mathematics, music, physics, and astronomy.

Articulating and arguing your opinions has another familiar benefit: stating and defending a view is a way of making it your own. Too many students, in reading and studying philosophy, look at the various statements and arguments of the great philosophers as if they were merely displays in some intellectual museum, curiously contradicting each other, but, in any case, having no real relevance to us. But once you have adopted a viewpoint, which most likely was defended at some time by one or more of the philosophical geniuses of history, it becomes very much your own as well. Indeed, doing philosophy almost always includes appealing to other philosophers in support of your own views, borrowing their arguments and examples as well as quoting them when they have striking things to say (with proper credit in a footnote, of course). It is by *doing* philosophy, articulating and arguing your views, instead of just reading about other people's philosophy books, that you make your own views genuinely your own, that is, by working with them, stating them publicly, defending them, and committing yourself to them. That is how the philosophies of the past become important to us and how our own half-baked, inarticulate, often borrowed, and typically un-digested ideas start to become something more. Philosophy, through reflection and by means of articulation and argument, allows us to analyze and critically examine our ideas, and to synthesize our vision of ourselves and the world, to put the pieces together in a single, unified, defensible vision. Such a synthesis is the ultimate aim of philosophical reflection, and scattered ideas and arguments are no more philosophy than a handful of unconnected words is a poem.

The Fields of Philosophy

For convenience and in order to break the subject up into course-size sections, philosophy is usually divided into a number of fields. Ultimately, these are all interwoven, and it is difficult to pursue a question in any one field without soon finding yourself in the others, too. Yet philosophers, like most other scholars, tend to specialize, and you, too, may find your main interests focused in one of the following areas:

Metaphysics: the theory of reality and the ultimate nature of all things. The aim of metaphysics is a comprehensive view of the universe, an overall worldview. One part of metaphysics is a field sometimes called **ontology**, the study of "being," an attempt to list in order of priority the various sorts of entities that make up the universe.

Ethics: the study of good and bad, right and wrong, the search for the **good life**, and the defense of the principles and rules of morality. It is therefore sometimes called **moral philosophy**, although this is but a single part of the broad field of ethics.

Epistemology: the study of knowledge, including such questions as "What can we know?" and "How do we know anything?" and "What is truth?"

Logic (or **philosophical logic**): the study of the formal structures of **sound** thinking and good argumentation.

Philosophy of religion (or **philosophical theology**): the philosophical study of religion, the nature of religion, the nature of the divine, and the various reasons for believing (or not believing) in God's existence.

Political (or **sociopolitical**) **philosophy**: the study of the foundations and the nature of society and the state; an attempt to formulate a vision of the ideal society and implement ideas and reforms in our own society to better achieve this.

Aesthetics (a subset of which is the **philosophy of art**): the study of the nature of art and the experiences we have when we enjoy the arts or take pleasure in nature, including an understanding of such concepts as "beauty" and "expression."

Concepts and Conceptual Frameworks

The basic units of our philosophical projects and viewpoints are called **concepts**. Concepts give form to experience; they make articulation possible. But even before we try to articulate our views, concepts make it possible for us to recognize things in the world, to see and hear particular objects and particular people instead of one big blur of a world, like looking through a movie camera that is seriously out of focus. But in addition to defining the forms of our experience, concepts also tie our experience together. Concepts rarely occur in isolation; they virtually always tie together into a conceptual framework.

An example of a concept would be this: As children, we learn to identify certain creatures as dogs. We acquire the concept "dog." At first, we apply our new concept clumsily, calling a "dog" anything that has four legs, including cats, cows, and horses. Our parents correct us, however, and we learn to be more precise, distinguishing dogs first from cats, cows, and horses and then later from wolves, coyotes, and jackals. We then have the concept "dog"; we can recognize dogs; we can talk about dogs. We can think about and imagine dogs even when one is not actually around at the time, and we can say what we think about dogs in general. We can refine our concept, too, by learning to recognize the various breeds of dogs and learning to distinguish between dangerous dogs and friendly dogs. On certain occasions, therefore, the concept takes on an undeniably practical importance, for it is the concept that tells us how to act, when to run, and when to be friendly in turn. But the concept "dog" also becomes a part of our vision of the world—a world in which dogs are of some significance, a world divided into dogs and nondogs, a world in which we can contemplate, for example, the difference between a dog's life and our own. (One of the great movements in ancient philosophy was called **Cynicism** after the Greek word for "dog." The cynics acquired their name by living a life of austerity and poverty that, to their contemporaries, seemed little better than a "dog's life.")

Some concepts have very specific objects, like "dog." These specific concepts, derived from experience, are often called empirical concepts. We have already seen this word *empirical* referring to experience (for example, knowing the various breeds and behaviors of dogs). We will see it again and again; the root *empiri-* means having to do with experience. Through empirical concepts we make sense of the world, dividing it into recognizable pieces, learning how to deal with it, and developing our ability to talk about it, to understand and explain it, and to learn more and talk more about it. In addition to such specific concepts, we make use of a set of much more abstract concepts, whose objects are not so tangible or empirical and which cannot be so easily defined. These are *a priori* (Latin, "from the earlier") concepts, because they are conceptually *prior to* empirical concepts. One example is the concept of "number." However important numbers might be in our talk about our experience, the concepts of arithmetic are not empirical concepts. Mathematicians talk about the concept of an "irrational number," but there is nothing in our everyday experience that they can point to as an example of one. To understand this concept requires a good deal of knowledge about mathematics because this concept, like most concepts, can be defined only within a system of other abstract concepts.

Types of Knowledge

Empirical knowledge: knowledge based on experience (whether your own experience or the observations and experiments of others), for example, "The temperature in Chicago today is 17°F."

a priori knowledge: knowledge that is independent of ("before") any particular experience, for example, "2 + 3 = 5" or "$A + B = B + A$."

The a priori concept of "number" raises problems far more difficult than the empirical concept of "dog," and it is with the most difficult concepts that philosophy is generally concerned. Because philosophical concepts are abstract, there may be far more room for disagreement about what they mean. For example, the concepts of a "good person" and the "good life" seem to mean very different things to different people and in different societies. So, too, the concept of "God" creates enormous difficulties, in fact so many difficulties that some religions refuse to define God at all, or even give him (and not always "him") a name. Within the Judeo-Christian and Islamic traditions, there are very different conceptions of God, even within the Bible. When we begin to consider some of the other conceptions of God—for example, the Greek conception of Zeus and Apollo; the Hindu ideas of Vishnu and Shiva; or some modern conceptions of God as identical to the universe as a whole, or as a vital force, or as whatever a person takes to be his or her "ultimate concern in life"—you can see that simply agreeing on the word still leaves open the hardest questions: What is God like? What can we expect of God? What is involved in believing "in" God? What is our concept of God?

Oxen Gods?

The Ethiopians make their gods black-skinned and snub-nosed; the Thracians say theirs have blue eyes and red hair. If oxen and horses had hands and could draw and make works of art as men do, then horses would draw their gods to look like horses, and oxen like oxen—each would make their bodies in the image of their own.

— Xenophanes, circa 570–circa 475 BCE,
Greek Asia Minor

The concept of "freedom" is particularly difficult. Some people think that freedom is being able to do whatever you want to do; others think that freedom makes sense only within the rules of your society. But it is not as if the word *freedom* already means one or the other; the word and its meaning are open to interpretation, and interpretation is the business of philosophy. This is not to say, however, that what we might disagree about is simply the meaning of a word. What we disagree about is the *concept*, and the concept in turn determines the way we see the world.

The concept of "self" is like this, too. In a purely grammatical sense, the word *self* just points to a person—for example, to *myself* when I say, "I presented myself to the dean." But what is this self? Again, it is not defined by the word, which only points. Is my self just the *I*, the *voice* that is now speaking, or does it refer to a whole human being? Does it include every trivial and insignificant fact about me? (For example, the fact that I forgot to brush my teeth this morning?) Or does it refer just to certain *essential* facts—for instance, the fact that I am a conscious being? Is my self a *soul*? Or is my self perhaps a social construction, which must be defined not in terms of one person alone but in terms of my society and my particular role in it?

The concept of "truth" is an important concept in philosophy. Is the truth simply the "way things really are"? Or does it depend on the nature of what and how we believe as well? Could it be the case that we are all caught up in our limited view of the world, unable to see beyond the concepts of our own language and our own restricted range of experiences?

The most abstract and controversial concepts of all are not those through which we divide up the world into understandable bits and pieces but rather those grand concepts through which we try to put it all together. Religion is the traditional vehicle for this total understanding, but in our culture religion has been challenged by science, by art, by the law, and by politics for this ultimate role, as well as by philosophy.

These all-embracing pictures and perspectives are our ultimate **conceptual frameworks**—that is, the most abstract concepts through which we "frame" and organize all of our more specific concepts. The term *conceptual framework* stresses the importance of concepts and is therefore central to the articulation of concepts that makes up most of philosophy. But what we are calling a "conceptual framework" can also be viewed, from a more practical perspective, as a set of values and a way of looking at life, expressed as a way of living, or, in our contemporary vocabulary, as a **lifestyle**. If the emphasis is shifted to politics and society, the framework can be called an **ideology**—that is, a set of ideas about the nature of society and our political roles within it, which themselves are reflected in one's lifestyle. If we shift to a more historical viewpoint, we find that historians sometimes refer to the same thing as a **climate of opinion**. If we shift the emphasis away from the concepts through which we give form to our world and emphasize instead the view of the world that results, we can use a popular philosophical term, **worldview** (which is often left in German, *Weltanschauung*, because a number of German philosophers used this term quite often in the last century or so). But whether we use one term or the other, with one emphasis or another, the important point is that we in some sense already have such viewpoints, through which we give shape to our world and define our lives within it. When we articulate them in philosophy, we are not just creating an arbitrary structure of ideas; we are making explicit and clarifying what we already believe—to be more aware of our ideas, to be able to defend them, and, sometimes, to be able to change them.

Religion and Science: Einstein

*It is easy to see why the churches have always fought science and perse-
cuted its devotees. On the other hand, I maintain that the cosmic religious
feeling is the strongest and noblest motive for scientific research. Only those
who realize the immense efforts and, above all, the devotion without which
pioneer work in theoretical science cannot be achieved are able to grasp
the strength of the emotion out of which alone such work, remote as it is
from the immediate realities of life, can issue. What a deep conviction of the
rationality of the universe and what a yearning to understand, were it but
a feeble reflection of the mind revealed in this world, Kepler and Newton
must have had to enable them to spend years of solitary labor in disentan-
gling the principles of celestial mechanics! Those whose acquaintance with
scientific research is derived chiefly from its practical results easily develop
a completely false notion of the mentality of the men who, surrounded by
a skeptical world, have shown the way to kindred spirits scattered wide
through the world and the centuries. Only one who had devoted his life to
similar ends can have a vivid realization of what has inspired these men and
given them the strength to remain true to their purpose in spite of countless
failures. It is cosmic religious feeling that gives a man such strength. A contemporary has said, not unjustly, that in this materialistic age of ours the
serious scientific workers are the only profoundly religious people.*

— Albert Einstein,
"Religion and Science,"
New York Times Magazine
9 Nov. 1930.
(German-born American
physicist, 1879–1955)

Our conceptual framework, our lifestyle, our ideology, our climate of opinion, or our worldview is usually taken for granted as the intellectual ground that
we walk on. But sometimes it is necessary to examine that ground, to look carefully at what we usually take for granted. If we are planning to construct a house,
it is a good idea to investigate the ground we will build on, especially when something seems wrong—the soil is too soft, or it is on a fault and susceptible to earth-
quakes. This is often the case, too, with our conceptual frameworks; as soon as we
look at them, they may seem to be soft, ill formed, perhaps in danger of imminent
collapse, or liable to disruption by a well-placed question or confrontation with
someone who disagrees with us. This is a common experience among college
freshmen, for example; they come to school with certain religious, moral, political, and personal views that they have always taken for granted, which they have
never questioned or been forced to defend. Then they meet someone—a roommate, a teacher, a friend in a course—and these lifelong views are thrown into
chaos. Students who are not prepared for intellectual confrontation may find that

they are no longer so sure; then they get defensive, even offended and belligerent. But with time and some philosophical thinking, the same students again become clear about what they believe and why. Before the ground was examined, it might have been soft or near collapse, but once they see where they stand, they can fill in the holes, make it solid, protect themselves against unexpected "idea-quakes," and renew or revise their beliefs, which they now hold with a confidence much greater than before.

It is possible, of course, that you will find yourself using two or even more conceptual frameworks—for example, a scientific framework in school, a pleasure-seeking (or **hedonistic**) framework for Saturday night, and a religious framework on Sunday morning. The question then becomes, How do these different frameworks tie together? Which is most important? Are they actually inconsistent with one another? If our lives are to be coherent, don't we have to unify our various beliefs so that they all hang together? Ultimately, what makes an understanding of concepts and conceptual frameworks so important and rewarding is the fact that in understanding them, we are also in the process of *creating* them, and in so doing enriching them, developing them, solidifying them, and giving new understanding and clarity to our everyday lives.

Three Important Names to Know

Plato (427–347 BCE) was a student of Socrates and the leading spokesman for Socrates's ideas. He was shocked by Socrates's execution and dedicated his life to developing and spreading his philosophy. In 385 BCE he set up the Academy to educate the future leaders of Athens in morality and philosophy in general.

Aristotle (384–322 BCE), a student of Plato, strongly disagreed with many of his teacher's theories. Aristotle was an accomplished scientist as well as a philosopher, and his ideas ruled most of the sciences—especially biology—until modern times. He was the tutor of Alexander (who became "the Great") and later founded his own school (the Lyceum) in Athens. When Alexander died, Aristotle was forced to flee, commenting that he would not let Athens "sin against philosophy a second time."

Immanuel Kant (1724–1804) was, in the opinion of many philosophers, the greatest philosopher of modern times. He spent his entire life in a small eastern Prussian town (Königsberg). He was famous for his simple, regular life. (He never married, and his neighbors were said to set their clocks by his punctual afternoon walks.) And yet this apparently uninteresting professor was also an enthusiast of the French Revolution—and a revolutionary in his own way, too. His ideas turned many of the traditional views of knowledge, religion, and morality upside down.

Doing Philosophy with Style

The quality of a philosophy depends on the ingenuity with which its ideas are presented, the thoroughness with which they are worked out, the care with which one idea is tied to another, and the vividness with which the entire view comes across to the reader. Many of views of the greatest philosophers in history—for example, Plato, Aristotle, and the German philosopher Immanuel Kant—were not so different from those of most of their contemporaries, including other philosophers whom they knew and regularly talked with. But they became the great philosophers of our tradition because they presented their ideas with eloquence, defended them so brilliantly, and put them together in monumental constructions that are wonderful (if also very difficult) to behold. Philosophy is first of all articulation and argument, but it is also articulation and argument *with style.* Every philosophy, and every essay or book in philosophy, is essentially *making a case.* That is why philosophical training is so valuable for students going into law, or politics, or business, or—ultimately—almost every career where articulation and argument are important.

Disjointed articulation and argument not aimed at making a case to some particular audience (even if that audience is only your roommate or philosophy instructor) is without a point or purpose. Philosophy should be persuasive. That means that, in addition to evidence of hard thinking and a display of wisdom, philosophical writing should be somewhat entertaining, witty, dramatic, and even seductive. It is working out common views in ways that are not at all common. But whether philosophy is the somewhat modest thinking of a first-year philosophy student or the hundreds of pages that make up the classic texts of the great philosophers, the activity is the same—to try to articulate and clarify and present one's own view of the world as coherently and attractively as possible. It is possible to appreciate philosophy only by participating in it, by being a philosopher, too. And by the time you have completed this course, you too will be a part (if a small part) of that long tradition that has come to define the world of Western philosophy, perhaps non-Western, too. To be part of the extended conversation that is philosophy, you will need the following:

1. *Your ideas:* Without ideas, articulated clearly, there is nothing to think or write about.

2. *Critical thinking:* Ideas unqualified and uncriticized, undeveloped and unargued, are not yet philosophy. One of the most valuable tools you can carry away from a philosophy class is the ability to read and think critically, to scrutinize ideas as well as gather information.

3. *Argumentation:* Philosophy is not just stating your opinions; it is providing arguments to support your opinions, and arguments against objections to your views. The best philosophy always includes a kind of

point–counterpoint format. Don't just state your views. Argue for them and anticipate the kinds of objections that will probably be raised against you, countering them in advance. ("Now you might object that . . . , but against that I want to point out that . . .")

4. *A problem:* Philosophy does not consist of random speculations and arguments about some topic or other. It is motivated by a problem, a real concern. Death and the meaning of life are philosophical problems because—to put it mildly—we are all concerned with questions about life and death, *our* lives and deaths. Problems about knowledge arise because someone somewhere challenged our ability to know as much as we think we know, and philosophers ever since have been trying to answer that challenge. (For example, how do you know that you are not dreaming right now? Or, how do you know that the world wasn't created five minutes ago, with all of its fossils and supposedly ancient relics, and with us and all of our memories of the alleged past?) Philosophy may begin by wondering about life and the world in general, but it comes into focus through attending to a problem.

5. *Imagination:* A list of your ideas with qualifications and arguments might count as philosophy, but it would be uninspiring and dull. Don't be afraid to use metaphors and analogies. As you will see, some of the greatest philosophers developed their views of the world into visions that are as much poetry as philosophical essays.

6. *Style:* Anything in writing is readable only if it is written in a lively style. The rules of good essay writing apply to philosophy, of course, but so do the rules of entertaining—be exciting, attractive, appealing, persuasive. No matter how exciting an idea or incisive a criticism, it always gets across better when presented with eloquence, with a personal touch and an elegant turn of phrase.

Socrates might have said, "Everyone should think about his or her life because at least sometimes that helps us out of hard situations and makes life more valuable," but probably no one would remember it. Instead, he said, "The unexamined life is not worth living," and a hundred generations have been struck by the boldness and bluntness of his statement, whether or not, on examination, they have agreed with it. Socrates's aphorism is only a summary statement, not the whole body of Socrates's philosophy, with all of its ideas, images, and arguments. Your philosophy, too, is nothing less than the entirety of what you believe, articulated and argued as convincingly and as elegantly as you can.

For more on philosophical style—and writing a philosophy essay or exam—see Appendix A.

A Little Logic

*The central problem of logic is the
classification of arguments, so that all those
that are bad are thrown into one division,
and those which are good into another.*
— *Charles Sanders Peirce*

❧

Philosophy consists of ideas, grand theories, and visions, articulated in speech or in writing and presented in the clearest way possible. In the presentation, therefore, it is crucial to give **reasons** for your ideas, to *support* your theories with a variety of examples and considerations that will show that your philosophy is more persuasive than its alternatives (or at least as persuasive). Accordingly, the key to good philosophical presentation development is what we call an **argument**. In ordinary language, we sometimes think of an argument as a violent quarrel, filled with hostility and mutual resentment. This need not be the case, however; an argument is nothing more than the process of supporting what you believe with reasons. "I know that I am not dreaming right now because I never dream this vividly, I just pinched myself, and besides, if I were dreaming I'd probably be snoring right now." An argument ties your belief to other beliefs and helps persuade someone else to accept what you believe. A good argument can be presented in a perfectly coolheaded and amiable manner. Indeed, the best arguments are always defined by a process of careful thinking that we call **logic**, often described as the "science (and the process) of proper reasoning."

Philosophers use a variety of arguments and argument types. So, of course, do politicians, salespeople, television talk show hosts, and each of us, every time we are trying to convince someone of something we believe or trying to think something through for ourselves. There are arguments by **example** ("Let's look at a particular case,") and arguments by **analogy** ("Life is like a novel. There is a beginning and an end; it can be dull or exciting; there will surely be conflicts and bad scenes; there is suspense; the plot thickens. Therefore, the most important thing in life is to live an interesting life, develop your character, and don't just play it safe."). There are arguments based on extensive scientific research, and there are arguments that are very abstract and largely verbal (concerned more with the words used to describe a phenomenon than with the phenomenon itself). There are arguments based on nothing more than a vicious attack on one's opponents, and there are arguments that—despite their appearance—are not really arguments at all. In general, we might divide arguments into two classes—good arguments and bad arguments—depending on the *relations* between various statements. (*Truth* and *falsity,* on the other hand, apply to the statements themselves, never to the arguments.)

What counts as a good or a bad argument depends on what kind of an argument it is. As a useful way to understand arguments and what it is that makes them good or bad, it is convenient to divide them into two very general categories, to which philosophers and logicians (that is, those who study logic as their essential interest) apply the names **deduction** and **induction**.

Deduction
꙰

In a deductive argument, one argues for the truth of a conclusion by deducing a statement from a number of others. An example that might be familiar to you is any proof of a theorem you learned to formulate in high school geometry. Some statements are assumed to be true from the outset (for example, statements that are true by definition and statements so obviously true that they need not be proved at all, called **axioms**). Then, new statements are **deduced**, or **inferred**, by means of a number of established **rules of inference**—that is, the laws of thought, such as "A statement cannot be both true and false at the same time" or "If either *A* or *B*, but not *A,* then *B.*" A deductive argument is thus a progression from one true statement to another. The second statement is established as true, too; in fact, a deductive argument is sometimes defined as an argument whose final statement—or **conclusion**—is guaranteed to be true by the truth of the previous statements—or **premises**.

The best known deductive arguments are called **syllogisms**. An example of a syllogism is:

> All philosophers are wise.
> Socrates is a philosopher.
> _____
> Therefore, Socrates is wise.

What is important in such arguments is the form of the component statements:

> All Ps are Qs.
> S is a P.
> _____
> Therefore, S is a Q.

When a deductive argument proceeds correctly according to this form, we say that it is **deductively valid**, or simply **valid**. Arguments that are not valid are **invalid**. Deduction guarantees that our conclusions will be at least as certain as the premises. If the premises are certainly true, then the conclusions will certainly be true as well. But it is important to emphasize that an argument can be valid even if its premises and conclusion are false. For example, the following syllogism correctly follows the above form and is therefore valid:

> All cows are purple.
> Socrates is a cow.
> _____
> Therefore, Socrates is purple.

This is a valid argument, even though both the premises and the conclusion are false. But without true premises, even a valid argument cannot guarantee true conclusions. A good deductive argument must also have premises that are agreed to be true. Notice that, contrary to common usage, philosophers restrict their use of the words *valid* and *invalid* to talking about correct and incorrect arguments; the words *true* and *false* apply to the various statements that one makes in an argument—its premises and its conclusion. Thus, the claim that "3 + 2 = 8" is false, not invalid; and the argument "If Socrates is a man and all goats eat cabbage, then Socrates is a goat" is invalid, not false (whether or not its premises or conclusion are false). When an argument is both valid and has true premises (a good argument, in other words), it is called a **sound** argument. An argument is **unsound** (a bad deductive argument) if one or more of its premises are false, or if it is invalid. A good deductive argument, then, has two essential features:

1. It is a valid argument.

2. Its premises are true.

A detailed discussion of valid argument forms can be found in Appendix B.

Induction

Inductive arguments, on the other hand, do not guarantee the truth of their conclusions, even if all the premises are agreed to be true. The most familiar form of **induction** is **generalization** from a number of particular cases—for example, noting that every animal we have seen with sharp front teeth eats meat and concluding that *all* animals with sharp front teeth eat meat. But notice that although we might be absolutely sure that we are correct about the particular cases—that every such animal we have seen does in fact eat meat—we might still be wrong in our generalization, our conclusion that *all* such animals are meat eaters. Thus, it is essential in any inductive argument to begin with a well-chosen number of particular cases and to make sure that they are as varied as possible (that is, to approximate what social scientists call a random sample). Inductive arguments can be **strong** or **weak**, depending on the weight of the evidence for the conclusion, the quality of the sample, and the plausibility of the generalization. Inductive arguments are not evaluated as valid or invalid; in fact, given the definition of validity as the guarantee that the conclusion is true if the premises are true, *no* inductive argument is ever deductively valid. (That is not a mark against it, of course. Inductive arguments have other functions; they are not supposed to be deductively valid.)

Deductive and Inductive Logic

Deductive logic guarantees the truth of the conclusion, *if* the premises are true.

Example: If Moriarty didn't do it, then the Spiderwoman did. We know that Moriarty was in prison at the time, so the Spiderwoman must have done it. (Premises: "If M didn't do it, S did," and "M was in prison at the time.")

Inductive logic does not guarantee the truth of the conclusion, but only makes it more reasonable for us to believe the conclusion (compared with other possible conclusions).

Example: The pipe tobacco is the same kind he uses, and the footprints match his shoes. He was seen in the neighborhood only an hour before the crime, and he was heard to say, "I'm going to get even with her if it's the last thing I do." The best explanation of the evidence in this case seems to be the conclusion that he is guilty.

Although generalization is the most familiar example of induction, inductive arguments can be used to support virtually every statement of fact. For example, if you believe that Julius Caesar was murdered in Rome on March 15, 44 BCE, that is a statement of fact that you cannot directly observe today. The argument for its truth must therefore be inductive, based on information you have read in history books, colored by imagery from a play by Shakespeare, to be further verified—if you are curious—by an investigation into the **evidence** available in chronicles of the period, records of Roman politics, and perhaps a few relics from the times. In such inductive arguments, it is the **coherence** of the evidence that provides the argument—that is, the various elements of the argument fit together well. In a criminal trial, for instance, evidence is presented in favor of two contradictory statements of fact ("The defendant is guilty" versus "The defendant is not guilty"). The inductive question in the minds of the judge and the jury—and probably earlier in the minds of the detectives who worked on the case, too—is whether the evidence for conviction is more coherent than the evidence against. It is worth noting that what Sherlock Holmes and Dr. Watson continuously point to as Holmes's "amazing powers of deduction" are for the most part powers of

inductive reasoning, drawing factual conclusions from scattered and sometimes barely noticeable evidence.

One of the most important ingredients in inductive reasoning is the **hypothesis**, the statement that an experiment is supposed to prove or disprove. You are probably familiar with hypotheses in science, but we use hypotheses throughout our lives. Induction would be a waste of time if we did not have some hypothesis in mind. Just as scientists try to organize their research around a particular topic and a specific claim, we organize our attention around particular concerns and specific hypotheses. "Who killed the judge? It must have been either Freddy or the thug. Which hypothesis is the more plausible?" Not only science but almost everything we know and want to know depends on hypotheses and inductive reasoning, from looking for the car keys in the morning ("Now, I probably left them somewhere near my books") to speculating on the existence and the nature of black holes in space.

From the preceding discussion, it should be clear that much of what passes for argument is not that at all. For example, many people seem to think that simply stating and restating their opinion—forcefully and with conviction—is the same thing as supporting it with arguments. It is not. Stating your opinion clearly is the essential preliminary to formulating an argument, but it is not the same thing. An argument goes beyond the opinion itself; it involves supporting the opinion by deduction from other statements or with evidence based on experience. Some people seem to think that a single example will serve as a complete argument, but, at most, a single example serves as *part* of an argument. Most inductive arguments require many examples, and they must deal with examples that *don't* fit the hypothesis, too. Every argument is bound to meet up with several counterarguments and objections, so even a single argument is rarely enough to make one's case.

Similarly, many people seem to think that an appeal to **authority** will settle the case, but in most philosophical disputes, it is the nature of authority itself that is in question. If someone insists that God exists because it says so in the Bible, the question immediately shifts to the authority of the Bible. (A person who does not believe in God will probably not accept the authority of the Bible either.) If someone defends a political position because his mother said so or, for that matter, because Thomas Jefferson said so, the question then moves to the authority of the arguer's mother or Jefferson. One of the main functions of philosophy is to let us question authority and see for ourselves what we should believe or not believe. Appeal to authority does not necessarily show respect for that authority, but it does show disrespect for ourselves. **Legitimate** authority has to be earned as well as respected.

Criticizing Arguments

One of the most crucial philosophical activities—but by no means the only one—is **criticism**. Criticism does not necessarily mean—as in everyday life—negative remarks about someone or something; it means carefully examining a statement, testing it out, seeing if in fact the arguments for it are good ones. But this does mean that, whether it is our own statements or other people's statements that are being examined, it is important to find out what is *wrong* with them so that they can be corrected or strengthened. One way to criticize a deductive argument, for example, is simply to show that its premises are not true; if it is an inductive argument, one can do so by showing that the evidence on which it is based is false or distorted.

Another way to criticize an argument is to show that it consists of invalid deductive arguments or weak **inductive generalizations**. A particularly powerful way to do this is by the use of **counterexamples**. For instance, if someone claims, "All American men love football," he or she can be refuted if we can find a single American man who does not like football. Any claim that takes the form "All X's are Y's" or "No A's are B's" can be refuted if we can point out a single counterexample—that is, a single X that is not Y, or a single A that is a B. If a philosophy student says, "No one knows anything for certain," a familiar response might be to hold up your hand, stick out your thumb, and say, "Here is a thumb: I know *that* for certain." This may not be the end of the argument, but it is through such general claims and counterexamples to them that philosophical arguments are made more precise.

Even if all of its arguments seem to be sound, a philosophy can be shown to be in trouble if it is **inconsistent**, that is, if the conclusions of its different arguments **contradict** one another. In the same way, one can raise doubts about a philosophy's acceptability if it can be shown that it results in paradox and consequently must be thoroughly reexamined. For example, suppose a philosopher argues that God can do absolutely anything. For instance, God can create a mountain. He can move a mountain. But now a critical listener asks, "Can God create a mountain so large that even he can't move it?"—and we have a paradox. Either God can create such a mountain but then can't move it (and so cannot do everything) or God cannot create such a mountain (and so cannot do everything). The paradox forces us to reexamine the original claim that God can do

---

Paradox

A **paradox** is a **self-contradictory** or seemingly absurd conclusion based on apparently good arguments. Sometimes the paradox is merely apparent and requires restating; on occasion a well-formulated paradox has brought about the total rethinking of the whole of a branch of science, philosophy, religion, or mathematics. Some examples of paradoxical statements are:

"This sentence is false." (If that is true, then it is false.)

"There is a barber who shaves everyone in town who does not shave himself." (Does he shave himself?)

"God is all-powerful, so he could create a mountain so huge that even he could not move it."

If Achilles shoots an arrow from point *A* toward point *B*, it first must cover distance *A–C*, which is half of *A–B*; then it must cover distance *C–D*, which is half of *C–B*, and then *D–E*, which is half of *D–B*, and so on, each moment covering half the distance it has covered in the moment before. The paradox is that if the arrow keeps moving forever, it will never reach point *B*.

© Cengage Learning 2014

absolutely anything. (Perhaps it can be revised to say something like, "God can do anything that is logically possible.") Notice that the argument just given is takes the form of what is called **reductio ad absurdum**, Latin for a reduction to absurdity, in which a position is rejected because it results in a paradox.

A philosophy that does not contain outright inconsistencies or lead to paradoxes may still be unsuccessful, however, if it is **incoherent**. This means that the various claims have virtually nothing to do with each other, or mean very little, or can be interpreted only in an absurd way. A philosophy can be accused of **begging the question**, repeating as a supposed solution the very problem that it is attempting to resolve. An example of begging the question is the argument, "Other people exist. I know because I've talked to them." And a philosophy can be accused of being silly or trivial, which is just about the most offensive thing you can say, indicating that it is not even worth your time to investigate it further. It is much better to say something false but interesting than to say what is silly or trivial. (A common way in which philosophical claims can turn out to be trivial is when they express what logicians call *tautologies:* for example, "A is A." A **tautology** is a statement that is so necessarily true, so obviously correct that a statement claiming the opposite would be self-contradictory.) An argument can be **ad hominem** (Latin, "to the man," or "to the person," from the phrase *argumentatum ad hominem*) (or **ad feminam**, "to the woman," when referring to a woman), aimed at discrediting the person but ignoring the issue completely. Accusing

---

The Basic Concepts of Logic

An *argument* is a sequence of assertions, or statements, to back up a viewpoint or idea. The *conclusion* is an assertion that is supported by all the other assertions. These assertions are thus the *reasons* for accepting the conclusion. The assertions that are assumed to be true (for the sake of that argument) are called *premises*. Arguments can be either *deductive* or *inductive:* Deductive arguments *guarantee* the truth of their conclusion if they are both valid and have all true premises; inductive arguments do not guarantee the truth of their conclusions, no matter how impressive the evidence. Deductive arguments are said to be *valid* or *invalid*. (Arguments are never true or false.) Invalid arguments are also called *fallacies*. Individual assertions or statements are *true* or *false*. (They are never said to be valid or invalid.) A deductive argument that is both valid and has true premises is said to be *sound*. (Otherwise, it is *unsound*.) An inductive argument that is well supported by its evidence is called *strong;* a poorly supported argument is called *weak*. *Logic* is the use and the study of good arguments and the means of differentiating these from bad arguments.

---

someone who disagrees of being an atheist, a communist, or a Nazi is an all-too-familiar example of an ad hominem argument. Such bad arguments, in general, are called **fallacies**, whether or not they are formally invalid. (A *formal* fallacy is one that violates the proper rules of inference. An *informal* fallacy may not break the rules of inference but "cheats" by sneaking in ambiguous terminology, biased language, evasion of the facts, and distraction.) A list and discussion of such fallacies can be found in Appendix C.

In emphasizing criticism, it is important to point out, as a matter of balance, that philosophy is nevertheless an especially *cooperative* enterprise. Argumentation and criticism are not hostile or defensive. They are ways of making your ideas and their implications clear—clear to yourself as well as to other people. Socrates used to say that his truest friends were also his best critics. Indeed, we would distrust a friend who was never critical and never argued. ("If you were really my friend, you would have told me!") Arguments and objections take place within an arena of shared interest and with a common concern for reaching the truth. But, just as important, arguments and objections and mutual respect between people who disagree are absolutely essential in a pluralistic democracy such as our own, in which everyone's opinion is respected and it is most unlikely that we will all agree. But to say that everyone's opinion is respected is not to say that everyone's opinion is of equal value; the depth

Tautology

A **tautology** is a trivially true statement. Some examples:

A man is free if he is free.

You can't know anything unless you know something.

I wouldn't be here if I hadn't arrived.

What about the following? Are they tautologies?

Business is business.

Boys will be boys.

"A rose is a rose is a rose." (Gertrude Stein)

"Become who you are." (Friedrich Nietzsche)

of thinking and the quality of argument make some opinions better and more plausible than others. At the same time, cooperative respect, mutual concern for the importance of argument, and honest disagreement are indispensable to life as we want to live it.

In developing your own thoughts about the various questions of philosophy, you will inevitably find yourself using both deductive and inductive arguments, and it is perfectly normal to catch yourself—or your friends—using some incorrect arguments as well. What is important, however, is that you can recognize these forms when they appear and that you are aware—even if only in a preliminary way—of what you are doing when you argue for a position or an idea. Arguments aren't the whole of philosophy; an argument can't be interesting if the statements it is intended to support are trivial or uninteresting. But the best ideas in the world can be rendered ineffective and unheeded if there are no good arguments used to present them.

Closing Questions

Examine the following arguments. Are they inductive or deductive arguments? Are they valid and sound? If they are invalid or unsound, why? Is there anything else wrong with them? (You may want to consult Appendixes B and C.)

1. The philosopher from northern Greece is a well-known homosexual. Therefore, his claim that the universe is ultimately made up of atoms should be ignored.

2. Every event in the world is caused by other events. Human actions and decisions are events in the world. Therefore, every human action and decision is caused by other events.

3. If God exists, then life has meaning. God does not exist. Therefore, life has no meaning.

4. All cows are purple. Socrates is purple. Therefore, Socrates is a cow.

5. William James and John Dewey both called themselves pragmatists. They are the leading American philosophers. Therefore, all American philosophers are pragmatists.

6. Believing in God makes people moral—that is, believers tend to do good and avoid evil.

7. If I try to doubt that I exist, I realize that I must exist if I am doing the doubting. Therefore, I must exist.

8. We haven't seen a fox all day. Therefore, there must be no foxes in the area.

9. If you don't agree with me, I'm going to hit you.

10. God must exist; the Bible says so.

11. He must be guilty; he has a criminal face.

12. If she were innocent, she would loudly proclaim her innocence. She is loudly proclaiming her innocence. Therefore, she must be innocent.

13. "The state is like a man writ large." (Plato)

14. "I have terrible news for you. Mary is going out with Frank. I called Mary on Saturday night, and she wasn't home. Then I tried to call Frank, and *he* wasn't home, either!"

Suggested Readings

Three good introductions to logic are Robert J. Fogelin and Walter Sinnott-Armstrong, *Understanding Arguments,* 7th ed. (Wadsworth, 2005); Patrick J. Hurley and Joseph P. DeMarco, *Learning Fallacies and Arguments* (Wadsworth, 2001); and Patrick J. Hurley, *A Concise Introduction to Logic,* 10th ed. (Wadsworth, 2007). The standard introductions to symbolic logic are Irving Copi, *Introduction to Logic,* 12th ed. (Pearson Education, 1961) and W. V. O. Quine, *Methods of Logic,* 4th ed. (Harvard University Press, 2006). A good and very practical book, with many good examples, is Merrillee Salmon, *Introduction to Logic and Critical Thinking,* 5th ed. (Wadsworth, 2006). A good discussion of fallacies is S. Morris Engel, *With Good Reason,* 6th ed. (St. Martin's, 1999). A wonderful student handbook on logic is Anthony Weston, *Rulebook for Arguments* (Hackett, 1987). An excellent introduction to critical thinking is Larry Wright, *Critical Thinking: An Introduction to Analytical Reading and Thinking* (Oxford University Press, 2001). Albert Einstein's "Religion and Science" appeared in the *New York Times Magazine,* November 9, 1930.

Caspar David Fredrich, *Wanderer Uber Dem Nebelmeer.*
© Bildanchiv Preussischer Kulturbesitz/
Art Resource, NY.

1
Philosophical Questions

It is now some years since I detected how many were the false beliefs that
I had believed to be true since my earliest youth. And since that time, I have
been convinced that I must once and for all seriously try to rid myself of all
the opinions which I had formerly accepted, and begin to build anew, if I
wanted to establish any firm and permanent structure for my beliefs.

—René Descartes, *Meditations*

Philosophy begins with nagging personal questions. Quite often, our philosophical awareness begins in disappointment or tragedy, when we first start wondering whether life is fair or whether we are really learning anything in school. Sometimes, philosophy begins when we find ourselves forced to make difficult decisions that will affect the rest of our lives and other people's lives, too—for example, whether to attend college or enter a trade or the military, whether to get married, or whether to have children. We all feel a need to justify ourselves from time to time—living in relative luxury in a world in which millions are starving, attending college when it sometimes seems as if we are not really getting much out of it (or not putting very much into it), saying that we believe in one thing when our actions (or inaction) would seem to indicate that we believe something quite different.

Our philosophizing can begin with a trivial incident: we catch ourselves lying to a friend, and we start thinking about the importance of morality; we suffer from (or perhaps enjoy) a momentary illusion or hallucination, and we begin to wonder how it is that we know anything is real or even that we are not dreaming all the time; we have a quick brush with death (a near car wreck, a sudden dive in an airplane), and we start thinking about the value and meaning of life. In such moments, philosophy takes hold of us, and we see and think beyond the details of everyday life. *Doing* philosophy, in turn, is thinking further about these dramatic questions, which can suddenly become so important to us. In this chapter we will consider some of these questions and some of the possible answers.

What Is Philosophy?

〜〇〜

Philosophy, simply stated, is the experience of asking and seeking to answer such grand questions about life, about what we know, about what we ought to do or believe in. It is the process of getting to the bottom of things, questioning ideas that, most of the time, we simply take for granted and probably never put into words. We assume, for example, that some acts are right and some are wrong. Why? We know that it is wrong to take a human life. Why is this? Is it always so? What about in wartime? What about the life of a person who is hopelessly sick and in great pain? What if the world were so overcrowded that millions would die in one way if others did not die in another?

However you respond to these difficult questions, your answers reveal a network of beliefs and doctrines that you may never have articulated before you first found yourself arguing about them. Not surprisingly, the first time an individual tries to argue about issues he or she has never before discussed, the result may be awkward, clumsy, and frustrating. That is the point behind philosophical questions in general: to teach us how to think about, articulate, and argue for the things we have come to believe in, to clarify and perhaps revise our views, and to present them in a clear and convincing manner to other people, who may or may not agree with us. Very often, therefore, philosophy proceeds through disagreement, as when two philosophers or philosophy students argue with one another. Sometimes the dispute seems trivial or just a matter of semantics. However, because what we are searching for are basic meanings and definitions, even arguments about the *meaning of words*—especially such words as *freedom, truth,* and *self,* for example—are essential to our philosophical positions. With that in mind, let's begin our study with a series of somewhat strange but provocative questions, each of which is designed to get you to think about and express your opinions on a variety of distinctly philosophical issues. (It will help enormously if you write down your answers to the questions before you read on in the text.)

René Descartes was born into the French aristocracy in 1596. As a young man he discovered the connections between algebra and geometry (a field that we now call analytic geometry), established the mathematical basis for a number of sciences, and used mathematics-like thinking in philosophy and theology. An early Enlightenment thinker, he developed a method of thinking based on individual reason that did not allow for appeal to any authority except the "clear light of reason" itself. His approach was to doubt everything until he could prove it to his own satisfaction. The first premise of his philosophy was the indubitability of his own existence (see Chapter 6). He died in 1650.

Opening Questions

1. Is there anything you would willingly die for? If so, what?

2. If you had only a few minutes to live, what would you do with them? What if you had only a few days? Twenty years?

3. A famous philosopher once said that human life is no more significant than the life of a cow or an insect. We eat, sleep, stay alive for a while, and reproduce so that others like us can eat, sleep, stay alive for a while, and reproduce, but without any ultimate purpose at all. How would you answer him? What purpose does human life have, if any, that is not to be found in the life of a cow or an insect? What is the purpose of *your* life?

4. Do you believe in God? If so, for what reason(s)? What is God like? (That is, what is it that you believe in?) How would you prove to someone who does not believe in God that God exists that your belief is true? (What, if anything, would change your mind about this?)

   If you do not believe in God, why not? Describe the Being in whom you do not believe. (Are there other conceptions of God that you would be willing to accept? What, if anything, would change your mind about this?)

5. Which is most "real"—the chair you are sitting on, the molecules that make up the chair, or the sensations and images you have of the chair as you are sitting on it?

6. Suppose you were an animal in a psychologist's laboratory but that you had all the mental capacities for thought and feeling, the same "mind," that you have now. You overhear the scientist talking to an assistant, saying, "Don't worry about that; it's just a dumb animal, without feelings or thoughts, just behaving according to its instincts." What could you do to prove that you do indeed have thoughts and feelings, a "mind"?

   Now suppose a psychological theorist (for example, the late B. F. Skinner of Harvard University) were to write that, in general, there are no such things as "minds," that people do nothing more than "behave" (that is, move their bodies and make sounds according to certain stimulations from the environment). How would you argue that you do indeed have a mind, that you are not just an automaton or a robot, but a thinking, feeling being?

7. Suppose that you live in a society in which everyone believes that the earth stands still, with the sun, the moon, and the stars revolving around it in predictable, if sometimes complex, orbits. You object, "You're all wrong: The earth revolves around the

sun." No one agrees with you. Indeed, they think that you're insane because anyone can *feel* that the earth doesn't move at all, and you can *see* the sun, moon, and stars move. Who's right? Is it really possible that only you know the truth and everyone else is wrong?

8. "Life is but a dream," says an old popular song. Suppose the thought were to occur to you (as it will in a philosophy class) that it is possible, or at least conceivable, that you are just dreaming at this moment, that you are still asleep in bed, dreaming about reading a philosophy book. How would you prove to yourself that this is not true, that you are indeed awake? (Pinching yourself won't do it. Why not?)

9. Describe yourself as if you were a character in a story. Describe your gestures, habits, personality traits, and characteristic word phrases. What kind of a person do you turn out to be? Do you *like* the person you have just described? What do you like—and dislike—about yourself?

10. Explain who (what) you are to a visitor from another planet.

11. We have developed a machine, a box with some electrodes and a life-support system, which we call the "happiness box." If you get in the box, you will experience a powerfully pleasant sensation, which will continue indefinitely with just enough variation to keep you from getting too used to it. We invite you to try it. If you decide to do so, you can get out of the box any time you want to; but perhaps we should tell you that no one, once they have gotten into the happiness box, has ever wanted to get out of it. After ten hours or so, we hook up the life-support system, and people spend their lifetimes there. Of course, they never do anything else, so their bodies tend to resemble half-filled water balloons after a few years because of the lack of exercise. But that never bothers them either. Now, it's your decision: Would you like to step into the happiness box? Why or why not?

12. Will a good person (one who does no evil and does everything he or she is supposed to do) necessarily also be happy? Will a wicked person surely suffer, at least in the long run? In other words, do you believe that life is ultimately fair? (If not, why should anyone bother trying to be good?)

13. Do you believe that it is wrong to take a life under *any* circumstances? *Any* life?

14. Have you ever made a decision that was *entirely* your own, that was no one's responsibility but yours? (That is, it was not because of the way your parents raised you, not because of the influence of your friends or television or books or movies, not

because you were in any way forced into it or unduly influenced by someone or by certain circumstances.)

15.   Is freedom always a good thing?

16.   Do you want to have children? If so, why?

Some of these questions seem frivolous; others are clearly "profound." But they all are aimed at getting you to articulate what you believe about yourself and the world. More important than your beliefs, however, are your **reasons.** Your philosophy will begin to unfold in your reasons for believing what you believe.

Let's look at the questions one by one, and you can compare your answers with those of some of the famous philosophers of history as well as with the responses of other students. (It may also be a good idea to compare and contrast your answers with those of your friends and your own classmates. They may well have thought of angles that did not occur to you, and you may have some answers that did not occur to them.)

1. Is there anything you would willingly die for?

The philosopher **Socrates** went willingly to his death because he believed he had an obligation to respect the laws of his city even when those same laws condemned him to death (see the excerpt from Plato's account of a discussion of these views between Socrates and his student Crito in the "Living Well" box later in this chapter). (Socrates died by poisoning. He was forced to drink a cup of hemlock and was dead within half an hour.) His friends tried to convince him to escape. He himself thought he was condemned unjustly. But his respect for the laws and for his own sense of honor were so strong that he decided that the most important thing for him to do would be to show his belief in his own principles by dying for them. In modern times, in our own country, the young patriot Nathan Hale went down in history during the Revolutionary War. As he was about to be hanged by the British, he said, "I only regret that I have but one life to give for my country."

Some students say that they would willingly die to save the lives of members of their immediate family. (Some cautiously qualify their answers, adding that they would do so only if risking their own lives would mean a fairly good chance of saving the others' lives.) Some students say they would give their lives "for Jesus," but they are not very clear under what circumstances such a sacrifice would be called for. A few veterans have said they would give their lives for freedom but some, disillusioned by certain U.S. military involvements, were highly skeptical about what would count as a fight for freedom. It is worth noting that very few students in our classes have written that they would die for "honor" as such. Socrates did, though, and most of his fellow Greeks also would have considered death preferable to shame in the eyes of their countrymen. Quite a few students have said that there is really *nothing* they would willingly die for. What does that indicate about their values and what they think is most important in life?

Living Well

Socrates is in prison, condemned to die. His friend Crito has arranged an escape.

CRITO: . . . I do not think that what you are doing is right, to give up your life when you can save it . . .

SOCRATES: My dear Crito, your eagerness is worth much if it should have some right aim. . . . We must therefore examine whether we should act in this way or not . . . I ask you: when one has come to an agreement that is just with someone, should one fulfill it or cheat on it?

CRITO: One should fulfill it. . . .

SOCRATES: Look at it this way. If, as we were planning to run away from here, or whatever one should call it, the laws and the state came and confronted us and asked: "Tell me, Socrates, what are you intending to do? Do you not by this action you are attempting intend to destroy us, the laws, and indeed the whole city, as far as you are concerned? Or do you think it possible for a city not to be destroyed if the verdicts of its courts have no force but are nullified and set at naught by private individuals? . . . Surely," they might say, "you are breaking the undertakings and agreements that you made with us without compulsion or deceit, and under no pressure of time for deliberation. You have had seventy years during which you could have gone away if you did not like us, and if you thought our agreements unjust. . . . It is clear that the city has been outstandingly more congenial to you than to other Athenians, and so have we, the laws, for what city can please if its laws do not? Will you then not now stick to our agreements? . . .

"Be persuaded by us who have brought you up, Socrates. Do not value either your children or your life or anything else more than goodness. . . . Do not let Crito persuade you, rather than we, to do what he says." . . .

CRITO: I have nothing to say, Socrates.

SOCRATES: Let it be then, Crito, and let us act in this way, since this is the way the god is leading us.

— Plato, Crito,
abridged, fourth century BCE. (Trans. G. M. A. Grube.)

2. If you had only a few minutes (a few days, twenty years) to live, what would you do with them?

There is an old quip that there are no atheists in foxholes. The idea is that when faced with death, we all search for some ultimate source of support. Of course, the foxhole example can represent desperation and terror as well as some latent religious impulse, but the point has been made again and again that the thought of death brings out the philosopher in all of us. Would your last thoughts turn to God? If so, why? Would they turn to your best friends? Your family? Your work? Your frustrated ambitions for the future? Unfinished business? Sex? A final meal? A last listen to your favorite music? A farewell note to the world? In the 1970s movie *The King of Hearts,* the hero says in panic, "We've only got three more minutes to live!" The heroine replies with excitement, "Three whole minutes. That's wonderful!"

3. What purpose does human life have that is not to be found in the life of a cow or an insect? What is the purpose of *your* life?

The question of the "meaning of life" is, perhaps, the biggest question of philosophy. There is an enormous difference, we suppose, between the significance of the life of a mosquito, for example, and a person. But what is this difference? One suggestion is that we alone have a special place in God's creation and a special role to play. But what is that role, and why are we so sure that mosquitoes don't have it, too? Can life lack meaning even if we are God's creations? How does one know what one's assigned role is?

Can life have meaning if there is no God?

It is sometimes suggested that human life is meaningful because we, unlike cows and insects, are *reflective*. What does this mean—and what difference does it make? Does being reflective—even being thoughtful and philosophical—guarantee that life is meaningful? What are we asking for when we ask about the "purpose" or "meaning" of life?

4. Do you believe in God?

Most college students have no trouble answering this; even those who aren't sure what to believe are quick to say that they aren't sure what to believe. Of all philosophical questions, this one is perhaps the most thought about because it is obviously so important—even if it is, compared with most of our concerns in life, distinctly philosophical. But what is much more difficult is to say *why* we believe and *what* it is that we believe in. Many people will recognize that they believe in God, if they do, because they were brought up to do so. Is that a legitimate ground for believing? Many Americans seem to feel that a reason for believing in God is that it makes them happier and more secure—a reason that would have horrified the original Christians. *Is* this a reason? Doesn't it imply that it really doesn't matter what you believe in so long as you're happy?

If you believe in God, what does that signify about the rest of your life? For example, there has been a dispute in Christianity ever since the third century CE about whether what is most important for believers is having faith (as argued by the philosopher **Saint Augustine**, for instance) or taking the initiative in moving toward salvation by performing good works (as argued by the monk Pelagius, Augustine's contemporary). If you believe in God, does that mean that other people should, too? Do you have an obligation to convince them to do so? Or is belief in God your own personal concern and nobody else's business? If you believe in God, how do you account for the amount of evil and suffering in the world? If you don't believe in God, can you still think that life has some ultimate meaning? In fact, if you don't believe in God, can you believe there is any reason for the universe to exist at all?

5. Which is most "real"—the chair you are sitting on, the molecules that make up the chair, or the sensations and images you have of the chair as you are sitting on it?

   We tend to think of "reality" as what is most true, most obvious, most evident to our senses. But sometimes what is evident to our senses turns out to be an illusion, and what is obvious turns out to be untrue. Scientists tell us that our belief that the chair is obviously and evidently a solid object is in fact not correct. Instead the chair is an enormous complex of invisible particles, atoms, and molecules in various arrangements, electrons whizzing around at tremendous speeds, and mostly empty space. On the other hand, a philosopher or psychologist might tell you that what is so obvious and evident to your senses is not the chair itself but rather your sensations, particularly those of sight and touch, from which you *infer* the existence of something causing these sensations. If this is so, how can you be so sure that the chair you experience is real?

6. What could you do to prove that you do indeed have thoughts and feelings, a "mind"?

   One of the basic but continuously debated distinctions in philosophy is the one between those aspects of us that are *physical,* tangible and explainable through the techniques of physics, chemistry, and biology—our *bodies*—and those that are *mental,* that have to do with our *minds.* The problem is that mental events and processes—such as our feelings and our thoughts—can be known directly only to the person who has them, whereas our physical traits can be observed by almost anyone. But how, then, can anyone ever *know* that anyone else has a mind as well as a body, if all that one can ever observe is another's body? Usually, of course, we *assume* that the visible movements of a person's body (his or her behavior, gestures, speech) are expressions of mental processes, which are not visible. But how could you prove this? And how could you prove that you have a mind (thoughts and feelings) to someone who did not assume that your bodily movements were expressions of mental processes? How would you argue with someone who claimed that you (and he) did not have a mind at all?

7. Suppose you alone believe that the earth moves around the sun, rather than vice versa. Is what you believe true?

There was a time, about five hundred years ago, when only a few people believed that the earth moved around the sun, the most famous being **Copernicus**. The heliocentric theory is now accepted by all scientists (and virtually everyone else). But it is worth noting that our ordinary way of talking is still riddled with words and phrases such as "sunrise," "sunset," and "summer constellations," as if the earth were indeed stationary. The fact is that even in this scientific climate, most students are incapable of giving any convincing reasons for believing the Copernican theory rather than what would seem to be the obvious testimony of the senses. If you were not surrounded by an entire society that kept insisting that the earth does in fact move around the sun, what reasons would you have for believing it at all?

But let us return to our question. You are stubborn, and you insist on the geocentric view. Is what you believe—against everyone else and against most facts of common sense—*true*? Well, that depends on what we mean by "truth." If the truth is "the way things really are," then it doesn't matter how many people know it or deny it. But suppose that part of what we mean by "truth" has to do with what people believe and agree to? For example, it is impossible that only one person should know the meaning of a word in English; a word has meaning in English because English speakers agree on its meaning (more or less). Truths of arithmetic—such as "2 + 5 = 7"—depend in part on **conventions**, general agreement about the meaning of certain symbols (such as "2" and "+"). Could this be true of scientific theories about the world, too?

8. Suppose the thought were to occur to you that it is possible, or at least conceivable, that you are just dreaming right now, that you are still asleep in bed, dreaming about reading a philosophy book. How would you prove to yourself that this is not true, that you are in fact awake?

This has long been one of those standard questions that philosophers use to the rigor of their theories of knowledge. Or, as the French philosopher **René Descartes** states the question in his *Meditations,* "How often has it happened to me that in the night I dreamt I found myself in this particular place, that I was dressed and seated near the fire, whilst in reality I was lying undressed in bed!"

Of course, there are very few philosophers who would actually say that they are dreaming right now, but having to **prove** it forces them to be very clear about what they think knowledge is, what they think reality is, and how we can in fact know anything at all. If you say, for example, that reality is "what you experience" or "what you believe" at any given time, then it may be impossible to prove that what you now think is real might not be just a dream.

What implications does this problem have for all of the other things that you believe?

9. Describe yourself as if you were a character in a story.

Part of the problem of finding an adequate conception of ourselves is that we spend almost all our time seeing ourselves from the inside rather than as others see us. From the inside, however, it is all too easy not to see ourselves at all. We do not see the gestures or hear the words that would give us a strong impression of someone we were meeting for the first time. For just this reason, people are often shocked to see themselves in a video or hear recordings of themselves. Many, in fact, think of themselves as if in a kind of daydream, with very little contact with what—to anyone else— would be their most obvious characteristics. This exercise is designed to correct such tendencies, to get you to look at yourself as others look at you and to try to say what is *essential* about you. But it is also a way of asking what it is that you really value, in others as well as in yourself. What do you admire? What sort of person do you want to be?

A German philosopher once said that the test of who you are is whom you admire. Do you admire athletes more than artists? Do you admire people with wealth or power? Do you admire a person who stands up for what he or she thinks is right and becomes a martyr as a result? Do you admire a person because you wish you were like him or her? Or for some other reason? Some people admire athletes because they are enjoyable to watch, for instance, but they do not emulate them. Some people admire Jesus, not so much because of the kind of person he was (about which we know very little) but because he was the Son of God. But if you admire people who are very different from yourself, that raises the possibility that you admire people who make you feel inferior; why would a person do that? Do you admire people in order to provide inspiration and perhaps a measuring stick for yourself? Or just to be amused? Or in order to *discourage* yourself? What would you have to do to become a person you would admire? (Or are you already such a person?)

Writing up a list of virtues (see Aristotle's list on p. 277) is a way of seeing what we value in ourselves and what kind of a person we think is ideal (assuming, of course, that you aren't just thinking like a babysitter, for whom the virtues in one's wards are that they sit quietly and do nothing bothersome). Try to arrange your list in order—that is, with the most important virtues first. Is being honest, for example, as important as being considerate? Is being neither a borrower nor a lender as important as helping friends in need? Is being cautious as important as being courageous? Or is being polite as important as being entertaining or provocative?

10. Explain who you are to a visitor from another planet.

"A student at the university" will obviously not be very informative. (The creature will look up *university* and *student* in its American dictionary, but what will this tell it?) You say, "I am a human being." What does that mean? The creature pulls out a weapon that you guess to be a ray gun, and you hurriedly try to talk it out of disintegrating you. What would you say? What reasons can you give that are not just of personal importance (that is, reasons that would be understood only by you and people like yourself—for example, "I have to take my midterm exam in two days," or "I've still got books out from the library")? What is particularly impressive about being human, being a student, being *you*?

11. Would you like to step into the happiness box?

The point of the question is obvious enough. What do you value? If it is pleasure and contentment, you obviously ought to get in the box. (Are pleasure and contentment the same thing as happiness?) If, on the other hand, you think life is about relationships with other people, fulfilling ambitions, and *doing* something, you certainly won't get in the box. But then again, if the reason you like to have friends and lovers is because you *enjoy* them, if the reason you like success and accomplishment is because they give you pleasure, then why not just get in the box? There you'll find genuine enjoyment and pleasure, without the hassle of other people, and without having to work, sweat, or worry about the possibility of failure. After all, isn't that what you really want?

12. Will a good person necessarily be happy, too? Is life ultimately fair?

One of the central ideas in our way of looking at the world is our belief that virtue should be rewarded and evil should be punished. In fact, of course, this does not always occur. Governments try to catch and punish criminals, but they do not always succeed. The events of life sometimes punish the wicked and reward the good, but—unfortunately—not all that often. In order to preserve the belief that life is fair, many religions invoke God (or karma) to provide some assurance that things will come out right. Yet even among theologians, the question arises whether we can believe that God does fulfill this function (see "The Problem of Evil" in Chapter 3). Still, even if we can't be sure that justice will triumph, it doesn't follow from this that there is no reason to be good—or not to be wicked—if there are no guarantees of ultimate reward and punishment. The ancient Greeks, for example, did not believe in ultimate rewards and punishments, but they did believe in the importance of honor, and for them, we might say, this was its own reward.

13. Do you believe it is wrong to take a life under any circumstances?

Two contexts in which this question comes up immediately are the controversial question of abortion and the age-old quandary of when war is justified. But what the question also provokes is a sense of the very nature of morality. Do moral principles hold *no matter what*? Suppose you had a chance to save an entire city by sacrificing one innocent child (as in the ancient Greek tragedy *Iphigenia,* in which the warrior Agamemnon sacrifices his daughter Iphigenia to assure victory in the Trojan War). Or suppose God said to you—as he says to Abraham in the biblical account—that he wanted you to take the life of your child to prove your faith? On the other hand, would it be right to artificially extend the life of a person suffering horribly from incurable cancer? Is life by itself worth more than anything else under all circumstances? What if we discover that another society has different views from our own about when it might be appropriate to take a life? This raises the general question of whether we have the right to impose our moral laws (even if we consider them absolute for ourselves) on other cultures. If a band of cannibals has long practiced the custom of killing and eating the weakest among them, do we have the right to say that they are wrong? You can't just reply, "Yes, because killing is immoral," if you already accept some exceptions to this rule. Why pick on the poor hungry cannibals?

14. Have you ever made a decision that was *entirely* your own?

Most of our students have come down hard on the word *entirely.* Some of them have said, "Well, of course, not *entirely* my own." They admit that there were always at least some influences on every decision—from family and friends, something recently read or some half-hidden influence, some nagging feeling, or some half-forgotten childhood fear that is nevertheless still effective. But then opinions begin to split into two opposite sides. Some students have argued that this set of influences, taken all together, wholly determined their decision. That is, they could not have chosen to do otherwise, and anyone who knew them well would have recognized that. On the other side, some students have argued that no matter how powerful or numerous the influences on a person, he or she is *always* free to choose. If nothing else, we can always choose exactly the opposite of what everyone else expects, even the opposite of what we know we ought to choose, just to prove that we are free to choose for ourselves.

This question has become one of the most controversial in philosophy. It is commonly called the **free will** and **determinism** problem, and many philosophers consider it the central issue of their entire philosophical worldview. On the one side, there are philosophers who call themselves **determinists**; they believe that everything that happens—even our most carefully deliberated and (apparently) freely chosen actions—is totally caused, or determined, by a set of prior conditions and influences. This means that there is no such thing as a "free choice," because no one ever "chooses" to do anything that he or she is not determined to do anyway. On the other side are the philosophers who believe that our apparently free choices actually are free. One term for those who hold this view is **libertarians**. (This term, however, can be confusing because *libertarianism* is also a term for a very different kind of view about freedom, the political position that emphasizes freedom from government restrictions on individuals' freedom); we can also call them by more cumbersome phrases, such as "defenders of free will." According to the determinist's view, we are mainly victims of forces beyond our control; according to the libertarian view, we are always responsible for our actions. From the rivalry between these two views, some of the most important differences in philosophy have emerged.

15. Is freedom always a good thing?

Suppose there were a society in which the people have to act according to the orders of a dictator, but they obey happily and things run smoothly without many of the problems—such as crime, unemployment, and economic scarcity—that plague most modern nations. The only problem is that no one (except perhaps the dictator) is free. There is no freedom of speech or freedom of the press. Everyone is raised in the same religion, and the punishments for any form of eccentricity or unusual behavior or belief are severe (often the death penalty). How could you convince the members of such a society that they were missing out on something essential? We routinely speak so highly of "freedom," without qualification and without any attempt to understand its meaning, that, when called upon to do so, we often find ourselves simply insisting that "freedom is good." Good for what? It is not necessary for happiness or a well-run society; indeed, it is easy to find or imagine societies in which people are both happy and prosperous but not, in our sense, free. But what is "our sense," and does it always make sense? Is freedom a *means* to happiness and prosperity? Or is freedom an end in itself, one feature of human life that should be defended no matter what? Why would this be? What if freedom is sometimes harmful (for example, the freedom *not* to wear seat belts)? What if one person's freedom threatens the freedom of others (for example, freedom of speech for Nazi advocates of violence and intolerance or the freedom of an unstable and potentially dangerous person with schizophrenia)?

16. Do you want to have children? If so, why?

Many people have children for terrible reasons—or for no reason at all. They have them to keep a floundering relationship together. They have them because they are temporarily lonely. They have them because they forgot to use a contraceptive or miscalculated the time of the month. But choosing to have children is one of the most important decisions anyone can ever make, and it is a decision with the longest-lasting personal consequences. It is a decision that reveals a great deal about the way we deal with the world—or fail to deal with it. Do we want to provide some future for the family name? Why? Do we need more hands around the house to help with the chores? (Don't bet on it.) Do we look forward to having absolute authority over someone? (It won't last very long.) Do we need someone to inherit the throne after we're dead? (Not applicable to most of us.) Do we think that having children will give us a sense of immortality? Could it just be a matter of curiosity? Vanity? Are we willing to sacrifice that much of our time and energy? Or do we not consider it a sacrifice at all?

We can look at another account involving Socrates, this time a bit of his interaction with Diotima, an imaginary wisewoman to whom Socrates claims to have been talking. This brief dialogue is from Plato's *Symposium:*

DIOTIMA: *All men, Socrates, have a procreative impulse, both spiritual and physical, and when they come to maturity they feel a natural desire to beget children. . . . There is something divine about the whole matter; in procreation and bringing to birth the mortal creature is endowed with a touch of immortality. Procreation is the nearest thing to perpetuity and immortality that a mortal can attain.*

SOCRATES: *Diotima, am I really to believe this?*

DIOTIMA: *Certainly, and if you will reflect you will see that the ambition of men provides an example of the same truth. You will be astonished by its irrationality unless you bear in mind that the love of fame and the desire to win a glory that shall never die have the strongest effects upon people. For this even more than their children they are ready to run risks, spend their substance, endure every hardship and even sacrifice their lives. Consider the great poet Homer, for example. Who would not envy him the children, that is, the great poems, The Iliad and The Odyssey that he has left behind, children who have won for their parent immortal fame and glory?*

Diotima suggests that not only having children but other important adult aspirations are motivated by the same desire for some kind of immortality. We earlier considered the question of what is worth dying for. Diotima asks the converse question: what is worth living for? This is a question about what makes life meaningful, and it may be the biggest and most important philosophical question of all. We will consider it in the following chapter.

Suggested Readings

Plato's *Symposium* is available in a delightful translation by A. Nehamas and Paul Woodruff (Hackett, 1989). René Descartes's *Meditations,* the standard starting point for a great many introductory philosophy courses, is translated by Donald Cress, 4th ed. (Hackett, 1998). The last days of Socrates—his arrest, trial, imprisonment, and execution—are described by

Plato in the dialogues *Apology, Crito,* and *Phaedo,* all of which are translated by G. M. A. Grube, with revisions by John M. Cooper, in *The Trial and Death of Socrates* (Hackett, 2001). (The source of the excerpt in this chapter is the previous edition of this work.) For a delightful but very biased general introduction to philosophical problems, see Bertrand Russell, *A History of Western Philosophy* 2nd ed. (Routledge, 2004) or the same author's shorter but more difficult *Problems of Philosophy* (Book Jungle, 2008). Or, see Robert C. Solomon and Kathleen M. Higgins, *A Short History of Philosophy* (Oxford University Press, 1996).

Jacques-Louis David, *The Death of Socrates*.
© Francis G. Mayer/CORBIS.

2
The Meaning of Life

"Maybe I did not live as I ought to have done," it suddenly occurred to him.
"But how could that be, when I did everything so properly?" he replied, and
immediately dismissed from his mind this, the sole solution of all the
riddles of life and death, as something quite impossible.
— Leo Tolstoy, *The Death of Ivan Ilych*

Opening Questions

1. Fill in the blank: "Life is _____." Some examples:

   Life is a puzzle, except that you don't know what the picture
   is supposed to look like, and you don't even know if you've
   got all the pieces.

   Life is a maze, except that you try to avoid the exit.

   Life is a poker game. (It requires luck, but you can win with
   a high pair and you can lose with a flush.)

   Life is win or lose. A few people win. Most are losers.

   Life is an adventure.

   Life is a learning experience.

   Life is a blessing.

   Life is suffering.

   What does your answer say about you and how you see yourself?
   What are your ultimate goals? Expectations? Hopes? Fears?

2. Suppose an angel is sitting on a cloud, watching the parade of
   human activities below—the way we would watch a colony of
   ants hurrying along in their daily business. What would the
   angel say about the flurry of activity? What would it amount to,
   in the angel's eyes?

3. Name three or four things that you would not like to leave
   undone at your death. How many of these things have you
   already accomplished or begun? Which of these things could
   you now be doing, but are not? (Why not?)

4. The philosopher Albert Camus suggested that life is like the task of the Greek mythological hero Sisyphus, who was condemned to roll a rock up a mountain, only to have it fall back again; and he had to do this over and over, forever. Is life indeed like this? If so, how?

What is the meaning of life? This is *the* big question—the hardest to answer, the most urgent and at the same time the most obscure. Careful thinkers often avoid it, aware that the question is vague, that the meaning of the word *meaning* is itself ambiguous, that the answers are not always literal truths that can be defended by argument and reason. Yet, it is reason that makes an answer possible, and it is reason that makes the question necessary. In this chapter we will consider some possible foundations for meaning in life and then some candidates for the type of life that would be meaningful.

What Kind of Meaning?

For most of us, the question about the meaning of life is most likely to arise in a time of confusion, when we are depressed or when some incident has upset our values and expectations. In everyday life, when we aren't studying philosophy or thinking in general about things, life seems crammed full of meanings—there's a term paper to write, an oil filter in the car to change, a good party to look forward to or remember, the prospect of an important job interview sometime in the next few weeks. But when we begin to think abstractly, as we inevitably do at times, it becomes obvious to us that none of these small goals and expectations could possibly count as the meaning of life. And so we look at bigger things—happiness in general, doing well in life, success, influence, love. But then the ominous message of the biblical Book of Ecclesiastes hits home: "All is vanity," and soon to pass away. And so we begin to look beyond life itself for the meaning of life—the ultimate question of philosophy.

What is the meaning of life? First we should ask, what is the meaning of *meaning* in this question? Sometimes, the meaning of something (a sign, a word) is what it refers to, something beyond itself. Thus, the sign "Beware of the dog" presumably refers to some dog, probably unseen, presumably large, and possibly ferocious. The name *Socrates* is the name of Socrates. Thinking of meaning this way, we would say that the meaning of each of our lives is whatever our individual lives refer to. But what would this be? One might say that each of our lives in some sense refers to other people around us—family, friends, associates—so that the meaning of life is other people. Or one might say that each of our lives refers to the larger community, to the nation, or to humanity as a whole. Or one might say that our lives refer to our Creator, so that the meaning of life is God. But the concept of "reference" becomes stretched very thin here, and one might well object that a life doesn't refer to anything at all. It just *is*. This seems to leave us without an answer to the question of the meaning of life. Perhaps the problem is with the notion of *meaning* as reference.

The Meaning of Life: From the Book of Ecclesiastes

Vanity of vanities, saith the Preacher, vanity of vanities; all is vanity. What profit hath a man of all his labour which he taketh under the sun? One generation passeth away, and another generation cometh: but the earth abideth for ever . . . All things are full of labour; man cannot utter it: the eye is not satisfied with seeing, nor the ear filled with hearing. The thing that hath been, it is that which shall be; and that which is done is that which shall be done: and there is no new thing under the sun . . .

I said in mine heart, Go to now, I will prove thee with mirth, therefore enjoy pleasure: and, behold, this also is vanity. I said of laughter, it is mad: and of mirth, What doeth it? I sought in mine heart to give myself unto wine, yet acquainting mine heart with wisdom; and to lay hold on folly, till I might see what was that good for the sons of men, which they should do under the heaven all the days of their life. I made me great works; I builded me houses; I planted me vineyards: I made me gardens and orchards, and I planted trees in them of all kind of fruits: I made me pools of water, to water therewith the wood that bringeth forth trees: I got me servants and maidens, and had servants born in my house; also I had great possessions . . . Then I looked on all the works that my hands had wrought, and on the labour that I had laboured to do: and, behold, all was vanity and vexation of spirit, and there was no profit under the sun. And I turned myself to behold wisdom, and madness, and folly: . . . I saw that wisdom excelleth folly, as far as light excelleth darkness. The wise man's eyes are in his head; but the fool walketh in darkness: and I myself perceived also that one event happeneth to them all. Then said I in my heart, as it happeneth to the fool, so it happeneth even to me; and why was I then more wise? Then I said in my heart that this also is vanity . . . Therefore I hated life; because the work that is wrought under the sun is grievous unto me: for all is vanity and vexation of spirit.

But let us hear the conclusion of the whole matter: Fear God, and keep His commandments: for this is the whole duty of man. For God shall bring every work into judgment, with every secret thing, whether it be good, or whether it be evil.

—Ecclesiastes 1:2–9, 13–14; 2:1–17
(book of both the Hebrew Bible and the
Christian Bible, third century BCE,
unknown author, King James Version)

We can say that particular words and signs refer, but they do so only within the context of a language, a community of shared meanings. The written word *pepino* doesn't mean anything to a person who doesn't speak Spanish. The word *fore* may be meaningless to someone who doesn't play golf. Reference is a contextual affair, and so it is in life, too. The meaning of our particular acts can be explained by reference to goals and conventions ("He did that in order to impress the recruiter," or "He did that in order to signal a left-hand turn"). But can we similarly explain the meaning of our whole lives? A rare person does dedicate his or her entire existence to a single goal—winning the revolution or finding a cure for cancer—but most people are not so single-minded, and their lives don't have a meaning in this easy-to-define sense. Still, this doesn't mean that their lives lack meaning. In linguistics, we can ask the meaning of the word *pepino,* but we cannot intelligibly ask for the meaning of the whole language. The question "What is the meaning of Spanish?" is nonsense. So, too, we might say, asking for the meaning of life *as a whole* is nonsense—but this seems to deprive us of any possible answer to our all-important question.

In any case, when people ask about the meaning of life, however, they often have in mind just such reference to something beyond them, something outside of their lives. These references may be extremely important. They may even be the most important things *in* life. But it is worth pointing out that, in a sense, these references do not fully answer the question; they only postpone it. Four such answers along these lines are worth mentioning: thinking of one's children, or God, or an afterlife as the meaning of one's life, or, in despair, concluding too quickly that life has no meaning.

Children as Meaning

Many people would say that the meaning of life lies in their children and their children's children. But this answer has an odd consequence as soon as you start to think about it. If the meaning of life lies not in these children's own lives, but in someone else's life, what is it that makes *their* lives meaningful? *Their* children. But what makes their *children's* lives meaningful in turn? *Their* children, and so on. In this way people always have tended to project abstractly into the future, to a place of total peace and happiness—what philosophers call a **utopia**. And this is how they would like their children, or their children's children, or their children's children's children, to live. But how does this make their *own* lives meaningful? And what is the meaning of life for those distant relatives happily living in Utopia? They face the same question. Successful couples often look back to their years of struggle together and agree that *those* were the best years of life. How does this square with the idea that an eventual peaceful Utopia is the meaning of life? And is happiness itself so obviously the meaning of life?

God as Meaning

A traditional answer to the question of the meaning of life is God. In fact, it often has been suggested that for people who believe in God the question does not even arise, and that in the days before many people doubted his existence, the meaning of life was never in question. But this simply is not true. The great philosopher Saint Augustine, a most devout Christian, asked that question more persistently than most atheists. So did Martin Luther and an enormous number of

Christian thinkers before him and since. To think that believing in God by itself *answers* the question of the meaning of life only pushes the question back one step further. Why has God created us? What does he expect from us? Why did he create *us*? Some people think that God created us as something special, not only "in His own image" but with a mission to accomplish for him here on earth. But why would he do that, if he can do anything? To prove a point? (To whom?) To satisfy his vanity? (The God of the Old Testament was, after all, a jealous God; perhaps he was a vain God, too.) Furthermore, why should we think that we have been created for a special mission or purpose? If we are, what is that mission? What is that purpose? The question thus repeats itself, as the great thinkers of Christianity have long recognized; what is the meaning of our lives? Belief in God seems only to make the question more urgent; belief does not solve it.

Afterlife as Meaning

Some people believe that the meaning of life is to be found in another life that is our reward or punishment for this one. But whether or not you believe in such an afterlife, this answer to the question is odd, too. To say that this life has meaning only by reference to the next one is to say, as is openly claimed in the Book of Ecclesiastes, that this life itself is insignificant, meaningless. But what is it that we are to do in this insignificant life so that we will be rewarded in the next one? Simply have faith? Do good works? Live life to the fullest? Realize our artistic or social potential? Convert the heathens? Learn to cook? Again the question repeats itself, and one might also ask: If this life is so insignificant, what would make the next one any more meaningful? Is it that this one is so short and the next one is so long? But if life—even a few minutes of life—has no significance in itself, then what significance can eternal life have? If you're bored by sitting in a class for an hour, it won't make you any less bored if you are told that the class will be extended for ten more hours. On the other hand, Christian thinkers, especially in the past several centuries, often have argued that the rewards of the next life will be available only to those who live *this* life to the fullest. This brings up our question once again: What is it to live life to the fullest? What is it to find this life meaningful?

No Meaning at All

On the other side of the question, there are those philosophers—and a fair number of today's students—who would say that life has no meaning at all. The word that is often used to express this view is **absurd**. "Life is absurd," they say, which means that it has no meaning. Again, this is a view that has been held both by people who believe in God and by people who don't, although it is clear that the most troubling and final statements have come from those who do not. For example, the French philosopher **Albert Camus** said in his book *The Myth of Sisyphus* that the absurd had become a widespread sensibility in our times.

At any street corner the feeling of absurdity can strike any man in the face. . . .
It happens that the stage sets collapse. Rising, streetcar, four hours in
the office or the factory, meal, streetcar, four hours of work, meal, sleep, and
Monday Tuesday Wednesday Thursday Friday and Saturday according to the
same rhythm—this path is easily followed most of the time. But one day the
"why" arises and everything begins in that weariness tinged with amazement.

Albert Camus was born in Algeria in 1913. He was an outspoken journalist
and throughout his life adopted a difficult middle stance in politics, between
the radicals and revolutionaries on his left and the harsh authorities of Nazi
occupation and perpetrators of colonial injustices on his right. His first
published novel, *The Stranger*, made him an instant celebrity in Europe;
it is still one of the most popular novels on American college campuses.
His philosophy was based on his view that life is essentially "absurd," that
the universe will never satisfy our expectations for meaning and justice. His
reaction, however, was not that life is therefore not worth living, but rather
that we have to *make* it worth living by rebelling against this absurdity, by
refusing to participate in the injustices of the world, and by living life to the
fullest. He died in a car crash in 1960.

It is important to emphasize that each of these answers may have great importance in a person's life. One certainly can dedicate oneself to one's children,
and many people always have done so. It is possible (though more rare than
people usually say) to devote one's life to God, and many people do. But it is
just as important to realize that these noble answers leave our question open, for
they just transfer it one step down the line. What is the meaning of our children's
lives? What kind of life would amount to life in the service of God? We need an
answer *in* our lives, not just beyond them.

The same might be said of the reply that life has no meaning, that it is all
absurd. Camus sometimes argues that position on the basis of his atheism; if
there is no external meaning, then there can be no meaning at all. But an external
meaning may not be the meaning of life, and it does not follow from the absence
of God (if, in fact, he does not exist) that life is without meaning.

The Thought of "External Recurrence"

The greatest weight.—What if some day or night a demon were to steal after
you into your loneliest loneliness and say to you: "This life as you now live
it and have lived it, you will have to live once more and innumerable times
more; and there will be nothing new in it, but every pain and every joy and
every thought and sigh and everything unutterably small or great in your
life will have to return to you, all in the same succession and sequence . . ."

Would you not throw yourself down and gnash your teeth and curse the demon who spoke thus? Or have you once experienced a tremendous moment when you would have answered him: "You are a god and never have I heard anything more divine." If this thought gained possession of you, it would change you as you are or perhaps crush you. The question in each and every thing, "Do you desire this once more and innumerable times more?" would lie upon your actions as the greatest weight. Or how well disposed would you have to become to yourself and to life to crave nothing more fervently than this ultimate eternal confirmation and seal?

—Friedrich Nietzsche,
The Gay Science §381,
1882, trans. Walter Kaufmann

The Myth of Sisyphus (as Told by Camus)

The gods had condemned Sisyphus to ceaselessly rolling a rock to the top of a mountain, whence the stone would fall back of its own weight. They had thought with some reason that there is no more dreadful punishment than futile and hopeless labor.

If this myth is tragic, that is because its hero is conscious. Where would his torture be, indeed, if at every step the hope of succeeding upheld him? The workman of today works every day of his life at the same tasks, and this fate is no less absurd. But it is tragic only at the rare moments when it becomes conscious. Sisyphus, proletarian of the gods, powerless and rebellious, knows the whole extent of his wretched condition: it is what he thinks of during his descent. The lucidity that was to constitute his torture at the same time crowns his victory. There is no fate that cannot be surmounted by scorn.

The struggle toward the heights is enough to fill a man's heart. One must imagine Sisyphus happy.

—Albert Camus,
The Myth of Sisyphus, 1942

It is worth noting that linguists now insist that meaning must be found *within* the context of language. A word has meaning not just because of its reference but, more important, because of its sense in the language. Thus, we might say, by way of analogy, that the meaning of life is to be found in the context of our lives—the sense they make and the sense we give to them—rather than in reference to anything outside of life. Devotion to God answers the question of the meaning of life insofar as one actually *lives for* God. Having children answers the question insofar as one actually lives for one's children. Ironically, **nihilism**—the view that life has no meaning—also can provide life with a meaning, if one actually dedicates one's life to the proposition that life has no meaning and deflating the false and sometimes self-righteous and vicious meanings that people think it has. Camus seems to have lived his life that way.

The Meanings of Life

Life is like the Olympic games; a few strain their muscles to carry off a prize, others sell trinkets to the crowd for a profit; some just come to look and see how everything is done.

— Pythagoras, sixth century BCE

Life is like playing a violin in public and learning the instrument as one plays.

— Samuel Butler, 1612–1680

Life is just a bowl of cherries.

— Anonymous

Life is a bowl of pits.

— Rodney Dangerfield

The question of the meaning of life is not one of those questions that require or allow for a specific answer. Indeed, what is required is a metaphor, an image, a vision of life in which you can see yourself as having a definite role, a set of reasonable expectations, and—what makes this so important—your vision in many ways determines the life you will lead. For example, suppose you go into business, or perhaps to school, with the attitude that life is "dog eat dog" and everyone for himself. You will greet everyone as a threat and a rival; you will not be wholly honest, and in any case generally you will not enjoy others' company. People will begin to sense your competitive hostility and distrust you, perhaps even testing your intentions with small acts of provocation. And soon you will find yourself indeed in a "dog eat dog" atmosphere—one that you largely have created yourself. So the question of the meaning of life is not just a matter of discovery but also an important act of creation. Your own philosophy is only in part the expression and clarification of the view you already have of the world, for the philosophy you formulate also will be an instrument for shaping and revising that view. Thus, some philosophers who have had a gloomy or pessimistic temperament willfully have formulated rather cheerful and optimistic philosophies, not to deceive themselves but to *change* themselves, and some of them have succeeded remarkably well.

The images we use to talk about life define the meaning we find, or don't find, in it. Thus, your answers to Opening Questions 1 and 4 in particular should give you a fairly clear indication about the general view of life you seem to accept, even if your answer is playful or poetic. (We reveal our views through play and poetry, as well as in doing serious philosophy.) If you claimed that "Life is a game," for example, then you said that you think life shouldn't be taken very seriously (whether or not you yourself do take it seriously), that it doesn't add up to anything in the end, and that the best way to live is to enjoy it. On the other hand, if you stated that "Life is a gift from God, to be used wisely," you said that you think life is indeed serious, with a more or less definite mission (which you have to discern) and a fairly clear-cut sense of success and failure (in God's judgment). In what follows, we have listed and briefly described a number of grand images of life and its meaning (or lack of it) that have appeared in history and in students' papers. Of course, the list is not at all complete; you will want to add some images of your own, which may be even better than the ones we have listed here.

Life as a Game

If life is a game, it is not to be taken so seriously, as we said above. A game is a self-contained activity, and even if it does add up to something (as playing basketball increases your coordination or as running track increases your endurance), the significance of the game lies in the playing itself. ("It's not whether you win or lose, but how you play the game.") But then again, some people see games as fiercely competitive. (Thus, Vince Lombardi's famous line, "Winning isn't everything; *it's the only thing!*") And to see life that way is to see it as a perpetual con in which you win or lose. If you think life is a game, it is therefore also important to ask what kind of game. Some games are played for fun alone. Some games are played to prove your superiority (arm wrestling); others are played to kill time (solitaire). Some games are distinctively social (bridge); some are intentionally anxiety producing (high-stakes poker); some are aimed at hurting the opponent (boxing); and some are aimed at helping others (turning charity into a game, for example, to see who can collect the most money for a cause). The notion of life as a game has been used by many writers—Eric Berne's *Games People Play* spent time on the best-seller list—and some philosophers have suggested that language, economics, and philosophy itself are games. To think of life as a game is to put it in a certain perspective, in order not to take it *too* seriously, in order to emphasize the importance of obeying the rules and, perhaps, the centrality of being a "good sport," enjoying oneself, and, if possible, winning. But we tend to use the words *winner* and *loser* in a dangerous way. For example, what kind of standards are we setting for ourselves when we declare that the second-best football team *in the world*—the team that just lost the Super Bowl—"is a bunch of *losers*"?

Life as a Story

"Life imitates art," wrote the Irish dramatist and essayist Oscar Wilde, reversing Plato, who claimed that art is an imitation of life. It is obvious that we do not live just moment to moment or for some single great goal, but rather we follow a rather detailed script, a story, a narrative, which (to at least some extent) we make up as we go along. The outlines of the story and our roles in it probably are provided first by our families and our culture, then by the circumstances in which we find ourselves. To think of life as a story is to think of life in a particular temporal way, as a plot unfolding, as the development of character and personality. (The German philosophers of the nineteenth century talked about life as a *Bildungsroman*, a story of personal development as an individual goes through the various quests, disappointments, and discoveries of life.)

We often find ourselves making decisions about our lives using the standards we also use in evaluating literature or a movie: Is it interesting? Is it boring? Does it have enough suspense? Is it in good taste? Is it well timed? Is it carried out dramatically—or overdramatically, "overacted"? Is this action in line with the character of the hero (namely, *you*)? The American novelist John Barth (in *The End of the Road*) suggested that each of us is the hero of his or her own story: "The character Polonius," he writes, "did not consider himself a minor character in *Hamlet*." One could rewrite *Hamlet* from Polonius's point of view (as, indeed, playwright Tom Stoppard has rewritten *Hamlet* wonderfully from the point of view of two even more minor characters, Rosenkrantz and Guildenstern, in his play *Rosenkrantz and Guildenstern Are Dead*). *Hamlet*, of course, is a tragedy. But some people live their lives as comedies, as farce, and others as adventure stories—choosing glamorous jobs or dangerous hobbies— doing whatever is required dramatically to add to their list of swashbuckling episodes. According to this view, it is not the end goal or outcome of life that gives life meaning, but the quality of the story, the quality with which one lives out and develops his or her role or roles. To choose the wrong role (one for which one is unsuited and untalented) or not to recognize one's role—or to have too many roles or incoherent roles—is to damage the meaning that one finds in life.

Life as Tragedy

One incontrovertible fact is that we all die. But this fact can be ignored; or death can be viewed as an inconvenience, as a passage to another life, or as ultimate disaster. If we look at our lives as less dramatic and less well-written versions of *Hamlet, Macbeth, Othello,* or *Faust,* we indeed can find the crucial ingredients of tragedy in every one of us—some tragic flaw, some error in judgment, some fatal contradiction—that get played out through life until everything ends in death. The philosopher Camus ends his novel *The Stranger* with a character declaring, "All men are brothers, and the same end awaits them all—death." As opposed to the game metaphor, the tragedy metaphor makes life into a serious and unhappy process, punctuated by pleasures, perhaps, but ultimately an inevitable progression of a tragic plot that can have only one end. To live well, in this view, means to play one's tragic role well—to bear it heroically, perhaps making some grand soliloquies along the way.

Life as Comedy

"Life is a joke." Well, perhaps not, but it may be refreshing to think of life that way in contrast to the idea that life is tragic. Laughter too often is ignored as an essential ingredient in life, perhaps even as *the* essential ingredient in the good life. Plato does not write much about laughter, but he certainly displays a profound sense of humor throughout his Socratic dialogues. The sixteenth-century Dutch philosopher **Erasmus** wrote one of the most profound books about human life, which he called *In Praise of Folly*, a celebration of human foolishness. Nietzsche's fictional prophet Zarathustra teaches that we should not be so serious, but instead enjoy laughter and levity.

From the Stranger

[In prison, awaiting execution, Meursault:]

Then all day there was my appeal to think about. I made the most of this idea, studying my effects so as to squeeze out the maximum of consolation. Thus, I always began by assuming the worst; my appeal was dismissed. That meant, of course, I was to die. Sooner than others, obviously. "But," I reminded myself, "it's common knowledge that life isn't worth living, any- how." And, on a wide view, I could see that it makes little difference whether one dies at the age of thirty or three-score and ten—since, in either case, other men and women will continue living, the world will go on as before. Also, whether I died now or forty years hence, this business of dying had to be got through, inevitably. Still, somehow this line of thought wasn't as consoling as it should have been; the idea of all those years of life in hand was a galling reminder! However, I could argue myself out of it, by pictur- ing what would have been my feelings when my term was up, and death had cornered me. Once you're up against it, the precise manner of your death has obviously small importance. Therefore—but it was hard not to lose the thread of the argument leading up to that "therefore"—I should be prepared to face the dismissal of my appeal.

— Albert Camus, 1942
From: Stuart Gilbert, trans. Copyright 1946 by Alfred A. Knopf, Inc.

Of course, there are many kinds of humor. There are jokes, including both good and bad jokes, offensive jokes, and "shaggy dog" (tediously protracted) jokes. Some thinkers would emphasize the importance of sophistication in hu- mor, but others would say that laughter itself is what is important, not what the laughter is about. (Offensive jokes, as opposed to merely bad or silly jokes, on the other hand, perhaps should not count as "humor" at all.) Jokes, however, tend to be rather contrived and limited in time, and a person who spends all of his or her time playing or telling jokes (a "jokester") too easily becomes a tedious and pathetic person to have around. But then there are more serious comedies, not one-line, stand-up humor but protracted stories of ambition and frustration, desire and disappointment, all treated not in terms of what Camus called "The Absurd" but rather as absurdity in a humorous sense.

Tragedy and comedy can be combined, in "black humor" or in irony. At the end of a classic Humphrey Bogart–John Huston movie, *The Treasure of Sierra Madre,* the old man (played by Walter Huston, John's father) has lost everything, but he breaks out in uproarious laughter and encourages the others to do the same. It provides the only possible "happy ending" to a story of greed, disappointment, and death. It is hard to deny that all of us could use a little more humor, not so much in our lives (television provides more than enough of that) but *about* our lives, in the way we see our own faults and foibles.

Johann Wolfgang von Goethe (1749–1832) is still considered to be the greatest German man of letters. He was also a scientist, a lawyer, a civil servant, an artist, an adventurer, a physicist, and a politician. He made important discoveries in botany and wrote essays on Newtonian physics. Goethe wrote in virtually every literary genre, from simple love poetry to long and involved epic plays, the most famous of which is *Faust,* which he worked on for over sixty years. He once claimed to "teach poetry to speak in German," and Hegel followed him in philosophy. Both the poet and the philosopher used the biological imagery of growth as the basis of their work, combating the largely mechanical imagery that dominated the age after Newton.

Life as a Mission

Christianity has often taught that life is a mission, the mission being to get others to become Christians, too. But not only Christians accept this view of life as a "calling." The German poet **Johann Wolfgang von Goethe**, for example, described his mission in life as the creation of poetry to give the German people a sense of cultural identity, and the philosopher Hegel took it as his mission (about the same time as Goethe) to use philosophy to clarify for everyone the meaning of the world in the wake of the French Revolution. Political extremists often talk of their life as a mission—to liberate oppressed people or to get rid of tyranny in their homeland. Scientists sometimes feel they have a mission to fulfill in the expansion of knowledge or the development of a cure for some dread disease, and people with children often feel that their mission is to raise their children well and do what they can to make the world a better place for them to live in. If one's mission is primarily moral, it will be manifested according to one's moral philosophy. A utilitarian like Bentham would aim to change things to promote the greatest happiness of the greatest number. An ethical rationalist like Kant would urge that our goal should be to cultivate our moral personality and to practice our duty as prescribed by reason.

Life as Art

The German philosopher **Friedrich Nietzsche** urged that we live our lives as works of art. He was comparing life not so much to a story but to an art like sculpture, suggesting that one live by creating a shape for oneself, "building character," developing what we call "style." The German philosopher **Friedrich von Schelling** saw the whole of life as God's work of art (with us as in effect God's apprentices). Artists often describe their sense of mission in life as simply "to create," but it is the activity itself that counts for them as much as the results of their efforts. The ideal of this view is appropriately to live *beautifully* or, if that is not possible, to live at least with style, "with class" we might say. From this point of view, life is to be evaluated as an artwork—as moving, inspiring, well designed, dramatic, or colorful, or as clumsy, uninspired and uninspiring, or easily forgettable.

German philosopher **Friedrich Nietzsche** (1844–1900) is known especially for his attack on Christianity and Christian morality, and some unflattering comments about women. He declared himself an "immoralist," and insisted instead on the *aesthetic* value of life. Yet, he is generally recognized as one of the great moral philosophers of all times (see Chapter 8).

Friedrich von Schelling (1775–1854) was a German philosopher who was a friend and great admirer of the romantic poets of the early nineteenth century. His philosophy places unusual emphasis, accordingly, on the importance of creativity and the centrality of art. Indeed, he interprets God not only as a creator but ultimately as the Great Artist, who is still creating the universe, through us. Schelling was one of Hegel's best friends in college, and the two developed their philosophies together until they quarreled and went their separate ways.

Life as an Adventure

Life as a story, life as art—these are inspiring images, but the virtues of life then become the virtues of literature or sculpture: their shape and timing, their appeal to onlookers. But life can be aesthetic and exciting without being like art, without the necessity of always thinking about the shape of the whole or what it looks like to an observer. There is also the thrill of living "to the fullest," taking chances, enjoying challenge and the rush of adrenaline. These are the concerns of those who see life as an adventure. Their sense of living is to take risks, even risking life, and to thrill in their sense of both skill and uncertainty. This is certainly not an image for everyone. (There is an old Chinese curse: "May you live in interesting times!") But for those who see life this way, there may be no other way to live. The alternatives are too boring and tedious. And unlike those who view life as art or as literature, those who see life as adventure never plan a proper ending. When it's over, it's just—over.

The Meaning of Life: Nietzsche

Concerning life, the wisest men of all ages have judged alike: it is no good. Always and everywhere one has heard the same sound from their mouths—a sound full of doubt, full of melancholy, full of weariness of life, full of resistance to life. . . . Even Socrates was tired of it. What does that evidence? What does it evince? Formerly one would have said (—oh, it has been said, and loud enough, and especially by our pessimists): "At least something of all this must be true! The consensus of the sages evidences the truth." Shall we still talk like that today? May we? "At least something must be sick here," we retort. These wisest men of all ages—they should first be scrutinized closely. Were they all perhaps shaky on their legs? late? tottery? decadents? Could it be that wisdom appears on earth as a raven, inspired by a little whiff of carrion?

When one finds it necessary to turn reason into a tyrant, as Socrates did, the danger cannot be slight that something else will play the tyrant. Rationality was then hit upon as the savior; neither Socrates nor his "patients" had any choice about being rational: it was de rigueur, it was their last resort. The fanaticism with which all Greek reflection throws itself upon rationality betrays a desperate situation; there was danger, there was but one choice: either to perish or—to be absurdly rational. . . . One must be clever, clear, bright at any price: any concession to the instincts, to the unconscious, leads downward.

— From *Twilight of the Idols*, 1889

Life as Disease

Life viewed as tragedy has a sense of grandeur about it; life viewed as a disease is rather pathetic. **Sigmund Freud**, for example, said that "the goal of all life is death," a view that has been around since ancient times. Not many years ago, Kurt Vonnegut said that we are "terrible animals," and that the earth's immune system is trying to get rid of us. The "disease" metaphor has been applied to modern life, to Western civilization, to capitalism, and so on. But to be "sick" presupposes some sense of what it is to be well, and the all-important question for anyone who uses this metaphor is: what would count as a *healthy* life? Immortality? A life of antlike social productivity? A life of unblemished happiness? A life of continuous love without a hint of hostility? These all may be desirable, of course, but to desire them does not mean that the lack of them makes life a disease. And yet, much of our language these days is caught up in such "health" metaphors. (Another word for much the same view is the word *natural; natural* is healthy, *unnatural* means disease or deformity.) We talk about a "healthy economy," and we think of what we used to call games now as "exercise" to promote health. And life itself, viewed through the health metaphors, beginning with the expression "a healthy economy." If we take the metaphor of health too seriously, life itself is bound to seem like a fatal disease, at least ultimately, because there seems to be no cure for it and it ends in death.

Austrian-born **Sigmund Freud** (1856–1939) is not usually thought of as a philosopher. As one of the greatest thinkers of modern times, though, he has changed our conception of ourselves and our minds as much as any orthodox philosopher, even while rejecting some of the favorite premises of most philosophers. For example, he argued that the clarity of self-knowledge discussed by such thinkers as Descartes may often be an illusion, that most of our ideas and desires are in fact the product of the *unconscious*, in which forbidden urges and wishes are repressed and often distort what we think we know so clearly. And yet Freud himself continued to be the great defender of rational thinking, and his whole technique of psychoanalysis, he once wrote, was aimed at nothing less than making the unconscious conscious and so putting its contents within the realm of rational understanding and control.

Life as Desire

The view of life as desire is often coupled with the **Sisyphus myth** of life as constant frustration. The Greek allegory in this case is **Tantalus** (from whose name we get the word *tantalizing*), who was condemned by the gods to be tied just out of reach of a bunch of grapes; he spent all eternity reaching for the fruit, but he never managed to get any. A more modern version of the life as desire story is the legend of Faust, the subject of some of the greatest plays in Western literature—*Dr. Faustus*, by the English writer Christopher Marlowe in 1589, and *Faust*, by Goethe, already mentioned. Faust lived for his desires; when one was satisfied, it was immediately replaced by another. This image of life is that of continuous wanting, one craving succeeding another, with no end in sight. A person wants to earn "just enough money to support myself," and does so, only to find that now he or she wants something more, which becomes the focus of life until it is acquired, but then it, too, is not enough. Now the person wants something else. And so on and so on. This is not necessarily a life of frustration, for such desires usually can be satisfied. It is rather the life of desire after desire, in which nothing is ever ultimately satisfying. On this view, desire, as well as the satisfaction of desire, gives life meaning; not to desire is to be already dead.

Life as Nirvana

The opposite view of life as desire is life as *not* desiring, as the overcoming of desire. Freud called the effort to maintain psychological equilibrium the "constancy principle" in his early psychoanalytic works, the "nirvana principle" later on (though he thought of it as governing our psyches independent of conscious effort). In his view, the goal of life is to attain as restful a state as possible, without tension or desire. The word *nirvana*, a Sanskrit word meaning "extinguish," is used in Buddhism to refer to the state of liberation from selfish cravings. The goal of Buddhism is to loosen the hold our desires have on us and to reach a state of tranquility. In Buddhism nirvana includes an equanimity toward death, and Freud even sometimes referred to his principle as the "death wish." The Western counterpart to the Buddhist nirvana is the peace of mind that some schools of thought have promoted as the goal of philosophical activity, which they characterize as **contemplation** (unperturbed learning and thinking).

What We're Here For

We are put on this earth to help others, but what the others are here for I cannot say.

—John Foster Hall (1867–1945)
(a.k.a. The Reverend Vivian Foster,
the Vicar of Mirth), English comedian

Life as Altruism

Altruism is acting for the benefit of others, even if there is no benefit whatsoever to oneself. Some people see themselves as being here on earth to help others less fortunate than they are. It is a view of life that has a very definite sense of mission, as well as quite clear-cut views of success and failure and of what ought to be done. For some people, life as altruism is a one-way enterprise; they help others in order to give their own lives meaning, but they expect nothing in return. For other people, life as altruism is a *general* ideal, and their hope is that, some day, everyone selflessly will help everyone else.

What Do You Value Most?

Do not value either your children or your life or anything else more than goodness.

—Socrates, in Plato's *Crito*,
trans. John Madison Cooper

Life as Honor

Honor is a concept that has changed over time, but for the Greeks in Homer's *Iliad,* for instance, life was essentially a matter of living up to the expectations of your community, of proving yourself in battle, and of not disgracing yourself in any way. This was not to say that you couldn't behave badly: Achilles went sulking to his tent like a child when the king took one of his favorite slave girls away from him. But he established his honor again when he returned to the field of battle to avenge the death of his best friend. For the Greek heroes, honor was more important than life itself, and given the choice between death with honor and life without it, they would not have hesitated for a moment. But the concept of honor has not been limited to military heroes. Socrates died for his honor, too, not in battle but in a prison cell, to show that he valued his principles more than life itself. Our own concept of honor is not so clear, however. American soldiers have died with honor, of course, but the more general sense of honor—as the guiding principle of life—is surely not so evident in daily American life as it supposedly was in ancient Athens. But we do have a sense of *duty,* and many people would say that, whatever else, the meaning of life is doing your duty—to God, country, family, friends, and employer.

Stoicism

Stoicism is a philosophy that flourished for centuries, from 300 BCE (not long after the death of Aristotle) to the fourth and fifth centuries CE (near the end of the Roman Empire). The Stoics viewed most human desires and emotions as irrational, and held that, in order to live in harmony with the universe, we need to control our passions and live a simple life of integrity and duty. Seneca (4 BCE–65 CE), a member of the court of the emperor Nero, was the most famous of the later Stoics; like Socrates, he was condemned to death (allegedly for plotting to kill Nero, but this is unlikely). The Stoic school also included a Roman emperor, Marcus Aurelius (121–180), and hundreds of lesser figures who were powerful spokesmen in their times. Most of the Stoics did not share Seneca's fate, but virtually all of them stressed the importance of maintaining one's honor and integrity even at the expense of one's life.

Life as Learning

A common image is the view of life as a learning experience. Of course, *why* we are learning all of this is an open question; but some learning, at least, is satisfying for its own sake. This satisfaction, presumably, is what the learning of life is all about. We have a bad experience (being walked out on by a boyfriend or girlfriend, being thrown out of school for smoking), and we "chalk it up to experience." Some people feel compelled to experience as much as possible, to "try everything at least once," just in order to know what it is like. For them, "living life to the fullest" means doing everything. But notice that this same expression means something very different from other viewpoints: the person who sees life as a mission lives life to the fullest by taking every opportunity to carry out his or her mission, and the person who sees life as tragedy takes that phrase to mean to suffer dramatically. These days the learning theme is evident in talk of "developing your human potential." This view of life was also popular in Germany almost two hundred years ago, and it can be found, too, in Greek philosophy—for example, in Aristotle. Does it make sense to ask what we are learning for? The age-old answer is that learning leads to **wisdom**, and accordingly, the life of contemplation has been the suggestion of philosophers ever since ancient times.

"Four Noble Truths" of Buddhism

1. Life is marked by suffering.

2. Suffering arises from desire.

3. Desire can be eliminated.

4. One can eliminate desire by following the "right way."

Life as Suffering

"Life is suffering," says the first noble truth of Buddhism, according to one translation. The last word might be better translated as "troubled" or "dissatisfying," but the gist is that life is filled with turmoil and stress, The great pessimist **Arthur Schopenhauer**, who was strongly influenced by Buddhism, also thought that life is frustration. Our desires are ultimately irrational and pointless, he says. The answer, he proposes, is **detachment** as a result of recognizing that any lasting satisfaction is unavailable. Schopenhauer's answer is somewhat similar to that of Stoicism, which also taught that most of our passions are irrational and are best overcome through detachment.

The myth of Sisyphus pushing his rock up the mountain only to have it fall back again reflects this idea that life does not bring lasting fulfillment. We sometimes look at life as just one repetition after another, ultimately adding up to nothing. A character in one modern novel commits suicide when she looks at her toothbrush and realizes that she will have to brush her teeth again and again for the rest of her life, a prospect that, when thought of all at once, indeed seems pointless. Sometimes you fix something, knowing that it will break again soon; you learn how to do something for the seventeenth time, knowing that you will have forgotten it in a week. You get a high school diploma just to go to college, just to get a B.A., just to get into medical school, just to get an M.D., just to intern, just to study surgery, just to practice surgery, just to live the good life you wanted to live while you were in high school, but then you find you are too old and too busy to enjoy it. This perspective on life is a form of seeing life as absurd. But it is worth recalling that Camus thought Sisyphus's life was meaningful, despite the absurdity of his task, because he reacted to his frustration with a kind of defiance. Is there anything analogous to this in our lives?

The Only Serious Philosophical Question

"There is only one serious philosophical question, and that is suicide. Whether life is worth living or not amounts to answering the fundamental question of philosophy. All the rest . . . comes afterwards . . . One first must answer."

— Albert Camus,
The Myth of Sisyphus

Life as an Investment

Business plays such a major role in our society that sometimes we are inclined to think of life as business. ("The business of America is business," said Calvin Coolidge, a businessman who happened also to be president.) To consider life this way is to think of the years of our lives as so much capital, which we invest in various enterprises—a career, a particular school, marriage, and children—to get a certain return. What it is that is returned is not so clear, and so the standards for a good investment versus a poor one are a matter of considerable dispute. A father might consider his son to have "wasted his talents" (that is, to have made a poor investment) because he decided to be a poet, whereas the son may accuse the father of having "sold out" for going into business as he did. It is fairly easy to confuse this metaphor with its most prominent manifestation and think of the actual money a person earns in life and the estate he or she accumulates as a of success. A moment's reflection, however, will show that this is not always a dependable measure. If a good investment is measured by what one has at the end, there is a very real question about how this could be the meaning of life, since this payoff is definite only when the life of which it is the supposed "meaning" has ended.

Aristotle, on Friendship and the Good

The excellent person is of one mind with himself, and desires the same things in his whole soul. . . . The excellent person is related to his friend as he is related to himself, since the friend is another himself. Hence friendship seems to be one of the features of the good life.

—Aristotle, *Nicomachean Ethics*,
Book IX, Chapter 4. Trans. Terence Irwin

Life as Relationships

We have said too little directly about love and marriage and friendship, but it has been obvious to many people what is most obviously important in their lives is human relationship—not the grand and abstract sense of being part of humanity or a citizen of a great nation, but the very particular relationship one has with another person or a few other persons. Thus, people say that what really counts in life is friendship, or the most important thing in life is love. But why do we describe something so important with a word that is as bland as "relationship"? Why do we think of the union of two people as a "relating" of one separate being to another, rather than thinking in terms of a union to begin with? Indeed, much of our language about "relationships" presents us with this unflattering picture of two lonely souls trying to "get through" to one another, trying to "communicate" or "break down the barriers." On the other hand, there is a much more inspiring picture of all of us already connected, perhaps—as Hegel argued—in one all-embracing Spirit. In this view, it is the distance between us, not intimacy, that is the aberration. The meaning of our lives is our network of relations with other people; ideally, the meaning of life is love.

Closing Questions

1. Give your preference for the following images of life. Rate them on a scale of 1–5, with 5 indicating that you wholeheartedly agree, and 1 indicating near-total disagreement. Are there some (for example, life as disease or frustration) that you think may be right even though you do not like them? Mark these with an X. Feel free to add other images of your own.

   Life is
a game	_____
a story	_____
a tragedy	_____
a mission	_____
comedy	_____
art	_____
an adventure	_____
a disease	_____
desire	_____
nirvana	_____
altruism	_____
honor	_____
learning	_____
suffering	_____
an investment	_____
relationships	_____

2. Suppose one of your friends tells you that the meaning of life is nothing other than "get yours while you can." What would you think of this view of life as selfishness? Would you try to talk him or her out of this position? If so, how would you do so?

3. A traditional Native American saying goes "Leave the earth as you found it." Many contemporary Americans, by way of contrast, are told that they should "make their mark on the world." What are the comparative virtues and vices of these two very different ways of thinking, and how would you try to reconcile the two? What are the two very different "meanings of life" that they offer?

Suggested Readings

We have used the King James Version of the Book of Ecclesiastes. Johann Wolfgang von Goethe's *Faust* is translated by Walter Kaufman (Doubleday, 1961). Friedrich Nietzsche's view of life as art begins with his study of the Greeks in *The Birth of Tragedy*, trans. Walter Kaufman (Random House, 1967); his attack on Socrates and the life of reason is best summarized in *The Twilight of the Idols* in *The Viking Portable Nietzsche*, trans. Walter Kaufman (Viking, 1954). Kaufmann is also the translator of Nietzsche's *The Gay Science* (Random House, 1974). Albert Camus's *Myth of Sisyphus*, trans. Justin O'Brien (Vintage, 1955), is one of the classic books of the absurdist tradition in modern literature, and should profitably be read along with Camus's powerful short novel *The Stranger*, trans. Stuart Gilbert (Vintage, 1946). Aristotle's *Nicomachean Ethics,* translated by Terence Irwin, is available from Hackett Publishing 1985. The quotation from John Barth comes from his *The End of the Road*, available in *The Floating Opera and The End of the Road* (Doubleday, 1988). Freud's vision of life is perhaps best argued in his classic *Civilization and Its Discontents*, trans. James Strachey (Norton, 1962). Plato's *Crito* is available in *The Trial and Death of Socrates: Euthyphro, Apology, Crito, Death Scene from Phaedo,* trans. John M. Cooper, 3rd ed. (Hackett, 2001). Arthur Schopenhauer's pessimism is exemplified and expounded in his *The World as Will and Representation*, trans. E. F. J. Payne, Vol. I (Dover, 1969). Sigmund Freud's vision of life is perhaps best argued in his classic *Civilization and Its Discontents*, trans. James Strachey (Norton, 1962). Kurt Vonnegut expresses his views on the meaning of life and other matters in *A Man without a Country*, ed. Daniel Simon (New York: Seven Stories Press, 2005). For a variety of views on the meaning of life, see David R. Cheney and Steven Sanders, *The Meaning of Life* (Prentice-Hall, 1980). See also, for a good popular approach, Thomas Moore, *Care of the Soul* (HarperCollins, 1992).

William Blake, *God.*
© The Pierpont Morgan
Library/Art Resource, NY.

3

GOD

Opening Questions

1. Do you believe in God?

   If your answer is yes, you are a **theist** (no matter what particular conception of God you believe in).

   If your answer is no, you are an **atheist**.

   If you answer, "I don't know," you are an **agnostic**.

2. What are the most prominent features of God? (This question is just as important if you are an agnostic or an atheist as it is if you are a theist; it is important to know what it is you *don't* believe in or don't know. Even if you believe in God, there may also be some conceptions of God you don't believe in. Perhaps you don't believe in a fatherly God who looks after us but do believe in some vital force or "prime mover" that got the universe going in the first place, for example.)

   Is God all-powerful (**omnipotent**)?

   Is God all-knowing (**omniscient**)?

Did God create the universe?

Does God care about human beings?

Does God have emotions?

If so, which ones?
  Love,
  Jealousy,
  Anger (wrath),
  Hatred,
  Vengeance,
  Mercy,
  Others?

Is God distinct and separate from the world he created?

Is God knowable to us?

Can God take or has God ever taken human form?

3.   Why do you believe in God? Or why *don't* you?

Søren Kierkegaard (1813–1855), one of the most important philosophers of modern times, is often recognized as the father of **existentialism**. He lived his entire life in Copenhagen, and after a short period of wild living and then a brief engagement to be married he devoted his life to spelling out "what it means to be a Christian." His basic point: To be religious is to make a passionate, individual choice, a *"leap of faith"* against all evidence, even against reason itself. Faith is something personal, not a matter of doctrine, churches, social groups, or ceremonies.

The thing is to understand myself, to see what God really wishes me to do; the thing is to find a truth which is true for me, to find the idea for which I can live and die.

— Søren Kierkegaard, *Journals*
(at the age of twenty-two)

Believing in God

In most Western philosophies, the idea of God is one of the most important single concerns. It is God who ultimately makes sense of the universe, who gives life meaning. If we believe that life ought to be fair, for example, many thinkers hold that it is important to believe that there is some powerful being who will make things come out in some fair way—if not in this life, then in another. To believe in God allows a person to have that confidence; not to believe takes it away. Thus, the French philosopher Camus believed passionately in justice but felt that, because he was also an atheist, there could be no guarantee (in fact there was little likelihood) that justice would ever be realized. And so he concluded that life is "absurd," and that any meaning to be found in life must come from our struggling against the unfairness and rationality we found in it.

On the other hand, many people believe in God just because they cannot see, from their perspective, any ultimate justice in the universe. Again, it is God who makes sense of things, despite the apparent "absurdity" of life. The book of Job, in which God allows all sorts of misfortune to afflict a completely innocent man, makes this point powerfully, and the Danish philosopher Søren Kierkegaard used it to prove that "the absurd" that we encounter—far from leading to **atheism**—is the premise of true faith in God.

We begin this chapter with a brief discussion of what it means to believe in God, which is followed by a review of various traditional Western conceptions of God, as well as a few nontraditional alternatives. We then consider one of the major reasons that some people do not believe in God, the problem posed by the presence of evil in the world, and some of the solutions proposed by theists. Next we will look at some of the "proofs" that have been offered for the existence of God as well as arguments against using this strategy to bolster belief.

How Do I Think About Religion?

For the following questions, check each statement that applies to you.

I believe what I do (about religion) because

☐ **1.** I have thought about and justified it to myself.

☐ **2.** It gives my life meaning.

☐ **3.** It sounds good to other people.

☐ **4.** I've never really thought about it.

☐ **5.** My parents told me so.

When I go to a religious service, I feel

☐ **1.** Awed and overwhelmed by emotion.

☐ **2.** Peaceful and joyful.

☐ **3.** Comfortable and secure.

☐ **4.** Nothing in particular.

☐ **5.** Uncomfortable, bored, or angry.

(continues)

How Do I Think About Religion? (*continued*)

Hearing talk or reading about "spirituality"

☐ **1.** Makes me think long and hard about what it means.

☐ **2.** Reminds me of what is really important.

☐ **3.** Makes me think less of the speaker–author's intelligence.

☐ **4.** Turns me off.

☐ **5.** Makes me crazy.

Organized religion and religious institutions

☐ **1.** Are the only true vehicles for spiritual values.

☐ **2.** Embody the spiritual identity of a community.

☐ **3.** Are important social, not spiritual, institutions.

☐ **4.** Are contrary to the true idea of religion.

☐ **5.** Are socially irresponsible, parasitic institutions.

Adapted from George Fowler's
"Religious Consumer Index."

To believe that God exists is not the same as to believe in God. The eighteenth-century philosopher Voltaire, for example, said he believed in God as a hypothesis for physics because there had to be some initial force to start up the universe, which Voltaire believed to be like a giant watch, ruled over by Isaac Newton's laws of motion. But Voltaire also said that "God is no more just or moral than he is blue or square." In other words, God played no role in his view of life and its values at all; God had nothing to do with justice or reward and punishment, nothing to do with the rules of morality, and nothing to do with the meaning of life. But the book of Job and Kierkegaard's philosophy make it quite clear that belief in God is not necessarily tied to a conviction that the just will be rewarded and the wicked punished. According to Kierkegaard, believing in God gives life meaning even if we can't make sense of apparent unfairness in life; meaning must be found in a profound and passionate faith, not in a mere factual belief in the existence of some superior being. Kierkegaard's view suggests that believing in God, as a matter of great importance to our view of life, is not just a matter of intellectually accepting the proposition that God exists. It is also having a matter of passion, a sense that God that somehow matters to us and that we in turn matter to God, too.

Voltaire (1694–1778) was the leading philosopher of the French **Enlightenment**. He was a skilled critic and a dedicated political reformer who used his connections with the courts of Europe and the aristocracies of France and England to promote religious tolerance and other enlightened reforms. He was continuously at war with the Catholic Church in France. Although he was not an atheist but rather a **deist** (see p. 80), he rejected Christianity as an institution and once bragged, "I am tired of hearing how only twelve men established the Christian church; I should like to show that only one can destroy it."

Gods and Goddesses

This feeling, that the universe is not a mere It to us but a Thou, forced on us we know not whence, that by obstinately believing that there are gods (although not to do so would be so easy both for our logic and our life) we are doing the universe the deepest service we can, seems part of the living essence of the religious hypothesis.

—William James, 1902

When a Western person says he or she does or does not believe in God, we can usually assume that the God in question is some loosely defined Supreme Being drawn from the the Christian or the Hebrew Bible or the Qur'an. According to this traditional conception, God is a spiritual being, infinitely intelligent and infinitely powerful. God knows everything (including everything that will happen at any time in the future), and God can do anything—change the course of history, make the sun stand still, bring the dead back to life, part the waters of the Red Sea, enter into the human world as a seemingly ordinary person, and so on.

To gain some perspective on our own religious beliefs, it is important to appreciate the variety of beliefs, and the variety of gods and goddesses, that have satisfied the religious urge throughout history. There are religions—Buddhism, for example—that do not include a concept of God in anything like our own sense. There are a great many religions that place far more emphasis on ritual and community activity than our sometimes very contemplative and faith-oriented religions. There are religions that distribute the various functions of our God among a large number of gods and goddesses—for example, the gods and goddesses of the ancient Greeks, Romans, and northern European peoples.

In some ancient religions, the question "Who is your God?" had a very specific meaning: it meant, which gods or goddesses do you particularly pray to and rely upon? This might depend, in turn, on the city you lived in because each town or city had its own patron deity. It might depend on your family and what you did for a living. Farmers would tend to worship the goddess of the harvest;

a blacksmith would tend to worship the god of metalworking (Vulcan, in Roman mythology). In times of war, the gods and goddesses would typically choose sides; for instance, in the Trojan War, according to Homer, some chose the cause of the Greeks, others the side of the Trojans, and they often intervened in the battle itself, directing an arrow to its mark or otherwise helping or hindering one side or the other.

In the Judeo-Christian and Islamic traditions, there is only one God, not several. (This is called **monotheism**, as opposed to the **polytheism** of many other cultures.) But our conceptions of the one God have changed significantly over the past two thousand years, and even within the Bible, which was written over the course of a thousand years or so, the conception of God changes dramatically. Even in the Hebrew Bible, the Old Testament, despite the emphasis on God as the Supreme Being, the existence of other, lesser deities is acknowledged in the commandment, "I am the Lord your God, and you shall not have strange gods before me." Our ideas about how a person relates to God have changed even more significantly. To say that a person "believes in God," therefore, is not enough. We must also know which *conception* of God he or she has in mind.

Greek God(dess)	Roman God(dess)	Norse God(dess)	Function
Zeus	Jupiter	Odin	King
Hera	Juno	Freyja	Queen
Ares	Mars	Tyr	War God
Athena	Minerva	—	Wisdom
Aphrodite	Venus	Frija	Love Goddess
Poseidon	Neptune	Aegir	Sea
Hermes	Mercury	Loki	Trickster God
—	Janus	Heimdall	God of Beginnings

The Traditional Western Conceptions of God

It is essential to see our own conception(s) of God in social, historical, and cultural perspective. This does not mean that one should no longer believe that his or her God is the "true" God, but it does mean that one should not pretend that his or her conception is the only one possible. Even a religious belief has a particular set of origins, a set of social interests, and a distinct cultural perspective.

Does God Look Human?

In a 1987 poll, *People* magazine reported that 55 percent of its readers stated they thought that God looked human, 27 percent said "not at all"; only 18 percent admitted that they "didn't know."

In the Judeo-Christian and Islamic traditions, there is but one God (although in most sects of Christianity God is characterized as a "Trinity" of "Father, Son, and Holy Spirit"). He is distinctively a male God. And our conception of God is inevitably **anthropomorphic**, at least to some extent—that is, we describe God in terms of our own attributes. The Greek and Roman gods and goddesses were almost wholly anthropomorphic, in the sense that they had almost all the usual human characteristics, except that they were more powerful, they were immortal, and they could do some things that most humans wouldn't dream of doing. (Zeus could change himself into a swan or a bull, for example, and all of the gods and goddesses used their powers at times to transform people into different kinds of plants and animals.) The Greek gods and goddesses often misbehaved—they became jealous and vengeful when their love was thwarted; they sulked and behaved childishly.

Syncretism: The Merger of Religions

Religions do not remain the same when they travel. Here is an account of "syncretism" (a kind of merger) in the arrival of Christianity into Mexico.

In the area of religion, syncretism refers to the developmental process in which different or originally contradictory beliefs and practices are combined into new religious doctrines or belief systems. The conversion of the indigenous people of the New World to Christianity was not a simple affair in which the ancient religious beliefs completely disappeared while the Christian doctrines were accepted wholeheartedly. Instead, a syncretism between native and Christian beliefs occurred, which gave rise to a new religious perspective that included doctrinal and ritualistic elements of both traditions. The impetus for this syncretistic process often came from the efforts of mestizo (people of mixed Indian and Spanish blood) or Indian communities. The reason for this may lie in the fact that members of these communities had a stronger need to find a basis for identifying with the new religion; or perhaps it was an attempt to retain some measure of dignity and cultural solidarity in a situation in which they were politically, economically, and culturally disfranchised.

(continues)

> **Syncretism: The Merger of Religions (*continued*)**
>
> *One of the most prominent cases of syncretism involves the appearance of the Virgen de Guadalupe to a poor Indian named Juan Diego at the hill of Tepeyac near Mexico City. The dark-skinned Virgin spoke to him in Nahuatl, the language of the Aztecs, and told him that a shrine should be built on the site of her appearance. When Juan Diego notified the archbishop of his experiences, his story was met with skepticism. But the Virgin appeared to him a second time and instructed him to pick some roses in a nearby area (even though it was not the season when roses could bloom) and take them to the archbishop as proof of her appearance. Juan Diego followed her instructions and placed the roses in his cloak. When he extended his cloak to show the archbishop the roses, both men were amazed to see that the image of the Virgin was miraculously imprinted on it. This incident convinced the archbishop of the truth of Juan Diego's story, and what is now the most famous basilica in Mexico was built at the bottom of the hill of Tepeyac. Juan Diego's cloak now hangs on the high altar of the basilica of the Virgen de Guadalupe.*
>
> — Jorge Valadez, American philosopher, 1993

The God of the Judeo-Christian and Islamic traditions still retains essential anthropomorphic features. As children, some of us are taught through illustrations in Sunday school books that God is a kindly old man with a long white beard much as he is shown in Michelangelo's famous painting on the ceiling of the Sistine Chapel in Rome. And even as adults, we are taught to attribute some very human emotions to God—for example, in the Bible, God is sometimes said to be a "jealous God," who wreaks vengeance on those who do not believe in him or listen to his commandments. Lot's wife, for instance, is turned into a pillar of salt for disobeying the command not to look back at the burning city, and Jonah is devoured by a "big fish" for not obeying God's order to warn an offensive city that it should change its ways. Yet God is said to be characterized by infinite love, compassion, and patience.

Throughout the Bible, it is made clear that although God has many human attributes, some of these differ from our own not only in degree but also in kind: God feels not just a sense of love and justice but also an *infinite* sense of love and justice, which we cannot comprehend. Indeed, one of the features of Christianity as it has developed is the strong emphasis on the **mystery** of God, the fact that it is impossible for us to understand him or comprehend his ways. And yet, it is also part of the traditional conception of God in the major Western religions that he listens to our prayers and cares about us. God is also described as a rational being. Yet perhaps the most blatant evidence of the continuing anthropomorphizing of God is our insistence on using the pronoun *he* to refer to *him*. Why should we think that God has sex (or gender)? Many men and women are now challenging this traditional, patriarchal conception of God, charging that thinking of God as male is more a matter of politics than religion.

Despite the fact that the central tenet of the Judeo-Christian and Islamic traditions is the existence of *one* God, we must be fully appreciative of the rich variety of conceptions of this one God throughout our long history. From the somewhat picture-book image of God as a kindly old man who is prone to jealousy and rage and has his "chosen people," we have evolved an enormous variety of complex and abstract philosophical ideas about God. Among these are the idea that "God is love" in 1 John 4:8; the image of God as a continuously active creator in the philosophy of Saint Thomas Aquinas; and the conception of God as merely the first principle of physics in the thinking of Voltaire, Thomas Jefferson, and some other eighteenth-century deists (see p. 80). Some people conceive of God as a distant mystery, an ideal we long for through our lives, but never encounter or really "know." Other people conceive of God as an immediate presence that they feel in their lives virtually every waking moment. Some people claim to know God through a personal relationship (for instance, through the person of Jesus); for others, God is an abstract force, an impersonal cosmic power, perhaps simply identical to the universe itself. To say that one believes in God is therefore not yet to say which conception of God.

Both as the author of the Declaration of Independence and as the third president of the United States, **Thomas Jefferson** (1743–1826) wrote on many subjects, some of which are philosophical.

German religious reformer **Martin Luther** (1483–1546) was a Roman Catholic monk, priest, and theologian who led the Protestant Reformation. Stressing personal faith over church ritual, he was excommunicated from the Roman Catholic Church in 1521.

God as Transcendent

Much of our traditional conception of God emphasizes God as **transcendent**— that is, *beyond* the ordinary world of human experience, outside of ourselves and distinct from the world he created. In the Old Testament, God existed before creating the universe and still exists outside of it. But if God is outside of ordinary human experience, intervening in human affairs only on rare instances, how is it that we are able to know of God's existence, and how are we able to relate to God at all? Some people would not see knowing God as a problem because they would also see God as present everywhere and all-knowing, revealing himself to anyone who believes in him. Others see it as a serious problem, and find the effort to reach out to God to be one of the monumental tasks of life. Still other people, though believing in God, would say that we cannot know him at all but simply must have faith. And some people would say that, in general, we cannot know God, but, on rare occasions, we can indeed have a more or less direct experience of God, and those experiences—**mystical** experiences—are enough to sustain us, even for a lifetime. (*Mystical* does not mean *mysterious;* it refers to an immediate experience of a direct, intimate union with God. [See p. 96.])

Relating to God is another question. One view is that we cannot know God personally but that we can know him and relate to him through his earthly representations—the church, certain important people (the pope for Catholics, the king in some national conceptions of religion), through the Bible or other scriptures, or through the teachings of certain more recent figures. Another view is that the knowledge of God and our relationship to him must be direct and personal. The German churchman **Martin Luther** (1483–1546), who initially sought to reform the Catholic church from within, initiated the **Reformation** in Christianity, for example, partly because he saw the church as interfering with the direct relationship between the individual and God. The Danish philosopher Søren Kierkegaard, on the other hand, rejected even the influence of Luther's Reformation because, in his mind, the Lutheran Church still interfered with what he considered to be the most crucial element in religious belief, the purely *personal* relationship between the individual and God, not based on or helped along by any church or community of believers.

Certain recent Christian thinkers have interpreted the idea of having a relationship to God in terms of relationships to other human beings. The Jesuit theologian Karl Rahner (1904–1984), for example, describes God as an "absolute mystery" that we cannot understand and cannot properly be conceived of as a "person" in our finite sense. Nevertheless, we can relate to God because we have been created in such a way that being inclined toward God is a structural aspect of what we are as human beings. This is evident in our continual tendency to keep moving our (metaphorical) gaze beyond what is immediately in front of us toward something beyond it and our reaching, ultimately, toward God. We have the choice of accepting or rejecting God through our choices in everyday life, especially in relation to other people. A critic of this view might consider Rahner's account as reducing religion to ethics, but Rahner would respond that the reverse is the case: he shows ethics to have a spiritual dimension. Although his conception of God is transcendent, our way of responding to God is through our thoroughly immanent responses to other human beings.

God as Immanent

Although he claims that we relate to God in our everyday acts and encounters with others, Rahner considers God to be transcendent. His view can be classified as an instance of **panentheism**, the belief that although God transcends the world, God nevertheless dwells within every part it. Protestant theologian Marcus Borg has recently defended panentheism as offering a conception of God that draws attention to God's nearness and putting the focus of religion on relationship, not on belief as such. Borg explicitly rejects the idea that God cannot be both transcendent and immanent, and he sees panentheism as a coherent theory that can do a better job of informing spiritual life than do traditional concepts that consider God to be distant from us.

Some people, however, do not believe that God is transcendent in any respect. They hold, rather, that he is an **immanent** God, a God *not* outside of us or distinct from the universe. The view that God has an immanent reality has been formulated in many different ways, including the Christian conception of the incarnation of God as a man and the idea of a Holy Spirit that infuses us all. Some thinkers, however, hold a more extreme position, according to which God is simply identical to the cosmos as a whole.

If one holds that God is completely immanent, the problem of our knowledge of God and relation to him more or less resolves itself because we do not have to "reach out" at all, but can simply look within ourselves to find God. Difficult questions still arise, however. What aspects of our experience are relevant to perceiving God? Loving another person? A deep experience of faith? (And how do you know when it is really faith, as opposed to some nonreligious but still very powerful, experience?) Feeling a pang of conscience? Feeling awe during a thunderstorm or while gazing at the Grand Canyon?

Which Side Is God On?

The Divine Law is against communism.

— E. F. Landgrebe

Fascism is God's cause.

— Arthur Cardinal Hinsley

God did not mean for women to vote.

— Grover Cleveland

God loves you. God doesn't want anyone to be hungry and oppressed. He just puts his big arms around everybody and hugs them up against himself.

— Norman Vincent Peale

God ordained the separation of the races.

— Reverend Billy James Hargis

Who says I am not under the special protection of God?

— Adolf Hitler

(continues)

Which Side Is God On? (*continued*)

God has marked the American people as His chosen nation.

— Senator Albert Beveridge

There never was a lawgiver who did not resort to divine authority.

— Machiavelli

None of us is here by accident. Behind the diligence of our staffs, supporters, and our own individual campaign efforts, behind the votes of the people, we recognize divine appointment.

—Reverend Richard Halverson,
opening the predominantly
Republican United States
Senate session of 1981

Other Religions—Other Alternatives

More than three thousand years old, **Hinduism** does not place the unique emphasis on the one God that the Semitic religions do; in fact some Vedantic (Hindu) sects do not include any conception of God. There is simply a conception of ultimate reality (**Brahman**), which is impersonal, with no special concern for human beings. Hinduism is often thought to be a polytheistic religion, but in fact theistic Hinduism stresses a singular divine reality that can take many forms. Instead of the all-important emphasis on historical revelation (to Moses, to Saint Paul, to Muhammad), Hinduism stresses revelation and wisdom within each individual, which involves the recognition and the feeling of being "one" with the whole of the cosmos (*samadhi*).

Buddhism developed from Hinduism (Buddha was the son of an Indian king in the sixth century BCE). It teaches that dissatisfaction is the universal condition of human existence because of our continuous insistence on self and individuality. Relief from suffering and ultimate peace (nirvana) becomes possible when we give up these notions. **Zen Buddhism**, a more recent development (seventh century CE), evolved first in China and then moved (with great success) to Japan. Zen stresses the importance of meditation and direct master-student teaching. It has become quite popular in the United States in the past half century.

God as Totally Immanent: Pantheism

There have been a number of conceptions of God as immanent, as within us or as identical to the universe. Perhaps the simplest and most powerful of these conceptions is a view called **pantheism**. The most famous Western defender of pantheism is the seventeenth-century Jewish philosopher **Baruch Spinoza** (1632–1677), who insisted, in a simple phrase, that God is *everything*, identical to the universe itself. Spinoza's aim was to develop a conception of God that would not involve that terrible distance between ourselves and the Supreme Being, and that would leave room for any number of different religions and conceptions of God without insisting that any one of them was the only "true" religion. In Spinoza's view, *we* are God, though not as individuals, nor even humanity as a whole; we are an integral part of the whole of the universe (or what Spinoza called the "One Substance") and thus an integral part of God as well. (According to Spinoza, God has an infinite number of attributes, of which we know only two—mind and body.) In one of his more striking images, Spinoza suggested that each of us is like a tiny worm in the blood inside the body of some great being. We see only our immediate surroundings and tend to treat that alone as reality, with some vague idea of some greater being "outside of us." But, in fact, we are *part* of that great being, and once we appreciate this, we transcend our limited perceptions and our idea of something outside of us and instead come to see ourselves as part and parcel of that great being. The being, in this case, is the whole of the universe. And believing in God, for Spinoza, is actually coming to realize what we really are, not discovering the existence of something beyond our experience that we ourselves are not part of.

It is worth mentioning, however, that Spinoza's views were not well received, even in his native Holland, in his time the most liberal and religiously tolerant nation in Europe. His insistence on religious tolerance was too extreme, and his own views too unusual. He was exiled from the orthodox religious community in which he had grown up, and his works were banned for Christians and Jews alike until well after his death. And despite his devout beliefs, he was called an "atheist" because, in his view, God could not have created the universe (because he was the universe) and praying to God—as opposed to simply believing in God— makes no sense. One lesson to be learned from Spinoza, more than anything else, is that intolerance has, throughout history, greeted virtually all innovations in conceptions of God, even those that are proposed by unquestionably religious people. For most people, it is not just believing in God that counts, but believing in the "right" God—that is, the right conception of God, even if, as Spinoza argued, it is one and the same God for all of us.

Spinoza's pantheism has its parallels in some Eastern religions—in some forms of Buddhism, for example, in which the idea of a God separate from the universe is not even intelligible because nothing exists as a separate reality; all is connected. In Hinduism, too, Brahman (the fundamental divine reality) is everywhere, even in animals and in lower forms of life. But the religious perspective of pantheism renders somewhat confusing our usual question, "Do you believe in God?" If God is identical to the universe as a whole, then what is the difference

God in Everyday Life

The ordinary believer does not, however, report an awareness of God as existing in isolation from all other objects of experience. His consciousness of the divine does not involve a cessation of his consciousness of a material and social environment. It is not a vision of God in solitary glory, filling the believer's entire mind and blotting out his normal field of perception. . . . The believer meets God not only in moments of worship, but also when through the urgings of conscience he feels the pressure of the divine demand upon his life; when through the gracious actions of his friends he apprehends the divine grace; when through the marvels and beauties of nature he traces the hand of the Creator; and he has increasing knowledge of the divine purpose as he responds to its behest in his own life. In short, it is not apart from the course of mundane life, but in it and through it, that the ordinary religious believer claims to experience, however imperfectly and fragmentarily, the divine presence and activity.

—John Hick,
Faith and Knowledge, 1957

between believing in God and believing in the existence of the universe? Perhaps an atheist can respond: "I believe in the universe, but I do not see any reason for calling it 'God.'" But the religious attitudes and discipline of Spinoza, the Buddhists, and nontheistic Hindus show that such a view cannot be sufficient, for there is an enormous difference between an atheist who simply believes in the existence of the universe and a pantheist who believes that the universe is divine. What is this difference? One might say that it is a difference of *attitude.* What the atheist and the pantheist believe in (namely, the existence of the universe) might in a narrow sense be the same, but the way they look at it and act in it is entirely different. But this changes religious *belief in something* into a religious *attitude toward everything,* and the idea of believing in God, accordingly, changes radically.

Baruch Spinoza was born in an Orthodox Jewish community in Amsterdam in 1632. His parents had been refugees from the Spanish Inquisition, and Spinoza spent his entire life fighting for religious tolerance. He was thoroughly educated in both Jewish and medieval Christian philosophy, but his unorthodox opinions caused him to be banished from his native Amsterdam, despite the fact that Holland was then the most liberal country in Europe. His books were banned and he spent much of his life working as a lens grinder. The lens dust made him fatally ill and he died in 1677. His whole philosophy is based on the conception that the world and God are a single unity, and all of us are part of that unity. (See also Chapter 4.)

God as Universal Spirit

A related conception of God—the idea of God as **Spirit**—was defended by G. W. F. Hegel. But where Spinoza argued that God is identical to the universe in an eternal way, Hegel painted a much more dynamic and complex picture, in which we humans are essentially the primary *expressions* of spirit, which acts *through* us and even *uses* us for its own purposes. But spirit is, at the same time, not to be thought of as different from us. To make sense of this, think of yourself as being on the football team or even as one of the loyal fans at the game. You are imbued and inspired by what we call "team spirit." You find yourself caught up by the enthusiasm of the game, as if something has taken hold of you, and indeed it has. What we call "spirit" is not some alien force that invades you but rather the emotional connection you feel with everyone else in the stadium, the excitement of the game, your shared enthusiasm. Now imagine that picture enlarged to include all of humanity and a shared "team spirit" of sorts that you share just by being human, a kind of enthusiasm for life. That is what Hegel meant by "Spirit"; it is bigger than any of us, but not something distinct from us. And that, for him, is God.

Hegel on Spirit

The significance of that absolute commandment; Know thyself—whether we look at it in itself or under the historical circumstances of its first utterance— is not to promote mere self-knowledge in respect of the particular capacities, character, propensities and foibles of the individual self. The knowledge it commands means that of man's genuine reality—of what is essentially and ultimately true and real—of Spirit as the true and essential being.

—*Encyclopedia of the Philosophical Sciences*, 1817

The goal, which is absolute Knowledge or Spirit knowing itself as Spirit, finds its pathway in the recollection of spiritual forms as they are in themselves and as they accomplish the organization of their spiritual kingdom.

—*Phenomenology of Spirit*, 1807

God as Process

Hegel's notion of Spirit was not only all-expansive with regard to the universe, it was also expansive in the dimension of *time*. One of Hegel's bold suggestions was that God as universal spirit cannot be comprehended just in terms of God's present existence—as a being of a certain sort at a certain time—but must be comprehended through a long period of development, as a **process**. In other words, it is not as if God has always been what he is now, but he is rather in the process of **becoming**. One might say that God is constantly creating himself—and the universe as well. This means, for example, that the continuing battle between "creationists" and "evolutionists" may be a false fight, for God's own existence is an evolutionary process. In some respects, this is an extremely ancient religious idea. The ancient Egyptian monotheist **Akhnaton** (1353–1336 BCE) argued that God was continually self-creating. Buddhism has long argued that ultimate reality (they would not call this God) must be understood in terms of process and not in merely static, eternal terms. In contemporary times, the process view of God has been defended by philosopher **Charles Hartshorne**.

> More than three thousand years separate the births of Egyptian thinker **Akhnaton** (1353–1336 BCE) and American philosopher **Charles Hartshorne** (1897–2000), but both believed that God was constantly self-creating.

> Teacher of Napoleon, the French mathematician and astronomer **Pierre-Simon Laplace** (1749–1827) rejected the attenuated conception of God put forward by the deists.

God as Transcendent Creator: Deism

The perspective of the French philosopher Voltaire was far removed from that of such thinkers as Rahner and Borg, whose conceptions of God emphasized relationship. Voltaire defended a conception of God as a necessary hypothesis for physics. Although he considered himself an enemy of the church, Voltaire found atheism unthinkable, and he sharply criticized his intellectual friends who did not believe in God. But Voltaire's belief in God was, from most Christian points of view, extremely limited. Not only did he not believe in Christ and most of the doctrines and dogmas of Christianity, but he also did not even believe that God had any personal or human-like attributes. God could not be said to be just, or wise, or merciful. He could not be said to be loving, or jealous, or concerned with what happens to us. Voltaire would not be impressed by arguments from believers that "we simply can't understand God's nature." If you believe in God and defend yourself in this way, Voltaire can respond, "See, you agree with me. God is not just, merciful, loving, and so on." You might want to qualify your statement and say that "God is just, but God's justice is infinite, and we can't always understand his ways." To say, instead, that we cannot understand God at all, that our human word *justice* does not apply to him in any sense, and that "his ways" are beyond our comprehension is to raise the question of how we are to characterize our belief. Voltaire insists that we give up the "superstitions" of anthropomorphism, but with this he loses the conception of God as a moral being and as a *personal* God. The view that God created the world but has no further role in it is called **deism**.

Voltaire's view reduced the conception of God to the minimum, and it was not long before another Frenchman, the great scientist **Pierre-Simon Laplace**

(1749–1827), was heard to say (to the emperor Napoleon), "I have no need of any such hypothesis." To believe in God simply as an initial creative force is to believe much less than what is required even for what many of us would consider the most rudimentary religious belief. A God who is conceived of as an impersonal force, indifferent to the concerns of human beings, is not a God to be worshipped, not a God who gives meaning to our lives. In many people's opinion (both theists and atheists), such a force is not worth the name "God" at all.

God as the Unknown Object of Faith

As we noted earlier, **Søren Kierkegaard** rejected the idea that the Christian church (or any church) is a necessary intermediary between ourselves and God. He attacked what he sarcastically called "Christendom" and the "Christian hordes" for their hypocrisy. For them, he complained, "being a Christian" just meant that their parents were Christians, that they went to church occasionally, and that they nodded their unthinking assent whenever anyone asked, "Do you believe in God?" According to Kierkegaard, being a Christian or being "religious" in general was not *something* in your life; it had to be *everything*. Believing in God was not a matter for intellectual debate; Kierkegaard had nothing but disdain for those theologians who spent their time trying to prove that God exists. In one of his powerful aphorisms, he commented, "To stand on one leg and prove God's existence is a very different thing from going down on one's knees and thanking Him."

God as the Unknown: Kierkegaard

But what is this unknown something with which the Reason collides when inspired by its paradoxical passion, with the result of unsettling even man's knowledge of himself? It is the Unknown. It is not a human being, in so far as we know what man is; nor is it any other known thing. So let us call this unknown something: the God. It is nothing more than a name we assign to it. The idea of demonstrating that this unknown something (the God) exists, could scarcely suggest itself to the Reason. For if the God does not exist it would of course be impossible to prove it; and if he does exist it would be folly to attempt it.

— From *Philosophical Fragments*, 1844

For Kierkegaard, being a Christian was a matter of total **commitment**, requiring what he called a **leap of faith**. One could not *know* God. One could not know that God existed or anything about him. But one had to act as confidently *as if* one were absolutely certain of his existence, in an intimately personal relationship (like a son and his father or even, Kierkegaard suggested, like two lovers). God is the great unknown, Kierkegaard said, but at the same time one had to believe that God was totally familiar and immediately present. Indeed, Kierkegaard was so vehemently against the idea of *knowing* God (that is, in an abstract, intellectual way) that he rejected the whole of Christian **theology** and its attempts to develop a rational and comprehensible conception of God. Instead, he said that any adequate conception of God is thoroughly incomprehensible and irrational. What is important is therefore not our conception of God but the *passion* with which we believe in him. Again, we can raise the question, "Believe in *what*?" But Kierkegaard would say that such questions are not only irrelevant but also contrary to religious feeling. He stated, "If anyone succeeded in making Christianity plausible, on that day Christianity would be squashed," and "When faith begins to lose its passion, proof becomes necessary in order to command respect from unbelief." In other words, trying to understand God is antithetical to believing in him, and rationality only gets in the way of faith. Nevertheless, although Kierkegaard rejected the idea of having a conception of God, he had a distinctive conception of what it is to be religious. So despite his attacks on philosophy, he was very much a philosopher, offering us a radical conception of what it is to believe in God.

God as a Moral Being

Of all the characteristics that have been attributed to God, one set stands out above the rest. Whether you believe that God created the universe, that he once entered into human form as Christ, that he once parted the Red Sea, or that he is a transcendent being or an immanent spirit, what makes religion so important in many people's lives are the *moral* features of God, his care for justice and his concern for us. This is what makes Voltaire's conception of God so unimportant and trivial; it is what makes Kierkegaard's conception so all-important and vital. In terms of the Hebrew Bible or the Old Testament, perhaps the single most important lesson, repeated on virtually every page, is that God is a moral being who has given us laws—the Ten Commandments in particular but thousands of other commands, too. In the New Testament, the most important message, again repeated on almost every page, is that God *cares*, that God is the Divine Judge, concerned with virtue and evil on earth, who punishes the wicked and rewards the good. Indeed, even if one doesn't believe in God as primarily a divine judge who issues rewards and punishments, it is basic to the traditional idea of God to consider God as a moral being, as a being who cares, not an indifferent force in the universe.

Thus, in virtually all conceptions of God, among the most important questions (apart from whether you believe or not) are: What *moral* characteristics does God have? How much does he care about us? What will he do for us? Will he answer our prayers? (And which ones? Probably not our angry childhood prayer that the kid down the block be struck down by lightning. But what about our prayers for a more peaceful world, or for the strength to carry on through some ordeal, or to be cured of some terrible affliction?) What are God's laws? (He says, "Thou shalt not kill." Does that mean never? Except in war? Except in some [so-called just] wars?) And, perhaps most important of all, what is God's role in controlling the amount of suffering and evil here on earth? Indeed, this problem has struck most philosophers and religious thinkers as so important that an entire field has grown up around it: it is generally known as the **problem of evil**.

The Problem of Evil

The problem of evil begins with the main ingredient in most of our conceptions of God: simply stated, God is good. But this conception seems to be at odds with one obvious fact about the world—evil and suffering flourish. Now, it doesn't much matter how you understand "God is good," whether you think that means that God watches over us every minute and protects us from harm, or that God created us and so cares for us in some general way. The point of the conception is that God does care about us and therefore cares what happens to us. But if this is so, why is there so much evil and suffering in the world, even among young and innocent children?

The argument can be filled out in the following way. First, we can summarize the traditional Western conception of God in three statements:

1. God is all-powerful;

2. God is all-knowing; *and*

3. God is good.

But if there is evil in the world, then, so the argument goes, one of three things must be true:

1. He can't do anything about it;

2. He doesn't know about it; *or*

3. He doesn't care about it.

But all of these possibilities are contradictory to the traditional conception of God, and so our problem remains unresolved.

Denial of God

This argument has prompted an enormous number of responses. One is to conclude that God does not exist because to deserve the name "God" a Supreme Being must have all three features in the first list. But there are many ways of defending belief in God against this argument, and it is fair to say that every theistic philosopher who has ever written has felt obliged to respond to the problem of evil in one way or another.

Two Kinds of Evil

The first move for many philosophers has been to distinguish *moral* from *nonmoral* evil, in which moral evil is the product of our actions and intentions and nonmoral evil consists of natural disasters and "acts of God." The evil of the Holocaust and the murder of millions of Jews, Gypsies, Catholics, and other minorities was a moral evil. The great earthquake of Lisbon in 1755, in which thousands of innocent people were killed while they sat in church on Sunday morning, is a nonmoral evil. Most arguments aimed at solving the problem of evil focus on one or the other of these.

The Death of God: Nietzsche

The Madman.—Have you ever heard of the madman who on a bright morning lighted a lantern and ran to the marketplace calling out unceasingly: "I seek God! I seek God!"—As there were many people standing about who did not believe in God, he caused a great deal of amusement. Why! is he lost? said one. Has he strayed away like a child? said another. Or does he keep himself hidden? Is he afraid of us? Has he taken a sea-voyage? Has he emigrated?—the people cried out laughingly, all in a hubbub. The insane man jumped into their midst and transfixed them with his glances. "Where is God gone?" he called out. "I mean to tell you! We have killed him—you and I! We are all his murderers!"

— From *The Gay Science,* 1882
— From *The Complete Works of Nietzsche,* ed.
Oscar Levy, vol. 10 (T. Foulix, 1910).

Denial of Evil

One answer to the problem of evil is to say that, contrary to appearances, there is no evil or suffering. This response requires pretending that nothing is wrong. (It is always easier to do this regarding other people's troubles rather than your own, of course.) For example, there have been people who have asserted—despite all evidence to the contrary—that the Nazis did not in fact murder millions of Jews. (Others, not surprisingly, have responded that such denials are themselves evil and cause irreparable harm.) Some people deny that war is evil, even insisting that *everyone* killed or injured in a war—not only soldiers but civilian adults and children—somehow *deserved* it. But this is a solution that becomes more and more implausible and insensitive the more we look at it.

Many people who suffer do so because of their own errors, of course, so arguably this suffering does not reflect on God's goodness. But many who suffer did not bring their problems on themselves, especially children who starve to death or are murdered in war. You might say, "They are being punished for their parents' sins," but this would hardly count as justice. Justice, whether human or divine, means punishing the person who deserves it, not someone else. Would you think it fair if one of your parents or grandparents got a reckless-driving citation from the police, and the authorities took away *your* driver's license? Justice, whether human or divine, means punishing the person who deserves it, not someone else.

A Few of God's Commandments: Old Testament and New

Old Testament

Honour thy father and thy mother . . .
Thou shalt not kill.
Thou shalt not commit adultery.
Thou shalt not steal.
Thou shalt not bear false witness against thy neighbour.
Thou shalt not covet thy neighbour's house, thou shalt not covet thy neighbour's wife, nor his manservant, nor his maidservant, nor his ox . . . nor any thing that is thy neighbour's.

— From Exodus 20:12–17

New Testament

"You have heard that it was said [to the men of old], 'An eye for an eye and a tooth for a tooth.' But I say to you, Do not resist one who is evil. But if any one strikes you on the right cheek, turn to him the other also; and if any one would sue you and take your coat, let him have your cloak, as well."

"You have heard that it was said, 'You shall love your neighbour and hate your enemy.' But I say to you, Love your enemies and pray for those who persecute you, so that you may be sons of your Father who is in heaven; for he makes his sun rise on the evil and on the good, and sends rain on the just and on the unjust . . . You, therefore, must be perfect, as your heavenly Father is perfect."

"Judge not, that you be not judged."

"So whatever you wish that men would do to you, do so to them; for this is the law and the prophets."

"You shall love the Lord your God with all your heart, and with all your soul, and with all your mind. This is the great and first commandment. And a second is like it. You shall love your neighbour as yourself. On these two commandments depend all the law and the prophets."

— Matthew 5:38–40, 43–48;
7:1, 12; 22:37–40

The Least of the Evils

Some people have said that God, in his wisdom, saw all the different ways the world could be and deemed that a certain amount of evil and suffering was required in all of them. Pain is needed, for example, to indicate when we are in danger, as when our skin comes in contact with fire. God chose the world with the *least* amount of suffering, or, in German philosopher Gottfried Wilhelm von

Leibniz's positive terms, "the best of all possible worlds." This solution requires a good deal of faith on our part because it is easy to imagine any number of small changes in the world that might make it a better world and would not appear to throw off the balance of things. One way of saying this is to agree that there must be *some* evil and suffering in the world, but *why so much*?

The least-of-all-evils position is that there is no more evil in the world than is necessary except, perhaps, for the evil that we bring on ourselves—that is, moral evil. (See "The Free-Will Solution" that follows shortly.) As for nonmoral evil—the catastrophes of nature or the "acts of God" that wreak havoc on so many lives—theologian-philosopher John Hick suggests that such events are "soul-building." They may make our lives less predictable and more tragic, but they also make us better people. This is a common interpretation of the book of Job, in which a good man is made to suffer to "test" his faith. A very different version of the "least of the evils" suggestion has been popularized by the American Rabbi Harold Kushner, according to which it is God's limited power that explains, as he puts it, "why bad things happen to good people." God is not omnipotent. says Kushner; neither is he cruel. His power is limited by the laws of nature, the extent to which human nature has evolved, and the moral freedom of human beings. Most traditional theists, however, would rather find the explanation in us or in our limited understanding than in God himself.

The Aesthetic Solution

An elegant variation on the least-of-the-evils type of solution—which is sometimes defended by those who argue that God is a process or, in the case of some nineteenth-century Romantics, a kind of cosmic artist—is the vision of a world that is defined by dramatic and aesthetic categories rather than by our rather limited insistence on personal well-being. Once again, this solution urges us to take in "the big picture" in order to see that the beauty and goodness of the whole depend in part on the shadows and tragedies that seem to us to be evil. By considering God as a process, what we consider evil in the world can be taken as essential steps in God's (and the world's) development. Traditionally such efforts to explain how the existence of evil is compatible with the existence of God have been termed **theodicies**. If we include the whole of history in our vision instead of simply the particular concerns of the present, we would see, according to the process view, that the evil in the world is in some sense a necessary part of the story and not an argument against God's existence or his goodness.

The Free-Will Solution

Another solution, perhaps the most powerful and controversial of all, is the so-called **free-will** solution—the argument that God created us with free will, the ability to do what we wanted to do. Accordingly, we have created the evil and suffering in the world ourselves, and it is no reflection on God's goodness. But the problems that have been pointed out in this solution are these: First, again, why so much evil and suffering; couldn't God have created us a little bit wiser and less reckless to begin with, still with free will but with a little more intelligence, compassion, and self-control? Second, if God created us with free will does that mean that he cannot interfere? If so, then that would seem to mean that he is not all-powerful. If he can interfere, then the question is why he does not (since our suffering often far outweighs our errors). And if he does interfere, then the question, once again, is whether we are really free at all. Third, if God is all-knowing and knew in advance what terrible misfortunes we would bring on ourselves, then why did he give us free will in the first place? Wouldn't we be much better off without it, preprogrammed by God to be good, kind, and considerate to each other? And fourth, even if one accepts the free-will solution, it still seems most unlikely that all the evil and suffering in the world are due to our own errors and abuse of our freedom. Innocent children have been killed by natural disasters while they sleep or even while they are praying in church. How could God have allowed (or caused) this to happen?

Justice in the Afterlife

Another solution is the appeal to some further court of justice, not in this life but later on, in which the good are rewarded and the wicked punished. But this raises problems, too: even if you believe in divine reward and punishment, the question of justice reemerges. Is it fair to allow an innocent man to suffer even if you intend to give him an elaborate reward later on? Is it fair to reward some people who have not had a chance to prove themselves (for example, infants who are killed in war), while other people have to spend a lifetime proving their moral worth? And if you believe that this life is in some sense a "test" for the next one, it is important to ask whether the is entirely fair (since some people in some societies do not even know that they are being tested) and whether a truly good God would his believers at all.

Consider the story of Job, mentioned above, one of the most celebrated case studies in the problem of evil. According to the biblical story, God permitted all kinds of terrible sufferings to afflict Job, who was a good man and believed in God wholeheartedly. Job's wife and children died, his life was ruined, and he developed all kinds of painful diseases. And why? Just to test him? Just to win a bet with the devil (as the biblical story suggests)? Is this justice? And does it make everything all right again if God at the end of the story restores to Job all that he has lost? Job's equanimity in the face of hardship may be one of the great expressions of faith of all time, but it does not answer—it only intensifies—the problem of evil.

God's "Mysterious Ways"

Some people have handled the problem of evil by an appeal to God's "mysterious ways." We do not understand why God does as he does, and we should not question him. But this answer is very much at odds with the need to know something about God in order to have reason to believe in him. Furthermore, is there *any* just interpretation of some of the more brutal stories in the Bible (for instance, the Job story or God's destruction of whole cities)? Sometimes we can understand what it is for a wise person to do something that we do not understand; he or she seems more in command of the situation than we are. But there are limits to how far we can stretch this sort of explanation, and when we cannot even imagine a sense in which a course of action is just, appealing to "mysterious ways" is no longer an answer to the problem but an admission that we have no idea how to deal with it.

Working Out an Answer

None of these responses is adequate in itself, but none of the objections given is final either. Indeed, the whole history of religion—Judaism and Islam, Buddhism and other Asian religions as well as Christianity—has been taken up with various attempts at answering this problem. So if your philosophy includes belief in God, it is essential that you determine what moral qualities you believe God has and whether these can be made compatible with the existence of evil and suffering in the world. If you do not believe in God, of course, the problem of evil will seem to you to be a final reply, a proof that there cannot be a God who is powerful and all-knowing and just and caring as well. But then you have to face the question of whether there is *any* reason for the evil and suffering in the world and any way for us to deal with it besides simply accepting it at face value.

Italian-born **Saint Anselm** of Canterbury (1033–1109) produced several influential texts of philosophical theology. His famous ontological argument for the existence of God in *Proslogion* (1078) borrows from **Augustine's** in *On the Free Choice of the Will* (395).

Faith and Reason: Grounds for Believing

For many believers, belief in God and knowledge of him was a matter of pure **reason**. Reason did not in any way contradict faith but rather supported it. The eleventh-century theologian **Saint Anselm**, for instance, developed a famous and ingenious "proof" of God's existence (which we will discuss shortly). The philosopher **Saint Thomas Aquinas** also developed a number of ways of proving God's existence and nature (which we will discuss also), and indeed much traditional theology and scholarship is dedicated to this view that knowledge of God is essentially **rational** and that we can know that he exists by examining our thoughts about him. On the other hand, there are believers, as we indicated before, who have insisted that God cannot be rationally known at all. As we have also already mentioned, there are mystics who believe that we can know God only through a special kind of experience that most people might never have and in which, if only for a moment, God seems to present himself to us directly. But how we believe we can relate to God of course depends on our conception of him. If we believe in a largely anthropomorphic, personal conception of God, then relating to him through prayers and reasonable requests makes perfectly good sense. If, on the other hand, our conception of God is of an all-embracing universal love or a great spirit who watches over the universe, then personal requests may be quite out of line.

Does It Matter Why It Is True?

Sophisticated computer calculations indicate that the biblical parting of the Red Sea, said to have allowed Moses and the Israelites to escape from bondage in Egypt, could have happened almost precisely as the Bible describes it in Exodus.

A moderate wind blowing constantly for about ten hours could have caused the sea to recede about a mile and the water level to drop ten feet, leaving dry land in the area where biblical scholars believe the crossing occurred. An abrupt change in the wind would have then allowed the waters to come crashing back in a few brief moments.

Does this support or undermine religious belief in the religious significance of this spectacular event?

— From an article from the
Los Angeles Times Service,
March 1992, and the
*Bulletin of the American
Meteorological Society*

Most of what we have said applies primarily to those who believe in *some* conception of God, but everything we have said applies just as well to atheists. If you do not believe in God, *which* conceptions of God do you *not* believe in? If you take references to God to indicate a wise old man who grants prayers and answers requests somewhat capriciously, your disbelief might well be justifiable by virtue of ordinary common sense. But suppose someone insists, rather, that the proper conception of God is of a vital force that keeps the world in existence or perhaps the existence of the universe itself; what would it be *not* to believe in God so conceived? To be an atheist, in other words, presupposes a conception of God just as much as to be a believer; it is just as much a question of what one does *not* believe as it is a question of what it is that one does believe.

The Cosmological Argument: Saint Thomas Aquinas

In the world of sense we find there is an order of efficient causes. There is no case known (neither is it, indeed, possible) in which a thing is found to be the efficient cause of itself; for so it would be prior to itself, which is impossible. Now in efficient causes it is not possible to go on to infinity, because in all efficient causes following in order, the first is the cause of the intermediate cause, and the intermediate is the cause of the ultimate cause, whether the intermediate cause be several, or one only. Now to take away the cause is to take away the effect. Therefore, if there be no first cause among efficient causes, there will be no ultimate, nor any intermediate cause. But if in efficient causes it is possible to go on to infinity, there will be no first efficient cause, neither will there be an ultimate effect, nor any intermediate efficient causes; all of which is plainly false. Therefore it is necessary to admit a first efficient cause, to which everyone gives the name of God.

—From *Summa Theologica,*
1266–1273

One of the most important Christian philosophers of all time, Italian-born **Saint Thomas Aquinas** (1225–1274) synthesized Neoplatonic Christian theory and the newly rediscovered work of Aristotle.

The Cosmological Argument

A good example of a philosopher who believed in God as the most reasonable thing to believe is **Saint Thomas Aquinas.** In the thirteenth century he introduced some of the proofs, or what he called the "Five Ways," which are still standard in rational approaches to religion. (In fact, almost all of these ways had been invented long before Aquinas—some of them by Aristotle.) For example, it was Aquinas who defended the proof that you are probably quite familiar with; it is sometimes called the **cosmological argument**. It has many variations, but the simplest one is this: Everything has to be caused by or created from something else. Therefore, there must have been a first cause, or what Aristotle called a "prime mover," and this is God.

Of course, one might object that the universe has always existed and thus does not need to be explained by a "first cause" that supposedly created it. Or one could admit that God created the universe but then argue (as many deists did) that having set it in motion God lets it exist without any further interference on his part. To answer such objections, Aquinas makes it clear that he thinks of God as a first cause in two senses, as both the cause of the universe's coming into existence, and the cause of its being preserved in existence from one instant to the next.

The Argument from Design: Saint Thomas Aquinas

The fifth way is taken from the governance of the world. We see that things which lack intelligence, such as natural bodies, act for an end, and this is evident from their acting always, or nearly always, in the same way, so as to obtain the best result. Hence it is plain that they achieve their end, not fortuitously, but designedly. Now whatever lacks intelligence cannot move towards an end, unless it be directed by some being endowed with knowledge and intelligence; as the arrow is shot to its mark by the archer. Therefore some intelligent being exists by whom all natural things are directed to their end; and this being we call God.

—From *Summa Theologica,*
1266–1273

A Reply: David Hume

In a word, Cleanthes, a man who follows your hypothesis is able, perhaps, to assert or conjecture that the universe sometime arose from something like design; but beyond that position he cannot ascertain one single circumstance and is left afterwards to fix every point of his theology by the utmost license of fancy and hypothesis. This world, for aught he knows, is very faulty and imperfect compared to a superior standard and was only the first rude essay of some infant deity who afterwards abandoned it, ashamed of his lame performance; it is the work only of some dependent, inferior deity and is the object of derision to his superiors, it is the production of old age and dotage in some superannuated deity and, ever since his death, has run on at adventures from the first impulse and active force which it received from him. You justly give signs of horror, Demea, at these strange suppositions; but these, and a thousand more of the same kind, are Cleanthes's suppositions, not mine. From the moment the attributes of the Deity are supposed finite, all these have place. And I cannot, for my part, think that so wild and unsettled a system of theology is, in any respect, preferable to none at all.

—From *Dialogues on Natural Religion,* 1778

The Argument from Design

A very different argument for rationally believing in God is one that is probably also familiar to you. If we look at the world, we can see that it is intricately designed, everything with its place and its purpose. There are bugs for birds to eat, bark for bugs to eat, rain so trees can grow, clouds to produce rain, and so on.

In fact, the universe is so perfectly designed, with the stars in their orbits and our brains in our skulls, that one cannot believe that this all came about by chance. So one must believe that behind the design of the universe is a designer, namely, God. The British philosopher William Paley defended this argument, which is often called the **argument from design**, by drawing the analogy between our finding a watch in a field, and assuming that some person must have been there, and our seeing the intricate design of the world and concluding that some intelligent creator must have made it. Voltaire, who despised the argument from design, made fun of it in his novel *Candide* with such quips as, "Isn't it wise of our creator to give us noses; otherwise we wouldn't have any way of wearing our eyeglasses." On a more serious note, the argument from design seems to be in conflict with **Charles Darwin's** theory of evolution and natural selection because the Darwinian theory makes an attempt to explain exactly how a complex world *could* come into existence over time without assuming a divine creator. But Darwin himself believed in God and saw no incompatibility between his theory and his religious beliefs.

One of the advantages of the process conception of God is that it makes this conflict entirely avoidable. But the idea of an evolving God-in-process does tend to threaten if not undermine the premise of the argument by design, if only because it shifts the analogy from a fine and finished mechanism (the watch in the field) to a partially completed, still imperfect, and in-process world. The argument from design is a particularly good and dramatic example of the use of *arguments from analogy* in philosophy (see p. 15 in "A Little Logic"). Paley's argument depends on the similarity between the watch and the world in a great many crucial aspects, whereas the Scottish philosopher David Hume points out that there are many critical points at which the analogy breaks down.

English theologian and philosopher **William Paley** (1743–1805) propounded a version of the design argument. His moral theory combines utilitarianism and supernaturalism.

English naturalist **Charles Darwin** (1809–1882) changed the world when in 1859 he published *The Origin of Species,* which elaborated the theory that species evolve as a consequence of natural selection. Darwin rivals Aristotle as the most influential biologist of all time.

The Ontological Argument

Besides the cosmological argument and the argument from design, the **ontological argument** is a fascinating philosophical argument for rational belief in God's existence, formulated by the eleventh-century monk Saint Anselm. The word

ontological means "having to do with the nature of existence," and the argument, which has been developed in hundreds of variations, is essentially this:

1. We cannot conceive of God except as an infinite and most perfect being.

2. A being who had all perfections (justice, omnipotence, omniscience, and so on) except for the perfection of existence, would not be "most perfect."

3. Therefore, the most perfect being necessarily exists.

So stated, the argument is peculiar and somewhat crude, but new versions of the ontological argument are still being produced today, using all the resources of modern logic. The point behind the argument in all of its variations, however, is to prove by logic alone that, from the very idea we have of God, it is necessary that God exists. And if this is so, then belief in God is rational belief, justifiable on the basis of strict logical considerations.

Needless to say, many philosophers have questioned this logic, even if they themselves devoutly believed in God's existence. The most famous of these was Immanuel Kant, who argued that the flaw in the argument was its second premise—the idea that existence was a "perfection or any other kind of property." Existing, Kant argued, just isn't like being just, being omnipotent, and being all-knowing. Although a being can exist without being just, it makes no sense to say that a being is just if it doesn't exist. Indeed, it doesn't make sense to say that it is a "being" at all.

The Ontological Proof: Saint Anselm

. . . I began to ask myself whether one argument might possibly be found, resting on no other argument for its proof, but sufficient in itself to prove that God truly exists, and that he is the supreme good, needing nothing outside himself, but needful for the being and well-being of all things . . . And so, O Lord, since thou givest understanding to faith, give me to understanding—as far as thou knowest it to be good for me—that thou dost exist, as we believe, and that thou art what we believe thee to be. Now we believe that thou art a being than which none greater can be thought. Or can it be that there is no such being, since "the fool hath said in his heart, 'There is no God'"? But when this same fool hears what I am saying—"A being than which none greater can be thought"—he understands what he hears, and what he understands is in his understanding, even if he does not understand that it exists. For it is one thing for an object to be in the under-standing, and another thing to understand that it exists. When a painter con-siders beforehand what he is going to paint, he has it in his understanding, but he does not suppose that what he has not yet painted

(continues)

The Ontological Proof: Saint Anselm (*continued*)

already exists. But when he has painted it, he both has it in his under-standing and understands that what he has now produced exists. Even the fool, then, must be convinced that a being than which none greater can be thought exists at least in his understanding, since when he hears this he understands it, and whatever is understood is in the understanding. But clearly that than which a greater cannot be thought cannot exist in the understanding alone. For if it is actually in the understanding alone, it can be thought of as existing also in reality, and this is greater. Therefore, if that than which a greater cannot be thought is in the understanding alone, this same thing than which a greater cannot be thought is that than which a greater can be thought. But obviously this is impossible. Without doubt, therefore, there exists, both in the understanding and in reality, something than which a greater cannot be thought.

—From *Proslogion,* 1078

From: A Scholastic Miscellany. Vol. 10. *The Library of Christian Classics.* Ed. and trans. Eugene R. Fairweather. Philadelphia: Westminster Press, 1956.

Rational Faith

Some attempts to show that belief in God is rational are of a very different kind. Kant, for example, rejected all three arguments (the cosmological argument, the argument from design, and the ontological argument) and instead tried to show that belief in God is rationally necessary for anyone who would be a morally good person. The result is a *moral proof* for God's existence, the aim being not so much to prove God's existence as a matter of knowledge (on a par, for instance, with our scientific beliefs) but rather as a necessary feature of our moral outlook on the world. The argument is familiar: in order for virtue to be rewarded and vice to be punished, there must be some all-powerful, all-wise judge who can—if not in this life, then in another one—make justice prevail, reward the good, and punish the wicked. Kant called our belief in such a God **faith**. But by this he did not mean an irrational feeling or a belief that we hold despite all evidence to the contrary. Faith in God was, for Kant, every bit as justified as knowledge, and not simply a matter of feeling; a purely rational attitude that can be defended with reasons, with arguments, and with proofs. Without belief in God, Kant argued, our sense of morality and justice would be without foundation.

The Moral Argument for Belief: Kant

Happiness is the condition of a rational being in the world, in whose whole existence everything goes according to wish and will. It thus rests on the harmony of nature with his entire end and with the essential determining ground of his will . . . Still, the acting rational being in the world is not at the same time the cause of the world and of nature itself. Hence there is not the sligh ground in the moral law for a necessary connection between the morality and proportionate happiness of a being which belongs to the world as one of its parts and as thus dependent on it . . . Nevertheless, in the practical task of pure reason, i.e., in the necessary endeavor after the highest good, such a connection is postulated as necessary: we should seek to further the highest good (which therefore must be at least possible). Therefore also the existence is postulated of a cause of the whole of nature, itself distinct from nature, which contains the ground of the exact coincidence of happiness with morality . . . Therefore, the highest good is possible in the world only on the supposition of a supreme cause of nature which has a causality corresponding to the moral intention . . . Therefore, the supreme cause of nature, insofar as it must be presupposed for the highest good, is a being which is the cause (and consequently the author) of nature through understanding and will, i.e., God . . . Therefore, it is morally necessary to assume the existence of God.

—From *Critique of Practical Reason,* 1788

Pascal's Wager

A different kind of proof is an argument formulated by the French philosopher-scientist **Blaise Pascal**. Pascal's argument presents us with a kind of betting situation, and the argument is therefore called **Pascal's wager**. It runs like this: Either we believe in God or we do not. If we believe in God and he exists, we will be rewarded with infinite bliss. If we believe in God but he does *not* exist, then the worst that has happened is that we have given up a few sinful pleasures that we might otherwise have enjoyed. But even if God doesn't exist, the edifying feeling of having faith in him is rewarding in itself. If we do not believe, however, and God does exist, we may enjoy a few pleasurable sins, but we will be punished with eternal damnation. If we do not believe and God does not exist, then there is of course no problem. Now you don't have to be much of a gambler to figure out which alternative is the better bet; it is to believe. Any rational person will therefore believe in God: why risk eternal damnation in return for a few sinful earthly pleasures?

Blaise Pascal (1623–1662) was a French polymath of great fame. Making his first contribution to geometry at sixteen years of age, he is perhaps best known for his "wager."

Pascal's Wager

The Possibilities:	If God exists,	If God does not exist,
We believe	ETERNAL REWARD	We've missed a few pleasures but edified ourselves through prayer.
We do not	ETERNAL DAMNATION	We're OK, and we've had some good times.

Irrational Faith

Not all arguments for believing in God are rational arguments, however, and not all belief need be backed up by an argument aimed at convincing anyone else. The most prominent example of a philosopher with this view of religious belief is Kierkegaard, whom we have already discussed. For Kierkegaard, unlike Kant, for instance, *faith* is distinctively **irrational**, and proofs of God's existence are utterly irrelevant. For Kierkegaard, faith in God is an intensely personal, passionate concern, not prone to "proof" by any means. Faith is a kind of *commitment*; it is precisely the fact that one cannot simply know that God exists—Kierkegaard calls this an "objective uncertainty"—that requires us to make the "leap of faith." A very different sort of irrationalist approach to religious belief is that ancient tradition called **mysticism**, which says that one can come to believe in God by way of a special experience or vision that cannot be described or communicated to anyone else. (Such experiences are said to be **ineffable**.)

A mystic might agree that this experience has proved to him that God exists, but he need not say anything at all. In fact, a mystic does not even have to insist that what he has "seen" is *true* at all, but only that it is extremely significant *personally*. Thus, there is no argument with a mystic, for he doesn't have to tell you anything, and there is nothing you can say to refute him. And yet, mystical experiences are so powerful, according to those who have had them, that doubting God's existence becomes difficult or impossible afterward. Furthermore, the mystical experiences reported by many different people from many different

Mystical Experience: Koestler

If anyone thinks that mysticism consists in useless dreaming, or in the ideal and selfish enjoyment of wonderful experiences without any practical and valuable effects in life, they have here their answer. It is the universal testimony of those who know that mystical experience transforms human life, and alters character—often from the squalid and mean to the noble and selfless. I was standing at the recessed window of cell No. 40 and with a piece of iron-spring that I had extracted from the wire mattress, was scratching mathematical formulae on the wall. Mathematics, in particular analytical geometry, had been the favourite hobby of my youth, neglected later on for many years . . . Now, as I recalled the method and scratched the symbols on the wall, I felt the same enchantment.

And then, for the first time, I suddenly understood the reason for this enchantment: the scribbled symbols on the wall represented one of the rare cases where a meaningful and comprehensive statement about the infinite is arrived at by precise and finite means. The infinite is a mystical mass shrouded in a haze; and yet it was possible to gain some knowledge of it without losing oneself in treacly ambiguities. The significance of this swept over me like a wave. The wave had originated in an articulate verbal insight; but this evaporated at once, leaving in its wake only a wordless essence, a fragrance of eternity, a quiver of the arrow in the blue. I must have stood there for some minutes, entranced, with a wordless awareness that "this is perfect—perfect"; until I noticed some slight mental discomfort nagging at the back of my mind—some trivial circumstance that marred the perfection of the moment. Then I remembered the nature of that irrelevant annoyance: I was, of course, in prison and might be shot. But this was immediately answered by a feeling whose verbal translation would be: "So what? is that all? have you got nothing more serious to worry about?"—an answer so spontaneous, fresh and amused as if the intruding annoyance had been the loss of a collar-stud. Then I was floating on my back in a river of peace, under bridges of silence. It came from nowhere and flowed nowhere. Then there was no river and no I. The I had ceased to exist.

—Arthur Koestler, Hungarian-born British author, 1905–1983

countries at many different times have such similar features that one must wonder whether this in itself is a demonstration of the "truth" of such experiences. But for the mystic, this or any such demonstration is unnecessary, for he or she is not claiming to have "proved" God's existence. It is enough to have experienced God directly, if only for a moment or two; compared with that, what kind of proof would be more convincing?

Mystical Experience: Eckhardt

These three dimensions represent three kinds of knowledge. The first is sensual: the eye sees things at a distance. The second is intellectual and is much higher in rank. The third represents [the function of] that aristocratic agent of the soul, which ranks so high that it communes with God, face to face, as he is. This agent has nothing in common with anything else. It is unconscious of yesterday or the day before, and of tomorrow and the day after, for in eternity there is no yesterday nor any tomorrow but only Now, as it was a thousand years ago and as it will be a thousand years hence, and is at this moment, and as it will be after death.

— Meister Eckhardt, German philosopher, circa 1260–1328

Religious Tolerance: Ritual, Tradition, and Spirituality

*If there were only one religion in England, there would be a danger
of tyranny; if there were two, they would cut each other's throats;
but there are thirty, and they live happily together in peace.*
—Voltaire, *Philosophical Letters*

Religion plays a central role in many people's outlook on the world and in many people's lives. But it does not play a central role in everyone's view of the world or life, and within the same religion (for example, Christianity) there may be many religious outlooks and very different religious practices. We need to understand religion and appreciate both its power and its importance, but we should not presume that everyone has or should have a religion or a religious outlook. Nor is it enough to believe. In a complex and pluralistic world, it is necessary to learn to articulate and understand not only our own religious beliefs but also those of other people as well. Indeed, the fact that religion is usually thought to be a matter of *belief* and not a kind of *knowledge* that can be demonstrated or proven (whether or not religion is, as Kierkegaard argued, irrational) means that religious **argument** has its limits. One can prove a mathematical theorem. One can adduce evidence for an empirical hypothesis. But one can only, at best, *explain* one's religious outlook and the important role it plays in one's life. When one really believes something of great personal importance, it may be natural to want to convince others to believe it as well. But attempting to demonstrate that one's religious outlook is the *right* one is at the same time risky business, for it can lead to irresolvable conflict in this multicultural world with its many different religions and outlooks, some of which are not religious at all.

And yet, mere logic would suggest that it is hard to believe something without believing that it is *true*. Thus, believing that one's religion is the "true religion" would seem to follow just from the fact that one believes in its doctrines. There is something odd about saying "I really believe that God is X, but perhaps it isn't so." Moreover, the admirable effort to bring all religions under one umbrella and argue that "we all ultimately believe in the same thing" tends to water down belief to the point where words like *God* or *a Supreme Being* designate very little, and this is even before one tries to include those religions (for example, Buddhism) that do not involve a concept of God. Many people object to the idea that the God of the Hebrew Bible, the Christian God, and Allah are the same God (although all Muslims are taught this in the Qur'an). Are the beliefs of a Taoist or a Confucian in any significant way similar to the beliefs of a Christian or a Zoroastrian? That is by no means obvious. Some great philosophers have tried to establish shared ground among the various religions, but for the most part they have not been very persuasive. People tend to identify with the very particular aspects of their religion, and they easily find even minor differences in belief odd, alienating, or offensive.

So, how is religious tolerance possible? Part of the problem is that the philosophical understanding of religion tends to put far too much emphasis on religious doctrine and belief. To be sure, belief is an important part of religion, but it is not the whole of religion. We can point out at least two things that are also important and are by their very nature particular to one's religious affiliation in ways that are not readily sharable but nevertheless do not prove to be a threat to religious tolerance.

The first of these features of religion is *ritual*, in all of its variations. Rationalist philosophers like Kant tried to eliminate ritual from what is essential to religion, dismissing it along with superstition as one of those things that was not rational and therefore weakened the status of religion. Irrationalist philosophers like Kierkegaard, too, did not consider ritual as essential to religion, emphasizing instead irrational passion and commitment. But what Kant and Kierkegaard failed to appreciate in their philosophies was the extent to which religion is a social phenomenon, not just a matter of belief, and religious practices and rituals are of primary and not merely secondary importance. Here we should note those "heartfelt" routines whose virtue is their familiarity and intimate association with the most spiritual passions. (We will discuss the Confucian emphasis on the importance of ritual in Chapter 10.) Ritual is not merely something one *does* (that is, "just going through the motions"), but rather something one lives. It can involve everyday behavior (for instance, being respectful to your parents), as well as those special ceremonies in life (for example, getting married). But rituals have meaning whether or not they are universal. It is the particularity of the prayers, rituals, and ceremonies that give life to a person's religion. But engaging in the rituals of one's religion need not be experienced as divisive.

The other aspect of religion that is not just a matter of belief is closely connected to the first. It is *tradition,* that sense of history that informs a person's religion. Christianity, Islam, Buddhism, Zoroastrianism, and Confucianism all trace themselves back to a single person who is their founder, and it matters a great deal who that founder is, where he lived, and how the religion has developed. Christianity—and the various kinds of Christianity—are distinctive because of their distinctive histories, in part because of the different cultures in which they have developed. It is not irrelevant to Christianity that it grew out of Judaism within the Greco–Roman world. Islam, although it now has many non-Arab believers, is inextricably tied to Mohammed's historical effort to unify the Arab people. Confucianism grew out of the cultural context in which Confucius lived, and it has flourished in the region of East Asia. To ignore this would be to rob Confucianism as religion of much of the meaning it has for its adherents. Rituals are of course products of tradition. A ritual counts as a ritual because of its established history in a religion. Thus, rituals tend to allow for only small variations, and it is virtually impossible to simply invent a new ritual. (Try it.) Officials of churches sometimes create rituals (or renovate old ones), but they usually have the whole weight of tradition on their side.

Tradition, too, is particular. Different people have different histories, and these differences, again, are not necessarily matters of conflict (although the histories themselves may be filled with conflict). Nevertheless, the particularities of history and tradition make each culture and every religion what it is. Although one might postulate certain beliefs and rituals that go all the way back to primitive people (some way of dealing with the dead, for instance), the history of religion divides early on into very different and distinctive stories and accounts. Historically, it is certainly not the case that "all religions are the same."

But there is one thing that all religions do seem to have in common, and that is the general sensibility that we call *spirituality,* the feeling that we are part of something much greater than ourselves. Spirituality, unlike religion, is not the province of one group or another. It is as much a product of individual piety as it is the result of organized religious training. It is available to hermits and loners, and it can be shared by millions of people. Spirituality is nonsectarian. It is by its very nature appreciative of the wonders of the universe and the miracle of existence, with or without belief in a creator. It need not involve any hint of an "us" versus "them" mentality. Spirituality is not confined to religion; scientists experience it when they contemplate the wonders of the world. We all feel it, in a transient way, when we are moved or "swept away" by a powerful piece of music or a beautiful piece of art. Spirituality does not require doctrines (though doctrines may be brought in to supplement or explain it), and so one person's or group's spirituality is not in conflict with any other person's or group's spirituality. Spirituality may involve any number of traditions, practices, and rituals, but these need not become the basis of conflict. Religion and spirituality do not, like science, primarily provide us with explanations of the world. Rather, they provide us with edification, meaning, and significance, which are essential to our humanity.

Doubts
꘠

Doubt isn't the opposite of faith: it is an element of faith.
—Paul Tillich, 1886–1965

If God plays any significant role in your philosophy, it is important to come to terms with these various conceptions, attitudes, and arguments. What or who is the God you believe in? What do you expect of God? What does God expect of you? Why do you believe in God? Should other people believe in God, too, or is that none of your business? Can you or should you prove that your belief in God is rational? If not, why would you accept an *irrational* belief? Psychiatrists, beginning with Sigmund Freud, define irrationality not only as believing what cannot reasonably be believed but also as believing what it is harmful to believe. Freud argued that belief in God is irrational because it is a childish illusion that gives us unwarranted and sometimes destructive attitudes and expectations toward life. Other philosophers—for example, **Karl Marx**—have argued that belief in God is like a drug, which soothes our suffering but prevents us from seeing the ways in which we could actually improve the world we live in. ("Religion is the opium of the people," he said.) The emphasis on divine justice and on an afterlife, he charged, is rationalization and compensation for our own injustice here on earth. So one cannot simply say without thought, "I just believe in God on faith, that's all." Even if you accept the idea of an irrational belief, it is important to show why that belief is something more than mere illusion (as Freud argued) or escapism (as Marx argued).

The Rejection of Religion: Karl Marx

The basis of irreligious criticism is this: man makes religion; religion does not make man. Religion is indeed man's self-consciousness and self-awareness so long as he has not found himself or has lost himself again. But man is not an abstract being, squatting outside the world. Man is the human world, the state, society. This state, this society produced religion which is an inverted world consciousness, because they are an inverted world.

(continues)

The Rejection of Religion: Karl Marx (*continiued*)

Religion is the general theory of this world, its encyclopedic compendium, its logic in popular form, its spiritual point d'honneur, its enthusiasm, its moral sanction, its solemn complement, its general basis of consolation and justification. It is the fantastic realization of the human being inasmuch as the human being possesses no true reality. The struggle against religion is, therefore, indirectly a struggle against that world whose spiritual aroma is religion.

Religious suffering is at the same time an expression of real suffering and a pro against real suffering. Religion is the sigh of the oppressed creature, the sentiment of a heartless world, and the soul of soulless conditions. It is the opium of the people.

The abolition of religion as the illusory happiness of men, is a demand for their real happiness. The call to abandon their illusions about their condition is a call to abandon a condition which requires illusions.

— Karl Marx, from "Contribution to a Critique
of Hegel's *Philosophy of Right*," 1844

The Rejection of Religion: Freud

. . . if we turn our attention to the psychical origin of religious ideas. These, which are given out as teachings, are not precipitates of experience or end results of thinking: they are illusions, fulfillments of the oldest, strongest and most urgent wishes of mankind. The secret of their strength lies in the strength of those wishes. As we already know, the terrifying impression of helplessness in childhood aroused the need for protection—for protection through love—which was provided by the father, and the recognition that this helplessness lasts throughout life made it necessary to cling to the existence of a father, but this time a more powerful one. Thus the benevolent rule of a divine Providence allays our fear of the dangers of life; the establishment of a moral world-order ensures the fulfillment of the demands of justice, which have so often remained unfulfilled in human civilization; and the prolongation of earthly existence in a future life provides the local and temporal framework in which these wish-fulfillments shall take place. Answers to the riddles that tempt the curiosity of man, such as how the universe began or what the relation is between body and mind, are developed in conformity with the underlying assumptions of this system.

It is an enormous relief to the individual psyche if the conflicts of its child-hood arising from the father-complex—conflicts which it has never wholly overcome—are removed from it and brought to a solution which is universally accepted.

When I say that these things are all illusions, I must define the meaning of the word. An illusion is not the same thing as an error; nor is it necessarily an error . . . we call a belief an illusion when a wish-fulfillment is a prominent factor in its motivation, and in doing so we disregard its relations to reality just as the illusion itself sets no store by verification.

— Sigmund Freud, from *The Future of an Illusion*, 1927

The Rejection of Religion: Nietzsche

The deity of decadence, gelded in his most virile virtues and instincts, becomes of necessity the god of the physiologically retrograde, of the weak. Of course, they do not call themselves the weak; they call themselves "the good."

~⳹~

The Christian conception of God—God as god of the sick, God as a spider, God as spirit—is one of the most corrupt conceptions of the divine ever attained on earth. It may even represent the low-water mark in the descending development of divine types. God degenerated into the contradiction of life, instead of being its transfiguration and eternal Yes! God as the declaration of war against life, against nature, against the will to live! God—the formula for every slander against "this world," for every lie about the "beyond"! God—the deification of nothingness, the will to nothingness pronounced holy!

— Friedrich Nietzsche, from *The Antichrist*, written in 1889

Closing Questions

1. Give a general description of God, noting those characteristics without which you would not be willing to use the word "God." If you don't believe in God, say with some precision what it is that you don't believe in.

2. If you believe that there is a God who is all-powerful, all-knowing, and concerned with justice and the well-being of

humanity, explain how there can be so much evil and suffering in the world. Pursue as far as you can the responses and objections to *one* of the various attempts to answer the problem of evil. (A good way of doing this is to have a friend act as devil's advocate and try to refute your efforts to defend a solution to the problem.)

3. If you believe in God, try to explain to an atheist friend (real or imagined) *why* you believe in God.

   - If you think there are good reasons for believing, state them.

   - If you think there are good arguments for, or a proof of, God's existence, state the arguments or the proof and defend it against your atheist friend's objections.

   - If you think that the only way to believe in God is through faith, answer your atheist friend's objections that you are being irrational, that you are simply indulging in "wishful thinking," and that you are escaping from your responsibilities to change the world and, instead, are accepting a fantasy in which God will take full responsibility.

4. Choose one of the traditional proofs of God's existence and work it out in some detail, answering objections and making the argument as irrefutable as you can. (See the following section for further readings.)

5. If you don't believe in God, what would convince you that God does exist? If you do believe in God, what would convince you that God does not exist?

Suggested Readings

William James's *Varieties of Religious Experience* (Longmans, 1902) is probably the best-known work in the philosophy of religion by an American philosopher. The essential text of the Judeo-Christian tradition is of course the Bible, although surprisingly few students who proclaim their belief or their interest have actually read it through. St. Thomas Aquinas's arguments for the existence of God appear in *Summa Theologica*, trans. Fathers of the English Dominican Province (Benziger, Bruce & Glencoe, 1948). Martin Luther's Wittenberg theses, which initiated the Reformation, are available in *Luther's Ninety-Five Theses,* ed. G. W. Sandt (Fortress, 1957). Spinoza's pantheism is spelled out in his very difficult book *The Ethics,* trans. Samuel Shirley (Hackett, 1992), but is well explained in Stuart Hampshire's exposition and analysis *Spinoza* (Penguin, 1961). Hegel's conception of Spirit is elaborated in *The Phenomenology of Spirit,* trans. A. V. Miller (Oxford University Press, 1977). See also his *Encyclopedia of the Philosophical Sciences*, Part I, Logic, trans. William Wallace (Oxford University Press, 1892). Karl Rahner's views are explored in The Cambridge Companion to Karl Rahner, eds. Declan Marmion and Mary E. Hines (Cambridge University Press, 2005). Marcus Borg defends his panentheistic view of God in *The God*

We Never Knew: Beyond Dogmatic Religion to a More Authentic Contemporary Faith (Harper Collins, 1997). Karl Marx's "A Contribution to the Critique of Hegel's *Philosophy of Right*" appears in *Karl Marx: Early Writings*, trans. and ed. T. B. Bottomore (McGraw-Hill, 1963). Søren Kierkegaard's works almost all concern themselves with the nature of faith and personal belief in God, but perhaps the best place to start would be a short book called *Philosophical Fragments*, trans. David Swenson (Princeton University Press, 1962), as well as his larger *Concluding Unscientific Postscript*, trans. D. Swenson and W. Lowrie (Princeton University Press, 1941). Kant's discussion of God as a moral being is in his *Critique of Practical Reason*, trans. L. W. Beck (Bobbs-Merrill, 1956). For some examples of contemporary formulations of the ontological argument for God's existence, see *The Many-Faced Argument: Recent Studies on the Ontological Argument for the Existence of God*, eds. John Hick and Arthur McGill (New York: Macmillan, 1967). The problem of evil is discussed in Marilyn McCord Adams and Robert Merrihew Adams, eds., *The Problem of Evil* (Oxford, 1991), and a broad range of philosophical problems of religion are discussed in John Hick, ed., *Philosophy of Religion*, 4th ed. (Prentice-Hall, 1989) and Steven M. Cahn, ed., *Ten Essential Texts in the Philosophy of Religion* (Oxford, 2004). See also John Hick's *Faith and Knowledge* (Cornell University Press, 1961). Some of the most blistering attacks on religion in general can be found in David Hume's *Dialogues on Natural Religion* (Bobbs-Merrill, 1947) and Friedrich Nietzsche's *The Antichrist* (together with *Twilight of the Idols*), trans. R. J. Hollingdale (Penguin, 1990). Freud's attack on religion as an illusion is in his *The Future of an Illusion* (Doubleday, 1953). Arthur Koestler's account of his mystical experiences was published in *The Invisible Writing* (Collins, 1954). A classic summary of the teachings of various religions outside of the Judeo-Christian tradition is Huston Smith, *The World's Religions* (HarperOne, 1991). An excellent account of African religion and philosophy is found in John S. Mbiti, *African Religions and Philosophy* (Praeger, 1969), and in Jacqueline Trimier, "African Philosophy" in R. Solomon and K. Higgins, eds., *From Africa to Zen*, 2nd ed. (Rowman & Littlefield, 2003). Jorge Valadez's discussion of syncretism also appears there in "Pre-Columbian and Modern Philosophical Perspectives in Latin America." For an account of the basic philosophical premises of Buddhism, see Peter Hershock, "Buddhist Philosophy," in *From African to Zen*. Stephen Phillips's "Indian Philosophies," in the same book, provides a good summary of India's various philosophical traditions. Barbara Stoler Miller has done a good translation of the Bhagavad Gita (Bantam 1986). For a general introduction to Confucianism, see David L. Hall and Roger T. Ames, *Thinking Through Confucius* (State University of New York Press, 1987). (We will consider African, Chinese, and Indian religious and philosophical traditions further in Chapter 10.)

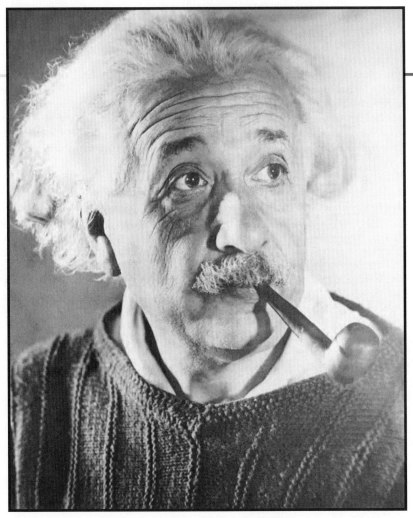

Albert Einstein, © Behman/CORBIS.

4

The Nature of Reality

Humankind cannot bear very much reality.
—T. S. Eliot, "Burnt Norton"

༄

Opening Questions

1. How "real" are the following items? (Rate them on a scale from 1 to 10, where 10 is most real, 1 is least real.)

    The person sitting next to you   _____

    The chair you are sitting in   _____

    God   _____

    The planet Uranus   _____

    Beethoven's music   _____

    The headache you had last night   _____

    Human rights   _____

    Electrons   _____

    The woman or man in (*not* "of") your dreams   _____

    Angels   _____

    The number 7   _____

    Water   _____

    Ice   _____

    Love   _____

    Beauty   _____

    Genes   _____

    The theory of relativity   _____

    Einstein's brain (when he was alive)   _____

    Einstein's ideas   _____

    Your own mind   _____

    The color red   _____

A red sensation (in your own mind)   _____

"Unreal numbers"   _____

The NFL   _____

Your own body   _____

Your soul   _____

2. Do you believe that the earth is flat and does not move, while the stars, sun, moon, and planets circle around it in more or less regularly shaped orbits? If not, why not? (If so, why?)

3. If a tree falls in the forest when there's no one around to hear it, does it make a sound? Why or why not? If no one ever sees, hears, or touches the tree itself, what sense does it make to say that the tree is "real"?

4. Does the universe itself have a purpose? If so, what is this purpose? If not, is it, as some modern philosophers have argued, just a universe of "matter in motion"—particles and electromagnetic fields acting according to the laws of physics?

The Real World

Much of what we believe about the world we believe on faith. As children, we believed what our parents told us, often without understanding it and only rarely testing their answers for ourselves. Most people most of the time throughout most of history have believed that **reality**—the ultimate nature of the world—was pretty much what their religious leaders told them it was, whether the world was a flat island or a plate on the back of an elephant supported on the back of a tortoise supported by another turtle (and from there on, "turtles all the way down," according to a traditional Indian tale) or an infinite expanse bounded only by God.

In this chapter we consider basic philosophical questions about reality, beginning with the one we have just raised: what is real? We proceed to discuss the traditional view that reality admits of degrees, so that some things are more real than others. The exciting philosophical question then becomes: what is most real? The next several sections comprise an historical survey of some of the answers of ancient Greek philosophers, who were divided on the issue of whether ultimate reality is material or immaterial. We devote particular attention to Plato's two-worlds theory, which attempts to explain the connection between the immaterial world that he takes to be ultimately real and the everyday appearances of material things. From this we segue into the questions of whether minds, physical bodies, or both are real, and if the latter, how minds and bodies are related. Taking the latter question first, we discuss Descartes's view that mind and body are separate substances, and then the alternative views of Berkeley and Leibniz. We then return to the question of what is most real and consider the arguments given by modern German philosophers in defense of idealism (the view that ideas and minds are ultimately real) along with the modern resurgence of the two-worlds theory. We next consider the question of teleology, the issue of whether the world has any ultimate purpose, and close with some observations about two general beliefs shared by virtually all Western philosophers: the belief that reality endures and that reality coheres into a unity.

Today most of us believe that reality is what our scientists tell us it is. None of us has ever seen or felt an atom. Very few of us could even offer any evidence that there is such a thing as our solar system, despite the fact that we have been looking at charts and drawings of it ever since we were children. When students are asked why they think that the sun doesn't move around the earth (as our very language, with words like *sunrise* and *sunset*, would seem to indicate), only a small number of them may be capable of giving any half-convincing answers.

Contemporary scientists do theorize about what is ultimately real, but such theories often make use of mathematically subtle concepts that are scarcely de-scribable from a layperson's point of view. String theory, for example, postulates that the fundamental reality consists of tiny vibrating "strings," which may be a closed loop or, alternatively, open. Furthermore, although themselves simple par-ticles, the strings have reality in nine or ten spatial dimensions (or 26 dimensions according to some versions of the theory) and can vibrate along any of these di-mensions. We find ourselves puzzling over this idea if we try to visualize it. The main merit of string theory is that it unifies a number of theories of basic physical forces in a way that is consistent with both quantum mechanics and Einstein's theory of general relativity. However, most of us are not able to follow the compli-cated mathematics that demonstrate these theoretical gains, and as yet no one has provided any experimental verification of the theory.

Science and Reality

The learned physicist and the man in the street were standing together on the threshold, about to enter a room.

The man in the street moved forward without trouble, planted his foot on a solid unyielding plank at rest before him, and entered.

The physicist was faced with an intricate problem. To make any move-ment he must shove against the atmosphere, which presses with a force of 14 pounds on every square inch of his body. He must land on a plank trav-elling at 20 miles per second around the sun—a fraction of a second earlier or later the plank would be miles away. He must do this while hanging from a round planet, head outward into space. . . . He reflects too that the plank itself is not what it appears to be . . . it is mostly emptiness, very sparsely scattered in that emptiness are myriads of electrical charges dashing about at great speeds. . . . It is like stepping on a swarm of flies.

—Sir Arthur Eddington,
English astrophysicist, 1882–1944

In any case, such theories indicate that even if we think the "real" thing is the material object, there are many levels on which that material thing might be described: such as the chair you are sitting on, for example. Is it the wood or other material it is made of, the molecular structure of that material, the atoms that compose them, the subatomic particles? Or is it something immaterial—the idea of a chair, which guided the chair's designer and anyone involved in its construction?

Before science came to claim complete domination over our picture of reality, during the past several centuries the ready answer to the question of what is ultimately real was *God*. According to this view, the material universe is real only insofar as it is kept in existence by God. (In fact, for hundreds of years it was considered heresy to believe that what was ultimately real were the "illusory speculations" of the scientists.) Also real were souls, angels, and other spiritual beings, whether or not these could be observed or tested by science. In the modern scientific worldview, which most of us accept without question, on the other hand, what is real is the physical universe.

The reality of such nonphysical things as numbers, spirits, minds, souls, angels, and even God is at least questionable—and if they are to be believed in, they must be justified somehow, preferably by appeal to the physical universe. Thus, minds are believable because they explain why various bodies behave as they do. And belief in God can be defended, for example, by the so-called argument from design, from the intricacy of the physical universe (see pp. 91–92).

God as Reality

The perennial Philosophy is primarily concerned with the one divine reality-substantial to the manifold world of things and lives and minds. But the nature of this one Reality is such that it cannot be directly and immediately apprehended except by those who have chosen to fulfill certain conditions, making themselves loving, pure in heart and poor in spirit. Why should this be so? We do not know. It is just one of those facts we have to accept, whether we like them or not and however implausible and unlikely they may seem.

—Aldous Huxley,
The Perennial Philosophy, 1946

We can see from the start that an answer to the question "What is real?" might begin with two very different starting points: an appeal to science on the one hand and an appeal to religion on the other. A religious person might still accept the findings of science, of course; philosophers such as Pascal and Leibniz were religious men as well as scientists. But for the religious person, the order of the universe is first of all a sign of the infinite wisdom and goodness of God. The scientist, however, approaches reality as being measurable and testable.

What Is Most Real?

In Opening Question 1, the point of asking you to rank as "real" various entities (the more proper philosophical word for "things") was to make some preliminary, crude attempt to get you to order your own sense of reality. This is what philosophers call an **ontology**. Ontology is essentially the study of what is real and the effort to establish a hierarchy of levels of reality; an ontology is a specific taxonomy of entities in accordance with such a hierarchy. Some people will formulate a commonsense ontology, with the most real entities being chairs, bodies, people; some will take a more scientific viewpoint and say that what is most real are those things discovered (or postulated) by science, like rons and genes. Other people will take a more spiritual approach and rank God highest, along with soul; some will always take people to be most real. Most people have the most trouble figuring out where to place such peculiar entities as Beethoven's music and the number 7.

Some people say that *nothing* is real and give a low ranking to virtually every entity on the list. We might then ask, "Real—compared to what?" For what becomes evident in such an exercise is the fact that "reality" is an **evaluative** term, a way of weighing what is most basic to our view of the world. To say that nothing is real is to say, in effect, that we don't believe in the world at all or, for that matter, in the existence of our own minds believing in the world. Surely, there is something odd about this. On the other hand, some people (including some important philosophers) have said that *everything* on the list is real. In fact, one might say this: everything is "real" for the kind of thing that it is. (Thus, the number 7 is real as a number; Beethoven's music is real as music; angels are real as angels; and the person sitting next to you is real in the way that people in general are real.) But this clever answer tends to miss the point of ontology, which is to discover what is *most* real, what is *most* basic, and what is to be accounted for in terms of what. If we say that in their own way Sherlock Holmes, or the Loch Ness monster, or the pot of gold at the end of the rainbow are just as real as you, me, and other people, as your own dog, or as the pots and pans in your friend's kitchen, then we seem to have lost our grasp of the notion of "reality" altogether. The whole purpose of thinking about reality is to somehow separate what is most basic and undeniable in the world from what is less so.

Appearance and Reality

The distinction that causes the most trouble in philosophy is the distinction between "appearance" and "reality," between what things seem to be and what they are. The painter wants to know what things seem to be, the practical man and the philosopher want to know what they are . . . but if reality is not what appears, have we any means of knowing whether there is any reality at all?

—Bertrand Russell,
The Problems of Philosophy, 1912

The Reality Behind the Appearances

Now, why should this question "What is real?" be so important? Consider this: Our dog (and your dog, too) couldn't conceive of such a question. The dog certainly learns a complex series of causes and effects (when the can opener whirs, he learns to expect dinner). He might also learn to ignore certain experiences as unimportant or untrustworthy. But what he never seems to learn is *explanation*. He never asks, "Why?" He apparently has only expectations, not theories. The connection between the can opener and dog food is enough for him; his life is seemingly a sequence of events, most of them expected, a few of them unexpected, but he cannot account for the connections between them, or presumably even follow such an account.

A child, on the other hand, asks "Why?" persistently. "How does a watch work?" for example. We could, if we wished, take it apart and show the child the mechanism. The surface movements are not enough for us; we want to know what is inside. Simply being aware of the sequence of lightning–thunder is not enough for us: we want to know what causes them, whether it is the bad temper of Zeus or the collision of convection currents in the atmosphere. And so we begin to postulate a **reality behind the appearances**, an attempt to account for the sequence of events that are seen in terms of other events unseen. "Primitive" mythologies populate this world behind the scenes with spirits, demons, gods, and goddesses. Science populates it with atoms and electrons and electromagnetic forces. Christianity fills it with God and a spiritual world only dimly perceived by those of us in this one—that eternal world is far more important than the mere passing appearances of this one.

The distinction between what we simply see, what *appears* to be the case, and the "deeper" picture that allows us to explain it, forces us to introduce the concept of "reality." This concept enables us to distinguish the ways things appear to us and their inner reality, and we learn to explain things to ourselves and make sense of them.

Essence and Appearance

Only as creators!—*This has given me the greatest trouble and still does: to realize that what things are called is incomparably more important than what they are. The reputation, name, and appearance, the usual measure and weight of a thing, what it counts for—originally almost always wrong and arbitrary, thrown over things like a dress and altogether foreign to their nature and even to their skin—all this grows from generation unto generation, merely because people believe in it, until it gradually grows to be part of the thing and turns into its very body. What at first was appearance becomes in the end, almost invariably, the essence and effective as such. How foolish it would be to suppose that one only needs to point out this origin and this misty shroud of delusion in order to destroy the world*

*that counts for real, so-called "reality." We can destroy only as creators.—
But let us not forget either: it is enough to create new names and estima-
tions and probabilities in order to create in the long run new "things."*

— Friedrich Nietzsche,
The Gay Science, 1882

From: Trans. W. Kaufman. New York: Vintage, 1974. §58.

The Basis of Metaphysics

In what we have said already in this chapter, we have anticipated some of
the main themes of what philosophers call **metaphysics.** Metaphysics is the attempt to say what reality is. **Cosmology,** or how we think the most real things
have come into being, is one of the components of metaphysics; another is ontology, the study of what is. In developing an ontology, as part of our attempt to
formulate our metaphysical views, we have to evaluate the different entities in the
world, picking out those that are most basic.

We have already anticipated two of the tests that often are imposed on this
notion of what is "most real." First, that which is most real is that upon which
all else is dependent. For a religious person, God is most real because all else depends on him; for a scientist, what is most real are the principles and particles on
which all of reality can be reasoned to be based. Second, that which is most real
is that which itself is not created or destroyed. It does not change. Thus, God created the earth, and he can destroy it, but God was neither created nor can God be
destroyed. You can destroy a chair, by burning it up or chopping it to pieces, but
you cannot destroy the basic particles and forces out of which the chair is made.
When we look back to the very beginnings of Western philosophy and metaphysics, when people first made the attempt to formulate their view of the world in
terms of what was most real and what was not, we find these same two tests being
invoked. Indeed, both modern science and modern theology, as well as Western
philosophy itself, are continuations of this same ancient metaphysical tradition.

In this chapter we will primarily consider the basic metaphysical question of
what is real. However, we should note that the range of matters covered by the
term "metaphysics" is considerably broader, and that different issues have been
given more or less prominence at various times. Some metaphysical questions—
such as the question of how the mind and the body are related (considered in
Chapter 6) and whether our actions are really free (considered in Chapter 7)—
have been longstanding issues, but some answers have been proposed fairly recently as a consequence of developments in the sciences. Other topics have been
taken up or recast in recent times, such as the relationship between time and
space, how parts make up wholes, what could and what could not have been different from the way it actually is, and how we should understand our ideas about
possibilities (which may or may not be actualized).

The First Metaphysicians

Thales

The disciplines of metaphysics and philosophy, as these are practiced in the Western tradition, began in the Aegean region about 2,600 hundred years ago. The first Western philosopher is generally agreed to have been a man named **Thales**, who lived from about 624 to 546 BCE. He was said to be somewhat eccentric: he once fell into a well while thinking about philosophy, but he also made a fortune on the olive oil market. His philosophy in a sentence was this: *water* is the ultimate reality.

This sounds simpleminded, but it was a momentous achievement, and it is not as silly as we might initially think. Try to suspend your knowledge of modern science—of the hundred-plus elements that have been discovered. Try to look at the world yourself; try to understand it in your own terms. And suppose you have the idea that, in order to make sense of the world, the first thing to do is to discover which element is most basic. (Remember that Greek science identified only four elements—earth, air, fire, and water.) And now try to imagine what the world is *ultimately* made up of.

What, you may ask, is so monumentally important about this? Whether the world is actually made of water is not really the issue. What Thales saw, and what we now take for granted, is a difference between the way the world *seems* to be and the way it *really* is. The world seems to be made of all kinds of different materials; it took a stroke of genius to suggest that all of these might be made out of a single basic element. Think how difficult life would be, to take but one simple example, if no one had ever noticed that water and ice were actually the same material under different conditions or if no one had ever discovered that basic food substances could be transformed (through mixing and heating) into an almost infinite variety of different things to eat. Modern scientific theory, which replaces Thales's initial theory about water with a complex system of elements and subatomic particles, is nevertheless an extension of the same strategy, to distinguish the way the world appears to be from the way it really is and to explain why it appears be as it does. Once we have made this basic distinction, a whole new world opens up to us, a "real world," behind (or above or below) appearances.

The Pre-Socratic Materialists

After Thales, a number of other pre-Socratic philosophers challenged his view of water as the basic reality of the world and suggested theories of their own. A student of Thales named **Anaximander** went one step further than his teacher and suggested that everything was made of some basic "stuff" (his word was *apeiron,* or "indefinite") that we could never experience as such; we could only know its manifestations.

The West's Oldest Philosophical Fragment, from Anaximander

The Non-limited is the original material of existing things; further, the source from which existing things derive their existence is also that to which they return at their destruction, according to necessity; for they give justice and make reparation to one another for their injustice, according to the arrangement of time.

— Sixth century BCE

From: Freeman, Kathleen. *Ancilla to the Pre-Socratic Philosophers.* Cambridge, MA: Harvard University Press, 1948.

Anaximander had a student named **Anaximenes** who thought that everything was made of *air*, so water was thickened air and earth was thickened even more than that.

A philosopher named **Heraclitus** suggested alternatively that everything was more like *fire* than it was like the other elements—always changing and consuming.

Before those thinkers, called the pre-Socratics, philosophers both in Greece and in other societies had also made the distinction between the world of appearances and the real world—for example, by appealing to gods and goddesses behind the scenes. But the pre-Socratics made a monumental step forward: they now tried to explain the world, as it normally appeared to them, in a systematic way, not by appeal to the moods and whims of invisible deities. With the Greek philosophers, the daily world of appearances, in which different things simply happen one after another, is supplemented by another world, a world in which the world of appearances can be explained.

Today perhaps none of us has an ontology as simple as that of the pre-Socratics. It is clear to us that there is more to the world than earth, air, fire, water, and the possibility that there is some fifth element, "stuff," which we have never seen. But the pre-Socratics, too, were aware that the world of ultimate reality might be more complex than at first they had imagined. Another pre-Socratic philosopher, **Democritus**, developed a picture of the world that is remarkably close to our current scientific views. He suggested that the world consisted of tiny indestructible elements, which he called **atoms** (derived from roots meaning "not cut" or "not divided"), that combined and recombined in various ways to give us the different elements and all the complex things of this world. These things might change, be created, and be destroyed, but the atoms themselves are eternal.

Only a little imagination is required to see that we debate the ultimate nature of reality in much the same terms as these ancient philosophers did. Democritus's view is still very much with us; we no longer believe that atoms themselves are these most basic particles, but we still postulate some such basic elements. A few decades ago, protons, electrons, and neutrons were said to be the basic building blocks of reality. Today, physicists refer to even more basic building blocks, electrons, quarks, and leptons, or, according to string theory, vibrating strings that manifest as electrons and quarks. But even if the particles are still smaller, the idea is the same.

Eternal Fire

This world that is the same for all, neither any god nor any man shaped it, but it ever was and is and shall be ever-living Fire that kindles by measures and goes out by measures.

—Heraclitus

Ancient Materialism ‑

Thales (624–546 BCE, Miletus)—Reality is ultimately water.

Anaximander (610–546 BCE, Miletus)—Reality is indefinite "stuff" (*apeiron*).

Anaximenes (585–528 BCE; Miletus)—Reality is essentially air.

Heraclitus (536–480 BCE; Ephesus)—Reality is like fire.

Democritus (460–371 BCE; Abdera)—Reality consists of tiny atoms.

*All dates are approximate.

So, too, we can understand Heraclitus in modern terms as the view that the nature of ultimate reality is not matter but energy. This view, which became as powerful as it is now only in the late nineteenth century, rejects the traditional emphasis on physical matter (whether tangible matter such as earth or water, or microscopic building blocks such as atoms) and instead declares ultimate reality to be power and forces and energy states, which somehow produce matter as their effects. A still more modern concept would be the view that reality consists of neither matter nor energy as such but some more basic element—matter-energy—which can manifest itself as either matter *or* energy. This, of course, is much like the view of Anaximander.

Laypersons often talk as if modern science has established what the ultimate nature of reality is. But the basic debate—whether reality should be thought of in terms of basic building blocks or rather, perhaps, in larger, more holistic terms, whether matter or energy should be primary—still goes on. Some people clearly do interpret the universe as Democritus understood it, consisting of an elaborate order of singular elements that can be understood by taking them apart and analyzing them. Some people do see the world as Thales did: comprehensible, solid, and substantial, like a pool of water, like the Mediterranean. Some people see the world with Anaximander, as unknowable, mysterious, beyond everyday experiences. And some people see the world as constant energy and change, with excitement and enthusiasm being among its manifestations. Metaphysics is not just an ancient, unsophisticated set of views about science. Metaphysics is a basic outlook on the world, and its terms are much the same today as they were 2,500 years ago.

Early Nonphysical Views of Reality

You have no doubt noticed that all five of the pre-Socratics we have named suggested that the basic element of reality was one of the *physical* elements (including "stuff" and "atoms," even though we can't sense them). But there were also pre-Socratic philosophers who thought that ultimate reality was not physical at all. One of them was **Pythagoras**; he believed that the ultimate elements of reality were *numbers*. (If he had answered our opening questions, he would have given the number 7 a "10.") For Pythagoras, numbers were eternal and indestructible; the things of this world were in some sense dependent upon numbers for their existence. The heavens, in particular, were divine examples of the mathematical order of the universe. (Pythagoras said that "the whole of heaven is a musical scale and a number.") He and his followers also believed in the immortality of the soul and in reincarnation.

Why did Pythagoras think that numbers were more real than trees and tables? Because numbers were eternal; they never changed, whereas trees and tables could be chopped up, used for firewood, and destroyed. Reality, according to the view that has been dominant from then until now, is what underlies all change, what does not itself change. Another pre-Socratic philosopher, **Parmenides**, went so far as to suggest that the world of our everyday life, because it was so filled with changes and things coming into being and disappearing, could not be real at all. The other pre-Socratics had said that the things of our world were only *less* real than some more basic reality. Parmenides said that our world was actually *unreal*.

Pythagoras of Samos (ca. 570–490) was the leading mathematician of the ancient world, as well as a philosopher who, in southern Italy, led a powerful religious cult whose views were at odds with most of the philosophy of pre-Socratic Greece. He believed in the immortality of the soul and in reincarnation, and he established a brotherhood of religious believers in which numbers and mathematics, as the basis of all things, held a special place in the universe. His discoveries in mathematics are still central to the sciences of geometry and acoustics. The Pythagorean theorem is named after him: "The sum of the squares of the two sides of a right triangle is equal to the square of the hypotenuse," or "$a^2 + b^2 = c^2$." He was the first to prove it.

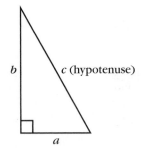

The Pythagoreans also placed great importance on the connections between mathematics and music. They noted, for instance, that if you halve the length of a vibrating string you produce the "same" note at a higher pitch (a discovery you can test for yourself on a guitar).

The principle, that what is real is eternal and unchanging, formed the framework within which most of the pre-Socratics, and almost all modern individuals (including scientists and religious people) developed their view of the universe. One of the pre-Socratic philosophers, however, challenged this basic principle. This was Heraclitus, whom we have already met as the philosopher who believed that fire was the basic model for reality. But fire is a violent element, always changing and never the same. So Heraclitus came up with the suggestion that must have upset the other early philosophers even more than Parmenides telling them that the world they lived in wasn't really real. Heraclitus said that *change is real,* thus contradicting the basic principle that reality is what doesn't change. (One might say that the only thing that doesn't change is change itself, but this is a good way of tying yourself up in logical knots.) Heraclitus expressed the idea that everything is constantly in flux by saying that you cannot step in the same river twice. Some of his more radical followers claimed that in actual fact you cannot step in the same river once because there is no moment when the water is not in the process of flowing past. (On the other hand, it has been pointed out by some of his more facetious critics that you *can* step in the same river twice if, having stepped in once, you jump out, run downstream, and jump in again!)

We should note, however, that the Heraclitean view of reality is so radical that not even Heraclitus actually held to it. He may have believed that reality was change, but he also believed that underlying all change was an eternal principle, **logos**, that did not change. Thus, he did believe in eternal reality after all. In our own era, Einstein reiterated this view when he claimed that, although nature may change continuously, the laws of nature stay forever the same. But some philosophers and many scientists now believe that not even the laws are permanent; does this mean that nothing is real? Philosophers have argued about this for 2,500 years.

From our abbreviated discussion of the earliest Western philosophers, we can already see many of the possibilities for a metaphysics, an account of ultimate reality, according to which you can articulate your own understanding of the world.

The Law of Logos

Listen . . . not to me, but to the Logos.

— Heraclitus

First, a metaphysics may hold that reality consists of purely *physical* or *material* components, whether these are elements such as water or fire or modern components such as atoms, electrons, quarks, and electromagnetic and intranuclear forces. This is called **materialism**.

Ancient Immaterialism

Pythagoras (c. 570-c. 490, Samos)—Reality is ultimately numbers.

Parmenides (539–492 BCE, Elea)—Reality is unchanging and unknown to us.

Zeno of Elea (fifth century BCE)—Reality is unchanging and motion is unreal. ("Zeno's paradoxes" were intended as proofs of this. See, for example, the paradox of the arrow on p. 21.)

Heraclitus (540–480 BCE, Ephesus)—Reality is change, but with an underlying *logos,* or logic. Thus, Heraclitus is sometimes interpreted as saying that reality is *logos.*

*All dates are approximate.

Second, and opposed to materialism, is the view that the basic components of reality are not physical or material at all, but are, for example, spirits, or minds, or numbers. This is called **immaterialism.**

The whole history of Western thought, in fact, has tended to be split between these two sets of views. Most scientists are materialists, whereas many religions defend immaterialism. But many scientists are also religious, and they recognize the importance of immaterialism, too. And most religious thinkers recognize the material nature of the physical world. So one of the most enduring problems of philosophy is the reconciliation of the two.

Plato's Forms

The ancient philosopher Plato (see p. 12) tried to have both materialism and immaterialism, but he clearly thought that what was more real were the immaterial entities, which he called **Forms.** The Forms represent Plato's attempt to capture the mathematical insights of Pythagoras and to correlate *being* and *becoming,* following Parmenides and Heraclitus. Like Pythagoras, Plato emphasized the importance of form over material content. Like Parmenides, he emphasized the idea that ultimate reality must be changeless; accordingly our ordinary world of experience cannot be ultimate reality. But like Heraclitus, Plato also appreciated the importance of apparent change, and the need for some underlying *logos* or ultimate principle, to make sense of it all. Plato's Forms are his version of the *logos.*

An example of a Form is this: Suppose you draw a triangle on this piece of paper and attempt to prove a theorem of Euclidean geometry about triangles. Now the first thing to notice is that this particular triangle, as you have drawn it, is not even close to being an accurate triangle; but even if you used the most precise instruments in the world, it would still not have exactly straight sides, the lines would still have some thickness (which a true line does not have), and the angles would be slightly in error. In other words, *it is impossible to draw a true triangle.* Second, even if the triangle were much better drawn, how is it possible that by proving something about *this* triangle you have thereby proven something about *all* triangles? Plato's answer is: Because, what you are really dealing with here is not this triangle at all, which is only a poor material example. You are really dealing with the Form *triangle,* an immaterial perfect triangle that does not exist anywhere in this material world.

Where does the Form *triangle* exist? Today most people would say, "In our minds" or "It doesn't." But Plato thought that it does exist. Indeed, his whole philosophy is based on the view that there are *two worlds,* this world of ordinary material existence, in which we spend most of our time and energy, and another world, a world of pure Forms, which is eternal, immaterial, and more real than this one. The first world consists of material things that change, die, and disappear; Plato called it the **World of Becoming.** It is not *un*real, but it is *less* real than the other world, the truly real world, which he called the **World of Being.** In his book *The Republic,* Plato gives us a dramatic account of the relationship between these two worlds in terms of a myth, "the myth of the cave." The cave represents the world of shadows, the World of Becoming, in which we all live. The sunlight represents the truth, the World of Being, which we can know only through *reason,* not through experience.

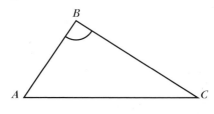

The Myth of the Cave (excerpt)

SOCRATES: *Imagine men to be living in an underground cavelike dwelling place, which has a way up to the light along its whole width, but the entrance is a long way up. The men have been there from childhood, with their neck and legs in fetters, so that they remain in the same place and can only see ahead of them, as their bonds prevent them turning their heads. Light is provided by a fire burning some way behind them, and on a higher ground, there is a path across the cave and along this a low wall has been built, like the screen at a puppet show in front of the performers who show their puppets above it. . . . See then also men carrying along that wall, so that they overtop it, all kinds of artifacts, statues of men, reproductions of other animals in stone or wood fashioned in all sorts of ways, and, as is likely, some of the carriers are talking while others are silent. . . . Altogether then . . . such men would believe the truth to be nothing else than the shadows of the artifacts?*

(continues)

The Myth of the Cave (excerpt) (*continued*)

GLAUCON: *They must believe that.*

SOCRATES: *Consider then what deliverance from their bonds and the curing of their ignorance would be if something like this naturally happened to them. Whenever one of them was freed, had to stand up suddenly, turn his head, walk, and look up toward the light, doing all that would give him pain, the flash of the fire would make it impossible for him to see the objects of which he had earlier seen the shadows. What do you think he would say if he was told that what he saw was foolishness, that he was now somewhat closer to reality and turned to things that existed more fully, that he saw more correctly? . . . And if one were to drag him thence by force up the rough and steep path, and did not let him go before he was dragged into the sunlight, would he not be in physical pain and angry as he was dragged along? When he came into the light, with the sunlight filling his eyes, he would not be able to see a single one of the things which are now said to be*

GLAUCON: *Not at once, certainly.*

SOCRATES: *I think he would need time to get adjusted before he could see things in the world above. . . . Then, at last, he would be able to see the sun, not images of it in water or in some alien place, but the sun itself in its own place, and be able to contemplate it . . . After this he would reflect that it is the sun which provides the seasons and the years, which governs everything in the visible world, and is also in some way the cause of those other things which he used to see.*

From Plato. *The Republic*. Bk. VII. Trans. G. M. A. Grube. Indianapolis, Hackett: 1974.

In Plato's view, people who devote all their attention to things in the physical world—the world we experience through our senses—are like people who spend their entire lives watching television. They deal only with images, never with the reality that lies behind those images. To come to know this reality is the work of the intellect and the ultimate task of philosophy.

Now you can see how Plato has saved both sides of his predecessors' philosophical views: he has the Heraclitean notion of constant change but also his *logos*, which lies in the Forms; he has Parmenides's spectacular claim that the things of our ordinary experience are not truly real; and he has Pythagoras's view that the most real things are eternal patterns and principles, such as those of mathematics. Now notice what Plato has done: he has taken the parts of all those views he agrees with, and he has integrated them into a single dramatic and compelling picture of the way they fit together in a single worldview. Lesser philosophers might have said, "Well, I believe in material things, of course; I also believe in numbers, and in some eternal principle underlying them." But Plato has worked out a view in which all of this *ties together*. The views themselves, as you have seen, are not particularly original. But almost everyone would agree that Plato is one of the greatest philosophers not only of Greece but of all times, and the reason is the brilliance and imagination with which he has put his views together.

Aristotle's Metaphysics

It is at this point in our history that Aristotle (see p. 12) enters the scene. Aristotle, who was Plato's student, found Plato's two-world view implausible. Aristotle was a far more commonsense thinker, who insisted that reality has to be the everyday world of things, trees, and people, not some other world that we never actually experience. So in effect he brought Plato back down to earth; he rejected Plato's World of Being and the Forms and insisted, along with what philosophers usually call the "ordinary person" (in other words, all of us as nonspecialists when we are thinking about philosophy), that this world is the real world and there is no other.

However, although Aristotle insisted that our everyday reality is reality, he did not therefore reject the all-important distinction between reality and appearances that had been developing over several centuries. But whereas Plato separated them into two different worlds, Aristotle instead said that the *forms* of things are in the things themselves and have no separate existence. (Let's use the lowercase letter *f* to show that there is nothing "otherworldly" here.) And in Aristotle, the ultimately real things—to which he gave the very important name **substances**—are nothing other than particular things in the world—horses, flowers, people, rocks, and so on.

The distinction between reality and appearances stays intact, however, for it is not always true that we understand the essential nature, or what Aristotle called "the essence," of these individual substances. For example, just because we are all familiar with people-substances (that is, people), we don't necessarily understand what it is to be human, what it is to be a person. And, to take a far more dramatic example, just because we are familiar with our small part of the universe in everyday life, it does not follow that we understand the universe as a whole. Indeed, Aristotle's picture of the universe is arguably even more dramatic than Plato's; he envisioned the universe as a gigantic organism, growing and restless, seeking knowledge of itself.

The conflict between their starting points, between Plato's view that reality is something other than our everyday world and Aristotle's view that the ultimate realities are the substances of our daily life, is one that has continued in philosophy until the present day. (In fact, both views became models for Christian thinkers. Plato's view of another, immaterial and eternal world, different from the material world of daily life, became the central thesis of Saint Augustine's philosophy and the main doctrine of Christian theology for centuries to come. Aristotle's view of a living, growing, goal-directed universe played an important role in the thought of Saint Thomas Aquiniz, and it is still an important part of Christian theology.)

We can now say quite clearly what we are trying to do. Philosophy—and metaphysics in particular—is an *interpretation of the world*. It is our attempt to make sense of it, our attempt to explain it. Some of our efforts will be directed toward specific issues—for example, what things can we properly consider real? Or, when are a person's actions to be considered as free and as his or her own responsibility? Some of our efforts will be aimed at the whole picture, and we'll ask such questions as "What is the origin of the universe?" and "Why is there a universe at all?" One way to answer such questions is by the pre-Socratic technique: pick out an essential element or set of elements and show how the world can be explained in terms of the chosen element(s). Another way is the Platonic approach: postulate and design a world "behind" this one, which explains why things are the way they are. A third way is the Aristotelian way: assume the commonsense world but then show that there is much in it that we do not yet understand and that the whole picture cannot be grasped from the details of life alone.

The choice largely depends on your views; the pre-Socratic way is initially attractive for its simplicity, but you will find that there is much that cannot be easily accounted for with a single element or set of elements. The Platonic and Aristotelian pictures are much more difficult, but it is for good reason that many philosophers consider virtually all philosophy done in the past 2,500 years to be modeled after Plato, after Aristotle, or after both. Between Plato's imaginative synthesis of the variety of views before him and Aristotle's hardheaded analysis of individual things and their properties, our concept of reality has continued to be formed and re-formed, from generation to generation, and whatever we decide to say about such matters, we can be certain that one or both of them had already anticipated it.

Mind and Metaphysics

Consider this table in front of us, which has hitherto roused but the slightest thought in us. It is full of surprising possibilities. The one thing we know is that it is not what it seems. Beyond this modest result, we have the most complete liberty of conjecture. Leibniz tells us it is a community of souls; Bishop Berkeley tells us it is an idea in the mind of God; sober science, scarcely less wonderful, tells us it is a vast collection of electric charges in violent motion.

—Bertrand Russell, 1912

You may have noticed that one familiar answer to our question of what is real has not been raised. That is the idea that, ultimately, *mind* or **consciousness** is real. Today most of us would insist that mind be at least part of the answer, and some people—called **idealists**—would insist that it be the whole answer. An idealist believes that the basis of the existence of all things is the mind (whether our own minds or the mind of God). We realize that we know of the existence of material things only through their effects on our minds. Numbers exist because we think them, according to idealists. Beethoven's music exists because we can hear it when it is played, hum it to ourselves, read it from the score if we have had some musical training. According to an idealist, such things are real *only* insofar as they are experienced in the mind; in other words, it is mind that is most real, and other entities are dependent on mind or minds. Why did none of the Greeks mention this? The fact is they had no such concept of something being "in the mind" but not in the external world; the idea would never have occurred to them. This, more than anything else, marks the greatest single difference between their metaphysics and most of ours.

Even if you don't accept the idealists' view that the ultimately real entities are minds, it is still hard to deny the claim that minds are part of reality (although materialism is still alive and well in many quarters, and there are many philosophers and scientists who hope to be able to explain the existence of minds in strictly physical and physiological terms). Others, however, believe minds to have their own kind of existence. Three different views of minds and their place in reality have dominated Western thinking for the past several hundred years. All three begin with the idea that mind is a substance (or an aspect of a substance), which is precisely the concept that the Greeks did not have. But in one view, minds are but one *kind* of substance; in another view, minds are but *part* of a substance; and in yet another view, minds are the *only* substances. These three views were represented by three European philosophers from the seventeenth and eighteenth centuries—the French philosopher René Descartes, the Dutch philosopher Baruch Spinoza, and the German philosopher Gottfried Wilhelm von Leibniz.

René Descartes

René Descartes (see p. 28) was a **pluralist**, in the sense of being a philosopher who believes in more than one substance. ("**Pluralism**" can have other meanings, too; for example, it can refer to someone who is tolerant of various methodological approaches within philosophy.) Descartes is usually referred to as a **dualist** because he accepts two basic substances—mind and body—but in fact he thought there were three kinds of substances: physical bodies, minds, and God. God created the other two substances, and except by God, they could be neither created nor destroyed.

The overriding problem of Descartes's metaphysics was how to connect the various substances—in particular, mind and body. It is obvious that each of us is, in some sense, a complex of both mind and body, mental and physical properties and therefore mental and physical substance. But if substances are by definition ultimate and totally independent of anything else, then how can they possibly interact? How is it possible for events happening to your body (a nail in your foot, for instance) to produce an effect in your mind (pain)? How is it possible for events in your mind (drive to the grocery store, for instance) to have an effect on your body (you walk to your car, put the key in the ignition, and start the engine)?

One suggestion might be that the two substances infiltrate one another, as copper and zinc combine (but don't chemically interact) to form brass. Descartes sometimes suggested this. But the interaction between mind and body still seems to go unexplained. In fact, it gets even more complicated when we see that Descartes defined mental substance as that which is not in space (or **unextended** as opposed to physical things, which are **extended** in space). Once we have defined mind and body as two different substances, there seems to be no way of getting them together. And this is even before we begin asking how God as a separate substance can interact with the substances he has created.

Descartes never solved the problem of how substances interact. To solve the problem, there seem to be only two solutions: Either (1) mind and body are not separate substances but parts of the same substance, or (2) they are separate substances, all right, but they don't interact after all. Spinoza would choose the first way; Leibniz chose the second. (We talk about this mind-body problem in Chapter 6.)

There are two important points to make about all of this right away. First, don't think that what we are debating are just the complexities of a technical word (that is, *substance*). The word is merely a convenient way of referring to what is ultimate reality—whatever you think that might be—and the debate between Descartes, Spinoza, and Leibniz is about the nature of reality, not about a word. Second, don't think that these debates about reality are not connected to the more urgent questions about the meaning of life and belief in God: these debates about the nature of reality and substance are in fact attempts to answer just those questions, different ways of conceiving of God and his relation to us, and different ways of conceiving of ourselves.

A Question of Substance

	Descartes	*Spinoza*	*Leibniz*
Nature of substance(s)	Mind, body, and God	The Universe (God)	Monads (minds)
Number of substances	Three types: many minds, many bodies, one God	One	Indefinitely many, plus God (the supermonad)
Interaction between substances	Causal interaction	Substances do not interact. Mind and body are two of the many attributes of the one substance.	Substances do not interact. Monads only appear to interact, orchestrated by God.

Baruch Spinoza

Baruch Spinoza (see pp. 77–78) saw that Descartes, having defined mind and body as separate substances, could not explain how they interact. Very well then, he said, the solution to this problem is that the are not separate substances, but different aspects—or what he called **attributes**—of one and the same substance. Furthermore, if God is a substance separate from the substance of which mind and body are attributes, then God cannot interact with the world, which is nonsense. Therefore, Spinoza concluded, God must be that same substance and, in fact, "God" is just another name for that substance. Indeed, the starting point of Spinoza's whole argument is that, because substance is ultimate and totally independent, and because substances cannot interact, there can be only *one* substance. A philosopher such as Spinoza who believes in one substance is a **monist**.

Spinoza's Metaphysics, From *Ethics*

Spinoza presented his metaphysical system in the style of Euclid's geometry, with definitions, axioms, and a sequence of "propositions" (theorems) that he proved one at a time. Here are some sample definitions, axioms, propositions, and proofs.

Definitions

I. *By that which is* self-caused, *I mean that of which the essence involves existence, or that of which the nature is only conceivable as existent.*

II. *A thing is called* finite after its kind, *when it can be limited by another thing of the same nature; for instance, a body is called finite because we can always conceive another greater body. So, also, a thought is limited by another thought, but a body is not limited by thought, nor a thought by body.*

III. *By* substance, *I mean that which is in itself, and is conceived through itself: in other words, that of which a conception can be formed independently of any other conception.*

IV. *By* attribute, *I mean that which the intellect perceives as constituting the essence of substance.*

V. *By* mode, *I mean the modifications of substance, or that which exists in, and is conceived through, something other than itself.*

VI. *By* God, *I mean a being absolutely infinite—that is, a substance consisting in infinite attributes, in which each expresses eternal and infinite essentiality.*

(continues)

Spinoza's Metaphysics, From *Ethics* (*continued*)

Axioms

I. *Everything which exists, exists either in itself or in something else.*

II. *That which cannot be conceived through anything else must be conceived through itself.*

III. *From a given definite cause an effect necessarily follows; and, on the other hand, if no definite cause be granted, it is impossible that an effect can follow.*

IV. *The knowledge of an effect depends on and involves the knowledge of a cause.*

V. *Things which have nothing in common cannot be understood, the one by means of the other; the conception of one does not involve the conception of the other.*

VI. *A true idea must correspond with its ideate or object.*

VII. *If a thing can be conceived as nonexisting, its essence does not involve existence.*

Propositions

Prop. I. Substance is by nature prior to its modifications . . . .

Prop. II. Two substances, whose attributes are different, have nothing in common.

Proof.—*. . . evident from Def. III. For each must exist in itself, and be conceived through itself; in other words, the conception of one does not imply the conception of the other.*

Prop. III. Things which have nothing in common cannot be one the cause of the other.

Proof.—*If they have nothing in common, it follows that one cannot be apprehended by means of the other (Ax. V.), and, therefore, one cannot be the cause of the other (Ax. IV.).* Q.E.D. [Latin, quod erat demonstrandum, a phrase used in traditional logic meaning "which was to be demonstrated."]

Prop. IV. Two or more distinct things are distinguished one from the other either by the difference of the attributes of the substances, or by the difference of their modifications. . . .

Prop. V. There cannot exist in the universe two or more substances having the same nature or attribute.

Prop. VI. One substance cannot be produced by another substance . . .

From Spinoza, Baruch. "Ethics." *The Rationalists*. Trans. R. H. M. Elwes New York: Doubleday, 1960.

In Chapter 3, we pointed out that Spinoza was a pantheist because he believed that God and God's universe were identical. Now we can see why that must be so. But Spinoza's metaphysical view has other dramatic results as well: because mind and body are attributes of the one substance, our everyday division between ourselves as individuals is arbitrary and ultimately unreal. We are in fact all "one" (as some Asian mystics have long taught, too). Individuality is an illusion. So, too, is what we call "freedom." Because we are all an integral part of the one substance, we are wholly *determined* in our thoughts and our behavior by what goes on in the rest of the one substance. (We will consider the issue of freedom and determinism in Chapter 7.) So Spinoza's philosophy, which turns on the concept of substance, ultimately presents us with a picture of reality very different from our everyday views; it is a reality in which we are all a unity, in which individuality doesn't count and in which free choice is an illusion. It is a reality in which we are identical to (or part of) God and should not take ourselves as individuals at all seriously.

Gottfried Wilhelm von Leibniz

Gottfried Wilhelm von Leibniz, on the other hand, agreed with Descartes that there is a **plurality** of substances—that is, more than one. But Leibniz also agreed with Spinoza that substances cannot interact. Therefore, Leibniz postulated a world in which there are many substances, all of them created by God. These substances are all immaterial, and Leibniz called them **monads**. (God, too, is a monad, but something of a supermonad.) Monads, as substances, do not interact. How then, does it *seem* as if the world is composed of interacting substances?

Gottfried Wilhelm von Leibniz (1646–1716), who has been called "the last of the universal geniuses," grew up in Leipzig and traveled frequently. A philosopher of the highest caliber, Leibniz also was one of the inventors of the calculus, the father of modern formal linguistics, the inventor of a primitive computer, a military strategist, and a physicist who, in his own time, was the main rival of **Newton**.

Leibniz, like Spinoza, used his metaphysics as a basis for an imaginative and unusual view of the world. But where Spinoza believed that all things are a unity and that there is no individuality, Leibniz was very much an individualist, and it is for that reason that his pluralism of monads is so important to him. For Leibniz it was also important that God is not simply identical to the universe, but separate from it and watching over it, guaranteeing that this is "the best of all possible worlds" (see pp. 86 and 399). Spinoza saw the world as wholly determined and without freedom; Leibniz thought that what is most important—and what in fact defines each monad—is its individuality and spontaneity. To prove this, he developed the following view of reality.

An Introduction to Monads: Leibniz

1. *The Monad, of which we will speak here, is nothing else than a simple substance, which goes to make up composites; by simple we mean without parts.*

2. *There must be simple substances because there are composites; for a composite is nothing else than a collection or aggregatum of simple substances. . . .*

8. *Still Monads must have some qualities, otherwise they would not even be existences. And if simple substances did not differ at all in their qualities, there would be no means of perceiving any change in things. Whatever is in a composite can come into it only through its simple elements and the Monads, if they were without qualities, since they do not differ at all in quantity, would be indistinguishable one from another. For instance, if we imagine a plenum or completely filled space, where each part receives only the equivalent of its own previous motion, one state of things would not be distinguishable from another.*

9. *Each Monad, indeed, must be different from every other. For there are never in nature two beings which are exactly alike, and in which it is not possible to find a difference either internal or based on an intrinsic property.*

—*Monadology*, 1714

Each monad is something like an individual mind. There are no physical substances as such, only appearances of them. Moreover, the monads don't interact; they only appear to do so. Imagine yourself in a room, not merely surrounded by television screens but by the most sophisticated equipment of virtual reality. Television offers visual experiences that are limited to two dimensions and audio experiences that are limited by the placement and range of the speaker system. But a virtual-reality room, such as the holodeck in *Star Trek: The Next Generation*, provides holistic experiences. You can travel to distant lands, test your ability to be a good parent, or even indulge in a sexual fantasy that you would never consider in "actual" reality. The equipment does not intrude itself: you see no wires, tubes, or boxes, and you can sense no difference between the apparent world and the real world. On the holodeck, you experience the world or, rather, images of the world, and each of us—each in our own little rooms—experiences on the holodeck our own perspective on the world. God has programmed all of us to have the right perspective and the right images so that it seems as if we are all looking at the same world and at each other, but in reality we are not. Like all other monads, we never actually see each other, and there is no world as such. There are only our individual perceptions, within our individual monads, created and cared for by God in a "preestablished harmony."

Idealism
꒰ꑘꜟ

Idealism is the philosophy that says that what is real is mind, that all else—material objects, numbers, ideas—are in the mind or in some essential sense dependent on minds for their existence.

Descartes himself was not an idealist, but he established the framework for most later idealists when he said, in his *Meditations*, that one's own ideas are the only things one can know directly. From that, it is a short but spectacular leap to the claim that only ideas are real. Leibniz, for example, was an idealist; he said that physical reality is nothing but "perceptions" within immaterial monads—including the mind of God. According to idealism, however, there is nothing beyond us, except perhaps God (who is immaterial). The universe is made up of minds and of things dependent on minds, and nothing else.

Bishop George Berkeley (1685–1753) was a brilliant Irish philosopher-theologian who is still the leading representative of subjective idealism, the view that nothing exists except ideas and minds. When we do our utmost to conceive the existence of external bodies, we are all the while only contemplating our own ideas. "To be is to be perceived," Berkeley argued. All objects exist only in the mind (including the mind of God). Late in life, Berkeley became an educational missionary, visiting early America. Berkeley, California, is named after him.

Another early-eighteenth-century idealist was the Irish bishop **George Berkeley** 1685–1753. Berkeley held the extreme position of **subjective idealism,** which, simply summarized, insisted that "to be is to be perceived" (*esse est percipi*). According to Berkeley, it makes no sense to believe in the existence of anything that we cannot experience. (We will consider the underlying view, called empiricism, in Chapter 5.) But all that we can experience, Berkeley argues, are our own ideas. We know that a stone exists because we have ideas (experiences) about it, ideas of the visual appearance, touch, and weight of the stone, as well as of the sound it makes when we scrape it, the pain it causes when we kick it, its visible effects on other things (which are also nothing but ideas in our minds). We know that our minds exist, Berkeley argues, because ideas depend on minds. And we can know that God exists (as an infinite Mind) because, Berkeley argues, our finite minds require God's infinite Mind as a "presupposition." In other words, our minds don't arise on their own and they didn't exist from eternity; they depend for their existence, we must suppose, on something whose existence is eternal and dependent on nothing else, namely, the immaterial mind of God. (God is entirely spiritual, and thus an infinite mind.) Beyond that there is nothing else. No material objects. No world outside of our (and God's) knowledge and ideas.

This may sound counterintuitive. What could be more obvious than the existence of material things? We encounter material things all the time. But what is it to say that we encounter a thing? According to Berkeley, it is that we have an experience of it, which is to say, it is a mental phenomenon, an idea in our minds. But don't we experience a *material* object? No, says Berkeley. We only experience the thing's "properties," its characteristics. In the case of a rock, for example, we experience its properties of hardness, durability, weight, dimensions, shape, color, and so forth. These properties are all ideas, which are joined together with our idea of the rock. In the thing, these properties all appear together; but we can separate them as ideas.

What we never really experience is the rock's matter. "Matter" is just an abstract concept that we've imposed on what we experience. In the case of the rock, we postulate some substance, which we call its matter, to which these various properties are attached. "Substance" is our idea of what holds the properties all together in the rock. But this is to say that matter itself is only an idea. So-called material objects are ideas through and through.

Idealism in such extreme forms may sound far-fetched and hard to believe, but it is important to emphasize that such positions are not argued lightly. They are based on careful consideration and a large number of sound, hard-hitting arguments. Idealism can be argued, for example, from the seemingly undeniable premise that the only things we can know are based on experience and that nothing other than experience—for example, material objects existing "outside of us" in the world—can be known. Or, idealism might be argued from the nature of God and his works; if God is infinite Mind, then his creations will be thoughts. Or, idealism might be argued from Platonic considerations about the formal properties of things (such as the angles in a triangle. A thing is triangular-shaped because we recognize the form of triangularity in it, for example—but this is to say that we recognize an idea.) But, in any case, idealism is not just the frenzied assertion of a mad person—"Nothing exists but my mind!" It is a philosophical position of long standing for the very reason that it is based on arguments that many people have found convincing. If idealism seems to contradict common sense, it is nevertheless advanced—by Berkeley, for example—as nothing other than a more adequate account of commonsense experience. The idealist still believes in the reality of rocks and the blueness of the sky. But idealism is an attempt to reason about what these must *really* be like, if we are to know them at all.

Three German Idealists

Immanuel Kant (1724–1804)

Arthur Schopenhauer (1788–1860)

Georg Wilhelm Friedrich Hegel (1770–1831)

The emphasis on argument in the defense of metaphysics cannot be under-estimated. Indeed, much of the history of metaphysics since Plato has been based on the idea that reality is ultimately to be discovered not by the senses but by reason—through that abstract and perhaps "godlike" ability we possess to figure things out despite the bewildering confusion of appearances. But idealism has another source of inspiration, too. Many idealists are also devout theists. Both Berkeley and Leibniz invoke God in their idealism as the all-knowing Mind. One reason for this connection between their idealism and belief in God is the neces-sity of having an all-knowing Mind to perceive things when we do not. But God is not, in these idealists' views, just a corollary to epistemology (that is, the theory of knowledge and how we can "know" something). They are also devout believ-ers, and idealism suits their religious sensibilities as well as their epistemological theories. Idealism, in general, is a combination of vision and rigorous argument. Like most metaphysical theories, it is a worldview, in German, a *Weltanschauung*, which is supported and structured by careful and often ingenious arguments about why the world *must really be that way.*

Perhaps the most spectacular forms of idealism were developed in the nineteenth century in Germany, by a diverse group of philosophers known, appropriately, as **German Idealists.** The founder and unchallenged leader of this group was the great East Prussian philosopher **Immanuel Kant.** Kant, like Berke-ley, begins with the epistemological premise that everything we know must be based on experience, but he takes this easily agreed-on premise to astounding lengths. The world, he argues, is essentially *constituted* (*set up,* as in the word *constitution*) by us, through categories that our minds impose on them. There is no space, no time, and there are no objects apart from our experience of them.

However, the nature of objects is not up to our own individual fancy. Our minds are constructed in such a way that there are certain universal and neces-sary principles that ensure that space *must* be a certain way for us, and as a con-sequence, time and objects must be a certain way, too. The formatting that our mind applies to things might be compared to the formatting that is necessary for a computer to "read" a disc, except that our minds impose the formatting them-selves. If our minds did not automatically structure the input in accordance with this basic formatting, we would be unable to make sense of it. What Kant argues, in summary, is that there is a way the world must be, but it is a necessity based on the nature of our minds, not on the world itself. We *impose* laws on nature; we do not, like scientists, merely find them.

Kant's radical and exhilarating vision of the world gets coupled in Kant with another, even more dramatic, idealist vision. We live, he says, not just in one world, but in two. When we are concerned with knowledge—for example, while studying science or just checking out what buildings are down the street—we perceive the world through the concepts of our understanding, constituted ac-cording to certain rules. But when we are involved in practical matters, for ex-ample, or matters of religious belief, those concepts and rules no longer apply. Instead, we use a completely different set of rules. For example, a physician or a physiologist can explain what we do in terms of nerves and muscles, bones and movements. That gives us knowledge. But when we *act* and actually *do*

Three Worldviews

Kant—Two worlds ("standpoints") are equally "real" and rational.

The World of Nature (which we perceive)	*The World of Action, Morals, Faith*
Physical objects	Rational principles (morality)
Cause and effect	Freedom to choose
Self as object of knowledge	Self as agent
Science, technology	God, immortal soul, faith
Facts to be known	Duty to be done

DUTY TO BE DONE:

Schopenhauer—The world is illusion; only Will is real (but irrational).

Representations *Will* (irrational, without purpose)

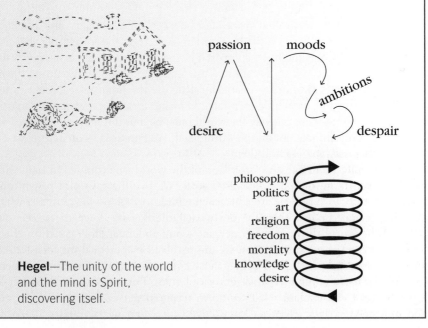

Hegel—The unity of the world and the mind is Spirit, discovering itself.

something, we don't see our bodies in terms of nerves and muscles; our bodies are simply the means by which we carry out our *intentions*, obey certain *principles*, achieve certain *ends*. So, too, when we think about God, we are not thinking of a Being who can be known through the concepts of scientific knowledge; and we already saw (in Chapter 3) that Kant instead defends a *moral* conception of God's necessary existence. Kant once said that he saw his mission in life as being to "limit knowledge to make room for faith." By dividing his idealism into two separate but equal realms, Kant succeeds in giving us a picture of reality in which science and religion are no longer at odds with one another.

After Kant, a considerable number of young German philosophers followed his lead and became idealists, too. Some preserved his "two world" vision; others rejected it. **Arthur Schopenhauer** considered himself a dedicated student of Kant, but where Kant tended to perceive the world with hope and considerable respect for humanity, Schopenhauer was a self-proclaimed pessimist. He didn't think much of people, and he didn't think much of life. His idealism, accordingly, spelled out his pessimism. But it was also based on a long train of sometimes brilliant arguments, some of them in defense of Kant's idealism, others pointing out where he thought Kant had gone wrong.

Arthur Schopenhauer (1788–1860) was possibly the crankiest philosopher in the history of Western thought. He was, perhaps ironically, an extremely willful person. He heaped scorn on most of his contemporaries, purposely announced his lectures at the same time as Hegel's at the University of Berlin in order to steal his students (an unsuccessful effort), and got involved in a lawsuit by knocking his landlady down the stairs. His philosophy, not surprisingly, takes the form of **pessimism**, the view that life in general is no good and has no purpose. Aptly, too, the central concept in his philosophy is "will." Yet he defended an ambitious system, modeled after Kant's, in which "will" is the driving force of everything in nature and, indeed, of reality itself. Despite his pessimism, Schopenhauer himself had a taste for good living, living very well until the age of seventy-two.

Kant divides metaphysics into two worlds—one of nature and knowledge, and one of action, morals, and faith. But both worlds are, in Kant's vision, *rational*. They operate according to necessary laws. Schopenhauer, by contrast, says in effect that both sides of this metaphysical dualism are *irrational*, a fitting conclusion for his pessimism. The world of knowledge is in fact a world of *illusion*, he claims. What is real is inside of us, our willful aspect with its desires and other passions, driving us to act. But where Kant, too, believed in the reality of an inner force, which he called the **Will**, this Will was, Kant believed, rational and obeyed the rules of reason. Schopenhauer disagreed. The Will, he said, is irrational. It was not "ours"; instead, it is a violent force operating through us, creating desires and passions and provoking us to act but, ultimately, to no purpose at all.

Schopenhauer's answer to this tragic vision of human life is escape from being driven by the Will—through either aesthetic detachment (the quiet enjoyment of art, literature, and music—unfortunately a temporary respite) or ascetic renunciation (the rejection of desire that characterizes many saints and mystics).

Kant employed an idealist metaphysics to envision the world as rational and to separate science and religion, because he was devoted to both of them. Schopenhauer used idealist metaphysics to portray his gloomy view of the world, in which both science and human passions were pointless. A third German idealist, G. W. F. Hegel (whom we met in the Preface and considered again in Chapter 3), used idealism once again to establish a picture of the world as rational and to reconcile his interests in science and religion and to establish a picture of the world as rational. But where Kant's idealism was largely static, a vision of two realms of human life each ruled by a priori principles, Hegel envisioned a single cosmos with constant internal conflict within which an all-embracing **Spirit** develops itself through all of us and throughout history. As Spirit, the world is a kind of cosmic consciousness, a universal mind, trying to understand itself. (Hegel borrowed heavily from Aristotle here.) For Hegel, the spheres of science, moral activity, and religion are all ways in which Spirit moved toward self-understanding. Hegel developed this vision through many arguments, some of them defending the general idealist position, some of them attacking the other idealists and saying why his particular vision was preferable to theirs. Whatever the particular version, idealism always remains an exciting mixture of basic visions and hopes for the world, coupled with hardheaded arguments about why this particular vision is the right one. Whatever else it may be, idealism is the view that our ideas define our world, and that the most essential thing in the world is—the mind.

Teleology

Hegel's view of the universal Spirit developing through history is a dramatic illustration of another ancient but still modern orientation premised on what we call **teleology** (from the Greek word for "purpose," *telos*). A teleological view of the world is one that thinks the world has an ultimate goal, a purpose, toward which it continually develops. In ancient times, Aristotle defended a teleological vision of the universe struggling to recognize itself—"thought thinking itself," he called it. So, too, Hegel's vision was universal Spirit struggling through human history to know itself *as* Spirit.

Modern science tends to discourage such thinking in terms of ultimate aims, urging instead explanations in terms of prior causes, which Aristotle calls "efficient causes"—that is, causes that bring something about. (Aristotle considered teleological goals to be causes, too, in that they helped to determine a course of events or behavior. He called these goals "final causes.") Indeed, since the seventeenth century we have been taught to think of the universe as something of a giant machine, a mechanism that operates according to the causal laws of nature. But this vision of the universe as a machine has always seemed incomplete to a great many thinkers, including even those at the forefront of its formulation. Both Descartes and

---

The Mutual Necessity of Truth and Falsity

The more conventional opinion gets fixated on the antithesis of truth and falsity, the more it tends to expect a given philosophical system to be either accepted or contradicted; and hence it finds only acceptance or rejection. It does not comprehend the diversity of philosophical systems as the progressive unfolding of truth, but rather sees in it simple disagreements. The bud disappears in the bursting forth of the blossom, and one might say that the former is refuted in the latter; similarly, when the fruit appears, the blossom is shown up in its turn as a false manifestation of the plant, and the fruit now emerges as the truth of it instead. These forms are not just distinguished from one another, they also supplant one another as mutually incompatible. Yet at the same time their fluid nature makes them moments of an organic unity in which they not only do not conflict, but in which each is as necessary as the other; and this mutual necessity alone constitutes the life of the whole.

—G. W. F. Hegel, *Phenomenology of Spirit*, 1807

From: Trans. A. V. Miller.
Oxford: Oxford University Press, 1977.

---

the great physicist Sir Isaac Newton, for example, defended a mechanistic, causal account of the universe, but also insisted that God provided purpose to his creation. So, too, Kant—who was an enthusiastic devotee of Newton—supplemented his causal view of the natural world with a teleological vision of the cosmos, and Leibniz taught that all monads unfolded according to God's purpose.

English-born **Alfred North Whitehead** (1861–1947) coauthored *Principia Mathematica* with **Bertrand Russell** before emigrating to the United States, where he developed his process theory.

The idea of the universe as a great machine is relatively new in history, but teleology is almost as old as Western civilization itself. The ancient Greeks were mostly **animists**—that is, they attributed some sort of lifelike activity to all things. Aristotle's teleological metaphysics was just a very sophisticated expression of this, a theory of the purpose *of* nature as well as of purposes *in* nature. So, too, Native Americans have long believed in a vision of the universe that is not mechanical (or "dead") but very much alive. Many Asian and African religions and philosophies also hold animistic and teleological views of the world, in contrast to our more mechanical, "scientific" models.

In contemporary times, such process philosophers as **Charles Hartshorne** and **Alfred North Whitehead** defend a teleological view of reality as **process** in place of the more static concept of substance, once again synthesizing science and teleological metaphysics. Whether or not the purpose of the universe is God's purpose, or the purpose of some other sort of Spirit or spirits, the idea that the universe *means* something and is itself striving for some sort of completion has always been an exhilarating philosophical view. In contemporary ecological context, many people employ the Greek term *gaia* to refer to a contemporary concept of the earth itself as a living organism, which they call the Gaia Theory.

A Theological "Mistake": Hartshorne

God Is Absolutely Perfect and Therefore Unchangeable. *In Plato's Republic one finds the proposition: God, being perfect, cannot change (not for the better, since "perfect" means that there can be no better; not for the worse, since ability to change for the worse, to decay, degenerate, or become corrupt, is a weakness, an imperfection). The argument may seem cogent, but it is so only if two assumptions are valid: that it is possible to conceive of a meaning for "perfect" that excludes change in any and every respect and that we must conceive God as perfect in just this sense. Obviously the ordinary meanings of perfect do not entirely exclude change. Thus Wordsworth wrote of his wife that she was a "perfect woman," but he certainly did not mean that she was totally unchangeable. In many places in the Bible human beings are spoken of as perfect; again the entire exclusion of change cannot have been intended. Where in the Bible God is spoken of as perfect, the indications are that even here the exclusion of change in any and every respect was not implied.*

—Charles Hartshorne,
Omnipotence and Other Theological Mistakes, 1984

By contrast, many people believe that the universe itself does *not* have a purpose, that it is simply "matter in motion" and not here for any particular reason. Indeed, it is in this vision of the purpose of the universe that our question about the meaning of life and our question about the ultimate nature of reality come together as a single problem. Does the universe have a purpose? Is this purpose provided by God? If so, what is it? And if the universe as a whole has no purpose, does human life have a purpose? Those are the ultimate questions that we all must ask ourselves at one time or another, for our various answers to them are with us all the time anyway. How we live and what we do, what we can hope for, and even our day-to-day attitudes toward our jobs, ourselves, and each other, ultimately fall within the framework of these ultimate metaphysical questions, and are accordingly affected by them.

But if the word *reality* is an evaluative term for what we consider most basic to our experience, as we suggested earlier, does reality have to be primarily scientific or religious? Suppose we give up the age-old presupposition that what is real must itself be most durable and eternal. Suppose, for example, one were to propose—as Hegel suggested—that what is most real is neither the world discovered by science nor the world believed in by religion but our *social* world, and that the primary structures of reality are not atoms or electrons or gods and other spirits but other people, tied together in bonds of kinship and community. Knowledge, in this interpretation of reality, becomes those views that are commonly shared and considered provable to anyone—or "objective"; religious belief consists of those doctrines and rituals held in common, which help hold the community together. Or suppose someone else were to say that *passion* is most real, that reality is what you feel when you're in love or extremely angry and everything else is but a pale shadow of this. Reality, in these views, is a function of *our* purposes, our passions, and our collective social goals.

The possibilities for metaphysics are more expansive than traditional Western philosophy has tended to suggest. It is a very real question, in other words, whether science and religion have been traditionally overemphasized in our view of ourselves. Are they really what's so important? What about *morality*? As we close this chapter we should open up the concept of "reality" to encompass further dimensions. Perhaps the stuff of the real world is none of the entities we have been talking about, but rather it is other people, or art, or music, or whatever—as Paul Tillich said of God—that is our "ultimate concern." The question of reality thus turns into the question of the meaning of life, which for some people may be answered in terms of God, for others in terms of science, but for many of us, once we start really to think about it, the answer might lie in an entirely different, perhaps even unexpected, place.

Metaphysics and the Everyday World

Philosophers frame our everyday experience in a larger vision so that their views about life and its meaning can be used to understand our ordinary experience in a different way. For Spinoza, for example, philosophy was a source of great consolation; it allowed him to see everything that happens as just another mechanical movement of the "One Substance," over which he had no control and in which, in any case, he didn't really matter. For Leibniz, on the other hand, philosophy was a source of optimism and confidence: he saw himself as an individual consciousness developing a view about the whole of the universe, assured from the outset that this view is programmed and guaranteed by God, who is watching over the whole process. These eminent writers were engaging in a great imaginative effort. To read them as if they were just solving some technical puzzles or, as some people complain, "just playing with words" is to misunderstand the way that they—and all of us—see the world. For we all need a vision, a conceptual framework, to give facts and things meaning and make our lives worthwhile. Spinoza and Leibniz were spelling out their vision of the world for themselves, for us to share, or for us to react against. Their success as philosophers depends on whether we do in fact react at all and whether we try to rethink their visions in our own terms.

You might object that Plato's vision of two worlds or the cosmic visions of Spinoza and Leibniz are poetic metaphors rather than philosophy. The German metaphysical views we have briefly explored—Hegel's grand view of the Spirit developing itself through all of us and Schopenhauer's dramatic view of a Will in all of us, driving us through our passions for no reason whatever—do indeed seem more like the images of poets than the hardheaded philosophical systems. But great philosophy is almost always poetry as well as sharp thinking, vision as well as argument, imagination as well as intelligence.

From our examinations of Western philosophers' ontologies and metaphysics, you should be starting to recognize certain basic suppositions that are common to most of them. First, there is an underlying assumption in most Western metaphysical views that *what is ultimately real* is that which endures throughout change. A second basic assumption is that reality is somehow a unity. If you believe that there are different ultimate units, or substances (like Descartes) or different worlds (like Plato or Kant), it is necessary to show how they somehow fit together. Scientists, too, have always sought the most elegant theory, which would tie together the most material under the simplest principle, and the ultimate goal of science, from Thales to Newton to Einstein, has been what Einstein called a "unified field theory"—that is, a single theory that would sum up and integrate all the laws of nature. And in religion, too, it is no surprise that some of the most dominant religions in the world, and all of the major religions in the West, are monotheistic—believing in one God—because a single deity, like a single explanatory principle, is more powerful and more compelling than a collection of gods or principles fighting among themselves for domination. Again, this assumption can be challenged, but to do so is to oppose the whole intellectual history of the West, and perhaps to be left with a sense of two or more realities that do not tie together in any coherent way.

We reiterate these two assumptions, not because they are beyond question (nothing in philosophy is beyond question), but because it is important to be aware of how powerful they are. The whole history of Western philosophy, science, and theology has struggled toward eternity and unity, so if you try to defend some other view you'd better have some good arguments for doing so. Still, these assumptions have been attacked, and brilliantly, for example by the philosopher Friedrich Nietzsche, who rejected the whole metaphysics of eternity and unity and thus rejected (he thought) the whole of metaphysics as well. If you think reality is to be found in the details of life, however, or in passions, or fleeting desires, then you might well be forced to reject these time-honored assumptions. But you cannot simply dismiss them. (Nietzsche spent his whole career trying to challenge them.) And whatever you do in your philosophy, it is at least important to take account of them. Is it possible that the world in reality is fragmented through and through?

Is it possible that life is essentially conflict and antagonism—what philosophers following Hegel and Marx call **dialectic**? Is it possible that there is no single, coherent viewpoint that will make sense of our lives? Even these are viewpoints to be defended, paradoxically, in a coherent, unified framework. Whatever else it is—visionary, speculative, inspiring—philosophy is also hard thinking, and imagination is its accomplice, not its substitute. Mutual tolerance of opinions is indeed a virtue, but not when it is lazy indifference or simply the insecurity that most of us have about defending our own ideas. When Socrates said that "the unexamined life is not worth living," what he really meant was "know yourself and your ideas; and criticize your ideas in order to revise them and be confident of them." What you think about reality isn't just "your opinion"; it is also basic to the way you live, and the foundation of everything that you do. And a flimsy foundation is no more secure for being unexpressed, unexamined, and unargued.

Closing Questions

1. Choose *one* of the elements defended by the pre-Socratic philosophers (water, fire, numbers, and so on) and argue for it as well as you can, preferably with a friend or a few friends who will try to prove you wrong. For example, if you choose *fire,* an immediate objection would be that fire could not possibly be the essential element in cold objects—a block of ice, for example. A reply might be that cold objects simply contain *much less* fire than hot things. You might also argue that not all fire manifests itself as flame, and soon, no doubt, you will find yourself moving into more modern-day talk about energy instead of fire as such. The point of the exercise is (1) to see how very much alive we can still make these ancient theories in our own terms and (2) to show how any theory, if it has even the slightest initial plausibility, can be defended, at least to some extent, if only you are clever enough to figure out how to answer the various objections presented to you and modify your theory to meet them.

2. Describe the Form of some ordinary objects around you, in accordance with Plato's theory. How do you know whether an object is defined by one Form or another? What can you say about the Form of an ordinary object, in the fashion of Plato's discussion of the Form of *triangle*? If an object changes, does it change Forms as well? Can an object have conflicting Forms? Can we understand our recognition of objects without some conception of Forms to explain how it is that we recognize them?

3. Categories in philosophy often seem too rigid or too simple-minded to classify the complexity of our views, but perhaps the following checklist will help you understand your own position in relation to the history of philosophy:

    a. Are you a materialist? An immaterialist?

Do you believe that ultimate reality can be discovered by science?

Do you believe that ultimate reality is a matter of religious belief?

b. What are the basic entities in your ontology? What is most real?

c. Are you a monist? A pluralist?

If you are a pluralist, what is the connection between the different entities in your ontology? Rank them in order of their relative reality, or explain their relationship.

d. Are the basic entities in your ontology eternal? If not, how did they come into being?

e. Are you an idealist? (Do you believe that the basic entities of your ontology are dependent on the existence of minds?)

f. How do you explain the existence of (or how do you deny the existence of) the following: minds, numbers, God, tables and chairs, the law of gravity, evil, moral principles, dreams, Santa Claus?

g. Does the universe have a purpose? Or one might ask, along with Martin Heidegger (see Chapter 6), "Why is there something rather than nothing?"

h. What does the word *real* mean to you? Using your definition, run once again through the items in Opening Question 1 and rate them for their reality in your view.

i. Do you think this world is the real world? Or do you believe that there is an existence more real than our own?

Suggested Readings

A good short introduction to metaphysics is Richard Taylor's *Metaphysics*, 4th ed. (Prentice-Hall, 1991). A good introduction to the pre-Socratic philosophers is John Burnet's *Early Greek Philosophy* (Adamant Media, 2005). Plato's *Republic* is available in a translation by G. M. A. Grube and revised by C. D. C. Reeve (Hackett, 1992). For a general introduction to Plato and his philosophy, see A. E. Taylor, *Plato, the Man and His Work* (Dial, 1936). A good contemporary introduction to Aristotle is Mortimer Adler's *Aristotle for Everybody* (Touchstone, 1997). The main works of the three philosophers René Descartes, Baruch (Benedict) Spinoza, and Wilhelm Leibniz are included together in *The Rationalists* (Doubleday, 1960). In that volume, Spinoza's *Ethics* is translated by R. H. M. Elwes, and Leibniz's *Monadology* is translated by George Montgomery. An exciting history of metaphysics is Arthur Lovejoy's *The Great Chain of Being* (Harvard University Press, 1976). Good surveys of the pre-Socratics, Socrates, Plato, Aristotle, Descartes, Leibniz, Spinoza, and other figures mentioned in this chapter are included in Paul Edwards, ed., *The Encyclopedia of Philosophy* (Macmillan, 1967), the *Routledge Encyclopedia of Philosophy* (Routledge, 2002), and the online *Stanford Encyclopedia of Philosophy*, ed. Edward N. Zalta. These are useful reference works for all philosophical topics. A good short introduction is John Searle's *Mind: A Brief Introduction* (Oxford University Press, 2005). An account of the German Idealists through imaginary interviews is Robert C. Solomon's *Introducing the German Idealists* (Hackett, 1981). Good articles on the German Idealists can be found in the *Cambridge Dictionary of Philosophy*, ed. Robert Audi, 2nd ed. (Cambridge University Press, 1999) and in Robert Solomon and Kathleen Higgins, eds., *The Age of German Idealism* (Routledge, 1993). For further consideration of Charles Hartshorne's process philosophy, see his *Omnipotence and Other Theological Mistakes* (State University of New York Press, 1983).

Madame Marie Curie, © Hulton Archive/Getty Images.

5
The Search for Truth

It is now some years since I detected how many were the false beliefs that I had from my earliest youth admitted as true, and how doubtful was everything I had since constructed on this basis: and from that time I was convinced that I must for once and for all seriously undertake to rid myself of all the opinions which I had formerly accepted and commence to build anew.

—René Descartes, *Meditations*

Opening Questions

1. Some of the information you have been given in your courses in school is, inevitably, not true. How would you start to prove to yourself that *all* of it is not false?

2. Suppose a friend were to challenge you, "How do you *know* that 2 + 2 = 4?" How would you answer?

3. Suppose another friend, in a provocative mood, were to ask you how you know that you are not dreaming at this very moment. What can you say? How would you prove to yourself that this is not true?

4. Is thinking rationally always the best way to think? Is the scientific answer to a question always the truest?

What Is True?

One unerring mark of the love of truth is not entertaining any proposition with greater assurance than the proofs it is built upon will warrant.

—John Locke, 1689

In the previous chapter, you were introduced to a wide variety of views of reality. Which of them do you believe? Which of them is *true*? It won't do to say "All of them," because some of them contradict the others; nor will it do to say "It's just a matter of opinion," because you still have to defend the one that you believe to be true. And because these various opinions are all *about* something—namely, the world—it is reasonable to ask whether they do or do not represent the way the world *really* is. But here we run into a more general problem, no matter what particular metaphysical view of the world we support: What is it for a set of beliefs to be true? How will we know when our beliefs are true? Sometimes a belief seems to be **obvious** (**self-evident**): But what if the "obvious" is not always so? These questions are the basis of the discipline called **epistemology**, the theory of *knowledge*, which is the focus of this chapter.

We will begin by indicating some of the reasons why the notion of a belief being true is not as straightforward as it seems. We follow this by distinguishing two types of truth, empirical and necessary, and then considering the related question of whether experience or reason is our primary basis for knowing the truth. Next, we will note that in our efforts to determine the truth, we inevitably begin with certain presuppositions, such as the ideas that the world exists and that every event has a cause. This raises the question of whether these presuppositions are defensible, and we will consider the skeptical challenge that suggests that they are not and the ways that Descartes, Hume, and Kant deal with skepticism. We then make note of the privileged position of science in what we take to be true and the extent to which this position is justified. We return to our opening question of what it means for an assertion to be true and discuss three theories of truth: the correspondence, coherence, and pragmatic theories. We then ask what it means to be rational and how rationality relates to the truth. We close the chapter by considering the problem of subjectivity (the possibility that truth depends on and varies with the subject) and the issue of relativism (what to make of the divergence of subjective interpretations of experience and the questions this prompts about whether anyone knows the truth).

Let us start by considering the question "What is it for an assertion or a belief to be true?" A seductively easy answer seems obvious: an assertion or a belief is true if (and only if) it corresponds to the facts. Thus, your belief that you have at least 75¢ in your pocket is true if and only if you do *in fact* have 75¢ or more in your pocket. Your belief that the Philadelphia Phillies have won the World Series is true if and only if, *in fact,* the Phillies actually did win the World Series. The great astronomer Galileo's belief that Jupiter has four moons is true if and only if, in fact, Jupiter has four moons, and so on. A belief is true if it corresponds to the facts. But that turns out not to help us at all.

First, consider the statements "$75 \times 3 = 225$" and "The cube root of 64 is 4." Are these statements true if and only if they correspond to the facts? What facts? Suppose it happens to be the case that there are not, in fact, any actual combinations of 3 sets of 75 things in the world; would that make the statement "$75 \times 3 = 225$" false, at least until such a combination occurs? Of course, you might say that *if* there were 3 sets of 75 things in the world, *then* they would add up altogether to 225 things. But "$75 \times 3 = 225$" seems to be true even if there are no facts in the world for the statement to correspond to. Therefore, presumably, there are true statements that do not (or need not) correspond to any facts.

Just the Facts?

Facts get in the way of truth.

—Miguel de Cervantes, *Don Quixote,* 1605

Facts are only the shadows of truth.

—Muhammad Ali, twentieth-century American boxer

Second, consider the status of a great many statements of "common sense." For example, going out in cold, damp weather causes us to "lower our resistance" and get sick. Doctors dispute this on the basis of scientific evidence, and yet we hold to such beliefs until they are *conclusively* refuted—and some continue to hold on to them even then. How do we know that what we believe as a matter of common sense is in fact justified and not just a set of plausible falsehoods that have been handed down uncritically from person to person, generation to generation?

Third, compare such statements as "There is a crystal vase here on the table," which is the report of an immediate and particular perception, and the natural law in science that "There is gravity between any two masses." Both statements are allegedly based on experience, but the latter obviously involves a much more complicated process of confirmation than the former. Between the two there are any number of generalizations based on experience—of **hypotheses**—that are formulated and confirmed by inductive argument, such as "Water freezes at 32°F" and "Cats run away when you put a German shepherd in front of them." But must all statements in science be confirmed by experience? Could it be that two very general theories might have no observation or experiment that could distinguish between them and verify one while refuting the other? String theory and other theories of subatomic particles might furnish examples. And what about religious truths—not only "God exists" but such claims as "Moses parted the Red Sea with the help of God"? Are these true because they "correspond to the facts"? Because they can in any sense be verified? Or is there a kind of truth that depends on faith and is very different from scientific truth?

Finally, what about very general truths or truisms, such as "All things will pass" and "Boys will be boys"? Tautologies are true (indeed, necessarily true), even though they don't seem to tell us anything about the world. And what are we to make of those grand statements uttered by the philosophers: "It is the Forms that are most real" and "There is only one substance"? Are they true or not? Are any of them true? How can we tell? What does our knowledge of such matters ultimately depend on? What is truth, and how will we know it when (or if) we find it?

Two Kinds of Truth

In the introduction to this book, it was suggested that true statements (or, simply, truth) might be divided into two separate categories: (1) true because of the facts and (2) true because of reasoning. Examples of the first would be the true statement that there is no change at all in your pocket, the true statement that Switzerland did not fight in a war in the twentieth century, and the true statement that water boils at less than 100°C on the top of a mountain. Examples of the second would be the true statement that "2 + 2 = 4," the true statement that "A + B = B + A," and the true statement that "No bachelor is married." These "truths of reason" are called necessary truths for they could not possibly be false.

Empirical Truth

A statement that is true because of the facts is called an **empirical truth**—that is, true because of experience. (The word *empirical* means having to do with experience.) Empirical truths can be known to be true only when we have actually looked at the world. (Of course, we don't always do this ourselves; most of our empirical knowledge depends on the observations and experiments carried out by other people. We take their word for it.) But because an empirical truth can be known only by looking at the facts of the world, a statement such as "There are no trees on the University of Texas campus" might—for all we know before we actually go out and look around—be false. Philosophers refer to such a statement (and the circumstances to which it refers) as **contingent**, or as a **contingent truth** (if it is true; if it is false, it is a **contingent falsehood**). Thus, the statement that there are no trees on the University of Texas campus, which happens to be false, is contingently so. We can *imagine* what it would be like otherwise; if someone were to cut down all the remaining trees, then the statement would become true, but only contingently true because there might someday once again be trees on the campus. As a general rule in philosophy, all empirical statements are, if true, only contingently true.

Two Kinds of Truth

Empirical, or factual, truth: "There are no rabbits in Antarctica."

Empirical, or factual, truths are true *as a matter of fact*, but it is possible that they might be otherwise and we can imagine what circumstances would make them false. They can be known only on the basis of experience (our own or someone else's).

Necessary truth: "2 + 2 = 4." Necessary truths cannot possibly be false, nor can we imagine circumstances in which they might be false.

Necessary Truth

A statement that is true because of reason, on the other hand, is *necessarily* true; it is a **necessary truth**. *Necessary* is here the opposite of *contingent*: we can always imagine what it would be for a contingent truth not to be true (or a contingent falsehood not to be false). We cannot even make sense out of the suggestion that a necessary truth might not be true (or that a necessary falsehood might not be false). "2 + 2 = 4" is a necessary truth, in that we cannot imagine—no matter how imaginative we happen to be—what circumstances might make that statement false. (Suppose you add together two drops of ink and they combine to form one drop; would this prove the statement to be false? Why not?) For example, the necessary falsehood "1 + 1 = 1" cannot be imagined to be true under any circumstances. Necessary truths can be said to be true, accordingly, *prior to* experience, or (in Latin) **a priori**. (It is important to note again that *a priori* does not mean "before" in the sense of temporally "before any experience"—that is, it does not mean that we knew these things before we were born. Some philosophers do believe that there are ideas "born into" us, or *innate* ideas. Nevertheless, we must come to recognize these truths after we have learned a language and presumably, acquired considerable intellectual sophistication.)

So long as we restrict ourselves to a limited number of standard examples— the statement that there is so much change in your pocket or the statement that "2 + 2 = 4"—the distinction between empirical, contingent truths, on the one hand, and what some philosophers call "truths of reason," or necessary truths, on the other, seems adequately clear. The distinction becomes extremely problematic, however, when we try to consider the status of the all-important philosophical questions we have been raising in the preceding chapters. Does God exist? What is reality? Is there a meaning to human life? Are the answers to these questions empirical or necessary truths, and should we appeal to our experience or reason (or both, or neither) to answer them?

Believing in the existence of God, for example, would seem to be a belief in a fact; indeed, many philosophers have argued (by means of the considerations we discussed in Chapter 3) that the existence of God is the ultimate fact. But suppose we imagine an argument between a theist (who believes in the existence of God) and an atheist (who does not). What facts can the theist show the atheist that would compel the atheist to believe in God? The theist can show the atheist one of the many passages in the Bible in which the existence of God is forcefully asserted; but of course the atheist will not accept this as evidence because an atheist does not accept the authority of the Bible on what is true. A few theists may even be able to claim that they have direct evidence of God's existence because he has actually talked with or presented himself to them. Again, the atheist will not think anything of this alleged evidence either, because he or she will dismiss such experiences as mere delusions. The theist brings up the miracles that have been recorded in history as evidence of God's presence on earth; the atheist dismisses these as accidents or as unexplained (but not unexplainable) occurrences. The theist points to the intricacy of the world (by way of the argument by design) as evidence that there must be a God to create such a masterpiece; the atheist insists

What Facts Will Prove the Existence of God?

Theist's Proof	Atheist's Reply
Stated in the Bible.	Not all statements in the Bible are true.
Experiences God in a vision.	Mere hallucination, doesn't prove anything.
Miracle of the Red Sea.	Geophysical quirk, not a miracle.
Delicate order of nature.	Product of natural selection and chance occurrences.
The existence of the world.	It just happened; otherwise, we wouldn't be here to discuss it.
The victory of the good over evil (in World War II, for instance).	Superiority of Allied forces (in the case of World War II) and a few lucky turning points.

that it is all chance, and, anyway, the world isn't such a "masterpiece" after all. It all depends on how you look at it.

The futility of this debate shows us that believing in God is not simply a matter of accepting the facts, but of something more. What more? "Faith" is one traditional answer, but faith is not so much a claim to know the truth as it is a matter of *confidence* that what one believes is true. It has been argued, however, that believing in the existence of God is perfectly rational and demonstrable, not as a matter of fact but through abstract reasoning. (We saw such reasoning, for instance, in the ontological argument for God's existence in Chapter 3.) If such an argument is successful, then "God exists," though it looks like a statement of fact, is a necessary truth.

Consider in the same way a statement about the meaning of life—whether life is meaningful or not and what that meaning might be. Suppose a friend of yours insists, without going into details, that human life is meaningful. What facts make this true? Your friend points out the pleasures of love, the joys of knowledge, the thrills of skiing, the delights of a good glass of wine in front of a fireplace. "Life is good," your friend concludes, as if having proved it. But you, who think life is absurd, disagree. "Love never lasts," you insist; statistically, at least, you are certainly right. You point out the futility of knowledge, the number of broken legs among skiers, the high cost of decent wine and firewood. You go through the crudest facts of human history, the atrocities of war, and the cruelties and the dead ends, even in those societies that lived under the illusion that life was "getting better all the time." You point out the tragedies in life and, in any case, how short life is. You conclude, "Life is no good." You and your friend each have facts on your side. Who is right? Once again, it is clear that the facts won't tell us. Your friend can insist that even wars and tragedies serve their purpose, to remind us of the value of life and to show us that some things are important enough to fight for. Your friend can insist that life is intrinsically meaningful no matter how long it lasts or how many misfortunes should befall us. In other words, it is the **interpretation** of the facts that matters, not the facts themselves.

Finally, consider the statement that what is most real are Plato's Forms (from Chapter 4), not the things and facts of everyday experience. If this is true, is it true because the statement corresponds to the facts? No, because the theory itself says that the facts of our experience are not the basis of truth. Could you say that this theory in turn does—or does not—correspond to the facts? If you do, then you generate a paradox—namely, that the theory is true because it corresponds to facts that it denies are the basis of truth. Once again, we can see that this philosophical statement, if it is true, must be true in such a way that the facts are not the central consideration.

Perhaps the statement "the Forms are most real" is defensible through pure thinking and without regard for whether the apparent facts of the world support it. Indeed, most philosophers would say straight out that the facts of ordinary experience (or, for that matter, the facts of extraordinary experience) may have very little to do with philosophical truth. But then are all philosophical truths necessary truths—the product of reasoning? Can reason deliver on such an enormous promise? Some philosophers have certainly thought so; others have denied it. But almost all of them (until fairly recently) thought that if there were an answer to any philosophical question (or any other question of knowledge), it would have to be *either* an empirical truth based on experience *or* an a priori truth that was both necessary and a product of reason.

It is one thing to say that a statement is true or false and something else to say what *kind* of truth it is and how we would know that it is so. Many philosophers have argued that knowledge is "justified true belief." Truth is only one of the necessary conditions of knowledge. It is also necessary to be able to *justify* our belief. We need to believe something on grounds that are justified in order to appropriately claim to know it.

We should note that even justified true belief can fall short of knowledge, as contemporary philosopher Edmund Gettier has pointed out. He considers cases in which someone believes something true on grounds that are usually good evidence, but in the particular case the evidence turns out not to be. An example of this sort would be your believing that a particular classmate is in the library because you saw her—but in fact you saw her twin sister. Nevertheless, the classmate is in another part of the library. In cases such as this, you have a justified true belief, but not knowledge. Still, such cases are unusual. Most of the time our main concern in attempting to determine whether or not we have genuine knowledge is to ascertain whether or not a belief we hold is justified. And it is the attempt to justify philosophical beliefs that has given rise to perhaps the single biggest split in modern philosophy.

Rationalism and Empiricism

In the past few centuries, two schools of philosophy have come to dominate much of the discussion of these questions about the kind of truth to be found in philosophy. They are usually given the names *rationalism* and *empiricism*. The names alone should give you a good indication of the positions they represent.

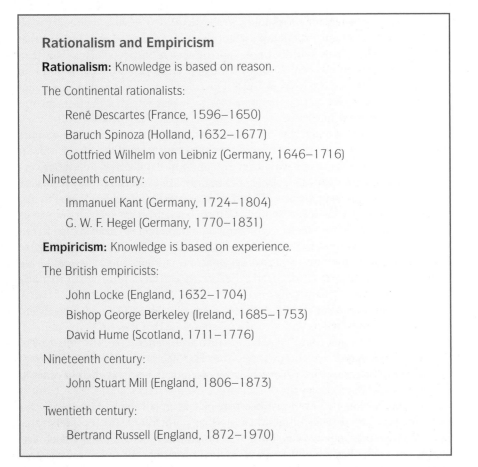

Rationalism and Empiricism

Rationalism: Knowledge is based on reason.

The Continental rationalists:

    René Descartes (France, 1596–1650)

    Baruch Spinoza (Holland, 1632–1677)

    Gottfried Wilhelm von Leibniz (Germany, 1646–1716)

Nineteenth century:

    Immanuel Kant (Germany, 1724–1804)

    G. W. F. Hegel (Germany, 1770–1831)

Empiricism: Knowledge is based on experience.

The British empiricists:

    John Locke (England, 1632–1704)

    Bishop George Berkeley (Ireland, 1685–1753)

    David Hume (Scotland, 1711–1776)

Nineteenth century:

    John Stuart Mill (England, 1806–1873)

Twentieth century:

    Bertrand Russell (England, 1872–1970)

Rationalism is a broad designation for a variety of theories, all of which have in common the confidence that human *reason* can provide the final answers to the most basic and essential philosophical questions. Furthermore, these answers all will be necessary truths. Great rationalists in modern times include the philosophers Descartes, Spinoza, Leibniz, Kant, and Hegel; in ancient and medieval times, most of the great philosophers were rationalists, including Plato, Aristotle (with qualifications), Saint Augustine, and Saint Thomas Aquinas (with qualifications). They all believed—in one way or another—that philosophical reasoning can give us the answers, and that these answers are all necessary truths and are to be found through our thinking processes themselves—whether inspired by God, radiated by "Forms," built into the structure of our minds, or "born into" our brains (that is, innate). Experience might provide some of the material for our thinking, as well as some clues and perhaps the trigger to the answer, but experience cannot by itself, according to the rationalists, teach us anything at all. Truth is not subject to the vicissitudes of experience.

Empiricism, on the other hand, is a philosophical method that rejects this conception of **innate ideas** and insists, in the words of John Locke, that "all knowledge comes from experience." According to Locke, the human mind at birth is a "blank tablet" (Latin: **tabula rasa**), on which experience writes the general principles as well as the details of all our knowledge. Other empiricists include David Hume, whom we will discuss further, the nineteenth-century thinker John Stuart Mill, and the twentieth-century philosopher Bertrand Russell.

Empiricists still believe in *reason*, of course, especially in the well-defined activities of calculation and logic—as in mathematics, for example. But they do not believe that reason has anything of importance to say about the big philosophical questions; indeed, the most radical empiricists of the twentieth century even insisted that reason can tell us nothing about the world but only about the structure of the language we use to describe the world.

Rationalists, on the other hand, do not reject the testimony of the senses either, but they do insist that observation and experiment—in short, *experience*—cannot give us philosophical truths. Both rationalists and empiricists would agree that the question "How much change do you have in your pocket?" is to be answered only by appeal to experience, and that the statement "If *A* is a *B* and all *B*'s are *C*'s, then *A* is a *C*" is a necessary truth by virtue of reason. What they disagree about is how the fundamental questions of philosophy are to be answered, and whether they can be answered.

Rationalists believe that they can be answered and answered with certainty—that is, as necessary truths. Empiricists generally believe that, if they can be answered at all, they will have to be answered either as trivial statements about the meaning of our words (for example, the word *reality* simply *means* "that which is material and sensible") or as generalizations based on extensive experience (for example, the empiricist John Stuart Mill thought that even such statements as "2 + 2 = 4" were in fact very general claims about experience and not "truths of reason" at all). Because, for empiricists, all knowledge is based on experience (and inductive arguments), knowledge is (at best) highly probable and not certain. Not surprisingly, many empiricists have argued that some of the big questions of philosophy are not answerable, and much of empiricism has been a reexamination of the questions themselves, an attempt to show that they cannot be answered and, perhaps, that they do not make much sense in the first place.

One of the main points of debate between the rationalists and the empiricists—both in the seventeenth century and today (for instance, in the debate between linguist Noam Chomsky, who contends that we have an innate aptitude for language, and such contemporary empiricists as Nelson

Goodman)—concerns the existence of innate ideas. We have already seen that innate ideas are those "born into" us, but this does not mean (what would be absurd) that newborn infants already "know" that 437 multiplied by 73 equals 31,901 (as if he or she just hasn't yet acquired the language to express this). Briefly put, rationalists generally accept the idea of innate ideas; empiricists usually reject it. Descartes, a rationalist, tried to begin with such intuitively certain truths as the idea that God is a perfect being and then tried to deduce from this other truths that would (by virtue of a valid deduction) be equally certain. John Locke, an empiricist, rejected this idea of innate ideas. Because our minds are blank tablets at birth, all of our ideas must therefore be derived from experience, for none of them are innate.

The problem here is that all of our knowledge does not consist of individual perceptions ("Here is a coffee cup"). Much is based on universal statements such as "Every action has an equal and opposite reaction." How do we get from the individual perceptions and our limited experience to such universal claims? The rationalists insist that it is only by way of some innate ideas or rational **intuitions** that this is possible—and that the most necessary truths about the world (the statements of mathematics) could not possibly be based on experience but must be based on innate ideas.

The Presuppositions of Knowledge
༺ঔ༻

Reason already persuades me that I ought no less carefully to withhold my assent from matters which are not entirely certain and indubitable than from those which appear to me manifestly to be false, if I am able to find in each one some reason to doubt.

—René Descartes, 1641

We have seen that there are two kinds of truth; we have also seen that it is not at all clear which (if either) kind of truth we will find in philosophy. But at this point in our discussion, we should also point out that other principles share this problematic status with such big questions as the existence of God, the meaning of life, and the nature of reality. Unlike the big questions of philosophy, these principles are not usually considered a matter of debate; they are rarely, if ever, suggested to be a matter of mere opinion or faith, and so they are often not thought of as principles of philosophy at all. But they are. These are philosophical principles that lie at the foundations of virtually all of our knowledge and beliefs. They are the **presuppositions** of our thinking, without which we could believe nothing, know nothing, think nothing else.

For example, the basic philosophical belief that the *world exists* is the presupposition of anything that any scientist wants to say about the world. It is presupposed, too, in our most ordinary statements, such as "We ought to paint the door of the house green instead of red," because that presupposes that there is a door, a house, paint, and the world. Similarly, one of the philosophical principles that has long been discussed and debated is the principle that *everything that happens has a cause* (sometimes called the **principle of universal causality**). We cannot imagine chemistry without this principle, in fact, and we cannot imagine even the most everyday occurrences without it. Consider what you would think of a garage mechanic who told you, when your car wouldn't start, "Nothing's wrong: this is one of those events without a cause." You wouldn't call into question the principle that everything that happens has a cause; you would go to another mechanic.

Are There Innate Ideas?

The Empiricist View

It is an established opinion among some men, that there are in the understanding certain innate principles, some primary notions, stamped, as it were, upon the mind of man which the soul receives in its very first being, and brings into the world with it. It would be sufficient to convince unprejudiced readers of the falseness of this supposition, if I should only show how many men obtain to all the knowledge they have, without the help of any such innate impressions. . . . Let us suppose the mind to be a blank tablet; how comes it to be furnished? To this I answer in one word, from experience.

—John Locke, *Essay Concerning
Human Understanding,* 1689

The Rationalist Reply

Is the soul empty, like a tablet upon which nothing has been written? Does all truth depend on experience, that is to say, on induction? . . . The senses, although necessary for all our actual knowledge, are not sufficient to give us the whole of it, since the senses never give anything but examples. And it would seem that necessary truths, such as are found in pure mathematics and especially in arithmetic and geometry, must have principles the proof of which does not depend on examples, nor, consequently, on the testimony of the senses, although without the senses it never would have occurred to us to think of them.

— Gottfried Wilhelm von Leibniz,
New Essay on Human Understanding, 1704

In moments of uncertainty, most of us wonder whether there is a God or whether life has meaning. Many people wonder from time to time—though only rarely to the extent of the philosophers—what the world is really like. But no one in his or her right mind ever really wonders whether the world exists; indeed, when philosophers debate such curious topics, it is usually only to out a theory they have about truth or reality, not to see whether in fact the world exists. But however obvious such principles as the existence of the external world or the principle of universal causality may seem to us, their status as knowledge is questionable. These statements are not clearly about matters of fact. They are not provable through experience. (That is why we know *before* we go to the garage, or a priori, that something must be the cause, though we do not know what.) Neither are they evidently true by virtue of reason. It is not contradictory to think that the outside world might not exist. Yet surely the existence of the world is not a mere matter of opinion. So what are we to say about philosophical truth? How can we prove, beyond a doubt, that these obvious truths are indeed true?

Skepticism

> *Nothing exists. If anything did exist, we couldn't know it. If we could know it, we couldn't communicate it.*
>
> —attributed to Gorgias

It may not be a question we ever ask in real life, but suppose someone were to ask you how you know that you're not dreaming right now. Suppose the same person—a friend taking his or her first philosophy course, perhaps—were to ask you how you know that the world even exists or has ever existed, how you know that all the things you have ever experienced, from your mother's breast to the car you call your own, have not been just ideas in your own mind. How would you answer? What would you say?

It is important to notice the assumption lying behind these questions, not necessarily because the assumption is false, but rather because it is indeed the assumption of most of our metaphysical thinking, as well as our way of talking about ourselves. The assumption is that there are two distinct realms of reality, one "outer"—the physical world—and one "inner"—the world of our experience. The physical world would exist, we presume, even if we were not here to experience it, but the world of our experience might be the same, according to this assumption, even if we were just dreaming about it, and even if, as Leibniz suggested, each of us were nothing but a mind, programmed by God to have certain experiences at certain times, *as if* there were a physical world "outside" us.

How do we get into this rather odd and troubling assumption? It seems quite obvious, given the way we have been talking—that each of us knows the world, from our own perspective, through our own personal experience. Both the empiricists and the rationalists would agree that what we know directly (whether through reason or experience) is first of all our own ideas and sensations. But these ideas and sensations are in our minds. The world, obviously, is outside of our minds, an external world. We assume, naturally, that our ideas or representations correspond to the things in the world, but how do we know this? Many empiricists, following John Locke, would argue that the things in the world affect our sense organs in ways that cause us to have certain sorts of experiences, and that we infer from the nature of these experiences what the things that caused them must be like. Rationalists, on the other hand, might assume that there is some inherent connection between our ideas and the world—perhaps, as Descartes argued, guaranteed by God.

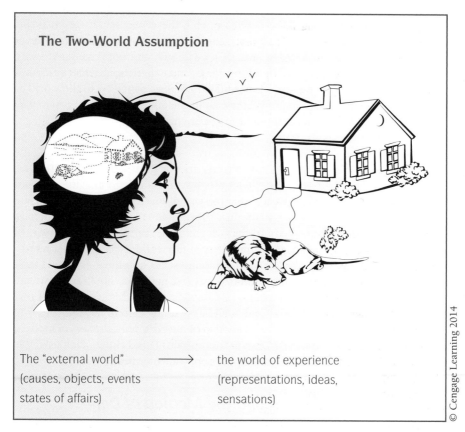

The Two-World Assumption

The "external world"	$\longrightarrow$	the world of experience
(causes, objects, events		(representations, ideas,
states of affairs)		sensations)

© Cengage Learning 2014

The two-world assumption, however, leads us into a serious conundrum about the relationship between our ideas and the things in the world. We can see the nature of the problem if we restate our assumption in the form of two apparently reasonable claims: (1) there is an external world—that is, a world beyond our beliefs and experiences, which is not affected by what we happen to believe about it, and (2) we cannot ever make direct contact with the world itself but only with the contents of our own minds—with our ideas, our beliefs, our various experiences, and the principles that we find to be necessary truths (such as the principles of logic and arithmetic).

The two preceding statements have been accepted by a great many thinkers of the past several centuries (though the second would not have been acceptable to most philosophers in ancient times). And they are still accepted by a great many philosophers today. Indeed, in everyday life we seem to accept both of them, too; the idea that the world actually exists seems so obviously true that, except in a philosophy class, we wouldn't even think of questioning it. And the idea that what we know directly are our own experiences, not the world itself, also seems indisputable; don't we often have experiences without knowing whether they are true? And we sometimes have experiences that do not in fact match up (or correspond) to the world (dreams and hallucinations, for example). Could we know anything whatsoever about the world if we did not first experience it in some way? Nonetheless, however reasonable these two statements may be, together they give rise to an intolerable conclusion: namely, that we can never know—or at least we can never be sure that we know—the world at all.

What we know are our own opinions, ideas, and experiences; what we cannot know is whether those opinions, ideas, and experiences match up to the world as it really is. The world we thought we knew so intimately suddenly seems far away from us, unreachable by either thought or experience.

Now if anything is to be true, it must be true by reference to the facts and objects of the world, or it must be true as a "truth of reason." But according to the two-world assumption, what we know directly are our own ideas and experiences, not the physical world itself. This is why it is possible for us to imagine, without changing anything in our experience, that the world might not exist or that we are now dreaming. Furthermore, we might raise the question of whether the principles we believe a priori—our necessary truths—might in fact be true only of our way of thinking, or true of our language, but not true of the world itself—in other words, not true. But now we have raised an embarrassing set of questions, for could it be that the world of our ideas, beliefs, and experiences, no matter how certain we are of them, is not at all like the physical world outside of us? This set of doubts that we might not actually know the world at all is generally referred to as **skepticism**. In the sections that follow, we will see how two of the great philosophers of modern times, the rationalist René Descartes and the empiricist David Hume, each used this set of doubts as the engine of his entire philosophical enterprise.

René Descartes and the Method of Doubt

The first rule is to accept nothing as true which I do not clearly recognize to be so; that is to say, carefully to avoid precipitation and prejudice in my judgments, and to accept in them nothing more than what was presented to my mind so clearly and distinctly that I could have no occasion to doubt it.

—René Descartes, 1641

The philosopher best known for his deliberations about all of this is the French philosopher **René Descartes** (1596–1650; see p. 28). He wrote a series of essays, the *Meditations*, generally considered to be the foundational text of modern philosophy. Descartes accepted both of the statements above (p. 157); in fact, he considered them both to be obviously true. But Descartes was a rationalist. He insisted on proof. Descartes was so concerned with *proving* his beliefs to be true, in separating his true beliefs from his opinions and false beliefs, that he decided, as a matter of method, to suspend his belief in everything. This is referred to as Descartes's "**method of doubt**." Doubt everything, Descartes resolved; assume that everything one believes is false until one can prove it to be true. Indeed, one of the things Descartes doubted was the very existence of the external world. "Suppose I am now dreaming," we might paraphrase him. "After all, I have found myself dreaming before, when I thought (in the dream) that I was awake. Could I be dreaming all of the time? In fact, probably not. But if I cannot know this for certain, then I must doubt it, for until I can prove that a belief *must* be true, I do not have the right to believe it at all."

Now you might think that once one has made such a drastic move, there is nothing in the world that cannot be doubted. But this is not the case. It is our second statement, in fact, that provides Descartes with his first absolutely **indubitable** belief (that is, beyond doubt or unquestionable): what we know directly are the contents of our own minds. "Suppose," we might paraphrase him again, "I try to doubt the existence of my own mind. What I find is that I doubt that I am now doubting. But if I doubt that I am doubting, then, as a matter of necessity, I must indeed be doubting." Descartes's conclusion: "I cannot doubt that I'm doubting." More generally he concluded, "I cannot be wrong about the fact that

"My feeling is that while we should have the deepest respect for reality, we should not let it control our lives."

I'm thinking, for the fact that I'm thinking about thinking already proves that I'm thinking." From this simple logical principle emerges Descartes's most famous statement, "I think, therefore I am" (in Latin, *Cogito ergo sum*—this argument is often referred to as simply "the *Cogito*"). Here is a statement that cannot be doubted. Here, therefore, is a statement that can be used as a premise with which to prove beyond a doubt the objective truth of other beliefs, too, including our belief in the existence of the external world.

The rest of Descartes's proof remains one of the most heatedly debated arguments in the history of modern philosophy. In brief, it is this: given the certainty of the statement "I think, therefore I am," Descartes then proved (or tried to prove) the existence of God, by way of one version of the ontological argument. We have a clear and distinct idea of "a supremely perfect being." We also clearly and distinctly perceive that part of the nature of this being is that it necessarily exists. A supremely perfect being has every perfection, and one such perfection is existing necessarily. It would be an imperfection to depend on anything else for its existence, so a supremely perfect being cannot be contingent for its existence on any other thing. Our reason enables us to infer that the supremely perfect being exists, claims Descartes.

So now Descartes had two **certain** statements: "I exist" and "God exists." But God, we know, is by definition a perfect being who includes within his perfections perfect goodness. And if this is so, God would not allow us to be fooled about the existence of the world. Therefore, if God exists, the world must exist, for otherwise "I do not see how God could be understood to be anything but a deceiver if the ideas were transmitted from a source other than corporeal things." So, too, Descartes could now argue that all of the basic principles of which I seemed so certain can now be shown to be true, necessarily. To paraphrase him, he argues, "God would not fool me; so I can know that I know the world, after all."

Note that Descartes has overcome his doubts entirely through reasoning. Reason is our firm basis for knowledge, while the senses can lead us astray. Descartes is convinced that our knowledge even of things in the world comes from our reason, not through the senses. To demonstrate this, he suggests that we take a piece of wax from a honeycomb. What do our senses tell us about the wax? They inform us that the wax is a pliable solid of a certain color, hardness, and shape. But now let us take the wax and put it near a fire. The wax melts and all its sensory properties are now different than they were before. It is no longer solid or hard; it is fluid and translucent; its shape is not even stable any longer. Our senses do not even enable us to say that the wax is changeable, Descartes tells us; they cannot even track that we are dealing with the same piece of wax. How, then, do we know that the wax is the same despite the change in its properties? We recognize this through our intellect, through reason, not the senses.

David Hume's Skepticism

Skepticism has been a powerful philosophical position ever since ancient times. It is not an answer to the big questions of philosophy so much as the disturbing reply that there are no answers. Where the basic questions of knowledge are concerned, this does not seem tolerable. Can we really doubt that the world exists or the ordinary presupposition that everything that happens has a cause? Because it seems we can't, skepticism has usually been considered more of a problem to be avoided or a challenge to be answered than a philosophical position to be accepted for its own sake. In your own thinking, it is a signal of danger that should keep you on your toes and wary of too easy, dogmatic answers that in fact you can't defend. Indeed, what makes Descartes's method of doubting everything and Hume's skeptical conclusions so valuable to us is, more than anything else, the fact that they make us so aware of how easily we simply presume that the obvious is objectively true. And the point of philosophy, in answering the big questions, is precisely to allow us to go beyond what we first think is obvious and to think things through to the point where we can actually defend what we believe—even against so brilliant a skeptic as Hume.

How much of what we believe is merely personal opinion? How many of our beliefs do we share only with our family or our friends but not with the larger community? Which of our beliefs might be generally accepted in our society but not believed by people in many other societies? Are there beliefs that are built into the human mind as such but that may nonetheless be false, beliefs that other intelligent creatures—perhaps highly intelligent beings from another planet— would know to be based on faulty evidence and misleading ideas, which for some reason seem to be particularly prevalent on earth? Are there beliefs that are built into our language but not into other languages?

This last idea is defended in the theory of linguists Edward Sapir and Benjamin Whorf, who contend that the patterns of one's native language shape the way one thinks about the world. Language carves up the world, not the other way around, and the categories that one's language provides are the categories through which one thinks. People who speak different languages, it follows, might be led by their languages to think very differently about the world. For example, languages like ours, which emphasize enduring objects, might lead us to experience the world quite differently from the way the speaker of a language that emphasizes processes might. The view that language structures the way we experience the world is sometimes called *linguistic determinism*. The Sapir–Whorf hypothesis predominated in linguistics in the early half of the twentieth century, and although it has since been challenged by Noam Chomsky and others, who contend that we have an innate knowledge of a universal grammar underlying all languages, it continues to be influential.

To ask questions about how much language and culture affect our understanding of the world is not to reject any possibility of our knowing the truth, any more than Descartes's method of doubt was an admission on his part that he could never know anything. But it is to make us more sensitive to the limitations of our knowledge and the need to support our beliefs on more solid footing than the fact that we, personally, find them to be "obvious."

In the eighteenth century, Scottish empiricist **David Hume**, like Descartes, pondered the extent to which we simply take our basic ideas about the world for granted, but unlike Descartes, he drew some disturbing conclusions. Hume accepted the two statements—that there is an external world existing independently of us and that each person is in direct contact only with the contents of that person's own mind—as obviously true, but he, too, insisted on proof of them. As an empiricist, he accepted John Locke's principle that all knowledge comes from experience; so for him the question was whether our belief in the existence of the external world could be proven to be true by appeal to experience. Or, if not, could it be shown to be true as a "truth of reason"? And this would be true of all our other philosophical questions, too, about the principle of universal causality, the existence of God, and the nature of reality. But whereas Descartes emerges from his *Meditations* with the positive conclusion that we *can* know the answers to these questions, and know them with certainty (that is, a priori, or as necessary truths), Hume emerges from his study with the most negative of conclusions—that we cannot know the answers to any of these questions, that the most basic principles of our everyday knowledge as well as the most important guiding principles of our lives are without justification.

David Hume (1711–1776) was, according to many British philosophers, one of the outstanding geniuses in philosophy. He spent most of his life in Edinburgh, Scotland, where he was born, but he traveled frequently to both London and Paris, where he was a celebrity. While still in his twenties (after a vacation in France), he wrote his *A Treatise of Human Nature* (1739), which became one of the great philosophical works in the English language. The book was not well received, however, so Hume wrote two more "popular" books on the same subjects, *An Enquiry into Human Understanding* (1748) and *An Enquiry Concerning the Principles of Morals* (1751). He was an avid historian as well as a philosopher, a jovial partygoer, and one of the most popular men in Europe. Because he was also an atheist, however, he was not allowed to teach his philosophy in any university.

Hume's Strategy (Hume's Fork)

Every justifiable true statement is either a

"truth of reason" (a priori)   or   "matter of fact" (empirical)

"2 + 2 = 4"   **"There are tigers in India."**

Which are the following philosophical statements?

   "God exists."

   "Life has meaning."

   "Everything that happens has a cause."

Hume's argument was elegantly simple, and philosophers have been trying to refute it ever since. (Bertrand Russell once wrote that in his opinion no one had yet succeeded and that "Hume's conclusions . . . are equally difficult to refute and to accept.") Hume's position is skepticism, and it amounts to the negative claim that we cannot know the answers to questions to which we once thought the answers were obvious. The argument "**Hume's Fork**," simply presses home the idea that there are two (and only two) kinds of truth, **matter of fact** and **truth of reason**, and any belief that cannot be proved one way or the other is therefore without justification. So Hume asks, with regard to any belief, "Is this a matter of fact, to be defended by appeal to experience or experiment? Or is this a truth of reason, the truth of which can be demonstrated by an abstract calculation of the kind we find in mathematics or logic?" If the answer is "Neither," then Hume insists that the judgment in question has no grounds for our continued belief, because it is without rational justification.

Hume's skepticism began, as Descartes's rationalist proofs had begun, by accepting the second of our two statements (which says that we cannot ever make direct contact with the world itself but only with the contents of our own minds). He might doubt the existence of the world, but he did not for a moment doubt that our knowledge begins with experience, and that what we know directly are our own ideas and experiences (or what Hume called "impressions"). From this starting point, Hume shows us why we are not justified in believing principles that no sane person would actually doubt (except in philosophical investigations). Let's look first at his argument against the principle of universal causality, then at his argument against our supposed knowledge of the external world.

Is the principle of universal causality a matter of fact, known through experience? Or is it a relation of ideas known through calculation and logic? Let's take the second possibility first: the principle of universal causality essentially says that everything that happens has a cause. Can we imagine a world in which it is not the case that everything that happens has a cause? Seemingly so; contemporary physicists frequently talk about random subatomic emissions as having no cause (not simply no *known* cause, but *no* cause). We can imagine a particle in space, significantly isolated from all other particles, simply shooting off in one direction with no cause whatsoever. And regarding all particular causes, this is certainly not a matter of reason. We know, for example, that the collision of one moving billiard ball with another causes the second to move; but this, Hume argues, we learn entirely from experience, not on the basis of reason. The first human being, Hume suggests, could not possibly have figured out that water could drown him or that fire would burn him, until he actually had the experience of trying (unsuccessfully) to breathe under water or the painful experience of putting his hand in the fire.

Knowledge of causes and effects, it seems, is a matter of experience, not reason. And so, we presume, is our knowledge that everything that happens has a cause. But this, it turns out, is not the case either. In our example with the metaphysically perverse garage mechanic, the key to our illustration was the fact that we knew before we entered the garage that something had to be the cause of the car's failure. (In other words, we knew it or thought we knew it, a priori.) But this means that we do not learn the principle of universal causality *from* experience; in some sense we carry it *to* experience. No number of unexplained events in the world would ever lead us to give up this principle, and in fact it is only because we already expect a cause that we know how to look for and find one.

What is a *cause*? We might say that one event causes another if the first event brings about the second. But if we look at the previous sentence, we see that it is an utterly trivial statement; "brings about" is just another phrase for "causes," so we have not yet explained what a cause is. Let's take a particular example: the example of the two colliding billiard balls. The movement of the first causes a certain movement in the second. (If we know the speed and direction of the first, we can calculate in advance the speed and direction of the second.) But what we actually see, Hume points out, is not the cause at all. What we see are just the two events—(1) the movement of the first ball and (2) the movement of the second ball. Indeed, the first time (or first several times) we watch, we may have no way of predicting the movement of the second ball at all. We might expect the first ball to come to a complete stop or bounce backward, or we might expect both balls to break or explode. This means that knowledge of causes is not a matter of reason. But no matter how many times we watch, all that we ever actually see are the two events—the movement of the first ball, the movement of the second ball—and we never see the connection between them, the actual *cause* of the second event. Hume concludes that we never actually see the cause of an event at all; we only see that two events are regularly found together, in "constant conjunction." Here, too, Hume's conclusion is skeptical: something we thought we knew for sure turns out not to be justifiable through experience or reason.

What Do We Do with Metaphysics?

When we run over libraries, persuaded of these principles, what havoc must we make? If we take in our hand any volume of divinity or school metaphysics, for instance, let us ask, Does it contain any abstract reasoning concerning quantity or number? No. Does it contain any experimental reasoning concerning matter of fact and existence? No. Commit it to the flames, for it can contain nothing but sophistry and illusion.

–David Hume, *An Enquiry Concerning Human Understanding*, 1748

Regarding the existence of the external world, Hume's argument is equally devastating and of much the same form. Can our belief in the external world be shown to be a matter of reason? Clearly not. We can imagine ourselves simply dreaming, as Descartes suggested. Is it a matter of experience? No, for just the same reason that pinching yourself to see if you are dreaming doesn't tell you if you are dreaming. Any experience is itself a part of that world being experienced. So long as we accept the two-world assumption, which seems quite irrefutable, it surely is possible that the world of our experience exists but the physical world does not. Within that world of experience there is no experience by which we can tell that this is not so.

The Resolution of Skepticism: Immanuel Kant

We end our discussion of skepticism, however, not with Hume and the apparent victory of the skeptic, but with Hume's greatest successor, the German idealist Immanuel Kant. Kant read Hume's arguments in defense of skepticism and was deeply shocked—"awakened" from his "dogmatic slumber," as he put it. He considered Hume's "fork" and realized that so long as one accepted the exclusivity of the "matters of fact" and "relations of ideas" dichotomy and, even more, so long as one accepted the seemingly innocent two-world assumption, there would be no getting around skepticism—and that meant no way of justifying those basic presuppositions upon which all our knowledge is based. So what Kant does, put simply, is to deny the two-world assumption.

We already saw (in Chapter 4) that Kant insists that we constitute or set up the world according to a priori rules. But then it is not true, he says, that we first of all and directly know only our own experiences, and that we know the things of the world only secondarily or by inference. To the contrary, the world we know *is* just the world of our experience. The mind, Kant suggests, imposes its forms and categories on our experience, and among these forms and categories are those that provide the presuppositions of our knowledge (for example, causality and substance). These presuppositions, accordingly, are neither empirical truths nor relations of ideas, but a special and new kind of truth that Kant calls *synthetic a priori*. In calling them "synthetic" Kant claims that these truths are not mere tautologies, not merely trivially true, but true of the world we experience. They are a priori because, like all necessary truths, we know them prior to experience.

What would our experience of the world be like if we didn't impose these forms on it? The answer is that we would not have anything we could really call experience. We would not be able to identify objects, recognize similarities or differences between our sensations, or even have any sense of self as the subject of different experiences succeeding one another in time. Thus, the presuppositions of our knowledge can be said to be necessarily true because they are the rules according to which any experience at all is possible. And because they are *our* rules, skepticism about them—or whether they correspond with the world they constitute—is utterly pointless. Or so Kant argued, and after him, Hegel.

Knowledge, Truth, and Science
ᘐᗡᘏ

When most people (including philosophers) look for the truth today, they look to **science**. For several centuries, science and its methods have been the royal road to finding out how the world really is. Empiricists and rationalists both tended to be scientists or to have great admiration for scientists. Skeptics often tended to defend their skepticism as "scientific." Educated religious critics of science did not usually reject it but only questioned some particular scientific theory or the intrusion of science into some concern where it was inappropriate. One need not attack science, for example, to question Darwin's theory of evolution or to insist that the experience of love is not something that social scientists should try to study. On the other hand, science does presume a certain worldview that may well be judged to be too limiting or too impersonal for many questions about human life. In any case, this much seems undeniable: science is today our touchstone of truth. To say that something is "scientifically established"—whether it is a theory about the surface of the planet Saturn or the effectiveness of a new, improved brand of toothpaste—is to imply that we have come as close to the truth as we can expect to get.

Science has been a word connoting praise for several centuries. The German equivalent, *Wissenschaft* (which includes systematic inquiry in fields beyond the natural sciences), was used by such figures as Kant and Hegel to emphasize the seriousness and thoroughness of their thinking about all sorts of matters, from physics to metaphysics. Today, however, the scope of the term *science* tends to be limited to those questions that can and must be answered by reference to **experience** and extrapolations from experience. Thus, it might be said that science is an *empirical* discipline—as opposed to logic and mathematics, for example. Physics, chemistry, geology, and biology—the natural sciences—are the standard examples. Somewhat more controversial are the social sciences—psychology, sociology, anthropology, and economics—but there is no doubt that, whatever else they may be, they are also empirical disciplines based on observation and, to a more limited extent than physics and chemistry, on experiment. To say that a science is empirical is to insist that its theories and hypotheses must be tested in experience and can be shown to be true or false by way of experience. Our measure of truth is largely a matter of whether or not this can be done, and philosophers called **logical positivists** once argued that any statement that could not be so tested was simply "meaningless" (unless, of course, it was a trivial truth or a statement in mathematics or logic).

It would be a mistake, however, to think of science as nothing but the gathering and testing of facts through experience. It would be a very limited and boring science indeed that did nothing more than collect large numbers of facts. Chemistry would be nothing but an enormous laboratory and catalog filled with specimens and names of different substances. Biology would be nothing but garden tending and zoo keeping. But these are not chemistry or biology and never were. Chemists since the ancient Babylonians—and probably long before that—operated not only with observed facts but with hypotheses and theories. The facts served the theories by *confirming* them—showing them to be probably true—or by disproving them—showing them to be probably false. A caveman searching for a mammoth and trying to avoid a saber-toothed tiger is operating with hypotheses about where each of those creatures should be (behind the bushes, in the swamp, asleep in the cave), and his experience had better confirm his hypotheses.

Modern chemists do not just collect chemicals but formulate hypotheses about how different chemicals relate to one another, how one is produced from another, why some chemicals cannot be further broken down, and so on. To do this, they need a whole language of chemistry that is not merely descriptive of what we can see, touch, and pour into bottles. In addition to such a descriptive **observational language** ("a fine red powder that easily bursts into flame"), chemists also need a **theoretical language**, a technical language for concepts generated by the theory itself ("atoms," "molecule," "element," "chemical bond," "oxidation"). Strictly speaking, no one has ever seen an electron. Yet electrons are among the most important particles ever discussed by chemists, and it is by talking about electrons (and other subatomic particles) that chemists can describe most of what they know about the world.

Science is an empirical discipline, but like metaphysics it involves speculation, imagination, the specification of things unseen. Besides the observation of facts and the carrying out of experiments, the scientist or the science student needs to *think* to formulate theories, to go beyond what can be observed and suggest what might explain it. Mathematical models, for example, play a central role in many sciences—physics and economics, for example. Truth in science is not just the truth of facts. It is also the truth of theories. A scientist without a theory and without a hypothesis for guidance would not have anything to do. Like a child with a new chemistry set, of course, a chemist could just throw together one substance after another and see what would happen. But in addition to being dangerous, this would be an aimless activity and as unlikely to produce an insight into truth as a monkey on a computer is to produce a novel.

Hypotheses and theories guide observation and experiment. A scientist might notice something by accident that leads to the formulation of a hypothesis and a sketch of a theory, but this is possible only after the scientist has been thinking about and working with the same subject for some time. A hypothesis tells us what facts to look for. A theory tells us how to understand these facts. The hypothesis that water is a combination of oxygen and hydrogen tells us what kind of experiments to perform (those that combine the two elements, those that divide water molecules into their components). It is atomic theory, however, that tells us how to interpret such results. Indeed, without atomic theory it is not even clear how we would interpret the idea that water is a "combination" of anything—much less the combination of two gases that cannot even be seen.

The importance of hypotheses and theories in science raises enormous problems about truth. We are not very confused about what is meant by *truth* when the claim is observationally straightforward: "The frog is sitting on the stone," for example, or "The powder just changed to blue." But when a large theory is under consideration, its truth, by its very nature, cannot be simply discerned. Darwin's theory is a complex and ingenious scheme for describing an enormously wide variety of observations—many of them not yet made. It is not the only scheme that explains these observations, even within the realm of evolutionary theory. So what does it mean to say that it is "true"? It might be shown that it is the simplest, the most far-reaching, the best-confirmed theory. Nevertheless, we want to say that *truth* means something more than "very well confirmed"; it means "the way the world really is." Are we ever justified in saying this of a theory?

Indeed, are we justified even in saying that a particular fact is true? We have seen how the skeptic tries to throw into doubt *all* our knowledge of the world, except, perhaps, the most basic facts of our senses ("I am seeing green right now"). The importance of theories in science points to a different way in which the truth of science might be doubted. Facts get gathered to confirm or disprove a hypothesis; the selection of hypotheses, in other words, determines what we will look for. But observations in general get made in the light of theories. To call something a "sunset" is to see what we observe in relation to a certain astronomical theory—a false theory, in fact. To call a streak of a cloud in a chamber an "electron" is to interpret what we see in the light of a certain theory. One might say, "There are no electrons; they are only postulations of a theory." But so, too, one might object, "There are no sunsets; there is only a certain position of the earth vis-à-vis the sun, with some peculiar refractions of light as the result."

Facts get interpreted according to theories. Without a theory, there would not even be certain facts. Some philosophers of science, on the basis of such considerations, have argued that there are no facts as such, only facts as viewed in the light of theories. Every observation in science presupposes a theoretical framework, just as every theory presupposes some facts to make it empirically plausible. But suppose, as we look through the history of science, we find that scientists have held very different theories, and interpreted the same facts in very different ways. What, then, are we to say about truth in science? How do we compare theories to tell which, if any, are true?

The question here is whether science really does give us the truth or perhaps only a truth of its own making. For example, many scientific observations are possible only by means of specially invented scientific equipment—a telescope, a microscope, a cloud chamber, or a cyclotron. Could it be that the truth we discover is in fact the creation of the implements we use? Imagine yourself in Galileo's laboratory several hundred years ago, looking through some weird-looking invention called a telescope. Through this strange tube, you see what look like moons around the planet Jupiter, and you see what look like mountains on the face of the moon. Do you trust your eyes? If you were living at the time, you might well refuse to accept what you saw, on the grounds that the tube distorted your vision, much as a red-colored lens will make the world look red. What would convince you that the tube really had improved your vision rather than distorted it? Or could it be that any implement in science, even while it allows us to learn something, nevertheless interferes with and distorts precisely the subject it seeks to study? (Imagine a traffic cop—in uniform—studying the ordinary behavior of drivers. What the cop sees, for the most part, is not the ordinary behavior of drivers at all but the behavior of drivers when they are in the presence of a police officer.)

Why do we take science as a paradigm of truth? Isn't it possible that the results of science can be doubted? Isn't it possible that even the observations described by science can be doubted? The answer to both questions is yes, but nevertheless science has two impressive claims in support of its current status as the road to truth:

1. Science has been highly successful in predicting nature and in giving us the ability to invent instruments to alter nature to our will. One might question whether science has allowed us to understand nature better than ancient religious or Renaissance artists, but one can hardly question the success of science in predicting how chemicals that were until recently unknown will react or in putting a man on the moon.

2. Science has both empirical and intellectual integrity. Scientific hypotheses can be and must be tested and tested again. No scientific theory is ever simply accepted; it must be supported over and over again with new research. It must always stand up to new questions, new challenges. No one ever has the authority to force a theory on science against the evidence, and no opinion is considered influential enough to prompt rejection of a theory that better explains the evidence. Any scientist will admit that these standards are sometimes violated; scientists are only human, after all. But the ideals remain and are accepted by everyone. Because of the rigor of these ideals, science has earned, and keeps, its place in our philosophy.

Even if we accept all this, however, we can still ask whether science deserves what often looks like an *exclusive* right to the honorable word *truth*. What about human feelings—are they true or not? What about art and beauty—how do they fit into the scientific world? What about human relationships and international politics—are they made better through science? When we pride ourselves on approaching all questions scientifically, is it possible that we are harming more than helping ourselves?

Consider the recent debate between defenders of the theory of evolution (not necessarily Darwin's) and those who accept the creationist view of the world based on Genesis. To their discredit, evolutionists have sometimes dismissed the religious view of creation altogether, not even trying to see how the two views might be fitted together, even if the words in Genesis are taken more or less literally. To their discredit, creationists have at times defended some appallingly bad "science" in trying to refute the evolutionists, and they, too, have not always been willing to see how the two apparently antagonistic views might be put together. One could interpret evolution as God's means of creation; one can invoke God as the explanation of how the whole process got started. But without entering into the tangled web of emotions and beliefs that make this controversy so intractable, we can make two points in favor of a cease-fire:

1. Whatever the plausibility of creationism as a scientific hypothesis, it must be understood that the thrust behind creationism is not scientific curiosity; it is an attempt to stop science and its exclusive claim to truth from encroaching on territory where it has no business—the domain of religion. The origin of species is the border between the two domains.

2. Whatever one might think of any particular theory of evolution, science is nothing if it is not empirical. A scientific theory must be confirmed by observed facts, not just accepted on the basis of authority. A theory must be falsifiable by facts; that is, we must at least be able to say what kinds of findings would undermine the theory. On the basis of its importance as a religious viewpoint, creationism may have as convincing grounds for belief as evolutionary theory has. But it is not and should not claim to be a scientific theory. (If the existence of fossils doesn't undermine it as a scientific theory, what could?) Indeed, given its religious motivation, why would creationism prefer to compete as bad science rather than present itself as solid and established religious doctrine?

The Nature of Truth

To say of what is that it is not, or of what is not that it is, is false, while to say of what is that it is, or of what is not that it is not, is true.

—Aristotle, fourth century BCE

We have already seen that some statements are true whether or not they correspond to the facts. We have also seen that basic principles of philosophy are of this sort; they are not matters of fact but something else—perhaps (according to the rationalists) truths of reason, perhaps (according to the skeptics) mere matters of opinion that cannot be justified at all. But in either case, what has become clear to us is that our initial conception of truth—the idea that a statement is true if and only if it corresponds to the facts—is inadequate. Let's give this conception of truth a name: the **correspondence theory of truth**. But there are other kinds of truth, as we have seen, such as the true statements of mathematics and logic, that don't obviously correspond to "facts" about the world. We need a more general theory that will include them.

So far we have talked primarily about the basic means for reaching the truth, setting aside the question as to what truth is. But the statement of the correspondence theory of truth and its presupposed two-world view forces us to take this secondary question much more seriously. Indeed, what good is a theory of truth if it gives us no indication of how—or even whether—we can ever *know* the truth? With that in mind, philosophers have often shifted their attention from a statement or belief *being* true to our *reasons* (or justification) for accepting it *as* true.

Consider this. In a detective story, a man is murdered out in the country on a dark and cloudy night. There are no witnesses, only a small scattering of clues (a footprint, some fabric from a raincoat made in Transylvania, some suspicious marks on the neck of the victim). Now, if you are the detective investigating the case or if you are a member of the jury at the trial, it won't help much to be told that you know that D is the killer if and only if you know that the statement "D is the killer" is true. What interests you are the *reasons* for believing that D is the killer—the perfect match of the footprints, the fact that D has recently "lost" his raincoat, and the curious toothy smile D occasionally displays in the prisoner's box. But such reasons never add up to a complete picture. They are always no more than evidence, which point to a conclusion but never actually reach it. (This is so even if D confesses; a confession is sometimes an excellent piece of evidence, but it is not in itself the fact that we are looking for.) We can't directly see whether or not the claim that D is the killer matches the facts. The facts we are concerned with are in the past; all we have now is the evidence.

Now, given that the facts themselves seem lost to us, a number of very different conclusions follow. Suppose that you, as detective, have developed an airtight case against D. What does this mean? Not that the claim that D is guilty could not possibly be false (because it is, after all, a *contingent truth* that D is the killer), but that the alibis that D would need to convince anyone that he was not the killer would seem so ridiculous and so unreasonable that no one would believe them—for example, stories to the effect that he has a twin brother who is always getting him into trouble or that he is the victim of a collective conspiracy on the part of you, the police, and all the witnesses. The evidence still adds up to less than the truth we are looking for. Can we *know* that D is the killer, that this is an objective truth instead of a merely subjective opinion? Some people would say, "Yes, of course; all you need to claim that your belief is true is the best available set of reasons; there is nothing else you can have." But others would say, "No, you never actually know what is true; at most, you have the best belief under the circumstances, and you have to make do with that." The first claim asserts that we still have objective truth, but it depends not on a property of the object but on the reasons we provide for our beliefs. In the second view, there is no objective truth as such; it is simply a matter of competing opinions and sets of evidence, some of which are more persuasive than others.

The situation is even more difficult with philosophical truths. If we are concerned with the existence of God, for example, it is clear that the same problem exists. If God appears directly to us, perhaps that would seem to settle the question. (But even then, how do we know that we are seeing *God*, as opposed to a delusion, or as opposed to the devil who is trying to fool us?—only by appeal to the *reasons* for believing one interpretation of the apparition rather than another.) We claim to have some evidence that God exists (the existence of Scripture, for instance, and the existence of the world as a designed masterpiece). But the evidence never adds up to the indisputable fact. To say that one *knows* that God exists is to assert that one's belief is both justified and true. But we have already seen that there are serious questions about what should *count* as a justification for belief in God. It seems that one must accept the truth of God's existence not because of but rather prior to any evidence or argument that would confirm it. This is why Kierkegaard holds that belief in God requires a "leap of faith."

How Do We Learn?

But how will you look for something when you don't in the least know what it is? How on earth are you going to set up something you don't know as the object of your search? To put it another way, even if you come right up against it, how will you know that what you have found is the thing you didn't know?

— Plato, *Meno*,
fourth century BCE

Protagoras and Meno. Trans. W. C. K. Guthrie.
Harmondsworth, UK: Penguin, 1957

This apparent need to have the truth *before* one collects adequate evidence and argument is not just a problem in connection with the very special belief in God's existence. It would seem that any claim to know the truth—whether coming from a rationalist or an empiricist—requires that we know the facts *independently* of our claim to know the truth in order to be able to justify our claim to the truth. This would mean, according to the correspondence theory of truth, that we first need the truth (the facts) to justify our claim to truth. In other words, we can't say that a statement is true without having justifying reasons—but this would seem to suppose (on the correspondence theory) that we can know the world apart from our own knowledge, a bizarre contention, to put it mildly.

Here we meet the skeptic face-to-face: Is it the case that we can't know the truth because we can never be certain, because we must always make a leap to get from our evidence and our reasons to the "facts"? Or is it even worse, that we can never know the truth because somehow we have to know the truth before we can have any reasons for claiming to know the truth? But perhaps the problem isn't truth but rather this particular, seemingly obvious theory of truth—the correspondence theory. Perhaps there are other conceptions of truth, which have the twin virtues of both accounting for the various kinds of truth we have discussed and answering the skeptic.

Two such theories have predominated in the past few centuries. They both shift the emphasis away from the "facts" to the *reasons* for accepting a certain belief. One is called the coherence theory of truth; the other is called the pragmatic theory of truth.

The Coherence Theory of Truth

The **coherence theory of truth** begins by rejecting the correspondence theory, insisting that the very notion of correspondence to the facts not only fails to account for truth in mathematics and logic but even fails (as our detective story example showed) to account for ordinary factual truth. All we have are reasons for believing—evidence, arguments, principles, and our various beliefs themselves. Why do we need anything more? Indeed, when we talk about truth, what we mean is simply this: what is true is simply that statement or belief that best *coheres* with the overall network of our experience and beliefs. We accept a principle as true because it fits with our other principles. We accept an argument because it follows from what we believe and leads to conclusions we can accept. We agree on the evidence because it fits into our hypotheses, because it hangs together, because it adds up to a coherent picture. Nothing else is needed to give us the truth.

Of course, our evidence is always incomplete, and the beliefs that we already accept are not always sufficient to allow us to know with certainty whether some new belief should be accepted. In fact, there may be occasions (for instance, a religious conversion) in which the whole network of our beliefs exhibits a significant shift or turnaround or disruption. But this is not to be taken as our inability to ever reach the truth; quite to the contrary, what it means is that the truth is within our grasp, and that with experience we change our beliefs precisely in order to grasp it more exactly.

The Pragmatic Theory of Truth

Grant an idea or belief to be true, what concrete difference will its being true make in anyone's actual life? . . . What, in short, is the truth's cash-value in experiential terms?

—William James, 1907

Of Fact and Truth

In the realm of truth-processes facts come independently and determine our beliefs provisionally. But these beliefs make us act, and as fast as they do so, they bring into sight or into existence new facts which re-determine the beliefs accordingly. So the whole coil and ball of truth, as it rolls up, is the product of a double influence. Truths emerge from facts; but they dip forward into facts again and add to them; which facts again create or reveal new truth (the word is indifferent) and so on indefinitely. The "facts" themselves meanwhile are not true. They simply are. Truth is the function of the beliefs that start and terminate among them.

The case is like a snowball's growth; due as it is to the distribution of the snow's growth, due as it is to the distribution of the snow on the one hand, and to the successive pushes of the boys on the other, with these factors co-determining each other incessantly.

—William James, *Pragmatism*, 1907.

New York: Longmans, Green, 1907. 225–26

Born in New York City, **William James** (1842–1910) received a degree in medicine from Harvard University before beginning his career teaching philosophy and psychology there.

The **pragmatic theory of truth** supplements the coherence theory with a practical proviso—namely, that among the reasons for accepting a statement or a belief as true is whether it allows us to function better, whether it suggests fruitful lines of inquiry to be pursued in the future—whether it "works," in the words of its famous defender, the American pragmatist **William James**. One hypothesis in science, for instance, may not have any more evidence for it than another, and it may fit into our overall beliefs no better than do a number of others; but it may well be more easily able, encourage further experimentation in the same field, or suggest interesting possibilities not suggested by other hypotheses. To say that a view is true, therefore, is to say that it is the most useful and most promising explanation available to us. We get the most benefit out of it in dealings with the world. But the value of a view is not just its scientific promise. It might be its social or spiritual value as well—for example, in the case of a view about morality or religion.

Rationality

With the shift of attention to reasons for believing something to be true, the virtue of having good reasons, or what we call **rationality**, has become increasingly important. Throughout most of the history of philosophy, from Plato to the modern rationalists, rationality and the search for truth were considered absolutely identical. But where truth seems to refer only to the "way the world is," without any reference to our ways of knowing it, rationality clearly refers to our mental activities, to our methods of finding the truth, and so provides us with a much more tangible and less evasive topic of discussion.

Rationality means "accordance with reason"; to be rational in our thinking and acting is to make use of reasons, good reasons. What is a "good reason"? If thinking is based on "facts," then the facts must be well confirmed, not simply hearsay or wild guesses. (We do not have to say that the facts are necessarily "true" in the correspondence sense; someone might have very good reason to accept them but, by some twist of circumstances, they turn out not to be true.) If thinking is based on deductive reasoning, then the reasoning must be valid. Of course, a "good reason" must make sense; appeals to mysterious forces or mystical insights will not do in rational argument. And a good reason must be relevant to the case at hand; a brilliant argument and a number of facts do not constitute rationality if they are not directed at the matter under consideration. But this last point is derived from the most important general characteristic of rationality: rationality depends most of all on coherence. To be rational is to provide as many reasons, dig up as many facts, and call up as many beliefs as are necessary to provide a comprehensive logical web in support of any given belief.

Since Kant, this ideal of rationality has ruled in philosophy. But what is the relationship between rationality and truth? In one sense, it is important that we insist that rationality does not require that our beliefs be true. For example, you might think that the belief that the earth is flat, motionless, or made of water is a false belief, and, in terms of the system of beliefs that we all share today, any of these beliefs certainly is not *rational*. But had you lived in earlier times, in ancient Greece, for example, these beliefs would not have seemed false at all but completely rational. And in the context of their system of beliefs, what you now believe would have been utterly irrational. This does not mean that it is always rational to believe what everyone around you believes and irrational not to; it *is* possible that everyone's beliefs are irrational, founded on bad reasons, lack of evidence, refusal to think about them clearly or carefully, and unspoken prejudice or superstition. But this is not always or even usually the case. In the example

Theories of Truth

Correspondence theory: True beliefs (or sentences) correspond to the facts.

"The cat is on the mat."

Coherence theory: True beliefs (including beliefs about experience) and sentences cohere with each other.

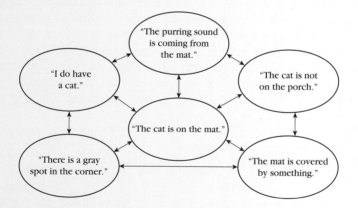

Pragmatic theory: True beliefs (or sentences) are those that "work."

"It's time to feed the cat."
"Get the cat off the mat."
"Why can't we burn the mat?"
"Why is the mat so heavy?"

mentioned, we may suppose that the Greeks had the best of reasons for believing what they did about the earth. Being rational, therefore, does not require or demonstrate that one has "the truth"; it requires only that a person make the best possible use of all of the information and "reason" at his or her disposal.

How does this conception of rationality relate to the commonsense idea that truth is correspondence to the facts? It is hard to deny that what makes the statement "The cat is on the mat" true is just that the cat is in fact on the mat. But what the preceding considerations and arguments suggest is that we can't simply take this correspondence of statement to fact at face value. What lies behind it is the entirety of our language and our ways of conceiving and referring to the world.

In isolation, the words (or more properly, the sounds or the scribbles) "The cat is on the mat" mean nothing at all, refer to nothing at all, and are neither true nor false. They make a true statement only by virtue of the conventions that connect words with ideas and those that allow words to operate systematically with each other. And what justifies the statement or belief that the cat is on the mat is not the fact but the array of evidence, both visual and from the other senses—the coherence of that statement or belief with all manner of other statements and beliefs and the implications for various practical concerns. In other words, even if one wants to insist that what makes the statement true is the relevant fact, we can say that we *know* that the cat is on the mat only because it is the most rational thing to believe.

Thus, although we can distinguish between rational thinking and truth in some particular cases, the truth is that which is most rational to believe at a given time and in a given situation, on the basis of the best available evidence and the most careful thinking possible. According to many philosophers, there is no other sense to be given to the words *true* and *truth,* unless we are to fall back again into the intolerable doubts of Hume's skepticism.

Why Be Rational?

By now you might well ask, why be rational? First, we have to be clear about what we mean by "being rational." Sometimes, the term has a familiar negative connotation, such as when you accuse a friend or lover of "being overly rational," meaning insensitive, not in touch with his or her emotions, or abusing thought as a way of escaping from an emotionally charged situation. In this sense, we can quickly agree that there is good reason not to be too rational. Similarly, if you think of rationality as "thinking something into the ground" so that you never act upon it at all or always too late, then we can willingly give up rationality in that sense, too.

What Is Knowledge?

To realize that you know something when you do, and to realize that you do not when you do not, this is knowing.

— Confucius, *Analects*, sixth century BCE

However, if we dispense with these negative associations with the term "rationality," we can answer the philosophical question "Why be rational?" straightforwardly: rationality is the most efficient way to comprehend the world and the best guarantee that you know what is going on around you. "Rationality" is not purely a matter of understanding, as important as it is for thinking well. It is also a matter of action and of living. And as soon as we add this pragmatic dimension, the answer to the question "Why be rational?" becomes extremely persuasive. To act rationally is to act in such a way that you are more likely to get what you want (including knowledge as well as enjoyment, satisfaction, and an occasional ego boost).

The best way to get something is not always "the most rational" in the colloquial sense of being the "most efficient." In this machine-and-consumer society, it is often more efficient to buy something than to make it with your own hands; that doesn't make it more rational. And it is not necessarily rational to think everything out and plan ahead, for sometimes what we want is novelty and adventure, in which case it may be most rational not to think it all out and plan ahead. But, in any case, rationality, in this sense, is hardly objectionable.

Subjective Truth and the Problem of Relativism

*The objective accent falls on WHAT is said,
the subjective accent on HOW it is said.*

—Søren Kierkegaard

Rationality is tying our knowledge and our lives together in the most coherent and effective way. But if we focus on the coherence of our knowledge and not on "the way the world really is," this raises questions about how secure our knowledge really is. This has been a problem facing Western philosophy since Kant, with his denial that we have any grasp of the way the world is independent of the way our minds construct our experience. We are also well aware that different societies and even different individuals can tie their experiences and their lives together in very different ways. Does this mean that we are forced to accept any system, no matter how bizarre, as rational and even true, just because it is coherent and satisfies the person or people who believe in it?

As our conception of truth moves further away from correspondence with "the way the world really is," it moves nearer and nearer to the subject, to the person trying to learn the truth. In other words, we move further from **objective truth** (that is, truth independent of our personal opinions) toward what has sometimes been called **subjective truth**, truth *dependent on the subject* and his or her beliefs. We might say that the paranoid person's view of the world is a subjective truth; true for him, but not objectively true—that is, not true of the world. We might say that an entire society's view of the world is subjectively true for that society, even if we know that its view is objectively false. The problem is that with this conception of subjective truth, we have moved far away from the basic concept of truth—that is, that there is but one truth, one true set of facts that is true for everybody whether they know it or not. Subjective truth seems to allow for a different truth, a different set of facts, for everyone. But isn't this just saying that *nothing* is true?—that there is no truth but only different perspectives and different ways of looking at the world? In other words, can we call anything *true* if it is true only for one person or one society? Doesn't truth, if it is truth at all, have to be objective?

Contemporary philosophy has dealt with this question in many different ways, but all of them are attempts to come to terms with **relativism**, the claim that what is true for one person or one people might not be true for another person or another people. At its most extreme, the claim is that every idea is as good as any other, something that even the most die-hard relativist cannot possibly take seriously (as attractive as this view may sound to unprepared or uninformed students). Probably we can all agree that some ideas are simply ridiculous. Others are incoherent, ill-formulated, wrong on the facts, insensitive to the context, ignorant of history, inappropriate in the conversation, or some combination of several or all of the above. One might add that if every idea is as good as any other, then the claim that every idea is as good as any other is no better than the claim that any one idea is the absolute truth. But if truth is not so straightforward as "the way the world really is," and if rationality depends largely on mere coherence and contextual appropriateness, there are nevertheless a number of persuasive ways to understand the search for truth and the seeming variability of truths.

One of these is to shift the emphasis from science and factual truth to a different kind of truth. Poet John Keats famously wrote that "beauty is truth, truth beauty," and the philosopher Friedrich Nietzsche, despite his respect for science, argued at considerable length that art and beauty give us a more profound type of truth than science does. We will see in a moment that the philosopher Søren Kierkegaard made much the same argument with regard to religious truth. Kierkegaard was perfectly willing to talk about objective truth with regard to science, but there were more important truths, he argued, personal or "subjective" truths that were not about how the world is but rather concerned our personal commitments in the face of "objective uncertainty."

Nietzsche sometimes argued a more radical thesis, summarized in the slogan "There is no truth." What he was arguing against, in a very polemical and exhilarating manner, was the correspondence theory of truth. That is, there is no truth "in itself," independent of our experience. Nevertheless, Nietzsche was not about to abandon truth altogether. When he insists, "There are no facts, only interpretations," he is suggesting that we cannot ever remove our own perspectives from the reading of "the facts" and that therefore it is the quality of our interpretations and the acuity of our perspective that gives us the truth. Thus, personality and style enter in whenever we try to state the truth. It is never a matter of simply disclosing the bare facts.

Following Nietzsche in the twentieth century is Michel Foucault, a French philosopher who defended a series of radical ideas about truth and knowledge. He argued, first of all, that truth is a historical matter and in that sense relative

---

There Is No Truth: Nietzsche

Ultimate Skepticism.—*But what after all are man's truths?—They are his irrefutable errors.*

—*The Gay Science*, 1882

Truth is the kind of error without which a certain species of life could not live. The value for life is ultimately decisive.

—*The Will to Power*, a collection of notes from 1883 to 1888

---

to particular times and places. More accurately, truth is relative to what he called an *episteme* (pronounced: eh pis teh MAY; from the Greek work for "knowledge," or "science" in a broad sense), a particular system of knowledge and an associated discourse that a society uses in presenting facts and formulating problems. Like Nietzsche, Foucault rejected the idea of bare facts, free of interpretation. But whereas Nietzsche left a lot of room for individual interpretations and perspectives, Foucault insisted that these interpretations and perspectives are *imposed* on us by the culture, by the discourse and within an episteme. He further argued that these discourses and epistemes are not continuous through history, so he rejects the common assumption of *progress*, particularly in the social sciences. The discontinuity of history, he argues, means that we have no warrant for believing that we have made continual progress in coming to know our world. Our sciences may not represent a real improvement on the science of ancient times. Perhaps, he suggests, they are only more oppressive.

Finally, Foucault argues that knowledge is essentially a matter of **power**. He borrows this emphasis on power, too, from Nietzsche, who argued for an exciting notion that he called the *will to power*. The idea is that we are always motivated by the desire for power (by which Nietzsche means self-assertion and self-expression, which may or may not involve dominating or manipulating others). For Foucault, the will to power becomes the centerpiece of his theory of knowledge. The episteme and the discourse that prevail are those of the ruling class, and so knowledge is what works to the advantage of those who are in power. (Given that the formulations of the social sciences have the potential to support particular political agendas, Foucault was particularly concerned about these disciplines.) Foucault makes a cynical argument that goes back to Plato. In *The Republic*, a thug named Thrasymachus argues that justice is nothing but what serves the interests of the strong. For Foucault, likewise, truth is what the powerful declare it to be.

A much more modest approach to dealing with the diversity of societies' conceptions of what is true also comes out of Europe, this time out of Germany rather than France. The philosopher Jürgen Habermas has argued for many decades that truth and knowledge are indeed relative to what Foucault calls discourse, but whereas Foucault insists that this is imposed on us, Habermas insists that discourse is something we *do*. He makes the notion of discourse more interpersonal, and it is

> *Nietzsche declares that it is the philosopher who is the most likely to be wrong about the nature of knowledge, since he always thinks of it in the form of congruence, love, unity, and pacification. [But] if we truly wish to know knowledge, to know what it is, to apprehend it at its root, in its manufacture, we must look not to philosophers but to politicians—we need to understand the relations of struggle and power.*
>
> —Michel Foucault, "Truth and Juridical Forms"

exemplified by concrete conversation and debate rather than an abstract *episteme*. Moreover, Habermas insists that it is in conversation that we cultivate rationality, which, again, is not to be conceived of as an abstract system but as something dynamic and in progress. Thus, he returns to the old Greek idea of *dialectic* (which literally means "conversation"). Habermas retains the faith that through dialectic or conversation we can still talk meaningfully of truth and knowledge.

> *In discourse the unforced force of the better argument prevails.*
>
> —Jürgen Habermas

From the United States and within the domain of scientific philosophy, we get yet another approach to the question of relativism. Willard van Orman Quine (1908–2000) was one of America's leading contemporary philosophers. Holding William James's old chair at Harvard, Quine considered himself a pragmatist, and he came out of a rigorous empiricist tradition. Yet he deeply challenges empiricism and rejects the idea that our truths refer directly to facts. He argues for a thesis he calls "the inscrutability of reference," which says that we cannot determine, just on the basis of empirical evidence, what a speaker is referring to. He suggests that someone pointing in the direction of a rabbit might be referring to the rabbit, rabbits (in the plural), the availability of meat from the rabbit, or the momentary appearance of the rabbit (as it comes out of the bushes, for example). In other words, how we put the facts together (what Nietzsche called an interpretation) is a matter not settled by the facts themselves.

Given any set of facts, there are any number of very different theories that will accurately describe those facts. But there is no way to differentiate these theories on the basis of the facts alone, for the facts are already accounted for in the theories. What is more, we can defend almost any theory if we are willing to adjust our language sufficiently. On the basis of this reasoning, Quine suggests that knowledge is an organic and systematic process, and that we can accept or give up virtually any theory if we are willing to make enough changes in the rest of the system. As a gung-ho defender of science, however, Quine insists that this is far from implying that we should give up on truth and knowledge. We should, however, recognize that our knowledge is holistic, not a collection of piecemeal observations.

Finally, let us return to Kierkegaard's idea of subjective truth. As we suggested, he thinks that this becomes important in talking about religious matters, where we face "objective uncertainty." In such cases, there are no "facts" of the matter. Instead, the truth in this case is an important *personal* truth, a truth "for which I am willing to live or die." Kierkegaard insisted that this is the kind of truth that makes life meaningful. His sense of "truth" in this context is that of being *true to* one's commitment to God. But subjective truth also applies to other aspects of life where science cannot give us an answer, such as ethics or religion. Kierkegaard also thought, however, that subjective truth is irrational, that it follows no rules and may require blind faith rather than careful thinking and planning. He never argues that subjective commitment is involved even in objective truth, but a number of contemporary philosophers, some of whom embrace the title **postmodernists**, have argued something very much like this.

Where are we to find truth, that is, objective truth? Current thinking on this issue is both confusing and exciting: On the one side, philosophers are generally agreed that subjective truth (being committed to a belief) is, in the realm of science in particular, not sufficient. Truth, if it is truth at all, must be generally believable, confirmable by any number of persons, true not just for some particular individual, and true even despite what people believe about it. On the other hand, the arguments of the skeptics and the alternatives to the correspondence

The notion lingers that to each statement, or each synthetic statement, there is associated a unique range of possible sensory events such that the occurrence of any of them would add to the likelihood of truth of the statement, and that there is associated also another unique range of possible sensory events whose occurrence would detract from that likelihood. My counter suggestion is that our statements about the external world face the tribunal of sense experience not individually but only as a corporate body.

The totality of our so-called knowledge or beliefs, from the most casual matters of geography and history to the profoundest laws of atomic physics or even of pure mathematics and logic, is a man-made fabric which impinges on experience only along the edges. . . . A conflict with experience at the periphery occasions readjustments in the interior of the field. Having re-evaluated one statement we must re-evaluate some others, whether they be statements logically connected with the first or whether they be the statements of logical connections themselves. But the total field is so undetermined by its boundary conditions, experience, that there is much latitude of choice as to what statements to re-evaluate in the light of any single contrary experience. No particular experiences are linked with any particular statements in the interior of the field, except indirectly through considerations of equilibrium affecting the field as a whole.

—Willard van Orman Quine, "Two Dogmas of Empiricism"

Subjective Truth: Kierkegaard

When the question of truth is raised in an objective manner, reflection is directed objectively to the truth, as an object to which the knower is related. . . . When the question of the truth is raised subjectively, reflection is directed subjectively to the nature of the individual's relationship; if only the mode of this relationship is in the truth, the individual is in the truth even if he should happen to be thus related to what is not true.

ᗯᗣ

. . . An objective uncertainty held fast in an appropriation-process of the most passionate inwardness is the truth, the highest truth attainable for an existing individual.

—From Concluding Unscientific Postscript, 1846

---

theory of truth—including the coherence theory, the pragmatic theory, and the more radical theories—have made philosophers (and scientists, too) more humble than they used to be, no longer so sure that they are finding out the facts of the "world as it really is." They have been prompted to wonder just how many of their "discoveries" are indeed the product of an order that they themselves have imposed on nature, through their theories, their concepts, and their experiments. Does this mean that we will never know the "way the world really is"?

Does this mean that two alternative ways of looking at the world might both be *equally* true? However we answer these very difficult questions, our conclusion cannot be "It's all subjective," which is more often than not a sign of lazy thinking or of a refusal even to attempt to answer the hard questions. The answer is, rather, that whatever the claims we make for truth, the rules of rationality retain a persistent hold on us. We might have a powerful insight or mystical vision; we might be suddenly inspired or emotionally moved. But in general what we say and believe nevertheless requires something more to count as true: It requires *reasons*. It requires working out. It requires development into a systematic understanding of what this insight, vision, inspiration, or emotion amounts to.

And that's the truth.

Closing Questions

1. Does it make sense to say that a statement or belief is true for a particular person? Can a truth be simply subjective? Give some examples, and explain what significance to give to the above expression "is true for."

2. If a belief makes a person who believes it happier and more secure, does that make it true in any sense?

3. If there were facts, what would they be?

4. Bertrand Russell once wrote, "Better the world should perish than I or any other human being should believe a lie." Discuss. Is truth all *that* important?

5. Are there electrons?

6. Could a scientist give an adequate account of the biblical story of the raising of Lazarus?

Suggested Readings

Simon Blackburn gives an extended discussion of the topic of truth in *Truth: A Guide* (Oxford University Press, 2007). David Hume's theory of knowledge is summarized in his *Enquiry Concerning Human Understanding*, 3rd ed. (Oxford University Press, 1975); the more complete argument is his *Treatise on Human Nature*, ed. L. A. Selby-Bigge (Oxford University Press, 1980). The main works of the British empiricists John Locke, Bishop George Berkeley, and David Hume can be found together in *The Empiricists* (Doubleday, 1960). An excellent general study of the history and strategy of skepticism is Richard Popkin, *A History of Skepticism: From Erasmus to Descartes* (Oxford University Press, 2003). Peter Unger offers a challenging defense of modern skepticism in *Ignorance* (Oxford University Press, 1979). A good study of Descartes and his methods is Anthony Kenny, *Descartes* (Random House, 1968). A number of fine translations of Descartes's *Meditations* are available, including John Cottingham's (Cambridge, 1996), from which we cite in this chapter. A very good general discussion of the problems of knowledge is Robert Audi, *Epistemology*, 2nd ed. (Routledge, 2002). A variety of topics in epistemology are considered in Jonathan Dancy and Ernest Sosa, ed., *Companion to Epistemology* (Blackwell, 1994) A classic study in the philosophy of science is C. G. Hempel, *Philosophy of Natural Science* (Prentice-Hall, 1966). For a modern, though controversial, view of science, see Thomas S. Kuhn, *The Structure of Scientific Revolutions*, 3rd ed. (University of Chicago Press, 1996). For detailed studies of the creationism–evolution debate, see Philip Kitcher, *Abusing Science: The Case against Creationism* (MIT Press, 1982). For an example of an effort to reconcile evolution and religion, see John F. Haught's *Making Sense of Evolution: Darwin, God, and the Drama of Life* (John Knox Press, 2010). A number of good translations of Nietzsche's *The Gay Science* are available, including Walter Kaufmann's (Random House, 1974). Kaufmann also collected some of Nietzsche's notes (including many about truth) in *The Will to Power*, trans. and ed. Walter Kaufmann (Random House, 1968). W. V. O. Quine's "Two Dogmas of Empiricism" appears in *From a Logical Point of View*, 2nd ed. (Harvard University Press, 1961). Michel Foucault's "Truth and Juridical Forms" is translated by Robert Hurley in *Power: The Essential Works of Michel Foucault, 1954–1984*, Vol. 3 (Penguin, 1994). Kierkegaard's *Concluding Unscientific Postscript* is translated by Howard V. Hong and Edna H. Hong (Princeton, 1992). Michel Foucault's "Truth and Juridical Forms" is translated by Robert Hurley in *Power: The Essential Works of Michel Foucault, 1954–1984*, Vol. 3. (Penguin, 1994).

Pablo Picasso, *Girl Before a Mirror*. © 2004 Estate of Pablo Picasso/Artists Rights Society (ARS), New York / © Superstock

6
Self

I think, therefore I am. . . . But what then am I? A thing which thinks.
—René Descartes, *Meditations*

Though man is a unique individual,—he is equally the whole, the ideal whole, the subjective existence of society as thought and experienced. He exists in reality as the representation and the real mind of social existence, and as the sum of human manifestations of life.
—Karl Marx, manuscript of 1844

〜

Opening Questions

1. Who are you? Compare the descriptions or profile you would provide:
   a. On a job application.
   b. On a first date.
   c. On your Facebook page.
   d. In a talk with your parents, as you are trying to tell them what you have decided to do with your life.
   e. In a trial with you as the defendant, trying to convince the jury of your "good character."
   f. As the "I" in the statement "I think, therefore I am" (Descartes).

2. Explain who you are to a visitor from another planet.

3. Describe yourself as a character in a novel. Describe the gestures, postures, revealing habits, characteristic word phrases you use. Try to imitate yourself, by way of parody. What kind of person would you describe yourself as being?

4. Is it ever possible to know—really know—another person? Imagine what it would be like to suspect that you can never know another person's true feelings, that all his or her movements and

gestures are intended to fool you and that you can no longer assume that what the individual means (for example, by a smile or a frown) is what you mean by the same outward movement. How do you feel about this?

5. What is involved in being a "human being"? What (or who) would be included in your characterization? What (or who) would be excluded?

6. You say to yourself, "I am going to move my arm." You decide to do it, and—lo and behold—your arm moves. How did you do that?

The Essential Self

With the concept of rationality, we found ourselves moving away from questions about pure reality and back to questions about ourselves and our own activities. Indeed, with the concept of subjective truth, we found a renewed emphasis on *personal* questions, questions about the self rather than questions about the world. So we find ourselves raising a new set of issues, questioning what seemed to us so clear and unproblematic before. What is the *self*? What is it to be a person? What do you know when you "know yourself"? What is someone telling you to do when he or she tells you "just to be yourself"?

Confucius on Becoming Human

To discipline oneself through ritual practice is to become authoritatively human. If for the space of one day one were able to accomplish this, the world would appear to be as a model of humanity. However, becoming human emerges out of oneself; how could it emerge out of others?

— Confucius (sixth century BCE). *The Analects of Confucius: A Philosophical Translation*. Trans. Roger T. Ames and Henry Rosemont, Jr. New York: Ballantine, 1998

Our conceptions of self, like our conceptions of God, religion, and the nature of reality, turn out to be extremely varied, different not only for different people and cultures but for each of us from time to time and in different contexts. For example, in Opening Question 1, you probably described yourself on a job application as an industrious worker, with so many years of school and so much experience, with a certain grade point average and a certain amount of ambition. In defending yourself in court, on the other hand, you probably thought very little of your achievements in school; rather, you tried to define yourself in terms of your good deeds, your good intentions, the number of your friends, and the fact that you tend to be gentle with children and animals. To see how bound up with their context such descriptions tend to be, we need only switch them, with shocking results. Imagine yourself giving an employer the information you would more appropriately give to a person on a date. What would your Facebook friends make of it if your postings only described your work experience and grade point average, the sorts of things you might list in a job application? Potential employers, on the other hand, have sometimes been appalled by what they discover about job candidates on Facebook—does this mean that you *should* only put on Facebook descriptions of yourself and your activities that would be appropriate to mention at a job interview? Or consider how you would feel about a supposedly close friend who told you at great length only about his or her achievements in school. What we think of ourselves and consider to be significant about ourselves—and others—depends to a great extent on the context in which we are trying to explain who we are.

Yet we all have an undeniable sense that, beneath the various descriptions of ourselves that we produce for various occasions, there is within us a "real self," a self that does not vary from context to context. In the Judeo-Christian tradition (and before that, in some ancient religions and in the thinking of the Greeks, among others) this invariant self, our "real self," has been called the **soul**. Philosophers have called the "real self" the **essential self**—that is, the set of characteristics that defines a particular person.

The experience of our real, or essential, self is familiar to us in a great many circumstances. For example, if we are forced to go to a party with people we don't like and do not feel comfortable with, if we are forced to behave in an artificial way, to talk in language that is more vulgar than usual or more sophisticated than usual, to talk about subjects that do not interest us at all, we might well describe our experience in phrases such as "I couldn't be myself" or "I felt like a phony." As another example, picture yourself filling out one of those dozens of questionnaires that are forced on you at so many junctures, requiring you to list your birth date, home address, sex, major and perhaps grades, military service, awards, marital status, and so on. A natural reaction to such forms is that they are irrelevant to knowing who you really are. They don't ask the "right" questions, and they leave out any reference to what you and your friends think is most important about you. In other words, they don't even begin to get at your essential self, the personal self that is the "real you." This chapter is about the nature of this "real you" and your relationships with other people.

As we have found in other philosophical investigations, the most obvious answer often disappears as soon as we begin to follow our thinking to its consequences, and what once seemed simple turns into a wide variety of answers that sometimes compete with one another. For example, one answer to the question, "Who am I?" or "What is my real, essential self?" is the religious answer; you really are just a soul before God, and all else—your worldly goods and accomplishments, even your physical body and its various pleasures and pains—is insignificant, unimportant. Some people, on the other hand, think that to be a human being is to be just another animal, caught up in the process of staying alive and enjoying itself. A very different answer emerges from Descartes and

many other modern philosophers; they say the real self is the conscious self—
that is, the thinking self, the self that is aware of itself. A powerful contemporary
view of the self that insists that there is, ultimately, no set self, that "the self" is
a process of creation that goes on as long as we are alive. Another view (this one
from Buddhism) teaches us that the self is ultimately unreal, that there is no self
at all, only an illusion of one. Finally, there are views that suggest that the self is
not an individual entity at all but rather part of a larger Self or the product of an
entire society. Your self, in other words, is not really your own, after all.

In this chapter we will consider some of these accounts of the nature of the
self, beginning with the debate about whether the self can be identified with
the body or with consciousness, and going on to consider the extent to which
emotions are essential to who one is conscious. In everyday contexts, we tend
to refer to ourselves as both minds (with personalities) and as bodies (as when
we say, "I was in the computer store"), and this raises a major philosophical
questions: how are our minds and bodies related to each other? Accordingly, we
will proceed to consider various proposals regarding the connection between
the body and the mind and the implications these answers have for what "the
self" amounts to. Observing that many of these accounts fail to account for "the
whole self," we conclude by considering alternative pictures of the self that
might do justice to this broader idea of our identity, including Sartre's idea of the
self as a choice, the no-self view of Buddhism, the multilayered self, the social
self, and the relational self.

Self as Body, Self as Consciousness

*What am I? A thing which thinks. What is a thing which thinks? It is a
thing which doubts, understands, affirms, denies, wills, refuses, which
also imagines and feels.*

—René Descartes, 1641

A person's **self-identity** is the way he or she characterizes his or her essential
self. This includes both a general characterization—as a human being, as a man or
woman, as a creature before God, as an American, as a Christian, Muslim, Hindu,
Buddhist, or Jew, or as a member of any other large organization or group—and
a particular description—as the tallest person in the class, as the winner of the
Olympic gold medal in pole vaulting in Athens in 2004, as the person who is
lucky enough to be married to J, and so on. Sometimes we make these essential
characteristics explicit, but even when we don't, they almost always enter into
our behavior and our attitudes toward ourselves. Most of us would not think of
naming our height as part of our essential self-identity; but, in fact, if we think
of the way we stand or walk and if we pay attention to our feelings when we are
with people considerably taller or shorter than we are, it becomes evident that
such seemingly unimportant characteristics may indeed enter into our conceptions of our essential self. So, too, a person's physical condition is usually a key
ingredient in his or her conception of self and his or her self-identity, a fact that

becomes obvious, for example, when a person has been ill for an extended period of time.

But to what extent should we equate the self with the body? **Derek Parfit**, a contemporary British philosopher, offers a science-fictional scenario involving *Star Trek*'s teleporter as a means of considering how we understand the relationship between self and body. The teleporter is a computerized machine that conveys a person from one place to another without passing through the space between the two locations. It first "dematerializes" the person's body, turning it into an energy pattern. The teleporter then "beams" the energy to the new location, and reconstructs the person's body, particle by particle. Now imagine, Parfit proposes, being transported from one location to another by means of the teleporter. When you arrive, are you still you, even though every one of your original particles was destroyed? Would you still exist (Parfit doesn't think so), or is what now exists a clone (Parfit's view)?

Keep in mind that over the course of our lifetime, we lose cells and new cells take the place of (at least most) of the cells we have lost. Would it make sense to say that at the point at which all of your cells have regenerated, you are actually a clone of the person you were when you were born? What if the teleporter malfunctioned (as it sometimes does in the *Star Trek* series) and your original self gets left intact but a duplicate is reassembled, particle by particle, in another location. Does this mean that you now have two bodies, and that you are two places at once?

Even the idea of you "having two bodies" takes the self to be essentially something other than our physical nature. This is in keeping with much of the Western philosophical tradition and much of Western religious thought, which plays down such physical traits, emphasizing the more spiritual and mental aspects of our existence. Do your intuitions agree? Suppose, to choose an extreme example, your best friend turned into a frog. (Kafka's *The Metamorphosis* and both versions of the film *The Fly* present similar cases, in each case with tragic results for the person transformed.) What characteristics would your friend have to retain in order for you to still consider this frog as your friend? The frog would certainly have to display signs of having your friend's mind, most clearly by continuing to talk, if that were possible; then you could recognize that it was indeed your friend, trying to communicate with you and explain what it is that he or she was thinking.

We tolerate considerable changes in a person's physical appearance as long as his or her mind seems to remain the same; in fact, we are used to stories, cartoons, and imaginative examples of a person turning into almost anything, from a frog to a cloud to any of a large variety of plants, as long as somehow the person's mind remains intact. (Indeed, the idea that the person has endured despite the physical transformation is the premise of *The Metamorophosis* and *The Fly*.) On the other hand, it takes very little alteration in a person's mental capacities for us to complain that he or she seems like a different person or that we don't know that person at all anymore.

The theory that the essential self of self-identity is the mind, or self-consciousness, can be traced back to ancient times, but its best-known defender is the philosopher René Descartes, who presented a simple but elegant argument that the individual self is the first thing that each of us can know for certain, and that this self, whose existence is indubitable (see pp. 125–126; 158–160) is nothing else but the **thinking self**, the self that is aware of itself. But it was in Descartes, too, that we saw the origins of the dilemma that would lead to Hume's skepticism—the position that we in fact never know anything but our own ideas and experiences. Now, with reference to the self, a related problem emerges—can we ever know that there is any other self besides ourselves? We find here, too, a stance comparable to Hume's skepticism about knowledge of the world; it is the position called **solipsism**, which says that indeed nothing exists but one's own mind. And like skepticism, solipsism is a position that most philosophers find intolerable. The problem is this: if one agrees that one's self should be identified with one's consciousness and that each person can know only his or her own consciousness, how is it possible to reach out beyond ourselves to anyone else? Our bodies can touch each other and make contact, but our minds cannot. We will return to this concern below, after discussing the basic view that the self is consciousness.

The Sameness of Self

The identity of the same man consists in nothing but a participation of the same continued life, by constantly fleeting particles of matter, in succession vitally united to the same organized body. . . . If the identity of soul alone makes the same man; and if there is nothing in the nature of matter why the individual spirit may not be united to different bodies, it will be possible that those men living in distant ages and of different tempers may have been the same man. . . .

But to find wherein personal Identity consists, we must consider what Person stands for;—which, I think, is a thinking intelligent being, that has reason and reflection, and considers itself as itself, the same thinking 'thing,' in different times and places; which it does only by that consciousness which is inseparable from thinking, and, as it seems to me, essential to it: it being impossible for anyone to perceive without perceiving that he does perceive. When we see hear, smell, taste, feel, meditate, or will anything, we know that we do so. Thus it is always as to our present sensations and perceptions: and by this every one is to himself that which he calls self. For, since consciousness always accompanies thinking, and it is that which makes every one to be what he calls self, and thereby distinguishes himself from all other thinking things, in this alone consists personal identity, i.e. the sameness of a rational being: and as far as this consciousness can be extended backwards to any past action or thought, so far reaches the identity of that person; it is the same self now it was then; and it is by the same self with this present one that now reflects on it, that the action was done.

—John Locke, *Essay on Human
Understanding*, 1689

The theory that the self is consciousness has several ingenious variations. The English philosopher John Locke, for example, argued that the self was not the whole of consciousness but a specific part of the mind—namely, our memory. Thus, the self is that part of the mind that remembers its past. This explains how it is that we think of ourselves as the same person over time, despite even radical changes. Our friend-turned-frog is certainly still our friend if the animal

What Is It Like, to Be a Bat?

I assume we all believe that bats have experience. After all, they are mammals, and there is no more doubt that they have experience than that mice or pigeons or whales have experience. I have chosen bats instead of wasps or flounders because if one travels too far down the phylogenetic tree, people gradually shed their faith that there is experience there at all. Bats, although more closely related to us than those other species, nevertheless present a range of activity and a sensory apparatus so different from ours that the problem I want to pose is exceptionally vivid (though it certainly could be raised with other species). Even without the benefit of philosophical reflection, anyone who has spent some time in an enclosed space with an excited bat knows what it is to encounter a fundamentally alien form of life.

I have said that the essence of the belief that bats have experience is that there is something that it is like to be a bat. Now we know that most bats . . . perceive the external world primarily by sonar, . . . detecting the reflections, from objects within range, of their own rapid, subtly modulated, high-frequency shrieks. Their brains are designed to correlate the outgoing impulses with the subsequent echoes, and the information thus acquired enables bats to make precise discriminations of distance, size, shape, motion, and texture comparable to those we make by vision. But bat sonar, though clearly a form of perception, is not similar in its operation to any sense that we possess, and there is no reason to suppose that it is subjectively like anything we can experience or imagine. This appears to create difficulties for the notion of what it is like to be a bat. . . .

Our own experience provides the basic material for our imagination, whose range is therefore limited. It will not help to try to imagine that one has webbing on one's arms, which enables one to fly around at dusk and dawn catching insects in one's mouth; that one has very poor vision, and perceives the surrounding world by a system of reflected high-frequency sound signals; and that one spends the day hanging upside down by one's feet in an attic. Insofar as I can imagine this (which is not very far), it tells me only what it would be like for me to behave as a bat behaves. But that is not the question. I want to know what it is like for a bat to be a bat. . . .

—Thomas Nagel, 1989

remembers all the experiences it had as a person before its transformation. On the other hand, we could certainly be suspicious—at the least—if someone who claimed to be our friend could not remember any of the experiences we had shared in the past. (There are, of course, cases of amnesia, or loss of memory; but what is also true of such cases is that the person no longer knows who he or she is, so it is not a question of having a different set of memories but rather of having no self-identifying memories at all.)

The theory that self-identity is determined by memories has its curious difficulties. To take a far-fetched but thought-provoking example, suppose Mr. Jones has an emergency operation in which his injured brain is replaced by the brain of Mrs. Smith (just deceased). The resulting person has the body, face, and general appearance of Mr. Jones, but the consciousness, memories, and knowledge of Mrs. Smith. Who is the resulting person? It doesn't seem to make sense to say that it is Mrs. Smith, but neither does it make sense to say that it is Mr. Jones. The example becomes even more complicated if you picture yourself in the position of Mrs. Smith, who awakens after a mysterious lapse in consciousness to find herself with the body of a man; would she know for certain (as the self-consciousness theory would suggest) that she still is, indeed, the same person? Or has her self-identity broken down entirely here?

Monty Python on Descartes

Detective-Inspector René "Doubty" Descartes absentmindedly flicked grey-white ash from the sleeve of his only vicuña jacket and stared moodily across the pigeon-violated rooftops of Whitehall. "I muse," he thought. "Therefore . . .

The ginger telephone shrilled its urgent demand. Descartes, rudely awakened from his reverie, snatched the receiver to his ear.

"Descartes here," he posited.

"Sorry to interrupt, sir." The familiar tones of Sergeant Warnock floated down the line. "Sergeant Warnock here."

"How can you be sure?"

"I think I am Sergeant Warnock, therefore I am Sergeant Warnock," replied Sergeant Warnock confidently. Some of Doubty's thinking was beginning to rub off.

—Monty Python, twentieth-century
English comedy troupe

Questions of self-identity give rise to paradoxes of this sort, for what they show us is that our sense of self-identity is far more complex than it seemed at first. If a single characteristic was all there were to the essential self, then self-identity would be that characteristic, no matter what else changed. If memory alone gave us our self-identity, then any being with the same memories, even in a different body, even a frog's, or even in two different people, would be the same. But we tend to have serious reservations about these cases, and the reason is that we can see that many different aspects of a person enter into our concept of self-identity. "I think, therefore I am," in all of its variations ("I remember, therefore I am who I am") is too simplistic to capture the whole of our sense of ourselves.

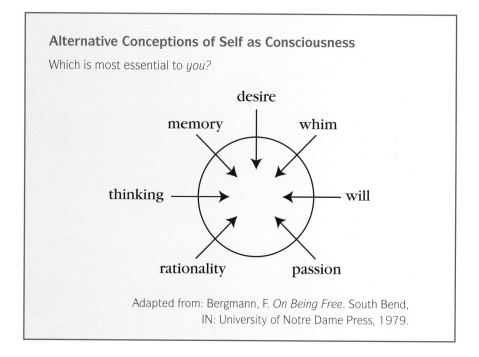

Alternative Conceptions of Self as Consciousness

Which is most essential to *you?*

Adapted from: Bergmann, F. *On Being Free*. South Bend, IN: University of Notre Dame Press, 1979.

The Self and Its Emotions

Although the views that the self is defined primarily through thinking and memory have dominated most self-consciousness theories, other aspects of consciousness might also define the self. Danish philosopher Søren Kierkegaard, for example, defined the self in terms of the passions. He thought that one's most important mission in life was to cultivate the self by cultivating one's passions, in particular, a passionate commitment to God.

Other philosophers have suggested alternative, nonreligious goals in the project of building a self. Friedrich Nietzsche, for instance, insisted that we organize our various traits on the model of an artwork, with every part contributing to the aesthetic value of the whole, and philosophers ever since Aristotle and Confucius have urged us to cultivate our ethical sensibilities, our virtues. (See Chapters 8 and 10.) But the idea of cultivating our passions, or we would say, our emotions, is subject to a serious objection. Our emotions are often thought to be **irrational**. (Kierkegaard thought that this was one of their virtues.) It is common knowledge that our emotions sometimes make us misperceive the way things really are and motivate us to do things that, with just a moment's clear thinking, we certainly would not do. But the idea that emotions are irrational—and therefore the self that is cultivated through them would be irrational too—is itself subject to objection. Not all emotions are irrational, and thus the self we create through them is not (or not entirely) irrational either.

The Passionate Self: Kierkegaard

It is impossible to exist without passion, unless we understand the word "exist" in the loose sense of a so-called existence. . . . Eternity is the winged horse, infinitely fast, and time is a worn-out nag; the existing individual is the driver. That is to say, he is such a driver when his mode of existence is not an existence loosely so called; for then he is no driver, but a drunken peasant who lies asleep in the wagon and lets the horses take care of themselves. To be sure, he also drives and is a driver, and so there are perhaps many who—also exist.

—From *Concluding Unscientific Postscript*, 1846

A long tradition sees the emotions as foreign to the self or as an inferior part of the self. Freud, for example, located emotions in the *id* ("it") as opposed to the *ego* ("I"), suggesting that they threaten the integrity of the self rather than being part of it. Plato had a more modest view. He thought that the emotions are the spirited part of the soul that needed to be governed by reason. (He suggested the famous image of a charioteer reining in the unruly horses of appetite and emotion.) Aristotle had a more conciliatory view; he insisted that emotions are an essential part of the good life—that is, having the *right* emotions in the right circumstances. And that means that the emotions are not separate from the self or soul, but essential constituents of it.

Reason is and ought to be the slave of the passions.

—David Hume, *Treatise of Human Nature*, 1739–40

As if every passion did not contain its quantum of reason.

—Nietzsche, *The Will to Power*. (Compendium of unpublished notes, 1906)

Nevertheless, the opposition of emotion and rationality continues to cast doubt on the desirability of emotion in the cultivation of the self. The eighteenth-century Scottish philosopher David Hume, for example, defended the radical view that "reason is and ought to be the slave of the passions," thus turning the Platonic view (that reason should govern the passions) upside down. But the opposition of emotion and rationality remains. Are they in fact opposites? Or does every emotion, as Nietzsche writes, "contain its quantum of reason"?

The question is, what is an emotion? It is commonly thought that emotions are *feelings* and that feelings by their very nature are unintelligent and irrational. Perhaps we should say that they are nonrational, without any intelligence at all. This view, however, has been often challenged. Recent research and thinking about emotions has dramatically changed this picture. Today we talk about the "intelligence" of emotions, and good evidence shows that, without emotion, we would not be capable of rational decision making. Individuals who have brain lesions that interfere with normal emotional activity are not more rational—but instead are incapable—of making sound decisions. Emotion is what enables us to determine which considerations are more important than others. Our emotions give us insights, even knowledge. Sometimes, as Blaise Pascal said, "the heart has its reasons, of which reason knows nothing." Moreover, the very idea that our emotions "make us" do such and such is under scrutiny. To a larger extent than we usually realize, we are *responsible* for our emotions. Psychologists talk of everyday efforts we make to "regulate" our emotions; and probably in our own experience, we have had experiences of nursing an emotion (anger, for example) by dwelling on thoughts that intensify it (for example, recollections of slights and annoying features of the target of anger).

Modern debate about the emotions begins with the philosopher-psychologist William James, who wrote a famous essay called "What Is an Emotion?" James argued that emotions are feelings, but a very specific kind of feeling. They are the feelings caused by changes in the body—for example, the heart pounding faster, hormonal changes, changes in skin sensitivity—that in turn were caused by some upsetting perception.

> *Our natural way of thinking about emotions is that the mental perception of some fact excites the mental affection called the emotion, and that this latter state of mind gives rise to the bodily expression. My thesis on the contrary is that the bodily changes follow directly the perception of the exciting fact, and that our feeling of the same changes as they occur is the emotion. Common sense says, we lose our fortune, are sorry and weep. The hypothesis here says that we feel sorry because we cry.*
>
> —William James,
> "What Is an Emotion?" 1884

James was immediately challenged by others, including fellow pragmatist John Dewey, who argued that the variety of emotions was much more impressive than such simple physiological changes would indicate. The differentiation of emotions could not depend on mere feelings, but required some reference to the situation and the person's engagement in it. So anger, for instance, is not just the feeling of energized aggression, but the perception of, for example, someone who has been offensive or insulting. Love is not just a soft mushy feeling, but necessarily directed at someone who is its object, one's beloved. This aspect of emotions, by which they are directed to the world, is called their intentionality. Every emotion, it is now thought, consists of both feeling and intentionality, typically together with an impulse to action as well. Thus, Aristotle defines anger as "a distressed desire for vengeance in return for a conspicuous and unjustifiable contempt of one's person or friends." Anticipating the modern notion of intentionality, he adds that "anger is always directed towards someone in particular, e.g. Cleon, and not towards all of humanity."

Intentionality

Intentionality is "aboutness." Emotions and other mental states are always about—or "directed toward"—things, people, or states of affairs. (The term "intentionality" comes from the scholastics and is derived from intentio, Latin: "I point at, I turn my attention to.") Intentionality is sometimes taken to differentiate the mental from the physical, as only mental states (and mind-related matters such as representations and language) have it.

Emotion is a certain way of apprehending the world. . . . An emotion is a magical transformation of the world.

—Jean-Paul Sartre,
"The Emotions," 1939

But if emotions essentially involve an engagement with the world, this in turn requires a certain modicum of intelligence. One has to recognize that a situation or a person is offensive, that a person is lovable, or that one is oneself blameworthy (for example, in guilt and shame). But recognition implies both the possibility of getting it wrong and the possibility of getting it right. Thus, an emotion is rational when one accurately recognizes and evaluates the situation or the person. An emotion is irrational when one gets it wrong, perhaps because one is deceiving oneself about the true nature of the case. Of course, an emotion could be irrational for other reasons as well. One might accurately recognize the situation but be imprudent in expressing the emotion. Overtly getting angry with one's boss or professor (during the term), for example, is usually a bad idea.

Emotions play an important role in shaping our identity. A person's identity is not determined just by what he or she knows or remembers or how he or she thinks. A person's identity is also determined by what he or she *cares* about. It is determined by which emotions are most prevalent and how they get expressed. Who we are depends, at least in part, on how we feel about things.

The Egocentric Predicament
~U~

Given our seemingly intimate knowledge of ourselves, we might wonder whether we can ever really know if the experiences we have in our minds in fact correspond to the world outside us—the problem of skepticism we discussed in the preceding chapter. This problem also gives rise to the awful possibility of *solipsism,* which we introduced at the beginning of this chapter as the view that only one's own mind exists. What, then, of other people? This odd question has been designated by philosophers as the **egocentric predicament.** *Egocentric* because it begins with the claim that the individual self is at the center of all our experience; *predicament* because it is indeed an intolerable idea that we cannot ever get beyond our own self to know the existence of others (or of the external world). In recent Anglo-American philosophy, the same problem has been called the "problem of other minds," which is, essentially, "How can I ever know of the existence of any mind other than my own?"

This curious problem begins with an assumption we have taken for granted throughout most of this book: we know our own mind directly and beyond any doubt. (There may be—according to Freud, for example—certain aspects of our mind that are unconscious, or unknown to us, but even Freud accepted the claim that we *generally* know what directly is in our mind, which is why the idea of unconscious mental processes became such a startling discovery.) Descartes's "I think, therefore I am" is essentially a statement of this direct and indubitable knowledge we have of our own consciousness; but even Hume, who rejected the existence of the self, and Sartre, who thought that the self is created, began with this assumption. ("Consciousness is transparent," wrote Sartre. "It has no corners and nothing in it can hide from us.") But if we know our own mind directly and without any doubts, it does not follow that we know other people's minds directly at all. We have to *infer* what other people are thinking or feeling; we have to figure it out. How can we do this?

A standard answer, first formulated as a theory by John Stuart Mill over a century ago, is that we know what is going on in other people's minds—indeed, that we can figure out that other people have minds at all—by **analogy.** An analogy is a comparison in which certain similarities are pointed out with the conclusion that there must therefore be other similarities as well. For example, if someone draws an analogy between a college and a business (because, let's say, both need some principles of good management), we may expect other similarities to appear as well: the fact that both produce something that is purchased by consumers, for example, and the fact that both employ a workforce whose responsibility it is to produce the product as efficiently as possible. But, of course, there are **disanalogies**, too, comparisons in which the apparent similarities break down. Knowledge, for example, isn't like most products; any number of people can have the same knowledge, whereas only a limited number of people can share a particular automobile, television set, or toothbrush.

The argument that we can know of other people and their minds by analogy proceeds according to the comparison between our bodies and other people's bodies or our own faces and gestures and other people's faces and gestures. Our bodies, faces, and gestures are quite obviously similar; this similarity is the basis of the analogy. You sometimes frown; another person sometimes frowns. You sometimes wince in pain; the other person sometimes winces, too, and in much the same circumstances in which you would wince. Now, you know that when you frown it is usually because you disapprove of something or because you are worried about something. You know therefore that your mental state is correlated with certain features and movements of your body. You also see that the other person has similar features and makes similar movements with his or her body, and so you infer from these similarities a further similarity: namely, that the other person is feeling or thinking as you are when that person's features and movements are similar to your features and movements. That is, you know that, in your own case, your mental states (M) and your bodily movements (B) are correlated like this:

M:B ("M is related to B.")

You also know that the other person's bodily states are similar to yours:

M:B::*x*:B ("My M is related to my B as the M of another person, *x*, is related to that person's B.")

What you must infer, then, is the *x*, and what you infer, of course, is the other person's M. By analogy, from the similarities between your bodies and the correlation between your mental states and your body, you infer that the other person has similar mental states. The other person, too, has a mind.

This argument seems persuasive until we consider the possibility of disanalogies. Is it possible, for example, to imagine a being with human form who does everything that I do and in the same circumstances, but who does not have a mind? Many philosophers have argued that robots could be like this; they can be programmed to behave just as we do and designed to look just like us, but they have no mind (at least no conscious mind). (Some people turn the argument about robots the other way, too: because robots can be made to behave as we do in similar circumstances, the argument goes, robots may have the same thoughts and feelings we do.) But at least this much is clear: we can imagine without difficulty that the people who surround us are not in fact human and do not have minds. I cannot doubt the existence of my own mind, according to Descartes. But we can, by this argument, doubt the existence of other minds. Because we can never get into the position of another person to see if indeed he or she has a mind, how can we ever check our analogy? How can you ever know that you yourself are not the only conscious being, the only mind, the only self, in the universe? On the one hand, this solipsistic conclusion is obviously absurd; on the other hand, the argument that we know of other people and their minds by analogy seems to leave it, at least in theory, an open question. What has gone wrong here?

One possibility is that the argument from analogy goes wrong in the very place we most expected it to be unquestionable, in its very first premise, in the idea that we know our own mind directly and beyond any doubt. Let's take another look, therefore, at the assumption we have so far nowhere questioned. Are we indeed "directly" and indubitably aware of our own minds? Is the existence of our own self indubitable, whereas the existence of all other selves is an open question? What is the presupposition of this seemingly unassailable assumption, "I think, therefore I am"?

A number of philosophers have suggested that the proper formulation of Descartes's famous slogan ought to be just "There are thoughts." Descartes was not justified, they have argued, in assuming that if there are thoughts, there must be a thinker. But this of course is just what we have been assuming, too, in talking about the individual self. Each of us, the assumption goes, must have a self. We will return to this assumption later on when we discuss alternatives to the theory of self as consciousness.

The Mind-Body Problem

The identification or the location of the self in consciousness, as opposed to the identification of the self with your physical body, raises a tantalizing and very difficult metaphysical and scientific question: what is the relationship between our minds and our bodies; how do they interact? You remember that Descartes believed that mind and body were two different *substances*, but substances, by their very nature, cannot interact. What's more, Descartes insisted that he could conceive of his mind existing without a body, and it was clear that human bodies could exist (for example, as corpses) without minds. If mind and body are separable in this way, what is going on when they are conjoined? This question is referred to as the **"mind-body problem."**

Descartes never solved this problem to his satisfaction, and the elaborate metaphysics of Baruch Spinoza and Gottfried Wilhelm von Leibniz were, in part, attempts to solve it for him. If substances cannot interact, then it must be that either (1) mind and body do not interact, or (2) mind and body are not separate substances. Leibniz defends the first option, arguing that mental events and physical events only *seem* to interact. They in fact stand in "pre-established harmony," like a film and its soundtrack (not his analogy). The two are perfectly coordinated and seem to be causally related, but in fact they are two separate "tracks" on the same tape. Spinoza chooses the second option, suggesting that mind and body are not in fact distinct but rather are two different attributes of one and the same substance. His theory, accordingly, is sometimes called *dual aspect theory*— that is, mind and body are two different aspects of one and the same substance (according to him, the only substance).

These metaphysical speculations seem to us somewhat quaint, but they can be readily translated into extremely troubling questions with which contemporary science and philosophy continuously struggle. Mind and body may or may not be two different substances, but in our experience mental events (for example, a pain) are very different from the physical events occurring in the brain. Moreover, the question of how an occurrence in the body might cause an experience in the mind (or vice versa) seems to be as much a mystery to us as it was to Descartes.

Since the seventeenth century, however, there have been some momentous advances in science, and the terms of the question have altered accordingly. First, it was only in the twentieth century that we gained any substantial knowledge about the workings of the brain and the central nervous system. Second, and even more recently, advances in computer technology (only dimly envisioned by Descartes and some of his contemporaries, notably Pascal) have provided a promising analogue to the traditional mind-body problem. These recent discoveries have tended to shift attention to updated versions of Spinoza's solution to the mind-body problem—his idea that mental events and physical (brain) events are not in fact so different but rather intimately related, perhaps even identical.

Yet the old questions remain, and it is by no means clear exactly what it means to say that a mental event and a physical event are identical. Indeed, one can still find defenders of each of the five traditional solutions to the problem, once discussed in the metaphysical language of substances but now debated in the contemporary terms of neurology, cognitive science, and computer technology:

1. Mind and body in fact do interact; physical events (a pin in the finger) do cause mental events (a pain) and mental events (deciding to go to the store) do cause physical events (walking toward the store) (Descartes). The question is how they do this.

2. Mind and body do not interact; mental events and physical events occur simultaneously, perhaps coordinated by God in a "preestablished harmony" (Leibniz).

3. There are no mental events (the materialist solution). There are only brain processes, and "mental events" are just descriptions of these brain processes from the unusual perspective of the person who has the brain.

4. There are no physical events (the idealist solution). Brain processes, too, are only ideas in the mind.

5. Mental events and physical events are in fact the same (Spinoza's solution).

All five solutions are clumsy and obscure, though most of them still have adherents. There are still a great many **dualists** around—that is, those who continue to argue that mental events and physical events are wholly separate, and there are still committed idealists. Today, views about the mind-body problem, however, tend to fall into one of three general categories, each of them a version of the thesis that mind and body are not really separate substances. Not surprisingly, Spinoza is often invoked as the ancestor of all such solutions. The three types of solution, each to be discussed in turn, are behaviorism, identity theory, and functionalism.

Behaviorism

The claim that there are no mental events may initially sound nonsensical, but great philosophers (and psychologists), driven to desperate lengths by Descartes's problem, have sometimes chosen this solution as the most palatable alternative. One sophisticated theory denying that there are any mental events, coupled with the insistence that there are only various patterns of behavior (some of which we label with mentalistic names such as *belief, desire,* and *anger*), is called **behaviorism.** This view had strong adherents in the early to middle twentieth century, and although its popularity has declined, there are still some behaviorists who flatly insist that there are no mental events, or at least, no such events that can legitimately function in a scientific theory.

The crude behaviorist might simply deny the existence of mental events, but it is obvious to anyone who thinks that thoughts exist in some sense, at least while he or she is thinking them. (Thus Descartes's famous "I think, therefore I am," in which he denies that it is possible to think and intelligibly deny that one is thinking.) The modern behaviorist is more subtle. Of course mental events "exist" after a fashion—that is, we have experiences that we call desires, beliefs, emotions, moods, impulses, and the like are real and undeniable—but they don't exist in the way that most people think they do. Philosophical behaviorist Gilbert Ryle, rejecting Cartesian dualism, which he describes as positing "the ghost in the machine," also denies the existence of "mental" events in the sense of "occult," that is, "mysterious," inner occurrences. What we call *mental,* he claims, is a pattern or a disposition to behave in certain ways. To name a mental event is actually to make a prediction about a person's behavior. Thus, to say a man is thirsty is not to name some unseen event in his mind but rather to predict that he will get a drink as soon as he can. To say that a person is in love is not to name a feeling but to predict a familiar sequence of activities, from agitation in the presence of the loved one to writing long letters in the middle of the night. That some reality corresponds to what we call mental events is not denied; but this reality is relocated, no longer in some mysterious place called "the mind," but in the perfectly tangible body of an acting organism.

Gilbert Ryle (1900–1978) was an Oxford don, the author of *The Concept of Mind* (1949), and a leading proponent of philosophical behaviorism. According to Ryle, mental-type terms in fact refer to *dispositions to behave,* not to "ghostly private occurrences." A disposition is a tendency that can be triggered in certain circumstances. "Glass is brittle" refers to a disposition such that glass, when struck, will shatter into tiny pieces. "People fall in love" refers to a disposition such that men and women, when together in certain circumstances (called "romantic"), will begin to act ridiculous, a prelude to spending their lives together.

Behaviorism

Behaviorism is the view that all talk of mental events should be translated into talk about tendencies to behave in certain ways.

For some mental events, behaviorism is perfectly reasonable. For example, a person's intelligence is not anything he or she experiences; it is a tendency to perform well in certain kinds of tests. A person's motives—we know since Freud—might not be known at all, but we can tell what they are by the acts they motivate. Behaviorism runs into more of a problem with such sensations as pain, seeing bright light, or hearing a tune in the key of C. We can agree that these sensations may be manifested in dispositions to behave in certain ways—wincing, putting on sunglasses, or starting to whistle—but we will probably insist that there is still something irreducibly mental that lies behind these dispositions, that behaviorism can't be the whole story. Much of what we call the mind may indeed be better understood as dispositions to behave in certain ways. But some mental events seem to be *felt,* and with them the mind-body problem emerges once again, as tough as ever.

Today, even most behaviorists tend to defend the view that what we call mental events are really a special category of physical events. The main difference between behaviorists and eliminative materialists is that the former claim that our mentalistic terms really refer to patterns of behavior (much of which is observable at a distance and describable in everyday terms such as "carried the catalogue to the counter"), while the latter claim that these terms really refer to neurological states (which are more difficult to observe but more describable in precise terms than everyday external behavior).

Identity Theory and Eliminative Materialism

For many years, the increasingly refined research in neurology has made clear something Descartes and his friends could not have known: specific mental events have correlated with specific brain events. This picture is made much more complicated by the fact that several alternative brain events may be linked to the same sort of mental event, and in the case of brain damage, it is even possible for new mental pathways to be related to mental events that had previously been associated with others. Nevertheless, we now know that there is a strict correlation between mental events, from simple pains to raging ambition, and certain processes in the brain. The mind-body problem is evident here: How are these connected?

Correlation is not the same as connection. Two things can be correlated (the mayor of New York eats lunch every day at exactly the same time that the mayor of San Diego eats breakfast) without having any connection. Correlated mental and brain events might be like that, but if they were that would make any scientific understanding of the mind from the physical (as opposed to psychological) standpoint impossible. Perhaps mental events and physical events do cause one another, but then we are still faced with the question of how such different things can do so. The **identity theory** cuts through all such questions and says that mental events (pains, for example) and brain processes are *the same thing.* They have different properties and deserve different descriptions ("It hurts" versus "The sodium level is back down now"), but they are nevertheless the same. Here is another case of identity:

Water is H_2O.

Now, it is clear that a description of water—as "wet," as "cold," as "filling the basin"—is quite different from the description of hydrogen and oxygen atoms and the way they combine to form a certain molecule. Nevertheless, it makes perfectly good sense to say that water is H_2O, even if the properties of water—as we normally describe it—and the properties of the molecules—as a scientist would describe them—are different.

Identity theory is still much debated. It solves the mind-body problem, but it raises other questions just as perplexing. For example, it is usually argued that two things are identical only if they have *all* properties in common (a principle propounded by Leibniz and sometimes called *Leibniz's law*). But it is clear that pains and brain processes do not have most properties in common; for example, we can locate a brain process at a certain place in the brain. There is no such exact localizability for pains. (But then again, if you are in Seattle, it is clear that your headache is not in Portland.) On the basis of such arguments, some theorists have rejected the identity theory. They would say that water and H_2O *can* be described in the same terms, even if they often are not, but that there is no way to describe a pain in the language of brain science and no way to describe a brain process in the language of sensations.

Still other theorists have suggested that terminology we use to talk about pains and other mental states is just a curious remnant from the old days, when people knew much less about brains. In the future, they suggest, we will drop the language of sensations and perhaps talk comfortably about something such as "having an F-stimulation of my cerebral cortex, process 4.21-B." The view that our everyday talk that makes reference to mental events is actually referring to physical, i.e., neurological, states and that we should replace the former with the latter is called **eliminative materialism**. Eliminative materialists argue that we have absorbed misleading ideas about mental events (the "occult" ideas that Ryle dismissed) through our language, which enshrines many primitive notions about the world. Now that we have learned more about the physical processes that are involved in what we call "mental states," however, we should endeavor to replace our everyday mentalistic language with more precise neurological terminology.

Critics of eliminative materialism have questioned the view's supposition that the mentalistic terms we use are really pointing to the same thing that neurological language describes. When we use everyday mentalistic terms in everyday life, saying, for example, that a person "desires" or "intends" something or is in a certain mood, we are not usually making scientific or quasi-scientific statements about that person's physiological circumstances, but referring to how that person is disposed to act or concerning ourselves with how the world appears from the other person's first-person point of view. We might, for example, want to know how a person feels (perhaps to determine whether we have pleased or insulted him or her). It is not clear that our neurological descriptions, which are always third-person accounts, can substitute for mentalistic talk if we want to know what an experience is like from the standpoint of the person who has it. Whether we go the route of adopting neurological description in our everyday life, the central claim of identity theory is this: what we call a mental event is not a special type of event but just a particular way of describing some brain process.

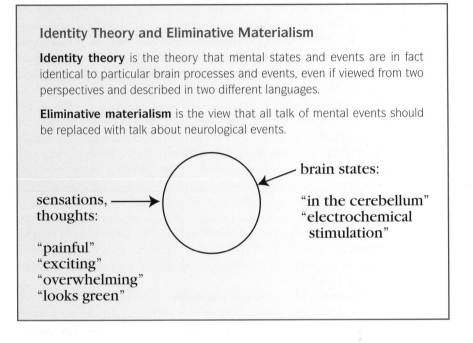

Identity Theory and Eliminative Materialism

Identity theory is the theory that mental states and events are in fact identical to particular brain processes and events, even if viewed from two perspectives and described in two different languages.

Eliminative materialism is the view that all talk of mental events should be replaced with talk about neurological events.

sensations, ⟶
thoughts:

brain states:

"in the cerebellum"
"electrochemical
    stimulation"

"painful"
"exciting"
"overwhelming"
"looks green"

Functionalism

Dissatisfaction with both behaviorism and identity theory as well as the rejection of all the old dualist theories of mind and body, coupled with recent discoveries about the workings of computers and the manufacture of artificial intelligence (AI), have led to another proposed solution to the mind-body problem, called *functionalism*. Behaviorism stresses the importance of behavior, but it cannot account for the nature of such sensations as pain and does not talk about the brain and its functions at all. Identity theory emphasizes the sameness of mental events and brain events, but it does not address the question of why this one particular organ should have such remarkable properties. One might ask, what is so special about the brain? Does the possibility of mental events depend on the special material of the brain? Or might various kinds of material (brains, but also computers) support mental event processes?

The **functionalist** answers these questions by insisting that the brain is not the only type of physical basis where minds and mental events can occur. The brain is special because it is such a marvelous piece of machinery—or "hardware." But other pieces of hardware not made out of brain material may someday do just as well and may have minds to match. Thirty years ago, skeptics were confidently insisting that no computer could ever win at chess; now computers are beating chess masters. Today, skeptics say that no computer will ever feel or think for itself; ten years from now, they may be apologizing to an indignant laptop.

Functionalists consider mental activity to be identical to certain processes, but they claim that the *function* is what counts as having a mind, not the material in which the function takes place. There is no reason to suppose that a computer exactly duplicating the human brain and capable of its various functions could not be built, and if it could, this computer would have a mind. There is no reason, apart from practicality, why one could not build a brain out of paper clips and rubber bands, so long as it included all the circuits needed to perform all proper functions. Functionalists solve the mind-body problem by saying that having a mind is equivalent to performing certain functions (for example, absorbing certain input and responding with certain output), and that although some kind of body is needed for these to occur, the exact kind of body does not matter so long as it can subserve the relevant functional roles. Whether or not a particular body can support mental functions will depend on the relationships among its parts; but the same kind of relations can in principle occur in bodies made of very different material.

Although both functionalism and identity theory try to solve the mind-body problem by asserting that the one thing is the other, their basic claims are quite different. The identity theorist claims that mental events simply *are* physical events, specifically events localized in the brain. The functionalist claims that mental events are functional *processes*, and these can occur on the basis of bodies of various types, brains being only one of these types.

Functionalism, it might be noted, still leaves open some questions. How do pain and other sensations fit in? Does the theory of functions explain how it is that one sees red or hears a melody? And might not a confirmed dualist come back once again and ask, "I agree that there is an impressive correlation between certain functions and mental events, but how does that explain how the one *causes* the other?" The functionalist asserts that mental activity is identical with performing certain functions. But couldn't it be that pains and great ideas are not identical to anything but themselves and that their place in a material universe is still a mystery our immaterial minds can't quite grasp?

Functionalism

Functionalism is the theory that mental activity consists of certain functions of the brain—which might well be duplicated in nonbrain material. There is nothing necessarily unique about the brain.

Against the Mind-Body Problem

Functionalism, its advocates argue, is a great advance in the efforts to solve the mind-body problem because it expands our vision to consider increasingly complicated processes of the brain (and its computer analogs), replacing older, more atomistic image of some comparatively simple event in the brain causing (or being identical to) some discrete mental event. But this same argument can be expanded further, and several philosophers in America and Europe have argued that the whole idea of reducing the mind-body problem to questions about the brain is a step in the wrong direction. We cannot understand human consciousness, the argument goes, apart from the *whole human being*. The dichotomy of "the mind and the body" is already a mistake, given this way of thinking, for what we are is *embodied consciousness*—not a mind *in* a body—and to argue about interaction and identity is already to misunderstand the terms that we use to describe human beings.

This argument against the mind-body problem is also a powerful argument against many of our favorite ideas about the self. To think of the self as an isolated individual consciousness, aware primarily of itself, is, according to similar arguments, a serious misunderstanding of selfhood. The self must be conceived of in terms of the *whole person*. (The position is sometimes called *holism*, accordingly.) In ancient times, Aristotle argued for such a view of the self as nothing less than the *complete* person; today, too, there are many philosophers who argue that nothing less can give us an adequate understanding of the self. The self is not just consciousness aware of itself but the flesh-and-blood person who is part of a family and a community and a soldier or a shoemaker or a politician. One is not a self not just for oneself, but with and for other people as well. We will proceed to consider various theories of the self that address broader notions of what it is to be a whole person.

Other Theories of the Self
〜❦〜

The Self as a Choice

What existentialists have in common is that they believe that existence comes before essence. . . . man first of all exists, encounters himself, surges up in the world—and defines himself afterwards. . . . to begin with, he is nothing.

—Jean-Paul Sartre, 1945

If self-identity is defined by our answer to the question "Who am I?" one possible answer is "Nothing yet, still in progress." If one sees the self not as an inner soul that is in us from birth (or perhaps from conception), but rather as a *product* of our actions and thoughts, then self-identity is something to be *earned*, not an already existing fact to be discovered. Thus, the existentialist **Jean-Paul Sartre** (1905–1980) would say that all those theories that take the self to be found in consciousness are misconceived. The self is not simply thinking, nor is it memory of the past. The self lies always in the future; it is what we aim toward, as we try to *make* ourselves into something. But this means that as long as we are alive there is no self—at least, no fixed and finished self. The self is an open question.

Self-Reliance

These are the voices which we hear in solitude, but they grow faint and inaudible as we enter into the world. Society everywhere is in conspiracy against the manhood of every one of its members. Society is a joint-stock company, in which the members agree, for the better securing of his bread to each shareholder, to surrender the liberty and culture of the eater. The virtue in most request is conformity. Self-reliance is its aversion. It loves not realities and creators, but names and customs.

Whoso would be a man, must be a nonconformist. . . . Nothing is at last sacred but the integrity of your own mind.

— Ralph Waldo Emerson,
"Self-Reliance," 1841

American transcendentalist **Ralph Waldo Emerson** (1803–1882) has influenced scores of important writers and artists, including philosophers **Friedrich Nietzsche** and John Dewey.

The first reply to the idea that the self is our own creation is usually that it neglects the fact that we are in fact a certain person with a fixed identity from the moment we are born, and facts continue to define us all through our lives. Consider, as an example, a person who is born in the year 1959, born female, born blond, born of a Scandinavian family, born poor; all these facts define this person and have nothing to do with "becoming." At the age of 3, the child is injured at play and loses a finger; at the age of 8, the child luckily finds herself in a class with a sympathetic and inspiring teacher, who interests her in science and starts her off on the road to a brilliant career in chemistry. At the age of 27, she by chance meets a fellow on an airplane; they fall in love and are soon married. He is kidnapped and killed by terrorists. She is hounded by the press, and a popular writer turns her story into a best-selling book. She retreats to her chemistry laboratory, thinks about her life as she runs her experiments, and comes to realize that it all consists of accidental facts—the fact of her birth, her childhood accident, walking into a certain classroom, taking a certain airplane flight, and so on. Those facts are her self. There seems to be nothing else.

Sartre's response to this portrait is that it leaves out an essential dimension at every turn. What is missing is choice. What is left out is the possibility, at any point in this story, of saying no to the facts as they stand. In Sartre's words, "No matter what is made of one, one is always responsible for what one makes of what is made of one." A person with an injury cannot wish away the injury, but he or she can make of it a badge of courage, a stigma of shame, a cocktail party curiosity, an excuse to stay out of the army, a handicap to be overcome. A person who is born blond and Scandinavian can be proud of that fact, embarrassed by it, or indifferent to it. One falls in love (something which itself has an enormous amount of choice built into it), but one can choose to ignore it, turn it into a tragedy, turn it into a marriage, even turn it into a joke of sorts.

Sartre called this dimension of our existence that enables us to choose what to make of the facts of our lives **transcendence**. We can always transcend, or go beyond, the facts that are true of us, or what Sartre called our **facticity**. Transcendence means that the self is defined not by the facts about us but by what we make—and continue to make—of these facts. But because we can change our minds throughout our lives about what to make of these facts (even those that are true of us for the whole of our lives), the self—which is the outcome of these interpretations and the actions based on them—is an unfinished process until the end of our lives. Only with death do our interpretations and our actions come to a halt.

French philosopher **Jean-Paul Sartre** (1905–1980) gained celebrity in his own time as a novelist, playwright, revolutionary journalist, and lifelong companion of feminist philosopher and writer **Simone de Beauvoir**.

To see what Sartre means by *transcendence*, consider, for example, a student who had once been extremely ill as a child and now (in college) intends to be a doctor. The facts of his illness are simply true; he cannot now do anything to change them. But he is obviously using those facts to motivate and justify his decision for the future, to become a doctor to cure other children who are afflicted as he was. But suppose in his senior year he becomes caught up in local politics, finds that he enjoys this, and, furthermore, that he does quite well in his new activities. He postpones his plans to go to medical school and spends a year campaigning for a political ally. Then he runs for office himself and wins, postponing medical school for another four years. His political career flourishes. Answering reporters when they ask, "How did you get into politics?" he finds himself remembering his childhood talent for negotiating and arguing well. What happened to the importance of his childhood illness? The fact of it remains true, of course, but it is no longer of significance for him; it no longer fits into the political project he has made for his life. Now suppose that the age of 43 he loses a critical election. His political career is finished, and, not surprisingly, he remembers his old ambition to become a doctor. The fact of his childhood illness is reinstated as a crucial fact about his life, and his projected self is once more a medical self, not because of the facts, but rather because of his renewed intentions.

Choosing Oneself

Man simply is. Not that he simply is what he conceives himself to be, but he is what he wills, and as he conceives of himself after already existing—as he wills to be. . . . Man is nothing else but that which he makes of himself. That is the first principle of existentialism.

Man is responsible for himself, not only for his own individuality but for all men.

Man chooses himself, and in choosing for ourselves, we choose for all men.

—Jean-Paul Sartre,
Existentialism as a Humanism, 1945

Sartre's view is that there is no "real self" other than the self that we make for ourselves. Certain facts are true of us, of course, and we cannot make them untrue. But we can make of them what we will, albeit that what we are able to make of them is also limited by the facts of our circumstances. Even prisoners, Sartre said, are free to make of their imprisonment what they choose; imprisonment can be injustice, martyrdom, an excuse for not doing anything, a challenge to escape, a symbol to the world, a way of amusing oneself, or just plain boring. But this also means that there are no "correct" choices; or, in Kierkegaard's language the "right" choice is a subjective truth, true for the person who makes it but not necessarily true for anyone else. The self is what each of us chooses *for ourselves,* our projection into our future, our intentions to *become* a particular kind of person. But as we never wholly achieve this—for even when our ambitions are fulfilled we can always change our mind, formulate new ambitions, and so on—the self never really exists in full. It is always at best our image of what we want to be, to which we strive with more or less success and persistency. And this striving, this sense of oneself as always incomplete and responsible for itself, is the **authentic self.**

Bad Faith: Are You Ever Just What You Are?

Let us take an example: A homosexual frequently has an intolerable feeling of guilt, and his whole existence is determined in relation to this feeling. One will readily see that he is in bad faith. In fact it frequently happens that this man, while recognizing his homosexual inclination, refuses with all his strength to consider himself "a homosexual." His case is always "different," peculiar. He refuses to draw from the facts their obvious conclusion. But then, his friend asks that [he] recognize himself and . . . declare, "I am a homosexual." But we ask, who is in bad faith? The homosexual or the champion of sincerity?

—Jean-Paul Sartre,
Being and Nothingness, 1943

If the authentic self for Sartre was something created, rather than something found, then the traditional theories that say that the self simply is are not only mistaken but, in a very important sense, self-deluding ways of not recognizing our responsibility for creating the self that we create. Sartre called this denial of responsibility for one's self **bad faith**. Bad faith (French: *mauvaise foi*, pronounced moh-vay FWAH) includes trying to excuse yourself from responsibility for what you are and what you will become by pretending that your life has been defined by the facts (by your facticity) instead of recognizing that you can try to make what you wish of those facts. Bad faith, in other words, is the negative side of having to create your self; it is the rejection of this responsibility—in effect, giving up even before you try.

No Self, Many Selves

There is nothing that can be called a "Self," and there is no such thing as "mine" in all the world.
—The Buddha, sixth century BCE

In reality, every self is far from being a unity; it is a constellation of selves, a chaos of forms, of states and stages, of inheritances and potentialities. Man is an onion made up of a hundred layers, a texture made up of many threads.
—Hermann Hesse, 1932

We have assumed throughout the whole of our discussion so far what would seem to be the most indubitable and undeniable thesis, that every person has one, and only one, self. But this assumption, too, can be challenged, and at least one of the major religions of the world—Buddhism—rejects as an "illusion" the very idea of the self.

The rejection of the self can be found in Western philosophy, too. In his *Treatise of Human Nature*, the skeptic David Hume turned his critical attention to Descartes's and Locke's claims to have found the self within consciousness, and he said, with his usual irony, that he found no such self in himself; all he found was a complicated cluster of different experiences and ideas, but nothing that could be called a self:

> *There are some philosophers who imagine that we are every moment intimately conscious of what we call our self; that we feel its existence and its continuance in existence; and we are certain, beyond the evidence of a demonstration, both of its perfect identity and simplicity. . . . But for my part, when I enter most intimately into what I call myself, I always stumble on some particular perception or other of heat or cold, light or shade, love or hatred, pain or pleasure. I never can catch myself at any time without a perception, and never can observe anything but the perception.*

As a consistent empiricist, Hume therefore concluded that we aren't really justified in talking about a self because the concept can't be related to something encountered in experience.

Jean-Paul Sartre, as we have seen, also rejected the idea of the existence of the self in the traditional sense. One way of reinterpreting his philosophy is to say that he, too, denied that we can find any self in ourselves; that for him the self, if it is not an illusion, at least always escapes us, always lies ahead of us in the future.

But let's take these arguments several steps further. Hume's skepticism is essentially a negative thesis: he could not find what most philosophers too confidently refer to as a self. But the negative thesis can be turned into a positive thesis, and this is what happens in Buddhism. For the Buddhist, not being able to find the self is not a philosophical inability; rather, seeing through the illusion of the individual self is the highest form of enlightenment and the most important single conceptual achievement. The self, in this view, is itself a false idea, a dangerous notion that cuts us off from the rest of the world, from the entirety (which Mahayana Buddhists call the "Buddha-nature"). The idea, then, is that our real self-identity is not individual *self*-identity at all but rather our unity with the whole of the universe. But this is to say that, in our sense, there is no self, that the self is an idea that has been imposed on us by our tradition and appearances instead of a fact that is true of us or of a soul inside of us.

The Buddhist view of self was formulated in opposition to an alternative view that was offered by Hinduism. As we will discuss further in Chapter 10, according to this Hindu view, we do have an identity as an individual, embodied self, but this is not the real self. The real self is a transpersonal self, a self that is the same within all individuals. This is yet another way of considering the self: the individual is an illusion, but the self is not.

The rejection of the individual self in favor of an all-embracing cosmic sense of self appears in Western philosophy, too. The nineteenth-century German philosopher G. W. F. Hegel also rejected our emphasis on the personal, individual self. He showed, in his *Phenomenology of Spirit*, that our true self-identity is indeed a universal self-identity—all of us as One—which he called "Spirit" (Chapters 2 and 3). For Hegel, too, the individual self is an illusion fostered by our society's particular way of thinking, and our true identity breaks through these limited boundaries to include all of us together.

The Unimportance of the Individual

At a time when spiritual life has become so very much emphasized and strengthened and the mere individual has become correspondingly a matter of indifference, . . . the individual must forget himself; he must simply become and do what he can, but less must be demanded of him and he should expect and ask less for himself.

—G. W. F. Hegel,
Phenomenology of Spirit, 1807

The rejection of the idea that each person has a distinct self leads to an even more astounding conclusion, found in some of the other philosophies of both East and West as well, which has been defended in the writings of the German author Hermann Hesse. According to this view, there are indeed selves, but not, as we have assumed, one self per person. Each of us is a multitude of selves. We may be different selves in different circumstances, and it is only a philosophical mistake that makes us think that we have to tie all of these selves together into a single coherent package, as a single self.

In a striking image, Hesse tells us that "man is an onion," with hundreds of different layers (selves). The traditional Western view, on the other hand, is that man is a peach, with a solid, single pit in the center (the soul). But if you peel away the layers of an onion, you know that you find more layers; when you reach the last layer, there is nothing more, no pit, no core, no soul. There are only the layers, the many roles we play in different parts of our lives, the many selves, which is to say, no individual "self" as such at all. (A similar view of the self is implicit in Confucianism.) A person is defined by the various roles he or she plays, and the model of self is Hesse's onion, not the peach with its pit.

The rejection of the atomistic self in any of these senses is not just a philosophical trick; it quickly becomes a way of life. Most of our plans and our behavior are based on the assumption that we have to *be* somebody or that we ought to make something of ourselves. But according to the views just discussed, this picture of the individual as the unit of selfhood breaks down, and self-realization becomes instead the recognition of being part of something much greater than one's (individual) self, or, in Hesse's view, the realization of the multitude of selves that are in us all.

The Self as Social

Man is by nature a social animal. . . . Anyone who is unable to live a common life or who is so self-sufficient that he has no need to do so is no member of society, which means that he is either a beast or a god.

—Aristotle, fourth century BCE

No doubt, each of us has a conception of our self as an individual self, and we do indeed have some sense of having an authentic, or real, self beneath the roles and postures we are taught to adopt in work and society, which sometimes make us feel uncomfortable, not ourselves. But we have concluded too quickly that our real self is an individual self and that the social roles we play and the conventions we learn in society are distortions and distractions from our true self. Indeed, this is a very old view; it is central to the Christian teaching that the inner soul before God is the real self and that our social position and power are, by comparison, of no real significance. Descartes taught this view when he declared that the real self is oneself as a "thinking thing," as opposed, for instance, to a social being, a son, a father, a daughter, a mother, and so on. The French philosopher Jean-Jacques Rousseau set forth the same thesis again in the mid-eighteenth century when he declared with vehemence that natural, individual human beings are good and innocent until society "corrupts" them, and we in America are still sympathetic to this philosophy, that what is natural and individual is essentially good.

Jean-Jacques Rousseau (1712–1778) was a stormy Enlightenment philosopher from Geneva, Switzerland, who fought throughout his life with virtually all his friends and supporters. An extremely troubled and unhappy man, he found in his solitude a conception of humans as basically and naturally good, before the conventions and artificialities of society "corrupted" them. His writings were often censored and at times he had to flee arrest. He died in total poverty, but only a few years later, his ideas became the philosophical basis for the French Revolution.

Paradoxically, the image we have of ourselves as *individuals* is an image that we have been taught collectively, by society, precisely because we are not mere individuals. Consider a common view in our society, that the general welfare will best be served by everyone pursuing his or her own interests. This is a premise that is still much debated, of course, yet it serves in particular as one of the assumptions behind **capitalism** and is certainly central to much of American thinking. But this is a very recent idea; indeed, it would not even have been considered plausible until the middle of the eighteenth century. The point to be made again is that, although the idea emphasizes the importance of individuals (and individual initiative, individual interests), it is an idea created and promoted by a specific kind of society. Our confidence that we are individuals in the way we think we are, in other words, is based on our having been brought up in a society that understands selfhood in a particular (modern) way. And if today we see our individual existence as indubitable, that is itself a matter that deserves philosophical curiosity and investigation.

Even in early Christianity, despite its emphasis on the individual soul, there was a powerful emphasis on the spiritual community, within which that soul could discover itself and through which it could earn its salvation. Before Christianity, Judaism was far more concerned with the integrity of the Jewish community than with the isolated identity of its members; indeed, Jewish identity was identity in the community and nothing more. Until modern times, our idea of individual identity would have been unintelligible. Today, too, when we think about the question "Who am I?" we are all too likely to forget that we are something more than our individual characteristics and talents, more than an isolated atom cut off from the community within which our existence, our characteristics, and our talents acquire their significance. What does it mean to be "attractive" or "good-looking," for instance, outside of the context of a particular society? What does it mean to be "smart," "charming," or "fun to be with" except among other people who have similar conceptions of these traits? What does it mean to

Harmony Rather Than Agreement

The exemplary person seeks harmony rather than agreement; the small person does the opposite.

— Confucius, *Analects*, sixth century BCE

The Importance of the Individual

The view that a society of individuals, each working only with his or her own interests in mind, might collectively serve to improve society as a whole and increase the general welfare was not seriously proposed as a theory of society until 1776, when Scottish thinker **Adam Smith** *(1723–1790) published his epoch-making* The Wealth of Nations. *Smith is universally considered to be the "father of capitalism" and the first great spokesman for laissez-faire ("leave alone") economics. Smith hypothesized that an "invisible hand" would guarantee the overall good of society through the workings of a free and competitive market. But such a market itself was not possible until modern times, when the medieval suspicion of "usury" and profit seeking was replaced by the recognition of money making as a legitimate activity, and the desires of the individual—by way of supply and demand—would be allowed to determine what was produced and in what quantities.*

be "trustworthy" or "generous" except within a community in which these traits make sense and are generally praised? In other words, most of the characteristics we ascribe to ourselves as individuals already presuppose the existence of other people and our living with them.

This observation can be repeated at a deeper philosophical level, too. Recall Descartes's argument that we are indeed directly and indubitably aware of our own self, our own mind, prior to our knowledge of the existence of other people. We pointed out that Descartes's claim that we have indubitable self-awareness is questionable; we may be aware of thoughts, but it does not follow that we are aware of the self, the "I" that thinks. How do we recognize thoughts, however? It can be argued that we recognize thoughts only because we have words and concepts that allow us to. (Ancient peoples, some archaeologists claim, did not have such words and concepts and so could only refer to what we call "thoughts" as "voices," presumably from the gods.) But where did we get these words and concepts? From our language, which we could have learned only within a community of other people who taught us the language, who gave us these concepts, who taught us to say, in effect, "I think, therefore I am"—and not to doubt it.

What this means is that we know of our own existence only because we have been taught by our society to recognize our own existence. But this also means that the existence of other people is not in question; it is not a doubtful belief that needs to be backed up with a problematic and probably inadequate argument from analogy. The existence of others, along with the existence of ourselves, is in fact one of the *premises* of our thinking, not one of its doubtful conclusions. Thus the German existentialist **Martin Heidegger** says that we are originally part of a community "with others"; the challenge is to learn within this context how to be an individual, how to be "authentic."

Similarly, Hegel wrote that we find our true identity in "Spirit." Making a more political point, Karl Marx tells us that we are essentially social beings and gain our identity only within a society (of a particular kind) and, ultimately, within the whole context of humanity. (He called us "species-beings," beings who live and work not just for ourselves, but for the whole.) So we all find, as we push our thinking further, that no matter how important our existence as individuals may seem to us, this individual existence gains its significance only through the picture of ourselves in a larger society and through our relations with other people.

Martin Heidegger (1889–1976) was a German existentialist who has had a profound influence on many philosophers around the globe. His best-known book is *Being and Time* (1927). The concept of "authenticity" (or "authentic self") has become popular largely because of his work.

> *Everyone is the other, and no one is himself. The "they" which supplies the answer to the question of the "who" . . . is "nobody."*
>
> *The Self of everyday [man] is the they-self, which we distinguish from the authentic self, that is, from the self which has been taken hold of in its own way.*
>
> —Martin Heidegger,
> *Being and Time*, 1927

Karl Marx (1818–1883) is usually thought of primarily as a social reformer and revolutionary. In fact, he was an accomplished philosopher and one of the leading economic theorists of all times. He studied in depth the writings of **G. W. F. Hegel** (who had died just before Marx started college in Berlin) and borrowed Hegel's concept of "dialectic" as a way of understanding social evolution, through conflict and resolution. But where Hegel's main concept was "Spirit," Marx emphasized the more material aspects of human life—the need for food, shelter, and security, for instance. Nevertheless, Marx also stressed the spiritual needs of individuals, especially art and creativity and the appreciation of nature. (He did not include religion among these spiritual needs, however.)

As society itself produces man as man, so it too is produced by him. Activity and mind are social in their content as well as in their origin; they are social activity and social mind. . . . The individual is the social being.

—Karl Marx, Manuscript of 1844

The Self and Relationships

The essence of our relations with other people is conflict.
—Jean-Paul Sartre, 1943

Man is a network of relationships, and these alone matter to him.
—Antoine de Saint-Exupéry, 1900–1944

The vision we have of ourselves determines the relations we will have with others. Poets and philosophers have often written that love begins with self-love, and social critics have pointed out that hate often begins with self-hate. But it is a matter for serious reflection that in our self-absorbed, individualistic society so much is written and said on self-realization and individual self-identity, while somewhat less has been written, at least on the same level of self-conscious philosophical profundity, on the nature of our relations with one another. Of course, we know the reason for this: our Western conceptions of self are such that we tend to think that our real or essential or authentic self is ours and ours alone, while relations with other people are secondary to selfhood and, in some sense, external. We talk about "reaching out to someone"; our poets and psychiatrists tell us about the plight of our loneliness, each of us having been born into the world alone and trying desperately to find refuge with another person through love.

But if the self is social, then all of this way of putting things might very well be misguided; rather than reaching out to people, we may need to realize the bonds that are already there. And it is simply false that each of us is born into the world alone; it is a matter of biology that even our first grand entrance is staged with at least one other person (our mother), and often the delivery room is rather crowded. The question then becomes: what is the nature of these bonds between us, with which our conception of selfhood begins?

The bonds between us are of a hundred varieties, of course—love, hate, dependency, fear, admiration, envy, shared joy or suffering, kinship, parenthood, patriotism, competition, sexual attraction, team spirit, being in jail together, running on the same political party ticket, and sitting next to each other in class. Each of these deserves its own analysis and understanding. But in general, we can break our conceptions of relationships into two very broad views: "us versus them" (or "me versus them") on the one hand and "we" on the other. The first presumes some basic difference, even antagonism, between us and them; the second presupposes a shared identity (within which, of course, there can be any number of differences).

The us-versus-them view can be illustrated, as an extreme case, by most wars. There are wars, perhaps, in which one or both sides retain some sense of kinship with the other, but even in most civil wars the other side is conceived of as "the enemy" and is often depicted as inhuman, barbarian, and uncivilized. On a more personal and less belligerent scale, the us-versus-them view emerges at least temporarily in competition with strangers (for the same job, for the same seat in a bus, or at a track meet). In every case, the emphasis is on the differences between sides; the presumption is usually that one person's gain is very likely another person's loss, and the self-identity of one is defined independently of or in opposition to the other.

The second view, however, takes mutual identity to be primary and differences to be secondary. There is a presumption of cooperation: what helps one will help the other, and self-identity is defined by this mutual identity. A familiar example is the sense of shared identity we have when we are playing on the same team. There are differences between us, of course; we play different positions, and we have different skills and different personalities. But what is primary is the team; indeed, we have all seen how a team falls apart when individual players begin to think more of their own performance than of the performance of the team. A second example would be love, whether the love of a mother for her child, the love of a married couple, or the love of a person for a country. Love, too, is the presumption of a shared identity; a person defines self-identity in terms of the relationship (at least in part), and it is assumed that one person's interest is the other's, too. (Even when this is not the case, one person typically takes up the other's interest as his or her own.)

These two views have deep roots in philosophy. The first can be seen quite clearly, for example, in the "problem of other minds" and the "egocentric predicament" of the solipsist, for whom all other people are literally other, actually unknowable and unreachable. There is more than a hint of solipsism, for example, in those social speakers who urge us to "escape our loneliness" and "reach out to someone." The presupposition of this popular (American) message is that we begin alone and that we desperately try to overcome this aloneness. But imagine telling that to the seventh child in an enormous tribal family. The truth is that our sense of loneliness is not universal or part of the human condition, but an inevitable consequence of our extremely mobile and individualistic society. And yet, as we have seen, we tend to take the view that the isolated individual self is not only the real self, but the only thing of which we can be absolutely certain. Not surprisingly, our view of relations with other people therefore tends to be that knowing and relating to other people is a problem.

This view was brutally argued, for instance, by Jean-Paul Sartre in his book *Being and Nothingness* (and in many of his novels and plays). Relations with others, Sartre argued, are essentially conflict. But we can see how he must conclude that this is so. He began by defending a conception of self that is strictly individual, in which each of us tries to create ourselves in a certain image and to be authentic to ourselves. Other people, accordingly, tend to be external to this creation of self; or they serve as the instruments or raw materials for the creation of self; or they may become impossible obstacles to the creation of self. For example, other people often restrict our abilities by making their own demands and setting up expectations, and they therefore tend to interfere with our freedom of self-creation. In a relationship between a man and a woman, Sartre argued, this mutual interference and antagonism reach their pinnacle; sex and even love are but weapons in the competition for independent self-realization. Each person tries to force the other to agree with his or her conception of self. Thus, all our relations are essentially conflict, even when they seem to be perfectly pleasant and mutually agreeable. (It is worth noting that Sartre reconsidered these views later in his life and that he himself had a lifelong relationship—sometimes romantic—with Simone de Beauvoir.)

This tragic view of relationships, however, is based on a conception of the isolated individual self, which has its problems. If we turn to the second conception of relationships, the "we" view of already existing bonds between us, we solve some of these problems and discover a much less tragic conception of relationships. We refer to this second conception, for example, when we declare that "we were made for each other," in the sense that, before we met, the connection between us had already been established. Similarly, people say "marriages are made in heaven." As a sociological theory, this is seriously challenged by current divorce statistics, but as a philosophical viewpoint, it has much to recommend it. From the moment we are born, we establish and reestablish bonds with others, not just particular people, but *types* of people. Thus, one adult or one teacher replaces another in our lives; one friend takes the place of another, and one boyfriend or girlfriend seems remarkably like the last.

This is not to say, of course, that we are incapable of particular commitments or of sticking with a single friend or spouse, but it is to say that our relations with others are *types* of bonds that we carry from one person to another, some of which we have from infancy. Thus, Freud was not being perverse when he insisted that every man falls in love with his mother and every woman falls in love with her father. The bonds and expectations and likes and dislikes that one learns as an infant stay with us through life, usually much modified and even reversed in some significant ways. But, according to this view, we are not isolated individuals searching desperately for other people; we already have networks of relationships, which are fulfilled in different ways at different times by different people. Our conception of ourselves—our self-identity—is determined in turn by these networks, without which we are ultimately nothing.

How Two Become One: Aristophanes

And so, when a person meets the half that is his very own, . . . then something wonderful happens: the two are struck from their senses by love, by a sense of belonging to one another, and by desire, and they don't want to be separated from one another, not even for a moment.

From Plato, *The Symposium,*
fourth century BCE

A marvelous illustration of this second view of relationships, as "made for each other," is a short story told in Plato's dialogue *The Symposium*. Asked to tell his fellow dinner guests about the nature and origins of love, the playwright Aristophanes invents a wonderful fable, in which we were all long ago "double-creatures," with two heads, four arms, four legs, and enormous intelligence and arrogance (or what the Greeks called *hubris*). To teach humans a lesson, Zeus, the king of the gods, struck the creatures down and cleft them in two—"like an apple," Aristophanes says—so that each resulting half-person now had to walk around the world, looking for his or her other half. That is the origin of love, Aristophanes concludes, not the search of one isolated individual for another, but the urge to reunite with someone who is already, as we still say, one's "other half." The fable is pure fiction, of course, but the point is profound. Relations with others do not begin when people first meet; they began, in a sense, with the very beginning of our species. The complete self, in other words, is not just the individual person. It is people *together* and, sometimes, in love.

Closing Questions

1. When a person says, "I think such and such . . ." is there necessarily reference to a self there, or is the word "I" simply a function of grammar? Would it make sense to say, as Bertrand Russell once suggested, that "It thinks in me" or "There is a thought here" instead?

2. In his play *No Exit*, Jean-Paul Sartre had one of his characters exclaim, "Hell is other people." What he might have had in mind is that people interfere with each other to such an extent that hell might simply be people torturing each other forever with their comments and their gestures, just as we torture each other here on earth. Do you agree with this picture of human relationships? Why or why not?

3. If a teenager commits a crime and is sent to reform school for a few years, what justification might the individual have, twenty years later, in explaining, "I am an entirely different person now"?

4. Which aspects of your self (or self-identity) do you attribute directly to your upbringing in a particular family, in a particular society, or in a particular neighborhood, city, or other environment? Which do you attribute to "nature" (that is, to instincts and inherited characteristics)? Which aspects of your self (if any) would you say are entirely your own, independent of other people and your biological nature?

5. If you were told (perhaps in a science fiction story) that a certain "person" was a robot, how could you tell if this were true?

6. Does your race signify an essential part of your self? Why or why not?

7. Does your sex constitute an essential part of your self? Why or why not?

8. Marriage is sometimes described as a union of two people. Sexual coupling aside, what does this mean?

9. Does a newborn baby have a self? What kinds of theories and considerations would you bring to bear on this question?

10. Could a computer have a sense of humor? What would it have to do to have one? What would it have to do to convince you that it had one? (Would it be enough to print out "Ha Ha" and shake around a bit?) If the computer lacks a sense of humor, does it necessarily lack a "self"?

Suggested Readings

A good general study of the various approaches to self-identity in recent American and British philosophy can be found in John Perry, *Personal Identity* (University of California Press, 1975). An entertaining and useful discussion of the problem in dialogue form is John Perry's *Dialogue on Personal Identity and Immortality* (Hackett, 1978). Derek Parfit's ideas about teleportation as well as his defense of the "bundle theory" of personal identity can be found in his *Reasons and Persons* (Oxford: Clarendon press, 1984). The existentialist view of selfhood is classically summarized in Jean-Paul Sartre's short lecture, "Existentialism as a Humanism," available in Robert C. Solomon, *Existentialism*, 2nd ed. (Oxford University Press, 2004). This anthology also includes relevant selections from Heidegger's *Being and Time* (State University of New York Press, 1996). Marx's theory of the human being in relation to society can be found in *The Economic and Philosophic Manuscripts of 1844,* and the *Communist Manifesto,* trans. Martin Milligan (Prometheus, 1988). Sartre's magnum opus on existentialism is *Being and Nothingness*, trans. Hazel Barnes (Washington Square Press, 1956). David Hume's skeptical attack on the idea of self appears in his *Treatise of Human Nature,* ed. L. A. Selby-Bigge (Oxford University Press, 1980). Hesse's image of the self as an onion appears in his novel *Steppenwolf,* trans. Basil Creighton and Rev. Joseph Mileck (Holt, Rinehart and Winston, 1929). Aristophanes' tale is in Plato's *Symposium,* trans. Alexander Nehamas and Paul Woodruff (Hackett, 1989). A good selection of readings on the mind-body question is David Rosenthal, *Materialism and the Mind-Body Problem,* 2nd ed. (Hackett, 2000). A useful discussion of the mind-body problem and the various contemporary solutions is David Chalmers, *The Philosophy of Mind: Classical and Contemporary Readings* (Oxford University Press, 2002). A good contemporary account of the self in "cognitive science" is Owen Flanagan, *Self Expressions* (Oxford University Press, 1996). A handy collection of historical and contemporary sources on the emotions is Robert C. Solomon, *What Is an Emotion?* 2nd ed. (Oxford University Press, 2003). William James's "What Is an Emotion?" is included in this volume. Sartre's The *Emotions: A Sketch of a Theory,* was translated by B. Frechtman (Philosophical Library, 1984). Thomas Nagel's

"What Is It Like to Be a Bat?" appears in his *Mortal Questions* (Cambridge University Press, 1979). The script of Monty Python's spoof on Descartes, along with those for its other (often philosophical) vignettes, are available in *All the Words: The Complete Monty Python's Flying Circus* (2 vols., Pantheon Books, 1989). Blaise Pascal's famous line about the heart and reason appears in *Pensées*, trans. A. J. Krailsheimer (Penguin, 1995).

Horatio Greenough, George Washington. National Portrait Gallery,
Smithsonian American Art Museum, Washington, DC/Art Resource, NY.

7
Freedom

In short, the actions of man are never free; they are always the necessary consequence of his temperament, of the received ideas, and of the notions, either true or false, which he has formed to himself of happiness. . . .
—Baron Paul Henri d'Holbach, 1770

One's own free unfettered choice, one's own fancy, however wild it may be, one's own fancy worked up at times to frenzy. That is the "most advantageous advantage" which is always overlooked.
—Fyodor Dostoevsky, 1864

ᘏᑌᘏ

Opening Questions

1. It is one of the main themes of American literature and folklore that freedom (or liberty) is one of the few things worth fighting for, even dying for. What does this mean? Describe a set of circumstances in which you would accept this as true. Describe a set of circumstances in which you would not accept this as true. What are the important differences between the two cases?

2. Most of what you do and say reflects the influences, training, education, examples, and rules that have affected you all your life. Some of these come from your parents; there were prejudices and preferences taught to you when you were very young so that you have never even been able to consider the alternatives. Some have been imposed on you by force (through threat of punishment or nonacceptance), and other people have subtly influenced you through television, magazines, and other forms of mass communication. Does all this make your actions and decisions any less "free"? To what extent would you be more free if you could get outside of all these influences and make decisions without them?

3. Have you ever made a decision that was *entirely* your own? If so, describe it.

4. We often talk about a person in love being "captive" to that emotion; is this possible? Is a person who acts out of love less free than a person who acts out of deliberate reasoning?

5. If a person commits a serious crime, but is wholly determined or caused to do so by his or her upbringing, by criminal influences, or by drugs, should he or she be held responsible for the crime? Should society be held responsible? Friends? The drug dealer? Should anyone be held responsible? Or is that just "the way things had to happen"?

6. Is freedom necessary for living the good life in a good society? Can you imagine circumstances in which freedom would be undesirable, or at least irrelevant? Is giving people freedom always giving them something good?

7. Is a person alone more free than a person bound by obligations to other people? Is it true, as our love songs often say, that breaking up a relationship is "being free again"? Is a person caught up in a web of duties and obligations at work necessarily less free than a person who, by choice, does not work at all?

Freedom and the Good Life

"Give me liberty, or give me death," cried the early American patriot Patrick Henry. Most of us, too—whether or not we would go quite so far—believe that freedom is one of the most important things in the world. It is not only an ingredient of, but the presupposition of, the good life; indeed, it may itself be the good life. It is possible to live our life fighting for freedom, and there are few things that we would say are more important to fight for. What we mean by freedom in this context is political freedom, the right to make autonomous choices and the practical ability to act on them independent of coercion by other human beings or institutions.

On a deeper philosophical level, we encounter another sense of **freedom**, in which freedom seems to be not only the presupposition of the good life but also the logical prerequisite for morality and moral responsibility. This is metaphysical freedom, the capacity to make choices that are not determined by forces external to us. If we were not free to act as we choose—whether rightly or wrongly—then holding us responsible for what we do would not seem to make any sense, nor would there be much point in imposing upon us those moral rules and principles that tell us what we ought to do. After all, we do not praise or blame a person for obeying the law of gravity, nor do we see any point in telling a person that he or she ought to do so. "Ought implies can," wrote Immanuel Kant in his discussion of moral philosophy and freedom. Without freedom there could be no morality. Without freedom, we often say, life would hardly be worth living.

Obviously, metaphysical and political freedom have something important in common. Freedom in either sense implies the unconstrained power to act autonomously, without being forced by anything outside of us. Among the questions we will consider in this chapter is why we consider freedom to be so important and how important it actually is. We will also consider the merits of the view that our imagined metaphysical freedom is illusory or considerably more restricted than we tend to think. A powerful argument can be made for the view that there can be no human freedom of choice or action, that is, no metaphysical freedom. This view is called **determinism**. The argument, quite simply, follows from the tenet we have called the **principle of universal causality** (see Chapter 5)—namely, the universal necessity that every event must have its explanatory causes. But if human decisions and actions are events, then it follows that they, too, must have their explanatory causes. If an action or a decision is caused (which is to say, brought about, or determined beforehand, by earlier events or conditions), then how could it possibly be free? What would it mean to say that we have a "choice"?

Before we examine this troublesome matter in some detail, let's first raise two questions too rarely raised in our constant adulation of freedom. Why is freedom so important to us? And what is *freedom*?

Why Is Freedom So Important to Us?

> *We posit freedom and slavery as opposites. We imagine a polarity and think that liberty represents the one extreme and slavery the other. That makes the case for freedom categorical and simple. Who wants to be a slave? But is the difference between the master and his slave simply that one has freedom which the other lacks? Doesn't the master live in a mansion, and the slave in quarters? Doesn't the slave toil while the other drinks mint julep? Doesn't the master wield the whip that cuts the other's back? A preference for the master's life proves very little about freedom.*
> —Frithjof Bergmann, 1977

Fascism

Against individualism, the Fascist conception is for the State; and it is for the individual insofar as he coincides with the State. . . . Fascism is for liberty, . . . the only liberty which can be a real thing, the liberty of the State and of the individual within the State.

—Benito Mussolini, "The Doctrine of Fascism," 1934

Freedom—the word, that is—excites almost everyone, but it can mean almost anything. We generally define *freedom* as the absence of all (unreasonable) restraint in our movements, our speech, our beliefs, and our activities. But is simply being left alone the same thing as freedom? Is being alone in the desert being free? And what is to count as an *unreasonable* restraint? If we think of almost any controversial social issue—particularly those involving drug taking, sex, or other personal activities—the vagueness of this question becomes painfully obvious.

Freedom For and Against

Our culture has a schizophrenic view of freedom.

For the first school it is axiomatic that freedom is wonderful; freedom separates man from the beasts and raises him above nature. Liberty gives a man a unique and incommensurate status which is lost to him when it is forfeited. . . . This is the more "official" tradition. It views freedom as satisfying, as the natural and obvious object of every man's longing. . . . All sides fight for freedom. Even the Nazis declared that they were for it.

If one had to choose a single motto for the second tradition, one might pick the phrase "escape from freedom." . . . One has a choice, . . . happiness or dignity. . . . The terms are, one or the other—but not both. . . . From this point of view, liberalism looks like an impossible insistence on having both; it links happiness and freedom . . . so that there need be no choice. It is amazing that liberalism usually treats this as completely obvious, as if there had never been any question.

—Frithjof Bergmann,
On Being Free, 1977

In his book *On Being Free,* Frithjof Bergmann outlined what he called our "schizophrenic view of freedom." The first side of this is the familiar view that freedom is "wonderful." It is what gives human beings distinguished status and separates us from nature, *and* it is assumed to be the goal of everyone, in every society, even those who do not know the word and have never thought about being free. The urge to be free is not to be questioned; the value of freedom is absolute, even more important than life itself. But notice that this view already poses a dilemma: it says both that we are *already* (by nature) free and that we *aspire* to be free. (Rousseau wrote, "Man is born free, and yet everywhere he is in chains.") We might thus distinguish *intrinsic* (that is, metaphysical) freedom, or our natural free will, and *extrinsic* (political) freedom, the freedom for which we must fight.

The other side of our conflicted view of freedom, however, is that it is dreadful and that we want nothing more than to escape from it. It is terrifying to have to make decisions that will affect one's entire life—choosing a college, selecting a marriage partner, deciding whether to join the army. And so we feel relieved (or, at least, part of us does) when someone else makes the choice or, better, "fate" steps in and makes it for us. The existentialist Jean-Paul Sartre and the psychiatrist Erich Fromm have both argued, for example, that we all try to "escape from freedom"; we find it too painful. We retreat to the unquestioning obedience of authority; we fall into what Sartre called **bad faith** (see p. 210). The example Bergmann gave is the story of the Grand Inquisitor in Dostoevsky's novel *The Brothers Karamazov.* Jesus finally returns to earth, but he is arrested by the Grand Inquisitor, who is also head of the Christian church. The cause of the arrest is that Jesus offered freedom; the Inquisitor recognizes that what people really want is authority and mystery, and so he has given them the church. The people are left with the word *freedom,* but what they are taught is obedience and servitude.

Do We Want the Illusion, Not the Fact, of Freedom?

The Grand Inquisitor is talking to Christ, just returned:

"Didn't you often tell them that You wanted to make them free? Well then," the old man added with a grin, *"now you see before you free men. Yes, that business cost us a great deal,"* he continued, looking sternly at Him. . . . *"For fifteen hundred years we were pestered by that notion of freedom, but in the end we succeeded in getting rid of it for good. . . . And I want you to know that on this very day men are convinced that they are freer than they have ever been, although they themselves have brought to us their freedom and put it meekly at our feet."*

—Fyodor Dostoevsky,
The Brothers Karamazov, 1880

We think we want freedom, but do we really? And if we do, why? Imagine a life in a very happy little island village. Everyone is born into a role, which he or she will assume for life, with certain stages appropriate to his or her age. Everyone knows his or her identity; everyone knows what he or she is expected to do, and everyone sets about to satisfy these expectations. Life is sufficiently full to prevent boredom; it is sufficiently luxurious to prevent scarcity and selfish infighting. What would *freedom* mean in such a society? What would be the *value* of freedom in such a situation? If a ship of European sailors were to land on the island and destroy the structure and the harmony of this little village, force its members to make hard choices and restructure their lives in accordance with what we call *freedom,* would this necessarily have to be considered an improvement in their lives? Is freedom necessarily a boon? Or consider a person who has just been fired, whose employer says, "Now you are free to do what you want with your daytime hours." If this is freedom, what is so good about it? Unless the job in question were utterly intolerable, is there any virtue at all in this newfound freedom?

Choosing an Ori

[In Yoruba philosophy,] the most important element of personhood is the ori or "inner head." . . . The ori determines one's fate, and, contrary to most alternative cultural accounts of the soul, the Yoruba actually chooses his ori. In the creation myth Ajala, the "potter of heads," provides each body with a head. But before a person arrives on earth, he or she must go to the house of Ajala to choose a head. To make matters more complicated, Ajala has a reputation for being irresponsible and careless. As a result, Ajala molds many bad heads; he sometimes forgets to fire some, misshapes others, and overburns still others. Because it is said that he owes money to many people, Ajala commonly hides in the ceiling to avoid creditors and neglects some of the heads he put on the fire, leaving them to burn. When a person gets to Ajala's storehouse of heads, he or she does not know which heads are bad or good—all people choose heads in ignorance. If a person picks a bad head, he or she is doomed to failure in life. Yet, if a person picks a really good head, the person is destined to have a good, prosperous life. With hard work, he or she will surely be successful, since little or no energy need be expended in costly head repairs.

—From Jacqueline Trimier,
"African Philosophy," 1993

These examples, of course, are biased to present freedom in the worst possible light. But such examples are necessary in order to balance the examples of the other kind, involving people who are generally miserable and oppressed, who are abused by some powerful conquerors or some insufferable king or queen, and who revolt in the name of freedom. The emancipation of the slaves in the southern states in 1865 did not make life immediately better for many former slaves. The lack of freedom within many religious communities has not been considered a terrible disadvantage or an inhuman situation—at least, not by those members who conform to their sect's basic beliefs and practices. Indeed, one might argue that the history of the United States exhibits the breakdown of family and community values in which obedience and conformity is presupposed; the emergence of freedom of personal choice has threatened and sometimes destroyed the peaceful harmony of the conformist community.

This argument would seem to contradict everything that we in the United States claim to stand for; but today it is argued persuasively in the name of "American values" and even "freedom." Here we face the same dilemma again, hidden by the word *freedom:* Do we in fact want freedom above all things? Or is it the case that freedom is often destructive, undesirable, and unwanted? Is it true that the basic value of American life is freedom? Or is it rather the case that the basic values of American life are community values and the virtues of moral conformity? Despite familiar rhetoric, these are not the same values—in fact, they seem to be directly opposed to each other. Is it reasonable, then, for us to want both of them?

What Is Political Freedom?

When people are free to do as they please, they usually imitate each other.

—Eric Hoffer, 1955

Part of the problem in defining freedom and trying to say what is so good about it is that freedom is so often understood as a negative concept; it is a reaction *against* something, and what that "something" happens to be can be known only in a particular context. When a people are suffering daily under an oppressive and unreasonable government or when an adolescent suffers through six dreary hours of classes that he or she is forced to attend, the meaning of the word *freedom* is clear: it means "free from." If taxes are imposed and we pay them unwillingly, then relief from taxes would be a form of freedom. If we are prevented by government forces from speaking our opinions or practicing our religion, then our right to speak or our right to worship would be freedom.

What is far more difficult is pinpointing what freedom is in cases in which there is no evident oppressor, no obvious suffering, and nothing definite to react against. It is not at all clear, to return to the example of the little village, that a happy population has been made "free" if we destroyed the life within which its members were most content. Or we may say, if we wish, that people who have just been fired are "free," but the context doesn't really justify this conclusion. The former employees did not want to lose their jobs; there is nothing else they want to do instead. They may be free *from* the demands of that particular job, but it is not clear what they are free *to do*. And it simply will not do to say, "They are free to do anything." First, this is obviously false. (None of us has that much freedom.) Second, it is probably true that "free to do anything" is a fraudulent way of talking about their not having the faintest idea what to do.

The Darkness of the Cave: Martin Luther King Jr.

Most people are totally unaware of the darkness of the cave in which the Negro is forced to live. A few individuals can break out, but the vast majority remain its prisoners. Our cities have constructed elaborate expressways and elevated skyways, and white Americans speed from suburb to inner city through vast pockets of black deprivation without ever getting a glimpse of the suffering and misery in their midst.

(continues)

The Darkness of the Cave: Martin Luther King Jr. (continued)

But while so many white Americans are unaware of conditions inside the ghetto, there are very few ghetto dwellers who are unaware of the life outside. Their television sets bombard them day by day with the opulence of the larger society. From behind the ghetto walls they see glistening towers of glass and steel springing up almost overnight. They hear jet liners speeding over their heads at six hundred miles an hour. They hear of satellites streaking through outer space and revealing details of the moon.

Then they begin to think of their own conditions. They know that they are always given the hardest, ugliest, most [menial] work to do. They look at these impressive buildings under construction and realize that almost certainly they cannot get those well-paying construction jobs, because building trade unions reserve them for whites only. They know that people who built the bridges, the mansions and docks of the South could build modern buildings if they were only given a chance for apprenticeship training. They realize that it is hard, raw discrimination that shuts them out. It is not only poverty that torments the Negro; it is the fact of poverty amid plenty. It is a misery generated by the gulf between the affluence he sees in the mass media and the deprivation he experiences in his everyday life.

—Martin Luther King, Jr., American civil
rights activist and Baptist minister,
1929–1968

The question of context gives rise to the suggestion that we miss part of the idea of freedom when we consider it simply as "freedom *from*" some undesirable imposition, power, or rule. What we're forgetting is freedom *to do* or *have* something as well. People seek freedom *from* an oppressive government in order to form a government for themselves. The unhappy adolescent in class wants to be free from school in order to play baseball, to go fishing, or to just lie around in the sun. These two notions of freedom, freedom *from* and freedom *to do* something, have been called (since the eighteenth century) **negative freedom** and **positive freedom**. They always go together; the one always presupposes the other, even if only one is actually stated. Indeed, it is unthinkable that people would overthrow their government, no matter how intolerable, if they had no idea, however dim, about what they would do to replace it. And it is unimaginable that the adolescent would so desperately want to be free from school if he or she had no idea, however vague, of doing something else instead.

Three Freedoms

It is by the goodness of God that in our country we have those three unspeakably precious things: freedom of speech, freedom of conscience, and the prudence never to practice either of them.

—Mark Twain,
American humorist, 1835–1910

We can see now how it is that such different definitions of freedom have emerged in politics and history; the fascist who claims that freedom is obedience to the state is actually just giving us the positive notion of freedom and leaving out the negative notion. (This idea of being free to obey may sound peculiar. But a Catholic who was not allowed to obey the authority of the Catholic Church without being persecuted by the secular authorities, for example, would be lacking freedom of exactly this sort.) The civil libertarian, on the other hand, emphasizes the negative notion of freedom—as in the fight to be free from racial or political discrimination—but sometimes fails to mention the positive notion.

But leaving out the positive notion of freedom too easily leads to the absurdity of people demanding freedom from everything with no positive idea of what they want that freedom for. A person who demands **absolute freedom** of speech, for example, may not be thinking about what restraints may be required on speech. Yelling "Fire!" in a crowded theater may be asserting that person's absolute freedom from any restraint whatsoever, but it is not at all clear that there is any defensible claim for his or her freedom *to do* anything. And if we are looking only at the negative freedom *from* interference by government agencies and other people, this leads us to the absurd conclusion that the person who is most free is the person out in the middle of the desert, who is safely out of range of government interference and any restraints from other people. Of course, we might insist that this person, to be the freest, should also be free *from want,* but that is saying only that he or she must be free to *have* the necessities for human survival—but for most of us these necessities include human companionship and an orderly society as well as food, water, and shelter.

Two Kinds of Freedom

On negative freedom:

The history of liberty is the history of resistance . . . the history of the limitation of governmental power.

—Woodrow Wilson, twenty-eighth
U.S. president, 1856–1924

(continues)

Two Kinds of Freedom (continued)

On positive freedom:

Whoever refuses to obey the general will [of the people] shall be constrained to do so by the whole society; this means nothing else than that he shall be forced to be free.

—Jean-Jacques Rousseau,
The Social Contract, 1762

Concepts of Self and Our Notions of Freedom

The force we seek to be free *from* is often more obvious to us than what we want to be free *to do.* It is easy to be so caught up in fighting against something that the alternative, what you are fighting for, is neglected or becomes reduced to a buzzword (like *freedom*) whose content has not been thought about at all. What makes this particularly difficult is that most of us feel that, whatever we are fighting against, what we are usually fighting for is in some sense ourselves, a chance to improve ourselves, a chance to be what we want to be. But as we saw in an earlier chapter, what counts as oneself is not always so obvious either.

If what we mean by *self* is an isolated individual self, then we will tend to conceptualize freedom as freedom *from* other people and society, whatever it is that we want to be free *to do.* Thus, we get the idea that freedom to "find yourself" is often obtained by "getting away from it all"—in other words, by a purely negative freedom. On the other hand, if we understand by *self* a social entity that depends for its very existence on our relationships with other people, then what will count as freedom will necessarily involve our relationships with others, and the person who is alone would not be free in this sense. If, with the Buddhists, we see the *self* as an illusion, freedom will tend to mean freedom *from* this illusion and a consequent freedom *to* realize ourselves as being one with the entire interconnected reality that that Mahayana Buddhists call "the Buddha-nature." If we think of ourselves (with Descartes) as being essentially consciousness, then freedom will tend to mean the development of consciousness—and this indeed is what freedom has tended to mean most often in our Western tradition. But even this is too simple, for there are many aspects of consciousness, not all of them equally our *self.*

For example, suppose we identify ourselves with our feelings about other people, our social attachments, and our sense of ourselves as social beings. Our concept of freedom, accordingly, will be such that we are most free when we are acting those roles and participating in those relationships. We will be less free if we are prevented from performing those roles or if we are prevented from being with our friends. People in love will not feel free when they are away from their beloved, no matter what else they can do, because what counts as essential to their self-identity is that one relationship. A traveler in a foreign country may be totally free from any expectations or responsibilities or from interference from other people, but if he or she identifies self with friendship—and no friends are around—it makes no sense to call the individual free. Freedom, in such a conception of self as social, is the freedom *to* participate in society and the freedom *from* factors that would prevent this. We can call this *social* freedom.

More generally, we can say that freedom depends upon self-identity—namely, those aspects of a person with which he or she identifies and defines the self (see Chapter 6). Consider this alternative view of self and, consequently, of freedom. A person thinks of the true self as the rational self. (Plato would be a good example.) A person acts freely, then, whenever he or she acts in accordance with reason, does what he or she has *decided* to do after careful thought and deliberation. The same person would consider an act less than free, on the other hand, if prompted by a mere whim or sudden desire or obedience to the urgings of a friend or authorities (assuming, that is, that the person had not already decided that obeying this friend or authority was the rational thing to do). People with such a rational conception of themselves will consider action most free when it has been carefully planned and thoroughly thought out; the less the planning and the thinking, the less free the action and the less it is an expression of the person's true self. This is *rational* freedom.

Yet another example would be that of a person who identified most with his or her emotions. People in love would consider themselves most free when acting out of love, even if, on psychological analysis, those actions could be called compulsive and even if, according to more rational-minded friends, such obedience to emotion is the very antithesis of freedom. Individuals who so value their emotions will not feel free if forced to suppress violent feelings of anger, but will feel free when they "let it out." For such people, the expression of emotion—whatever emotion—is freedom; being unable or not being allowed to express emotions, even under the respectable guise of "being reasonable," would seem like being deprived of freedom. This is *emotional* freedom.

Finally, there is the most perplexing example, which Bergmann discusses at great length, based on a most curious character in Dostoevsky's *Notes from Underground*. The bizarre hero of that short novel considers freedom to be the most important thing in human life. In fact, not only is his notion of freedom based on his sense of self-identity, but his self-identity is his conception of his freedom. He is really himself only when he is acting completely freely. His problem is this: Whenever he acts in accordance with other people's demands, he does not feel free, so he shuns other people and spends much of his time entirely alone. But neither does he believe that acting according to reason is acting freely because reason is in fact a system of thinking imposed on us by our society. In acting rationally, in other words, we are actually following the demands of other people, and so we are not free. But neither are we free when we act out of emotion. Our emotions do not seem to be products of our free deliberation but of forces within us that stem from our animal natures and social conditioning.

Then what *does* count as a free action? The perverse answer of Dostoevsky's character is, acting entirely on whim, for no reason whatsoever. His character insists on *capricious* freedom. But even acting entirely on whim, how does one know that one is indeed the sole author of one's own action? How does one know that the expectations of society or the hereditary workings of one's brain have not in fact caused this particular whim, which thereby is not really one's own? One cannot know and so Dostoevsky's pathetic character becomes in fact totally paralyzed in his actions because he can never know for certain whether they are truly his own free actions or not.

The philosophical principle here is not unfamiliar to us. It is the idea that behind all our more superficial aspects there is some pure inner self—not our thoughts, emotions, or desires but the self itself. And acting out of this pure self is what constitutes the true nature of freedom. Thus, Christianity teaches us that true freedom is giving up the worldly interests we have and focusing wholly on our inner souls. Thus, philosophers such as Sartre tell us that consciousness itself is pure freedom, which means not only freedom *to act* in any number of different ways but freedom *from* determination by all other influences—those of other people and those of our own reason, our emotions, and our desires as well. But here we come to our troublesome philosophical argument about the principle that every event has its explanatory causes. If there is a cause for every event and therefore for every action, what could it mean to say, as Dostoyevsky insists, that a truly free action is one that is wholly undetermined by anything but the pure self, which in turn is not determined by anything else? With this question, we enter into one of the most difficult problems in philosophy, the so-called free-will problem, which is concerned with metaphysical freedom.

Free Will and Determinism

"The murderer had been raised in a slum. His father abandoned him when he was seven months old; he was beaten by his older siblings and constantly abused by his mother. He never had the chance to attend school; when he was able to get a job, he never could hold it. By the time he robbed the store, he was near starvation, addicted to hard drugs, without friends, and without help of any kind. His sister said, 'I've known since he was a child that he would do this some day.' His mother complained, 'I don't understand!' The prosecutor called it a 'cold-blooded, premeditated act.' The defense accused the whole of society, claiming that it had, through its neglect as well as its negative conditioning, made this man an inevitable killer." We know the rest of the arguments: what we don't know is their resolution. Should a man be held responsible for an act for which he has been conditioned the whole of his life? Or must we not hold out that, no matter what the circumstances, he could have resisted, he could have decided not to commit the crime, and therefore he must be held responsible?

Are we cogs in the machine that is the universe? Are we pawns of the fates? People have often thought so. Most of the ancient Greeks believed that our destinies were already decided for us; no matter what our actions, the outcome was settled. Powerful movements in Christianity have taught that God has predetermined or at least knows in advance every action we will perform, as well as our ultimate chances for salvation. And today most people believe that a person's actions and character are the causal result of genes and upbringing, and perhaps also the result of unconscious fears and desires that may never be recognized. Then, too, astrology and other theories of external determination have always been popular, and we can see why they would be. The more our actions are the results of other forces and not our own doing, the less we need feel responsible for them, and the less we need worry about deciding what to do. It is already decided, and not by us.

The determinist argument can be cast as a syllogism, the premises of which seem beyond doubt:

Every event has its explanatory cause.

Every human choice or action is an event.

Therefore, every human choice or action has its explanatory cause.

Then, by a second syllogism:

Every human choice or action has its explanatory cause.

To have explanatory causes is not to be free.

Therefore, no human choice or action is free.

What this conclusion means is that there are no real choices. If a person can choose only one course of action, and if there are no alternatives that he or she (given the explanatory causes) *can* choose, then it makes no sense to say that the person has a choice. To have a choice means to be able to do either *A* or *B*. To have chosen *A* means that one could have chosen *B*. According to the determinist, even if I (seem to) make a choice between *A* and *B*, what I choose is already determined by causes, including those involved in my character and the process of deliberation. On the other hand, one might want to reply that one could have done otherwise *if* one's character, motives, and deliberations had been different. This retains the determinist's insistence that the choice is caused by antecedent conditions but retains, too, the idea that the person certainly has something to do with the choice. But it would make no sense to suppose that a person could have chosen otherwise if everything else (character and the rest) stayed exactly the same. A different choice would imply something different, perhaps dissimilar personal traits or some alternative way of thinking through the decision.

We sometimes talk of a "free choice," as opposed to a choice made under coercion, but if either is a choice at all, it must be free in the sense that one could have chosen otherwise (whatever the cost). If a man holds a gun to my head and forces me to give him my wallet, I have nonetheless freely chosen; I could have chosen to fight and be shot. But this is only to say that some free choices are made under conditions that make certain alternatives extremely foolish. It doesn't affect the metaphysical question of freedom.

If it is true, however, that every choice or action is fully *determined* (that is, brought about by earlier events and conditions) and fully explainable (if only one knows enough about the earlier events and conditions), then even the most obvious case of a free choice would not be free and would not really be a choice. It would be as if someone said to you, "OK, here is *A;* there is no *B* or *C*. Which do you choose: *A, B,* or *C?*" If the whole of our history, our genetic makeup, our education, the influence of our parents, our character, and the workings of our brains already predispose us to make choice *A* rather than any other, if our makeup is such that we could not choose any other, then all of our talk about "choice" and "decision"—and therefore "responsibility," too—amounts to just so much nonsense. We may have the *experience* of making a choice, but we never actually choose. Indeed, the experience is just another event in the causal chain, brought about by earlier conditions and just as predictably leading on to other effects in our behavior.

Determinism is therefore the theory that every event in the universe, including every human action, has its natural explanatory causes; given certain earlier conditions, then an event will take place necessarily, according to the laws of nature, and that accordingly we lack metaphysical freedom. But we must fill out the determinist's first premise with at least one more step. It is not enough to say, "Every event has its natural explanatory cause(s)," because this would leave open the possibility that, although every event requires certain earlier events and conditions in order to take place, the event might still be a matter of chance, at least to some extent, or a matter of human choice. In other words, it might be that the earlier events and conditions limit the possibilities but do not fully determine them. To be determinists we must say, therefore, that "every event has its *sufficient* natural explanatory cause(s)." *Sufficient* means capable of bringing the event about by itself. Then there is no room for chance, no room for choice, and no room for human freedom. Without choice, there can be no freedom, and without freedom, there is no reason to hold a person responsible for his action, no matter how virtuous or how vicious it might be. According to the determinist thesis, we can barely be said to be "acting" at all, for our actions are nothing but the results of conditions and laws of nature that leave no room for our "doing something."

Some philosophers, called **libertarians** (that is, metaphysical, as opposed to political, libertarians) deny the claims of determinism outright. We have free will, the actual freedom to choose what to do, and our choices are not determined by antecedent conditions. Libertarians often suggest that there is a "gap" in the sequence dictated by causal laws so that, no matter how many causes operate on our decisions, there is always at least a little bit of room within which we are free to make choices. This may seem to fly in the face of scientific views, but some have found support for libertarian views in contemporary science. Quantum mechanics is based on probabilistic models of reality that do not presuppose that every event has a cause. Some libertarians conclude from this that there is no longer any reason to suppose that the scientific view of things is incompatible with belief in free will.

Determinism Versus Indeterminism

Are the libertarians right? Why should we accept the determinist's opening premise? Without it, determinism cannot get to first base. Well, in earlier chapters we have already seen the arguments traditionally advanced, even by philosophers who are not themselves determinists. The most general argument is that only by assuming from the outset that every event has its sufficient natural explanatory cause(s) can we ever understand anything. A much stronger argument was made by Kant, who said that the basic rule of determinism, the principle of universal causation, is one of the rules by which we must interpret every experience. But even Hume, who denied that this principle can be justified either through reason or through experience, insisted that it is a "natural habit" that is indispensable to us and that we could not give up even if we wanted to. The consensus, then, has been that the principle itself is inescapable.

Without the assumption that every event has its sufficient natural explanatory cause(s), human knowledge would seem to be without one of its most vital presuppositions. Not only scientific research but also even our most ordinary everyday apprehension of what is happening would be forced to an intolerable skeptical standstill. Our every experience would be unintelligible, and our universe would appear to be nothing but a disconnected stream of incoherent events, from which nothing could be predicted and nothing understood. So the answer to the question, "Why should we accept the determinist's first premise?" seems to be, "We cannot give it up; how could we possibly do without it?" For no matter how it is rephrased or philosophically altered, the assumption that every event in the universe, including our own actions, can be explained and understood, if only we know enough about it and its earlier events and conditions, is a presupposition of all human thinking that we cannot imagine doing without.

But even if the determinist's premise seems undeniable, it is not yet clear how we are to understand that premise. Many philosophers would defend determinism only as predictability on the basis of probability. To say that every event is determined, according to this view, means only that it would be predictable if we know enough about earlier conditions.

But it has been objected, against the determinist, that the fact of such predictability is not sufficient to defend determinism. It is one thing to say that all events, including human actions, are actually caused or compelled by physical forces. It is something quite different to say that all events, including human actions, are predictable. They might be predictable, for example, only on the basis of certain statistical probabilities. "Most people in this circumstance would do that." "The odds are for it," in other words. Or, in the case of human actions, the predictability might still be the result of human choices; we can predict each other's actions because we know how we would probably choose in the same circumstances. But there is no need here to talk about "causes" or compulsions. Nor, it has been argued, should we even talk any longer about "determinism," if this is all that we mean by it.

Another antideterminist argument has been made by defenders of a view called **indeterminism**. Indeterminism explicitly rejects determinism; it claims that not every event has a cause, and thus determinism is false. The advantages of this theory are obvious, for it would seem that as soon as we allow that there are some events that are uncaused, human actions might be among them. And that means that we can be held properly responsible for our actions and not simply explain them by appealing to certain antecedent conditions. Or does it? Is someone responsible for behavior if it is not caused by that person?

The indeterminist argument has received a boost from recent physics, the very science that gave rise to the determinist threat in the first place. Newtonian theory, which accounts for the behavior of physical objects in causal terms, gave determinism its strongest claims. The French Newtonian philosopher Pierre-Simon Laplace boasted that if he knew the location and motion of every particle in the universe, he could predict every future state of the universe at any time. But recent physics has shown that such knowledge is impossible. One of the most important discoveries of modern physics is that we cannot know both the location and the momentum of a subatomic particle. According to the Heisenberg uncertainty principle (named after Werner Heisenberg, the German theoretical physicist who discovered it), there is enormous uncertainty in the measurement of anything as tiny as an electron. If one can ascertain the position of the particle, its motion will be unknown. Or one can measure its motion, but then one will not be able to know its position. So this means, on a subatomic level, that it is impossible to predict what the future is. From this principle, the British physicist-philosopher Sir Arthur Eddington advanced the indeterminist argument that determinism is false on physical grounds. Every event in the universe is not predictable. Thus, Laplace's bold conjecture that he could predict the entire future of the universe if only he knew the present position and motion of every particle was an empty gesture.

But does the Heisenberg uncertainty principle refute determinism, or does it simply show that we cannot predict what may in fact be determined? Indeterminists use Heisenberg's principle to argue that the determinist premise, "Every event in the universe has its sufficient explanatory natural cause," is false. Some events—namely, those involving some subatomic particles—are not caused, not predictable, and therefore not determined by any interpretation. And because all events and objects involve subatomic particles as their basic constituents, it can therefore be argued that no event is caused or strictly predictable, or determined. But to be caused and to be predictable are not the same thing. And, of course, the indeterminacy–uncertainty thesis applies only to events with subatomic dimensions. What does this imply about macro events—a person making a decision about whether to marry, for example? At most, it appears, the Heisenberg uncertainty principle means that not all events are causally explicable. But if this is the case, perhaps human actions are among those events that cannot be completely explained by antecedent causal factors, not just because we don't know all the factors, but because some events are not caused. In that case, our actions would not be determined, but free.

The Heisenberg Uncertainty Principle

We can know the position of a particle, but then we will not be able to determine its motion.

We can know the motion of a particle, but then we will not be able to determine its position.

Therefore, we cannot predict its future states.

The object of indeterminism is to deny the determinist position in order to make room for human freedom. There are, unfortunately, two serious objections to the indeterminist argument.

First, even if we suppose that the conclusions of modern physical ("quantum") theory are correct (a matter still in dispute among physicists), it is clear that determinism is of importance to us primarily as a theory of macroscopic bodies (that is, of visible size—people, trees, cars), not subatomic particles. And no one has ever concluded that quantum theory and modern physics actually refute Newton's theories, which were formulated to explain the behavior of macro things. It might be true that it is impossible to predict what a subatomic particle in our bodies might do. But it does not follow that it is impossible to predict what our bodies will do. Falling out of a plane, we still fall at exactly the same speed as a sack of potatoes. And that is all that determinists need to continue their attack on our conception of freedom.

Second, even if the indeterminist view is correct, indeterminism is not the same as freedom. Suppose, all of a sudden, your legs started moving and you found yourself kicking a fire hydrant; surely this is not what we mean by a free action. Freedom means, at least, that we are free to choose what we will do and that our decisions are effective. Indeterminism, by suggesting that some events are uncaused, robs us of our freedom just as much as determinism. If we freely choose our actions, our choices themselves are causes. But if an action is uncaused, our choices are ineffective. The argument against determinism, in any case, is not yet sufficiently persuasive to allow for the indeterminist's conclusions.

On the other hand, although indeterminacy in the motion of subatomic particles may not help us understand how freedom of the will is possible, the acceptance of indeterminacy by scientists does have philosophical significance. When the scientific view of things was thoroughly deterministic, those who defended the idea of free will clearly contradicted the scientific attitude. They could therefore reasonably be accused of being antiscientific. But the acceptance of indeterminacy has required scientists to limit their predictions, at least in some spheres, to statements of probability.

Such probabilistic prediction is much closer to the sort of prediction we can and do make about people without thereby denying the possibility of individual freedom. We can safely predict, for instance, that a higher proportion of people from affluent backgrounds will attend college than will people from economically deprived backgrounds or that people from this latter category are more likely to spend time in prison. We even quantify such predictions, saying, on the basis of a person's class, race, or sex, what his or her chances are of eventually living past age 65, owning a home, having more than three children, committing a crime, or being addicted to cigarettes. This way of describing groups of people resembles probabilistic reasoning in the physical sciences. It is scientifically defensible, but it allows us to maintain in the case of each individual person within a given group that what they do is not determined by virtue of their group membership, but that it is, to some extent at least, up to them.

The Role of Consciousness

Determinism seems to hold true of us as physical bodies. But, you might insist, we are not just physical bodies. We are also conscious; we can make decisions; we have wills of our own. Whatever we are besides physical bodies, our physical bodies are still subject to all of the laws of Newtonian physics. At this point, you can see the problem. If our bodies are just cogs in the mechanism of the universe, what does it matter whether we are conscious or not? Our bodies are composed of bits of matter, various molecules undergoing chemical interactions and acted on by the various laws of physics. Once all the parts are determined in their various movements and activities, what is left for consciousness to do?

There are two possible replies to this problem, but both seem to support the determinist position and leave us without the freedom that we are trying to find room for. One possibility is that consciousness, unlike our physical bodies, is not part of the scheme of determinism. Consciousness, unlike our bodies, is free, free to make decisions, free to choose what to do. The problem with this response is that if our bodies are determined in their movements, then what can consciousness do, even if it is "free"? Whatever consciousness decides, it cannot have any possible effect on the movements of our bodies; in other words, it cannot affect our actions. Every human action has its sufficient natural explanatory causes apart from consciousness, and consciousness can make no difference whatsoever. If consciousness could intrude on the physical order of causes and effects, that would seem to violate the most basic physical laws (for example, the conservation of energy). Here we return to the mind-body problem (considered in Chapter 6). What is their relationship? How can the one affect the other?

Freedom and Determinism

Determinism (or "Hard" Determinism): Every event, including human thoughts and decisions, has a cause and is fully governed by the laws of nature. We are neither free nor responsible for our actions.

Indeterminism: It is not true that every event has a cause. Some events, possibly human decisions, are free.

Compatibilism (or "Soft" Determinism): Determinism is true, but this does not mean that we are not free and responsible for our actions.

Libertarianism: Human choices are free, not fully determined by antecedent causes.

Most determinists, in any case, would probably not agree with the idea that any event, even a nonphysical event such as an act of consciousness, could be "outside" the determinism of nature. Most determinists would argue that our thoughts and feelings, even our decisions, are caused by the states of our brains and nervous systems. Our decisions are nothing but the conscious effects of complex causal antecedents, most of which we still don't understand, but which are definitely embedded in the deterministic scheme of things. Consciousness itself might be a cause of our behavior—including the decisions we (seem to) make—but because consciousness itself is caused by earlier events and conditions, this does not make us free. At most, it explains why we might *think* that we are free. (Indeed, the thought that we are free may itself be wholly determined by earlier events and conditions—including the fact that we have always been taught to think of ourselves as free.)

Physiologist **Benjamin Libet** provided experimental evidence that challenges the idea that our sense of making free conscious choices is illusory. He measured the brain activity of subjects who were doing simple motor activities like pressing buttons. These actions would appear to be voluntary, but Libet found that an electrical charge in the brain (which he calls the "readiness potential") always preceded such an act, and that it consistently occurred before the subject became aware of intending to perform the act. Libet concludes that the action was begun before the conscious awareness that would be necessary for it to be entirely a result of "free" choice. Free will, at best, can halt an action that is already in progress; it does not initiate the action in the first place.

Libet's results are certainly interesting, but one can question whether they demonstrate what he claims. Perhaps the charge in the brain is not the originating cause of the action but itself a consequence of some choice. Libet is assuming that whatever initiates the action will appear as some activity within the brain, but what if free choice does not originate in the body but in a soul that is immaterial? In this case, the electrical charge could be a consequence of the choice. Even if one does not accept the idea of an immaterial soul, one might still argue that our awareness of making a choice is not decisive for whether or not we are making one. There could be a temporal gap between the choosing and being able to register our choosing. Nevertheless, this evidence is daunting for libertarians who take consciousness to be essential to our making free choices.

Compatibilism, or Soft Determinism

There have been many attempts, needless to say, to slip around determinism and defend the existence of free choices and actions. The basic principle of determinism, the principle of universal causation, seems too undeniable to give up, but the need to hold people responsible for their actions is also too important to abandon. Thus, there has developed a series of views that accept the determinist thesis and try to show that free will and determinism are compatible: these positions are sometimes called **compatibilism**. Those who accept determinism but refuse to accept its harsh conclusion are also referred to as **soft determinists** (as opposed to the **hard determinists**), who accept both determinism and the implication that we are not free or morally responsible. Soft determinists defend compatibilism in a number of ways. Two of them are worth mentioning in particular:

1. Even if we accept the determinist thesis, it can be argued, we can still believe in freedom. In fact, we *must* believe in freedom because we can never

know all the earlier events and conditions that brought about a particular decision or action, and thus we can never establish that actions are completely determined. It may be true that *if* we knew everything, we could predict a person's actions with certainty (or at least, a very high probability). But this big *if*, which is the heart of the determinist thesis, turns out to be unobtainable in practice; so although in theory we can be determinists, in practice we can continue to believe in free will and hold people responsible for their actions.

2. Even if we accept the determinist thesis, we can still distinguish between those causes that make a person's action free and those that make it unfree. There have been a great many suggestions of this kind. Aristotle long ago claimed that an act would be called *free* if it was not performed (a) from "external compulsion" (the actor was pushed or forced) or (b) out of ignorance (the actor didn't know what he or she was doing). Some philosophers have said that an act is free if it is caused by reason; others have said that it is free if it is caused by consciousness or by the will. David Hume, who was a soft determinist, believed that we could say that an act was free if it followed from a person's "character." This had the practical advantage of also explaining the purpose of praise and blame—namely, to mold or change a person's character such that he or she would in the future tend to perform more desirable actions. This is still determinism, but it is soft in that it carves out an area that can be called freedom, and thus it allows us to talk meaningfully of our actions both as being completely determined and as being our own responsibility.

Soft Determinism: Hume

Men are not blamed for such actions as they perform ignorantly and casually, whatever may be the consequences. Why? but because the principles of these actions are only momentary, and terminate in them alone. Men are less blamed for such actions as they perform hastily and unpremeditatedly than for such as proceed from deliberation. For what reason? but because a hasty temper, though a constant cause or principle in the mind, operates only by intervals, and infects not the whole character. Again, repentance wipes off every crime, if attended with a reformation of life and manners. How is this to be accounted for? but by asserting that actions render a person criminal merely as they are proofs of criminal principles in the mind. . . .

—From *An Enquiry Concerning Human Understanding*, 1748

A key motivation for defending compatibilism is to preserve the notion that we are morally responsible for your choices. Recall the objection to compatibilism that unless there is a set of (at least two) alternatives from which we can choose, the apparent choice is not a choice at all. Deciding to go to the movies is a decision only if it is possible that you choose either to go or not to go. If you are already determined by earlier events and conditions to go, then there is no decision, no matter how long you spend deliberating about whether or not to go. Thus the (hard) determinist concludes, presumably because he himself had no choice but to do so.

Philosopher **Harry Frankfurt** has challenged the view that one must have real options to be able to be morally responsible (which is sometimes called the **Principle of Alternative Possibilities**). Frankfurt thinks that we have control of and responsibility for our actions even in cases in which we aren't able to do otherwise. He considers a case in which one man plans to pull the trigger to kill someone and does so, even though a third man would have intervened if the gunman had hesitated to ensure that he fired the shot. Even though there is no situation in which the trigger will not be pulled, the gunman has acted freely because his shooting was the result of his own choice. What is decisive is whether I act from my own motives, not whether an alternative possible scenario is actually available.

Even if genuine alternatives are not essential for saying that someone has made a choice and is responsible, it would still seem odd to say that we would be free if we *never* had genuine alternatives. Many philosophers continue to seek ways to show determinism compatible with free choice among real options.

In Defense of Freedom

Compatibilists claim to defend freedom, calling an act free if it is willed by the agent. But defenders of both hard determinism and libertarianism question whether it can deliver what it claims: both a determined world and the moral freedom to choose among alternatives. These critics argue that the agent's will is either determined or it is not. If it is, then the situation is as the hard determinist describes it. All the compatibilist has done is apply the label "free" to a particular class of actions that are, at bottom, as fully determined as every other action or event. If it is not, then the compatibilist in fact recognizes that what we need is a breach in determinism, a conception of our actions, or at least our decisions, as truly free of determination by antecedent causes.

The classic statement of this claim to freedom and responsibility is to be found in the philosophy of Immanuel Kant. We have already seen that Kant (in his *Critique of Pure Reason*) gave an unqualified endorsement of determinism, arguing that the principle (of universal causation) on which it is based is nothing less than a necessary rule of all human experience. And this includes human actions:

Actions of men are determined in conformity with the order of Nature, by their empirical character and other causes; if we could exhaust all the appearances, there would not be found a single human action which would not be predicted with certainty.

This is surely a statement of the hardest of hard determinism. But Kant also appreciated, as much as any philosopher ever has, the importance of unqualified freedom for human responsibility. (He called freedom, as he had called God, a "postulate" [or presupposition] of **practical reason**, that is, reason applied to practical problems, especially moral ones.) But how could he defend both universal determinism and human freedom? Determinism is true of every possible event and object of human knowledge, Kant said, but it does not follow that it is the *only* way of viewing things: our acts of will can and should sometimes be viewed in a different way. Action is a wholly different matter from knowledge. Kant said that we adopt two different standpoints toward the world—one theoretical and the other practical. Insofar as we want to know something, we adopt the standpoint of science and determinism. Within that standpoint every event, including human actions, is determined, brought about by sufficient natural explanatory causes (including the states of our brains and various psychological factors). But when we are ready to do something, we switch to the practical standpoint.

The main point is this: when we are acting or deciding to act, we *must* think of our own acts or will and decisions as the sufficient explanatory causes of our actions, and we cannot continue the causal chain backward to consider whether those acts of will are themselves caused. When we act, in other words, we cannot think of ourselves except as acting freely.

Soft Determinism: Mill

Correctly conceived, the doctrine called Philosophical Necessity [determinism] is simply this: given the motives which are present to an individual's mind, and given likewise the character and disposition of the individual, the manner in which he might act might be unerringly inferred; that if we knew the person thoroughly, and knew all the inducements which are acting upon him, we could foretell his conduct with as much certainty as we can predict any physical event. . . . [But] this does not conflict in the smallest degree with what is called our feeling of freedom. . . . Our actions follow from our characters [but] we are exactly as capable of making our own character, if we will, as others are of making it for us.

(*continues*)

Soft Determinism: Mill (continued)

The free will doctrine, by keeping in view precisely that portion of the truth which the word "necessity" ["determinism"] puts out of sight, namely the power of the mind to cooperate in the formation of its own character, has given its adherents a practical feeling much nearer to the truth than has generally (I believe) existed in the minds of the [determinists].

—From *A System of Logic,* 1843

You are about to make a decision: You are finally going to give up smoking. A friend offers you a cigarette on the second day. Yes or no? Do you smoke it? Now it might very well be that, given your personality, your weakness for past habits, and any number of other psychological factors, you are clearly determined to accept the cigarette and thus break your resolution. Your friend, who knows you quite well, may even know this. But you can't think of yourself in this deterministic way, for you have to make a decision; you can't simply "find out" what you will do. In other words, you can't simply predict your own behavior, no matter how much you know about the various causes and factors that allow your friend to predict your behavior. If you were to predict, "I'm going to start smoking again anyway," you would not be simply predicting; you would be, in that very act, breaking your resolution—that is, deciding to break it. So, when your own acts and decisions are concerned, you have to act as if you were totally free. This in a way denies determinism. For, as you are the one who has to make the decision, determinism isn't relevant. (Kant said, "And to have to think yourself free is to be free.")

Kant's suggestion has been taken up in a very different way in more recent European philosophy, in particular by the existentialists. Like Kant, they accept (or at least do not bother to reject) determinism in sciences. But they insist that, even if determinism is true, we must always view *ourselves as agents* as necessarily free. When we have to decide what to do, all the knowledge of the possible factors determining our decision are not sufficient to cause us to decide, for we cannot predict our own decision without at the same time making it.

Jean-Paul Sartre, a leading proponent of existentialism, defended the Kantian claim for human freedom as far as it can possibly be defended. In *Being and Nothingness,* Sartre argued that we are always absolutely free. This means, as Kant had insisted, that insofar as we act (and Sartre said that we are always acting), our decisions and our actions cannot be viewed as having any causes whatsoever. We must make decisions, and no amount of information and no number of causal circumstances can ever replace our need to make them. We can of course refuse to make decisions, acting as if they were made for us. But even in these cases, we are making decisions, "choosing not to choose," in a classic Sartrean phrase. We are "condemned to be free," he says. Again, desires may enter into our deliberation about what to do, but only as "considerations." We can always act against a desire, no matter how strong, if only we are sufficiently decided that we will do so. A starving man may yet refuse food, if, for example, he is taking part in a hunger strike for a political cause to which he is dedicated. A mother may refuse to save her own life if it would be at the expense of her children. A student who has resolved to study for tomorrow's test may miss a favorite television show. Whether trivial or grandiose, our every act is a decision, and our every decision is free. And even if we fail to live up to them or find that we "cannot" make them, we are responsible nevertheless. There is no escape from freedom or from responsibility. But, as Sartre reminds us, freedom is always also an opportunity.

Absolute Freedom: Sartre

We were never more free than during the German occupation. We had lost all our rights, beginning with the right to talk. Every day we were insulted to our faces and had to take it in silence. . . . And because of all this we were free. Because the Nazi venom seeped into our thoughts, every accurate thought was a conquest. Because an all-powerful police tried to force us to hold our tongues, every word took on the value of a declaration of principles. Because we were hunted down, every one of our gestures had the weight of a solemn commitment.

—From *Situations*,
1947

Thus there are no accidents in a life; a community event which suddenly bursts forth and involves me in it does not come from the outside. If I am mobilized in a war, this war is my war; it is in my image and I deserve it. I deserve it first because I could always get out of it by suicide or by desertion; these ultimate possibles are those which must always be present for us when there is a question of envisaging a situation. For lack of getting out of it, I have chosen it. This can be due to inertia, to cowardice in the face of public opinion, or because I prefer certain other values to the values of the refusal to join in the war (the good opinion of my relatives, the honor of my family, etc.). Any way you look at it, it is a matter of choice. This choice will be repeated later on again and again without a break until the end of the war.

—From *Being and Nothingness*,
1943

Closing Questions

1. Define *freedom* in your own terms, specifically outlining those aspects of yourself that you consider the basis of your own conception of "acting freely." To what extent does your conception include playing roles and interacting with other people? To what extent do other people limit your freedom? To what extent can you be really free only when you are alone?

2   Imagine yourself trying to make a difficult decision (for instance, what job offer to accept, whether to get married, whether to enlist in the army). Now consider yourself a determinist and ask yourself, "What am I going to do in this situation?" How does this affect your deliberations?

3. Consider one of the two compatibilist (soft determinist) positions discussed in this chapter and defend it, or attack it, from the point of view of a hard determinist.

4. Aristotle said that we are not free if our action is caused by "external compulsion." What counts as external compulsion, in your opinion? Can compulsions be internal as well? Give some examples, and explain how it is that they interfere with our freedom.

Suggested Readings

Rousseau's account of the individual as free can be found in *The Social Contract and Discourses*, trans. G. D. H. Cole (E. P. Dutton, 1947). A good collection of essays on the legal and moral concerns of freedom is Herbert Morris, ed., *Freedom and Responsibility* (Stanford University Press, 1961). A number of Isaiah Berlin's essays on liberty, including "Two Concepts of Liberty," have been edited by Henry Hardy under the title *Liberty* (Oxford University Press, 2002). Dr. Martin Luther King, Jr., utilized the cave metaphor to describe the oppression of African Americans in *Where Do We Go from Here: Chaos or Community?* (Beacon Press, 1967). Frithjof Bergmann's provocative study is *On Being Free* (Notre Dame University Press, 1977). Dostoevsky's *Notes from Underground* appears in part in Robert C. Solomon, *Existentialism*, 2nd ed. (Oxford University Press, 2004). The complete *Notes from Underground* is translated by Ralph Matlaw (E. P. Dutton, 1960) and Dostoevsky's *The Brothers Karamazov* has been translated by Andrew R. MacAndrew (Bantam, 1970), among others. d'Holbach's deterministic vision is presented in his *System of Nature* (Kearsley, 1797). Hume and Mill present their soft determinism in their respective books, *An Enquiry Concerning Human Understanding*, 3rd ed. (Oxford University Press, 1975) and *A System of Logic* (Harper & Row, 1874). Sartre's view on freedom is found in virtually all of his writings, but in particular in his *Being and Nothingness*, trans. Hazel Barnes (Washington Square Press, 1956). See also Sartre's *Situations*, trans. Benita Eisler

(Fawcett, 1965). A more expanded discussion of the free-will and determinism problem than is presented here can be found in Clifford Williams, *Free Will and Determinism: A Dialogue* (Hackett, 1980). More recent studies of the freedom-vs.-determinism issue include Daniel C. Dennett's *Elbow Room* (MIT Press, 1984); Robert Kane's *A Contemporary Introduction to Free Will (Oxford University Press, 2005)*; and Richard Double's *The Non-Reality of Free Will* (Oxford University Press, 1990). Benjamin Libet's "Do We Have Free Will?" appears in *The Oxford Handbook of Free Will*, edited by Robert Kane (Oxford University Press, 2002). Harry Frankfurt's paper is available in his book *The Importance of What We Care About* (Cambridge University Press, 1988).

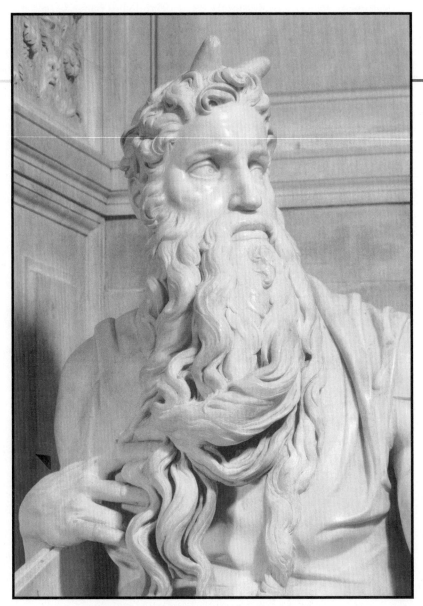

Michelangelo, *Moses*. San Pietro in Vincoli, Rome.
© Scala/Art Resource, NY.

8

Morality and the Good Life

What I really lack is to be clear in my mind what I am to do.
—*Søren Kierkegaard*

Opening Questions

1. We sometimes say that to be a good person, one must be "true to oneself." Do you think this is so? Give examples.

2. Do you believe that a morally good person will, at least in normal circumstances, also be assured of being a happy person? Why or why not?

3. If a sadist were to gain enormous pleasure from torturing his or her victims—in fact, more pleasure than the pain suffered by the victims themselves—would the sadist's cruelty be justified? Defend your answer.

4. Is there anything you would find worth dying for? What? (Camus, in his *Myth of Sisyphus,* said, "A reason for dying is also a good reason for living.")

5. Many religious commandments, in sexual and food prohibitions, tell us to abstain from the material, or bodily, enjoyments of life. Is it possible to be a religious person and deny yourself none of the pleasures of life? Or if a religion encourages us to make money, buy fancy cars, and indulge ourselves, is it thereby corrupting its status as a religion?

6. Do we always act selfishly, even in those instances in which we appear to be "selflessly" helping others?

7. Is it true that the "bottom line" of business is profit and profit alone? Or, even in business itself, are there other, less tangible goals that are intrinsic to and just as important as making money?

8. Do you believe that abortion is justifiable, even in cases in which the life of the mother is not threatened? How do you justify your answer, and how would you defend it against a person who disagreed with you?

9. Assuming that we agree on a list of injunctions that we all *ought* to obey, which we call *morality,* why should we be moral?

10. Would it be possible for a person to be perfectly good and yet cause harm to innocent people? Could a person be wicked even if he or she never caused any harm at all?

11. Which is more important to you, success or happiness? What if you are forced to choose between them?

12. We are a nation ruled "by laws, not men." What does this say about our view of "men"?

Moral Philosophy
〜⚘〜

What should we do? What should we not do? How should we treat other people? How should we ourselves live? These are questions of *value* rather than of truth and reality, the topics we have mostly been discussing so far. Of course, it should already be obvious that our discussions of truth and reality were heavily steeped in values (we frequently referred, for instance, to the meaning of life or the existence of God), and any discussion of values presupposes a thoughtful and informed view of the world. But **moral philosophy**—the search for the best way to live and the right principles for our actions—nevertheless deserves a chapter of its own.

Morality is a set of principles, or rules, that guide us in our actions. Moral rules tell us what to do—for example, "Tell the truth," "Treat others as you would

---

Kant's Good Will

The moral philosophy of Immanuel Kant (1724–1804) is wholly based on the concept of a "good will." To have a good will is to act on moral principles that are wholly justifiable by what he called practical reason, the result of which is *duty*. A good will is not directed by any ulterior motives. Kant believed will to be crucial for two reasons. First, he refused to accept the view that our actions are just another set of events in the physical universe, determined by factors beyond our control. *We* are responsible for what we do, he argued; otherwise, the very notion of morality doesn't make any sense, nor does the concept of human dignity, which Kant found all-important. Second, Kant was aware that it makes no sense to blame people for what is beyond their control; the consequences of what we do are often beyond our control, subject to accidents or interruptions that we could not possibly have predicted. Therefore, he said, "Nothing can possibly be conceived in the world, or even out of it, which can be called good without qualification, except a good will"—in other words, our good intentions and attempts to do our duty.

like to be treated yourself"—and what not to do—for instance, "Do not cheat," "Do not kill," and "Do not steal." The Ten Commandments, from the biblical Old Testament, and the injunction to love one another, from the New Testament, form the core of much of the morality of the Western tradition, which can therefore appropriately be called Judeo-Christian morality. Moral rules typically take the form of commandments, or orders, often with the words *ought* or *ought not* (or *Thou shalt* or *Thou shalt not*). Morality and moral rules—whether stated as law or not—form the basic structure of every society, defining the limits of what is not only permitted but also expected. The key to morality, according to the German philosopher Immanuel Kant, is **duty**—doing what you *ought* to do.

But morality is part of a much larger quest, which gives morality its importance. Why shouldn't we kill each other? Why should we help each other? What reasons can we give to defend one sexual ethic rather than another? And, in general, why should we be moral? The answer to this last question must be larger than morality itself, for it must supply us with the reasons for accepting moral principles and rules. That answer is, "the **good life**." This is a phrase without precise meaning, but we all know quite well what it signifies. How should we live? What do we want? What should we want? What do we most enjoy? What should we most enjoy? What is worth working for? And what is not worth the effort? What should we accept? What should we try to change? These are questions for which we all have answers before we enter philosophy, but philosophy sometimes has surprising results in changing them or at least in giving us better arguments to support them.

The goal of moral philosophy is to develop a set of principles and a view of our aims in life that will allow us to live with clarity and confidence. This general quest, which includes morality as well as the search for the good life, is usually called **ethics**. We will begin our discussion of ethics by considering various suggestions about the basis of living well. We will then take up the possible roles that self-interest and concern for the interests of others play in our motivational structure and in living a good life. Next we will consider the meaning of "morality" and several theories about what it involves (those focused on duty, consequences, virtue, and relationships, respectively). We will conclude with Friedrich Nietzsche's critique of traditional morality and his suggestion that as opposed to conforming to universal norms, we should develop our unique virtues, each in our own fashion.

The Good Life
~~✧~~
Hedonism

In Plato's dialogues in which Socrates is the leading character, the recurrent theme is the search for the good life. And from Socrates's discussions with his fellow Greeks, it is evident that this was not at all a new question but one about which virtually everyone had very strong opinions. And almost all of these opinions are still defended today. Most prominent among them is the philosophy called **hedonism,** the view that says the good life involves getting as much pleasure out of life as you possibly can.

Hedonism is an attractive candidate for the good life, but Socrates and people ever since have seen that it has certain limitations. You might notice that people talk a lot more about hedonism than they actually practice it. Students often talk about hedonism, but their ambitions and worries about school and careers show that they want something more than just pleasure—success, security, social standing, respect, power, money, freedom. This is not to deny that they also want pleasures, but more as distractions, entertainments, and enjoyments than as the goal of life. Compared with the average cat, for example, we are masters in self-denial. We put off meals when we are hungry because we have work to do or because we are on diets. We suppress our sexual impulses because it would be awkward or embarrassing to act on them in the middle of class or at the dinner table. We want much more than "just sex."

Many people argue that the reason they deny themselves pleasures now is in order to get more pleasure later. But, if that is so, then most people are surely fooling themselves, for we all know that work and responsibility breed more work and more responsibility. Social respect and manners require further refinements, more respectable behavior and more manners, and the idea that we are simply delaying our pleasure is usually disproved by our own actions. People also argue that the work itself, the respect, or the success is what gives them pleasure, but here philosophers have pointed out a crucial distinction—between acting for the sake of pleasure and acting for some other goal whose achievement gives pleasure. Hedonism is the first, not the second.

Perhaps the most famous philosophical hedonist in history was the Greek **Epicurus** (341–270 BCE). He argued that the good life was the love of pleasure, and we still refer to a person who spends his or her life living for pleasure (good food, enjoyable vacations, and so on) as an *epicurean.* In fact, however, Epicurus taught that not all pleasures are good; he encouraged simple pleasures, peace and quiet, and pleasures of the mind, and fellowship with friends.

> *The pleasant life is not the product of one drinking party after another or of sexual intercourse with women and boys or of the seafood and other delicacies afforded by a luxurious table. On the contrary, it is the result of sober thinking.*
>
> —Epicurus,
> *Letter to Menoeceus*

The classic argument against hedonism as the good life was formulated by Aristotle 2,500 years ago. He argued, as we have suggested, that pleasure is not an activity in itself but rather something that accompanies satisfying activities. Thus, the key to the good life is to be found in the notion of "satisfying activities," not in the pleasure itself. Our goal is not the pleasure but the activity, and the pleasure is more like a bonus, or what Aristotle called the "completion" of the activity. Forbidden activities or vulgar pastimes may be pleasurable, but the pleasure is more than balanced by the amount of pain and discomfort (for example, guilt) that they eventually produce. An activity may be extremely painful, on the other hand—running long distances or enduring a rigorous test—but, because the activity itself is admirable or challenging, it may nevertheless produce pleasure of a meaningful variety. But this means that pleasure itself, even if it is an essential component of the good life, cannot be the good life itself.

Life's Pleasure

One might think that all men desire pleasure because they all aim at life, but life is activity. Pleasure completes the activities and therefore life. It is with good reason then that they aim at pleasure too, since it completes life, which is desirable. . . . Without activity pleasure does not arise, and every activity is completed by the attendant pleasure.

—Aristotle, *Ethics*, fourth century BCE

There are actually very few hedonists among us. In one of our opening questions in Chapter 1, we discuss a certain imaginary invention (based on the research of a Cornell psychologist, James Olds), a box fixed with electrodes and capable of stimulating continuing waves of pleasurable sensations in the person strapped into it. The only hitch is this: Once you get into the box, you will never want to or have to get out of it (since arrangements have been made to take care of the bodily needs of the person who uses it). Here is the life of absolute pleasure, but in return for it you will give up your ambitions and your friends, sports, reading, sex, food, and television. Would you do it? When we have put this question to students over our many years of teaching, only a dozen or so have said they would. Most of us desire other satisfactions over and above sensory pleasures.

Success

The exclusive worship of the bitch-goddess Success is our national disease.
—William James, 1842–1910

Success is counted sweetest/By those who ne'er succeed.
—Emily Dickinson, 1830–1886

In our society, the good life is often equated with success. Success may mean money, but it does not mean only this. It involves social status and respectability as well (although these often go together). There are curious twists; for example, gangsters are sometimes admired as eminently successful, no matter how they acquired their wealth and status. Some creative people and hermits may be admired and idolized as successful despite the fact that they are, by any customary measure, total failures.

But once again, we must be careful not to confuse what people say they take to be the good life with the way they actually live. Many people who work very hard for success will say that they are working toward their retirement, to have enough security to enjoy themselves, or to have enough money to buy themselves lavish pleasures. But, again, their lives often demonstrate the opposite, as people work themselves into exhaustion long after they have "made it," to such an extent that they are no longer capable of enjoying the simplest pleasures. You might say that they are success addicts, just as people become money addicts, working at first to get something else but ultimately working simply for the work itself. Money addicts start earning money like everyone else—to buy homes, cars, and TV sets—but they end up needing the money itself so much that they work only for it. Success addicts work hard for security, social status, or wealth but end up working just for the success alone.

Confucius on Friendship

Confucius said, "Having three kinds of friends will be a source of personal improvement; having three other kinds of friends will be a source of personal injury. One stands to be improved by friends who are true, who make good on their word, and who are broadly informed; one stands to be injured by friends who are ingratiating, who feign compliance, and who are glib talkers."

—The Analects of Confucius, 16.4

The life of seeking success has its problems. There is always the real possibility of failure, of course, but this is equally an argument against almost every lifestyle. In any case, the threat of failure is not a good reason to reject a lifestyle—the problem is rather the threat of success. We all know stories of successful people in their mid-forties or fifties committing suicide, just when it would seem that they have achieved what they have been working for most of their lives. Why? Perhaps often because, once earned, their success proved not to be what they wanted after all. If a certain conception of the good life fails us, that doesn't mean that there is no good life, much less that life isn't really worth living. It does not even mean that success is not worth having or that success is wrong. It only means that success, by itself, does not seem to give us the good life.

Asceticism

In recent decades in our society, dissatisfaction with this success conception of the good life, the "success ethic," has given rise to a reaction in precisely the opposite direction. In place of success, some people demand simplicity and even poverty—freedom from the burden of possessions. At the extremes, this manifests itself in our choice of folk heroes, off in the wilderness as pioneers or rebels. More moderately, it manifests itself in the return to the country, life on the farm or in a small commune, largely by people who have been brought up in big cities and nurtured on the success ethic.

It is worth noting that this is not at all a new philosophy. It was in reaction to the decadent success ethic of the Roman Empire, for example, that simple Christian asceticism began. **Asceticism** is the proper word for this life of simplicity and self-denial. And even before Christianity, around the time of Socrates, a group of philosophers who called themselves Cynics defended a similar lifestyle. The most famous of them was Diogenes (circa 400–circa 325 BCE), who lived in a bathtub and owned little beyond a single lantern, with which he is said to have searched the faces of everyone, "looking for even one honest man." When Alexander the Great came to his city, he asked to see Diogenes, of whom he had heard much. On their meeting, Alexander asked Diogenes, "What can I do for you?" Diogenes turned to the ruler of most of the known world and said, "Move over, you're blocking the sunlight."

Many people have accepted the ascetic life as the means to the good life, but not as the good life itself. A great many religious people, for example, have accepted asceticism as a way to salvation or "purification." It is not the self-denial itself that they praise, but self-denial as a means to the holy life. Some artists adopt the ascetic life, but only because it seems to them the best way to achieve what they really consider the good life—namely, creativity. And it is important not to confuse asceticism, with its extremes of self-denial, with that familiar belief that the "simplest" pleasures in life are not only the best but the easiest to obtain. Some people try to simplify their lives just because society makes life so bureaucratically and socially complicated. But they do this "in order to enjoy life more," not for purely ascetic reasons. Here, too, asceticism is a means or a corrective, not an end in itself.

Freedom

Freedom can be singled out as a separate conception of the good life. Usually, freedom is considered a means, the freedom to do what one wants: to yield pleasures or satisfy ambitions, create or worship, retreat from society or live as one wishes. But, like other means, freedom may become an end in itself. The person who throws over a promising career and takes to the open road might be said to value freedom more than any pleasures or successes. Freedom from ties and responsibilities may be seen as preferable to an intimate relationship or marriage just because it offers more "freedom."

The life of freedom need not be any particular way of life because one might, within it, be religious, hedonistic, or ambitious. The question is ultimately: which is more important—the freedom itself or these other concerns? The extreme of this conception is the peculiar and extravagant conception of freedom portrayed in Dostoevsky's "underground man." (See Chapter 7.) He was willing to give up everything, not only success and pleasure but also his health, just to realize his "most advantageous advantage," his freedom.

Power and Creativity

There are many other conceptions of the good life. Indeed, there are as many possible conceptions as there are human goals. Some of the other most common conceptions of the good life are very close to those we have discussed so far; for example, the life in pursuit of great wealth or political power is very much like the life of the success ethic. But then there is another sense of power that is not political but personal. It is the power to grow as a person, to expand one's consciousness, to develop one's talents and to create. Friedrich Nietzsche, for instance, defended such a conception of the good life under the phrase the "will to power." Arguing against those many philosophers, particularly the British moralists, who argued that humans act only for pleasure, Nietzsche sarcastically quipped: "Man does not live for pleasure; only the Englishman does." What all people ultimately want, Nietzsche argued, is power:

> Not need, nor desire—no, the love of power is the demon of man. One may give them everything—health, nourishment, quarters, they remain unhappy; for the demon insists on being satisfied. One may take away everything from them and satisfy this demon: they then are almost happy.

All other seeming conceptions of the good life, Nietzsche added, are in fact different ways of seeking power—even religion, as well as the contemporary scramble for wealth. But the highest sense of power, Nietzsche argued, is reserved for those people who live autonomously and creatively, as artists, philosophers, or saints. The composer Mozart, for example, probably considered the good life to be the life of artistic creativity, which is not to deny that he enjoyed a great many of the pleasures of life along the way. The good life for Socrates was a life in accordance with the moral principles he had defended in his philosophizing, though he, too, had more than his share of pleasure as well. For him, the good life was the life of wisdom, the life of principles and creative thinking. And these were worth holding onto even when they meant his death.

Religion

Religion is our ultimate concern.
—Paul Tillich, 1957

The religious conception of the good life also deserves special consideration, not when it is simply intermingled with the other goals and ambitions of life and squeezed into Sunday mornings, but when it is truly the goal of life to which all other goals are subordinated. Still, it is never altogether clear how many people have completely endorsed this conception of the good life. There are millions of people who have said that they do, but whether their lives bear out their statements is something that we must always view, particularly in our own case, with a cautious eye.

The religious life is a life of devotion; in the Christian tradition, it is sometimes said to be "living with the fear of God in one's heart." The religious life need not be based on "fear," but the truly religious person lives with an emotional attachment to his or her religion that permeates and dominates everything else. This is not to say that the religious person performs only religious acts, but religious behavior must have the primary place in his or her life. In practice, the religious life is often in conflict with other conceptions of the good life.

Each of the conceptions of the good life we have itemized is fairly specific; it singles out one goal or type of goal among the many that we desire, and it claims one goal as the mark of the good life. But, once we have begun thinking about it, all of these seem one-sided. Who wants pleasure if it means giving up all friends and social ties? Who wants power or success if it makes us miserable? Who would even want to be creative if nothing but misery came from it? Wouldn't it be better to be both creative and enjoy life? Or be creative and successful as well? Wouldn't religious people have a better life if they did not devote themselves to God exclusively but also enjoyed the blessings of the secular world, without diminishing religious faith? The good life, in other words, seems to be something more general than any single goal, no matter how grand that single goal may seem to many people. Yet we should not conclude that the good life is simply "the best of everything," without further qualification. Even if we reject these one-sided views, we may still find that the good life has but a single goal.

Happiness

In the ancient world, Aristotle examined the different one-sided conceptions of the good life and rejected them in favor of a single conception with which most of us are probably in agreement—happiness. Happiness is the good life, claims Aristotle, although happiness itself is not a single activity but the result of a great many activities. Aristotle took personal development, or self-realization, as his goal. In his *Ethics*, Aristotle examined two one-sided conceptions of the good life, pleasure and success (which for him meant political success), and rejected them; yet he also insisted that they have their place in the good life. They are not the good life themselves; they are only necessary conditions for it.

Aristotle sees happiness as that which is wanted "for its own sake" and not "for the sake of anything else." As it turns out, happiness as Aristotle understands it includes a large number of advantages and virtues, including wealth, power, and community status as well as military courage, the ability to drink wine without getting too obnoxious, a sense of justice, good friends, and a good sense of humor. Happiness, in other words, was not just a sense of well-being, as it is for us; happiness for Aristotle meant the good life as a whole, an integrated life with all the virtues and good fortune and the philosophical wisdom to appreciate it.

Happiness is nothing less than an entirely good life, with all of its parts in balance. Indeed, Aristotle tells us, it makes no sense at all to say that a person is happy for a few hours or days or even months or years. A person can be called happy only on the basis of his or her entire lifetime. Aristotle even suggested, at one point, that a person can be made unhappy after death—for example, if an individual's children dishonor the family name.

The Highest Good

In view of the fact that all knowledge and every pursuit aims at some good, what is the highest of all goods achievable by action? Verbally there is very general agreement; for both the general run of men and people of superior refinement it is happiness; they identify living well and doing well with being happy.

—Aristotle, *Ethics*, fourth century BCE

These comments indicate an important difference between Aristotle's society and moral philosophy and our own. It seems to make perfectly good sense for us to say that a person could be happy for even ten minutes; for example, you can imagine waking one fine spring morning to the sun and the chirping of birds, feeling quite happy, only to find out ten minutes later that you have just been kicked out of school. But for Aristotle, happiness requires a lifetime of good living. Part of this might be attributed to a difference in language; Aristotle's word (*eudaimonia*) more accurately means "doing well" or objective "well-being."

But the difference in language reflects a profound difference in moral philosophy as well; we tend to think of the good life primarily in terms of inner satisfaction and a sense of well-being. Aristotle's Greeks would not have understood this at all (indeed, they would have considered a man who could keep a sense of well-being in the midst of misfortune to be insane, not happy). The good life for the Greeks was a public, social, objective life of achievement and good fortune; it had little to do with one's inner feelings. We, on the other hand, tend to believe a person to be happy if he or she is satisfied with what life has provided, whatever others may think—indeed, even if others think he or she is most unfortunate. So the ideal of happiness, which we would all agree is the key to the good life, nevertheless leaves a great many questions open. How important is inner satisfaction? How essential are our place in the community and our actual accomplishments? Is happiness available to everyone (as we like to think)? Or is happiness instead the privilege of the very powerful and very rich or very lucky, as the ancient Greeks thought? Would it be possible—in our sense—to be happy and to still not live the good life?

Egoism Versus Altruism

Of the various conceptions of the good life as pleasure, success, asceticism, freedom, power, creativity, religion, and happiness, some are available to virtually everyone (for example, the life of simple pleasures), and others are available only to a lucky few (the life of creativity). But it must have struck you by now that all of these conceptions of the good life have left something out. However radical the differences between hedonism and the religious life, the success ethic and the ascetic life, the life of seeking wealth and the life of freedom, creativity, or happiness in general, there is something that they all share. They are all self-centered; they make no mention of other people. They are all, in one form or another, varieties of egoism. This is not true of Aristotle's philosophy as he developed it, as we will see; nor is it true of Socrates's moral life. One might hesitate to include the religious life of an isolated monk or an ascetic as "selfish" in any sense, but the monkish life often does place its emphasis on the good life for a single person.

Egoism is the thesis that everyone always acts for his or her own advantage, that the only reason why people act respectfully or kindly toward each other is that courtesy and generosity, too, for one reason or another, are to their advantage. It might be fear of punishment that makes them act "correctly"; some have ulterior motives—that is, they expect other things later on, perhaps a favor in return, a reward in heaven after they die, the avoidance of guilt, or a feeling of self-satisfaction. In popular language, the egoist position is often called "selfishness."

Egoism and Altruism

Psychological egoism	*Psychological altruism*
"All acts are basically selfish."	"Some of our acts are 'naturally' altruistic."
Ethical egoism	***Ethical altruism***
"You ought to act selfishly."	"You ought to act for the good of others."

One of the most widely read contemporary egoists, Ayn Rand, has written of the "virtue of selfishness." According to her, we all should act for our own interests. At this point, we must distinguish two very different forms of egoism, although people often confuse them. The first is the position that everyone in fact acts according to his or her own interests, that our psychology is such that we cannot help but act in this way. Accordingly, this position is called **psychological egoism**. The second position must be defended or attacked independently of the first: it is the thesis that people *ought* to act to satisfy their own interests, and this presupposes that they have a choice about whether to act that way or not. This position is **ethical egoism**.

Both egoist positions are contrasted with what is usually called **altruism**—that is, acting for the sake of other people's interests. There are degrees of altruism. One may be altruistic because one recognizes an obligation to other people. Or one may be altruistic in actually taking another person's interests as being as important as or even more important than one's own interests; this is often the attitude of lovers or brothers and sisters. Altruism can also be divided into two distinct theses, although these are not so often distinguished. **Psychological altruism** is the view that people "naturally" act for each other's sakes. **Ethical altruism**, on the other hand, holds that people *ought* to act with each other's interests in mind. This is, of course, a basic statement of morality, best summarized in the so-called Golden Rule: "Do unto others as you would have them do unto you." Altruism need not mean self-sacrifice, however. Altruism means acting for the (intended) benefit of others—but not necessarily *against* one's own interests. So, too, acting in one's own self-interest is not necessarily *selfish*—that is, acting contrary to or without regard for other people's interests.

The Rule of Deference

Tzu-Kung asked, "Is there one expression that can be acted upon until the end of one's days?" The Master replied, "There is shu [putting oneself in the other's place]: do not impose on others what you yourself do not want."

—The Analects of Confucius, 15.24

The most familiar and most difficult question is about psychological egoism: is it true that people only act for their own self-interest? A famous story about Abraham Lincoln is an apt illustration of the thesis. As he was arguing the psychological egoist position with a friend, his carriage was passing a mudslide, where a mother pig was squealing as her piglets were drowning. Lincoln stopped the carriage, saved the piglets, and then moved on. His friend asked him whether that wasn't a clear case of altruism. Lincoln replied: "Why, that was the very essence of selfishness. I should have had no peace of mind all day had I gone on and left that suffering old sow worrying over those piglets. I did it to get peace of mind, don't you see?"

Many actions are based on self-interest and are selfish without any question. But are there also actions that are not based on self-interest? Lincoln's response indicates that this can be hard to tell. It would seem as if his action is not for selfish reasons at all. Yet according to him, he had a selfish reason for his actions— his own sense of satisfaction and "peace of mind." Could this be true of all our actions, as the psychological egoist claims?

Plato raised the question of whether psychological egoism is true in the *Republic*, when the character Glaucon tells the story of an ancestor of Gyges of Lydia who discovered a ring that would turn him invisible when he turned the setting inward and render him visible again when he turned it outward. Once he is convinced that he is really undetectable while the setting is pointed toward him, Gyges uses this new power to seduce the king's wife, kill the king, and take over the kingdom. Glaucon asks how many, if certain of evading detection, would persist in good behavior. Wouldn't anyone who had access to such a ring sooner or later take advantage of it and do wrong? And isn't the reason that most people do not act immorally because they fear the consequences of getting caught (itself a selfish motive)? Socrates' answer, which emerges after an extended discussion of the nature of goodness and the soul, is that being a just person, doing the right thing, actually benefits the individual and that Gyges's ancestor has a faulty idea of his own interests. Socrates does not, however, counter Glaucon's egoistic premise. In fact if one accepts psychological egoism, so much the better for Socrates's argument, since its purports to reveal what is truly in one's interests.

Among the many arguments that have been put forward against the view that all actions are essentially selfish, three in particular have been much repeated since they were formulated several hundred years ago by an English clergyman, Bishop Joseph Butler (1692–1752).

1. Many of our actions are motivated by desires that themselves are aimed at the good of others, whether or not they are of benefit to ourselves. Lincoln may have reflected beforehand and thought, "If I don't save those little pigs, I will be miserable all day." But it is unlikely that he did. At somewhat minimal inconvenience to himself, he acted out of a motive common to (almost) all of us, the urge to help another creature or person in trouble, or what we usually call **compassion**. In friendship and with those we love, in particular, we are often moved to act in such a way that it would be absurd to say that we acted for our own satisfaction or to avoid guilt. Of course, in every case in which we act out of desire, we satisfy a desire of ours to act. But this is not the same as being selfish or egoistic, which means not just satisfying my desire but satisfying my desire *with an eye to my interests alone.*

2. Many of our desires in life have to do with obtaining the approval and recognition of other people. Therefore, in acting to get what we want—namely, their approval—we act on their behalf and in accordance with their desires and needs as well. It is a tricky question, on occasion impossible to answer, to what extent we are moved by the urge for approval alone and to what extent we are truly motivated by the desire to serve others. But it is certainly not plausible to suggest that we *always* act just to get approval and not at all to help others. Indeed, one of the things most of us want most in life is self-respect, a sense of being a "good person," and this is utterly impossible unless we not only help others but also help them for their sake alone, even if, afterward, we may enjoy the self-satisfaction of having helped them.

3. Within all of us is a sense of right and wrong, or what we sometimes call conscience. It does not matter, for purposes of this argument, whether conscience is simply the voice of our parents within us (as Freud argued, calling this the superego), the voice of God (as many religious people believe), or simply the fear of punishment (as many psychologists have argued). The point is that we do have such a conscience, and to act in accordance with its demands is not to act in our own interests alone, even if we know that not obeying our consciences will very likely be followed by the pain of guilt. Further, it must be asked, why is this guilt so painful, except for reason of conscience and the fact that we do want to, or feel the need to, act on others' behalf without regard to (and sometimes even against) our own needs and desires? And even if, on rare occasions, some of us obey our consciences only with an eye to avoiding future self-punishment, it is surely not the case that we all do this all the time. But this is what the psychological egoist argues, and this, we can see, is plainly false.

The argument against the psychological egoist, in a single statement, is this: merely acting in accordance with our own desires—assuming that we always do this—does not make an action selfish, for all actions are in some sense based on our desires, but at least some of those desires are desires to serve someone else's interests. Thus, the "object" of desire is what makes an act selfish or unselfish, not merely the fact that one's own desire is acted on. The satisfaction that accompanies good acts is itself not the motivation of the act. Here is the answer to Lincoln. His act was, despite his philosophical claims, an altruistic one; his satisfaction was not the motive of the act but only its consequence. And, if psychological egoism is not always true, then altruism is at least possible.

But even if altruism is possible, whether it is desirable is still an open question. An ethical egoist, for example, would admit that altruism is possible but would attack it all the same. Ayn Rand, in her polemics on the "virtue of selfishness," argued that the strict definition of this word is "concern with one's own interest." She then launched into a diatribe against altruism:

> If it is true that what I mean by "selfishness" is not what is meant conventionally, then *this* is one of the worse indictments of altruism: it means that altruism *permits no concept* of a self-respecting, self-supporting man—a man who supports his life by his own effort and neither sacrifices himself nor others. It means that altruism permits no view of men except as sacrificial animals and profiteers-on-sacrifice, as victims and parasites—that it permits no concept of a benevolent coexistence among men—that it permits no concept of *justice*. (*The Virtue of Selfishness*, 1961.)

The argument here is extreme and utilizes the same kind of fallacy that the psychological egoist employs. The argument contrasts the notion of "acting in one's own interest" (that is, selfishness) with self-sacrificing and lack of self-respect. That is, if an act is for the benefit of others, then it cannot be to one's own benefit as well. Similarly, if an act is not in one's own interests, it is an act that denies one's self-respect. You can see how unjust this extreme contrast is, treating all human situations as if they must be either black or white. Our every action and intention is aimed at a large number of goals: some are immediate; others are long range; some are means; others are ends. But to pretend that every action and intention can be simply defined by a single goal—either self-interest or other people's interest—is to treat human action as we might treat the actions of rats or bees, as utterly simple-minded.

Ayn Rand (1905–1982) was a popular American novelist, a Russian immigrant whose defense of what she called "the virtue of selfishness" earned her an enormous following. She is the author of *The Fountainhead* (1943) and *Atlas Shrugged* (1957), among other novels.

It is true that people who follow the rules of morality without any exceptions may hurt themselves and other people as well. A person who refuses to tell a lie under any circumstances may well be self-sacrificing in just this way. However, from the fact that unnecessary self-sacrifice is undesirable it does not follow that acting for the benefit of others is equally undesirable. Even the paragon of self-sacrifice, the martyr, sees himself or herself as gaining at least self-respect. And the paragon of action in one's own interest, according to Rand's own ethic, the businessperson who dedicates everything to personal achievement, may end up "sacrificing" self *and* self-respect most of all.

To act strictly according to "your own self-interest" is to rob yourself of the richness of goals for both self and others that gives human action its complex social and personal textures. This is not to say that we should always—or even ever—act against our self-interests. Rather, it is to say that any philosophy of human life will have to begin with a far richer conception of morality and human motivation than this limited ethical egoism. This is the main thrust of Bishop Butler's arguments.

To make her thesis more palatable, Rand argued that acting in one's own self-interest, in an enlightened way, will result in the mutual benefit of us all. Now, in one sense, the notion of enlightened self-interest is an extremely respectable idea, and we will discuss it at length under the name *utilitarianism* later in this chapter. But it is important to distinguish the two positions, for the utilitarian is perfectly aware that the general welfare may require the sacrifice of personal self-interest in a great many cases. The utilitarian argument is that making such sacrifices is, in the long run, actually in one's own interests. Rand refused to acknowledge this. To suppose that acting in our exclusive self-interest without sacrifice or attention to the welfare of others will in fact turn out to be to our mutual benefit is so contrary to our very experience that it cannot be made into a convincing thesis, even in fiction. Psychological egoism is a problem; if it is true, then we have to teach people to consider other people's interests to be their own. But straightforward ethical egoism is more than a problem; as an ideology, telling us all to be even more selfish than we usually are, it may be a social disaster.

Psychological altruism in a universal sense has never had much of a following. The view that people always act for other people's benefit has never even been defended. At most, it is argued that we have the psychological capacity for altruism, that we at least sometimes feel pangs of sympathy for the other person, and that if certain misunderstandings and unnecessary social pressures are corrected, then people will act altruistically. But we must distinguish the claim that we *can* act altruistically from the claim that we *ought* to do so.

In any case, morality is not, strictly speaking, action for the sake of others, although that is typically a part of it. Morality is action for the sake of principle. And because moral principles are those we recognize as overriding our own interests, it makes little sense to suppose that morality itself is selfish. Of course, it may still be that people are moral only because of selfish reasons—out of fear of being punished, for example, or because they believe it will bring them reward in heaven. And we all know people who use morality to further their self-interests. But whether or not this is so, morality must be discussed in its own terms, even if there may be egoistic or selfish motivation behind it as well.

Morality and Theories of Morality

An action done from duty derives its moral worth, not from the purpose which is to be attained by it, but from the maxim by which it is to be determined, and therefore does not depend on the realization of the object of the action, but merely on the principle of volition by which the action has taken place, without regard to any object of desire.

—Immanuel Kant, 1785

Morality gives us the rules by which we live with other people. It sets limits to our desires and our actions. It tells us what is permitted and what is not. It gives us guiding principles for making decisions. It tells us what we ought and what we ought not to do. But what is this morality that sounds so impersonal and "above" us? It is important to begin with an appreciation for the metaphor that so well characterizes moral rules. Nietzsche described it this way: "A tablet of virtues hangs over every people."

This "tablet of virtues" is morality. Morality consists of the most basic values and rules of behavior. The prototypes of morality, in this sense, are those ancient codes, carved in stone, with commands that are eternal and absolute. Many of us in the West know best the two tablets allegedly inscribed by God and given to Moses, which we call the Ten Commandments. And they are indeed *commandments.* They are absolute rules that tell us what we must do or not do, no matter who we are, no matter what we want, and regardless of whether our interests will be served by the command or not. "Thou shalt not kill" means, even if you want to, even if you have the power to, and even if you can escape all punishment, you are absolutely forbidden to kill.

The image of morality as coming "from above" is appropriate. First, moral laws are often said, and not only in our society, to come from God. Second, we learn these laws from our parents, who do indeed stand over us and indoctrinate us with them through their shouts, commands, examples, threats, and gestures. Finally, and most important, morality itself is above any given individual or individuals, whether it is canonized in the laws of society or not. Morality is not just another aid to getting us what we want; it is entirely concerned with right and wrong. And these considerations are above tampering by any individual, no matter how powerful.

This characteristic of morality as independent of individual desires and ambitions has led many people to characterize morality simply in terms of some absolute and independent agency. Most often, this absolute and independent agency is God. But whether or not you believe in God, it is clear that something further is needed to help us define morality. Even assuming that there is a God, we need a way of determining what his moral commands must be. One might say that God has given these commands to various individuals, but the fact is that different people seem to have very different ideas about the morality that God has given them. Some, for example, would say that it explicitly rules out abortion and euthanasia. Others would argue that God does not rule these out, but makes it clear that they are, like other forms of killing (a "holy war," for example), justifiable only in certain circumstances. And in view of such disagreements, we cannot simply appeal to God but must, with reasons that we can formulate and defend, define our morality for ourselves.

There is the further question of whether we should follow God's laws just because they are God's commands or, rather, whether we recognize that God is good through the fact that his laws are good. Though expressed in polytheistic terms, this is the question raised in Plato's *Euthyphro*, a dialogue between Socrates asks his interlocutor, Euthyphro (a self-styled expert on piety). Socrates gets Euthyphro to admit that the goodness of the gods' commands is not based on the mere fact that it is the gods who give them; instead the gods command what is good. If this is the case, the question of what is good must be answered on some other basis than simply saying that God (or the gods) command it.

Even if one disagrees with Socrates and maintains that God's commanding certain rules is what's important, this doesn't settle the matter. We may have to decide whether to believe in God (or what is alleged to be God) precisely on

---

The Price of Happiness

Imagine that you are creating the fabric of human destiny with the object of making men happy in the end . . . but that it was essential and inevitable to torture to death only one tiny creature . . . and to found that edifice on its unavenged tears; would you consent to be the architect of those conditions? Tell me, and tell the truth!

—Fyodor Dostoevsky, *The Brothers Karamazov*, 1880

the basis of whether we can accept those commands. (We would presumably not believe in a god, for example, who ordered that we kill innocent people.) Either way we answer Socrates's question, we have to decide for ourselves what laws of morality we find acceptable.

Similar considerations hold true of that familiar appeal to conscience in determining what we ought to do or not do. Even if one believes that conscience is God-given, the same problems emerge again. Should we follow our conscience just because "conscience tells us to"? Or do we follow our conscience just because we know that what our conscience commands is good? And if we believe that conscience is simply the internalization of the moral teachings of our parents and society, then the question takes an extra dimension: should we accept or reject what we have been taught? Because our consciences often disagree, we must still decide which rules of conscience one ought to obey. Conscience doesn't determine what we ought to do; it only reminds us of rules we have already accepted.

We have talked about morality thus far as being defined in terms of rules and principles, but there is another conception of ethics and of "morals" that places its primary emphasis not on rules and principles but on questions of *character*— that is, the ethics and personality of the individual (and, perhaps, of an entire culture). Of course, one aspect of having a good moral character is obeying the rules of one's society, but there are several **virtues** of character that seem not to be governed by rules at all—for example, courage and kindness. A general rule to the effect "be courageous" or "be generous" not only seems uninformative and unnecessary but also seems to contradict the spirit of the virtues themselves, which are best displayed through spontaneous action and not deliberation and obedience. One of the questions that has become prominent in modern moral philosophy is how distinct and how important such questions of character and virtue are, as opposed to the concern with rules and principles in morality.

Whether it is a matter of principles or virtue, the basis of morality is an attempt to get straight about how we should lead our lives. How do we want to live? How *ought* we to live? But here we confront a problem that, since the days of Plato and Aristotle, has challenged moralists and morality alike—namely, why should one be moral? It is clear that moral principles—(for example, "Do not lie") sometimes go against our self-interests. Why, then, should we obey them? So, too, a virtue such as courage may, in certain circumstances, place one in severe danger. Why, then, should we be virtuous? When moral rules and virtues serve our self-interests, there is of course an easy answer to such questions: one acts morally because it is (perhaps in the long run) in one's own best interests to do so. But what of those cases in which such an appeal to self-interest is not even plausible (for example, when one is morally required to sacrifice one's life or career)?

What, in other words, is the justification of morality? What rules count as *moral* rules, and what sort of people should we be? These are the questions that define much of the work of moral philosophy. At the core of our concern, of course, are those central principles of morality taught by the Judeo-Christian tradition and many other traditions as well—"Don't kill," "Don't steal," "Honor your parents," and so on. We might disagree about what counts as killing, of course (or more precisely, what counts as *murder*—that is, intentional, wrongful killing). But we might also disagree about the reason behind the principle. Should we not kill because ultimately not killing is in our own best interests? Should we not kill because morality or being moral is desirable for its own sake, whether or not it is in our interests? Could it be that this principle is just one of the curiosities of our own society, a rule that we consider extremely important but that other societies may not?

Theories of morality are formulated to answer these questions of interpretation and justification. What is it for a principle to be a *moral* commandment in the first place? Is its purpose to make us happier and healthier? To guarantee a more orderly society? To please God and not have our city destroyed, like the biblical Sodom or Gomorrah? If the commandment not to kill, for example, is interpreted according to the theory that morality is a set of principles imposed upon us by God, then the interpretation of that principle is to be filled out, presumably, by looking for further information about God's intentions, whether in the scriptures or by appealing to the current authorities in whom such opinions are vested (the pope, a priest, an imam, a rabbi, or a guru, perhaps, or perhaps the church in general).

If, on the other hand, moral principles are taken to be efficient guides to promoting human happiness and the general welfare, then the law against killing has to be interpreted and defended by showing that obedience to such a law does indeed make more people happier and fewer people miserable than they would be if there were no such law. Abstract moral theories and the substantial principles and activities of morality are intimately connected. We often talk as if moral principles appear from nowhere. But in fact, all our moral principles are embedded in an enormous network of theory and practical observations, and that network allows us to interpret and make sense of what otherwise would be empty commands subject to any interpretation one pleased. (It was more or less clear to the Hebrews, for example, how the Ten Commandments were to be interpreted, because those were the key principles of a morality that they had more or less been following for centuries already.)

Over the 2,500 years or so in which scholars, preachers, and philosophers of all kinds have been formulating their moral theories, it has become evident that theories of morality tend to fall into a number of precise but overlapping categories. For our purposes here, we will classify moral theories into four groups: duty-defined moralities, consequentialist theories, virtue ethics, and feminist ethics.

Duty-Defined Morality

The least complicated example of a duty-defined morality would be the Ten Commandments, which simply give us a list of our duties. Immanuel Kant presents another when he asserts that all our moral duties can be summed up in a single principle that he calls the **categorical imperative**—an *imperative* simply being an order or a commandment and *categorical* meaning "without qualification." It is categorical, or without qualification, because it offers no reasons or conditions; it just tells us what it is that we must do or not do. We shall presently get the content of Kant's principle (actually, he presents several formulations), but first let us note that it is the authority of the principle itself—or the authority by which it is given to us—that is the sole reason needed to obey it. In addition, of course, obeying the principle might in fact be good for us; indeed, it might even be the precondition for the stability of our society. But any **duty-defined morality** insists that it is the status of the principle itself, whatever its consequences and whatever personal reasons we might find in addition for obeying it, that is its justification for us.

Duty-defined morality (which is also termed "deontological" morality) may appeal to a number of authorities, and these authorities may be either within us or outside of us. Traditional Judeo-Christian moral theory understands the authority and the source of morality (God) as being wholly outside of us (although there may be some inner reminder as well, such as conscience). But duty-defined morality may be secular as well as religious, and the king, the president, the state in general, or the local oracle or prophet may serve as the source and authority of moral principles. When people say, "You must obey; it's the law," they are appealing to the state (or the law) as an authority to be obeyed, even if the consequences of the law in question are such that we might all be better off if it were eliminated. And within families, it is often the case that, without understanding the purpose or the consequences of an order, young children are expected to obey the authority of their parents just because the parents are, in that small context, the authorities who define the rules, presumably in accordance with the established rules and values of their society.

Immanuel Kant and the Authority of Reason

The most complex and sophisticated theories of moralities of principles, however, are the ones that make the authority *internal* to us. According to such theories, moral rules and principles are not imposed upon us by God or by society but are to be found within us, as *conscience,* for example, or as the voice of *reason.* Kant insists that morality, whatever else it might be, is first of all a matter of reason and rationality, and that the source and justification of moral principles—however we might learn them as children—are ultimately in ourselves. He calls this **autonomy,** which means that every one of us is capable of figuring out what is right or wrong on his or her own, without appeal to external authority, just by using the faculty of reason. This does not mean that morality is whatever each of us decides it to be, a mere matter of personal, or subjective, opinion. Reason is an authority that is "in" us but yet transcends us. It is objective and prescribes universal and necessary laws and duties.

The authority of reason is what justifies moral principles, according to Kant. He adds the intriguing suggestion that the laws of God are justified because they, too, are clearly rational. Here he sides with Plato's Socrates as opposed to the traditional view that the laws of God are justified just because they are from God. Kant believed devoutly in God, but he also believed that morality has to be a matter of autonomy for us. This means that God cannot *give* us laws, that God can only tell us what our reason is already capable of justifying.

To Be Good

To secure one's own happiness is a duty, at least indirectly; for discontent with one's condition, under a pressure of many anxieties and amidst unsatisfied wants, might easily become a great temptation to transgression of duty.

Kant's formulations of the categorical imperative:

1. *Act only on that maxim [intention] whereby you can at the same time will that it should become a universal law.*

2. *Act as if the maxim of your action were to become by your will a universal law of nature.*

3. *Always act so as to treat humanity, whether in yourself or in others, as an end in itself, never merely as a means.*

4. *Always act as if to bring about, and as a member of, a Kingdom of Ends [that is, an ideal community in which everyone is always moral].*

—Immanuel Kant, *Grounding of the Metaphysics of Morals*, 1785

Kant's morality of principles theory begins with the insistence that it is always the rationality of the principles, not the consequences of our actions, that is morally relevant. Accordingly, he said, it is not so much our actions that are of moral interest (because any number of circumstances or events can interfere with them) but rather our *intentions,* which are completely within our control. (Someone who has good intentions is described by Kant as having a good will.) A person is moral insofar as he or she tries to be moral, tries to obey moral principles, and tries to do his or her duty. And though obeying these moral principles and trying to do our duty will, in most cases, benefit both us and other people, this is in no way relevant to their justification. The justification for being moral is simply that it is the rational thing to do. Nothing else.

If, as Kant maintains, consequences themselves are irrelevant, how are we to decide what the moral thing to do *is*? First of all, Kant doesn't say that consequences are in no way to be considered; what he says is that our acts are to be judged on the basis of our intentions (which includes a concern for the *intended* and *expected* consequences) and not on the basis of the *actual* consequences of our action, which in the case of an unpredictable accident may have nothing to do with the rightness of our intentions. Moreover, Kant holds that in a moral principle it is always the *type* of action that is in question (for example, a case of cheating) rather than the particular action as such.

For example, let's imagine that we want to know whether it would be moral to tell a lie in certain circumstances. Suppose I need $15 immediately, but I know that I cannot pay it back. I now consider, "Should I lie to you and tell you that I will pay you back when I know very well that I won't?" Because what concerns us here is the rationality of such action, rather than the consequences of this particular transaction, what I must ask myself, according to Kant, is whether such action should be carried out *generally,* by everyone in similar circumstances. Thus, I ask myself, "What if everyone were to borrow money under false pretenses, by lying about being able to pay it back?" Kant's answer is clear: if everyone were to lie about paying back money, it would be a very short time until no one would believe anyone else who promised to pay back money. If someone said to you, "Could you lend me $5? I'll pay you back tomorrow," you would simply laugh and consider it some kind of joke. This, Kant argued, is enough to show that the intended action is immoral and irrational. If it's not possible or clearly unacceptable for everyone to act similarly, then the action in question is immoral and should not be taken. (Some of Kant's examples can be found on pp. 388–389.)

Now we get a clear view of what is perhaps the most important feature of Kant's morality of principles theory. The test of a moral principle's rationality is its **universalizability**—that is, its capacity to be generalized for everyone, everywhere. What this also means is that one and the same *set* of specific moral principles (which amount to applications of the categorical imperative in specific types of cases) will apply to every person, in every society, at every time in history, regardless of the particular circumstances and interests of individuals or different societies. Of course, this is also sometimes said to be true of God-given moralities (though not, usually, of moralities whose authority resides within a particular society). Customs may differ, of course, but morality must be the same everywhere. Reason's authority, for Kant, was as powerful and as universal as God's when he gave us the Ten Commandments. Indeed, Kant said, these are ultimately one and the same authority.

Consequentialist Theories

"The road to Hell," we are told, "is paved with good intentions." What good is a good will, we might ask, if it does not produce good consequences—that is, if it does not make people (in general) happy or, at least, protect them from pain and suffering? Of course, because people usually do what they intend to do, even allowing for mistakes and the usual amount of stupidity in the world, good intentions usually lead to good consequences. But are the intentions good because of the consequences, or do the consequences count as good (at least in part) because of the goodness of the intentions? Kant insists on the priority of the good intentions. Consequentialist moral theorists, however, insist that it is what actually happens that makes an act (and its consequences) good or bad. A good act, whatever its intentions, is one that has the happiest (or at least the least miserable) results.

Utilitarianism: Jeremy Bentham and John Stuart Mill

The clearest case of a consequentialist moral theory in the modern Western world is a still dominant view called **utilitarianism**, first formulated in the eighteenth and nineteenth centuries by a number of British philosophers and social thinkers, including **Jeremy Bentham** (1748–1832) and **John Stuart Mill** (1806–1873). Utilitarianism is a goal-oriented moral theory because it places all of its emphasis on the actual consequences of moral rules and principles, and insists that they be justified only by appeal to how happy they make us. The duty-defined morality theorists, on the other hand, do not ask whether being moral will make us happier; they insist that we ought to be moral for the sake of being moral. Of course, duty-defined morality theorists also want to be happy and want us all to be happy, too, but they separate, as the utilitarians do not, moral questions of what is *right* from merely practical questions of what will benefit or harm us.

The Utility Principle

Always act for the greatest good for the greatest number of people.

For utilitarians, however, questions of what will benefit or harm us count for everything; as Mill said succinctly, "The sole evidence it is possible to produce that anything is desirable is that people actually do desire it." The goal of morality, according to Mill, Bentham, and almost all other utilitarians, is to make people happy, to give them pleasure and spare them pain. Indeed, Bentham developed a **happiness calculus** precisely in order to calculate, for any action or policy, what the consequences in terms of pleasure and pain would be. He considers a number of factors, such as how intense and how lasting the pleasure (or pain) produced by an action would be, how certain it is that we would attain it, how quickly it would result, how much ongoing pleasure (or pain) would result, how many people would be affected, and the extent to which pleasure and pain are

---

John Stuart Mill was born in London in 1806. His father was also a famous philosopher, and the young man was subjected to a rigorous education in virtually every field of knowledge. He became the leading logician, social scientist, and moral theorist of nineteenth-century England. His view of individual liberty (as the right not to be interfered with so long as you do not harm others) is still the basis of much of our own society's thinking about civil liberties, and his theory of morals—utilitarianism—is still taken by many contemporary philosophers to be the dominant moral theory. Mill died in 1873.

likely to be mixed. Thus, if we wanted to evaluate the previously described action that Kant rejected as immoral and irrational, we would not ask, "What if everyone were to lie?" but rather, "What would be the actual consequences of my lying in this situation?" Bentham would essentially add up the beneficial results of the action, using a quantitative point system, subtract the painful consequences from this, and see whether the action was therefore relatively desirable or not. Because this system is quantitative, it could also be used to compare the relative merits of alternative courses of action.

John Stuart Mill qualified Bentham's calculus in at least one important way. Mill claims that there were different *qualities* of pleasure and pain as well as differences in *quantity.* He insists that it is better to be only slightly satisfied with a higher pleasure than to be very satisfied with a lower pleasure—or, as Mill put it in his work *Utilitarianism:*

> It is better to be a human being dissatisfied than a pig satisfied; better to be Socrates dissatisfied than a fool satisfied.

Mill's qualification makes purely quantitative calculation virtually impossible, but the basic principle is still the same: seek the greatest good for the greatest number of people, the most happiness and the least pain for as many people as possible, in every act and every law or principle.

Why is Mill's alteration of Bentham's utility principle so important? Doesn't it unnecessarily complicate the question and make the elegant simplicity of Bentham's happiness calculus unworkable? Bentham himself said that "pushpin [a simple game of the time, a bit like shuffleboard] is as good as poetry," indicating that one activity was as good as any other if it provided as much net pleasure (or as little net pain). But Mill's qualification is not just a matter of defending his love of fine literature and philosophy against philistines who would just as soon drink beer or wallow in the mud. There is a much more serious objection to Bentham's purely quantitative calculus than its refusal to give adequate respect to the "finer things in life."

John Stuart Mill: Why Be Noble?

The utilitarian standard . . . is . . . the greatest amount of happiness altogether; and if it may possibly be doubted whether a noble character is always happier for its nobleness, there can be no doubt that it makes other people happier, and that the world in general is immensely a gainer by it. Utilitarianism, therefore, could only attain its end by the general cultivation of nobleness of character, even if each individual were only benefited by the nobleness of others, and his own, so far as happiness is concerned, were a sheer deduction from the benefit. But the bare enunciation of such an absurdity as this last renders refutation superfluous.

—From *Utilitarianism,* 1861

Morality, as we have noted, sometimes goes against our interests. Morality sometimes prohibits pleasures, and being moral sometimes causes pain. But if morality is not just a set of general rules for making people happy (and Kant, for one, certainly denied that morality had this ultimate purpose), then we can expect that there will be some cases, at least, in which the principle of utility will contradict even the most basic moral values. For example, suppose a sadistic dictator derives so much pleasure out of torturing his subjects that his pleasure outweighs their collective pain. Or suppose a group of rich people in a community devise a way to get even richer by legally depriving a great many poor and middle-class people of just a small amount of their income—and get more pleasure from their considerable gains than the others suffer from their modest losses. (They might not even know about the losses.)

In such cases many of us will think that the principle of utility should be abandoned in favor of considerations of fairness. The greatest good of the greatest number is not the only important consideration. There are also moral concerns like those that Kant defended, which constrain utility and provide rules that shouldn't be violated *even if* more people suffer than prosper because of them. Mill's qualification of the utility principle allows us to build such notions as justice and virtue into the notion of "quality" and thereby into the idea of utilitarianism—even if this means that we must give up the simplicity of Bentham's quantitative calculus. The pleasures of the sadist or the group of wealthy exploiters are not among the higher pleasures, and even if the happiness calculus would show that the numbers come out in their favor, these are not the kind of pleasures that utilitarians should use as a touchstone for what to do.

Mill does not resolve another problem with utilitarianism's quantitative approach to everyone's satisfaction, however. According to the principle of utility, the greatest good for the greatest number trumps the good of individuals or smaller numbers of individuals. What is to guarantee that this principle will not promote outcomes in which the minority or even one single individual pays dearly for the greatest good of the majority? Is it obvious that utilitarianism has a principled way to rule out slavery in cases, such as that of the antebellum American South, where the economic viability of the region depends on it? And even if economic survival is not a specifically "higher" pleasure, the activities that yield these higher pleasures surely depend on it. Shouldn't there be some protections for the minority against mistreatment, regardless of how much the majority may benefit? Mill, taking the criticism seriously, responds that the principle of utility can help us determine what arrangements are just, but this doesn't answer the question of whether some burdens imposed on the minority are unjustifiable even when they result in the greatest benefit for the majority.

Some empirical studies have tested subjects' moral intuitions about whether the good of the majority should be actively pursued even at great expense to the minority, and the evidence suggests that most of us do think this is morally appropriate. Some studies have focused on what is dubbed "the trolley problem," a thought experiment originally proposed by philosopher Philippa Foot about whether it is appropriate to harm someone in order to save a larger number of people from harm. In the basic version of the problem, we are asked to imagine seeing a runaway trolley that will kill five people if nothing is done to redirect it. You are in a position (and have just enough time) to pull a switch that will divert the trolley onto another track, but if you do so one person will be killed. Most people who were asked in studies what should be done think that diverting the trolley car would be morally acceptable. This might suggest that we are "naturally" consequentialists—perhaps even utilitarians—because we think that the number of people who are saved is relevant to whether harming another person is morally permissible. (What would we think about redirecting the trolley if only one person would be saved?)

Responses to another, related case, however, cast doubt on the idea that we are naturally consequentialists. When given an alternative version of the trolley problem, in which subjects were asked whether it would be morally permissible to push a heavy person onto the tracks from a bridge in order to stop the trolley and save the five people, most responded that this would be morally wrong. Some philosophers have interpreted this as an indication that we are naturally inclined toward views, such as Kant's, that take some types of actions (such as killing or otherwise violating the rights of an innocent person) to be morally wrong regardless of the greatest good for the greatest number. Others have said that the different responses reflect the fact that one is more emotionally distant from the person harmed when one pulls a switch than when one pushes a person to his or her death. Still others conclude that we consider it worse to harm someone directly, to *do* harm, than to harm someone indirectly by *allowing* harm to befall them.

The fact that such different conclusions can be drawn from the trolley case studies raises the question of whether the results of empirical studies can justifiably be used as support for philosophical views. Do studies of our unexamined intuitions about what is right and wrong have any relevance to the question of how we should determine what is right to do? Even if they reveal something about our moral psychology, we should be concerned with whether or not our moral views are justified. We should not just rely on our preconceptions; we should defend our views with reasons and abandon our preconceptions if we find that they are not well grounded.

Aristotle and the Ethics of Virtue

The function of man is a certain kind of life, and this is an activity of the soul embodying a rational principle, and the function of the good man is the good and noble performance of these.

—Aristotle, fourth century BCE

We have already mentioned (in our discussion of "The Good Life") Aristotle's view that happiness (or *eudaimonia*) is the ultimate good in human life. Aristotle, like Bentham and Mill, thought that what is good and right in human activity are those actions that aim at happiness. But Aristotle, unlike Bentham and Mill, did not equate happiness with pleasure; he insisted that the happy life is the life of *virtuous action*, a life filled with pleasure, too, admittedly, but not good *because of* the pleasure. For Aristotle, pursuing happiness would always further the well-being of the entire community. Bentham calculated the greatest good for the greatest number of people by adding up the individual advantages and disadvantages of an action or rule. But this seems to leave out entirely the intentions and the character of the actor. Kant, on the other hand, gives generous attention to the intentions but little attention to the consequences, and he says little about the community in which these actions take place. Aristotle simply assumes that the ultimate advantage of the individual is identical to the well-being of the community in which he or she lives. In fact, if one looks over Aristotle's list of virtues, it becomes clear that every one of them is aimed at strengthening and protecting the community as well as adding to the status and happiness of the individual.

Aristotle's List of Virtues

Courage—particularly courage in battle.

Temperance—which includes the enjoyment of pleasure as well as moderation; a man who abstained from sex, food, and drinking would not be considered virtuous by the Greeks, as he might be by some people today.

Liberality—what we would call charity.

Magnificence—spending lavishly and entertaining well.

Pride—being and feeling oneself to be deserving of great things, and of honor in particular.

Good temper—but it is important to get angry when appropriate.

Friendliness—a very important virtue for the Greeks, not just a personal pleasure or necessity.

Truthfulness—even when nothing major is at stake.

Wittiness—People who can't tell or take a joke aren't virtuous. Aristotle would not equate "seriousness" with being moral, as some people do.

Shame—being sensitive to one's honor and feeling appropriately bad when it is besmirched. "Feeling guilty," on the other hand, did not even seem to be worth talking about.

Justice—the sense of fair treatment of others.

For Aristotle the most essential virtue of all, not named on the list but rather presupposed by all the other virtues, was *honor*. We still use the word, but what we mean by it is a much watered-down version of what was in ancient Greek society the most important thing in life, even more important than life itself. Honor reflects the fusion between the individual citizen and the community. Because honor was bestowed on the individual by the whole of the community—and we must be careful to distinguish this general sense of honor from the occasional honors (medals, citations, commendations) that a person might receive—and because honor was the most important ingredient in the good life, it followed that it was wholly in the interest of every individual to maintain his or her honor. Individual interests and society's interests were therefore impossible to separate.

Aristotle is clearly concerned with consequences, but he includes within his theory elements that might rightly be considered part of a duty-defined theory. For example, like Kant, he considers reason and rationality essential to morality and the good life, and rationality, for him, includes the understanding and contemplation of principles. Moreover, the justification for these principles is authority (both the authority of reason and the authority of society as a whole). Ultimately, however, Aristotle defends as the best life one that is centered in the further virtue of wisdom. In his view, the good life is essentially the life of the philosopher, the "life of contemplation," and one of its main ingredients (as for Kant) is the wisdom of thinking about, as well as acting upon, the virtues.

Feminist Ethics: The Ethics of Care

Aristotle intended his list of virtues to apply to his specific audience, that of the free male citizens of Athens. He was not concerned to tell the slave population how they could be virtuous; nor did he theorize about the good life for women. Historically, his insinuation that *eudaemonia* was the province of (free) men is not atypical; nor is his idea that women are less capable of virtue than men because they, to a greater degree than men, are controlled more by their emotions than by reason. Much of the Western tradition followed him in the belief that men are better able to make moral decisions than women, and more capable of acting on them. Over the last two centuries, this view and others that denigrate the moral status of women have been challenged explicitly by feminists. Empirical evidence has in recent times been drawn in to support these feminist views beginning with work pioneered in the early 1980s by Harvard psychologist **Carol Gilligan**.

Armed with experimental evidence, Gilligan countered the views of her former teacher, the well-known psychologist, **Lawrence Kohlberg**, who had studied the development of moral reasoning in children. Kohlberg had concluded that as people mature, their method of moral decision making goes through certain stages. Moral thinking, he claimed, develops from the self-absorbed, purely personal, or "egocentric" framework of infants and very young children to become the completely abstract and principled framework of the mature adult. This last stage, as Kohlberg described it, is very much akin to Kant's version of moral reasoning, and to the philosopher, it sounds as though Kohlberg is claiming that we develop from pure egoists to Aristotelians to utilitarians and finally to Kantians.

Lawrence Kohlberg's Theory of Moral Development

Stage Six　Universal Ethical Principles (internalized principles, respect for human dignity and justice, willingness to challenge unjust rules).

Stage Five　Social Contract (legalistic and utilitarian).

Stage Four　Law and Order (authority-based and duty-oriented).

Stage Three　Good Boy/Girl Orientation (geared to social norms).

Stage Two　Instrumental Relativist Orientation (self-interested, concerned with reciprocity).

Stage One　Punishment and Obedience (geared to avoiding punishment).

Few people, according to Kohlberg, matured in their moral reasoning to the point of this Kantian level. But experimental data involving women suggested that women hardly ever did so. According to Kohlberg's criteria, most women remain "stuck" at the fourth stage, in which they make moral decisions according to social or familial norms. In her groundbreaking book, *In a Different Voice,* Gilligan takes a stand against Kohlberg (and so, indirectly, against Kant). She suggests that women make moral decisions according to different but equally mature and morally upright reasoning. Gilligan conducted her own studies, using many more women as subjects, and concluded that mature women, on the whole, understand moral problems in a different way than men and in a different way than that described by Kohlberg and Kant.

Rather than thinking of ethics in terms of impersonal, abstract, moral principles of right and wrong, claimed Gilligan, women tend to think of ethics in terms of personal moral responsibility. Whereas men commonly understood a moral dilemma posed by the experimenter as a problem having a right or wrong answer, women often understood such a dilemma as the result of an interpersonal conflict in need of resolution, not a right-versus-wrong answer. Gilligan hypothesized that, in addition to the moral reasoning grounded in abstract principles of right and wrong described by Kant and Kohlberg, there is also a more "feminine" but equally valid type of moral reasoning that is grounded in maintaining the stability of interpersonal relationships.

As we have listened for centuries to the voices of men and the theories of development that their experience informs, so we have come more recently to notice, not only the silence of women, but the difficulty in hearing what they say when they speak. Yet in the different voice of women lies the truth of an ethic of care, the tie between relationship and responsibility . . .

To understand how the tension between responsibilities and rights sustains the dialectic of human development is to see the integrity of two disparate modes of experience that are in the end connected . . .

Carol Gilligan, *In a Different Voice,* 1982.

Gilligan claimed that both types of moral reasoning are important to a fully developed person and society. Some detractors claim that Gilligan's data and her interpretations are dubious and that she cannot justify her claim to such a pervasive difference between the sexes.

Carol Gilligan's Theory of Moral Development

Stage Three   Caring for Self and Others (emphasizes relationships; avoids harm to self or others)

Stage Two   Caring for Others (concerned with self-sacrifice and responsibility)

Stage One   Caring for Self (concerned with individual needs and survival)

Some of Gilligan's defenders have gone further than she has. Philosophers such as **Nel Noddings** and **Sara Ruddick** argue that the *ethics of care*, more typical of women's moral reasoning than men's, is a superior, more mature type of moral reasoning than that which appeals to abstract principles. They cite the failure of "masculine" moral reasoning and the moral theories that advocate it to resolve moral dilemmas. Some of these feminists have drawn a comparison between this ethics of care and the **virtue ethics** of Aristotle. However, the specific virtues promoted by the ethics of care are *relational* virtues, geared to promoting good relationships between particular individuals, not the individualistic virtues that Aristotle defends. According to both Noddings and Ruddick, the virtues characteristic of good mothering are conducive to good relationships in general. Attentive love that respects the uniqueness of the other individual and is concerned with that person's specific needs, Ruddick claims, is the supreme virtue of mothering and a virtue that can guide us in all relationships and help us build a more peaceful world.

Morality—Relative or Absolute?

The content of ethics and morality seems to mean different things to different philosophers. Kant strictly defines morality when he equates it with duty and "the dictates of practical reason," whereas utilitarians tend to focus instead on the consequences of action. Aristotle did not even have a conception of morality as we know it (morality as a code of rules), but he certainly believed both that reason played a major role in ethics and that the consequences of our actions were just as important as our good intentions. Other cultures—some even more different from ours than was ancient Greece—display even greater differences in their conceptions of morality. Does this mean that there is no single set of absolute values, certain fundamental values that are essential to every system of ethics? Does this mean that all values are relative to a particular society or people?

Traveling around the world—or reading novels and books on anthropology—we quickly discover that people do believe and have believed in very different moral and ethical systems. One culture believes an action is right that another believes is wrong. A society suffering from a severe food shortage and overpopulation may believe it permissible to abandon newborn babies, who will almost certainly die; another, like our own, finds this practice horrible and condemns it in the strongest moral terms. Are we right and they wrong, or are they right, too? Who is to judge? (If we call in a third party, an "impartial" judge, wouldn't that just open up the possibility of a three-way rather than a two-way disagreement?)

Are There Absolute Values?

Moral Relativism: the thesis that there *are no* universal and essential moral values, that morality is relative to particular societies or peoples.

Moral Absolutism: the thesis that there *are* universal and essential moral values. If some societies or people do not accept these values, then they are not moral.

Many of the differences between us, of course, are merely superficial—for instance, differences in custom or etiquette (dress, table manners). Some are profound—such as differences in religion and philosophy—yet most cultures manage to coexist with others whose beliefs are startlingly different. Where the differences become something more than ethnic peculiarities and matters of tolerance, however, they become serious disagreements over basic ethical questions—questions about life and death, questions about the very nature of society. But even then we can ask whether the differences are in fact rock-bottom disagreements or premised on some more basic, shared value. For example, the overpopulated culture that abandons newborns presumably does so for the well-being of the already mature or maturing members of society. And this—the well-being of the society—is a value that we share with them even if we are horrified by their practice of abandoning babies.

But suppose that there are fundamental differences between our society and its morality and others—does this mean that morality must be relative? Let's distinguish two very different theses. **Cultural relativism** is the thesis that different people around the world (and even in the same society) in fact hold different values and believe in different moral codes. This leaves open the question as to which (if any) is correct. **Ethical relativism** is the thesis that whatever a culture or a society holds about right and wrong *is* therefore correct, at least for them. From an extreme individualist view, this could be interpreted as meaning that you are right if you sincerely think you are. Ethical relativism raises deep questions for philosophers. Cultural relativism—the thesis that different people have different moral beliefs—can be accepted as true without concluding from it that different people are correct in their different beliefs. It could still be that every society but one is wrong or even that every society is wrong.

Relativism: Facts and Values

Cultural Relativism: the thesis that different people *in fact* have different values. This leaves open the question as to which (if any) is correct.

Ethical Relativism: the thesis that whatever a culture or a society holds to be right *is* right, at least for them.

One immediate problem with ethical relativism is that it seems to render meaningless any moral judgments about another culture's behavior. If morality were truly relative, how could we continue to condemn the horrors committed against innocent civilians in Nazi Germany, or how could we have condemned apartheid in South Africa in the last century? We need some standard or standpoint from which we can affirm one morality and reject another, whether or not it is the generally accepted morality of the other society. Naturally, atrocities never are acceptable to all members of any society. The Jews, Catholics, and Gypsies who were herded into the Nazi death camps did not share their persecutors' moral values; nor did the large majority of black and other people of color in South Africa share the government's view of racial separation and privilege. On what basis did they criticize the views of their own society? Presumably they based their judgment on values that differed from those of (the majority within) their society, quite possibly values they held to be right regardless of societal views or contexts. Moral relativism appears to make such dissent from the dominant values within one's culture unjustified, but this hardly seems plausible. If any kind of moral relativism is defensible, it cannot be the simple-minded relativism that claims that whatever a society believes is right.

To defend moral absolutism, we should add, is not necessarily to affirm one culture-bound set of moral rules as applicable to everyone else on earth (which is sometimes called *moral imperialism*). At its most defensible, moral absolutism affirms some set of standards (possibly extremely broad ones) that transcends any one culture and applies equally to all cultures. It is at least possible, accordingly, that our shared sense of morality is inadequate or less moral than the values of some other people. To be a moral absolutist is not necessarily to be a moral imperialist.

Tolerance is one of the central values of our multiracial, multiethnic, polydimensional society. Ours is a **pluralistic** society, which means that we are not so much a "melting pot" as a "mixed salad" of a society, in which different groups have very different values, different religions, and different customs, and for us to get along together, it is essential that we tolerate these differences. We force ourselves to tolerate—which means that we must accept—behavior very different from our own and perhaps very different from what we think is right. Sometimes, though, we may feel that to be tolerant would be to abdicate our responsibilities. Consider issues such as human trafficking, genital mutilation, or sweatshop labor conditions. At some point, many people will start to argue that a certain practice is so reprehensible that the good of suppressing it overrides the imperative to be tolerant.

The question of moral relativism asks whether there is a limit to tolerance, an end point to how far differences are acceptable. Is it the case that even the most basic moral values will inevitably be points of contention and conflict? We should note that even to advocate tolerance is to defend at least one value as absolute (for example, the value of getting along with one another) and so to reject strict relativism.

Friedrich Nietzsche and the Attack on Morality

By morality the individual is taught to become a function of the herd, and to ascribe to himself value only as a function . . . Morality is the herd instinct in the individual.

—Friedrich Nietzsche, 1882

The theories of morality that take morality to be primarily a matter of duties and the consequentialist theories that take moral rules to be mainly guidelines to human happiness have in common most of their substantial moral principles. Indeed, John Stuart Mill and Immanuel Kant would probably have agreed on most major issues, though their reasons may have been quite different. Even Aristotle would have agreed with most of their recommendations.

But there is a further step that may be taken in moral theorizing, which is far more skeptical and far less respectful of our ordinary moral sentiments than any of the theories we have discussed thus far. Suppose we were to return to our initial question of this section and ask, once again, why an individual should act against his or her own self-interests and obey a moral principle. According to duty-defined moralities, the answer would be something like, "Because of the authority vested in the principle" (whether by God, by society, or by reason). The answer of consequentialist moralities would be something like "Because it will be best for most of us in the long run." But suppose a philosopher comes along who asks why he or she *should* personally respect the authority of God, or society, or reason. What would happen if it turned out in the long run that what is best for a single individual is not best for more of us? Why, then, should that person be moral?

Friedrich Nietzsche led an attack on morality—more precisely, Judeo-Christian morality. Nietzsche attacked the authority of the Ten Commandments; in fact, he declared that "God is dead," thus leaving traditional morality devoid of its divine justification, source, and sanctions. Nietzsche pointed out that societies of modern times were decadent, falling apart, and that their moral authority need no longer be binding on a creative individual who rejected that decadence and disintegration. And as for reason, he claimed, there are other things of importance in human life besides reason—passion, the love of adventure, and artistic creativity. Mere pleasure and happiness are not of ultimate importance either, he argued.

Rather, our primary goal in life is, in every case, what Nietzsche calls "power," but what might better be understood as "self-expression" or "making one's mark" on the world. The meaning of human life, according to Nietzsche, is creativity; to live a good life is to construct one's life as an artwork. But this ideal, he argued, is incompatible with what is now called morality, which dampens creativity, which tries to make all of us the same, which prevents us from being daring and inventive.

"Master" and "Slave" Morality: Nietzsche

Wandering through the many subtler and coarser moralities which have so far been prevalent on earth, I found that certain features recurred regularly together and were closely associated—until I finally discovered two basic types . . . Master morality and slave morality . . . The noble human being separates from himself those in whom the opposite of such exalted, proud states finds expression: he despises them. It should be noted immediately that in this first type of morality the opposition of "good" and "bad" means approximately the same as "noble" and "contemptible." (The opposition of "good" and "evil" has a different origin.) . . .

It is different with the second type of morality, slave morality. Suppose the violated, oppressed, suffering, unfree, who are uncertain of themselves and weary, moralize: what will their moral valuations have in common? Probably, a pessimistic suspicion about the whole condition of man will find expression, perhaps a condemnation of man along with his condition . . . Conversely, those qualities are brought out and flooded with light which serve to ease existence for those who suffer: here pity, the complaisant and obliging hand, the warm heart, patience, industry, humility, and friendliness are honored—for here these are the most useful qualities and almost the only means for enduring the pressure of existence. Slave morality is essentially a morality of utility.

Here is the place for the origin of that famous opposition of "good" and "evil": into evil one's feelings project power and dangerousness, a certain terribleness, subtlety, and strength that does not permit contempt to develop. According to slave morality, those who are "evil" thus inspire fear; according to master morality it is precisely those who are "good" that inspire, and wish to inspire, fear, while the "bad" are felt to be contemptible.

—Friedrich Nietzsche, *Beyond Good and Evil*, 1886

Interpreters have pictured Nietzsche in two entirely different ways, both probably partly correct. On the one hand, Nietzsche uses the most belligerent language imaginable. He sounds very much like an ancient barbarian out to destroy everything in modern civilized life, with all its comforts and conveniences, in order to return to a world in which the strongest, most creative people flourish and the weak tend to perish. This is the Nietzsche who outraged his contemporaries and has terrified some undergraduates and most Sunday school teachers ever since.

But Nietzsche himself, according to all reports, was a perfectly civilized, shy, witty gentleman. The other Nietzsche, accordingly, is a mild-mannered but outspoken defender of creative ideas, a critic of those who hid behind moral principles as an excuse for doing nothing and making nothing of themselves, an enemy of hypocrisy, laziness, and cowardice, but not of civilization and sanity. In fact, what Nietzsche envisions is a society more exciting and more civilized than our own, a society led by dynamic individuals rather than (according to his favorite metaphor) a herd of sheep. He calls the members of this ideal future society *Übermenschen*, or "superhumans." But to clear the way for this superior civilization, it will first be necessary to remove the false justifications of the reigning morality, Judeo-Christian morality.

Nietzsche's moral theory is, therefore, an attempt to undermine morality, to get rid of it, to show it to be fraudulent. One part of his attempt is his rejection of God as "dead," by which Nietzsche means, essentially, that people no longer really believe in God as the center of their lives; they go to church and say a few prayers, but belief in God does not structure the way they actually conduct their lives. But if belief in God has died, why do people still endorse the morality that traditionally was associated with God? Morality, according to Nietzsche, is a kind of trick; it is a trick to gain power, a trick not needed by strong, creative souls (who already have power), but rather a trick perpetuated by the weak, as a way of protecting themselves against the strong.

If we consider once again the various rules of morality—for example, "Don't kill," "Don't steal," "Don't cheat"—we might notice that a significant proportion of such rules are *prohibitions*—that is, rules forbidding us to do something. Why is this? Suppose we change our approach to these questions and ask, "Who benefits from these prohibitions?" The answer is not "Everyone" but rather "Those who cannot protect themselves"—in other words, the weak. Now we can see why so many of the rules are prohibitions rather than positive virtues (as in Aristotle): the rules benefit the weaker members of society by preventing the stronger members from taking advantage of their strength. The strong can take care of themselves; morality is the protection of the weak.

We can understand, too, according to Nietzsche's view, why the idea that moral rules must be universal has been so important. Moral rules would not protect anyone if those people against whom the rules were formulated did not obey them, or if they thought that the rules did not apply to them. But once this has been pointed out, Nietzsche claims, those who are strong and creative will realize that, contrary to the utilitarian promises, obedience to the rules may not be advantageous to everyone—specifically, not to them. And ultimately, the rules are harmful to everyone, in that they obstruct precisely those who have most to contribute to culture. Nietzsche expects such arguments to eventually hold sway, with the result that traditional morality is undermined.

Yet, Nietzsche did not enjoy the idea that civilization as we know it might soon break down and give way to an orgy of violence and political chaos. In fact, he predicted such a future (that is, the twentieth century) with considerable horror. Nietzsche's idea seems to be that the creative hero for whom his philosophy is intended should be concerned primarily not with being a "good person" and being moral in a conventional sense, but rather with living life as an adventure, with making our own individual contributions to culture, and with each of us "giving style to one's character." We should develop our virtues in our uniquely individual ways, and this would require discipline and commitment to our own exacting standards, though not to universal moral principles. The problem that Nietzsche has left for us is this: how can we justify the rules of morality for all of us without quashing the individual creativity that is in the best of us? "Why should we be moral?" is no longer an immoral question to ask. In fact, it has become an essential part of the moral life itself.

Closing Questions

1. What is your conception of the good life? What goals or principles are primary? What are the roles of success, wealth, freedom, and friendship? Are they ends or means? If they are means, how do they lead to the end in question?

2. What qualities do you consider to be the most important virtues a person can possess? What are the qualities most valued by our society?

3. In our sense, is it always the case that everyone strives for happiness? Are there other goals or principles that might be more important?

4. What considerations do you use to tell whether someone's action is selfish? Is selfishness always wrong? Sometimes wrong? When? Be specific.

5. Under what circumstances, if any, is it permissible to lie? What does your answer indicate about the justification of the principle that one ought not lie?

6. How would you apply the first formulation of Kant's categorical imperative to a specific circumstance? Imagine, for instance, that you are considering stealing someone's iPhone when no one is looking. How would you decide, according to Kant, that this act is immoral?

7. A hungry cannibal chieftain looks you over and declares that you will indeed make a fine dinner. What can you say to him to convince him that cooking you would be *wrong*? (Convincing him that you won't taste good is not enough.)

8. The British philosopher Alfred North Whitehead once wrote, "What is morality in any given time and place? It is what the majority then and there happen to like and immorality is what they dislike." Do you agree?

9. In traditional India, some wives have been expected to share the funeral pyre with their just-departed husbands. In what terms is it possible for us to criticize or object to such a practice? In some parts of Africa, young women have been expected to undergo the painful operation of clitoridectomy. In what terms is it possible for us to criticize or object to such a practice? In many countries today, infant boys (or, sometimes, young men) are expected to undergo the painful operation of circumcision. In what terms would you criticize or defend such a practice?

Suggested Readings

A good introduction to ethics is Simon Blackburn, *Being Good* (Oxford University Press, 2003); see also his *Ethics: A Very Short Introduction* (Oxford University Press, 2009). A brief but comprehensive history of ethics is Alasdair MacIntyre's A *Short History of Ethics* (Macmillan, 1966), which can be followed by MacIntyre's exciting book on contemporary morality, *After Virtue* (University of Notre Dame Press, 1981). A schematic discussion of the various theories of ethics is Robert C. Solomon, *On Ethics and the Good Life* (Wadsworth, 2005). Epicurus's Letter to Menoeceus is included in *Letters, Principle Doctrines, and Vatican Sayings,* trans. and ed. Russel M. Geer (Bobbs-Merrill, 1964). Paul Tillich argues that religion is our ultimate concern in *Dynamics of Faith* (Harper & Row, 1957). The classic argument against egoism is in Joseph Butler, *Fifteen Sermons upon Human Nature* (Macmillan, 1900); a more recent set of arguments is Thomas Nagel's *The Possibility of Altruism* (Oxford University Press, 1970). Plato's *Republic* and *Euthyphro* are available in *Plato: Complete Works,* ed. John M. Cooper (Hackett, 1997). Aristotle's ethics are mainly to be found in his *Nicomachean Ethics,* trans. W. D. Ross (Oxford University Press, 1925). Kant's best summary of his moral philosophy is his *Foundations of the Metaphysics of Morals,* trans. L. W. Beck (Bobbs-Merrill, 1959). John Stuart Mill summarizes his utilitarian moral philosophy in his short book *Utilitarianism* (Bobbs-Merrill, 1957). *The Analects of Confucius* is translated by Roger T. Ames and Henry Rosemont, Jr. (Ballantine, 1998). Philippa Foot's article "The Problem of Abortion and the Doctrine of Double Effect" can be found in *Virtues and Vices* (Basil Blackwell, 1978). Judith Jarvis Thompson discusses the trolley problem in "Killing, Letting Die and the Trolley Problem," which is available in her book *Rights, Restitution, and Risk: Essays in Moral Theory*, ed. W. Parent (Harvard University Press, 1986). Lawrence Kohlberg defends his theory of moral development in "The Claim to Moral Adequacy of a Highest Stage of Moral Judgment," *Journal of Philosophy* 70 (18): 630–646. Carol Gilligan's *In a Different Voice* (Harvard University Press, 1982) is now the established statement of the new gender-specific moral theory. For a survey of feminist ethical views, see Hilde Lindemann, *An Invitation to Feminist Ethics* (McGraw-Hill, 2005). Nel Noddings's classic statement of care ethics appears in *Caring* (University of California Press, 1984), and Sara Ruddick formulates her maternal approach to care ethics in *Maternal Thinking: Toward a Politics of Peace* (Beacon Press, 1989). Nietzsche's quip about English morality appears in *Twilight of the Idols*, trans. Walter Kaufmann (Penguin, 1976). His most systematic study of morality is in his *On the Genealogy of Morals,* trans. Walter Kaufman (Random House, 1967), and his more positive ethical views are evident in *Thus Spoke Zarathustra*, trans. Walter Kaufmann (Viking, 1966). Peter Singer's *Ethics* (Oxford University Press, 1994) provides a good but controversial contemporary discussion of morality. More diverse perspectives on contemporary ethics appear in the *Blackwell Companion to Ethics,* ed. Peter Singer (Blackwell, 2000).

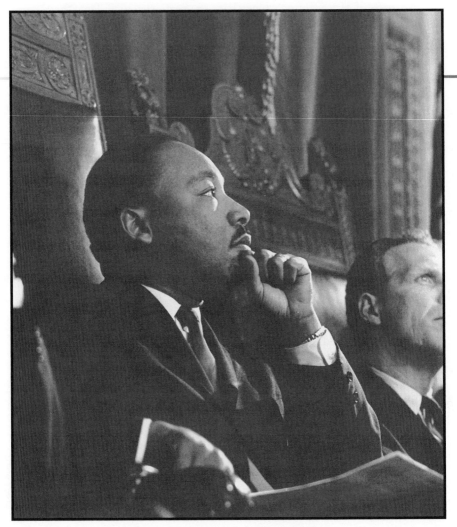

Martin Luther King Jr., © Behman/CORBIS.

9

Justice and the Good Society

Justice is that which is most primitive in the human soul, most fundamental in society, most sacred among ideas, and what the masses demand today with most ardour. It is the essence of religions and at the same time the form of reason, the secret object of faith, and the beginning, middle and end of knowledge. What can be imagined more universal, more strong, more complete than justice?

—Pierre-Joseph Proudhon

Opening Questions

1. In what kind of society would you prefer to live? A large urban society; a small rural society; some safe suburb; a bustling commercial city; a quiet, more or less homogeneous town in which people more or less share the same values; a multiethnic neighborhood with many different peoples?

2. Do you believe in the death penalty for the most heinous crimes? Why or why not?

3. Should a president of the United States be impeached if his or her subordinates break the law?

4. Should shelter for the homeless be provided at government (that is, taxpayer) expense? Should this be undertaken at the federal, state, or local level? If you say, "none of the above," what do you think should be done about the problem?

5. Is political power ultimately nothing but the rule of the strongest, the most powerful, the most persuasive on TV? Is a government anything more than the power of those who run it? Why are there governments at all?

6. Does the government have the right (rather than merely the power) to demand a percentage of your paycheck as taxes? Why or why not?

7. What is justice? What aspects of our society make it a just society? What aspects of our society are unjust?

8. Are there any reasons for paying one person less than another for the same measurable productivity?

9. Is there a "human right" to an education? Who (if anyone) has the obligation to make sure that you get one—your parents, the government, you yourself?

10. Do you believe that "all men [and women] are created equal"? What does this mean? In what respects are they equal?

Morals and Society

The Greeks had a saying: "To live a good life one must live in a great city." What counts as a "great city," of course, is always a matter of considerable dispute: New York or Omaha, Los Angeles or Austin? But what the Greeks had in mind, of course, was the idea that, to live a good life one had to live in a good community—one in which people respected one another and obeyed the rules, one that flourished and was not overwhelmed with problems of crime and poverty, one in which the happiness of one person was not to be gained at the expense of others. Aristotle's *Ethics* described the ideal citizen of such a community, and Bentham's and Mill's utilitarianism provided one description of the ultimate goal of such a community—the greatest happiness of the greatest number of people. Indeed, even Kant, in his final formulation of the categorical imperative, suggests that one should always act in such a way as to bring about a "Kingdom of Ends," an ideal community. There seems to be no doubt about it: for almost all of us, the good life presupposes residing in a good place to live with other people, and our ability to be a good person depends at least in part on those with whom we share our world and the society in which we live.

But although we can perhaps imagine a society in which everyone is wealthy and healthy, in which everyone at least respects everyone else and there is no crime and no poverty and plenty of everything for everyone, the world we live in is just not like that. It is worth noting that the imaginary perfect societies that some of the great philosophers and social thinkers have dreamed of and written about have been called **Utopia**—derived from Greek roots, meaning both "good place" and "nowhere," and referring to an imaginary, ideal place. Human life as we know it is burdened with misfortune and tragedy. There is not plenty for everyone, and sometimes there is not even enough to go around. People are born into poverty while others are born into riches. Some people are born with physical or mental disabilities, and most of us become seriously ill at some time or another. People of one race or religion look down on people of other races and religions, and crime runs rampant, not just in the streets of the city but all over the country, and not only because of poverty or need.

So the question of living in an ideal society remains but a dream; meanwhile, we have to figure out how best to live in the world we actually do inhabit. Given the fact that people are born into very different circumstances and enjoy or suffer very different fates during their lives, how should society take this into account?

What should we do with those who break the law and intentionally, or irresponsibly harm others? How should we organize society, and who should have the power to run things? Just as we asked in Chapter 8 how we ought to live as individuals, we must now ask how we ought to live as a society. Of course, the questions can never be kept wholly apart.

We will pursue these questions first by noting the fact that philosophers have typically sought to justify the organization of their own societies, then by discussing various conceptions of who should rule. We will then consider challenges to the idea that any government is necessary. In light of the fact that the nature of justice is, perhaps, the central question of social-political philosophy, we will devote the majority of the chapter to this topic, addressing the question of what justice is, the meaning of equality, and the theory of the social contract as the origin of justice. We will then consider issues of justice in connection with those beyond our own society, and different philosophical views of individual rights. We will conclude with a brief discussion of African-American and feminist critics of conditions within the status quo, both in social practices and in their philosophical underpinnings, suggesting that their insights might help us rectify past injustices and reshape our institutions accordingly.

The Nature of Society

People have always lived in groups, in large families or tribes that evolved into great cities and nations. "Man is a social animal," wrote Aristotle 2,500 years ago. If some caveman 25,000 years ago had been asked his opinion, he probably would have said pretty much the same thing. Apart from an occasional (usually fictional) hero alone in the wilderness, we are mutually dependent creatures. We need to live together. And with the exception of that one noisy neighbor, we usually *like* to live together. But any group of people, no matter how large or small, needs some form of organization, and organizations of people have not implausibly been compared to living organisms, in which a collection of individuals happen to live in one place. Every society has its own structures, its own culture, its history, its mode of organization, its rules. The questions are what kind of structures and rules these ought to be and what kind of people we are, such that we need these structures and rules.

Some Key Contrasts in Social Philosophy

Person as a social function ←——————→ Individual free to define him/herself

Social status/privileges ←——————→ Equality
(by virtue of birth, power,
talent, skill, achievement)

Obligations to society ←——————→ Rights (demanded of society)

The nature of the societies people have built and grown up in vary enormously, from the peasant- and family-based agrarian cultures we still find in many parts of the world to the bewilderingly mobile and fast-paced cities of New York, Paris, New Delhi, and Beijing. In some of these societies, a person is viewed strictly in terms of his or her place in the society—as a member of a certain family, as a member of a certain class, as one who will be trained to be a soldier, a shoemaker, a farmer, or a diplomat. In others, the concept of "the individual" is all-important, and a person's self-identity is to be distinguished from all of these "accidents" of birth and functions. In some societies, it is taken for granted that some people are "better" than others, by virtue of their birth or their abilities or their accomplishments; in others, it is said that everyone is equal and due equal respect and consideration.

The nature of society and the role of the person in society are essential considerations in social philosophy. It is not surprising that, as one reads the different philosophers who have written about the nature of society, philosophers tend to reflect or project the perceptions, preferences, and dissatisfactions with their own societies. Plato's imaginary Republic is easily recognizable as a variation on Greek society, and the philosophers of the late Middle Ages who lived under monarchies defended the "divine right of kings." The philosophers of eighteenth-century England—living during the Industrial Revolution and the boisterous birth of capitalism—not unnaturally defended the right to private property that capitalism presupposed. And most contemporary social philosophers in America defend first and foremost the rights of the individual, such as freedom of speech and religion. This is not necessarily because of any cowardice or lack of imagination on these various thinkers' parts, but rather because we are, no matter how free thinking and imaginative, a part of the society in which we were raised. Our conception of the good society and its structure is usually based on values we digested along with our mothers' milk. There will always be the occasional conversion—the repentant communist who turns into a vehement anticommunist and the successful capitalist who devotes the rest of his life to advocating socialism—but these are special stories just because they are so rare. Sometimes an entire society may undergo such a conversion—China rebelling against its Confucian heritage and embracing communism in the 1940s—but the enormous difficulties that such societies face in carrying out their conversion just goes to show how deep-set the old ideas will always be.

Who Should Rule? The Question of Legitimacy

What kind of a society do we want? Who should run things? Since prehistoric times, it seems that someone—usually the strongest or the wisest of the group—has taken charge, given orders to the others, and taken on certain privileges and status himself or herself. Looking beyond ourselves to the rest of nature, we can see similar high-status roles. A wolf pack is led by the strongest, smartest wolf, and without such a leader the pack usually perishes. A hive of bees or a nest of ants each has its queen, without which there could be no hive or nest. So it is easy to presume that the emergence of a leader in human society is just as "natural." Who the leader is, of course, will depend on the nature of the society. In a warrior society, it will probably be the best soldier; in an intellectual society, it may be the wisest scholar. In a society where money is power, the rule will be by the rich (a **plutocracy**). In a society that depends on certain specialized skills (for example, intimate knowledge of computers), power will depend on merit and ability (a **meritocracy**). In some societies, religion rules and those who hold power are the most powerful religious people (a **theocracy**; literally, "rule by God"). In some societies, those who rule come from the highest caste or class in society (an **aristocracy**; literally, "rule by the best")—whether one is born into this position or comes to adopt it by virtue of certain credentials, such as a sufficiently prestigious university degree. In some societies, the ruler will be one person (a **monarchy**); in others, it will be a few (an **oligarchy**); in others rule is shared, at least in theory, by everyone (a **democracy**).

But we are not, we keep telling ourselves, just animals. We are rational as well as social animals; we can figure things out although most animals cannot. Perhaps it is true that every society needs some authority and organization, but why should such power and direction be in the hands of one man or woman? Why not a group? Why not everyone, working and thinking together? And if there is to be some governing body, why should we simply let nature "take its course" rather than design it ourselves?

Varieties of Rule

Plutocracy: rule by the rich

Meritocracy: rule by virtue of merit and ability

Theocracy: rule by religion or by God

Aristocracy: rule by "the best"

Monarchy: rule by one person

Oligarchy: rule by the few

Democracy: rule by the people

Less Is Best

The best of all rulers is but a shadowy presence to his subjects. Next comes the ruler they love and praise; Next comes one they fear; Next comes one with whom they take liberties.

The sage says, I take no action and the people are transformed of themselves; . . . I am not meddlesome and the people prosper of themselves. . . .

Do that which consists in taking no action; pursue that which is not meddlesome . . .

Therefore it is because the sage never attempts to be great that he succeeds in becoming great.

—Lao-Tzu, *Dao de Jing* (*Tao Te Ching*), fifth century BCE

That gov't is best which governs least.

—Thomas Jefferson, 1776

Even in ancient times, the idea that the strongest deserve to rule was hard to swallow. To be sure, one had to accept such a leader if one wanted to survive oneself. But the idea that such power was **legitimate**, that such power was justified—that was a different matter. And throughout history, when those who have the power abuse it (**tyranny**, from ancient Greek, means such abuse of power), some people have banded together (the ruler's own inner circle, a popular uprising) to "throw the bums out" (in our distinctively American political vocabulary). Legitimate power—or **authority**—is not just a matter of strength or cleverness; it is a matter of justified power. That is why, for many centuries, monarchs claimed to rule by "divine right." In a religious society, who could provide a more powerful, more unassailable justification?

Might and Right

Political *power* is one thing, but *legitimate* power is *justified* power, or *authority*. A legitimate government has a *right* to rule. The extreme abuse of political power is *tyranny*.

What makes a government **legitimate** (that is, justified)? It used to be thought that rulers were justified by God. But although our own politicians may often invoke God in support of their own positions (see "Which Side Is

God On?" p. 75), we no longer think that God alone justifies a government; in any case, one has to prove God's support by winning an election or two. So, too, it may have once been the case that **might makes right**—that those who were strongest or otherwise most superior would rule—but we do not accept the idea that the fact that one has and can hold power gives one the right to power—that is, legitimate power or authority. We believe, in short, that governments are supposed to serve the people, and the legitimacy of a government depends on this.

But even here, there are hard questions. Does serving the people mean making them prosperous? Is a rich society therefore a good society? And is the ruler who makes people rich therefore a legitimate ruler? Or is there another consideration here—that it is not the overall wealth or well-being of a society that counts first and foremost but rather the prevalence of *justice* in society (an important concept that we will discuss shortly)? Is a legitimate government one that protects not only the rich but also the very poor as well? Or is a legitimate government one that defends justice in a different sense, by enforcing the various rules and customs of the society, by punishing wrongdoers and thus protecting the values of the culture? Or is the legitimacy of a government not at all dependent on what the government does *for* the people, but rather how the government is formed *by* the people? For example, is legitimate government first and foremost one that has been properly elected in a fair political contest?

Anarchism, the Free Market, and the Need for Government
~∞~

The Benefits of Capitalism: Adam Smith

If we examine, I say, all those things . . . we shall be sensible that without the assistance and cooperation of many thousands, the very meanest person in a civilized country could not be provided, even according to what we very falsely imagine, the easy and simple manner in which he is commonly accommodated. Compared indeed with the more extravagant luxury of the great, his accommodation must no doubt appear extremely simple and easy; and yet it may be true, perhaps, that the accommodation of a European prince does not always so much exceed that of an industrious and frugal peasant, as the accommodation of the latter exceeds that of many an African king, the absolute master of the lives and liberties of ten thousand naked savages.

—From *Wealth of Nations*, 1776

One possible, and in one sense not unappealing, suggestion is that no one should run things. We all know that governments typically make a botch of things, often assume too much power, and provide their citizens too little in return. The *Dao De Jing (Tao Te Ching)* of ancient China suggests that aggressive measures to reform things often end up making things worse, and the *Dao De Jing* encourages rulers to refrain from intervening in the day-to-day operations of the state. It claims that the best ruler would be just a shadowy presence to the people, for, having appointed competent ministers to run things, he could just sit back and watch the state's affairs unfold in good order.

A more radical response to the failures of governments would be just to let everyone do what they want, a state of affairs more pejoratively called **anarchy**—a state of confusion and social disorder. Not having a government would create certain obvious problems of organization (for example, establishing rules for safe driving and ensuring that essential goods and services are provided). But it is not at all obvious that a reasonably sized group of intelligent planners could not design an organization (for instance, a set of traffic rules and regulations, a system of supermarkets and service stations) that would be generally agreeable within the society. We generally accept the convention of driving (in the United States) on the right-hand side of the road, not because the government forces us to but because we all agree that we must agree to drive on one side or the other, to drive safely, to drive sober. To be sure, there will always be those who refuse to comply with such agreements, but one might ask whether we really need a government (a highway patrol, traffic courts, judges) to enforce such mutually agreed-upon rules. And, to be sure, the absence of any higher power to delegate responsibilities might cause certain temporary shortages of goods—if it happens that no one at the moment is producing such goods—but must we assume that governmental authority is the only means for preventing such shortages?

One of the most powerful arguments of our times insists that, indeed, we do not need government to organize society, at least with regard to our economic affairs. In a sense, we can just let each person do what he or she wants. It is the idea of the **free market**—that people will do what they need to do without being forced to do so by any law or government. If essential goods and services are needed, enterprising people will provide them—at a profit to themselves, motivated by self-interest. And if there are mutual agreements that must be made to make society better or safer, we will accomplish this ourselves, in our own interest, without the interference or the authority of anyone else. Of course, there may still need to be rules and restrictions (for example, regulations to ensure "fair play")—but there need be and should be no government interference or organization where freedom of the market is concerned.

The Invisible Hand

As every individual, therefore, endeavours as much as he can both to employ his capital in the support of domestic industry, and so to direct that industry that its produce may be of the greatest value; every individual necessarily labours to render the annual revenue of the society as great as he can. He generally, indeed, neither intends to promote the public interest, nor knows how much he is promoting it. By preferring the support of domestic to that of foreign industry, he intends only his own security; and by directing that industry in such a manner as its produce may be of the greatest value, he intends only his own gain, and he is in this, as in many other cases, led by an invisible hand to promote an end which was no part of his intention. Nor is it always the worse for the society that it was no part of his intention. By pursuing his own interest he frequently promotes that of the society more effectually than when he really intends to promote it.

—Adam Smith, *Wealth of Nations*, 1776

However, free markets have not shown themselves capable of solving some very pressing social problems. We need not question the value of individual freedom or the efficiency of the free market to satisfy at least some of our needs and desires in order to argue that certain basic needs are not well-served by such a market. Health care is one example much in the news today. The demand for health care is simply not like the demand for most consumer goods. When a person becomes acutely ill, he or she is in no position to "shop around," or to consider whether the services in question are affordable. And with the advances in medical science, the cost of effective care is now prohibitively expensive for even the reasonably well-to-do. Moreover, because illness is often a consequence of other deprivations—malnutrition or lack of adequate shelter—illness often strikes hardest at those who can least afford it.

"Alienated Labor": Karl Marx

What constitutes the alienation of labour? First, that the work is external to the worker, that it is not part of his nature; and that, consequently, he does not fulfill himself in his work but denies himself, has a feeling of misery rather than well-being, does not develop freely his mental and physical

(continues)

"Alienated Labor": Karl Marx (continued)

energies but is physically exhausted and mentally debased. The worker, therefore, feels himself at home only during his leisure time, whereas at work he feels homeless. His work is not voluntary but imposed, forced labour. It is not the satisfaction of a need, but only a means for satisfying other needs. Its alien character is clearly shown by the fact that as soon as there is no physical or other compulsion it is avoided like the plague. External labour, labour in which man alienates himself, is a labour of self-sacrifice, of mortification. Finally the external character of work for the worker is shown by the fact that it is not his own work but work for someone else, that in work he does not belong to himself but to another person. . . .

We arrive at the result that man (the worker) feels himself to be freely active only in his animal functions—eating, drinking and procreating, or at most also in his dwelling and in personal adornment—while in his human functions he is reduced to an animal. The animal becomes human and the human becomes animal.

—Manuscript of 1844

The free market has also shown too little ability to care for the poor. There is an old bit of market wisdom: the rich get richer, and the poor get poorer. There seems to be no correction built into the market to handle such increasing inequality, and so there is a need for some countervailing force—notably government—to ensure that the very poor are adequately protected and provided for. Some people get extraordinarily rich, and some people sink into a cycle of poverty from which there seems to be no escape without considerable outside assistance. There is always charity, perhaps, but what if it isn't adequate? What we are discussing here, of course, is that enormous political concept called **justice**. Insofar as the purpose and the legitimacy of governments is to promote justice, we want to know—as Plato asked long ago in his great book *The Republic*—"What is justice?"

What Is Justice?

Justice is the first virtue of social institutions, as truth is of systems of thought.
—John Rawls, *A Theory of Justice*, 1971

Life is never fair . . . And perhaps it is a good thing for most of us that it is not.
—Oscar Wilde, *An Ideal Husband*, 1895

In a good society, there will be something more than prosperity; there will also be justice. For example, one might insist that people who are good will be rewarded,

> ### Justice: Payback and Fairness
>
> **Retributive justice:** making sure that the wicked and wrongdoers get theirs
>
> **Distributive justice:** the fair arrangement of the goods, benefits, and responsibilities of a society

while those who are bad will be punished. One might insist that people who work hard will be held in esteem and paid well for their work. One might insist that people will get to keep what they have, without fear that it will be taken away, and that those in need are taken care of. The problem of justice arises when *all* these various demands cannot be satisfied, when there is not enough to go around, or when the demands simply contradict one another. How can we make sure that the needy are taken care of if there are no taxes on the rich? How can we make sure that innocent people are protected without letting go some of the guilty? Justice, accordingly, is concerned with the priority of these various concerns and their implementation in a society that is, we admit, something less than perfect.

Justice is often divided into two parts, one concerned with punishment and the other with the distribution of goods and responsibilities. The first is called **retributive justice**, coming from the word *retribution*; criminal courts and prisons are society's instruments of retributive justice, and in a just society criminals are caught and sentenced fairly. A harsh sentence for a minor crime is an injustice, but so is a light or a suspended sentence for a heinous crime. If the guilty party "gets off easy" because he or she is rich and powerful, justice is particularly ill-served, for one of the presuppositions of justice is that it is "blind" to particular individuals, their status, and their power. (That is why the Western depiction of justice traditionally shows a *blindfolded* woman holding balanced measuring scales.)

> ### Four Kinds of Equality
>
> - Every person has the same abilities, talents, and advantages (implausible).
>
> - Every person has the same status before the law (fundamental to the American conception of justice).
>
> - Every person deserves to be given the same goods, benefits, and responsibilities in our society (unworkable and contrary to our notions of merit and entitlement).
>
> - Every person should have the same opportunities for achievement and advancement in our society (a necessary ideal but difficult to achieve).

The other kind of justice is **distributive justice**—the distribution of goods—which includes salaries and bonuses for well-done work and education and medical care for the public. Distributive justice continues to be a source of deep controversy in contemporary life. For example, there is vehement disagreement, to say the obvious, over Karl Marx's famous suggestion: "From each according to his abilities; to each according to his needs." This is a summary of one theory of justice, but notice that it says nothing about what people *earn* or about their right to what they already have. It does not suggest that people might ever deserve more than they need, and some would find this in itself grounds for rejecting the theory. On the other hand, a great many people are outraged that some shiftless playboy can lead a life of luxury just because his father worked himself to death, leaving his fortune to this wastrel.

Such entitlement plays no role in the Marxist conception of justice, in which serving people's needs is the main concern of justice. Yet most Americans would say that the young man is *entitled* to the money, if only because his father was entitled to do what he liked with his earnings. The American sense of justice is more concerned with making sure that people get and keep what is theirs. In a Marxist society, justice would demand that the playboy be disinherited and sent out to work for a living. His unearned fortune would be distributed among the needy. In our society, the young man gets to keep his money, even though we think he doesn't deserve it, because he is entitled to what has been left to him by his father.

Of course, matters of justice are not so simple. Marxist societies find it necessary to reward people for their work, if only to give them *incentives* to work harder. The Marxist view does not grapple with problems of ensuring motivation. In our society, the shiftless young man may get to keep a substantial part of his fortune, but we can be sure that the government will take a good chunk of it for its own redistributive purposes (whether these are to to assist the needy, to build bombers, or to build roads). Indeed, every line on a tax return is in effect a miniature theory of justice—stating what people deserve and what activities are considered particularly worthy. Having children is rewarded with tax deductions; gambling losses are ignored. Return on investments may be rewarded with a low tax rate, lower than taxes on salaries. (What does this say about our concept of justice?) Distributive justice is an all-pervasive concern in our society: in every salary negotiation, in every commercial transaction, and in every grade assigned by a professor.

Four Concerns of Justice

- People should get what they need.
- People should give what they can.
- People should be allowed to keep what they have (**entitlement**).
- People should get what they deserve (**merit**).

Our concern for justice, however, is a never-ending balancing act among a number of very different and sometimes antagonistic factors. Most Americans probably agree with Marx that people should work up to their abilities and have their needs served, but we do not put these two considerations at the forefront of our sense of justice. Our system shows our concern that people get what they earn (just as, in criminal cases, we think they should get what they deserve). We also assume that taking risks and shouldering considerable responsibilities should be highly rewarded. And we apparently think—a matter worth pondering—that it is perfectly just that the highest paid, most honored and celebrated members of our society are those who entertain us—in sports, on film, or on the stage, for example.

The American sense of justice also insists, above all, on that sense of entitlement—that people deserve to keep what they have, no matter how little they have done to earn it, no matter what we may think of them. This makes our sense of justice largely conservative, as opposed to the radical redistribution of wealth urged in many revolutionary countries. Indeed, many prominent social theorists have argued that, whatever our emphasis on hard work and merit, our capitalist system of justice depends first of all on this conservative sense of entitlement (the inviolability of private property, for example) and only afterward on these other concerns.

The Meaning of Equality

The law, in its majestic equality, forbids the rich as well as the poor to sleep under bridges, to beg in the streets, and to steal bread.

—Anatole France, 1844–1924

What is most important for justice, however, in both Marxist societies and our own, is the concept of **equality**. On the one hand, it is obvious to everyone that all people are *not* equal in every sense. Some are born healthy, wealthy, and smart; others are born wretched, impoverished, and disabled. People have different talents, different looks, different capacities. Nevertheless, justice insists that they are all equal. What does this mean?

It means, first of all, that they are all equal *before the law*. Again, the blindfolded figure of justice signifies that justice does not recognize individual differences in rank and privilege; justice sees everyone as equal. In theory, at least, the same laws apply to everyone and in the same way. A judge is obliged to hand out the same sentence to a rich man as to a poor man, to a homeless person as to a movie star, if they have committed the same crime. Two people doing the same job deserve the same salary, and it does not matter if one is male and the other female, if one is black and the other white, if one is tall and the other is short. Indeed, this sense of "same job, same pay" is defended in American courts because it is so important to our sense of justice and the good society.

> ### A Principle of Justice
>
> *Inequalities are arbitrary unless it is reasonable to expect that they will work out to everyone's advantage and provided that the positions to which they attach are open to all.*
>
> —John Rawls, contemporary American philosopher

But many writers have argued equality cannot mean that everyone should be made equal in a more general sense. In a story by Kurt Vonnegut, the author talks about a society in which everyone is made equal by handicapping the advantaged. Strong people are made weak by being forced to carry heavy weights all the time; smart people are made dumb by wearing noisemakers that distract them from thinking; graceful people wear lopsided weights to keep them off balance. The outrageousness of the story is its suggestion that *inequality* is inevitable in any society. According to this view, some inequalities reflect real differences in accomplishment and make our whole society richer. People who work hard ought to live better, and people who can but refuse to work shouldn't have those same advantages given to them. And so the argument is that—above a certain subsistence level necessary for human existence—inequality should be tolerated as inevitable and, in certain ways, as desirable and advantageous to everyone.

But should there be *so much* inequality? (This is the very question that Marx raised when he complained that laborers were alienated even from a sense of their own accomplishment when the fruits of their labors were not theirs to sell but belonged to someone else, for example, a factory owner.) And even though we can understand why virtue and productiveness should be rewarded, why should we therefore accept the very different thesis that mediocrity and failure— or just plain bad luck and misfortune—should be punished? Could we not have incentives for hard work and productivity that nevertheless coexisted with material equality?

What equality means, many writers say, is **equal opportunity**. But here, too, there are problems. When we try to insist that everyone should be equal, we run up against the unavoidable fact that people are from birth unequal in abilities and advantages, and even the most radical and topsy-turvy restructuring of the society would leave this largely so. Besides that, our feeling that people ought to be rewarded (and punished) for what they do and our sense that people should get to keep what they have result in further inequalities among individuals. There is no equality of opportunity because the same circumstances that give some people ample advantage over others give them much greater opportunities, too. "It takes money to make money" goes an old piece of wisdom, and no one can doubt that even a mediocre, lazy child who goes to a first-rate prep school has a better chance at opportunities for the future than bright, energetic, but disadvantaged children in an inner-city school. Equal opportunity seems as elusive as equality.

One might think that such complications would be enough to render an ideal impractical, but that is to miss the point of moral ideals in society. There has probably never been a perfectly just society; perhaps there never will be. But what our ideals of justice and equality do is to remind us, all the time, of what we believe in and what we stand for. An overall scheme for assuring equality or equal opportunity might escape us, but we can, by virtue of our insistence on equality, be aware of *in*equalities that exist around us and do what we can to correct them. It is "natural," one might argue, for people to associate with people of their own age, race, religion, and political persuasion; nevertheless, when this "natural" inclination interferes with fairness—for example, when an employer is hiring, firing, or promoting, or when some workers are forming a union, or when a club is being formed—our sense of justice intervenes and reminds us (perhaps with the help of the law) that such discrimination is not fair. It is unsurprising, one might similarly argue, that in a complex corporation different people doing the same job with the same title might find that they have different salaries; but our concept of equality comes once again to the rescue, for it is under the power of that concept that we feel compelled—and the corporation will too—to make sure that people doing substantially the same job are paid the same salary. However difficult and controversial our concepts of justice and equality may be, they serve an invaluable purpose in our society. We may argue for another two centuries on exactly what they mean and how they apply, but in the meantime they will be the instruments we use to improve our society.

Two Principles of Justice: John Rawls

We may think of a human society as a more or less self-sufficient association regulated by a common conception of justice and aimed at advancing the good of its members. As a cooperative venture for mutual advantage, it is characterized by a conflict as well as an identity of interests. There is an identity of interests since social cooperation makes possible a better life for all than any would have if everyone were to try to live by his own efforts; yet at the same time men are not indifferent as to how the greater benefits produced by their joint labours are distributed, for in order to further their own aims each prefers a larger to a lesser share. A conception of justice is a set of principles for choosing between the social arrangements which determine this division and for underwriting a consensus as to the proper distributive shares.

The two principles of justice . . . may be formulated as follows: first, each person engaged in an institution or affected by it has an equal right to the most extensive liberty compatible with a like liberty for all; and second,

(continues)

Two Principles of Justice: John Rawls (continued)

inequalities as defined by the institutional structure or fostered by it are arbitrary unless it is reasonable to expect that they will work out to everyone's advantage and provided that the positions and offices to which they attach or from which they may be gained are open to all.

These principles regulate the distributive aspects of institutions by controlling the assignment of rights and duties throughout the whole social structure, beginning with the adoption of a political constitution in accordance with which they are then to be applied to legislation. It is upon a correct choice of a basic structure of society, its fundamental system of rights and duties, that the justice of distributive shares depends.

—*Philosophy, Politics and Society,*
Peter Laslett and James Fishkin, eds., 1979

One notion of equality, however, should stand in front of all these other notions. It precedes equality before the law and is more important than equality of incomes and even opportunities. And that is the notion of *equality of respect*—the presumption that we will view everyone we meet with the vague but immensely meaningful idea that he or she, like ourselves, is a human being with feelings and thoughts, hopes and worries, affections and concerns. It is not a political or even a social sense of equality as much as a deeply felt personal one, taught to most of us in the United States from childhood as an essential part of being a citizen of a classless society, whatever the inequalities in income, wealth, and power among us. But if we fully appreciate the importance of such mutual respect, perhaps some of the other inequalities in our social lives will gradually be corrected.

The Origins of Justice and the Social Contract

Outside of civil states, there is always a war of all against all.
—Thomas Hobbes, 1588–1679

Man is born free, and everywhere he is in chains.
—Jean-Jacques Rousseau, 1712–1778

Where does justice come from? And why should considerations of justice have any binding authority over us? Why do we have states and governments, and why (apart from fear of punishment) should we obey them? The most popular modern answer to these questions—which has come down to us primarily from the great social thinkers of the seventeenth and eighteenth centuries (especially Hobbes, Locke, and Rousseau)—is that justice and the whole of society as well have been produced by a general social agreement, a **social contract**. We are obliged to obey the rules of justice—and the governments that enforce them—because we (in some sense) *agreed to do so.* It is as if we made a contract with the state—or, more properly, with everyone else in (what is now) our society—to live together according to certain rules that, according to our best calculations, are in everyone's interest, including our own. In return for our obedience to the rules, everyone else will obey them too (or be threatened and forced to do so).

Just think of traffic rules alone to see how well this idea works as an account of both why there should be such general rules and how it is in our interest to obey them (at least most of the time) ourselves. And in return for our agreement to be fair and to support and participate in fair institutions—in particular the justice system but also the tax system (by willingly paying our "fair share"), the market system, and the system of contracts and ownership—others will participate as well. Society will be orderly and more or less peaceful; property will be safe and secured and our personal lives protected. Justice thus results from a mutual agreement according to which we all agree to abide by certain rules and principles.

We ourselves have signed no such contract, of course; although one can argue (as even Socrates did in the *Crito* almost 3,000 years ago) that one has made an implicit agreement with the society in which one lives simply by "choosing" to (continuing to) live there. And in the United States, in particular, there actually is something like a "social contract," an actual written document signed by representatives from the various then-existing states in order to set up a government and a set of general laws—our Constitution. But the appeal of the social-contract view, whether or not one believes that there ever actually was or is such a contract, is that it makes government conditional on our (collective) interests and dependent on our (collective) decisions. (Jean-Jacques Rousseau, one of the leading defenders of this theory, referred to our collective demands as the **General Will** of the people.) Governments, on this view, don't just appear "by nature" and impose themselves on us. We are in effect the ultimate source of their rules and laws, and it is our "will" that becomes the law of the land. As Rousseau profoundly put it, we collectively impose the laws on ourselves.

What was there before people got together to form society? Why did they get together? The most famous theory of the prior "state of nature" (that is, before the formation of society) is that of Thomas Hobbes, who argued that human life before society and justice was "a war of all against all" and, consequently, "nasty, brutish, and short." He suggested that people are naturally selfish and, in a world with too scarce resources, we would literally kill one another if there were no laws and governments to force us to behave ourselves. So why would we join a society and agree to such laws? Because each of us would be quite afraid of being hurt or killed by the others. And in return for our promise not to harm them, they agree in return not to harm us. Not a bad deal.

The implication, of course, is that human nature is still much the same and, without laws and governments, we too might return to that same brutal, mutually murderous situation. In *Leviathan*, published in 1651, at the time of the English Civil War, Hobbes regarded civil discord as the worst evil that could befall a society. The only way to avoid it, he argued, was for power to be given to a strong central authority, which could be either an individual or a collective body. On this view, the members of society voluntarily give up their rights to the sovereign power; but Hobbes believed this was a price worth paying in order to ensure peace.

The Social Contract

The **social contract** was a concept that became enormously popular and powerful in the eighteenth century as a theory of the nature of society, although it was typically presented instead as a view about the origins of society, which was most implausible. The social contract theory views society as based upon the shared agreement of all individuals who are its citizens; as citizens, they give up certain rights and privileges in return for the protection and the mutual advantages of the state. The best single example of a historical manifestation of such a contract is the U.S. Constitution, in which representatives of the various states and commonwealths got together and composed a contract setting up the federal government and its limitations. Moreover, the idea of a social contract was one of the basic justifications of the French Revolution (1789) and, a few years earlier, the justification used by the American colonies to break away from Britain. "We hold these truths to be self-evident, that all men are created equal, that they are endowed by their Creator with certain unalienable Rights, that among these are Life, Liberty and the pursuit of Happiness. —That to secure these rights, governments are instituted among Men, deriving their just powers from the consent of the governed. . . ."—(The Declaration of Independence, July 4, 1776)

The idea of a social contract was influenced by three authors in particular:

Thomas Hobbes (1588–1679) was an English philosopher who also defended the theory of **materialism** ("Everything is matter in motion"), which influenced Sir Isaac Newton.

John Locke (1632–1704) was an English physician and philosopher who became known as the father of British empiricism (see Chapter 5). He defended the idea of the social contract in his *Essays on Civil Government* in 1690, just after the English Revolution (1688).

Jean-Jacques Rousseau (1712–1778) was a Swiss philosopher. In 1762 he wrote the influential book titled *The Social Contract*.

A somewhat more cheerful theory of the social contract was defended by Hobbes's successor, John Locke. Locke suggested that in the state of nature we were basically hardworking creatures who tried to build things and cultivate the soil and by doing so claimed ownership of that property with which we had "mixed our labor." But ownership in the state of nature would be a tenuous business. For although one had earned the right of ownership through one's work, protecting what one owned was quite a different matter. We got together to form societies with laws and governments, therefore, to protect our hard-earned property. Locke's theory, needless to say, places a high premium on the importance of private property both in justice and in the workings of society.

An even more benign theory was defended by Jean-Jacques Rousseau, who saw society and justice (as we mentioned earlier) as the expression of the General Will of the people. But Rousseau did not see the state of nature as a brutal war, as Hobbes did, nor did he see it primarily as a world of hardworking individuals. Rousseau instead imagined a world of plenty, in which our presocietal ancestors could easily survive picking berries off the trees and sleeping in natural shelters. They left one another alone, and even felt pity for others in need. "Natural man," Rousseau argues, was happier and healthier than most of us. Why, then, did people in the state of nature ever decide to form societies? Well, much of the evolution of society, Rousseau tells us, is something of a tragedy, a product of our inventiveness but also our gullibility. Whereas nature finds us naturally good and happy, society, he says, "corrupts" us. Nevertheless, society properly conceived will not only restore something of our natural vitality and utilize our inventiveness but will actually make us into something more than merely "natural." Society will make us moral. Society will change a mere man or woman into a **citizen**.

These three thinkers' views of human nature differ considerably, but they all point to the same conclusion. For whatever reason, we got together and formed society, with laws and justice as its central feature. It is an exciting vision. And whether one gives any credence to its historical claims—either the theories of human nature presupposed or the story of the social contract itself—the vision exemplifies many of our most treasured demands regarding ourselves and the society we live in.

Justice beyond Our Borders
❧

The topic of justice raises questions not only about how one should treat one's fellow citizens, but also about how members of other societies should be treated. Some philosophers, in addressing this concern, have challenged some of our everyday assumptions about what it means to be a good member of society.

Being patriotic probably seems to most of us as an obvious virtue. But how does this seeming virtue square with the virtue of being just? The question becomes clearer when we translate the idea of patriotism into the attitudes that compose it. Does patriotism imply preferring the wellbeing of members of our own society to that of foreigners? If so, is that really fair? Leo Tolstoy analyzed patriotism along these lines and concluded that it is immoral because the preferential attitude it takes toward one's own society or nation is at the expense of all others. But is this really the right way to look at what we mean by being patriotic? Might we not say instead that patriotism is being loyal to the society that has supported us in many ways over our lifetime, as well as being loyal to the particular members with whom we have interacted?

How should we define "patriotism"? Does it just mean that we identify with our country? This seems too weak a definition. One can identify with one's country and be ashamed of it, and many people would consider such shame to be incompatible with patriotism. Others might say that shame under certain circumstances—when one's nation is not living up to its ideals, for example—is a manifestation of patriotism. If patriotism is a virtue, it is surely something other than mindless agreement with everything done by one's leaders, one's government, or one's compatriots. Patriotism, to be meaningful, involves participation in a larger community or society, and most defenders of patriotism would agree that patriotic participation sometimes may involve criticizing the very nation to which one maintains allegiance.

In any case, mere identification with one's nation falls short of patriotism. As most of us use the term, "patriotism" seems to require enthusiasm for one's nation and putting its interests first. Members of the military, who risk their lives on behalf of the nation, are often seen as the epitome of patriotism. But this idea of putting the interests of one's nation first brings us back to the question of whether such partiality can be morally justified.

One argument in defense of patriotism is that citizenship imposes special moral obligations on the citizen. This is the argument that Plato's Socrates gives to his disciple Crito when he claims that he has obligations to the state because it nurtured and educated him, and that by living in it he has made an implicit contract with it that require him to obey its laws. Seemingly, Socrates would see the partiality of patriotism as justified in that it is an outcome of this implicit contract with the state.

Some thinkers have denied that any kind of partiality is legitimate. The ancient Chinese philosopher **Mozi** (also Mo-Tzu) contended that any kind of preferential treatment, even that based on family ties, is immoral and also harmful to society as well as one's family members. Surely, he claimed, we would be more confident that our parents were well cared for if we lived in a society in which everyone cared for everyone's parents, not just their own.

The Confucian philosopher **Mencius** (Mengzi) countered that this approach would lead to a leveling of the concern we showed to a lowest common denominator, and (like Socrates) he argued that we have special obligations to those who have tended to us since our birth. It is natural that we have special concern for those who are closest to us, and the family is the context in which we first learn to care for others besides ourselves. While we have particular obligations to care for those who are closest to us, the cultivation of our natural sympathy for others naturally expands in a widening circle of concern for others. Contemporary communitarians such as Alasdair MacIntyre, while focusing on the community instead of the family, similarly argue that partiality toward those among whom one has developed one's sense of morality is not only acceptable, but morally required.

Situations in which one's country goes to war particularly raise questions about the moral standing of patriotism. When our nation declares war on another, it is targeting other human beings on the basis of their national affiliation, so partiality is evident in the extreme. The question of whether war is ever justified is a philosophical issue of long standing. In the Hindu scripture the Bhagavad Gita, Arjuna, the person who has the responsibility to give the order to commence the battle, has difficulty bringing himself to do so. He reflects on the fact that his order will lead to the deaths of kinsmen and others on both sides. (He ultimately does give the order, for reasons we will consider in Chapter 10.)

At the very least, war involves killing other human beings, perhaps the paradigm case of a type of action that is wrong (at least the vast majority of the time). Most people would claim that there are cases in which killing people is not wrong, and many would include kiling combatants in war among these exceptions. But if they are right, is this true of any war, no matter whether or not it is provoked or how aggressively or cruelly it is waged? And how does one ensure that one kills only combatants and avoids killing civilians (often chillingly and euphemistically referred to as "collateral damage"). Most philosophers think there must be at least some restrictions on when killing in war is morally acceptable (if it ever is).

Just-war theory tries to establish the circumstances under which it is morally permissible to go to war and what actions are acceptable when war is undertaken. Most just-war theorists take a nation's self-defense when attacked to be a just reason for going to war; there is more disagreement about whether a nation can legitimately go to war to protect innocent people who are not citizens. The questions become more complicated when a multinational alliance is involved, particularly when it goes to war to protect innocents in nations that are not part of the alliance. Some have argued that a first strike can be a form of defense against a looming threat, but this raises the question of when an attack is so obviously impending that this could be fairly called defensive. The notion that war should be undertaken only as a last resort, after efforts at negotiation have been attempted, is also an important principle in just-war theory. (Interestingly, although famous for his ingenious analysis of military strategy within war, the ancient Chinese military theorist **Sunzi** [or Sun-Tzu] is in agreement with just-war theorists on this point, although his grounds are prudential, not moral.) At every phase of war, just-war theorists insist that a party to the conflict is morally obligated to limit the amount of force employed to what is necessary to achieve its legitimate goal.

Qualms about the legitimacy of partiality motivate many who adopt the position called **cosmopolitanism**. Cosmopolitans (in the sense of those who hold this view, not the colloquial sense of being well-traveled or at home everywhere) take seriously the idea of global community. Typically they hold that we have moral obligations to all other human beings. They promote the idea of international political arrangements that would facilitate the welfare of all human beings, regardless of their national citizenship. Philosopher-economist **Amartya Sen** and philosopher **Martha Nussbaum**, for example, defend a cosmopolitan view according to which policies should be developed that help people develop their natural capabilities to thrive and provide them the freedom to make use of these capabilites.

Cosmopolitans differ with respect to the nature of the international institutions they defend and how much power such institutions should have, as well as on the extent (if any) to which citizens of specific nations have special obligations to their fellow citizens. Nevertheless, they concur that national sovereignty should be weakened at least to some extent so that neither the policies of particular states nor national borders should interfere with the satisfaction of human needs.

Rights and the Self

One of the most important ingredients in most contemporary theories of justice—some authors would insist it is the definitive ingredient in justice—is the notion of **rights**. A right, essentially, is a kind of claim. Employees have a right to their salaries, for example, by virtue of a prior agreement with the company. Students have a right to an A if they have done excellent work in a course. To say that a person has a right is to say that someone else (perhaps the whole society) has a duty or an obligation to that person. For example, if a child has a right to a decent education, society has an obligation to make such an education available. Needless to say, there may be considerable disagreement about who should be responsible for this and how it will be paid for. Nevertheless, the right exists, with the corresponding obligation. To be a self in a society is to have such rights, as well as the corresponding obligation (for example, to help see to it that others get an education, by paying taxes, by sending your children to school, perhaps by teaching school).

There are different kinds of rights and duties. For example, some are **contractual rights**—the right to be paid for one's work, the obligation to pay for what you buy, or the duty to keep one's promises. Some are **legal**—such as the right to drive (with certain reasonable restrictions) and the duty to drive (more or less) under the speed limit. Other rights and duties are **civil**, whether or not they are written into law—such as the right and the duty to vote or the right and the duty to speak one's mind about topics of political concern. Finally, there is the general category of **human** (or "natural") rights, which apply to every human being on earth, no matter what the society or the circumstances—for instance, the right not to be tortured and not to be imprisoned without reason, the duty not to torture and not to imprison without reason.

This conception of rights, however, gives rise to some notorious political problems about their scope and nature. For example, we can all agree that the right not to be tortured is a global human right, but what about the right to free medical care? Or the right to keep what one has earned, however one has earned it? How much power should society (through government, or the state) have over individual citizens? Indeed, how much of one's self is defined by citizenship? How much is one a self quite apart from one's membership in society?

A broad spectrum of answers to these difficult questions has emerged over the past several hundred years, as concern for the individual has increased and as the size and power of societies has increased. We may mention, for instance, three possibilities: libertarianism, liberalism, and communitarianism.

Libertarianism

Libertarianism is the view that people are defined as selves by a strong set of natural rights as individuals, including the right to be left alone and not to be interfered with, the right to keep what one has, or has earned, and the right to be free from government interference in all things except when absolutely necessary to the general good. Libertarians tend to be strongly against taxes and big government and strongly for individual freedoms of all kinds. For the libertarian, the self is largely independent, and people establish themselves as selves by what they do with this freedom. **Robert Nozick** defends a libertarian position in his *Anarchy, State, and Utopia.*

Liberalism

The view of **liberalism** also holds that people are defined as selves by a strong set of natural rights, but the set of rights is quite different from the rights defended by the libertarian. Whereas libertarians emphasize the right not to be interfered with and the "negative rights" that this implies (for example, the right not to be prevented from speaking one's mind), the liberal emphasizes people's "positive" rights to the benefits of society (decent housing, education, food, health care, security). Whereas libertarians stress minimal and local government ("That gov't is best which governs least"), contemporary liberals tend to support a strong centralized government to administer social programs. (This is in contrast to the "classical liberals" of the eighteenth century and beyond, whose focus was negative liberty and defense of private property.) For the contemporary liberal, the self is the bearer of rights to a decent life, which become the obligation of society. **John Rawls**'s *A Theory of Justice* presents a vision of the just society that is premised on liberal ideas. A cosmopolitan variant of liberalism is the view that the rights of all human beings, regardless of citizenship, should be promoted and defended on an international basis. In 1948 the United Nations General Assembly adopted along these lines a Universal Declaration of Human Rights that called for international justice and the defense of the dignity of every human being through the protection of both civil liberties (negative rights) and freedom from want (positive rights).

Communitarianism

The **communitarian** view rejects the one-sided liberal and libertarian emphasis on rights and stresses the concept of duty instead. What defines a citizen is not his or her rights but rather his or her duties ("Ask not what your country can do for you, but what you can do for your country"). In the communitarian view, the self sometimes becomes a function of society rather than an independent entity. G. W. F. Hegel, for example, attacked the very idea of a social-contract theory because such a theory claims that there are individual selves who are capable of entering into a contractual agreement before the origins of society in which such agreements are possible. This, he insists, is nonsense. The self must be defined by society; there is no self outside of society. At its extreme, this view sometimes leads to **totalitarianism** (or **fascism**), which holds that the individual self is literally nothing, that the whole self is defined by—and is the property of—the state. (Hegel himself rejected this conclusion.)

Justice Denied: The Problem of Race

[I]t doesn't mean that we're anti-white, but it does mean that we're anti-exploitation, we're anti-degradation, we're anti-oppression. And if the white man doesn't want us to be anti-him, let him stop oppressing and exploiting and degrading us. . . .
—Malcolm X, 1964

Each of us is a citizen of our nation, but this has not always guaranteed that our rights have been protected, particularly if we are members of a minority group. In the United States, African-Americans constitute one of the most important marginalized groups. The problem of institutionalized racism has been of crisis proportions in this country ever since the drafting of the Declaration of Independence in 1776, and even before, when the first slaves were brought over from Africa to toil in the fields of Virginia and the Caribbean Islands. Racism has become, over the last fifty years, an inescapable problem that threatens the very moral integrity as well as the social harmony of life in America. The question of how we are to resolve the injustices perpetrated against racial minorities is pressing, and political philosophy should help us to address it.

Philosophy itself, however, has been accused of collaborating with racist society in downgrading people of color. The fact that African-American writers, for instance, have traditionally been left unread and out of the curriculum in American universities has been challenged as a continuation of "cultural slavery," the marginalization of one people's ideas by another's. In this respect, we can ask whether our tradition's approach to intellectual history has itself been unjust in its neglect of African-American thinkers and its failure to attend to their (often political) concerns. The rise of African-American philosophy over the past half century represents a step toward redressing this unfairness and toward acknowledging the role that racial prejudice has played not only in our social practices, but even in our philosophical theories. The fact that African-American philosophy has emerged into greater prominence in the last half century is thus a step toward greater justice within the field and ideally a sanguine development for redressing past injustice.

Philosophy Must Consider Race

Thinking about how the facts of "race" and the demand for justice may be accommodated to each other and to the realities of our various identifications and identities: nothing could be a more recognizably philosophical project. And what [W. E. B.] Du Bois called the "social heritage of slavery; the discrimination and insult" as well as the contemporary meaning of "racial difference" need always to be borne in mind if these discussions are to hew to reality.

These issues, which are crucial for questions of race in public life quite generally, intersect with a more narrowly academic range of questions in what I suppose we could call not so much the philosophy of education as the philosophy of the academy, questions about how racial identities and racist histories have shaped our disciplinary heritages. Philosophers (like others) have not always been good at seeing clearly the historical formation of their own discipline.

Feminist philosophers have argued that the structure of philosophical discourse reflects the longstanding exclusion of most women and women's concerns, first from the life of intellectuals, then, as it developed, from the university; and their lesson is not simply that here, as elsewhere, sexism has damaged women and men, but that it has clouded our understanding. There has not been an equally extensive exploration of the question how racism has misguided our more abstract reflections; of how the absence of black voices has shaped our philosophical discourse . . . [I]t seems simply astonishing how little of the political philosophy of the philosophers explicitly acknowledges the distinctive and different significances of race and other kinds of collective identity as well as of gender to the questions that arise at the intersection of the state with morality.

—K. Anthony Appiah

From: *The Philosophical Forum: A Quarterly* V, xxiv, nos. 1–3 (Fall–Spring 1992–1993): 30–31.

We do not have the space here to go into all the various contributions of African-American thinkers over our country's history. But two African American thinkers from the 1960s have become extremely influential—**Martin Luther King Jr.** and **Malcolm X**—and so it may be helpful to devote our attention to them. The two men—who knew each other and both worked throughout their lives to enhance the position of blacks both in America and elsewhere in the world—held widely different political philosophies.

Martin Luther King Jr. advocated civil disobedience in the tradition of Gandhi and Henry David Thoreau. In other words, he sought to advance the position of African-Americans in this country through peaceful political protest. Such protest included breaking unjust laws and suffering the consequences of doing so, but never violence. King was also an integrationist, meaning that he believed that equality of the races required mixed neighborhoods, workplaces, and schools. His goal was full integration and the equal recognition of civil rights for black and white Americans, to be achieved through peaceful and ultimately "color-blind" means.

As Good as Anyone

My mother confronted the age-old problem of the Negro parent in America: how to explain discrimination and segregation to a small child. She taught me that I should feel "somebodiness" but that on the other hand I had to go out and face a system that stared me in the face every day saying you are "less than," you are "not equal to." She told me about slavery and how it ended with the Civil War. She tried to explain the divided system in the South—the segregated schools, restaurants, theaters, housing; the white and colored signs on drinking fountains, waiting rooms, lavatories—as a social condition rather than a natural order. She made clear that she opposed this system and that I should never allow it to make me feel inferior. Then she said the words that almost every Negro hears before he can yet understand the injustice that makes them necessary: "You are as good as anyone." At this time my mother had no idea that the little boy in her arms would years later be involved in a struggle against the system she was speaking of.

—Martin Luther King Jr.

From: *The Autobiography of Martin Luther King, Jr.* Ed. Clayborne Carson. New York: Warner Books, 2001.

Malcolm X, on the other hand, was generally taken to be a revolutionary, and he advocated Black Nationalism. Black Nationalism was a separatist movement that sought a unification of African-descended people all over the world into a separate society. Malcolm X is somewhat notorious for his claim that the interests of blacks throughout the world should be advanced "by any means necessary," meaning that violence was appropriate where peaceful means failed. And in general, Malcolm X believed that peaceful means had failed during the hundreds of years of white oppression of blacks. During much of his active life, Malcolm X was a Black Muslim, that is, a member of an American Islamic black separatist movement. The Islamic religion, the Black Muslims believed, lent itself particularly well to the project of worldwide unification for blacks. Although Malcolm X later qualified his strong views about violence and separatism, he defended them in much of his writing, and because he died young, he is largely remembered for them.

A Revolution of Self-Defense

No, since the federal government has shown that it isn't going to do anything about [the Klan] but talk, then it is your and my duty as men; as human beings, . . . to organize ourselves and let the government know that if they don't stop that Klan, we'll stop it ourselves. Then you'll see the government start doing something about it. But don't ever think that they're going to do it just on some kind of morality basis. No. So I don't believe in violence—that's why I want to stop it. And you can't stop it with love, . . . No! So, we only mean vigorous action in self-defense, and that vigorous action we feel we're justified in initiating by any means necessary.

Now, for saying something like that, the press calls us racist and people who are "violent in reverse." This is how they psycho you. They make you think that if you try to stop the Klan from lynching you, you're practicing violence in reverse. . . . Well, if a criminal comes around your house with his gun, brother, just because he's got a gun and he's robbing your house, and he's a robber, it doesn't make you a robber because you grab your gun and run him out. No, the man is using some tricky logic on you. . . . With skillful manipulating of the press they're able to make the victim look like the criminal and the criminal look like the victim.

—Malcolm X, Speech at the Afro-American Broadcasting Co.,
Detroit, 14 February 1965. *Malcolm X Speaks*. New York:
Grove Press, 1965. © Random House, Inc.

Although Malcolm X and Martin Luther King Jr. disagreed in their political orientations and analyses, they were both committed to pressing the cause of African-Americans. Both, however, made enemies, some of whom were not content to continue the conversation through words and symbolic actions. Malcolm X was assassinated in 1965, and Martin Luther King Jr. in 1968.

African Americans have sought to take the premise that all men are created equal as meaning what it says; but most whites in America in the latter 1960s, including many persons of good will, took equality to mean, roughly, some measure of improvement. Even now, white America does not seem organized (even psychologically) to close the gaps, but instead seems concerned only to make the situation less painful and obvious. It is worth asking what orientations and policies would really make a difference and which are geared, perhaps with window dressing, to retain the status quo.

Sexual Politics: The Rise of Feminist Philosophy
ᴖᴖ

*Remember all men would be tyrants if they could. If particular care
and attention is not paid to the ladies we are determined to foment
a rebellion, and will not hold ourselves bound by any laws in which
we have no voice or representation.*

—Abigail Adams, 1776

The exclusion of thinkers from the philosophical canon on the basis of race is paralleled by exclusion on the basis of gender. When we look at the list of major figures within the Western philosophical tradition, we should ask: Where are all the women? We know of female students in Plato's Academy and female thinkers in the Middle Ages, but why are they not part of the official canon of philosophy? The short answer, perhaps, is that most of them never got the opportunity to run their own schools, found it hard to have their ideas preserved in writing, and have been, for whatever reason, "written out" of the official history of the tradition.

According to recent critics, there has been an effort among philosophers and scholars to create and preserve an exclusively male, white, largely European Western intellectual tradition, which has marginalized or ignored the contributions of thinkers who were not male, white, and of European descent. Throughout the years of development of the current university curriculum in Europe and the United States, according to these critics of the university canon, the political interests of Europe—essentially a mixture of colonialism and industrialized capitalism—have influenced and distorted intellectual life throughout the world as well as in the university curriculum. They have argued that the traditional canon is propaganda for the industrialized world and its particular ideas of culture and philosophy.

Gendered Points of View

Would the world seem entirely different if it were pictured, felt, described, studied, and thought about from the point of view of women? A great deal looks altogether different when we notice the realities of class brought to our attention by Marx and others. Not only do economic activity, government, law, and foreign policies take on a very different appearance. "Knowledge" itself can be seen as quite a different enterprise when subject to the scrutiny of the sociology of knowledge. When connections are drawn between intellectual enterprise and class interests, social sciences claiming to be "value-free" can be seen to lend support to a capitalist status quo, and we can recognize how normative theories presented as impartial can be used to mystify reality rather than to contribute to needed change.

(continues)

Gendered Points of View (continued)

Gender is an even more pervasive and fundamental aspect of reality than class. If feminists can succeed not only in making visible but also in keeping within our awareness the aspects of "mankind" that have been so obscured and misrepresented by taking the "human" to be the masculine, virtually all existing thought may be turned on its head . . . a revolution is occurring that is as important as those that took place when the views of Copernicus, Darwin, and Freud changed so radically man's view of man. Some feminists think this latest revolution will be even more profound.

—Virginia Held, "Feminism and Epistemology," 1990

Women have been largely excluded from philosophical history. With only a few exceptions, they were long deprived of the chance to study, the opportunity to participate in philosophical discussions, and the venues for publishing their ideas. They and their ideas were not taken seriously, or they functioned, as the queen of Sweden functioned for René Descartes, as a good student who helped to sharpen *his* philosophy and provide an easy foil for *his* ideas. Because politics and inferior social status kept women out of philosophy, it is natural and understandable that feminist philosophy should first of all be social and political philosophy.

Nineteenth-Century Feminism

In 1851 English feminist **Harriet Taylor** (1807–1858) published *The Enfranchisement of Women*, in which she argued for the education, employment, and civic participation of women—for the sake of both men and women. Although many men and women assume that the submission of women is natural and beneficial, Taylor reasoned that their views do not recognize what is truly good for either men or women.

It is an acknowledged dictate of justice to make no degrading distinctions without necessity. In all things the presumption ought to be on the side of equality. A reason must be given why anything should be permitted to one person and interdicted to another. But when that which is interdicted includes nearly everything which those to whom it is permitted most prize, and to be deprived of which they feel to be most insulting; when not only political liberty but personal freedom of action is the prerogative of a caste; when even in the exercise of industry, almost all employments which task the higher faculties in an important field, which lead to distinction, riches, or

(continues)

Nineteenth-Century Feminism (continued)

even pecuniary independence, are fenced round as the exclusive domain of the predominant section . . . the miserable expediencies which are advanced as excuses for so grossly partial a dispensation, would not be sufficient, even if they were real, to render it other than a flagrant injustice. While, far from being expedient, we are firmly convinced that the division of mankind into two castes, one born to rule over the other, is in this case, as in all cases, an unqualified mischief; a source of perversion and demoralization, both to the favoured class and to those at whose expense they are favoured; producing none of the good which it is the custom to ascribe to it, and forming a bar, almost insuperable while it lasts, to any really vital improvement, either in the character or in the social condition of the human race.

Since the 1960s and even since the early suffragettes, feminists have sought first and foremost political equality for women. But political equality presupposes philosophical equality. A turning point in modern feminist political philosophy was **Simone de Beauvoir's** *The Second Sex*. Beauvoir's work was a groundbreaking analysis of the experience of women in Western society, in which a man is taken as the norm and a woman is viewed as "other." The book motivated women worldwide to reflect upon their social and political position and to work to improve it.

There have always been women. They are women in virtue of their anatomy and physiology. Throughout history they have always been subordinated to men, and hence, their dependency is not the result of a historical event or a social change. It was not something that occurred, . . . but it might seem that a natural condition is beyond the possibility of change. In truth, however, the nature of things is no more immutably given, once for all, than is historical reality. If woman seems to be the inessential which never becomes essential, it is because she herself fails to bring about this change. . . . [W]omen do not say "We," except at some congress of feminists or similar formal demonstration; men say "women," and women use the same word referring to themselves. They do not automatically assume a subjective attitude. . . . (Simone de Beauvoir, *The Second Sex*, 1949)

Following Beauvoir, **Kate Millett** claimed in her *Sexual Politics* that the political domination of women by men is evident in every institution, every economic relationship, every work of literature, every personal relationship, of our society, both currently and throughout history. Millett called this pervasive system of male domination "**patriarchy**," and gave analyses of how patriarchy was the norm in every arena of our lives.

A disinterested examination of the situation between the sexes now, and throughout history, is . . . a relationship of dominance and subordinance. What goes largely unexamined, often even unacknowledged (yet is institutionalized nonetheless) in our social order is the birthright priority whereby males rule females. Through this system a most ingenious form of "interior colonization" has been achieved. . . . Sexual domination obtains nevertheless as perhaps the most pervasive ideology of our culture and provides its most fundamental concept of power.

This is so because our society, like all other historical civilizations, is a patriarchy. The fact is evident at once if one recalls that the military, industry, technology, universities, science, political office, and finance—in short, every avenue of power within the society, including the coercive power of the police, is in male hands. (Kate Millett, *Sexual Politics*, 1970)

One of the most controversial arenas of the current debate has to do with the question of whether femininity and masculinity (as opposed to the physiological categories "male" and "female") arise from biology or upbringing, "nature or nurture." Many feminists hold that the categories of gender (that is, "feminine" and "masculine"), unlike the categories of sex ("male" and "female"), are created and defined by culture. They are not "natural," much less obligatory. Culture creates these categories and the social and political status that goes along with them, and culture can change those categories and their status. Beauvoir makes the point that gendered roles are culturally constructed when she announces, "One is not born a woman." Beauvoir is suggesting that to call someone "a woman" is not just to claim that she is anatomically female, but to project on her the various socially imposed roles and behaviors that serve as standards for judging women. (Philosophers such as Kwame Anthony Appiah make similar arguments about the category of race, contending that there are no biological "facts" that differentiate races; race is entirely culturally constructed.)

The Second Sex

French philosopher and novelist **Simone de Beauvoir** (1908–1986) left her position as teacher of philosophy when she published her first novel, but she did not abandon her interest. In 1949 she published *The Second Sex*, which is now considered to be one of the most important documents of feminism. Still controversial today, *The Second Sex* argues both that "woman" is a socially constructed category and that its meaning is derivative from the meaning of "man."

(continues)

> ## The Second Sex (continued)
>
> *If her functioning as a female is not enough to define woman, if we decline also to explain her through "the eternal feminine," and if nevertheless we admit, provisionally, that women do exist, then we must face the question: what is a woman?*
>
> *To state the question is, to me, to suggest, at once, a preliminary answer. The fact that I ask it is in itself significant. A man would never get the notion of writing a book on the peculiar situation of the human male. But if I wish to define myself, I must first of all say: "I am a woman"; on this truth must be based all further discussion. A man never begins be presenting himself as an individual of a certain sex; it goes without saying that he is a man.*
>
> *The terms masculine and feminine are used symmetrically only as a matter of form, as on legal papers. In actuality the relation of the two sexes is not quite like that of two electrical poles, for man represents both the positive and the neutral, as is indicated by the common use of man to designate human beings in general; whereas woman represents only the negative, defined by limiting criteria, without reciprocity. In the midst of an abstract discussion it is vexing to hear a man say: "You think thus and so because you are a woman"; but I know that my only defense is to reply: "And you think the contrary because you are a man," for it is understood that the fact of being a man is no peculiarity.*
>
> —Trans. H. M. Parshley (New York: Knopf, 1953), introduction.

Feminist philosopher **Sherry Ortner** has argued that the distinction between nature and culture is not itself a natural distinction but a distinction made in language and therefore within culture. She points out that "nature" has often been associated with women, while "culture" has been associated with men. Women are and have long been represented as "closer" to nature, as the bearers and caretakers of children, the cookers of food, the domesticators of households, while "culture"—the context of political power and distinctively human achievement—is mainly the domain of men. The nature-culture distinction itself—or at least what counts as "nature" and "culture"—should not be taken for granted, but instead should be recognized as a means by which women are deprived of power.

Other feminists, however, have celebrated the difference between feminine and masculine characteristics. Some have argued that the feminine virtues of nurturing and caring are far preferable and more conducive to a harmonious, peaceful civilization than are the abstract, more warrior-like virtues of masculine thinking. They do not deny the differences but instead insist that women should have more say in society—in part because women have something distinctive to say.

Mary Wollstonecraft (1759–1797), self-taught and a native of London, founded a school at Newington Green with her sister Eliza. She worked there as schoolteacher and headmistress and soon became convinced that the young women she and her sister taught had already been effectively enslaved by their social training in subordination to men. In *Thoughts on the Education of Daughters* (1787), Wollstonecraft proposed the deliberate extrapolation of Enlightenment ideals to include equal education for women.

In 1792 she published *A Vindication of the Rights of Woman*. In this landmark feminist work, Wollstonecraft argued that all human beings possess the faculty of reason and women must claim their equality by accepting its unemotional dictates. She rejected the notion that the natural condition of female existence *required* excessive concern for romantic love and desirability; these are, rather, the socially imposed means by which male domination gains a foothold.

In 1797 Wollstonecraft married radical activist and gothic fiction writer William Godwin. She died a few days after the birth of her daughter, Mary, who later married Percy Bysshe Shelley and wrote *Frankenstein*.

Women and the Body

The idea that women are more often represented as part of nature than men comes in part from the idea that women are more closely identified with their bodies. Culture is then defined as the domain of men. In earlier chapters, we studied the philosophical problem of mind and body. Ever since Plato, philosophers have found it important to distinguish the mind—as that with which we think and reason, from the body—as that with which we move and sense our surroundings and take up space in the world. It is also the body that is so easily injured, gets sick, disintegrates with age, and eventually dies, so it is not surprising that so many philosophers have tried to separate and protect the mind from similar calamities. In particular, seventeenth-century philosopher Descartes claimed that the mind was a separate substance from the body and that only the mind can be known for certain to exist. The body, according to Descartes, is a separate substance, known by way of inference.

In several recent articles and books, however, various feminist philosophers—notably **Susan Bordo** and **Genevieve Lloyd**—have taken philosophers such as Descartes and Plato to task on feminist grounds because, they claim, these thinkers dubiously associate the mind or reasoning faculty with masculinity and the body with femininity. In this way Descartes and Plato can be understood on one level to be justifying male authority over women. Not only in Descartes's metaphysics, but also in his theory of the passions, he puts mind or reason in authority over everything having to do with the body. This implicitly endorses the authority of men (the "specialists" in reason) over women (the "specialists" in bodily matters). Because Descartes and Plato are crucially important philosophers in the Western tradition, these feminists attribute some responsibility to them for the Western world's bias against women and the celebration of the supposedly more masculine virtues of pure thinking.

Aristotle, too, gives philosophical support to sexism, according to many feminist thinkers. In sexuality in particular, the roles of men and women seem to some extent to be biologically defined. But the obvious differences between men and women and their biological roles, particularly in the act of procreation, can be understood in various ways. In his *Generation of Animals,* Aristotle (fourth century BCE) argued:

> For there must needs be that which generates and that from which it generates . . . and in those animals that have these powers separate in two sexes the body and nature of the active and the passive sex must also differ. If, then, the male stands for the effective and active; and the female, considered as female, for the passive, it follows that what the female would contribute to the semen of the male would not be semen, but material for the semen to work upon.

Thus, Aristotle suggests that by nature women are more passive and men more potent, that the essence of reproduction comes from the male while the female provides mere matter. His analysis makes the woman's contribution akin to a blob of clay. It has the potential to become a statue, but it is inert matter that must be acted upon by the sculptor. In the creation of a human being the activity that brings about the change is the male contribution, according to Aristotle. Aristotle seems to extend to ethics as well his association of men and women, respectively, with activity and passivity, for he implies that the male is more fully able to actualize his potential as a human being than is the female.

This association of masculinity with action and femininity with passivity did not end with Aristotle. It is evident in many doctrines of the Christian church and in many religions. We find these associations also in Sigmund Freud's theories about men and women, and in many other theories of human nature, for example, in the ancient Chinese Confucian tradition. (They occur in Daoism, too, where the female is associated with passivity, although in that tradition the image of "female" passivity is held up as an ideal for everyone.) Many feminists have taken issue with these tendencies—and in philosophy Aristotle comes under particular scrutiny. Because Aristotle's worldview set the tone for both Christian theology and modern metaphysics, it must be considered a profound problem if he held a mistaken belief about women and femininity. There, as elsewhere, his views held sway for nearly 2,000 years, and many of them persist today.

Aristotle Challenged

So it is naturally with the male and the female; the one is superior, the other inferior; the one governs, the other is governed; and the same rule must necessarily hold good with respect to all mankind.

—Aristotle, *Politics*

The fact that the adult American Negro female emerges a formidable character is often met with amazement, distaste, and even belligerence. It is seldom accepted as an inevitable outcome of the struggle won by survivors, and deserves respect if not enthusiastic acceptance.

—Maya Angelou, *I Know Why the Caged Bird Sings*, 1969

Plato: Patriarch or Early Feminist?

Although Aristotle's views of women and femininity were fairly clear, those of his teacher Plato are much disputed among feminists and among philosophers in general. In some ways, Plato seems to have been radically egalitarian for his time, particularly regarding women. In *The Republic,* for instance, Plato has Socrates argue for the complete equality of women in the ideal city. The important class of rulers ought to be open, argues Socrates, to women as well to men, and promising girls should be educated accordingly. And he further claims that any two people who do the same job, whatever their sex, ought to be educated, brought up, and treated in the same way. In Plato's *Republic,* Socrates (fourth century BCE) argues:

> There is therefore no pursuit connected with city management which belongs to a woman because she is a woman, or to a man because he is a man, but various natures are scattered in the same way among both kinds of persons. Woman by nature shares all pursuits . . . All things . . . should be done in common.

These and similar claims in Plato's dialogues have led some feminists to the conclusion that Plato was sympathetic to their cause. One noted scholar of ancient philosophy, **Martha Nussbaum,** for instance, calls Plato "the first feminist."

Other feminists, such as **Elizabeth V. Spelman,** however, have taken these claims of Plato's to be only minor gestures in an otherwise typically "masculinist" Platonic philosophy. Plato's repeated claim, for instance, that reason ought to rule over the passions in the healthy soul indicates to many Plato's accession to the gender-imposed opposition between mind and body. This is reinforced by his tendency to identify women, along with slaves and animals, as beings in whom reason does not rule the soul. Because reason, as these feminists see it, is arrogantly associated with masculinity and passion with femininity, Plato's concept of the harmonious soul is basically that of a male soul.

The Greek poet **Sappho**, priestess of a feminine love cult that flourished around 590 BCE on the island of Lesbos, celebrated the love of women for other women. Her poetry, characterized by passion and simplicity, greatly influenced Catullus, Ovid, and Swinburne.

Sappho presents a very different picture of love from that of Plato and in a very different style. It is not hard to imagine that it was poets such as Sappho that Plato may have had in mind when he suggested banning them and their work from Athens.

Sappho's verse survives in papyrus fragments and in the quotations by later critics. Some six hundred years later, the geographer Strabo would write, "Sappho was something to be wondered at. Never within human memory has there been a woman to compare with her as a poet."

Feminist Epistemology and Feminist Science

Some feminists are also asking whether the very notion of knowledge, as it has traditionally been understood, is sex or gender based and whether women and men might view the world in fundamentally different ways. In the same vein as Gilligan, Beauvoir, and Millett, some feminist thinkers have claimed that scientific methodology and standards for knowledge have employed masculine models throughout their Western history. Some of them believe that a feminist model of scientific method—or at least the inclusion of women's observations—would yield a very different body of scientific knowledge as well.

Evelyn Fox Keller argues in her "Feminism and Science":

To see the emphasis on power and control so prevalent in the rhetoric of Western science as a projection of a specifically male consciousness requires no great leap of the imagination. Indeed, that perception has become a commonplace. Above all, it is invited by the rhetoric that conjoins the domination of nature with the insistent image of nature as female, nowhere more familiar than in the writings of Francis Bacon. For Bacon, knowledge and power are one, and the promise of science is expressed as "leading you to nature with all her children to bind her to your service and make her your slave . . ."

One might imagine how this could be so. We often **anthropomorphize** (that is, personify, or understand, in overly human terms) scientific concepts in order to understand them. You may have had a chemistry teacher who described a molecule as "seeking" another hydrogen atom, for example. But sometimes such anthropomorphisms make their way into scientific hypotheses. For example, a biologist talks about dominant and recessive genes, and these descriptions have been made to carry the same gender connotations of "activity" and "passivity" that some feminists have opposed in more general Aristotelian discussions of reproduction. There are also, of course, "male" and "female" fittings in electrical circuits, and various other oppositions used in modern science that lend themselves to feminist interpretations. One of the strongest feminist arguments, however, is that the topics that become the agenda in the various sciences can reflect a male bias. Feminists have pointed, in particular, to the relative neglect of women's health in medical research, an expression of the tendency to take the male to be the norm for the species. The concerns of serious science, particularly in medicine and the social sciences, are predominantly men's concerns.

Feminist Philosophy of Language

Keller's mention of the impact of rhetoric and vocabulary on the way we think recalls our earlier discussion of the **Sapir-Whorf hypothesis**, which claims that the patterns of one's native language structures the way one understands the world. Feminists have sometimes criticized linguistic practices on the ground that they support a sexist view of reality. For example, the allegedly gender-neutral use of male pronouns (such as the use of *he* to refer back to "the student," even though the student may be female), the use of terms like *chairman* or *policeman* to refer to individuals of both sexes, and the use of *man* to refer to humankind at large strike them as further instances in which the male case is presented as the norm. In response to the counterargument that English speakers recognize that such terms refer as much to women as to men, these critics point out that most people visualize a male when these terms are used and are at least momentarily startled when "he" or "the chairman" turns out to be female. In practice, these terms are not really gender neutral.

One solution to this problem is to avoid such dubiously "gender-neutral" usage, the strategy we have applied to this book. But this approach can be difficult. What if one wants to refer back to the individual student? One can, of course, say "he or she," but if one repeatedly refers with such pronouns, statements can become painfully convoluted. A common solution is to refer with a plural pronoun (for example, *they* and *their*) even when the referent is singular (for example, "the student"), but this is ungrammatical. Another possibility is to alternate between using *he* and *she* in examples.

Fortunately for feminists, language evolves. American English usage has started to reflect more sensitivity toward inclusion. Terms like *chair* have replaced *chairman* in many contexts, and *humankind* is beginning to sound natural, even if at first it seemed an odd substitution for *mankind*. Perhaps the most effective way to make language less sexist, however, is to change the reality that it is used to track. If women more routinely appear in roles of power and authority, language will need to reflect this.

Feminist epistemologists and feminist philosophers of science and language all draw attention to the ways in which the perspectives of those in the politically dominant majority become enshrined in our beliefs about the world. In this, they join African-American philosophers and other thinkers concerned about the ways that racism has narrowed our outlooks. The analyses of all these philosophers can help correct injustices of the past and present by undermining the self-serving theories that the powerful have used to support their position of privilege. More positively, they can enrich all our lives by helping us to make our society more just, something that can only happen if we recognize and acknowledge the women and members of minority groups among our fellow citizens.

Closing Questions

1. What does it mean to say that "might makes right"? In your opinion, what makes a government legitimate?

2. In your opinion, what is the single most important feature of justice? Is it serving the needs of the worst off? Ensuring that people are paid fairly for what they do? Ensuring that people may keep what they earn? Protecting people's rights? Making sure that everyone is treated equally?

3. Before the legal abolition of slavery, was it morally legitimate to own slaves? Why or why not?

4. What do you think human beings were like before the formation of societies as we know them? What would we be like if we were raised (and somehow survived) outside of any social or societal context? Do you think that such questions are relevant?

5. If you and several hundred other people were about to form a new society (let's say, as you plunged into space to populate a newly discovered planet), what principles of justice would you propose to your peers? What sort of principles (if any) do you think would gain general agreement? (Examples: "Finders keepers, losers weepers." "Everyone shares what they've got equally with others." "No one should be punished under any circumstances." "Anyone who breaks even the smallest law is exiled to space.")

6. If an already-rich person makes another fortune on a lucky stock market investment, does he or she have the right (entitlement) to the entire gain—or should this be subject to taxation? What does your answer suggest about your sense of justice?

7. Would it be fair to hire or fire a female TV news anchor on the basis of her age or appearance? Why or why not?

8. Is it just that people should receive better schooling, better health care, and better legal aid only because they have more money? If you think it is just, explain why; if you think it is unjust, say what you think should be done to remedy the situation.

9. In what sense is it fair and in what sense is it not fair to treat everyone equally—for example, in the distribution of salaries and payment for services? Should someone who works hard make more than someone who does not? Why do we believe that hard work should be rewarded? Should a twenty-year employee make no more than a novice? Why should "time on the job" make a difference? Should the owner of a company keep no more in profits than she pays her employees? Why should ownership make a difference? Should a person who desperately needs a good deal of money for a lifesaving heart operation be given more than another person who is in perfect health and has no particular need for the money? Do we in fact consider such need an important measure of "just desert"? Finally, should a person make more because he or she is particularly talented or skilled? After all, he or she was lucky enough to be born with talent or into a family where talent could be cultivated. So why should we treat people unequally just because of luck?

10. Do you think that African-Americans have made significant progress in their struggle for equality? Do you think that greater integration could be effective in bettering race relations in this country? Do you think that voluntary segregation could be as effective? Why or why not?

11. Do you think that patriarchy (rule by men) and racism are institutionalized in Western philosophy and culture? What reasons would you give in defense of your vies?

12. Do you agree that the various binary oppositions in our language are always or basically gender related? Why do you think so, or not?

Suggested Readings

For a general selection of views on social philosophy, see Joel Feinberg, *Social Philosophy* (Prentice-Hall, 1973). The first text for any study of justice and society is Plato's *Republic*, trans. G. M. A. Grube (Hackett, 1974). Two classic statements of the social contract are Thomas Hobbes, *Leviathan* (Hafner, 1926), and Jean-Jacques Rousseau, *Discourse on the Origins of Inequality* and *The Social Contract* (Hackett, 1981). For a selection of modern theorists on justice, see James P. Sterba, *Justice: Alternative Political Perspectives* (Wadsworth, 1979). For a complete (and somewhat overwhelming) look at the leading modern theory today, see John Rawls, *A Theory of Justice* (Harvard University Press, 1971). A very different sort of theory is defended in Robert Nozick, *Anarchy, State and Utopia* (Basic Books, 1974). For a fascinating discussion of the nature of the disagreement between Rawls and Nozick, see Alasdair MacIntyre, *After Virtue* (University of Notre Dame Press, 1981), esp. ch. 17; see also Robert C. Solomon, *A Passion for Justice* (Addison-Wesley, 1990). An excellent recent book on justice is Amartya Sen, *The Idea of Justice* (Harvard University Press, 2009). Adam Smith's analysis of capitalism is presented in his *The Wealth of Nations* (Modern Library, 1965). A very different picture of the ideal social arrangements can be found in the *Tao Te Ching*. One translation of this work, from which we quote in this chapter, is Lao Tzu, *Tao Te Ching*, trans. D. C. Lau (Penguin, 1963). The debate between Mozi and Mencius can be tracked in *Basic Writings of Mo Tzu, Hsün Tzu, and Han Fei Tzu*, trans. Burton Watson (Columbia University Press, 1967); and *Mencius*, trans. D. C. Lau (Penguin, 2005). For various views about the morality of patriotism, see Igor Primoratz, ed., *Patriotism* (Humanity Books, 2002). You can read more about just war theory in David Fisher, *Morality and War: Can War Be Just in the Twenty-First Century* (Oxford University Press, 2011). Sunzi's theories of warfare can be found in Sun Tzu, *The Art of Warfare*, trans. Roger T. Ames (Ballantine Books, 1993). For theories of cosmopolitanism see Kwame Anthony Appiah, *Cosmopolitanism: Ethics in a World of Strangers* (W. W. Norton, 2006), and Gillian Brock and Harry Brighouse, *The Political Philosophy of Cosmopolitanism* (Cambridge University Press, 2005). An outstanding defense of "rights" in contemporary thinking about justice is Ronald Dworkin, *Taking Rights Seriously* (Harvard University Press, 1977). On equality, see Bernard Williams, "The Idea of Equality" in *Problems of the Self* (Cambridge University Press, 1973), and Thomas Nagel, "Equality" in *Mortal Questions* (New York: Cambridge University Press, 1979). A selection of classic and contemporary readings on justice is Robert C. Solomon and Michael Murphy, eds., *What Is Justice?*, 2nd ed. (Oxford University Press, 2000).

Several of Martin Luther King Jr.'s most famous and influential speeches are collected in *Testament of Hope* (Harper & Row, 1986). *The Autobiography of Malcolm X* (with Alex Haley) has been republished (Ballantine, 1987), with an excellent film version by Spike Lee (1992). Some of Malcolm X's speeches are collected in *Malcolm X Speaks*, ed. George Breitman (Pathfinder, 1965). An excellent commentary on race in America is Cornell West, *Race Matters*, rev. ed. (Beacon, 2001). For a survey of African-American philosophy, see Tommy L. Lott and John P. Pittman, *A Companion to African-American Philosophy* (Blackwell, 2003). See also the provocative works of Patricia Williams, *The Alchemy of Race and Rights* (Harvard University Press, 1992) and *Seeing a Color-blind Future: The Paradox of Race* (Noonday Press, 1998).

For a historical introduction to feminism, see Janet McCracken, *A Historical Anthology* (Wadsworth, 1997). For an excellent and very readable book on feminism, see Linda Nicholson, *Feminism/Postmodernism* (Routledge, 1990); see also Linda Martin Alcoff and Eva Feder Kittay, eds., *A Companion to Feminist Philosophy*, 2nd ed. (Blackwell, 2006). Carol Gilligan's *In a Different Voice* (Harvard University Press, 1982) is now the established statement of the new gender-specific moral theory, but for a survey of feminist ethical views, see Hilde Lindemann, *An Invitation to Feminist Ethics* (McGraw-Hill, 2005). On feminist epistemology and philosophy of science, see Linda Martin Alcoff and Elizabeth Potter, eds., *Feminist Epistemologies* (Routledge, 1993), and Sandra Harding, *Whose Science? Whose Knowledge?* (Cornell University Press, 1991). The entirety of Virginia Held's "Feminism and Epistemology" is available in *Philosophy and Public Affairs* 14 (1985): 296–307. Evelyn Fox Keller's, "Feminism and Science," appears in *Signs* 7 (1982): 589–602. For considerations of perspectives on women in traditional Western philosophy, see Genevieve Lloyd, *Feminism and the History of Philosophy* (Oxford University Press, 2001), and Susan Bordo, *The Flight to Objectivity* (State University of New York Press, 1987). Maya Angelou's account of her experience as a black women in America appears in *I Know Why the Caged Bird Sings* (Random House, 1969).

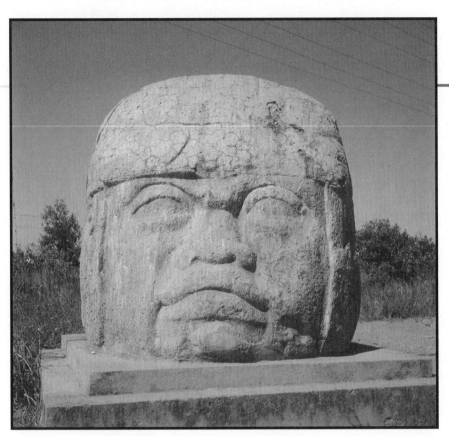

Colossal Head. Olmec culture. © Scala/Art Resource, NY.

10
Non-Western Philosophy

In dark Africa, people always dance because they feel. "To dance is to discover and to re-create, to identify oneself with the forces of life." It is, at any rate, the highest form of knowledge. The reason of classical Europe is analytic through utilization, the reason of the African Negro, intuitive through participation.

—Léopold Sédar Senghor, "On Negrohood"

[I]t doesn't mean that we're anti-white, but it does mean that we're anti-exploitation, we're anti-degradation, we're anti-oppression. And if the white man doesn't want us to be anti-him, let him stop oppressing and exploiting and degrading us. . . .

—Malcolm X, 1964

Remember all men would be tyrants if they could. If particular care and attention is not paid to the ladies we are determined to foment a rebellion, and will not hold ourselves bound by any laws in which we have no voice or representation.

—Abigail Adams, 1776

꩜

Opening Questions

1. Do you believe that men and women think differently? How do you know? If so, to what do you attribute the difference—nature, education, or choice?

2. What makes one culture different from another? How is it possible to translate a practice or a belief from one culture into another? Do you believe that all cultures could understand one another, if only they learned to "speak the same language"?

Beyond the Western Tradition
꩜

As we observed in the previous chapter, most of the philosophers mentioned throughout this book have something in common: they are white and male. (Saint Augustine and Confucius are among the few exceptions, and Augustine's

African origins are rarely explored in most philosophical discussions.) They also share a philosophical tradition that begins in the world of ancient Greece and develops through Judeo-Christian theology and the rise of science in Europe. In this book so far, although we have primarily focused on philosophical problems rather than figures as such, we have mainly traced this tradition and stayed within its bounds. But there is much more to philosophy and the story of human thought.

The great ideas of Western philosophy are found in a well-preserved written, argumentative, and more or less scientific, or at any rate literalist tradition—that is, one that demands literal truth in philosophy and does not rest content with metaphor or allegory. Philosophers who did not make their way into print (or who were not lucky enough to have Plato as a student or Aristotle as an admiring commentator) disappeared from the tradition. Thinkers who did not engage in active argument with the tradition were often ignored. (Thus, the mystical and esoteric tradition in the West is often confined to footnotes.) And nonliteral, nonscientific explanations of life and the universe through myth, heroic legends, and nonmonotheistic religions were simply dismissed as, at best, primitive or prephilosophical. The result is the rather well defined list of problems and sequence of philosophers that we have (mainly) discussed in this book. It is an admirable and noble tradition, but it is not the only one.

India and southern Asia have an ancient philosophical tradition—or actually, several traditions—dating back at least as far as the Western tradition, and there is a philosophical tradition in China that also stretches back thousands of years. Moreover, there is persuasive evidence that there were thriving schools of philosophy in the Americas and in North Africa before the arrival of the Europeans. Living oral traditions in Africa and many South Pacific islands have been passed down from generation to generation, and virtually every civilization we have ever heard of has some articulated conception of its origins and its place in the universe. It is therefore important that we not be so arrogant or provincial as to define "philosophy" to include only the ideas of ancient Greece and medieval and modern Europe.

A fuller view of philosophy should take into account the philosophical perspectives of those outside the West. In this chapter, we cannot hope to become more than casually acquainted with the various philosophical traditions of the world. But what we can do is to become aware of the peculiarities and limitations of our own ways of thinking and, especially, see how that thinking has been shaped and perhaps even distorted by the particular features of our tradition. Throughout the chapter, we will take a peek at authors and perspectives not usually included in standard Western philosophy courses.

In some instances, we may discover familiarities and contributions that we may not have expected—for example, some similarities between Confucian ethics in China and Aristotelian ethics in ancient Greece. We may recognize the enormous interaction of European Christian thinkers with medieval Arabic, Jewish, and Persian philosophers, many of whom interpreted and kept ancient Greek and Roman philosophies alive during that long period during which they were denounced as pagan by the very Western tradition that would later claim them as exclusively its own. In many instances, however, what we will notice are the enormous differences between our own thinking and the thoughts of others. Chinese philosophy, for example, is largely concerned with analogies and analogical thinking, what we would call metaphorical comparisons, rather than a logic of evidence and inference as such. The method of using stories to make philosophical points is a staple of Chinese philosophy, while Western philosophy, at least recently, shuns "anecdotal evidence" in favor of a more scientific model for ascertaining the nature of reality.

We will begin our brief tour of philosophy outside the West by considering some of the challenges involved in attempting to broaden our philosophical horizons. After noting the close connections between religious and philosophical traditions in most cultures, we will proceed to survey some of the important themes and issues in several traditions: native American philosophy, African philosophy, Latin American philosophy, Middle Eastern philosophy, South Asian philosophy, and East Asian philosophy.

The Challenges of Broadening Our Horizons

It would seem, perhaps, as if all that would be necessary to revise and expand the canon of philosophy would be to assign more books in our classes and extend our reading lists—with books by African-Americans, third-world philosophers, Native Americans, women, and other neglected philosophers. We could add some Indian philosophy, some Chinese philosophy, some Arabic or ancient Egyptian philosophy, and that, of course, is exactly what many of the current philosophical reformers are doing. But the project of inserting non-Western philosophy into the curriculum is more challenging than it may initially appear. Many of the texts that defined entire traditions are inaccessible because war and disease wiped out the entire culture, because the texts themselves were destroyed (as was the case in Mesoamerica), or because there never were any written texts, only oral traditions that have sometimes been grotesquely distorted or have disappeared (the situation of much traditional African philosophy).

Some have also alleged that the influence of the mainstream Western tradition has been so great that it has pervaded or transformed every other tradition that we might try to read, with the result that an "authentic" voice from another tradition is impossible to find. Some advocates of an African philosophy, for example, rightly complain that every attempt at such philosophy is already contaminated by the harsh history of colonialism and slavery, and that an authentic African perspective is no longer available to us.

A very different kind of problem is presented to us by Chinese philosophy. China has energetically protected its own traditions, sometimes even sealing itself off from the West, precisely in order to avoid that sort of compromise and contamination that has destroyed the original cultures and ideas in other parts of the world. But the Chinese have thus remained so distinctive that, even if we read the Chinese texts, we have great difficulty entering into the context within which those texts are comprehensible. Furthermore, the language is so different that it frustrates any attempt at mere translation. Chinese is wonderfully ambiguous, a feature of the language beloved and admired by Chinese scholars and philosophers but frowned on by many Western thinkers and frustrating to Western translators. In a sense, therefore, the texts are available to us and can be easily added to any reading list, but this does not mean that we will understand them or the world of which they are such an important part.

One of the most important and challenging projects for today's philosophers and philosophy students is to expand the number of contexts in which they feel comfortable and familiar. But it has also become more important to understand one's own texts and traditions in a different way, to understand the relation between a text—even in mathematics, epistemology, or religious philosophy—and its social and cultural context, and perhaps also the social and political position of its author and its initial readers. Western philosophers of race and feminist philosophers have emphasized the importance of recognizing the role of culture—often sexist and racist culture—in shaping our tradition's philosophical formulations.

As we have seen, much of philosophy consists of a kind of self-reflection, an attempt to understand oneself and one's place in the world. But it may do one little good—and perhaps a great deal of harm—to be forced to understand oneself in *another culture's* categories. As we noted in the last chapter, some female philosophers object that they have been forced to think of themselves in philosophy in male terms and therefore as inferior or inadequate men (literally Aristotle's conception of women). Third world philosophers similarly object that they have been forced to view themselves philosophically in Western terms and therefore as philosophically naive, primitive, or merely as developing societies. We should endeavor in our efforts to gain awareness of other philosophical traditions not to impose our categories on them. Instead, we should try as far as possible to understand their philosophical positions in light of their starting points and concerns, which may differ from ours, even while recognizing that our own standpoint will inevitably affect our interpretations.

Other Cultures, Other Philosophies

It is no easy task to understand the philosophy of another culture. If some of the concepts of Western philosophy seem a bit strange to the average American student, at least the ways of thought and thinking of which they are a part are quite familiar. The examples (usually) strike home. The questions sufficiently resemble those with which we have grown up to make sense, even if they sometimes seem extreme or strange. (For example, "Is my mind or soul distinct and separable from my body?" or "How can God allow evil in the world?") But to understand another culture's philosophy in any depth, we would really have to submerge ourselves in that culture as well. Philosophy is never a completely detached, timeless, or placeless set of ideas. It always has its roots in the people who ask the questions and seek the answers. The styles as well as the subjects of philosophy vary from society to society, and although we can be confident of always finding some familiar similarities—after all, we are all human beings and face some of the same basic problems in life—we will always be struck and sometimes stopped by the differences.

Just as much of Western philosophy gets its background and impetus from our religious traditions, so the source of culturally diverse philosophies is often found in different religious traditions. In India, for example, philosophy is much more difficult to distinguish from religious thought than it is in the modern, more secular traditions of the West. In many cultures, in Africa and China and many islands of the South Pacific and Southeast Asia, for example, religion is itself much less abstract, much more human than it has seemed in philosophical discussions in the modern West. Not only are its deities anthropocentric (a charge that can be made regarding many understandings of the Judeo-Christian God). A most important ingredient in the religion and philosophy of these regions is one that plays a very small role at best in Judaism, Islam, and Christianity, namely, the notion of the **ancestor.**

In many cultures, one's ancestors are considered, with varying degrees of literalness, to still be present and influential in ongoing life. In traditional African cultures, for example, ancestors form an essential part of every community. "The family" refers not only to living members, but also to deceased ones. This is true in the traditional Mexican understanding of the family as well. In China, tremendous emphasis is placed on the ancestral family and the community. While the ancestors are revered, less emphasis (if any) is placed on a godhead. Confucius and the Buddha, the founders of two of the great religions of the world, are not deified in the way that Jesus is viewed in Christianity. Just as some of the great religious traditions are not, in the Western sense, theistic, some of the great philosophies of the world begin with a very different set of concepts than those that have defined Western philosophy since Plato and before.

Clash of Cultures

From time to time I began to feel an awkwardness arising from the difference between my ways of thinking and feeling and those of my hosts (that is Americans). For example, not long after my arrival in America I visited the house of someone to whom I have been introduced by a Japanese acquaintance, and was talking to him when he asked me, "Are you hungry? We have some ice cream if you'd like it." As I remember, I was rather hungry, but finding myself asked point-blank if I was hungry by someone whom I was visiting for the first time, I could not bring myself to admit it, and ended by denying the suggestion. I probably cherished a mild hope that he would press me again; but my host, disappointingly, said "I see" with no further ado, leaving me regretting that I had not replied more honestly. And I found myself thinking that a Japanese would almost never ask a stranger unceremoniously if he was hungry, but would produce something to give him without asking.

—Takeo Doi, Japanese psychiatrist
and philosopher (1920–)

In what follows, we present a brief introduction to the various famous and influential philosophical traditions from some of the world's great cultures. But, before we begin, consider the box "Clash of Cultures," a statement by the well-known Japanese philosopher-psychiatrist Takeo Doi, who finds himself puzzled by one of the most ordinary gestures in American life. Similarly, we should find ourselves feeling somewhat out of place in our initial exploration of other philosophical traditions.

Native American Philosophy

In much of North America and in Africa, a major problem was that cultures had oral rather than written traditions (as did Greece, before the pre-Socratic philosophers we have discussed). But this meant that when the cultures died out or were overwhelmed by colonial conquerors, their history and philosophy usually died with them. Consequently, we do not know how long civilizations existed in Africa or the Americas or when or how they developed. We do not know the age of the abandoned ancient cities of the central African rain forest or how long the Navaho, the Hopi, the Ojibwa, the Apache, the Seminoles, the Iroquois, and hundreds of other Native American tribes lived in the northern Americas. Archaeological evidence shows that North America was populated thousands of years ago, and it is quite clear that Africa was populated top to bottom tens of thousands of years ago. The fact that indigenous cultures in these places seem to lack a history and philosophy simply reflects the lack of written records. What we do know and are learning, however tentatively, about these indigenous cultures is, nevertheless, rich and fascinating. We can only indicate our growing awareness with a few general points here.

Native American tribal societies, despite their differences, typically adopted a philosophical perspective that we in the West are just now beginning to appreciate. On this view, human beings have not been placed here on earth to "have dominion" over all other creatures and things, as promised in Genesis and reiterated by English philosopher Frances Bacon (1561–1626). We are a part of the earth, dependent on it, and it is dependent on us. We have ecological responsibilities, and the world around us, "nature," is not just a resource or a source of aesthetic fascination.

Instead, we have moral responsibilities to the earth and to other creatures. Native American tribes typically consider the natural world as a manifestation of "the Great Spirit," although the Great Spirit is not understood anthropomorphically. (Anthropomorphic gods do appear in mythological accounts, but these are also manifestations of the Great Spirit.) Human beings should treat the earth with reverence, which involves caring for and respecting it. We are caretakers of the earth, but we do not own it. Accordingly, on this view, we should not treat land as private property.

Animals, too, have moral dignity and should be treated, in effect, as persons. The hunting tribes among Native Americans acknowledged the debt that they had to the creatures that provided their food. In their view, killing other creatures is not a right but a necessity that should provoke gratitude and reverence. Saying prayers and thanking one's quarry may strike most supermarket shoppers as a bit odd, but the consciousness of the fact that another creature has been killed for one's benefit might better be seen as a fundamentally humane gesture. The act of prayer in thanksgiving reflects a feature common to most Native American traditions—the tendency to see everyday life as sacred, as part of a great spiritual circle.

The Circle of Nature

You know, it always makes me laugh when I hear young white kids speak of some people as "squares" or "straights"—old people, hardened in their ways, in their minds, in their hearts. They don't even have to be old. You can be an "old square" at eighteen. Anyway, calling these people "squares"— an Indian could have thought it up. To our way of thinking, the Indians' symbol is the circle, the hoop. Nature wants things to be round. The bodies of human beings and animals have no corners. With us the circle stands for the togetherness of people who sit with one another around the campfire, relatives and friends united in peace while the pipe passes from hand to hand. The camp in which every tipi had its place was also a ring. The tipi was a ring in which people sat in a circle and all the families in the village were in turn circles within a larger circle, part of the larger hoop which was the seven campfires of the Sioux, representing one nation. The nation was only a part of the universe, in itself circular and made of the earth, which is round, of the sun, which is round, of the stars, which are round. The moon, the horizon, the rainbow—circles within circles within circles, with no beginning and no end.

To us this is beautiful and fitting, symbol and reality at the same time, expressing the harmony of life and nature. Our circle is timeless, flowing; it is new life emerging from death—life winning out over death.

The white man's symbol is the square. Square is his house, his office buildings with walls that separate people from one another. Square is the door which keeps strangers out, the dollar bill, the jail. Square are the white man's gadgets—boxes, boxes, boxes and more boxes—TV sets, radios, washing machines, computers, cars. These all have corners and sharp edges—points in time, white man's time, with appointments, time clocks and rush hours—that's what the corners mean to me. You become a prisoner inside all these boxes.

More and more young white people want to stop being "straight" and "square" and try to become round, join our circle. That is good . . .

—John (Fire) Lame Deer and Richard Erdoes. *Lame Deer: Seeker of Visions.* New York: Pocket Books, 1976

African Philosophy

Africa contains hundreds of different cultures, of course—indeed, hundreds of different languages. Nevertheless, a good deal of precolonial African philosophy can be characterized by means of the twin notions of *tribalism* and a special sense of *identity with nature* (concepts that apply to Native American societies as well).

Tribalism establishes an individual's identity and significance as a person only in the context of his or her family and community. This idea may sound odd to those in the contemporary West who have relinquished such familial and **communitarian** sensibilities in favor of a radical individualism. But for those who live such a communitarian philosophy (and this would include the Confucian cultures of Asia as well as the many tribal societies of the Americas and the South Pacific), an isolated individual lacking the concrete presence and intangible ties of kinship would be understood as hopelessly lost or effectively dead.

We reject the power-based society of the Westerner that seems to be ever concerned with perfecting their technological know-how while losing out on their spiritual dimension. We believe that in the long run the special contribution to the world by Africa will be in the field of human relationships. The great powers of the world may have done wonders in giving the world an industrial and military look, but the great gift still has to come from Africa—giving the world a more human face.

—Steve Biko. "Some African Cultural Concepts."
The African Philosophy Reader. Eds. P. H. Coetzee and
A. P. J. Roux. New York: Routledge, 1998

Traditional African tribes tend to see personhood as something acquired over time, by means of becoming a part of one's community. To become a full-fledged person is an achievement. Birth and death do not mark the person's beginning and end. A newly born baby is not yet a full person, whereas a deceased person who lives in the memory of his or her descendents is a person still, despite physical death. Initiation rites are crucial to achieving full membership in most tribal communities and thus becoming a full person. Similarly, throughout a person's life span, rites and ceremonies keep the individual's life in rhythm with that of the community.

The Western conception of an individual, atomic soul for each person is alien to the thinking of most traditional Africans. In some tribes, such as the Yoruba (now mostly in Nigeria) and the Lugbara (now mostly in Uganda), the communal basis for personhood is reflected in a conception of the human being as composed of multiple spiritual elements, all of which are essential to the person's life. So far are the Yoruba from believing in an isolated individual soul that they believe that ancestors' souls can return in their descendants (sometimes even their grandchildren). In light of this sense of identity, members of African tribes typically emphasize the worship of ancestors, who are considered living inhabitants of the spirit world, capable of assisting their descendents.

African tribal societies (and many Native American ones as well) also often embraced **animism**, the belief that nature embodies numerous vital forces, sometimes understood as souls, that manifest ancestors who are no longer individually remembered. Nature, for most traditional Africans, is full of living forces. Spirits dwell throughout nature. Human beings can interact with them to some extent, utilizing these spirits' powers or driving them elsewhere. The African conviction that human beings are intimately connected to nature is part and parcel of the traditional belief that nature is essentially spiritual.

In recent decades many African thinkers have reconsidered their relationship to the philosophical tradition of Europe, which tended to colonize their philosophies along with their political and economic lives. Some have attempted to apply philosophical thought to the unique problems of African societies in the wake of colonialism. They have sometimes appealed to traditional ideas and values as resources for reconstituting societies that had been undermined or torn apart by colonialism. In this turn to tradition for resources to revive societies that had been damaged, they bear some resemblance to Confucius.

Other African thinkers have asked whether there is an authentic African philosophy and how philosophy in Africa should be approached. Both culturalist and universalist positions are represented among African philosophers. **Culturalists**, claim that a philosophy always arises in a concrete social context to deal with that context's own specific problems, while **universalists**, contend that philosophy involves the same concerns and the same methods wherever it is practiced. Culturalists would include thinkers such as Léopold Sédar Senghor (1906–2001), who sought to celebrate African difference from Europe. Senghor was one of the initiators of the "Negrohood" or "negritude" movement, which claimed that black Africans and their descendents had a spiritual unity, based on their relating to the world primarily through participation and emotion, in contrast with the European dependence on disinterested thought. Although Senghor's views did encourage self-affirmation on the part of Africans, his views were criticized for basing his cultural analyses on race, and for reinforcing the stereotypical view that Africans are less rational than Europeans. Other African thinkers have used different grounds for defending pan-Africanism, the belief in African solidarity and commonality. What Africans have in common, they claim, is a consequence of a shared history of colonialism and the problems they face in the aftermath.

Many of the culturalists among African philosophers argue that philosophy does not have to be expressed in writing to be genuine. Some attempt to explicate the philosophical positions implicit in traditional tales, myths, and practices (including artistic practices). Others, who insist that philosophy must critically assess, think that simply itemizing and elaborating on traditional beliefs does not amount to a philosophy. Nevertheless, they claim, Africa has traditionally had sages, who not only mastered their cultures' worldviews, but assessed them critically. These thinkers were true philosophers, whether or not their views were expressed in writing.

The universalists, by contrast, claim that African philosophy is no different in its methods or aims than philosophy elsewhere in the world. Some of these insist that philosophy must be written, so that formulations of views are sufficiently stable to lend themselves to criticism. Many universalist philosophers acknowledge that the specific concerns of African philosophers have some relation to their postcolonial problems. But they do not think that African philosophy is restricted to these issues, and many address issues that are of concern in European and American philosophy, not necessarily topics of particular pertinence to Africans.

Latin American Philosophy

Contemporary Latin American philosophers share some similar concerns with their African counterparts, and these grow out of two common circumstances: the absence of written records and the history of colonialism. In many cases, the cultures of the Americas had records, but colonizers destroyed them, often along with the civilizations themselves. The Aztecs of Mexico, for example, had a thriving school of philosophers called *tlamatinime* (which means "knowers of things"). But all we have left are fragments of their teachings, largely because their Spanish conquerors deliberately burned most of their books.

Aztec Philosophy: The Tlamatinime

Years before the Europeans arrived on the shores of the Americas, there were sophisticated civilizations with systems of thought. The Aztecs were one of them. Aztec philosophers were the *tlamatinime*, whose philosophy emphasized the ephemeral nature of life. The following is by Miguel León Portilla:

The tlamatinime's *point of departure was the ephemeral and fragile quality of all that exists. "Although it be jade, it is broken; although it be gold, it is crushed; although it be quetzal plumes, it is torn asunder." Obviously, "this is not the place where things are made; here nothing grows green," and "we only dream, all is like a dream."*

Convinced of the evanescence of earthly life, the Nahuatl wise men posed two questions, one of a practical nature, the other more speculative: "On earth, is the striving for anything really worthwhile?" "Do we perhaps speak any truth here?" Since truth is that which gives support or foundation to all things, the second question led to two even more urgent problems: "What is

---

(continues)

Aztec Philosophy: The Tlamatinime (continued)

it perchance that stands?" "Are men really true?" In other words, do things and men have a real truth or foundation, or are they merely dreamlike, as are those things which come into one's semiconscious mind at the moment of awakening?

The problems were formulated cosmologically in the language of the ancient myths, and they were given impetus by the need of finding an answer before the imminent end of the Fifth Sun. For man, here on earth without "a well-formed face and heart," the question of his own truth is the most pressing, since the reality embraces his origin, his personality, and his final destiny.

At the core of Latin American philosophy (in what is now Mexico and central South America) was a belief in three levels of time and reality—ordinary, mythical, and divine. The mythic and divine levels of reality exerted tangible influences on the ordinary plane of human experience, and they did so at predictable times. This belief motivated detailed attention to the construction of calendars and to astronomical observation. The balance between the different orders of reality was sufficiently fragile that human beings had to assume responsibility for maintaining the cosmic order. The continued existence of the universe itself depended on human actions and rituals, and, in particular, the willingness of humans to sacrifice themselves. The Mayans and the Aztecs believed that blood was the fundamental life force.

Such beliefs, taken together, suggest the logic behind the best known and most horrifying of ancient Aztec rituals, bloody human sacrifice on an enormous scale. Similarly, the Mayan kings and queens regularly pierced themselves and lost enough blood to cause them to have visions. They understood such relatively modest sacrifice as repayment to the gods, who had sacrificed themselves to create the world. For the Aztecs, the sacrifice was far less modest, involving wholesale killing of the best youths of their society along with captured enemies. It has been suggested that one of the reasons the warrior Aztecs lost so badly to the Spanish invaders was that, in desperation, they sacrificed so many of their best young warriors to the gods who had seemingly turned against them. Thus, philosophy can be the undoing as well as the strength of a great civilization.

Octavio Paz (1914–1998) was a Mexican poet and critic whose essays, including *The Labyrinth of Solitude* (1950), explore the Mexican identity. Distinguished for his insight, elegance, and erudition, Paz was awarded the 1990 Nobel Prize for literature.

Modern man likes to pretend that his thinking is wide-awake. But this wide-awake thinking has led us into the mazes of a nightmare in which the torture chambers are endlessly repeated in the mirrors of reason.

— From *The Labyrinth of Solitude*

Mexican Philosophy: Octavio Paz

Here Paz discusses the pre-Columbian attitudes toward death, which remain evident in Mexico's holiday *la Día de los Muertos*, or "Day of the Dead":

The opposition between life and death was not so absolute to the ancient Mexicans as it is to us. Life extended into death, and vice versa. Death was not the natural end of life but one phase of an infinite cycle. Life, death, and resurrection were stages of a cosmic process which repeated itself continuously. Life had no higher function than to flow into death, its opposite and complement; and death, in turn, was not an end in itself: man fed the insatiable hunger of life with his death. Sacrifices had a double purpose: on the one hand man participated in the creative process, at the same time paying back to the gods the debt contracted by his species; on the other hand he nourished cosmic life and also social life, which was nurtured by the former.

Perhaps the most characteristic aspect of this conception is the impersonal nature of the sacrifice. Since their lives did not belong to them, their deaths lacked any personal meaning. The dead—including warriors killed in battle and women dying in childbirth, companions of Huitzilopochtli the sun god— disappeared at the end of a certain period, to return to the undifferentiated country of the shadows, to be melted into the air, the earth, the fire, the animating substance of the universe. Our indigenous ancestors did not believe that their deaths belonged to them, just as they never thought that their lives were really theirs in the Christian sense.

Everything was examined to determine, from birth, the life and death of each man: his social class, the year, the place, the day, the hour. The Aztec was as little responsible for his actions as for his death.

—*The Labyrinth of Solitude.* Trans. Lysander Kempt, Yara Milos, and Rachel Phillips Belash. New York: Grove Press, 1985

After the Spanish invasion, philosophy as it developed in Latin America was for a long time dominated by European traditions. The initial European philosophical import was the tradition of Scholasticism (a dialectical tradition that sought to apply reason to the elucidation of Christian teachings). Much later, **positivism**, first developed by nineteenth-century French thinker Auguste Comte

(1798–1857), became attractive to some thinkers in Latin America who objected to the way that Christian thought had been used to justify imperialism. Positivism was a completely secular movement that sought to set aside religious and metaphysical accounts by explaining human behavior entirely in terms of natural laws. Social scientists should determine what these laws are, and then society should be organized in accordance with them. Positivism had not only theoretical but also practical impact when it provided the guiding principles behind political regimes in Mexico and Brazil. (In practice, the two regimes were quite different in character. In Mexico the government utilized positivistic principles to assert its own totalitarian authority, while in Brazil positivism served a progressive agenda, geared to economic and technological development.)

Some thinkers in the former Spanish colonies objected to the idea that all of human behavior could be accounted for through scientific laws, however. Mexican philosopher and politician José Vasconcelos (1882–1959), for example, complained that positivism did not acknowledge the importance of emotion, especially emotion experienced in connection with music and the other arts, for organizing our knowledge and putting us in touch with the rhythms of our world. Besides being a philosopher, Vasconcelos promoted education and literacy generally, serving at times as Minister of Public Education in Mexico, as well as directing the National University of Mexico.

In addition to Scholasticism and positivism, a third European philosophical movement that became influential in Central and Latin America was Marxism. The wide disparity in wealth and power between the poor and the rich in Latin America has prompted many thinkers to address questions of social justice, and some have found in Marxism useful analytic categories for considering political and economic issues. Others, however, have found Marx's analysis too focused on the historical conditions of industrialization in Europe and on the prospects for international revolution to be helpful in dealing with the specific circumstances of the descendents of those once colonized by the Spanish.

The issue of whether European models are appropriate for thinking about problems within these formerly colonized nations has itself become a significant recent debate in Latin American philosophy, much as in Africa. Some Latin American thinkers are universalists who argue that there is no particular reason why European models would be unserviceable in Latin American contexts. Other Latin American philosophers are culturalists among them Peruvian thinker Augusto Salazar Bondy (1927–1974), who argue that Latin American philosophy should develop its own philosophical identity in light of its distinctive concerns. One philosophical movement that has attempted to do so is called the **philosophy of liberation**, developed in Argentina in the 1970s. The philosophy of liberation seeks to address the needs of the disenfranchised by philosophizing from their viewpoint and articulating ways to bring about social change toward a more just state of affairs.

Middle Eastern Philosophy

The Middle East was one of the cradles of civilization and the birthplace of not only the three most influential Western religions, but some of the first great philosophies as well. The ancient capitals of Babylon, Assyria, and Persia, for example, nurtured systems of ideas that eventually gave rise to many of our own concepts in philosophy and religion. The ancient Persian religion of **Zoroastrianism**, for example, is generally recognized as a precursor of the other great Western religions and of many of our central philosophical conceptions as well (for example, the basic opposition between good and evil). The Middle East was also responsible, during medieval times, for keeping many of the great ideas of ancient Greece and Rome alive when they were dormant or suppressed in Europe. At the height of the medieval period, the interchange between Christian, Jewish, and Islamic philosophers was so intense that it is often hard to separate the various innovations and influences.

Islam, the third and latest of the three great Western religions, developed a theology and an accompanying philosophy that were in every way as profound and detailed as those of the other two. Although we often tend to collapse the various cultures of the Muslim world into the single concept of "Arabic," there were and still are vital differences between the very different cultures, some of them not "Arab" at all. In Persia, for example, there is an active tradition of theology and philosophy that goes back to Zoroaster. With the spread of Islam in the seventh century, Persia along with its Arabic neighbors turned to theology and questions that were also being asked by the Christians in Europe.

Medieval Islamic philosophers were conversant with ideas from ancient Greece and made use of them in their own thinking. Many of these thinkers were influenced by and elaborated on ideas in Aristotle, in particular, which they attempted to integrate with the teachings of Islam. Among them was Al-Kindi (circa 800–866), from present-day Iraq, who made use of Aristotle's ideas about causality to articulate his views about the relation between God and the natural world. One of his views was that only God acts in a full sense. All other beings act only in a secondary sense. God created the world from nothing, but everything else comes to be as a result of a chain of causes and effects that God set in motion. Even our current activity depends on the action of God.

Another Islamic thinker who considered God's relation to creation was the Persian philosopher Ibn-Sina (or Avicenna, as he came to be known in the West, 980–1037), an innovator in medical science as well as in philosophy. Ibn-Sina characterized God as pure thought, who, in his creation, "emanates" lesser intelligences. In other words, created beings flow forth from God's activity as pure thinking.

A central issue in medieval Islamic thought concerned whether reason or revelation should have primacy in coming to know the truth. al-Farabi (died circa 950), who was born in Turkestan, defended the primary importance of the intellect. His commentaries on Aristotelian logic were controversial for their apparent efforts to establish truth apart from revelation. Although al-Farabi considered revelation important as well, he did consider reason the most important means for attaining knowledge, and he defended it as the faculty of discernment on which the good ruler would rely. Ibn-Rushd (or Averroes, as he came to be known in the West, 1126–1198) sought to demonstrate that revealed truth and the conclusions of reason coincide, and he points out that the Qur'an (the Islamic scripture) itself encourages the use of speculative reason. Not only did these Arabic thinkers make use of earlier thought from the "Western" tradition; they themselves were important contributors to later Western thought through their influence on Thomas Aquinas.

In *Wisdom of the Throne,* the sixteenth-century Persian thinker **Mulla Sadra** (approximately 1571–1641) reflects on these questions of God's relation to the world and the relative importance of reason and revelation. Sadra argued that God shares his existence with lesser entities in creating the world. Drawing on an image used by twelfth-century philosopher Al-Suhrawardi, Sadra compares God's creation to light that spills from its source to illuminate other things. God's existence is eternal, but God has allowed his existence to overflow to grant limited existence to the beings within the world. God's existence is also manifested in each particular thing, though in a limited way. Sadra contends that intellectual pursuit of truth and mystical experience must complement each other, and ideally the philosopher should engage in both.

Philosophy from Persia (Iran)

Know that to attain the true inner divine knowledge one must follow a proof or "unveiling" by immediate vision, just as He—May He be exalted—said Say: "Bring your proof, if you are among those who speak truthfully!" *(2:111); and He—May He be exalted—said:* Whoever calls upon another god together with God has no proof for that *(23:117).* This proof is a Light that God casts on the Heart of the man of true faith, a Light that illuminates his inner vision so that he "sees things as they really are," as it was stated in the prayer of the Prophet—May God's blessings and peace be with him—for himself and the elect among his community and his close disciples: "O my God, cause us to see things as they really are!"*

Know, too, that those questions concerning which the commonality of the philosophers have disagreed with the prophets—May God bless them— are not matters that can easily be grasped and attained; nor can they be acquired by rejecting our rational, logical intellects, with their (intrinsic) measures and their contemplative activities of learning and investigating. If this were so, then there would never have been any disagreement (with the prophets) concerning these questions on the part of those intelligent men who were busy all their lives using the tool of thought and reflection to acquire a (true) conception of things; those (philosophers) would never have fallen into error in these questions and there would have been no need for the sending of the prophets (if these metaphysical realities were so easy to grasp). So it should be known that these questions can only be comprehended by taking over Lights from the Lamp-niche of Prophecy, and by

(continues)

South Asian Philosophy

The oldest philosophical text (even older than the Old Testament) was written in India, possibly as early as 1500 BCE. It is the *Rig-Veda*, a book of hymns that reflect on the origins and ultimate nature of the world and the personality of the gods and goddesses. It was one of many Vedas, or holy books. The philosophy of ancient India is bound up with Hinduism, but, strictly speaking, there is no single set of philosophies—or, for that matter, no single religion—called Hinduism. (*Hindu* is an Arabic word, referring not to a religion but a place, "east of the Indus River.") **Hinduism** refers to an enormous variety of beliefs based on the Vedas. Hinduism is also associated with a particular system of fixed social roles, the caste system, which Vedic philosophy was used to justify.

Traditional Hinduism is populated with fantastic creatures and divinities. A central trinity of gods is fundamental to classical Hindu mythology: Brahma (the creator god), Vishnu (the god who maintains the universe), and Shiva (the god of destruction). But these have come to be understood as faces of one divine reality. (This view that a single divine nature takes a variety of forms is called **henotheism.**) Familiar depictions of Vishnu (some of which show him with a boar's head) reveal a tradition in which the gods routinely take on various forms and manifestations, adopt different personae, serve multiple functions, and accordingly have many different names as well. Vishnu sometimes takes human form, playing a role that helps preserve the world. A god incarnating in human form is called an **avatar.** Krishna, one of the few Hindu divinities familiar in the West, is an avatar of Vishnu.

The Rig-Veda, Circa 1500 BCE

Hymn of Creation

1. *Non-being then existed not nor being:*

   There was no air, nor sky that is beyond it.

(continues)

Hymn of Creation (continued)

What was concealed? Wherein? In whose protection?
And was there deep unfathomable water?

2. *Death then existed not nor life immortal;*
Of neither night nor day was any token.
By its inherent force the One breathed windless:
No other thing than that beyond existed.

3. *Darkness there was at first by darkness hidden;*
Without distinctive marks, this all was water.
That which, becoming, by the void was covered,
That One by force of heat came into being.

4. *Desire entered the One in the beginning:*
It was the earliest seed, of thought the product.
The sages searching in their hearts with wisdom,
Found out the bond of being in non-being.

5. *Their ray extended light across the darkness:*
But was the One above or was it under?
Creative force was there, and fertile power:
Below was energy, above was impulse.

6. *Who knows for certain? Who shall here declare it?*

—Hymns from the *Rig Veda*. Ed. and trans. A. A. Macdonell
London: Oxford University Press, 1911

Throughout ancient Hindu thought we find the enduring themes of renewal, the continuity of life, and the oneness of the universe, however many its manifestations or appearances may be. Later philosophical texts appended onto the Vedas, the Upanishads or Vedanta (some of which are written as early as 800 BCE), further focus on the oneness of ultimate reality, called "**Brahman**" (to be distinguished from the god with a similar name). The theory of Brahman, like the rich mythology of earlier India, is the idea that one reality underlies infinitely many manifestations. The idea that there are many gods, all of whom are manifestations of the same God, is no doubt startling to monotheists and polytheists alike, if they think of being godlike as an inherently stable quality. Indian philosophy will also seem bewildering or incoherent to those who insist on not only the singularity but the ultimate rationality of reality and on its unchanging existence. Manifestations of Brahman are unchanging only in the sense that they are always changing.

Traditional Indian thought itemizes four aims of human life: material possessions (*artha*), pleasure and love (*kama*), moral and religious duties (*dharma*) that are specific to one's social position, and spiritual release (*moksha*), which is the ultimate aim. Moksha is achieved when one transcends the illusions involved in our everyday perspective on the world and recognizes the ultimate reality, Brahman.

The notion of dharma is emphasized in the *Bhagavad-Gita* (literally "song of the Blessed Lord"). The Bhagavad-Gita is an important philosophical text that is embedded in the Mahabharata, a great epic poem about two related families who are in conflict over who should properly inherit a throne. The scene described in the Bhagavad-Gita occurs just before a battle, when both sides have gathered and await the command to begin. The person who has been selected to give this order is Arjuna, an excellent archer who is one of five brothers on one side of the conflict. Arjuna looks out over the field, seeing friends and relatives on both sides, and hesitates to begin a battle that will result in the death of many.

Krishna, the ruler of a neighboring country, is serving as Arjuna's charioteer. Krishna tells Arjuna that it is his duty to begin the battle, for he is a member of the warrior caste. Moreover, the other side has usurped the throne in question by illegitimate means, so Arjuna is also obligated to avenge his family. Krishna also tells Arjuna that he should not fear death, which involves exchanging one body for another, much as one changes clothes.

Krishna then reveals himself to Arjuna as an avatar and advises Arjuna on the orientation he should take, that of **karma yoga** (the yoga of selfless action). *Yoga*, which literally means "yoke," is a method of spiritual discipline. According to the *Yoga-sutra,* a compendium on yoga traditionally said to have been compiled by Patanjali (second century BCE), the aim of yoga is to still the mind and thus eliminate mental activities that interfere with insight. Traditionally, yoga involved mental and physical practices very different from the activities of everyday life. However, the karma yoga that Krishna proposes involves engaging in everyday activities, but with a transformed attitude.

The idea of **karma** (which literally means "action") is that every action bears fruit. Besides obvious external results, every action leaves residues (or *samskaras*) in the mind, typically the unconscious mind that are mostly unconscious. Our actions build up tendencies that can become habitual. Although the term "karma" has become fairly familiar in the West, it is often misunderstood as implying that your just deserts eventually catch up with you in this life. Indian philosophy presupposes reincarnation, and the Hindu doctrine of karma does not claim that the fruits of an action will necessarily appear within the same life in which it was performed. The personalities we were born with are shaped by karma from previous lives. We will continue the cycle of rebirth as long as karmic tendencies continue. In Indian thought, however, continuing this cycle is not considered a good thing; instead it extends one's distance from the spiritual release that is one's ultimate goal. This being the case, the accumulation of further karma is undesirable.

Karma yoga, as Krishna presents it, involves acting without the accumulation of further karma. The practitioner of karma yoga goes about everyday activities in accordance with the moral law (*dharma*), but without concern about the consequences. He or she adopts an attitude of detachment, no longer considering the fruits of one's action as one's own possessions, but instead offering the fruits of one's actions to God, fixing one's thought on God. By acting without concern to possess one's actions and their results, one avoids accumulating additional karma. If Arjuna gives the command for battle (which he ultimately does) in the spirit of karma yoga, he will not assume more karma by doing so. He should offer his action to God, and not concern himself with whether the results will be to his liking.

Hinduism gave rise to two other great religions, which developed around the sixth century BCE. The first was **Buddhism**, founded by **Siddhartha Gautama** ("the Buddha," literally, "the enlightened one," 566–486 BCE). The other, founded by the Buddha's contemporary **Mahavira**, was **Jainism**, a religion thoroughly committed to the sanctity of life and to nonviolence (*ahimsa*). Both rejected the caste system, and both focused their attention on the problem of suffering in the world and how to escape, or "liberate," oneself from it. Buddhists refer to this escape as **nirvana**, which literally refers to "extinguishing" (that is, extinguishing selfish craving and the suffering that it causes) but is understood as blissful. Hindus refer to the ultimate liberation as *mukti*, which they also characterize as involving a state of bliss. For all three philosophies, liberation is achieved through proper living, through ritual practice (for example, yoga), and through meditation.

Central to all three religions is an emphasis on **mysticism**. Mysticism is the conviction of one's unity with a spiritual reality and the attempt to gain insight into this unity through direct experience. It would be an enormous mistake to think of Indian philosophy, even in its most ancient forms, as *nothing but* mysticism, the favorite excuse of many Western philosophers for ignoring Indian thought altogether. Indian philosophy uses rational accounts to defend religious views as well as to elaborate on the nature of reality. But the oldest Vedas express skeptical doubts that Brahman can be comprehended through reason or reflection alone. Knowledge of Brahman may come through an all-embracing, unifying mystical experience. The great Buddhist philosopher Nāgārjuna (circa 200 CE), however, thought that rationality could be used in the service of this possibility. He used brilliant rational argumentation to undermine his opponents' positions, making them less attached to their own views and more open to nonrational insight.

Buddhism split early in its history into a South Asian version, Theravada Buddhism, which remains dominant mainly in and near India, and which focused attention on personal enlightenment, and an East Asian version, Mahayana Buddhism, which spread to China, Korea, Vietnam, and Japan, where it became popular among the samurai warriors as Zen. The Mahayana Buddhists insist on the primacy of compassion and regard for the less fortunate. The spiritual aim within Mahayana Buddhism is to become a *Bodhisattva*. Bodhisattvas do not enter the state of nirvana when they reach enlightenment. Instead, they remain active in the world, as the Buddha did, to help others extinguish suffering.

Zen Buddhism: Dōgen

In such an unpredictable world, it is extremely foolish to waste time worrying about various ways of earning a living in order to postpone one's death—uncertain as it is—to say nothing of plotting evil against others.

Precisely because this is reality, the Buddha preached it to all living beings, the patriarchs taught only this truth in their sermons and writings . . . Impermanence is swift; life-and-death is the great matter. Reflect on this reality again and again in your heart without forgetting it, and without wasting a moment. Put your whole mind into the practice of the Way. Remember that you are alive only today in this moment. Other than that, [practice of the Way] is truly easy. You needn't discuss whether you are superior or inferior, brilliant or dull.

—From: Shōbōgenzō Zuimonki.
Trans. Shohaku Okumura. Kyoto: Kyoto Soto Zen, 1987

Reflection on the nature of the self pervades Indian philosophy. On the one hand, there is the conception of the individual soul, *jiva*, which distinguishes each individual as a unique being. Whether or not this *jiva* is ultimately real, however, or in any way sufficiently substantial to survive the death of the body, is a matter of fascinating debate. On the other hand, the self is also referred to as *atman*, which might be understood as the principle of life that exists in every human being. Atman is the same within each individual, and this implies that we all share the same self. The belief that our individual selves are completely distinct entities is an instance of *maya*, or illusion. Thus, one might see each and every individual as a jiva vitalized by atman, or, quite differently, one might come to see jiva as a false self and atman as the true self.

The Vedas make clear, however, that we are not to think of jiva and atman as two selves fighting for superiority within a person. The self that we recognize within ourselves is ultimately atman, and atman is not separate from Brahman, the fundamental reality. By looking within ourselves, we discover the fundamental reality that underlies and animates everything. The microcosm of our personal selves and the macrocosm that is Brahman are ultimately identical. In a passage from the *Chandogya Upanishad,* a teacher (a *guru*, literally, one who leads from darkness to light) draws his student's attention to the various phenomena in the world—the diverse creatures all animated by the same life, the manifold branches that share the life of a tree, the minute seeds that can grow into a gigantic tree, water in various locations that all has the same taste—and instructs the student in every case, "You are that." The student's own reality is, in other words, the same reality that gives being to these things.

Buddhists reject the idea of the self altogether. They believe that all of life is impermanent. According to the Buddhists, reality amounts to a series of momentary existences, and there are no enduring substances. It is only delusion that leads us to believe that our selves have an enduring reality. In fact, there is no permanent self or soul. A human being is just a series of temporary composites of physical form, feelings, thoughts, dispositions, and consciousness ("the **five aggregates**"). (We might compare this view to that of David Hume. See Chapter 6.) There is no underlying substance, a self or soul in addition to this composite. Nor is there a larger eternal self, what the Vedantists call *atman*. This Buddhist doctrine is termed ***anatman***, literally "no atman." Recognition of the impermanence of the "self" and all objects of desire, according to Buddhists, is a step toward insight and the end of misery.

From the *Dhammapada*

Let each man first direct himself to what is proper, then let him teach others; thus a wise man will not suffer.

If a man make himself as he teaches others to be, then, being himself well-subdued, he may subdue others; for one's own self is difficult to subdue.

Self is the lord of self, who else could be the lord? With self well-subdued, a man finds a lord such as few can find.

The evil done by one's self, born of one's self, begotten by one's self, crushes the foolish, as a diamond breaks even a precious stone . . .

The foolish man who scorns the instruction of the saintly, of the elect [ariya], of the virtuous, and follows a false doctrine—he bears fruit to his own destruction, like the fruits of the Katthaka reed.

By one's self the evil is done, by one's self one suffers; by one's self evil is left undone; by one's self one is purified. The pure and the impure stand and fall by themselves; no one can purify another.

Let no one forget his own duty for the sake of another's, however great; let a man after he has discerned his own duty, be faithful to his duty.

All forms are unreal—he who knows and sees this is at peace though in a world of pain; this is the way that leads to purity.

He who does not rouse himself when it is time to rise, who, though young and strong, is full of sloth, whose will and thought are weak, that lazy and idle man never finds the way to wisdom.

Watching his speech, well-restrained in mind, let a man never commit any wrong with his body! Let a man but keep these three roads of action clear, and he will achieve the way which is taught by the wise.

—Third century BCE

Jains, by contrast, hold onto the belief in an individual self or soul, not only in human beings but in every living thing. That is why their respect for all life is so uncompromising. They—like many Hindus—believe that human souls may be reborn in animals. Jains take as their primary principle "Do no harm," and they practice respect for life—all life—even to the point of taking care that they do not crush the insects on the ground beneath them or accidentally inhale those flying in the air.

Both Buddhists and Jains pay special attention to the nature of suffering and liberation from suffering, and their philosophies are centrally concerned with this problem. The Buddha denounced the caste system because it increased human suffering.

The Buddha's basic philosophy, however, is concerned primarily with the individual's *inner* transformation, achieved by means of insight into the Four Noble Truths of Buddhism:

1. Life is full of suffering.

2. Suffering arises from selfish craving.

3. Selfish craving can be eliminated.

4. One can eliminate selfish craving by following the right way.

This right way to liberation or enlightenment is called the Eightfold Path of Buddhism, which consists of (1) the right way of seeing, (2) right thinking, (3) right speech, (4) right action, (5) right effort, (6) the right way of living, (7) right mindfulness, and (8) right meditation.

The aim of Buddhism is to free oneself from deluded belief in the ego and all that goes with it—desire and frustration, ambition and disappointment, pride and humiliation—and to gain enlightenment and the end of misery. Because of ignorance, we each imagine that we have an individual existence, separate from that of others, and we seek to secure a good situation for this separate existence. But this is impossible. Everything changes and passes away, as the Buddhist doctrine of impermanence (*anitya*) asserts. We cannot sustain any situation, nor is there a distinct self to sustain.

Mahayana Buddhists stress the interdependence of all things in the doctrine of interdependent arising (*pratītyasamutpāda* in Sanskrit). Everything that exists in our world exists only in relation to other things, and its relative "existence" is constantly undergoing transformation. Our selfish cravings, accordingly, are based on a faulty view of reality, for they presuppose an enduring self that can be catered to. The Eightfold Path offers the practical means to overcome this ignorant understanding. By following it, one learns to perceive things accurately and to construct the right habits of motivation and action. Mahayana Buddhists also describe the status of our egos and the "things" we take so seriously as "empty." The Buddhist concept of emptiness (*śūnyatā*) is used in reference to the phenomenal world to indicate its illusionary character but also to refer to what underlies it, the Buddha-nature, which is the only reality.

Emptiness

The "being dependent nature" of existing things: that is called "emptiness."

That which has a nature of "being dependent"—of that there is a non-self-existent nature. . . .

All things prevail for him for whom emptiness prevails;

Nothing whatever prevails for him for whom emptiness prevails.

—Nāgārjuna (150–circa 250),
Averting the Arguments

East Asian Philosophy

The great Chinese philosopher Confucius (the Latinized name for Kong Fu Zi, "the honorable master Kong," 551–479 BCE) was active about the same time as the Buddha and Mahavira and the earliest Greek philosophers. In the sixth century BCE, China was already a highly advanced political culture. It was also a society in turmoil. Confucius's philosophy, called *Confucianism*, responding to these circumstances, was concerned with harmonious social and political relationships, good leadership, and getting along with others through cultivating personal virtue. The central question in Chinese thought generally is the ethical question of what is the good life. For Confucius, the answer was to live in harmony with other human beings, and his philosophy focuses on "the Way" (**Dao** or **Tao**) to do that.

Eight Chinese Thinkers and their Major Themes

Confucius (or Kong Fuzi, sixth century BCE)	Virtue, harmony in relationships
Laozi (or Lao-Tzu, sixth century BCE)	The importance of harmony with nature
Mozi (or Mo-Tzu, fifth century BCE)	Impartial benevolence (and a good army)
Sunzi (or Sun-Tzu, fourth century BCE)	The art of war
The Legalists (fourth century BCE)	People need rules
Zhuangzi (or Chuang-Tzu, fourth century BCE)	(Taoist) Emphasis on natural harmony
Mencius (fourth century BCE)	(Confucian) People are good (by nature compassionate)
Xunzi (or Hsün-Tzu, third century BCE)	(Confucian) People are bad (selfish, but culture makes them good)

Confucius proposed that society return to the rituals of an earlier time as a means of restoring social harmony. He suggested that ritual practices enable people to harmonize without coercion. Knowing what is called for, people direct their own energies into dignified interactions with others, gaining a sense of partnership with others in their society. For Confucius, therefore, practicing ritual (*li*) is an important virtue. Ritual is something like a vocabulary for social participation. By knowing the rituals—the way things are done—within one's society, one can take part fully in the life of the community.

Five Key Terms in Chinese Philosophy

dao (or *tao*, pronounced "dao") 道: "the Way," the process of living well.

ren (or *jen*, pronounced "ren") 仁 to be human–humanity–virtue.

li 禮: ritual.

he (pronounced "huh") 和: harmony.

yi 義: appropriateness.

Confucius also called for a sense of nobility based on moral excellence. In his society, important civil positions had been a matter of inheritance. Confucius claimed that aristocracy was a matter of personal character, not birth into the right family. (We have had a similar transformation of the notion of nobility in the Western world. We no longer think the term "gentleman" refers to a person born into an aristocratic family, but instead consider it to refer to a person's good behavior and manners.) Although Confucius defended traditional principles of succession to the throne, he thought that the ministers who served under a ruler should be chosen on the basis of their merits, even if this meant elevating a commoner to a position of authority. An itinerant teacher during much of his life, Confucius taught aristocrats and commoners all together, stressing the point that belonging to a prominent family did not impress him as much as the cultivation of a good character.

Confucius advised rulers to be moral exemplars to their citizens. This would involve genuinely acting in the role of a benevolent father toward the society. Too many rulers in his own time had failed to do this, instead hoarding the resources they secured through taxation to satisfy their own whims, and paying little attention to the concerns and needs of the people. The ruler who lived up to his role would, according to Confucius, be successful as a leader, for he would have the people's support. Such a ruler would be the "pole star" of his state, and he would have a kind of moral charisma that would motivate the people to follow his lead, a power completely lacking in those who ruled through coercion.

Confucius did not restrict his attention to rulers, however. He pointed out that the family is the context in which people learn cooperation and other political virtues. Political life begins at home. Ideally, the family should be a model of interpersonal harmony, in which members have various responsibilities with the common aim of fulfilling the needs of all members. Filial piety, respect for one's elders, is consequently a profoundly important Confucian virtue. To be filial, Confucius claims, is already a way of participating in the governing of the state.

Whether an official or not, everyone should live up to his or her roles. Confucius makes the startling suggestion that if he had power within the government, the first item on his agenda would be the "attunement of names." This may sound a bit eccentric, as it initially did to his disciples, but this idea is motivated by concern about human relationships, but actually relationships are the primary concern behind this idea. Attunement of names means that the name we give to something should match the reality. A king should really be a king. A father should really be a father. Part of Confucius's point is that the names for our roles are morally loaded. They indicate obligations we are committed to. These names can help us to evaluate whether someone is really living up to his or her commitments.

Confucius is also concerned about the way language functions as a medium for communication. Human beings relate best when their words mean the same things to all parties. Language enables us to coordinate our plans and intentions. Language that is used misleadingly or in an obscurantist manner fails to do the basic job for which it was designed.

To make sense of Confucius's point, consider some experience when you have had to deal with some bureaucratic office, let's say the parking office on your campus. You have lost your parking permit and need to get a new one. Imagine first of all that you do not know where the parking office is located, and that people keep giving you faulty directions for getting there. Suppose you eventually find the office and spend some time in line waiting to speak to someone. You finally get to the counter and say what it is you want. The person at the counter says that the parking office no longer issues parking permits but that it is now being handled by the registrar. You say, "But this is the parking office." The person at the counter says, "Yes, but the registrar really likes handling parking permits." A situation like this would not only be frustrating for you, it would indicate a system that is organized in a way that will mislead everyone who has any occasion to need a parking permit. Language should be an efficient tool of communication, not a mysterious code that only some people are in on. For institutions to run smoothly, words must refer to realities, and in a way that is clear to everyone.

It is easy to imagine that Confucius would object to euphemisms used to make circumstances seem more pleasant than they actually are. When killing innocent people is called "collateral damage," we are not facing up to the real situation. George Orwell made a point that is much in the Confucian spirit in his essay, "Politics and the English Language."

> In our time political speech and writing are largely the defense of the indefensible. Things like the continuance of British rule in India, the Russian purges and deportations, the dropping of the atom bombs on Japan, can be indeed defended but only by arguments which are too brutal for most people to face

and which do not square with the professed aims of political parties. Thus, political language has to consist largely of euphemism, question-begging, and sheer cloudy vagueness. Defenseless villages are bombarded from the air, the inhabitants driven out into the countryside the cattle machine-gunned, the huts set on fire with incendiary bullets. This is called "pacification." Millions of peasants are robbed of their farms and sent trudging along the roads with no more than they can carry. This is called "transfer of population" or "rectification of frontiers." People are imprisoned for years without trial, or shot in the back of the neck, or sent to die of scurvy in Arctic lumber camps. This is called "elimination of unreliable elements." Such phraseology is needed if one wants to name things without calling up mental pictures of them.

Confucius would see such euphemisms as an abdication of moral responsibility. We avoid the real circumstances that need to be dealt with if we refuse to let our language name them. Euphemisms aim to obscure even as they pretend to communicate. In a society in which names are attuned, words convey what they purport to convey. People who speak with each other can act in harmony because they share an apprehension of the situation by using the same words to describe it.

Confucius assumed that interpersonal relationships are hierarchical. He did not defend any form of egalitarianism. However, obligations within relationships are reciprocal. A parent has authority over a child, but also an obligation to care for the child. Later in life, the child will have obligations to take care of his or her parents. Someone in authority and a subordinate should each do what is possible to assist the other in fulfilling his or her role. In general, Confucius urges that everyone consider the situation from the other's point of view: "Do not do to others what you yourself would not want." At the same time, by enhancing others, one enhances oneself. The self, as Confucius understands it, is essentially relational. We are who we are because we are related to others, as children, parents, siblings, friends, coworkers, and so forth. The nexus of particular relationships we have with particular others is what makes us who we are.

Dao (or *Tao*, The Way): Laozi (or Lao Tzu)

The Way that can be spoken of is not the eternal Way;
The name that can be named is not the eternal name,
The nameless is the origin of Heaven and Earth;
The named is the mother of all things.

(continues)

***Dao* (or *Tao*, The Way): Laozi (or Lao Tzu) (continued)**

These two are the same,
But diverge in name as they issue forth.
Being the same they are called mysteries,
Mystery upon mystery, the gateway to all subtleties,

My mind is that of a fool—how blank and how muddled.
Vulgar people have clear ideas. They see clear-cut distinctions. I alone
make no distinctions. They all have a purpose. I drift like a high wind
and the ocean. They are alert and smart. I am uncouth and rustic.

The highest good is like water. Water is good; it benefits all things
and does not compete with them. It dwells in lowly places that all
disdain. This is why it is so near to the Way.

Human beings are supple and weak when living, but hard and stiff
when dead. Grass and trees are pliant and fragile when living, but
dried and shriveled when dead. Thus the hard and the strong are the
comrades of death; the supple and the weak are the comrades of life.

Therefore a weapon that is strong will not vanquish;
A tree that is strong will suffer the ax.
The strong and the big fall to the lower positions,
The supple and the weak take the higher positions.

—Dao De Jing (Tao te ching), 6th century BCE, trans. Thomas Seung

Around the same time as Confucius, a sage called **Laozi** (or **Lao-Tzu**) argued a very different vision of the Way (Dao, or Tao) to live a good life. According to Lao-Tzu we achieve the good life by living in accordance with the Way (Dao) of nature. The Dao for Laozi and other like-minded thinkers is the world in its constantly changing entirety. Because of their focus on the Dao in this sense, they are called **Daoists** (or **Taoists**). The Taoists urge us to set our course by attuning ourselves with the dynamic flow of energies within the world. Thus, they attempt to discern the energies and patterns that appear within this cosmic flow and adapt their own behavior to them.

Having a different sense of the best way to live, the Daoists have some basic disagreements with the Confucians. The Confucians, for example, think that governmental office is a desirable circumstance for pursuing the Way (understood in their sense). The Daoists, on the other hand, think that too often people wear down their health in a quest for political office or influence. From their point of view, social or political status is not worth the strain on one's body. Health is to be prized above social prominence.

Dao De Jing (or, *Tao Te Ching*)

Favor and disfavor have been called equal worries,

Success and failure have been called equal ailments.

How can favor and disfavor be called equal worries?

Because winning favor burdens a man

With the fear of losing it.

How can success and failure be called equal ailments?

Because a man thinks of the personal body as self.

When he no longer thinks of the personal body as self,

Neither failure nor success can ail him.

One who knows his lot to be the lot of all other men

Is a safe man to guide them.

One who recognizes all men as members of his own body

Is a sound man to guard them.

What we look for beyond seeing

And call the unseen

Listen for beyond hearing.

And call the unheard,

Grasp for beyond reaching

And call the withheld,

Merge beyond understanding

In a oneness . . .

—*Dao De Jing*, sixth century BCE

Daoism: Zhuangzi (or Chuang-Tzu)

Now, speaking is not simply discharging air. Speaking has that which it says, only that about which is spoken is never fixed. In effect, do we say something or have we never said anything? It is considered to be different

(continues)

Daoism: Zhuangzi (or Chuang-Tzu) (continued)

from the chirping of young birds, yet is there really any distinction or not? How is the dynamic pattern of things [Tao] so obscured that there is such a thing as "genuine" and "counterfeit"? . . . The dynamic pattern of things [Tao] is obscured by small contrivances, and what is said about it is obscured by embellishments on them. Thus we have the right and wrong of the Confucians and Mohists who contradict each other. If we really want to contradict them both, nothing can compare with enlightenment.

— Trans Roger T. Ames, fourth century BCE

The Daoists also think that the Confucian emphasis on ritual is misguided. The prescribed formulas of ritual make it too easy to go through the motions without being mentally and spiritually present, according to the Daoists. We should respect nature by acting naturally, allowing our own nature to express itself spontaneously. This does not mean that we should do anything that occurs to us. The Daoists think that we are overly influenced by social conditioning, and we must unlearn tendencies we have developed that obstruct our awareness of both external and internal nature. Again, this contrasts with the Confucian perspective, which stresses the importance of cultivating oneself by learning from the classics and the exemplary individuals of one's tradition. The Daoists encourage cultivation, too, but for them this is a return to the condition of unworked wood. Like wood before anyone has worked on it, we should once again employ the powers we had when we operated by instinct, before society gave shape to our habits. (We might see some similarity between the Daoist view of social conditioning and Rousseau's position.)

What is really important is clear perception of reality, according to the Daoists. This requires a receptive mind. Too often, we force our own preconceptions on things and discover in things only what we have projected onto them. Even the words we use to describe things can get in the way of real understanding. Once we have a word for something, we feel that we have grasped hold of it. Words are like fishing nets, according to the Daoist Zhuangzi (also Chuang-Tzu); they catch some things, but they allow much to slip through. Words are neither as subtle as reality, nor do they reflect the constant changes that reality undergoes. Even pronouncements about the Dao distort reality, seeming to fix what is continually in flux. According to Laozi's *Dao De Jing*, "The Dao that can be spoken of is not the eternal Dao; the name that can be named is not the eternal name."

The Daoists stress receptivity by using many surprising metaphors, including that of the infant. The infant is almost entirely potential, they suggest, and in that sense is stronger and more virile than the strongest man. A baby is a model of flexibility. Similarly, the Daoists use water as an image for the ideal state. Water conforms to its surroundings. In this respect it is "soft" or "weak," lacking a definite shape of its own. Yet water is strong enough to carve out great canyons, precisely because it does flow exactly where the ground is. The weakness of water is in fact its strength.

The seeming contradictions in such Daoist metaphors (the infant that is virile, the weakness of water being its strength) reflect an ideal that the Daoists emphasize, that of **wuwei**, which literally means "nonaction." In practice, *wuwei* does not mean literally doing nothing; instead it involves acting nonassertively, taking one's cues from one's situation. Consider the case of driving in heavy, obstructed traffic when you are in a hurry to get somewhere. When you find yourself in this situation, you are likely to feel aggravated, your frustration growing as every moment passes. This experience illustrates the useless expenditure of energy when your own desires do not adjust to the flow of energies in your situation. The Daoist would say that you are needlessly wasting your vitality. Instead, you would do best to exemplify wuwei, not trying to force your will on the environment, but going with the flow.

Again, what seems weak proves to be strong. Adopting the policy of wuwei results in tremendous power within the environment. Zhuangzi relates many stories of artists and craftsmen whose skill stems from their allowing the Dao—the energies inherent in the situation—to flow through them. The Dao directs their art.

To see the Daoist point, you might consider skills you have developed, perhaps in the context of sports or learning to play a musical instrument. In learning a skill, you initially practice particular movements (batting a ball, practicing fingering on the piano), very deliberately, over and over. When you have actually acquired the skill, however, you can perform the required movements without thinking about them. They seem to just come to you. They are simply there as you act. This nondeliberate acting is the essence of wuwei. The more positive way to characterize this kind of behavior is to say that it is spontaneous (**ziran**), the ideal according to the Daoists. This spontaneous way of being expresses one's inner nature.

Despite their differences, the ancient Confucians and the Daoists shared many views, however. They agreed in their overall emphasis on harmony as the ideal state of both society and the individual, and they insisted on an all-encompassing, or holistic, conception of human life that emphasizes a person's place in a larger context. For both Confucianism and Daoism, the development of personal character was the main goal in life, but the personal was not to be defined in individualistic terms. (For the Confucian, the personal was the social. For the Taoist, the ideal was living in accordance with nature.) Whatever their disagreements about the relative importance of nature and society, the Chinese thinkers were in considerable agreement concerning the need for harmony in human life and a larger sense of the "person" than merely the individual. When Mahayana Buddhism arrived in China early in the first century BCE, despite its being alien in many respects, the Chinese could recognize something familiar in the Buddhist doctrine that the separate self does not exist. Each of these three schools of thought contributed to the Chinese worldview and continue to exert their influence to this day.

Closing Questions

1. Do you think that universal truths underlie all religious belief? Do you think that the different religious traditions and their different views are incompatible? Why or why not?

2. In what sense are philosophies products of their culture? How or how not, or to what extent?

3. Do you agree with the universalists that philosophy everywhere in the world addresses the same problems and uses the same methods? Why or why not?

4. While reading about any of the non-Western traditions, were you prompted to compare anything to some theory in Western philosophy? If so, which features of the two traditions did you see as comparable?

Suggested Readings

For an introductory survey of world philosophy, see K. Higgins and R. Solomon, *From Africa to Zen,* 2nd ed. (Rowman & Littlefield, 2004). A parallel volume of original texts in translation is Higgins and Solomon, *World Philosophy* (McGraw-Hill, 1995). Takeo Doi analyzes human behavior from a Japanese cultural point of view in *The Anatomy of Dependence* (Kodansha, 1973). A variety of perspectives on African philosophy are presented in P. H. Coetzee and A. P. J. Roux, eds., *The African Philosophy Reader* (Routledge, 1998) and Emmanuel Chukwudi Eze, ed., *Postcolonial African Philosophy: A Critical Reader* (Blackwell, 1997). The entirety of Senghor's essay "On Negrohood" appears in *Diogenes* 32 (1962): 1–15. Kwame Anthony Appiah's *In My Father's House: Africa in the Philosophy of Culture* (Oxford University Press, 1992) is also an excellent examination of issues related to African identity and the philosophical concerns of contemporary Africa. Further discussion about philosophy in pre-Columbian Mexico can be found in Miguel León-Portilla, *Aztec Thought and Culture*, trans. Jack Emory Davis (University of Oklahoma Press, 1963). Further discussion of Native American philosophy can be found in *American Indian Thought: Philosophical Essays*, ed. Anne Waters (Blackwell, 2004). Octavio Paz's study of Mexican thought and identity is *The Labyrinth of Solitude*, trans. Lysander Kemp, Yara Milos, and Rachel Phillips Belash (Grove, 1985). Two fine surveys of Latin American thought are Jorge J. E. Gracia and Elizabeth Millan-Zaibert, *Latin American Philosophy for the Twenty-first Century* (Prometheus Books, 2004) and Ofelia Schutte's *Cultural Identity and Social Liberation in Latin American Thought* (State University of New York Press, 1993). Heinrich Zimmer's *Philosophies of India*, ed. Joseph Campbell (Princeton University Press, 1951) presents a broad range of classical Indian philosophical views in a particularly engaging manner. A lucid account of one nontheistic version of Hindu thought can be found in Eliot Deutsch, *Advaita Vedanta: A Philosophic Reconstruction* (East-West Center Press, 1969). Nāgārjuna's "Averting the Arguments" is translated by Frederick J. Streng in *Emptiness: A Study in Religious Meaning* (Abingdon Press, 1967). Portions of the Buddhist *Dhammapada* can be found in *The Teachings of the Compassionate Buddha*, ed. E. A. Burtt (New American Library, 1955). A good historical introduction to Chinese philosophy is Fung Yu-Lan's *A Short History of Chinese Philosophy*, trans. Derk Bodde (Free Press, 1977). Herbert Fingarette's *Confucius: The Secular as Sacred* (Harper & Row, 1972) offers an accessible interpretation of Confucius's basic project. David L. Hall and Roger T. Ames's *Thinking from the Han* (State University of New York Press, 1998) provides a useful comparison between Chinese and Western philosophical approaches. An easy-to-read introduction to Japanese Buddhism is D. T. Suzuki, *Zen Buddhism* (Doubleday, 1956). George Orwell's "Politics and the English Language," is available in *Modern British Writing*, ed. Denys Val Baker (Vanguard, 1947).

Sandro Botticelli, *The Birth of Venus*.
Uffizi Gallery, Florence. ©Foto
Marburg/Art Resource, NY.

11
Beauty

A man who has had no opportunity of comparing the different kinds of beauty is totally unqualified to pronounce an opinion with regard to any object presented to him.

—David Hume, 1757

Opening Questions

1. What is it that makes some human artifacts art (for example, a painting or a piece of music), while others (for example, the mass-produced classroom chair you are sitting in) are not art? Or are the latter (or might they be) art?

2. Is a copy of a great painting itself a work of art?

3. In what sense is art an imitation of reality?

4. Does the appreciation of beauty make us better (more moral) human beings?

5. What is your (personally) favorite work of art? How would you describe your relationship with it?

Aesthetics

The ideals of philosophy have often been summarized as "the Good, the True, and the Beautiful." In this book we have raised all sorts of questions about ultimate reality, what it is like, how we might know it, and about how we should live, what we should do, and what is ultimately good for us. But one of the best and most rewarding dimensions of human life is the aesthetic, which involves the appreciation of art and beauty. Plato and Confucius (and many other thinkers) have taken the ultimate good in human life to be characterized by its beauty. We often talk about the wonders of nature in aesthetic terms—the beauty of a complex organic molecule, a crystal, or the stars and planets in the sky. So, too, we describe scientific theories as "elegant." We exclaim of a particularly generous or courageous action that it is "magnificent" or "beautiful," and we characterize anything well done as "artful." Indeed, many people (including the philosopher Friedrich Nietzsche) have said that a well-lived life is itself a work of art. You might think of your life as a novel or a play in progress, of your situation as a scene in a film, and of course it is all accompanied by a soundtrack of one of the greatest of arts, music.

But beauty does not always fit well with truth and goodness. Our novels and stories do not always depict reality. When we say that a story is "fiction," what we mean is precisely that it is not true. When we look at paintings or doctored photographs that represent made-up situations or fantasy figures, our judgment is not primarily concerned with the fact that they are not "true." And then there is music, which often seems not to represent anything at all. What is the relationship between art and truth? Some philosophers and many poets (for example, John Keats) have insisted that beauty is its own kind of truth, even the ultimate truth, but to insist that art has "its own kind of truth" only seems to reinforce the suspicion that art is not always in accord with our more ordinary conceptions of what is true and what is false. And we all know how beauty can sometimes be seductive or distracting or even fatal (like Circe in Homer's *Odyssey*) and thus an obstacle to our search for the good. Beauty and art must be understood in their own terms, so **aesthetics** and the philosophy of art deserve a chapter of their own.

Why do people produce art, music, and stories? Why do we so appreciate them? Why are we so often *moved* by them? What makes a piece of work art? How do we distinguish between good art and bad art? What about *great* art? If I like a work, does that mean it is good? These are among the questions of aesthetics. Although some of them are as old as philosophy itself, the word *aesthetics* was coined only in the eighteenth century. Originally (and according to its Greek roots), it had to do with sensory perception in general; only later did it refer to the appreciation of beauty. Today the term is often used to refer to the study and appreciation of all the arts, and much that is not art as well— not only the beautiful but the sublime, the striking, even the silly and the ugly (for example, in comedy).

In this chapter we will consider several issues within aesthetics that have been historically prominent and remain important: whether beauty and truth go together (in nature or in art); why artistic presentations of some things that would be unpleasant in the real world can be enjoyable; whether taste is objective; and how art might relate to ethics and religion. We will then look at what makes something art, which became a pressing issue in the twentieth century, when contemporary artists abandoned many of art's traditional aims and presented works that much of the public found unintelligible. We will conclude by moving beyond the topic of art in the traditional sense, drawing attention to the ubiquity of aesthetic questions raised in the broader contexts of our everyday encounters with popular culture.

Beauty and Truth

"Beauty is truth, truth beauty,"—that is all / Ye know on earth and all ye need to know.

—John Keats, 1795–1821

One of the more enduring beliefs about art in both Western and Eastern cultures is that art reveals deep truths about the world, perhaps even truths that cannot be articulated by science or philosophy. But, of course, as different cultures have very different ideas about the nature of reality, so, too, their arts may differ. Looking through the history of Western art, you might be struck by a marked change in the place of beauty. Throughout a great deal of the art tradition, it is clear that the aim of art is to depict beauty. The beauty presented might be the subject matter of the work, all of those athletic young men—such as Michaelangelo's *David*—and shapely young women—such as Botticelli's *The Birth of Venus*. Or it might be in the depiction itself (for example, those gruesome medieval crucifixion scenes, which are by no means a "pretty picture" as subject matter but beautiful because of the religious connotations of the work and the skill in rendering the image).

The highest praise for a work of art throughout most of art history was, "It's beautiful." But no longer. With artistic realism in the nineteenth century and other shifts in taste, great art could even be ugly, in both its subject matter and its depiction. Think, for example, of the difference between classical music (at least before the twentieth century) and a great deal of contemporary popular music in which the aim is to be shocking, even painful. It is not hard to see the changes in philosophical outlook that accompany this change, from the faith of the Middle Ages and the optimism of the eighteenth century to the increasing cynicism and despair of the nineteenth and twentieth centuries. Throughout most of Western history, reality itself, created by God, was conceived of as beautiful. Today, our philosophical doubts about the order and the meaning of the universe are manifested in art that is no longer beautiful. Indeed, many contemporary aestheticians would insist that beauty in art is often sentimental or fraudulent, and that aesthetics no longer focuses on the appreciation of beauty.

Education in Beauty

He who would proceed aright in this matter should begin in youth to visit beautiful forms; and first, if he be guided by his instructor aright, to love one such form only—out of that he should create fair thoughts; and soon he will of himself perceive that the beauty of one form is akin to the beauty of another; and then if the beauty of form in general is his pursuit, how foolish would he be not to recognize that the beauty in every form is one and the same! . . . in the next stage he will consider that the beauty of the mind is more honourable than the beauty of the outward form. So that if a virtuous soul have but a little comeliness, he will be content to love and tend him, and will search out and bring to the birth thoughts which may improve the young, until he is compelled to contemplate and see the beauty of institutions and laws . . . and after laws and institutions he will go on to the sciences, that he may see their beauty . . . drawing towards and contemplating the vast sea of beauty, he will create many fair and noble thoughts and notions in boundless love of wisdom; until on that shore he grows and waxes strong, and at last the vision is revealed to him of a single science, which is the science of beauty everywhere.

—Plato, *Symposium*, fourth century BCE

For many centuries, the definitive voice in the identification of beauty with ultimate reality was **Plato**. As we saw in Chapter 4, Plato's conception of reality turned on the idea of unchanging **Forms**, perfect prototypes that gave rise to all of the things of the world. One of these Forms is Beauty, pure beauty, which manifested itself in all and only beautiful things. Thus, beauty itself is not just the truth of (beautiful) things, according to Plato. Beauty is a transcendent Form that stood behind every beautiful thing and made it beautiful. On a personal level, falling in love, Plato suggested, is finding ourselves entranced by Beauty, the Form of beauty manifested in a beautiful human being. But the beauty of another human being is not merely a property of the person. It is Beauty itself manifested and perceived in and through the particular person. Ultimately, therefore, the beauty of a beautiful horse refers to the same Form as the beauty of a beautiful statue of an athlete or a beautiful piece of music. Beauty is therefore *objective*. The idea that beauty is truth and truth beauty was, for Plato, quite literally true.

On the other hand, truth and beauty may not go together so easily. What makes those ancient Greek statues so beautiful, among other things, is their utter absence of blemishes—in other words, the fact that it is *not* an exact replica of a real person. Many of the most striking paintings in both Western and Eastern art depict mythological scenes that have no counterparts in reality, and, indeed, one could argue that what makes such paintings art is first of all the fact that they involve artifice—that is, something constructed or imagined and to that extent not real at all. Thus, art is said to present us with ideals, not reality.

The crucifixion scenes in medieval art were not intended to be accurate representations of Jesus on the cross. The face and body are caricatured, flat, and without depth or mass. Artists had known how to draft a good likeness of a human face and body since ancient times. (This is evident, for example, in the murals of the ancient Romans and even earlier in ancient Crete.) Clearly, the lack of realism in the medieval artists' depictions reflect their deliberate intention to depict Jesus and the scenes of his life and death as being "unnatural," rather than reflecting an inability to paint realistically. Many theorists have insisted that art is not about accurate representation but instead is concerned with expression. The "truth" of such art refers not so much to the accuracy of the representation. Rather "truth" inheres in the work of art, where it conveys something so meaningfully and effectively that it has emotional power, in this case inspiring faith. The primary purpose of medieval art is to express and inspire faith, not to provide a mere documentary. Besides, a wholly realistic crucifixion scene would just be grotesque, inspiring horror or disgust possibly, but not faith.

The divide between truth and beauty—or more generally between truth and art—is nowhere more evident than in the case of fiction. It is "fiction" just insofar as it is not true. Arthur Conan Doyle's detailed descriptions of his invented detective Sherlock Holmes are well known by every detective story fan. But those details, every one of them, are *not true*. This leads to some very curious questions. For example, it is true (in the world invented by Conan Doyle) that Sherlock Holmes's best friend is Doctor Watson and that Holmes smokes a pipe and lives in a flat on Baker Street. But there are no such persons as Holmes and Watson (and there never were), and the flat on Baker Street never existed. So, if asked, "Is it true that Doctor Watson was Holmes's best friend?" you might well be stumped about how to answer. Or you might say that it is true in that fictional world; or, on the other hand, you might say that Holmes had no best friend because he never existed.

The Danger of Poetry

We are ready to acknowledge that Homer is the greatest of poets and first of tragedy writers; but we must remain firm in our conviction that hymns to the gods and praises of famous men are the only poetry which ought to be admitted into our State. For if you go beyond this and allow the honeyed muse to enter, either in epic or lyric verse, not law and the reason of mankind, which by common consent have ever been deemed best, but pleasure and pain will be the rulers in our State.

— Plato, *The Republic*, fourth century BCE

Although a fierce defender of beauty—especially in philosophy—Plato takes issue with art and artists insofar as they deviate from the aim of providing a true picture of ultimate reality. Thus, at the end of *The Republic*, Socrates famously proposes that the poets be banned from his ideal city, because unlike the philosophers they do not tell the truth. Plato also holds that art and artists should be socially responsible and contribute to the virtues and not promote vice. So his character Socrates urges a ban on flute playing in his Republic because it inspires licentiousness. He suggests that poetry, even the works of Homer, can lead people astray by posing as factual when it is not and through its undignified portrayals of the gods. Poetry should be banned unless it can be shown to have some redeeming merit.

Plato remains one of the sources for the continuing demands for censorship in the arts. It is not enough, he suggests, that a work of art appeal to the public, for such a work might only excite the appetites, encourage bad behavior, purvey untruths, or inspire worthless fantasies (unlike Plato's fantasy of *The Republic*, of course). Contemporary demands for censorship employ similar arguments. Popular music and music videos are said to encourage licentiousness, as are movies and television shows unsuited for "prime time." The violence as well as the sexual content presented through these media are denounced as encouraging people (often young people) to act out what they see. Visual artworks displayed in museums, too, have sometimes been condemned for purportedly exciting prurient interests and encouraging antisocial and repugnant behavior. (Some of Robert Mapplethorpe's sexually explicit photographs, particularly those involving underage subjects have been criticized on these grounds.) And some people have objected to certain contemporary works on the grounds that they attack their religious beliefs. (Examples include Andres Serrano's *Piss Christ*, a photograph involving urine and a plastic crucifix, and Chris Ofili's *The Holy Virgin Mary*, which makes use of elephant dung.) Few contemporary Americans go so far as to propose direct governmental censorship of artworks, though some would argue that withholding all government funding from museums—a policy that has sometimes had strong advocates—can amount to the same thing, but many encourage policies such as rating movie and television shows for content, so long as it is undertaken by the producers. Their defenses of such policies are direct descendent of Plato's insistence that art should encourage the all-important values of truth and goodness, and that it is of dubious value unless it does so.

Enjoying Tragedy

Aristotle rejected Plato's theory of Beauty as a transcendent Form just as he rejected Plato's theory of Forms in general. What made a work of art beautiful was its form, all right, but the form was the form of the work in a straightforward sense. No transcendent Forms were necessary. Aristotle's philosophy of art was an attempt to analyze forms and structures to find out what made some art works "work" and others not. In particular, Aristotle was concerned with the art of theater and with tragedy, a type of drama that—along with comedy and satire—was among the classical forms of Greek theatrical art. (He also wrote on comedy, but his writings on this topic have all been lost.) In Aristotle's Athens, some of the greatest plays in Western literature already existed and were performed to great popular acclaim. Two examples were Sophocles's *Oedipus Rex* and Euripides's *Medea*. Aristotle wanted to understand the success of such plays and so he developed a detailed analysis of the essential ingredients of this type of drama.

Beginning, Middle, and End

We have laid it down that a tragedy is an imitation of an action that is complete in itself, as a whole of some magnitude; for a whole may be of no magnitude to speak of. Now a whole is that which has beginning, middle, and end. A beginning is that which is not itself necessarily after anything else, and which has naturally something else after it; an end is that which is naturally after something itself, either as its necessary or usual consequent, and with nothing else after it; and a middle, that which is by nature after one thing and has also another after it. A well-constructed Plot, therefore, cannot either begin or end at any point one likes; beginning and end in it must be of the forms just described.

—Aristotle, *Poetics*, fourth century BCE

Oedipus Rex is the well-known story of a king who has murdered his father and married his mother. In Sophocles's play, which is set after the fact as Oedipus is trying to understand the source of the plague that has devastated the city,

Oedipus's wife–mother commits suicide with a hair brooch, and Oedipus blinds himself with it. In *Medea,* a mother brutally murders her children. Despite the horrible subject matter, these plays were generally considered great works of art as well as popular entertainment. What made them "work" as works of art? According to Aristotle, they work because of the development of the characters, the pacing, and the structure of the plot. But most important, such plays work because they allow for the expression of some basic emotions, such as fear and pity, and the elements of character and plot are effective in evoking these emotions.

For example, the closure of the play—its completeness in itself and its clearly defined limits, its having "a beginning, a middle, and an end"—facilitates the focus of the audience on the events portrayed and their emotional significance. Closure is one of Aristotle's most important criteria for success in tragedy, many of which were applied by later theorists to other fine arts besides drama as well. Western artists have typically used fully shaped forms, clear boundaries, and (in the case of paintings) literal frames to mark the separation of the artwork from its environment. But the notion of closure may be operative even when such explicit demarcation is absent. In Japan, for example, artists only hint at closure, leaving some work for the imagination to do in filling out the complete form suggested by a work. (Gestalt psychologists claim that we naturally organize perceived elements into unified wholes in accordance with innate psychological tendencies, and one of these is what they call "the principle of closure," which is the tendency, exploited by Japanese artists, to perceptually fill-in incomplete forms).

Why Do We Cry at Movies?

There is something puzzling about the fact that we are so often moved emotionally by characters and events that we come across in works of fiction. For these are characters who never existed as persons and events that never actually took place! And typically we are well aware that this is so as we read or watch such works. After all, most of us would not think of climbing onto the stage during a performance of Othello *in an attempt to save Desdemona from Othello's clutches. And a person who tried to find the original copy of Tom Sawyer's birth certificate in the Missouri State Archives would simply have misunderstood the sort of things that Mark Twain's novels are. If we are to appreciate and respond appropriately to works of fiction, we have to appreciate and respond to them as fiction.*

But why does knowing that a work of fiction is fiction make our emotional responses to it puzzling? . . . Colin Radford argues that it is largely because in everyday circumstances beliefs and judgments appear to play a crucial role in our emotional responses. Part of what it is to be afraid for oneself, for example, is to judge the situation one is in to be dangerous or threatening. Similarly, I cannot feel pity for others unless I believe them to be

(continues)

> ### Why Do We Cry at Movies? (continued)
>
> *victims of misfortune. And beliefs of this sort would appear to depend on beliefs in the existence of the objects in question. For example, it will be difficult to make sense of my claim to be afraid of the burglar in the kitchen if I know that there is no such burglar. If I know that there is no burglar, how can I believe that a burglar (what burglar?) threatens me?*
>
> —Alex Neill, contemporary British philosopher,
> "Fiction and the Emotions"

Ever since Aristotle, aestheticians have been asking: why do people take pleasure in such gruesome portrayals of some of the worst things that could happen to a human being? Aristotle wanted to understand why people subjected themselves to such scenes as people blinding themselves and murdering children. Today, he could have asked the same question about popular horror movies and "thrillers." Why do people pay $10 or more to have the wits scared out of them for two hours?

Aristotle's answer has provoked endless discussion and debate. He suggests that the function of such drama was to allow us—both actors and audience—to express some of our most disturbing emotions, in order to achieve **catharsis**, release or sublimation. By allowing ourselves to feel fear and pity in the theater (or at the movies), we get rid of or purify some of those emotions. By vicariously facing a fictional situation and empathizing with the play's protagonists, we diminish the power of those emotions over us and lighten our own sense of vulnerability. Plato, by contrast, had argued that poetry (and theater as well) promotes acting out such passions rather than releasing them, which is why he suggested banning certain kinds of poetry. More than 2,000 years later, Sigmund Freud would pick up on Aristotle's conception of catharsis and, with many modern variations, make it one of the bases of his psychoanalytic theory.

Arguing About Taste

For those who like this sort of thing, this is the sort of thing they like.
—Max Beerbohm, 1872–1956

Plato and Aristotle agreed, however, that beauty is objective; that is, it resides either in works of art or (for Plato) "behind" them in another realm of ultimate realities. Thus, disputes about art had a solution. Either the artwork did or did not manifest beauty, did or did not manifest the ideal structure that Aristotle claimed to find in every great tragedy. But in modern times, however strict the standard of taste may be, there is no such confidence in the objectivity of beauty or the quality of an artwork. "Beauty is in the eye of the beholder," says one of the best-known bits of modern aesthetic theory, and "There is no disputing over tastes." The idea is that artistic beauty involves a person's emotional response, but not necessarily any particular objective feature of the artwork. There may or may not be agreement between people on the quality of an artwork. You might like it. She might not. But there is no way of proving which one of you is right.

Cross-Cultural Differences in Art

Insofar as art is an expression of culture, we would expect cultures to differ in their artistic expressions, even when the subject matter remains the same. Even in one of the most enduring arenas of art, the depiction of eroticism, cultural differences can be revealing. Here is Mara Miller's discussion of Shunga, a type of Japanese erotic art, usually in the form of woodblock prints.

In explicitly erotic prints women are not restricted to the role of passive object of male desire. They quite clearly appear as active desiring Subjects. Women are sometimes shown in positions of submission, but more often stand and sit upright or lie with a man who is also lying down. Either the woman or the man may be on top, they may be intertwined, with neither dominant. Poses characteristic of Western erotica—the woman lying on her back with her hands behind her head, fully exposed to the viewer, or lying with her head fallen back in abandon, as if her neck were broken—are not seen in Japan until after contact with the West.

These women are not only active, and avoiding either extreme of dominance or submission, but they are desiring. They actively reach out for the man and fondle his genitals. They curl their toes with rapture. It is impossible to mistake their enjoyment.

The disempowerment of the nude Western sex object is missing in the Japanese examples. Nudity is important in the Western context because it signals the permission given the male viewer: deprived of social status, her nudity indicating not merely her agreement to the male gaze/fantasy/ act but often a wantonness that makes her agreement beside the point, the woman is vulnerable. In Japan, on the other hand, the vulnerability of nudity is not only unnecessary but undesirable. (And nudity per se is not sexy in Japan; it was common in public bathing.) What is desirable in a woman to a Japanese man is a Subject with whom to interact, not an Object on whom to project one's own fantasy. Clothing—the choice and combination of patterns, the colors, the references—is vital to the revelation of one's Subjecthood.

—Mara Miller (contemporary American philosopher),
"Art and the Construction of Self and Subject in Japan"

David Hume (1711–1776) believed that everyone must judge for him- or herself whether a work of art is worth appreciating. Art appreciation, in other words, is a wholly *subjective* enterprise. An artwork is valuable, according to Hume, if it inspires a particular aesthetic emotion. You might take a course to teach you what works of art are out there, allowing you to look at (reproductions of) a great many of the greatest artworks in history and learn about the contexts in which they were produced, their symbolism, their means of production, their history as works of art (who ordered them, who owned them, what happened to them in various wars, and so on). Or you might take a music history course and learn about music that you did not hear growing up. But whether or not you like it—whether or not you find yourself moved by it—is not something you can be taught, although there will certainly be pressure on you to like those works that are generally thought of as "great." Taste is subjective, even if a great many people, including those who have had the most artistic and aesthetic experience, come to agree that certain works are great and others are mediocre or contemptible.

But if there were no disputing over artistic tastes—if there were no way to resolve the dispute between you (who love only progressive jazz) and your roommate (who likes only Norwegian death metal)—then how is it that differences in taste so often result in harsh denunciations and worse? Part of the reason may be that in the case of music you will inevitably be forced to listen to what the other person prefers, and in the case of the visual arts, you will have no choice but to look at the artwork or reproductions of artworks he or she hangs on the walls of your shared space. There is a deeper reason, however, and it has to do with the notion of taste itself.

Judging Beauty

But though all the general rules of art are founded only on experience and on the observation of the common sentiments of human nature, we must not imagine that, on every occasion, the feelings of men will be conformable to these rules.

Those finer emotions of the mind are of a very tender and delicate nature, and require the concurrence of many favourable circumstances to make them play with facility and exactness, according to their general and established principles. The least exterior hindrance to such small springs, or the least internal disorder, disturbs their motion, and confounds the operation of the whole machine. . . . A perfect serenity of mind, a recollection of thought, a due attention to the object; if any of these circumstances be wanting, our experiment will be fallacious, and we shall be unable to judge of . . . universal beauty.

—David Hume, "Of the Standard of Taste," 1757

When we speak of someone "having taste" or "not having taste," the question is not whether the person has preferences (in art, in music, in literature). The question is whether he or she has *good* taste, making *good* judgments in matters of art. But how can this be determined if taste is subjective? Hume concludes his argument by suggesting that even though taste is subjective, there is nonetheless a way of determining the worth of a work of art. One can and should turn to those who have had the most experience and who are relatively unbiased in their judgment. The great masterpieces of art, music, and literature are those that such people, over the course of time, have agreed on. Each of us will only consider a work of art good if it affects us subjectively. But those works that have compelled admiration over time are likely to move us as well. The true standard of taste, according to Hume, is the collective judgment of the best judges, an ideal standard that we approximate by turning to those critics who are recognized as having good judgment.

Indeed, the argument that there is a standard of taste might be made even stronger than this. **Immanuel Kant** (1724–1804) rejected Hume's account of taste as inherently individual. Just as Kant insisted that inherent structures of the mind provide the basic principles of knowledge (see Chapter 5) and ethics (see Chapter 8), so, too, these structures of the human mind establish the possibility of appreciating beauty. According to Kant, it is not emotional response that allows us to do this but an intellectual response. (This is why human beings, but not animals, have aesthetic taste. A dog can tell whether its dog food is yummy or awful tasting, but it does not judge the elegance of the presentation.) One difference between an emotional response and an intellectual response is that only the latter is "disinterested." If you are looking at a Cézanne painting of a bowl of fruit, for example, it is not an aesthetic response if you find yourself getting hungry and wanting a piece of fruit. An aesthetic response is free from such interests or any other practical concern. (A person might look at the painting and decide to try to buy it as an investment. But this intention shows that the attitude being taken is not disinterested, and thus not aesthetic.) From this disinterested aesthetic perspective, the very real possibility of sharing a beautiful experience with other people can be actualized. Because one is not observing with a personal agenda in mind, one responds as any other person would, using the mental faculties that every human being shares with every other.

Art, Ethics, and Religion

At the beginning of this chapter, we suggested that one of the enduring ideas about art is that it reveals in some sense deep truths about the world. But whether or not art shows us truths about external reality, it may well convey important truths about ourselves. The essence of art has often been taken to be the expression and the inspiration of basic feelings, and in this connection art has often played an important role in ethics and religion.

The Greek poet Sappho insisted that "what is beautiful is good and what is good will soon also be beautiful," suggesting an educational role for art insofar as it is beautiful. In China, the great philosopher **Confucius** argued that music appreciation is conducive to virtue. By appreciating music, with its harmonious interplay among voices, we learn how to construct harmony more generally in our lives. Plato employed much the same musical metaphor, which he borrowed from one of his most influential teachers, Pythagoras. The idea that music has a powerful influence on personality can be found in many of the cultures of the world, certainly in India as well as in Africa and many other tribal societies. It is said that music tames even wild beasts, but whether or not that is true, it has proven to provoke and soothe the feelings of most human beings. Anthropologists like to point out that despite the great variety in arts and customs of the peoples of the world, there is not a single culture in which music does not play a prominent role. So, too, with the other arts. Dance and the making of visual artworks are found more or less universally, and in virtually every culture—including ours—the arts are not merely thought to be entertaining but educational, culturally important, and inspirational as well.

Friedrich Schiller (1759–1805) is but one of many Western philosophers who have argued that appreciating art makes us better people. Like Confucius in ancient China, Schiller in modern Germany argued that beauty is not a distraction from the serious business of life but an inspiration to be a good citizen. Beauty, Schiller suggests, helps us to develop morally. As infants and small children, we are likely to experience other people as competitors for the satisfaction of our desires, even as adversaries with respect to our personal interests. But in the experience of beauty, we discover that our interests and those of others can coincide. This conviction is essential, according to Schiller, if one is to abandon the selfishness of small children and to be willing to cooperate harmoniously with others, an attitude that is essential to good citizenship. The practical consequence of this theory is that art and aesthetics are an essential part of every child's education.

The pessimist **Arthur Schopenhauer** (1788–1860) followed Kant in conceiving of art as essentially disinterested, but he nevertheless argues that art, more than any other human activity, gives us deep insight into ourselves and allows us to reconcile ourselves with an ultimately irrational and unsatisfying world. In Chapter 4 we presented Schopenhauer's fascinating but perverse theory that the world in itself is irrational Will, the source of our endless desires and ambitions and, accordingly, the source of our unhappiness. But art—music most powerfully—gets us "out of ourselves." Schopenhauer accepts Plato's notion of the Forms "behind" particular things, and in the case of representational art, the artwork reveals the Form of what is portrayed. Music, however, bypasses the Forms and is nothing less than the direct representation of the Will, the fundamental reality animating ourselves and the rest of the world. When we "get into" a piece of music we are in touch with the most basic truth about ourselves.

Besides revealing the truth of our nature, art can also facilitate ethical insight. When we appreciate any work of art, according to Schopenhauer, we are no longer conceiving of ourselves as particular individuals. We become "pure will-less subjects of knowledge," and we forget about our desires and ambitions, at least for a while. The appreciation of beauty, he says, "frees us from the penal servitude of willing," our virtually nonstop tendency to be captivated by one desire after another. When we forget about our own desires and ambitions this makes us much more sympathetic to other people, who, after all, are in the same situation we are. Schopenhauer's aesthetics may reflect in part his interest in Indian philosophy. Indian aesthetics emphasize art's power to help us transcend egotistical interests and to empathize with universal emotions.

One of the most radical suggestions concerning the relationship between aesthetics and ethics comes from **Friedrich Nietzsche**. Nietzsche does not argue that aesthetic values are conducive to ethical ones. (As we have observed, he rejects much of what we traditionally call "morality" altogether.) He rather argues that aesthetic values should *replace* standard moral principles; that is, instead of thinking of what we ought to do as a set of rules dictated by God or reason, we should pay attention to such values as beauty (and ugliness) as guidelines for action. One should live one's life as a work of art, he tells us. We ought to render our characters and our lives "beautiful," not simply do what is obligatory.

On the Aesthetic: Nietzsche

Only as an aesthetic phenomenon is the world justified eternally.

—Friedrich Nietzsche, *The Birth of Tragedy,* 1872

Nevertheless, Nietzsche famously distinguishes two different types of art and aesthetic experience, which he calls the **Apollonian** and the **Dionysian**. The first is named after the Greek god Apollo, the god of the sun and of classic beauty. Dionysus, by contrast, is the Greek god of wine and fertility, and the art associated with Dionysus is dynamic, inspiring a frenzied state of mind. A clear example of Apollonian art would be the elegant marble statues of ancient Greece. A clear example of Dionysian art, by contrast, is music, especially wild music that gets us dancing and makes us oblivious to ourselves. Apollonian art, focusing on individual things, depicts the world as orderly and harmonious. Dionysian art, by contrast, absorbs the individual in the vibrant frenzy of life. The Dionysian perspective involves an irrational state, and it has little to do with what is traditionally called ethics.

The greatest art, however, is neither Apollonian nor Dionysian alone, but both of these in combination. Nietzsche praises the art of the ancient Greeks, and Greek tragedy in particular, as having attained the ideal harmony between these two very different conceptions of art and reality. Similarly, he suggests that we need both of these ways of seeing the world to do justice to our own natures, which are both individual and transpersonal. Nietzsche challenges the traditional assumption that art has a single aim or purpose. He also defends the value of frenzy and chaos in art, as well as art involving objects for calm contemplation and appreciation. But this, Nietzsche argues, is the way the world is. The truth of art is not just the expression of our feelings or the accurate representation of the world, but both of these and more. Art offers us both insight into and intimate connection with the world and the love of life that goes along with this intimacy.

Why Is It Art?

Over the course of much of Western art, the aim has been to imitate the appearances of reality in some medium. According to Plato, this was one of the problems with art—it reinforces the human tendency to be caught up in appearances, as opposed to realities (which for him were the Forms). The ideal of imitating appearances began to change when new technologies made it possible to mechanically produce realistic representations of things. Some artists began to doubt the point of traditional painting in the age of photography. Philosopher Arthur Danto argues that even more than photography, cinema provoked shock waves among artists, since cinema could reproduce something no static image could manage, the appearance of things in motion.

Already in the early nineteenth century, Hegel had described the art of his era as being aware of its limitations and as becoming more reflective than straightforwardly mimetic (imitative). Paintings, for example, drew attention to what was not explicitly rendered, such as the inner life of the person presented in a portrait. Art was no longer to be associated simply with a beautiful object. It increasingly involved meditations on subjective experience. Much French painting in the early twentieth century certainly fits this description. The impressionists, for example, sought to suggest the movement of the eye as it took in now this, now that splash of color. But many philosophers think that a watershed moment for aesthetic theorizing occurred when artist Marcel Duchamp exhibited works that he called "readymades," objects that were objects found in everyday contexts, usually with minor modifications, if any. Among Duchamp's readymades were a pocket comb, a snow shovel, and notoriously a number of urinals (in some cases with a signature and date added by the artist).

In addition to shocking the art establishment and the general community, Duchamp's readymades provoked a new line of questioning among philosophers. If these things were art, what made them so? Was it because they were exceptionally well made? (Duchamp actually did claim that his urinals drew attention to the pristine beauty of the porcelain, but many interpreted this as tongue in cheek.) Were such things art because Duchamp was an artist and he said they were? Was it because galleries were willing to exhibit them? Was the whole thing a scam?

Philosophers took on this question of defining what it means for something to be art. Some have defended a functional definition, contending that something is art by virtue of some *function* that it performs. The traditional function of (at least visual) art had been the imitation of features of reality. Defining art on the basis of this function became harder to maintain when combs and shovels could be implements one day and artworks the next. Another traditional answer was that art should be beautiful, but this raises the question of whether there aren't artworks that are important and tremendously valuable but nevertheless not beautiful. A stroll around many contemporary art museums will give the impression that many current artists are not even interested in making beautiful works. Some alternative approach must be given if these works are to be covered by a functional definition of art.

Another approach is to seek a procedural definition of art, which counts a thing as art when certain procedures have been performed with respect to it. These might include an artist making the work, or the work being admitted into a gallery show or a museum exhibition, or the work being a subject in museum catalogues and art criticism. Many alleged artworks were not physically made by the artist (as was the case for Duchamp's readymades and is true of many contemporary works, such as those of Jeff Koons, who conceives the ideas for his works but hires craftspeople to construct the art objects), so some philosophers defending a procedural view contend that it is enough for an artist to simply declare an object art. Many who embrace this type of definition take the artist's activity to be only one factor, perhaps a minor one; they consider the question of whether something is art to be decided by formal institutions such as galleries and museums and art periodicals or by a more vaguely clarified collection of institutions and people who influence the way a society looks at or values art. (Arthur Danto has dubbed this latter group "the artworld.") Philosopher and artist Timothy Binkley considers anyone's simply calling something art ("indexing" it as such) to be enough to qualify it as an artwork—the more interesting question, he claims, is whether or not it is a good artwork. But perhaps we need to know what art is supposed to do or what other criteria apply in order to determine an answer.

Arthur Danto has another account of what makes something art. According to Danto, "an atmosphere of theory" is what makes it so. What he means is that some view of what is within the range of art is sufficiently shared by members of "the artworld" and that the thing in question is within this purview. This answer may not be very satisfying to the members of the general public, who are often mystified by exhibitions of contemporary art and unaware of the theories that reign in the artworld. Some have been offended by the feeling that these shows rub in the fact that they are "outsiders" to what is going on. The impression of elitism that many get from shows and exhibitions of contemporary art may turn off many potential audiences, further ensuring that in contemporary art the view of experts holds sway.

The Aesthetics of Popular Culture

Aesthetics is often thought of as a focused on the *fine arts:* classical music, opera, traditional theater, museum-quality paintings and sculptures, ballet, classical dance, and, perhaps, contemporary forms making use of electronic media. But art in a broader sense surrounds us. Much of this art is bad, even offensive, but that should invite rather than discourage aesthetic analysis. What makes bad art bad? More important, what makes good art so valuable and meaningful to us? What makes a movie great or good? Why do some movies that start out with so many advantages (well-known stars, award-winning directors, an exciting story line)

Popular Modern Art: A Critique

José Ortega y Gassett was an early-twentieth-century Spanish philosopher who was intrigued by the transformations that were taking place in the arts. His subject here is "the dehumanization of art," the move from naturalistic aspirations in art to a new sensibility.

Far from going more or less clumsily toward reality, the artist is seen going against it. He is brazenly set on deforming reality, shattering its human aspect, dehumanizing it. With the things represented on traditional paintings we could have imaginary intercourse. Many a young Englishman has fallen in love with Gioconda [Mona Lisa]. With the objects of modern pictures no intercourse is possible. By divesting them of their aspect of "lived" reality the artist has blown up the bridges and burned the ships that could have taken us back to our daily world. He leaves us locked up in an abstruse universe, surrounded by objects with which human dealings are inconceivable, and thus compels us to improvise other forms of intercourse completely distinct from our ordinary ways with things. We must invent unheard-of gestures to fit those singular figures. This new way of life which presupposes the annulment of spontaneous life is precisely what we call understanding and enjoyment of art. Not that this life lacks sentiments and passions, but those sentiments and passions evidently belong to a flora other than that which covers the hills and dales of primary and human life. What those ultra-objects evoke in our inner artist are secondary passions, specifically aesthetic sentiments.

—José Ortega y Gassett, *The Dehumanization of Art,* 1925

nevertheless disappoint us? What songs move us? What is it about them? The beat? Their lyrics? Does it please you? Or, thinking about it, does it make you depressed? What could you do to correct this? All of these questions are legitimate and immediate concerns of aesthetics. We will close this chapter by indicating some of the aesthetic aspects of phenomena we encounter in everyday life, many of them through popular culture.

The aesthetics of popular culture is a booming business these days, not only in magazines and online chat rooms but also in philosophy. Whole books offer philosophical analyses of such movies as *The Matrix* and television series like *The Simpsons.* Music criticism and appreciation is a regular part of every magazine from *Vogue* to *The Nation,* and we not infrequently encounter news coverage of the latest studies, and speculations about what music means and why it moves us, both in general and in particular works. (English singer-songwriter Adele's "Someone Like You" has been discussed along these lines.) The number of magazines on decorating homes and gardens demonstrate that domestic aesthetics is a subject of considerable interest to many people. Again, the philosophical questions are how where we live affects us and how we can design our living and work space to make us more comfortable, happier, and more productive, as opposed to feeling depressed or claustrophobic or cluttered.

Our environment is not just a matter of where and how we choose to live, and the aesthetic choices of our lives are not limited to our selection of movies, television shows, and music to listen to. The aesthetics that surround us are largely imposed on us. A good example, so pervasive that we hardly even take note of it, is the ubiquitous advertising that surrounds and attacks us at every turn. In the movie *Minority Report* (2002), a billboard scans the hero's retina and speaks to him individually, backed by a database that includes all of his personal preferences. This is only a little far-fetched. Today, targeted advertising and the seemingly endless exchange of personal marketing data and contact addresses mean that we all receive or are exposed to an avalanche of somewhat personalized commercial messages throughout the day. Just think of all of the product and manufacturers' logos that you see every day on packages, appliances, your friends' hats and T-shirts, billboards, and shopping bags. Think of all of the ads on radio (including "ad-free" National Public Radio), television, and the Internet. How many junk fliers and catalogs do you see every day? How many magazines are composed almost entirely of well-posed advertisements, a few of which are disguised as articles? What do you think this does to your daily experience and the way you think about yourself and your world? These questions are part of aesthetics, too.

Many movies have a philosophical theme or philosophical implications. Pick one film that you have seen and explain its philosophical implications and its aesthetic effectiveness.

The Matrix has been analyzed as a virtual treatise on the difficulty of ascertaining what is reality and what is only appearance. The aesthetic questions we might ask, however, are how the film provokes our emotions and what makes us respond. What, for example, is the significance of the special effects? To what extent are the outfits of both the heroes and the villains suggestive? Did you catch the many references to ancient epics and classical tragedies? Similarly, the first trilogy of *Star Wars* films is rich in classical images, including references to the classical Indian epic the *Ramayana*. Again, how did the special effects enhance or detract from your enjoyment of these movies? How do you respond to these films in terms of their **Manichean** structure (that is, their interpretation of the world in terms of a battle between good and evil)? Does it bother you when (as in Part VI of the *Star Wars* series) the line between good and evil is no longer clear (as so often happens in everyday life)? If so, why?

We all listen to a great deal of music. It is hard to believe that only a century or so ago hearing music was limited to live performance—singing within the family, orchestras playing on special occasions, sing-alongs at a tavern, perhaps a concert in the park. Today, students often entertain themselves with thousands of prerecorded songs as they walk between classes, as they jog or exercise, in the car, and, occasionally, even in large classes. We all have favorite pieces of music, but very few of us have asked ourselves what it is we like so much about them. This is quite difficult. When describing our reaction to a film, for example, we can explain in some detail the characters, the plot, and the settings; when describing a piece of music, however, getting hold of anything so tangible is difficult. Most people do not know much music theory and have limited knowledge of musical notation, and so the description tends to be analogical or metaphorical. Describing a passage in terms of natural phenomena (waterfalls, thunder and lightning, fast-moving streams) or bodily functions (heart pounding, slow dancing) is sometimes the best that we can do. But this is fine. Just putting our reactions into words is often a giant step toward understanding what it is we like (or don't like) and why.

Write a review of a piece of music that particularly moves you (or perhaps turns you off). What is moving (or bothersome or boring) about it? How much of this impact is due to the words (if it is a song with lyrics)? How much is due to the instrumentation, the melody, the harmony, the rhythm, or the quality or nature of the voice(s)?

Finally, an even more difficult subject in everyday aesthetics is the concept of humor. What is it for something to be "funny"? Aristotle once said that laughing at someone is prompted by a sense of his or her inferiority (and, accordingly, one's own superiority). Freud suggested that laughter expresses relief, the release of suppressed thoughts or desires in a slightly revised or displaced form. (This would explain the prevalence of sexual and flatulence jokes in popular comedies.) Other philosophers (for example, Kant and Schopenhauer) insisted that humor depends on a sense of *incongruity*, some sort of startling surprise. Sometimes, of course, laughter has nothing to do with humor (for example, when you are tickled or, sometimes, when you are embarrassed), just as crying may have nothing to do with sadness (for example, when you are chopping onions). Sometimes, laughter is essentially a fellow feeling—people enjoying one another's company, without there needing to be anything particularly amusing. But the question "What makes something funny?" is nonetheless an interesting and sometimes profound aesthetic concern.

Tell a joke that you find particularly funny. What is it about it that makes it so funny? Of course, the explanation will not (usually) itself be funny, and explaining a joke may even seem to ruin it. But as an occasional exercise, it can be quite revealing and instructive.

"Are the Three Stooges Funny? Soitanly"

Most people have (happily or unhappily) seen a group called the Three Stooges, particularly in their classic incarnation of Larry FineHoward brothers Moe and Curly (and later brother Shemp). They exemplify a certain sort of humor, often neglected by philosophical and literary theorists, called slapstick. We need to raise an ethical question, whether slapstick can be enjoyed without guilt, for the very notion of laughing at (as opposed to laughing with) someone, even if they fully intend to be laughed at, surely raises ethical questions. And this leads us into the heart of ethics: Why is it so important to have a good sense of humor? And what is that? Does laughing at Larry, Moe, and Curly count, or is it, to the contrary, evidence that one does not have a sense of humor or, at any rate, does not have a "good" one? Plato warned against the dangers of humor, and he urged censorship to protect the guardians of the republic from the distortions and distractions of laughter. He had the slapstick comedies of Aristophanes in mind. Among Aristophanes's other faults—obscenity, blasphemy, and political incorrectness—he had committed the worst sin of all, making fun of Socrates.

—Robert C. Solomon, *Entertaining Ideas*, 1992

Closing Questions

1. Is there a difference in quality between current popular music and so-called classical music? Is there any plausible argument that one *ought* to prefer one to the other?

2. In what sense do we believe in objects or characters in fiction? Does it make sense to say that a work of art (say, a novel) is "*total fiction*," that is, that nothing in it is true?

3. Do you believe that art and aesthetic appreciation can make one a better person? How?

4. Why does listening to music move us? Pick a piece as an illustration.

5. Aesthetically evaluate your dorm room or apartment. What are its flaws and virtues? How well does it express you and your sensibilities? How well does it express your attitudes toward school? Toward life?

Suggested Readings

We cite in this chapter from the following important historical works in aesthetics: Plato, *Symposium,* trans. Paul Woodruff and Alexander Nehamas (Hackett, 1989); Plato, *The Republic,* trans. G. M. A. Grube (Hackett, 1974); Aristotle, *Poetics,* trans. Ingram Bywater (Clarendon Press, 1940); Immanuel Kant, *Critique of Judgment,* trans. W. Pluhar (Hackett, 1987); David Hume, "Of the Standard of Taste," in *Essays on Morality, Politics and Literature,* ed. T. H. Green (Longmans, 1882); Friedrich Nietzsche, *The Birth of Tragedy,* trans. Walter Kaufmann (Random House, 1967); José Ortega y Gasset, *The Dehumanization of Art and Other Essays* (Princeton University Press, 1948); and Robert C. Solomon, *Entertaining Ideas* (Buffalo, NY: Prometheus Books, 1992). A useful historical anthology is Albert Hofstadter and Richard Kuhns, eds., *Philosophies of Art and Beauty* (Chicago University Press, 1964). Three general anthologies are David Goldblatt and Lee B. Brown, *Aesthetics: A Reader in the Philosophy of the Arts,* 2nd ed. (Prentice Hall, 2004); Susan Feagin and Patrick Maynard, *Aesthetics* (Oxford, 1998); and Kathleen M. Higgins, *Aesthetics in Perspective* (Wadsworth, 1996), which includes a version of Mara Miller's "Art and the Construction of Self and Subject in Japan" and Timothy Binkley's "Piece: Contra Aesthetics." The latter originally appeared in *The Journal of Aesthetics and Art Criticism* 35(3) (Spring 1977): 265–277. Alex Neill's discussion of tragedy appears in Alex Neill, "Fiction and the Emotions," in *Arguing About Art,* ed. Alex Neill and Aaron Ridley, 2nd ed. (McGraw-Hill, 2001). Karsten Harries offers an account of the significance of developments in contemporary art in *The Meaning of Modern Art: A Philosophical Interpretation* (Northwestern University Press, 1968). Arthur Danto's *Transfiguration of the Commonplace* (Harvard University Press, 1981) offers a fascinating treatment of what makes something art. Danto discusses the avoidance of beauty in much contemporary art in *The Abuse of Beauty: Aesthetics and the Context of Art* (Open Court, 2003). For an alternative take on beauty in art see Alexander Nehamas, *Only a Promise of Happiness: The Place of Beauty in a World of Art* (Princeton University Press, 2007). For a general introduction to specific topics in aesthetics, see the *Blackwell Companion to Aesthetics,* ed. David Cooper et al., 2nd ed. (Blackwell, 2009).

Appendix A
Writing Philosophy

The true form in which truth exists can only be the scientific system of it; philosophy must be systematic.
—G. W. F. Hegel, 1770–1831

The will to a system is a lack of integrity . . . a subtle corruption, a philosopher trying to appear more stupid than he really is.
—Friedrich Nietzsche, 1844–1900

Preliminaries

1. By now you should know fairly well which ideas form the basis of your philosophy. The question at this point is what to do with them. Write down in a short list (no more than ten lines) the ideas that you want to present and defend. Rank them according to their importance to you and rewrite the list in order of this ranking with the most important ideas first.

2. Imagine yourself with a particular reader. (It might be a friend; it might well be your instructor. It might be a wholly imaginary reader, such as one of the great philosophers in history.) Take your list again and rank your ideas, this time in order of their probable appeal to this reader. Which ideas may be wholly agreeable? Which ones may be disagreeable? In other words, which can you present rather matter-of-factly, and which ones will you have to argue for?

3. Take these two lists together and plan a strategy of presentation. Decide which idea or ideas to begin with, presumably on the basis of initial agreeability, and sketch out a series of arguments from idea to idea. Be sure you make it clear which ideas you consider most important, which are merely preliminary, and which you consider to be consequences of your main idea.

4. Write a one-page abstract—that is, a summary of your intentions—in which you describe to your imaginary reader what you ultimately intend to prove and how and why. (This will be the first of several such abstracts before you actually sit down to write a final draft of your paper.)

The Rules of Good Writing in Philosophy

Philosophers sometimes feel more strongly about the *form* of philosophy than they do about its *content*—in other words, the particular view of the philosopher. This is for good reason. We have already said that most people in a society will have most of their views in common, and therefore it is the form, the style, the personality of the writing that gives a philosophy its distinctive character. By this time you are probably getting ready to begin your own writing or wondering how to begin, so this appendix is devoted to various forms in which a philosophical viewpoint can be expressed. At the same time, it will give you a chance to see a bit more of the variety of actual styles of some of the great philosophers in history. But the main idea is to provide you with some models for your own work.

We can distinguish two basic categories of philosophical presentation, which we call *standard* and *indirect*. In the standard presentation, you simply present your main ideas at the very beginning and then proceed to argue for them, give examples that support them, and show how they tie together. Indirect writing can take a number of forms, from the still rather straightforward but more subtle technique of saving your more controversial ideas until later, building up to them from viewpoints that are less controversial or even apparently trivial, to the much more difficult and complex styles of dialogue and aphoristic presentation. The distinction between the standard and indirect styles—like most distinctions—is somewhat overstated; most philosophies combine the two. But, at least to begin, let's look at philosophical presentation that is as straightforward as possible.

The rules of good philosophical presentation are the rules of good essay writing in general.

Organize

Organize your thoughts *before* you begin to write. Be clear about your main points, answer the primary questions (such as "What is the meaning of life?" "Do you believe in God?" and "What is real?"), and arrange these, not necessarily in order of importance to you, but in the order in which you feel most prepared to argue for them. In a straightforward presentation, your essay itself should show this organization.

An outstanding example of straightforward, point-by-point organization is found in Ludwig Wittgenstein's book *Tractatus Logico-Philosophicus*. (You will probably want a simpler title for your own work.) Wittgenstein organized his entire work around seven points, numbered them from 1 to 7, and then numbered the arguments and qualifications by decimals, such as, 1.1, 1.2, 1.21, 1.22. His philosophy is rather technical, but it might be worthwhile to show some of his basic outline.

1. The world is everything that is the case.

    1.1 The world is the totality of facts, not things.

2. What is the case—a fact—is the existence of a state of affairs.

    2.1 We picture facts to ourselves.
    2.2 A picture has a form in common with what it depicts.

3. A logical picture of facts is a thought.

4. A thought is a proposition with a meaning.

    4.1 Propositions represent the existence or nonexistence of states of affairs.

. . .

7. What we cannot speak of we must pass over in silence.

In the *Tractatus* Wittgenstein's writing is heavily analytic, and he tries to avoid grand metaphors. Most of his main claims seem rather obvious, but what Wittgenstein derives from them is not obvious and becomes dramatically inspirational. But you can see how straightforwardly the outline (and therefore the work) moves from one point to the next, beginning with a statement that seems totally unobjectionable and arguing from point to point.

A much longer and more imaginative work in which the organization is made obvious in its structure is Baruch Spinoza's *Ethics* (see pp. 127–128). Spinoza's outrageous conclusions—that individuality is an illusion, that there is no freedom, and that God is nothing but the universe itself—are embodied in a long technical work that begins with a number of statements that are so obvious that no one would think of questioning them. In fact, Spinoza designed his whole philosophy along lines of geometry and the proof of theorems from axioms and definitions, from which we can then prove further theorems, and so on, just as you did with triangles, lines, and points in high school. But Spinoza was talking about nothing less than the meaning of life, the existence of God, and the nature of reality. All of this, however, begins (as we have seen) with the definition of a technical word, *substance.*

You may find the geometric rigor a bit too cold for your own tastes, but this is to be balanced against the drama of Spinoza's images. Spinoza's *Ethics* provides an excellent illustration of how well-organized the best philosophies tend to be. In any case, even if you are not so explicit in your writing, it is a good idea to write an outline of the main ideas you want to establish, the order in which you want to establish them, and a sketch of the kinds of arguments, examples, and considerations you want to use.

Write Simply

Many students seem to feel that because they are doing philosophy and writing about such "profound" topics as the meaning of life, they ought to be particularly pompous and obscure. Writing good philosophy is like good journalism or good short story writing; it consists of simple, straightforward sentences. Except for a few specialized terms, it uses 25¢ words, not $3 words that are to be found only in a thesaurus. Say clearly what you want to say so that your readers don't have to spend their time trying to figure out what you mean. Let your reader know what you think, so that he or she knows right away how to discuss things with you. For example, consider this beginning statement in Kant's theory of morality:

> Nothing can possibly be conceived in the world, or even out of it, which can be called good without qualification, except a *good will*. Intelligence, wit, judgment, and other *talents* of the mind, however they may be named, or courage, resolution, perseverance, as qualities of temperament, are undoubtedly good and desirable in many respects; but these gifts of nature may also become extremely bad and mischievous if the will which is to make use of them, and which, therefore, constitutes what is called *character*, is not good. It is the same with the *gifts of fortune*. Power, riches, honor, even health, and the general well-being and contentment with one's condition which is called *happiness*, inspire pride and often presumption, if there is not a good will to correct the influence of these on the mind, and with this also to rectify the whole principle of acting, and adapt it to its end. The sight of a being who is not adorned with a single feature of a pure and good will, enjoying unbroken prosperity, can never give pleasure to an impartial rational spectator. Thus a good will appears to constitute the indispensable condition even of being worthy of happiness. (*Fundamental Principles of the Metaphysics of Morals*, 1785)

Be Clear

The philosopher Wittgenstein said, "Whatever can be said can be said clearly." There are some notable exceptions among the great philosophers, but for every obscure philosopher who for some reason becomes idolized by his students, hundreds are quite properly ignored. Reading them is not worth the time. Why hack a path through a jungle when there is a clear road in the same direction?

A good example of what your philosophy should *not* look like is this:

> Individual Being of every kind is, to speak quite generally, "*accidental.*" It is so-and-so, but essentially it could be other than it is. . . . But the import of this contingency, which is there called matter-of-factness (*Tatsächlichkeit*), is limited in this respect that the contingency is correlative to a *necessity* which does not carry the mere actuality-status of a valid rule of connexion obtaining between temporo-spatial facts, but has the character of *essential necessity,* and therewith a relation to *essential universality*. Now when we stated that every fact could be "essentially" other than it is, we were already expressing

thereby *that it belongs to the meaning of everything, contingent that it should have essential being and therewith an Eidos to be apprehended in all its purity;* and this Eidos comes under essential truths of varying degrees of universality.

There is no need for so much technical jargon, without examples or clarification. There is no need for a foreign word (*Eidos* is the word Plato used for "Form") when a good English word is available. There is no need for quotation marks when their only function is to undermine the significance of the word they enclose.

It happens that this passage is from a very important twentieth-century philosopher (Edmund Husserl, *Ideas*), but it must also be said that no one would possibly take the time to read it if it had not been written by someone already known to be profound and important. Most of us are not so lucky. If we don't write clearly, we have no right to expect to be read or understood or—more immediately—given a high grade.

Be Human

Remember you are trying to court the attention of your readers and make your views attractive and appealing. That means that they first have to feel that you really believe what you say and that they are sharing your thoughts rather than being attacked by them. Personal anecdotes and examples can help a great deal. Consider again this famous opening of René Descartes's *Meditations*:

> It is now some years since I detected how many were the false beliefs that I had from my earliest youth admitted as true, and how doubtful was everything I had since constructed on this basis; and from that time I was convinced that I must once for all seriously undertake to rid myself of all the opinions which I had formerly accepted, and commence to build anew from the foundation, if I wanted to establish any firm and permanent structure in the sciences. But as this enterprise appeared to be a very great one, I waited until I had attained an age so mature that I could not hope that at any later date I should be better fitted to execute my design. This reason caused me to delay so long that I should feel that I was doing wrong were I to occupy in deliberation the time that yet remains to me for action. Today, then, since very opportunely for the plan I have in view I have delivered my mind from every care (and am happily agitated by no passions) and since I have procured for myself an assured leisure in a peaceable retirement, I shall at last seriously and freely address myself to the general upheaval of all my former opinions.

Another effective use of anecdote appears in this well-known passage from David Hume's *Treatise of Human Nature*:

> Most fortunately it happens, that since reason is incapable of dispelling these clouds, nature herself suffices to that purpose, and cures me of this philosophical melancholy and delirium, either by relaxing this bent of mind, or by some avocation, and lively impression of my senses, which obliterate all

these chimeras. I dine, I play a game of backgammon, I converse, and am merry with my friends; and when after three or four hours' amusement, I would return to these speculations, they appear so cold, and strain'd, and ridiculous, that I cannot find in my heart to enter into them any farther.

Use Examples

It is no good starting a string of abstractions that never touch earth. If you are discussing the possibility of God's entering into earthly affairs, consider using an example or two from the Bible, the Qur'an, or another sacred text. If you are discussing the meaning of life, don't be afraid to talk about life. If you are talking about explanations in science, don't be afraid to use some examples from science. Consider, for example, the following use of examples by Immanuel Kant. He has just finished arguing, in a very abstract way, that a moral action is one that would make sense if everyone were to act similarly (see Chapter 8). And so he presents us with a series of examples in which this thesis is demonstrated:

1. A man reduced to despair by a series of misfortunes feels wearied of life, but is still so far in possession of his reason that he can ask himself whether it would not be contrary to his duty to himself to take his own life. Now he inquires whether the maxim of his action could become a universal law of nature. His maxim is: From self-love I adopt it as a principle to shorten my life when its longer duration is likely to bring more evil than satisfaction. It is asked then simply whether this principle founded on self-love can become a universal law of nature. Now we see at once that a system of nature of which it should be a law to destroy life by means of the very feeling whose special nature it is to impel to the improvement of life would contradict itself, and therefore could not exist as a system of nature; hence that maxim cannot possibly exist as a universal law of nature, and consequently would be wholly inconsistent with the supreme principle of all duty.

2. Another finds himself forced by necessity to borrow money. He knows that he will not be able to repay it, but sees also that nothing will be lent to him unless he promises stoutly to repay it in a definite time. He desires to make this promise, but he has still so much conscience as to ask himself: Is it not unlawful and inconsistent with duty to get out of a difficulty in this way? Suppose, however, that he resolves to do so, then the maxim of his action would be expressed thus: When I think myself in want of money, I will borrow money and promise to repay it, although I know that I never can do so. Now this principle of self-love or of one's own advantage may perhaps be consistent with my whole future welfare; but the question now is, Is it right? I change then the suggestion of self-love into a universal law, and state the question thus: How would it be if my maxim were a universal law? Then I see at once that it could never hold as a universal law of nature, but would necessarily contradict itself. For

supposing it to be a universal law that everyone when he thinks himself in a difficulty should be able to promise whatever he pleases, with the purpose of not keeping his promise, the promise itself would become impossible, as well as the end that one might have in view in it, since no one would consider that anything was promised to him, but would ridicule all such statements as vain pretenses.

3. A third finds in himself a talent which with the help of some culture might make him a useful man in many respects. But he finds himself in comfortable circumstances and prefers to indulge in pleasure rather than to take pains in enlarging and improving his happy natural capacities. He asks, however, whether his maxim of neglect of his natural gifts, besides agreeing with his inclination to indulgence, agrees also with what is called duty. He sees then that a system of nature could indeed subsist with such a universal law, although men (like the South Sea islanders) should let their talents rest and resolve to devote their lives merely to idleness, amusement, and propagation of their species—in a word, to enjoyment: but he cannot possibly *will* that this should be a universal law of nature, or be implanted in us as such by a natural instinct. For, as a rational being, he necessarily wills that his faculties be developed, since they serve him, and have been given him, for all sorts of possible purposes.

4. A fourth, who is in prosperity, while he sees that others have to contend with great wretchedness and that he could help them thinks: What concern is it of mine? Let everyone be as happy as Heaven pleases, or as he can make himself; I will take nothing from him nor even envy him, only I do not wish to contribute to his welfare or to his assistance in distress! Now no doubt, if such a mode of thinking were a universal law, the human race might very well subsist, and doubtless even better than in a state in which everyone talks of sympathy and good-will, or even takes care occasionally to put it into practice, but, on the other side, also cheats when he can, betrays the rights of men, or otherwise violates them. But although it is possible that a universal law of nature might exist in accordance with that maxim, it is impossible to *will* that such a principle should have the universal validity of a law of nature. For a will which resolved this would contradict itself, inasmuch as many cases might occur in which one would have a need of the love and sympathy of others, and in which, by such a law of nature, sprung from his own will, he would deprive himself of all hope of the aid he desires. (*Fundamental Principles of the Metaphysics of Morals*)

One author who is particularly well-known for his examples is the French existentialist Jean-Paul Sartre. Sartre, as you may well know, was also a novelist, playwright, and journalist. His abstract statements are often extremely abstruse, such as, "Being for itself [consciousness] is what it is not and is not what it is." But his examples, befitting a novelist, are almost always insightful, and he used them to break up his abstract prose and at every turn to get the reader to see his point. As an illustration of his conception of "bad faith," for example (see p. 210), he gives us the illustration of an anti-Semite (though any racist or extremely prejudiced person would do). And with this example, what otherwise might be an abstract philosophical concept becomes a very real flesh-and-blood problem.

> The anti-Semite has created the Jew from his need. Prejudice is not uninformed opinion. It is an attitude totally and freely chosen. . . . The anti-Semite is a man who is afraid, not of the Jews, of course, but of himself, of his conscience, his instincts, of his responsibilities, of solitude, of change, of society, and the world; of everything except the Jews. He is a coward who does not wish to admit his cowardice to himself, . . . a malcontent who dares not revolt for fear of the consequences of his rebellion. By adhering to his anti-Semitism, he is not only adopting an opinion, he is choosing himself as a person. . . . He is choosing the total irresponsibility of the warrior who obeys his leaders—and he has no leader. . . . The Jew is only a pretext; elsewhere it will be the Negro, the yellow race. . . . Anti-Semitism, in a word, is fear. . . . (*Anti-Semite and Jew*, 1946)

A third use of examples can be found in another existentialist, Søren Kierkegaard (whom we discuss in Chapter 3). Kierkegaard was concerned about the relationship between what he called the *ethical* life ("Do not kill," "Do not steal," and so on) and what he called the *religious* life, which is a life of devotion to God. Most people assume that these are the same, but Kierkegaard wondered whether they can sometimes conflict. He shows us how this might occur in an example drawn from the Bible, which is much more powerful than any long-winded, abstract discourse could be. The story, from Genesis, is the one in which God commands Abraham to prove his devotion by killing his son Isaac. What could be a more immoral act than to murder your own son? But what would be more irreligious than to disobey a direct command from God? In the example, Kierkegaard proves his point, though in the end, he argued, the two views of life can still be understood as compatible. Elsewhere, in a book called *Either/Or,* Kierkegaard made a similar point about the antagonism between the ethical life and what he calls the aesthetic life, the life of pleasure. His example is marriage, and with this example he captures all the differences between the moral life of duty and obligation and the irresponsible life of just enjoying oneself, whatever the cost to others. But again, it is the example that makes his distinctions and arguments work; otherwise his discourse would just be a string of abstractions.

Argue Your Point

Arguing doesn't have to be belligerent or nasty. In philosophy, to argue is to establish your viewpoint and give reasons why you accept it and why others ought to accept it, too. An argument begins with a statement that you can assume your reader already accepts and proceeds to some other views that your reader may not accept at all. Thus, Spinoza starts out with some noncontroversial definitions of words such as *substance* and *God* and *freedom* and a few axioms that no one could possibly disagree with, and then goes on to prove some extremely controversial views about life and God and ourselves.

to have someone specific in mind as you write) who will respond to your views and your arguments with objections and examples designed to show that you are wrong. One argument is almost never enough. Consider the following passage from Bishop Berkeley's *Principles*, which in effect includes an imaginary dialogue with an opponent. (The opponent he has in mind is John Locke.)

> But, say you, though the ideas themselves do not exist without the mind, yet there may be things *like* them, whereof they are copies or resemblances, which things exist without the mind in an unthinking substance. I answer, an idea can be like nothing but an idea; a color or figure can be like nothing but another color or figure. If we look but never so little into our thoughts, we shall find it impossible for us to conceive a likeness except only between our ideas. Again, I ask whether those supposed originals or external things, of which our ideas are the pictures or representations, be themselves perceivable or no? If they are, then they are ideas and we have gained our point; but if you say they are not, I appeal to anyone whether it be sense to assert a color is like something which is invisible, hard or soft, like something which is intangible; and so of the rest.

Define Your Specialized Terms

If you introduce a technical term that is not part of ordinary speech or if you use an ordinary word in some special way, tell the reader what you mean, and *stick to that meaning*. If you use the word *substance* to refer to the ultimate units of reality, say clearly (as many great philosophers have failed to do) what will count as a substance and how you know whether something is or is not a substance. Do not at any point slip into our ordinary use of the word *substance* (to refer, for example, to gum on your shoe, or the unknown stuff in the pot in the garage). Do not feel compelled, though, to define your terms at every turn of the argument. You can take it for granted that your readers understand ordinary English, as long as you use ordinary English.

A straightforward but somewhat clumsy way of introducing your specialized terms is to define them right at the beginning, in a series of specialized definitions, as we saw in Spinoza's *Ethics* (pp. 127–128). A more graceful way of doing so is to introduce them as they appear in your essay, building the definition right into your discussion. For example, Immanuel Kant introduced the technical terms *empirical* and *a priori* into his discussion in this way:

> Is there any knowledge that is independent of experience and even of all the impressions of the senses? Such knowledge is called *a priori* and distinguished from the *empirical*, which has its sources in experience. (*Critique of Pure Reason*, 1781)

Whenever you use words such as *subjective* and *objective*, which have been defined in a variety of different ways (see Chapter 5), it is particularly important to be clear which definition you are using and *stick to it*. It is also important not to define words in ordinary English in ways that are at odds with that ordinary usage, for this is sure to cause confusion. For example, Ayn Rand defined the ordinary word *selfishness* as simply "acting for one's own benefit," whereas the ordinary word means "acting for one's own benefit and *against the interest of others*." Not surprisingly, then, Rand later had to defend herself by insisting, "If it is true that what I mean by 'selfishness' is not what is meant conventionally, then this is one of the worst indictments of altruism: it means that altruism permits no view of a self-respecting, self-supporting man." But, of course, Rand herself had defined the terms this way and the problem she raised is primarily of her own creation.

Use the History of Philosophy

Don't be afraid to bring in the opinions of other philosophers you have read to support your view. You can repeat their arguments (with an acknowledgment that you are doing so); you can quote them. You can use a particularly appealing phrase or description they use to amplify your own views. You can begin by quoting or representing other philosophers' views to which you are directly opposed. And as you argue your position, it is always a good idea to think of those philosophers who would certainly disagree with you and what they might say (or have already said) in reply. Of course, you can't know the whole history of philosophy when you're just beginning, but the more you know, the better. The more clearly you see yourself as part of that long tradition and other people's terms and ideas as influencing your own, the more confident you'll feel about what you say. The idea that each of us is supposed to have an "original" philosophy is utter nonsense. Indeed, an amusing exercise is to try to reduce the thoughts of the great philosophers down to slogans your grandmother might have said to you—such as reducing Kant's whole moral philosophy (see Chapter 8) down to the question "What if everyone else were to do that?" It is doubtful that there are any completely new ideas. Even Einstein's views have precedents among the ideas of the early Greek scientists. What makes philosophy worthwhile is not total newness but the ongoing conversation extending through a long tradition and the individual styles and personalities (including your own) that contribute to it.

The rules for using other philosophers are simple enough: When you represent them, be sure that you do so accurately. If you offer an interpretation of a philosopher that is unusual or controversial, say so. ("I am aware that this is not the usual view of Socrates, but I think I can justify it on the grounds that . . . .") If you follow some other commentator, it is usually a good idea to say so. ("According to the noted Spinoza scholar S. H., . . .") And whenever you borrow ideas or phrases and especially longer quotations, *name your sources*. A footnote will do, or in more informal writing you can mention your sources in the text. For instance, you could say "As Hegel argued in his *Phenomenology*, . . ." or "In the more dramatic expression suggested by Hegel, '. . .!'" Don't make oblique allusions to famous philosophers unless the references are so obvious to your readers that no one will be left in the dark. For example, in his *Phenomenology of Spirit*, Hegel freely alluded to "the philosopher of the One Substance" without naming him, but everyone would know he meant Spinoza. In other places, however, Hegel alluded to philosophers whose identities were not so readily known, and the result was confusion and wasteful scholarly controversy over whom he really meant.

Indirect Styles

Indirect styles are *much more difficult* to bring off than straightforward presentations, and you are *well advised to check with your instructor* before trying the indirect approach for your own project. **These styles are not, in general, recommended for introductory philosophy students, except, perhaps, as a personal experiment.** One form of indirect style, however, is safe enough, and we have already treated it as "standard"—namely, that seductive approach (as in Spinoza) in which you save your most important conclusions for last and begin with a far less controversial set of statements, designed to lead readers from what they will certainly agree with to what they most likely will not. The problem with this method, and the problem many students have reading an author like Spinoza, is that readers get bored long before they get to the best part. So if you attempt this strategy, you need to proceed as if you were writing a mystery novel: you have to attract the reader's interest right from the beginning, by presenting certain problems that will keep everyone puzzled, by making a personal appeal that will convince everyone that this is a worthwhile project to pursue. What usually does not work is continually promising the reader great things to come. ("Later on, we will see the exciting consequences of this.") Most readers (especially instructors who are reading dozens of papers) will get restless long before then and will probably be disappointed when they get there.

Dialogue Style

The first and most famous style of indirect presentation is the *dialogue* style, which is the style of Plato's accounts of Socrates's discussions with his friends—thus called "Socratic dialogues." (In fact, as we have already pointed out, Plato made up many of these dialogues, and Socrates probably never had any such discussions as they are presented.) The strategy of these dialogues is to get someone else to make a philosophical statement, so that Socrates can refute it. The sequence of statements and refutations is such that, by the end, Socrates (Plato) emerges with his own view, which has been demonstrated to be better than all of the rest. The following excerpt is from Plato's *Theaetetus*.

SOCRATES: *To start all over again, then: what is one to say that knowledge is? For surely we are not going to give up yet.*

THEAETETUS: *Not unless you do so.*

SOCR.: *Then tell me: what definition can we give with the least risk of contradicting ourselves?*

THEAET.: *The one we tried before, Socrates. I have nothing else to suggest.*

SOCR.: *What was that?*

THEAET.: *That true belief is knowledge. Surely there can at least be no mistake in believing what is true and the consequences are always satisfactory.*

SOCR.: *Try, and you will see, Theaetetus, as the man said when he was asked if the river was too deep to ford. So here, if we go forward on our search, we may stumble upon something that will reveal the thing we are looking for. We shall make nothing out, if we stay where we are.*

THEAET.: *True; let us go forward and see.*

SOCR.: *Well, we need not go far to see this much: you will find a whole profession to prove that true belief is not knowledge.*

THEAET.: *How so? What profession?*

SOCR.: *The profession of those paragons of intellect known as orators and lawyers. There you have men who use their skill to produce conviction, not by instruction, but by making people believe whatever they want them to believe. You can hardly imagine teachers so clever as to be able, in the short time allowed by the clock, to instruct their hearers thoroughly in the true facts of a case of robbery or other violence which those hearers had not witnessed.*

THEAET.: *No, I cannot imagine that; but they can convince them.*

SOCR.: *And by convincing you mean making them believe something.*

THEAET.: *Of course.*

SOCR.: *And when a jury is rightly convinced of facts which can be known only by an eye-witness, then, judging by hearsay and accepting a true belief, they are judging without knowledge, although, if they find the right verdict, their conviction is correct?*

THEAET.: *Certainly.*

SOCR.: *But if true belief and knowledge were the same thing the best of jurymen could never have a correct belief without knowledge. It now appears that they must be different things.*

A more modern example is Bishop George Berkeley's dialogue on idealism and materialism in "Three Dialogues":

PHILONOUS: *Either, Hylas, you are jesting, or have a very bad memory. Though indeed we went through all the qualities by name one after another; yet my arguments, or rather your concessions nowhere tended to prove, that the secondary qualities did not subsist each alone by itself: but that they were not at all without the mind. Indeed in treating of figure and motion, we concluded they could not exist without the mind, because it was impossible even in thought to separate them from all secondary qualities, so as to conceive them existing by themselves. But then this was not the only argument made use of upon that occasion. But (to pass by all that hath been hitherto said, and reckon it for nothing, if you will have it so) I am content to put the whole upon this issue. If you can conceive it possible for any mixture or combination of qualities, or any sensible object whatever, to exist without the mind, then I will grant it actually to be so.*

HYLAS: *If it comes to that, the point will soon be decided. What more easy than to conceive a tree or house existing by itself, independent of, and unperceived by any mind whatsoever? I do at this present time conceive them existing after that manner.*

PHIL.: *How say you, Hylas, can you see a thing which is at the same time unseen?*

HYL.: *No, that were a contradiction.*

PHIL.: *Is it not as great a contradiction to talk of conceiving a thing which is unconceived?*

HYL.: *It is.*

PHIL.: *The tree or house therefore which you think of, is conceived by you.*

HYL.: *How should it be otherwise?*

PHIL.: *And what is conceived is surely in the mind.*

HYL.: *Without question, that which is conceived is in the mind.*

PHIL.: *How then came you to say, you conceived a house or tree existing independent and out of all minds whatsoever?*

HYL.: *That was, I own, an oversight; but stay, let me consider what led me into it.—It is a pleasant mistake enough. As I was thinking of a tree in a solitary place, where no one was present to see it, methought that was to conceive a tree as existing unperceived or unthought of, not considering that I myself conceived it all the while. But now I plainly see, that all I can do is to frame ideas in my own mind. I may indeed conceive in my own thoughts the idea of a tree, or a house, or a mountain, but that is all. And this is far from proving, that I can conceive them existing out of the minds of all spirits.*

PHIL.: *You acknowledge then that you cannot possibly conceive how any one corporeal sensible thing should exist otherwise than in a mind.*

HYL.: *I do.*

PHIL.: *And yet you will earnestly contend for the truth of that which you cannot so much as conceive.*

HYL.: *I profess I know not what to think, but still there are some scruples remain with me. Is it not certain I see things at a distance? Do we not perceive the stars and moon, for example, to be a great way off? Is not this, I say, manifest to the senses?*

PHIL.: *Do you not in a dream too perceive those or the like objects?*

HYL.: *I do.*

PHIL.: *And have they not then the same appearance of being distant?*

HYL.: *They have.*

PHIL.: *But you do not thence conclude the apparitions in a dream to be without the mind?*

HYL.: *By no means.*

PHIL.: *You ought not therefore to conclude that sensible objects are without the mind, from their appearance or manner wherein they are perceived.*

HYL.: *I acknowledge it. But doth not my sense deceive me in those cases?*

PHIL.: *By no means. The idea or thing which you immediately perceive, neither sense nor reason inform you that it actually exists without the mind. By sense you only know that you are affected with such certain sensations of light and colours, etc. And these you will not say are without the mind.*

HYL.: *True: but beside all that, do you not think the sight suggests something of outness or distance?*

PHIL.: *Upon approaching a distant object, do the visible size and figure change perpetually, or do they appear the same at all distances?*

HYL.: *They are in a continual change.*

PHIL.: *Sight therefore doth not suggest or in any way inform you, that the visible object you immediately perceive, exists at a distance, or will be perceived when you advance further onward, there being a continued series of visible objects succeeding each other, during the whole time of your approach.*

HYL.: *It doth not; but still I know, upon seeing an object, what object I shall perceive after having passed over a certain distance: no matter whether it be exactly the same or no: there is still something of distance suggested in the case.*

PHIL.: *Good Hylas, do but reflect a little on the point, and then tell me whether there be any more in it than this. From the ideas you actually perceive by sight, you have by experience learned to collect what other ideas you will (according to the standing order of nature) be affected with, after such a certain succession of time and motion.*

HYL.: *Upon the whole, I take it to be nothing else.*

PHIL.: *Now is it not plain, that if we suppose a man born blind was on a sudden made to see, he could at first have no experience of what may be suggested by sight.*

HYL.: *It is.*

PHIL.: *He would not then, according to you, have any notion of distance annexed to the things he saw, but would take them for a new set of sensations existing only in his mind.*

HYL.: *It is undeniable.*

PHIL.: *But to make it still more plain; is not distance a line turned endwise to the eye?*

HYL.: *It is.*

PHIL.: *And can a line so situated be perceived by sight?*

HYL.: *It cannot.*

PHIL.: *Doth it not therefore follow that distance is not properly and immediately perceived by sight?*

HYL.: *It should seem so.*

PHIL.: *Again, is it your opinion that colours are at a distance?*

HYL.: *It must be acknowledged, they are only in the mind.*

PHIL.: *But do not colours appear to the eye as coexisting in the same place with extension and figures?*

HYL.: *They do.*

PHIL.: *How can you then conclude from sight, that figures exist without, when you acknowledge colours do not; the sensible appearance being the very same with regard to both?*

HYL.: *I know not what to answer.*

PHIL.: *But allowing that distance was truly and immediately perceived by the mind, yet it would not thence follow it existed out of the mind. For whatever is immediately perceived is an idea: and can any idea exist out of the mind?*

Ironic Style

The second strategy is even more difficult than the first; it is the style of *irony,* in which one attacks a view by stating it in such a way that it becomes ridiculous. Consider the following parody from Voltaire's *Candide,* in which Voltaire makes fun of Leibniz's view that this is the "best of all possible worlds":

Half the enfeebled passengers, suffering from that inconceivable anguish which the rolling of a ship causes in the nerves and in all the humors of bodies shaken in contrary directions, did not retain strength enough even to trouble about the danger. The other half screamed and prayed; the sails were torn, the masts broken, the vessel leaking. Those worked who could, no one cooperated, no one commanded. The Anabaptist tried to help the crew a little; he was on the main deck; a furious sailor struck him violently and stretched him on the deck; but the blow he delivered gave him so violent a shock that he fell head-first out of the ship. He remained hanging and clinging to part of the broken mast. The good Jacques ran to his aid, helped him to climb back, and from the effort he made was flung into the sea in full view of the sailor, who allowed him to drown without condescending even to look at him. Candide came up, saw his benefactor reappear for a moment and then be engulfed for ever. He tried to throw himself after him into the sea: he was prevented by the philosopher Pangloss, who proved to him that the Lisbon roads had been expressly created for the Anabaptist to be drowned in them. While he was proving this a priori, the vessel sank, and every one perished except Pangloss, Candide, and the brutal sailor who had drowned the virtuous Anabaptist: the blackguard swam successfully to the shore and Pangloss and Candide were carried there on a plank.

When they had recovered a little, they walked toward Lisbon; they had a little money by the help of which they hoped to be saved from hunger after having escaped the storm. Weeping the death of their benefactor, they had scarcely set foot in the town when they felt the earth tremble under their feet; the sea rose in foaming masses in the port and smashed the ships which rode at anchor. Whirlwinds of flame and ashes covered the streets and squares; the houses collapsed, the roofs were thrown upon the foundations, and the foundations were scattered; thirty thousand inhabitants of every age and both sexes were crushed under the ruins. . . .

Next day they found a little food as they wandered among the ruins and regained a little strength. Afterwards they worked like others to help the inhabitants who had escaped the death. Some citizens they had assisted gave them as good a dinner as could be expected in such a disaster; true, it was a dreary meal; the hosts watered their bread with their tears, but Pangloss consoled them by assuring them that things could not be otherwise. "For," said he, "all this is for the best, for, if there is a volcano at Lisbon, it cannot be anywhere else; for it is impossible that things should not be where they are; for all is well."

Aphoristic Style

The most difficult style of all is the *aphoristic.* Like acupuncture, it hits all the vital points, but it is, figuratively, like dozens or hundreds of little pinpricks in a body of views that are already well established. What is essential, therefore, is that it be extremely clear to your reader what the point of these pricks is supposed to be. And it is equally important that the pricks be sharp and *to the point*. A dull aphorism is like a dull needle; it either doesn't get through at all or else it is very painful. You might try your hand at a few of these, but it is not advisable that you make this the style of your overall project.

Two simple aphorisms that we can use as examples are the German aphorist Lichtenberg's remark—aimed directly at the argument from design—that it is lucky that God made slits in the cat's skin right where his eyes are and Nietzsche's comment on the phony obscurity of his contemporaries: "They muddy the waters to make them look deep." A good aphorism is very short—rarely more than a sentence; it is usually extremely clever and must go right to the heart of the matter. And it must be clear what the "matter" is. For instance, Kierkegaard's aphorism, "It is one thing to stand on one leg and prove God's existence and quite another to go down on one's knees and pray to him" strikes at the heart of the whole history of theology. Here is another of Kierkegaard's aphorisms, from his *Journal*:

> The two ways: One is to suffer; the other is to become a professor of the fact that another suffered.

This is an indictment of abstract learning as opposed to passionate participation. He makes the same point, too, against abstraction in this aphorism, also from his *Journal*:

> Like Leporello, learned literary men keep a list; while Don Juan seduces girls and enjoys himself, Leporello notes down the time, the place, and the description of the girl.

Here is another:

> People hardly ever make use of the freedom they do have, for example, freedom of thought; instead they demand freedom of speech as compensation.

Nietzsche was one of the great aphoristic philosophers of all times, but even he admitted that behind all of his aphorisms, he was much clearer about what he hated than what he was aiming for. Some of his aphorisms were a cutting sentence—for example, a whole theory of truth in a single line, "What after all are man's truths but his *irrefutable* errors?" Others were a full paragraph. A short set of selections follows:

> *One becomes moral—not because one is moral.* Submission to morality can be slavish or vain or selfish or resigned or obtusely enthusiastic or thoughtless or an act of desperation, like submission to a prince: in itself it is nothing moral.

> *Corruption.* The surest way to corrupt a youth is to instruct him to hold in higher esteem those who think alike than those who think differently. (*The Dawn*, 1881.)

A people is nature's detour to arrive at six or seven great men—and then to get around them. (*Beyond Good and Evil*, 1886)

From a doctoral examination. "What is the task of all higher education?" To turn men into machines. "What are the means?" Man must learn to be bored.

The natural value of egoism. Self-interest is worth as much as the person who has it: it can be worth a great deal, and it can be unworthy and contemptible. (*Twilight of the Idols*, 1889)

Finally, there is the later philosophy of Wittgenstein. Earlier in this appendix, we introduced you to the strategy of his *Tractatus Logico-Philosophicus*, which he wrote during World War I. By 1940 he had changed his mind, and produced several books of aphorisms, all of which presumed intimate knowledge with the whole of contemporary philosophy and his own philosophy in particular. The following aphorisms, from *Philosophical Investigations*, are carefully designed, for example, to challenge such standard philosophical beliefs as the idea that each of us has sensations that we can know better than anyone else:

Imagine a person whose memory could not retain *what* the word "pain" meant—so that he constantly called different things by that name—but nevertheless used the word in a way fitting in with the usual symptoms and presuppositions of pain—in short he uses it as we all do. Here I should like to say, a wheel that can be turned though nothing else moves with it, is not part of the mechanism.

The essential thing about private experience is really not that each person possesses his own exemplar, but that nobody knows whether other people also have this or something else. The assumption would thus be possible—though unverifiable—that one section of mankind had one sensation of red and another section another.

Look at a stone and imagine it having sensations.—One says to oneself: How could one so much as get the idea of ascribing a sensation to a thing? One might as well ascribe it to a number!—And now look at a wriggling fly and at once these difficulties vanish and pain seems able to get a foothold here, where before everything was, so to speak, too smooth for it.

Think of the recognition of facial expressions. Or of the description of facial expressions—which does not consist in giving the measurements of the face! Think, too, how one can imitate a man's face without seeing one's own in a mirror.

But isn't it absurd to say of a body that it has pain?—And why does one feel an absurdity in that? In what sense is it true that my hand does not feel pain, but I [feel pain] in my hand?

What sort of issue is: Is it the body that feels pain—How is it to be decided? What makes it plausible to say that it is not the body?—Well, something like this: if someone has a pain in his hand, then the hand does not say so (unless it writes it) and one does not comfort the hand, but the sufferer: one looks into his face.

The form of philosophy is as important to the ultimate presentation of the project as the particular opinions in it. But regardless of your choice of form, the most important thing is that your writing represent careful and clear-headed thinking and that it serve to introduce the reader and entice him or her to your own view of the world. Most philosophers—including the great aphorists—begin with a straightforward presentation, at least in order to make their ideas clear. (Even Plato wrote straightforward essays, but we have lost them.) The most sensible way to start is by straightforwardly setting down your main ideas, ordering them in a brief (one-page) argument, and then filling out the details, providing quotations and examples as you expand the presentation. Then, if you feel like experimenting, you might want to try your hand at a short dialogue, or at a short series of aphorisms to supplement what you have done. But the overall effect always must be an impression of clear thinking and passionate involvement in thinking. Philosophy, in any of its forms, is never anything else.

Suggested Readings

Ludwig Wittgenstein, *Tractatus Logico-Philosophicus* (Routledge & Kegan Paul, 1960). Immanuel Kant, *Fundamental Principles of the Metaphysics of Morals*, trans. T. K. Abbott (Longmans, Green, 1898). Edmund Husserl, *Ideas: General Introduciton of Pure Phenomenology*, trans. W. R. Boyce Gibson (Collier, 1931/1962). René Descartes, *Meditations on First Philosophy*, in *The Philosophical Works of Descartes*, trans. Elizabeth S. Haldane and G. R. T. Ross (Cambridge University Press, 1911). David Hume, *A Treatise of Human Nature*, ed. L. A. Selby-Bigge (Oxford University Press, 1888). Bertrand Russell, *A History of Western Philosophy* (Simon and Schuster, 1945). St. Thomas Aquinas, *Summa Theologica*, trans. Fathers of the English Dominican Province (New York: Benziger, Bruce & Glencoe, 1948). George Berkeley, *Treatise Concerning the Principles of Human Knowledge* (Doubleday, Doran, and Company, 1935). Immanuel Kant, *Critique of Pure Reason*, trans. Norman Kemp Smith (St. Martin's Press, 1929). Plato, *Theaetetus*, trans. Francis M. Cornford (Bobbs-Merrill, 1957). George Berkeley, *Three Dialogues between Hylas and Philonous* (Harvard Classics, 1909–1914). Voltaire, *Candide, or Optimism*, ed. Norman L. Torrey (Appelton-Century-Crofts, 1946), Søren Kierkegaard, *The Journals*, trans. Alexander Dru (Oxford University Press, 1938). Friedrich Nietzsche, *Beyond Good and Evil*, trans. Walter Kaufmann (Random House, 1966). *The Portable Nietzsche*, trans. Walter Kaufmann (Penguin, 1982). Friedrich Nietzsche, *The Gay Science*, trans. Walter Kaufmann (Random House, 1974). Ludwig Wittgenstein, *Philosophical Investigations*, trans. G. E. M. Anscombe (Macmillan, 1970).

Appendix B
Deductive Logic Valid Argument Forms

In "A Little Logic," we introduced the distinction between the truth (or falsity) of a statement and the validity (or invalidity) of a deductive argument. It is possible for an argument to be valid even if its premises and conclusion are false. For example:

All dogs are green

Socrates is a dog

Therefore, Socrates is green.

This is a valid argument, even though both the premises and the conclusion are false. For a deductive argument to guarantee the truth of its conclusion, the premises must be true *and* the argument must be valid. Here we will say a little bit more about what it means for an argument to be valid.

A valid argument has the right *form;* invalid arguments do not. The right form of an argument is based on a list of basic rules of inference, such as the following:

The syllogistic form

All Ps are Qs.

S is a P.

Therefore, S is a Q.

is a valid form, as we saw above. But

All Ps are Qs.

S is a Q.

Therefore, S is a P.

is not. How do we know? Because the definition of a (valid) deductive argument is that the truth of the premises guarantees the truth of the conclusion, we try to find an argument that fits the form that does indeed have true premises and a false conclusion. If there is no such argument, the form is a valid argument form.

If there is *any* such argument, then it is not a valid argument form. So, we know that the above form is invalid because we can make up an example such as:

> All lemons are yellow.
>
> Sam (the canary) is yellow.
> _____
> Therefore, Sam is a lemon.

When you suspect that an argument in philosophy is invalid, translate the argument into formal symbolism ("All Ps are Ss . . .") and then find another argument with true premises and a false conclusion that fits the form ("That's like arguing that . . ."). If even one such instance of an argument form is invalid, then the form itself is not a valid argument form.

The most familiar form of deductive argument, the form illustrated above, is the *categorical syllogism*. A syllogism consists of three lines—two premises and a conclusion—and contains three terms or categories. (The term that appears in both premises is called the middle term.) The form of the statements themselves is quantitative, preceded by "all," "some," "no . . . ," and "not all . . ."

But not all deductive arguments are syllogisms; others involve a variety of inferences and complexities. Two of the most frequently used and best-known have the Latin names **modus ponens** and **modus tollens**. Modus ponens has the form:

> If P then Q.
>
> P.
> _____
> Therefore, Q.

For example:

> If Socrates keeps annoying people, he'll get in trouble.
>
> Socrates won't stop annoying people.
> _____
> Therefore, he'll get in trouble.

Modus tollens has the form:

> If P then Q.
>
> Not Q.
> _____
> Therefore, not P.

For example:

> If you care enough, you'll send the very best.
>
> You are not sending the very best.
> _____
> Therefore, you do not care enough.

Although any argument that fits one of these forms is valid, whether or not it is also sound depends on the truth of its premises.

There are two arguments that superficially look like modus ponens and modus tollens but are in fact invalid. They are:

If P then Q.	If P then Q.
Q.	Not P.
————	————
Therefore, P.	Therefore, not Q.

For example,

If you stay up too late, you'll miss breakfast.
You missed breakfast.
————————————————
Therefore, you stayed up too late.

If you stay up too late, you'll miss breakfast.
You didn't stay up too late.
————————————————
Therefore, you didn't miss breakfast.

These two fallacies are called the *fallacy of affirming the consequent* and the *fallacy of denying the antecedent.* They must always be avoided!

One type of argument, which is really a kind of modus tollens, is of special use in philosophy. It is called the *reductio ad absurdum* or "reduction to absurdity." One philosopher argues that P (for example, "Justice is whatever the strongest person insists on."). Her opponent argues that if P, then Q (for example, "If justice is the will of the strongest, then it is just for the strongest to be unjust."). But Q in this case is obviously absurd and therefore false—so the original claim P must be false as well. (The example is a famous argument by Socrates.) One good way to attack a philosophical position is to show that regardless of the apparent logic, its consequences are absurd.

Hating Logic

There is one danger that we must guard against, Socrates said.

What sort of danger? I asked.

Of becoming misologic [hating logic], he said, in the sense that people become misanthropic. No greater misfortune could happen to anyone than that of developing a dislike for argument. Misology and misanthropy arise in just the same way. Misanthropy is induced by believing in somebody quite uncritically. You assume that a person is absolutely truthful and

(continues)

Hating Logic (continued)

sincere and reliable, and a little later you find that he is shoddy and unreliable. Then the same thing happens again. After repeated disappointments at the hands of the very people who might be supposed to be your nearest and most intimate friends, constant irritation ends by making you dislike everybody and suppose that there is no sincerity to be found anywhere . . .

The resemblance between arguments and human beings lies in this: that when one believes that an argument is true without reference to the art of logic, and then a little later decides rightly or wrongly that it is false, and the same thing happens again and again . . . they end by believing that they are wiser than anyone else, because they alone have discovered that there is nothing stable or dependable either in facts or in arguments, and that everything fluctuates just like the water in a tidal channel, and never stays at any point for any time . . .

But suppose that there is an argument which is true and valid but someone spent his life loathing arguments and so missed the chance of knowing the truth about reality—would that not be a deplorable thing?

—Plato, *Phaedo* 89d–90e, fourth century BCE

From: Tredennick, Hugh. *The Last Days of Socrates.*
(Harmondsworth, UK: Penguin, 1954).

Rules of Inference

$\supset$ = if, then

$\sim$ = not

$\cdot$ = and

$\vee$ = or

$\therefore$ = therefore

1. *Modus Ponens (M.P.)*

$p \supset q$

p

$\therefore q$

2. *Modus Tollens (M.T.)*

$p \supset q$

$\sim q$

$\therefore p$

3. *Hypothetical Syllogism (H.S.)*

    p ⊃ q

    q ⊃ r

    ∴ p ⊃ r

4. *Disjunctive Syllogism (D.S.)*

    p ∨ q

    ~ p

    ∴ q

5. *Constructive Dilemma (C.D.)*

    (p ⊃ q) · (r ⊃ s)

    p ∨ r

    ∴ q ∨ s

6. *Absorption (Abs.)*

    p ⊃ q

    ∴ p ⊃ (p · q)

7. *Simplification (Simp.)*

    p · q

    ∴ p

8. *Conjunction (Conj.)*

    p

    q

    ∴ p · q

10. *Addition (Add.)*

    p

    ∴ p ∨ q

Irving Copi, *Introduction to Logic.* 7th ed. New York: Macmillan, 1986. 311–12.

Appendix C
Common Informal Fallacies

Informal Fallacies
꧁꧂

Many intended arguments are fallacious even though they are, formally, valid arguments; that is, they do not violate the rules of inference and the proper forms of deductive argument. They are nevertheless bad arguments. A tautology, for example, is a straightforwardly valid argument ("If P, then P."). But obviously such an argument, in the context of a discussion or a philosophy paper, does nothing to further the point to be made. The following is a list of often-made but almost always bad informal fallacies:

Mere Assertion

The fact that you accept a position is not sufficient for anyone else to believe it. Stating your view is not an argument for it, and unless you are just answering a public opinion survey, every opinion always deserves a supporting argument. There are statements, of course, that everyone would accept at face value, and you need not argue those. But that does not mean that they cannot be argued, for even the most obvious facts of common sense must be argued when challenged— this is what much of philosophy is about.

Begging the Question

Another fallacy is something that looks like an argument but simply accepts as a premise what is supposed to be argued for as a conclusion. For example, suppose you are arguing that one ought to be a Christian and your reason is that the Bible tells you so. This may in fact be conclusive for you, but if you are trying to convince someone who doesn't believe in Christ, he or she will probably not believe what the Bible says either. As an argument for becoming a Christian, therefore, referring to the Bible begs the question because it assumes the authority of the Bible, when this is in fact part of what you are trying to prove (the truth of Christianity and its sacred scripture). Question begging often consists of a re-worded conclusion, as in "this book will improve your grades because it will help you to do better in your courses."

Vicious Circle

Begging the question is similar to another error, which is often called arguing in a vicious circle. Consider a more elaborate version of the above fallacy. A person claims to know God exists because she has had a religious vision. Asked how she knows that the vision was religious rather than just the effect of something she ate, she replies that such an elaborate and powerful experience could not have been caused by anyone or anything but God. Asked how she knows this, she replies that God himself told her—in the vision. Or another example: "He must be guilty because of the look on his face." "How do you know that he looks guilty rather than frightened or sad?" "Because he's the one who did it, that's why!" If you argue *A* because of *B*, and *B* because of *C*, but then *C* because of *A*, you have argued in a vicious circle. It is vicious because, as in begging the question, you have assumed just what you want to prove.

But this is worth remembering: ultimately, all positions may come full circle, depending on certain beliefs that can be defended only if you accept the rest of a great many beliefs. Debates between religious people and atheists are often like this or arguments between free marketers and Marxists, where many hours of argument show quite clearly that each person accepts a large system of beliefs, all of which depend on the others. Some logicians call this a virtuous circle, but this does not mean that there are no vicious circles. A virtuous circle is the development of an entire worldview, and it requires a great deal of thinking and organizing. Vicious circles, like begging the question, are usually shortcuts to nowhere that result from careless thinking.

Irrelevancies

You have seen people who argue a point by arguing everything else, throwing up charts of statistics and complaining about the state of the universe and telling jokes—everything but getting to the point. This may be a technique of wearing out your opponent; it is not a way of persuading him or her to agree with you. No matter how brilliant an argument may be, it is no good to you unless it is relevant to the point you want to defend.

Ad Hominem Arguments

The most distasteful kind of irrelevancy is an attack on your opponent personally instead of arguing against his or her position. It may well be that the person you are arguing against is a liar, a sloppy dresser, ugly, too young to vote, or too old to work, but the only question is whether what he or she says is to be accepted. Harping on the appearance, reputation, manners, intelligence, friends, or possessions of your opponent may sometimes give your readers insight into why he or she holds a certain position, but it does not prove or disprove the position itself. As insight into an opponent's motives or personal considerations may, in small doses, be appropriate. But more than a very small dose is usually offensive, and it will usually weigh more against you than against your opponent. Whenever possible, avoid this kind of argument completely. It usually indicates that you don't have any good arguments yourself.

Unclear or Shifting Conclusions

One of the most frustrating arguments to read is an argument that has a vague conclusion or that shifts conclusions with every paragraph. If something is worth defending at all, it is worth stating clearly and sticking with. If you argue that drug users should be punished but aren't clear about whether you mean people who traffic in heroin or people who take aspirin, you are not worth listening to. If you say that you mean illegal drug offenders, don't argue that "drugs" are bad for your body because this term applies to both legal and illegal drugs. If you say that you mean amphetamine users, then don't switch to talking about "illegal drugs" when someone explains to you the several medical uses of amphetamines. Know what you are arguing, or your arguments will have no point.

Changing Meanings

It is easy to miss a fallacy when the words seem to form a valid argument. For example, consider this:

People are free as long as they can think for themselves.
Prisoners in jail are free to think for themselves.

Therefore, prisoners in jail are free.

This paradoxical conclusion is due to the ambiguity of *free,* first used to refer to a kind of mental freedom, second to refer to physical freedom. An interesting example is the argument often attributed to the British philosopher John Stuart Mill: "Whatever people desire, that is what is desirable." But notice that this argument plays with an ambiguity in the English language. Not everything that is in fact desired (for example, alcohol by alcoholics) *should* be desired. (Mill makes the case, however, that the only evidence that *x* is desirable is that people in fact desire it.) Be careful that the key terms in your argument keep the same meaning throughout.

Distraction

Another familiar form of fallacy is the "red herring," the sometimes long-winded pursuit of an argument leading away from the point at issue. For example, in the middle of an argument about the relation between the mind and the brain, a neurologist may well enjoy telling you, in impressive detail, any number of odd facts about neurology, about brain operations he or she has performed, about silly theories that neurology-ignorant philosophers have defended in the past. But if these do not bear on the issue at hand, they are only pleasant ways of spending the afternoon, not steps to settling a difference of opinion. Distraction is a fallacy that is especially advantageous when the time for argument is limited. (For this reason, it is particularly prevalent in the classroom.)

Pseudoquestions

Sometimes fallacious reasoning begins with the very question being asked. For example, some philosophers have argued that asking such questions as "How is the mind related to the body?" or "Could God create a mountain so heavy that even he could not move it?" are pseudoquestions. In other words, they look like real questions—even profound questions—but are ultimately unanswerable because they are based on some hidden piece of nonsense. (In the first of these cases, it has been suggested that there is no legitimate distinction between mind and body, and therefore any question about how they are "related" is pointless; the second question presumes that God is omnipotent in the sense that he can do the logically impossible, which is absurd.) Pseudoquestions, like distractions, lead us down a lengthy path going nowhere, except that, with pseudoquestions, we start from nowhere as well.

Dubious Authority

We mentioned earlier that modern philosophy is based on the assumption that we have a right—and sometimes a duty—to question authority. Yet, most of our knowledge and opinions are based on appeals to authorities—whether scientists or "the people" are particularly wise or not. It would be extremely foolish, if not fatal, not to appeal to authorities, especially in a world that has grown so technologically and socially complicated. We ask an economist what will happen if interest rates fall. We ask Miss Manners which fork to use for the salad. The fallacy of dubious authority arises when we ask the wrong person, when we appeal to an expert who is not in fact an expert in the area of concern. For example, when physicians are asked questions about nuclear policy or physicists are asked questions about high school education, their expertise in one field does not necessarily transfer to the other. The authority behind opinions in books and newspapers depends on the expertise of the authors and publications in question. What is in print is not necessarily authoritative.

Slippery Slope

Metaphors often pervade arguments. One of the more common metaphors is the slippery slope, the greased incline that once trod inevitably carries us to the bottom. (In politics, it is sometimes called "the chilling effect" or "the domino theory.") For example, it is argued that any interference with free speech whatsoever, even forbidding someone to scream "Fire!" in a crowded auditorium, will sooner or later lead to the eradication of free speech of every kind, including informed, responsible political discussion. But is it the case that, by attacking an extreme instance, we thereby endanger an entire institution? Sometimes, this may be so. But more often than not, the slippery slope metaphor leads us to think that there is such inevitability when in fact there is no such thing.

Attacking a Straw Man

Real opponents with real arguments and objections are sometimes difficult to refute, and so the easy way out is to attack an unreal opponent with easily refutable arguments and objections. This is called attacking a straw man. For example, French existentialist Jean-Paul Sartre argued that human beings have absolute freedom, meaning that they could always find some alternative way of dealing with a difficult situation. But unsympathetic critics quickly interpreted his claim to mean that a person can do absolutely anything he wants to do—for example, fly to the moon by flapping his ears—believing they had refuted Sartre with such silly examples.

Pity (and Other Emotional Appeals)

Some forms of fallacy appeal to the better parts of us, even as they challenge our fragile logical abilities. The appeal to pity has always been such an argument. Photographs of suffering people may well be an incentive to social action, but the connection between our pity—which is an undeniable virtue—and the social action in question is not yet an argument. The appeal to pity—and all appeals to emotion—have a perfectly legitimate place in philosophical discussion, but such appeals are not themselves arguments for any particular position. An orator may make us angry, but what we are to do about the problem must be the product of further argument.

Appeal to Force

Physical might never makes philosophical right. Sometimes a person can be intimidated, but he or she is not thus refuted. Sometimes one has to back up a philosophical conviction with force, but it is never the force that justifies the conviction.

Inappropriate Arguments

The last fallacy we mention has to do with choice of methods. To insist on deductive arguments when there are powerful inductive arguments against you is a fallacy, too—not a fallacious argument, perhaps, but a mistake in logic all the same. For example, if you are arguing deductively that there cannot be any torture going on in a certain country because Mr. Q rules the country and Mr. Q is a good man (where the implicit premise is that "good men don't allow torture in their country"), you had better be willing to give up the argument when dozens of trustworthy eyewitnesses publicly describe the tortures they have seen or experienced. To continue with your deduction in the face of such information is foolish. This may not tell you where your argument has gone wrong: Perhaps Mr. Q is not such a good man. Or perhaps he has been overpowered. Or perhaps good men can't prevent torture if they aren't told about it. But in any case, the argument must now be given up.

The same may be true the other way around. Certain abstract questions seem to be answerable only by deduction. When arguing about religious questions, for example, looking for evidence on which to build an inductive argument may be foolish. Evidence, in the sense of looking around for pertinent facts, may be irrelevant. What is at stake are your basic concepts of religion and their implications. Very abstract questions often require deductive arguments only.

To be caught in one of these fallacies is almost always embarrassing and damaging to your overall argument. If you have a case to make, then make it in the most powerfully persuasive way. An intelligent combination of deductive and inductive arguments, coupled with analogies and proper criticisms of alternative positions, is the most effective persuasion available. If you think your opinions are important, then they deserve nothing less than the best supporting arguments you can put together.

Informal Fallacy Examples

Changing meaning:

> Power tends to corrupt (Lord Acton).
>
> Knowledge is power (Francis Bacon).
>
> Therefore knowledge tends to corrupt.

Begging the question:

> *She says that she loves me,*
> *and she must be telling the truth,*
> *because she certainly wouldn't lie to someone she loves.*

Pity and other emotional appeals:

> *Mr. Scrooge, I certainly deserve a raise in pay. I can hardly manage to feed my children on what you are paying me. And my youngest child, Tim, needs an operation if he is ever to walk without crutches.*

Irving M. Copi, *Informal Logic.* 7th ed. New York: Macmillan, 1986

Glossary

This glossary of key terms serves also as a subject index to the important philosophical concepts discussed in the book. The page numbers in brackets at the end of the entries refer to the major text discussion of the concept. A name index of the philosophers and their works appears at the end of the book. **Boldface** terms within a definition are also defined in this glossary.

absolute freedom: This term can mean freedom from *all* constraints (which is impossible). Jean-Paul Sartre uses the term to insist that a person is *always* free to choose, between options no matter how confined or restricted by circumstances, but he does not thereby mean that a person is ever free from constraints. [p. 231]

absolutism (in ethics): The thesis that there is a single set of correct moral standards, applicable to all societies. See **moral absolutism**. [p. 281]

absurd, the "absurd": Unreasonable, irrational, without meaning. Albert Camus uses the term to refer to "the confrontation of reasonable man and an indifferent universe," a world that seems unresponsive to our demands for justice and meaningfulness. [p. 47]

ad hominem: An argument aimed at criticizing the individual but ignoring the issue completely (called *ad feminam,* when directed toward a female individual). [p. 21]

aesthetics: The branch of philosophy concerned with beauty, especially as it appears in works of art, and with the judgments we make about the artistic value of such works. [p. 364]

agnostic: A person who refuses to believe either that God exists or that he does not exist, usually on the ground that there can be no sufficient evidence for either belief. [p. 65]

ahimsa: (Sanskrit.) Nonviolence. [p. 349]

altruism: The thesis that one ought to act for the sake of the interests of others, rather than one's own interests alone. See also **ethical altruism; psychological altruism.** [pp. 58, 262]

analogy: Similarity, comparison. An argument by analogy is a demonstration that two things are similar in certain crucial respects, combined with the suggestion that they are therefore probably similar in other respects. [p. 197]

analysis: Understanding an idea by distinguishing and clarifying its various components. For example, the idea of "murder" involves three component ideas: killing, wrongfulness, and intention. [p. 6]

anarchy: A state of confusion and social disorder where, in lieu of a ruling government, everyone is allowed to or is able to do whatever he or she wants. [p. 296]

anatman: (Sanskrit.) Buddhist doctrine that there is no separate self. [p. 351]

ancestor: A forebear. A most important ingredient in the religion and philosophy of many non-Western cultures shaped by religions other than Judaism, Islam, and Christianity. In these cultures, one's ancestors are considered, with varying degrees of literalness, to still be present and influential in ongoing life. [p. 355]

animism: The view that everything—perhaps even the universe as a whole—is alive. [p. 339]

animists: Philosophers and others who attribute some sort of lifelike activity to all things. [p.137]

anitya: (Sanskrit.) The Buddhist doctrine that everything is impermanent, everything passes away. [p. 352]

anthropomorphic or anthropomorphize: Humanlike. An anthropomorphic conception of God ascribes human attributes to him (i.e., *anthropomorphizes* him), usually personality traits, such as a sense of justice or jealousy, sometimes (as in Greek mythology or children's stories) physical attributes as well. [p. 71]

Apollonian: Nietzsche's term for the rational principle in art; form. [p. 375]

a priori (knowledge): "Before experience," or, more accurately, independent of all experience. A priori knowledge is always necessary, for there can be no imaginable instances that would refute it and no intelligible doubting of it. One might come to know something a priori through experience (for example, you might find out by dividing the circumference by the radius in thousands of circles that in each case the result is π), but what is essential to a priori knowledge is that no such experience is needed. [p. 9]

argument: A process of reasoning from one claim to another. An argument may be, but need not be, directed against an explicit alternative. A philosophical argument does not require an opponent or a disagreement. [p. 9]

argument from design (for God's existence): An argument that attempts to prove that God exists because of the intricacy and design of nature. The basis of the argument is that, because the universe is so well designed, it must have a designer. The analogy most often used is our inference from finding a complex mechanism on the beach (for example, a watch) that there must have been some intelligent being who created it. [p. 92]

aristocracy: Rule by (i.e., leadership roles accorded to) those who come from the highest class or caste in the society. (Literally, "rule by the best.") [p. 293]

articulation: Putting ideas in clear, concise, readily understandable language. [p. 6]

asceticism: A philosophy of rigorous self-discipline and abstinence, rejecting as much as possible the comforts, luxuries, and pleasures of the world. [p. 257]

atheism: The belief that there is no God. [p. 67]

atheist: A person who doesn't believe in God. [p. 65]

atman: (Sanskrit.) The transpersonal, supreme self, which is the same in everyone. Also see *jiva.* [p. 350]

atom: One of the smallest possible material bodies. (Literally, "indivisible.") Atoms are the building blocks of reality. Democritus is credited with the first atomic theory. John Dalton is the father of the modern theory, which is the basis of modern chemistry. [p. 116]

attributes: characteristics. Baruch Spinoza saw that Descartes, having defined mind and body as separate substances, could not explain how they interact. Spinoza then elected to treat them not as separate substances, but as different aspects—or what he called *attributes*—of one and the same substance. [p. 127]

authentic self: In existentialism, the genuine, individual self-identity, to be distinguished from the inauthentic, merely role-playing and public identity. The term has become prominent through the philosophy of Martin Heidegger in this century. See also **essential self.** [p. 209]

authority: Legitimate power. But note: although many people seem to think that an appeal to authority will settle a philosophical dispute, in most philosophical disputes, it is the nature of authority itself that is in question. [p. 294]

autonomy: Independence. *Intellectual* autonomy is the ability of a rational person to reach his or her own conclusions about what to believe and what not to believe. *Moral* autonomy is the ability of a rational person to reach his or her own moral conclusions about what is right and what is wrong. (This does not mean that they will therefore come to different conclusions.) [p. 270]

avatar: A god embodied in human form. [p. 346]

axiom: A statement that is true by definition or is so obviously true that it need not be proved and so may be used without further debate as a starting point of argument. [p. 16]

bad faith: Sartre's characterization of a person's refusal to accept himself or herself, particularly regarding the extent of his or her own freedom and limitations. This sometimes means not accepting the facts that are true about you. More often, it means accepting the facts about you as conclusive about your identity, as in the statement, "Oh, I couldn't do that, I'm too shy." [p. 210]

becoming: Passing into a new condition. One of Hegel's bold suggestions was that God as universal spirit cannot be comprehended just in terms of God's present existence—as a being of a certain sort at a certain time—but must be comprehended in terms of a long period of development, as a **process.** In other words, it is not as if God has always been what he is now; God is rather in the process of becoming. [p. 79]

begging the question: Assuming the truth of the point at issue in a question, for example, "How do I know God would not deceive me?" "Because the natural light of reason with which he endowed me tells me so." (In popular writing nowadays, the phrase "begging the question" is often used very loosely to mean something like "inviting the question." This is incorrect usage.) [p. 21]

behaviorism: The (philosophical) thesis that there are no mental events (or that they are of no scientific importance). What we call by mentalistic names (pains, emotions, motives) are actually patterns of behavior, misnamed and mistakenly supposed to be inner, "ghostly" occurrences. [p. 201]

Bodhisattva: (Sanskrit.) In Mahayana Buddhism, an enlightened person devoted to the enlightenment of others. [p. 349]

Brahman: (Sanskrit.) The One; ultimate reality; absolute being. [p. 76]

Buddhism: A religion founded in India by Gautama Buddha (circa 566–480 bce), originally derived from **Hinduism** and teaching that suffering is the universal condition of human existence. [p. 346] **Zen Buddhism:** A form of Buddhism that developed in Japan and that stresses the importance of meditation and work. [p. 76]

capitalism: An economic system based on private ownership and the freedom of producers and consumers to sell and buy as they choose. One of the presuppositions of capitalism is that the general welfare will best be served by everyone pursuing his or her own interests. [p. 213]

categorical imperative: In Kant's philosophy, the moral law, a command that is unqualified and not dependent on any conditions or qualifications. In particular, it is that rule which tells us to act in such a way that we would be willing for everyone else to act . [p. 269]

catharsis: Aristotle's term for the purging or purifying of emotion through art. [p. 370] certain: Beyond doubt. But it is important to insist that certainty in the philosophical sense is more than the common psychological use of "certain" ("feeling certain"). One can feel certain and yet be wrong or foolish. One can be certain, in the philosophical sense, only if one can prove that the matter is beyond doubt, that no reasons for doubt could be raised. [p. 159]

citizen: Member of an organized society. This term was used by Rousseau to contrast with his notion of "natural man." "Natural man" was healthier and happier than modern man, who has been corrupted by (defective) society. But Rousseau believed that society properly conceived will not only restore something of our natural vitality and utilize our inventiveness but will actually make us into something more than merely "natural." Society will make us moral. Society will change a mere man or woman into a *citizen*. [p. 307]

civil rights: Entitlements to exercise certain political or social freedoms, e.g., the right–duty to vote or the right–duty to speak one's mind about topics of political concern. (See also **contractual rights, legal rights,** and **human** or **natural rights.**) [p. 314]

climate of opinion: A shared set of ideas and beliefs and the intellectual atmosphere in which these are generally acceptable. [p. 10]

coherence theory of truth: The theory that a statement or belief is true if and only if it coheres with a system of statements or beliefs. Because we can never get outside our experience, the only sense in saying that a belief is true (according to this theory) is that it coheres with the rest of our experience. [p. 172]

commitment: A binding obligation formed voluntarily. [p. 81]

communitarianism: A theory of society that emphasizes the interdependence of individuals within the context of particular communities. A communitarian view understands the citizen not in terms of his or her rights but rather his or her duties ("Ask not what your country can do for you, but what you can do for your country"). In the communitarian view, the self is sometimes understood as a function of society rather than an independent entity. (See also **liberalism** and **libertarianism.**) [p. 311]

compassion: Fellow feeling, sympathy, the sharing of another's suffering. [p. 263]

compatibilism: The thesis that both **determinism** (in some interpretations) and free action can be true. Determinism does not rule out free action, and the possibility of free action does not require that determinism be false. They are *compatible* positions. [p. 242]

concept: An idea, usually of a kind of object or state of affairs, typically expressed by a word or phrase. (Concepts are sometimes said to be the meanings of words.) [p. 8]

conceptual framework: A system of concepts within which objects are classified and recognized in a certain way and in which certain interpretations and ideas are given priority. In a scientific conceptual framework, for example, we tend to talk in terms of *physical forces;* in a religious conceptual framework, we tend to talk in terms of *spiritual entities;* in an economic conceptual framework, we tend to talk in terms of price, cost, supply, and so on. (Compare, for example, the very different ways we would discuss the building of a new steeple on a church in scientific, religious, and economic terms.) [p. 139]

conclusion: The end of an argument; the final claim. [p. 16]

Confucianism: East Asian philosophy–religion based on the teachings of the Chinese philosopher Confucius (551–479 BCE). Confucianism is concerned with harmonious social and political relationships, good leadership, and getting along with others through cultivating personal virtue. The central question in Chinese thought generally is the ethical question of what is the good life. For Confucius, the answer was to live in harmony with other human beings, and his philosophy focuses on "the Way" (Dao or Tao) to do that. [p. 353]

consciousness: Mental awareness (not to be confused with conscience). [p. 124]

contemplation (the life of): According to Aristotle (and other philosophers), the happiest life, the life of thought and philosophy. [p. 58]

contingent: Not necessary; could have been otherwise. What we believe (or a state of affairs) is contingent if we can imagine its being other than it is. [p. 148]

contingent falsehood: A statement that is false but might not have been so. "The earth has two moons" is a contingent falsehood, for we can imagine what it would be for the earth to have two moons. [p. 148]

contingent truth: A true statement that could have been otherwise. It is contingent that heavy objects fall toward the earth because we can easily imagine what it would be like if they did not (particularly if we have seen images of astronauts who are weightless in outer space). This is so even though it is physically necessary that heavy objects fall. [p. 148]

contradict: To be in conflict with. Even if all of its arguments seem to be sound, a philosophy can be shown to be in trouble if it is **inconsistent,** that is, if the conclusions of its different arguments contradict one another. [p. 20]

contract: See **social contract.**

contractual rights: Entitlements established by means of agreements among parties; e.g., the right to be paid a specific price for specific work. (See also **legal rights, civil rights,** and **human** or **natural rights.**) [p. 310]

correspondence theory of truth: The theory that a statement or belief is true if and only if it corresponds with the facts. Even when restricting our attention to statements of fact, however, this commonsensical theory gets into trouble as soon as it tries to pick out what corresponds to what. How can we identify a fact, for example, apart from the language we use to identify it? And what does it mean to say that a statement corresponds to a fact? [p. 170]

cosmological argument: An argument (or set of arguments) that undertakes to prove that God exists on the basis of the idea that there must have been a first cause or an ultimate reason for the existence of the universe (the cosmos). [p. 113]

cosmology: The study of such questions as how the universe came into being, the nature of space and time, and the dimensions of the universe. [p. 113]

cosmpolitanism: The view that we ultimately are all citizens of a global community and that we therefore have moral obligations to those who are not citizens of our own nation or society. [p. 390]

counterexample: An exception to a general claim. Use of a counterexample is a way to criticize an argument by indicating that one of its premises does not hold in all cases. For instance, if someone claims, "All American men love football," he or she can be refuted if we can find a single American man who does not like football. [p. 20]

critical thinking, criticism: Thinking carefully. It does not necessarily mean attacking anyone else's ideas. [p. 13]

cultural relativism: The view that cultures, as a matter of fact, have different views about what is morally right and wrong. [p. 281]

culturalism: The view that philosophy reflects the concrete sociopolitical context in which it develops. [p. 339]

Cynicism: A movement in ancient Greek philosophy that emphasized virtue and living a "natural" life. The term stems from the Greek word for "dog." The Cynics acquired their name by living frugally and in some cases living in the streets, a life that, to their contemporaries, seemed little better than a "dog's life." [p. 8]

Dao (also **Tao**): (Chinese.) The Way. Confucians understand the Way as a matter of committing oneself to certain virtuous ideals, geared to interpersonal harmony. Daoists understood the Way as the flowing reality of nature. [p. 353]

Daoism (Daoists) (also **Taoism**): Chinese school of thought that seeks to restore one's attunement with the rhythms and energies of nature by eliminating the habits we have acquired through socialization and by a stance of receptivity. [p. 357]

deduce: To reason from one principle to another in accord with accepted rules of inference. What is crucial to deduction or deductive argument is that the conclusion is guaranteed as much certainty as the premises. [p. 16]

deduction: An instance of reasoning from one principle to another in accord with accepted rules of inference. Sometimes defined more narrowly as the inference from a general premise to a particular conclusion by means of a syllogism—for example, from "All men are mammals," and "Socrates is a man," to "Socrates is a mammal." This is not what is meant by deduction in general, however, and it is not what Descartes intends by that term. [p. 16]

deductive logic: The study of deduction and reasoning based upon it. See **deduction**. [p. 18]

deism: A variation of the Judeo-Christian tradition that was extremely popular in the science-minded eighteenth century. Deism holds that God must have existed to create the universe with all its laws (and thereby usually accepts some form of the cosmological argument), but it also holds that there is no justification for our belief that God has any special concern for people, any concern for justice, or any other anthropomorphic attributes. [p. 80]

deist: A person who believes that God created the universe and then abandoned it. See **deism**. [p. 80]

democracy: Rule by everyone (i.e., by the majority will of all the people). [p. 293]

detachment: Lack of willfulness or emotional concern. Detachment through ascetic denial (or, failing that, aesthetic contemplation) was proposed by the great pessimist Arthur Schopenhauer as a method of responding to the fact that life is filled with frustration due to our incessant irrational desires. Schopenhauer's answer is similar to that of the ancient philosophy called Stoicism, which also teaches that most of our passions are irrational and are best ignored through the detachment and commitment to reason. [p. 60]

determinism: The view that every event in the universe is dependent upon other events that are its causes. In this view, all human actions and decisions, even those we would normally describe as free and undetermined, are totally dependent on prior events that cause them. See also **hard determinism; soft determinism**. [p. 38]

dharma: (Sanksrit.) Moral laws, duties. These are typically understood in Hinduism as being associated with particular social roles. [p. 348]

dialectic: A philosophical method, used extensively by G. W. F. Hegel and Karl Marx, in which contradictions contend with one another and give way to a more comprehensive truth. The origins of dialectic are to be found in ancient Greek philosophy. [p. 190]

Dionysian: Nietzsche's term for the irrational, energetic principle within art, manifest particularly in music. [p. 375]

disanalogy: Comparison in which apparent similarities break down (cf. **analogy**). [p. 197]

distributive justice: The fair apportionment of goods and services. [p. 300]

dualist: A philosopher who accepts the existence of two basic substance, typically mind and body. [p. 200]

duty: What one ought to do, whether by virtue of his or her place or position in society (in Plato or Aristotle, for example) or by virtue of rational moral principles (as in Kant). See **duty-defined morality**. [p. 253]

duty-defined morality: The view that moral right and wrong are determined first of all by a conception of a person's duties and obligations. [p. 270]

egocentric predicament: The problem that seems to follow from the view that we know only our own *minds* directly—that is, that we might never know anything or anyone else. [p. 197]

egoism: The thesis that people act for their own interests. See also **ethical egoism; psychological egoism**. [p. 261]

eliminative materialism: the view that (at least some kinds of) mental states do not exist, and that we should attempt to replace our everyday "folk" terminology that makes reference to mental states with neurological terms that refer to the physical processes that are actually occurring. [p. 203]

empirical (knowledge): Derived from and to be defended by appeal to experience. Empirical knowledge can only be so derived and so defended (as opposed to **a priori** knowledge, which need not be). [p. 9]

empirical truth: A statement that is true because of the facts and knowable through experience. [p. 148]

empiricism: The philosophy that insists that all knowledge, except for certain logical truths and principles of mathematics, comes from experience. The term "British empiricism" is often used to refer specifically to the three philosophers John Locke, George Berkeley, and David Hume. This movement is still very much alive, however, and includes Bertrand Russell and other contemporary philosophers. [p. 153]

Enlightenment: The dominant cultural movement of the eighteenth century, characterized by the rejection of the church's authority in intellectual matters, enthusiasm for modern science, and faith in the power of human reason to attain knowledge and promote social progress. [p. 69]

entitlement: Having a right to something. A central concern of justice is entitlement—the right to keep what one already possesses, the right to keep what one earns or is given. [p. 300]

epistemology: The study of human knowledge and its nature, sources, and justification. [p. 7]

equality: In concerns of justice, having the same rights and status before the law as others, being given the same opportunities for advancement. [p. 301]

equal opportunity: Treating people without discriminating on the basis of traits such as ethnic group, race, or sex. What some regard as the meaning of **equality**. [p. 302]

essential self: The characteristics that make a person *that particular person*. See also **authentic self**. [p. 187]

ethical altruism: The thesis that people *ought* to act in the interests of others. [p. 261]

ethical egoism: The thesis that people *ought* to act in their own self-interest. [p. 261]

ethical relativism: The thesis that whatever a culture or a society holds about right and wrong *is* therefore correct, at least for members of that culture or society. See **moral relativism.** [p. 281]

ethics: The study of a way of life and its values, including a system of general moral principles and a conception of morality and its foundations. Sometimes the term simply refers to the study of moral principles. [p. 7]

eudaimonia: (Greek.) Aristotle's word for "happiness," or, more literally, "living well" in objective terms. [p. 260]

evaluative: Involving value judgments, as opposed to simply being descriptive. [p. 111]

evidence: Facts or information serving as bases for believing something. [p. 18]

existentialism: A twentieth-century philosophical movement that developed in France and Germany through the work of Martin Heidegger, Jean-Paul Sartre, and others. Its basic themes are human freedom and responsibility, the lack of any given rules, and our individual responsibility for our actions. [p. 66]

experience: Practical interaction with the world and the knowledge we gain through it. Today the term *science* tends to be limited to those questions that can and must be answered by reference to experience and extrapolations from experience. [p. 166]

extended: Taking up space. Descartes defined physical things as extended, while claiming that mental substance is **unextended,** or not in space. [p. 126]

facticity: Jean-Paul Sartre's term, borrowed from Martin Heidegger, for the totality of facts that are true of a person at any given time. [p. 208]

factual truth: See **empirical truth.**

faith: In the popular sense, a belief in something for which you have inadequate evidence or little good reason. In theology, faith usually refers to the trust a believer should have in God's ultimate grace and fairness. Sometimes, faith is defended as a rational belief in God (for example, in Kant). [p. 94] More often, faith is defended *against* rationality (as in Kierkegaard). [p. 96]

fallacy: An invalid argument or form of argument. [p. 22]

fascism: The view that the state has the right to control virtually every aspect of individual life because the state is of primary importance, the individual only secondary. (Also sometimes called **totalitarianism.**) [p. 312]

five aggregates: in Buddhist thought, the five elements that make up the personality: form (our physical nature), feelings (sensations), discrimination (our ability to distinguish objects of perception), compositional factors (thoughts, ideas, mental habits, desires, etc.), and consciousness. [p. 351]

Form: The structure of a thing, that which identifies it as a particular thing or kind of thing. In Plato, a Form is an independently existing entity in the World of Being, which determines the nature of the particular things of this world. In Aristotle, forms are merely the essential characteristics that idenify a thing as what it is, without independent existence. [pp. 120–123; p. 366]

freedom: The power to act without being coerced or restrained. The idea of metaphysical freedom holds that a human decision or action is a person's own responsibility and that praise and blame may be appropriately ascribed. The most extreme interpretation of *freedom* is the absence of any causes or determinations. Thus, an indeterminist would say that an event was free if it had no causes; some philosophers would say that a human act was free if it was only self-caused but not determined by anything else (including a person's character). Certain determinists, however (**soft determinists**), would say that an act is free only if it is "in character" and based on a person's desires and personality. Most generally, we say that a person's act was free, whether or not it was the result of a conscious decision and whether or not certain causes may have been involved, if we would say he or she could have done otherwise. [p. 224]

free market: A system of voluntary exchange in which every agent is free to produce, buy, and sell "as the market will bear," without interference or standards set by any outside authority. [p. 296]

free will: Among philosophers, a somewhat antiquated expression (as in "he did it of his own free will") meaning that a person is capable of making decisions that are not determined by antecedent conditions. Of course, there may be antecedent considerations, such as what a person wants or what a person believes, but free will means that such considerations never determine a person's decision. At most they "enter into the decision." [p. 38]

functionalism: The theory that mental events are identical to certain processes in the brain, but that similar processes in another medium (like a computer) would have similar mental manifestations. [p. 205]

General Will (Rousseau): The collective desires and determinations of a people. [p. 305]

German Idealists: A diverse group of philosophers in nineteenth-century Germany who held that minds and ideas are the ultimate reality. [p. 133]

good life: A life well-lived; the most desirable way to live. [p. 7]

happiness calculus: A technique developed by Jeremy Bentham to calculate right action in terms of the quantity of pleasure and pain it produces. Pleasures are weighed against one another and balanced against the pain produced by an action, and of alternatives, the action that produces the most pleasure for the most people and the smallest amount of pain is the action that should be done. [p. 273]

hard determinism, hard determinist: The uncompromised and unqualified view that every event is caused by antecedent conditions. [p. 242]

hedonism: The conception of the good life that takes pleasure to be the ultimate good. [p. 254]

Heisenberg uncertainty principle (in physics): The principle that one cannot determine both the motion and the position of a subatomic particle. [p. 239]

henotheism: The view that a single divine reality manifests itself in various forms. [p. 346]

Hinduism: Ancient religion of India that stresses the unity of all being and the ideal of oneness with ultimate reality. [p. 346]

human or natural rights: Claims to certain treatment and protections by others that one has by virtue of being a human being; e.g., the right not to be tortured and not to be imprisoned without reason. (See also **contractual rights, legal rights,** and **civil rights.**) [p. 310]

Hume's fork: David Hume's argument that every justifiably true statement is either a **truth of reason** or a **matter of fact.** [p. 163]

hypothesis: A statement to be confirmed—or disproved—by appeal to experience and the facts of the case, to be ascertained through experiment and observation. [p. 19]

idealism: The metaphysical view that the mind and its ideas are the ultimate reality. [p. 131]

idealist: A person who holds the metaphysical view that mind and ideas are the ultimate reality. [p. 124]

identity theory (of mind and body): The thesis that mental events are physical events, namely, aspects of neurological processes in the brain. [p. 202]

ideology: A system of values and ideas through which actions and events are interpreted and evaluated. [p. 10]

immanent (God): God defined as *within* the world and the human spirit, rather than distinct from humanity and the universe he created. [p. 75]

immaterialism: The metaphysical view that accepts the existence of nonmaterial entities. The weak version asserts merely that there are such entities. The strong version, idealism, asserts that there are only such entities (that is, there are no material objects). [p. 120]

incoherent: Lacking coherence; not fitting together in an orderly or logically agreeable fashion. Using fancy jargon that has no precise meaning may be a source of incoherence. So is a mere list of random beliefs, without any order or logic to hold them together. (They may even contradict each other as well.) An incoherent philosophy may be insightful and true in parts, but, because it never coheres into a single system, it may well appear to be nonsense or simply a jumble of words and phrases. In other cases, an incoherent philosophy may be one that makes no sense, whose terms are utter gibberish or whose principles are mere ramblings without intelligible connection or interpretation. [p. 21]

inconsistent: Maintaining or arguing contradictory positions. Even if all of its arguments seem to be sound, a philosophy can be shown to be in trouble if it is inconsistent. [p. 20]

indeterminism: The thesis that at least some events in the universe are not determined, not caused by antecedent conditions, and not predictable. [p. 238]

indubitable: Not susceptible to being doubted. [p. 159]

induction, inductive argument, inductive generalization, inductive reasoning: The process of inferring general conclusions (for example, "All swans are white") from a sufficiently large sample of particular observations ("This swan is white, that swan is white, and that one, and that one, and that one ..."). It is usually contrasted with **deduction** in that, while **deductive** reasoning guarantees that the conclusion will be as certain as the premises, induction never gives us a conclusion as certain as the premises. Its conclusions are at most, merely probable. (There might always be some black swans somewhere—and there are, in western Australia.) [p. 20]

inductive logic: The study of induction and inductive reasoning. [p. 18]

ineffable: Impossible to describe. [p. 96]

infer (inferred, inference): To reason from one set of principles to another, as in an argument. *Deductive inference* is but a single kind of inference. [p. 16]

innate ideas: Ideas that we are born with, which may include tendencies to think in certain ways that are hardwired into our minds. [p. 153]

interpretation: A way of understanding, a view of a set of facts, from a certain perspective. [p. 151]

intuition: Direct, unmediated awareness. As the word is commonly used—for example, when people talk of feminine intuition—some sort of mysterious mode of knowing is implied. As a technical philosophical term, however, *intuition* need not have this connotation. Thus, Immanuel Kant describes sense perception as a form of intuition. [p. 154]

invalid: Not valid; not correctly following agreed-upon rules of inference in an argument. Properly applies to arguments, not to statements. [p. 16]

irrational: Going against the rules of reason. (Not the same as nonrational, such as when we say that worms and fish are "not rational animals.") Only rational (that is, thinking, planning, calculating) creatures can be irrational. [p. 96]

Jainism: One of the three great Indian religions, committed to a life of nonharm. [p. 349]

jiva: (Sanskrit.) The individual self or soul. See also *atman*. [p. 350]

justice: The administration of fair rewards, punishments, benefits, and responsibilities in society. See also **distributive justice; retributive justice.**[p. 298]

karma: (Sanskrit.) The principle that every action bears fruit. [p. 348]

karma yoga: (Sanskrit.) The spiritual discipline of disowning one's own actions, with the consequence that one does not accumulate karma from them. [p. 348]

leap of faith: In Kierkegaard, believing on faith what one cannot prove. [p. 81]

legal rights: Entitlements conferred by legislation; for example., the right to drive (with certain reasonable restrictions). (See also **contractual rights, civil rights,** and **human** or **natural rights.**) [p. 310]

legitimate (power): Power of a leader or government that is justified. See **authority.** [p. 294]

liberalism: A philosophical view that holds that individuals' liberty is fundamentally important and that government must respect their citizens' rights. Although classical liberalism (like contemporary libertarianism) emphasizes "negative" rights to act freely so long as one's actions do not interfere with the rights of others, contemporary liberals often defend the idea that individuals also have a strong set of natural rights—"positive" rights—to the benefits of society (decent housing, education, food, health care, security). Contemporary liberals tend to support a strong centralized government to administer social programs. (See also **libertarianism** and **communitarianism.**) [p. 311]

libertarianism: A philosophical view that holds that individuals' liberty is fundamentally important and that government must respect their citizens' rights, understood as "negative" rights (that is, rights to act without interference so long as one's actions do not interfere with the rights of others). Among the negative rights libertarians defend are the right to keep what one has or has earned, and the right to be free from government interference in all matters except when absolutely necessary to the general good. (Cf. **liberalism** and **communitarianism.**) [p. 311]

libertarians: One term for persons who holds the metaphysical view that our apparently free choices actually are free. This term is also used for those who adopt the political position of libertarianism. (Cf. **determinism.**) [p. 311]

lifestyle: A way of living, informed by certain values and concepts. [p. 10]

linguistic determinism: The view that language shapes the way people understand the world. [p. 161]

logic: That part of philosophy that studies the structure of *rational arguments,* in particular the rules of valid inference and the rules of inductive generalization. [p. 7]

logical positivists: Philosophers who argued that any statement that could not be empirically tested was simply "meaningless" (unless, of course, it was a trivial truth or a statement in mathematics or logic). [p. 166]

logos: (Greek.) Word, reason, or logic. The term is sometimes used to refer to the eternal principle underlying reality, giving the world order or to the divine intelligence that is manifest in this order. [p. 119]

Manichean: Related or akin to an ancient philosophy that taught that there is an objective battle between good and evil in the world. [p. 380]

materialism: The metaphysical view that only physical matter and its properties exist. Seemingly nonmaterial entities are really physical bodies: to talk about energy, for example, is, in a way, to talk about physical potential; to talk about minds is, as a kind of shorthand, to talk about behavior; to talk about ideas is, in a misleading way, to talk about the various structures and interrelationships between objects. Numbers have no existence of their own but only represent sets of sets of objects (the set of all sets of eight things is the number 8, for example). Materialism has been a powerful worldview in modern scientific culture, but the idea that the basic building blocks of reality were physical also had adherents as far back as the pre-Socratic philosophers. [p. 119]

matter of fact: In Hume, an empirical claim, to be confirmed or disproved through experience. [p. 163]

maya: (Sanskrit.) Illusion. [p. 350]

merit: the characteristic of being deserving or worthy of something. In the philosophy of distributive justice, the idea that people should get what they deserve makes reference to merit. [p. 300]

meritocracy: Rule by (i.e., leadership given to) persons depending on their merit and ability. [p. 293]

metaphysics: Most simply, the study of the most basic (or first) principles. Traditionally, the study of ultimate reality, or "Being as such." Popularly, any kind of very abstract or obscure thinking. Most philosophers today would define metaphysics as the study of the most general concepts of science and human life—for example, reality, existence, freedom, God, soul, action, mind. [p. 113]

method of doubt: René Descartes's technique for discovering those principles of which we can be "perfectly certain"; namely, doubt everything until you discover those principles that cannot be doubted. [p. 158]

mind–body problem: The problem of how mental events (pains, thoughts, feelings) are related to the body—in particular, the brain. [p. 199]

might makes right: The idea that, when determining who has **legitimate power** to govern a society, those who are the strongest or otherwise superior should (or inevitably will) rule. In effect, this is to claim that the person who is strong enough to hold on to ruling authority has legitimate power merely by virtue of being strong enough to retain power. [p. 295]

modus ponens: A Valid Argument Form and a Rule for making inference. The form of modus ponens is as follows:

If P then Q.

P.

Q. [p. 406]

modus tollens: A Valid Argument Form and a Rule for making inference. The form of modus tollens is as follows:

If P then Q.

Not Q.

Not P. [p. 406]

monad: In Leibniz, the simple immaterial substances that are the ultimate constituents of all reality. God, the one uncreated monad, created all of the others as self-enclosed ("windowless"), predetermined entities. [p. 129]

monarchy: Rule by a single person, who embodies the sovereignty of the state in his or her person. [p. 293]

monist: A philosopher who believes in only one kind of substance. [p. 127]

monotheism: The belief in one God. [p. 70]

moral absolutism: The thesis that at least some moral values and rules are universal. See **absolutism**. [p. 281]

moral philosophy: The study of right and wrong actions, moral values, and principles. [p. 7]

moral relativism: The thesis that a morality is appropriately relative to the society that holds it and that therefore an action that is wrong in one cultural context may be right in another. See **relativism.** [p. 281]

morality: In general, the rules for right action and prohibitions against wrong acts. Sometimes the term is understood to refer to a single set of absolute rules and prohibitions that are valid for all people at all times and in all societies. More loosely, a morality can be any set of ultimate principles and practices basic to a society. [p. 252]

mukti: (Sanskrit.) The Hindu concept of bliss in liberation. [p. 349]

mystery: Something that cannot be understood. One of the features of Christianity as it has developed is the strong emphasis on the mystery of God, the fact that it is impossible for us to understand him or comprehend his ways. [p. 72]

mystical: A term descriptive of an immediate experience of a direct, intimate union with God. *Mystical* does not mean *mysterious* [p. 74]

mysticism: The belief that one can come to grasp certain fundamental religious truths (the existence of God, the oneness of the universe) through direct experience of a very special kind, different from ordinary understanding and often at odds with reason. [p. 96]

necessary truth: Something that cannot be otherwise, and cannot be imagined to be otherwise. In philosophy, it is not enough that something be "necessary" according to physical laws (for example, the law of gravity) or "necessary" according to custom or habit (for example, the necessity of laws against tax evasion or the felt necessity of having a cigarette after dinner). *Necessity* does not allow for even imaginary counterexamples; thus, it is a necessary truth that 2 + 2 = 4; not only do we believe this with certainty and find ourselves incapable of intelligibly doubting it, but we also cannot even suggest what it might be for it to be false, no matter how wild our imaginations. [p. 149]

negative and positive freedom: *Negative* freedom is freedom *from* constraints (such as not being in prison or threatened with imprisonment or, worse, not being prevented from doing what one chooses). *Positive* freedom is the freedom *to* realize one's potential (by following rules, getting a good education, learning through experience). These are opposite aspects of the same considerations; every instance of being free *from* constraints is at the same time the freedom *to* do something, and vice versa. [p. 230]

nihilism: The view that nothing has any value or that there are no values. [p.50]

nirvana: In Buddhism, the ideal state of peacefulness. Literally, the term means "extinction" and refers to the elimination of suffering through the elimination of selfish craving. [p. 349]

objective truth: Truth independent of our personal opinions and demonstrably true to anyone (who is in the proper position to observe, who has the right testing equipment, and so on). [p. 177]

observational language: Language used by scientists to describe what we can see, touch, and manipulate (e.g., in scientific experiments). (Cf. **theoretical language**). [p. 166]

obvious: Taken to be true without argument or proof; apparently **indubitable** or **self-evident.** [p. 146]

oligarchy: Rule by the few. [p. 293]

omnipotent: All-powerful, usually said of God. [p. 65]

omniscient: All-knowing, usually said of God. [p. 65]

ontological: Having to do with the idea of existence or reality. [p. 93]

ontological argument: An argument (or set of arguments) that tries to prove the existence of God from the very concept of "God." For example: *God,* by definition, is that Being with all possible perfection; existence is a perfection; therefore God exists. [p. 92]

ontology: The study of being: "What is most real?"; "What is it for a thing to exist?" [p. 7]

panentheism: The belief that although God transcends the world, God nevertheless dwells within every part it. [p. 74]

pantheism: The belief that God is identical with creation. Baruch Spinoza, for example, was a pantheist. Hinduism, in some interpretations, can be construed as a form of pantheism. [p. 177]

paradox: A self-contradictory or seemingly absurd conclusion based on apparently good arguments. [p. 20]

Pascal's wager: The argument that it is prudent to believe in God because, if he exists and you believe, you will be eternally rewarded; if you believe he exists but he does not, you lose (risk) nothing; but if he exists and you don't believe, you will be eternally punished. Suggested by the French philosopher Blaise Pascal in the seventeenth century. [p. 95]

patriarchy: The domination of social institutions by men and the social forces that maintain this arrangement. [p. 318]

pessimism: The view that life is no good and ultimately serves no purpose. Loosely speaking, a *pessimist* is a person who expects things to turn out for the worst. Arthur Schopenhauer, a nineteenth-century German philosopher and (to a large extent) a follower of Immanuel Kant (who was not at all a pessimist), was one of the most notable pessimists of all time. [p. 135]

philosophical logic: The study of the formal structures of sound thinking and good argumentation. [p. 7]

philosophy of art: The study of the nature of art and the experiences we have when we enjoy the arts, including an investigation of such concepts as "beauty" and "expression" A subset of **aesthetics**. [p. 7]

philosophy of liberation: Developed in Argentina in the 1970s, the philosophy of liberation seeks to address the needs of the disenfranchised by philosophizing from their viewpoint and articulating ways to bring about social change toward a more just state of affairs. [p. 343]

philosophy of religion (or philosophical theology): The philosophical study of religion, the nature of religion and the nature of the divine, including consideration of the various reasons for believing (or not believing) in God's existence. [p. 7]

pluralism: The view in metaphysics that many distinct substances or ultimate principles exist. (In ethics, the acceptance of the coexistence in a society of several different ethical value systems—whether or not they actually contradict one another.) [p. 125]

pluralist: A philosopher who believes in more than one substance. ("**Pluralism**" can have other meanings, too; for example, it can refer to someone who is tolerant of various methodological approaches within philosophy.) [p.125]

pluralistic (society): As a description of the society in the United States, comprising different groups that have very different values, different religions, and different customs, which require that people within this multiracial, multiethnic, polydimensional society exercise **tolerance** in order that everyone can get along together. [p. 282]

plurality: More than one (for example, more than one substance). [p. 129]

plutocracy: Rule by (i.e., leadership roles accorded to) the rich. [p. 293]

political (or sociopolitical) philosophy: The study of the foundations and the nature of society and the state; an attempt to formulate a vision of the ideal society with the aim of implementing ideas and reforms in our own society to better achieve this ideal. [p. 7]

polytheism: Belief in many gods and goddesses. [p. 70]

positive and negative freedom: *Positive* freedom is the freedom *to* realize one's potential (by following rules, getting a good education, learning through experience); *negative* freedom is freedom *from* constraints (such as not being in prison or threatened with imprisonment or, worse, not being prevented from doing what one chooses). These are opposite aspects of the same considerations; every instance of being free *from* constraints is at the same time the freedom *to* do something, and vice versa. [p. 230]

positivism: This term used to be used as a synonym for **empiricism.** It has also been used to refer to the philosophy of nineteenth-century thinker Auguste Comte, who held that human behavior followed scientific laws and that social policy should be constructed on the basis of these laws. In recent times, it has come to mean the outlook advanced by logical positivists who hold that only sentences capable of empirical verification are really meaningful. [p. 342]

postmodernists: Originally a somewhat amorphous group of French philosophers and cultural figures in the late 1970s who attacked universal and "objective" categories and celebrated differences and fragmentation. It later became linked with such figures as Jacques Derrida and Jean-François Lyotard. [p. 181]

power: The ability to get something done. It is sometimes defined as power *over other people,* but this applies only sometimes, when to get something done requires moving or getting around others. [p. 179]

practical reason: The application of our rationality to practical problems—particularly moral problems—the solution to which consists in action (as opposed to a statement or a theory). [p. 245]

pragmatic theory of truth: The theory that a statement or belief is true if and only if it works—that is, if it allows us to predict certain results or function effectively in everyday life or if it encourages further inquiry and helps us lead better lives. [p. 173]

pratityasamutpáda: (Sanskrit.) The Buddhist doctrine that all "things" are interdependent, and thus have no separate existence. [p. 352]

premise: A statement that is accepted from the start of an argument and is not itself argued. "I think" is the premise of the argument "I think, therefore I am." [p. 16]

presupposition: A principle that is assumed as a precondition for whatever else one believes but that itself may remain unexamined and uncriticized throughout the argument. For example, a lawyer presupposes that the court aims at justice and has some idea what is just. It is the philosopher, not the lawyer, who challenges those claims. [p. 154]

Principle of Alternative Possibilities: The view that one must have real options to be able to be morally responsible for one's actions. [p. 244]

principle of universal causality: The belief that every event has its cause (or causes). In scientific circles, "its sufficient natural cause" is usually added in order to eliminate the possibility of miracles and divine intervention (which are allowed in Leibniz's similar but broader principle of sufficient reason). [p. 155]

problem of evil: The dilemma that emerges from trying to reconcile the belief that God is omnipotent, omniscient, and just with the suffering and evil in the world. [p. 82]

process: A development over a span of time. Hegel and some recent thinkers have argued that God must be understood as a process, in other words, as becoming or developing. [p. 79]

psychological altruism: The thesis that people "naturally" act for the well-being of others. [p. 261]

psychological egoism: The thesis that people always act for their own self-interest, even when it seems as if they are acting for other people's benefit (for example, in giving to charity, the egoist would say, the person is simply making himself or herself feel self-righteous). [p. 261]

rational: In accordance with the rules of effective thought concerning coherence, consistency, practicability, simplicity, comprehensiveness, looking at the evidence and weighing it carefully, not jumping to conclusions, and so on. **Rationality** may not guarantee truth; all the evidence and everything we believe may point to one conclusion, and yet later generations, who know things that we do not, may see that our conclusion was incorrect. It was rational thousands of years ago to believe that the earth was flat, even though it was not true. It is not rational for us to believe the same thing, for our evidence and all sorts of other beliefs indicate, rather, that it is rational to believe that the earth is (more or less) spherical. [p. 88]

rationalism: That philosophy that is characterized by its confidence in **reason,** and **intuition** in particular, to know reality independently of experience. *Continental rationalism* is a term usually reserved for three great European philosophers: Descartes, Spinoza, and Leibniz. [p. 152]

rationality: Primarily, the ability to think and to act according to goals, plans, and strategies. Rationality is also thinking well and effectively and having good, well-conceived goals, plans, and strategies. In the first instance, rationality is to be contrasted with *non*rationality; in the second instance, it is contrasted with *ir*rationality. Worms are nonrational; fools and fanatics are irrational. [p. 174]

reality: Everything that actually is, as opposed to what merely appears to be, might have been, or is not. A term of metaphysical praise, as in "what is most real is ..." [p. 108]

reality behind the appearances: In metaphysics, a traditional contrast between things as they seem to be and things as they actually are. The question that logically follows is, how can we be sure that the appearances we know are an accurate representation of reality? [p. 112]

reason: The ability to think abstractly, form **arguments**, and make **inferences**. Sometimes referred to as a "faculty" of the human mind (a leftover from eighteenth-century psychology). In **metaphysics**, however, it often has a more controversial meaning—namely, that human ability to go beyond experience to determine, through thought alone, what **reality** is *really* like. [p. 15]

reasons: Evidence or arguments in support of a belief or statement. A belief or statement is *reasonable* if it is or can be supported by sufficient evidence or arguments. [p. 31]

reductio ad absurdum: (Latin.) A form of argument in which one refutes a statement by showing that accepting it as true it leads to absurdity. [p. 21]

Reformation: Sixteenth-century religious movement, initiated by Martin Luther in Germany, which resulted in the splitting of the Christian church and the establishment of Protestantism. [p. 74]

refute: To reject for good, convincing reasons. One refutes a statement by showing that it is false; one refutes an argument by showing either that it is invalid or that its conclusion is false, or both. [p. 3]

relativism (in ethics): The view that societies differ in their basic ethical values. *Cultural relativism* is the thesis that societies in fact so differ. *Ethical relativism* is the more radical thesis that what is considered right (or wrong) in a given society is therefore right (or wrong) in and for that society. See **moral relativism.** [p. 281]

relativism (regarding truth): The claim that what is true for one person or one people might not be true for another person or another people. [p. 178]

retributive justice: The fair use of punishment. [p. 299]

right: A claim or entitlement justified by law, custom, or **morality**. [p. 310]

rule of inference: A generally accepted principle according to which one may infer one statement from another. [p. 16]

samskaras: (Sanskrit.) Residues of past actions that reside in the unconscious mind. [p. 348]

Sapir-Whorf hypothesis: the view, formulated by Edward Sapir and Benjamin Whorf, that the patterns and forms of one's native language shape the way one understands the world. [p. 325]

science: Systematic inquiry into the nature of the natural world and physical reality that depends on empirical observation and experimentation. [p. 165]

self-contradictory: Indicates a **contradiction** within one and the same statement or set of statements. What I say may contradict what you say; but what I say might also contradict something else that I said, in which case I am being self-contradictory. Moreover, in a few strange cases, my own statement may be self-contradictory; for example, "I do not exist." [p. 20]

self-evident: Obvious and acceptable without **argument**. The Declaration of Independence deflects certain arguments, for example, by declaring certain truths to be "self-evident." [p. 146]

self-identity: The way you characterize yourself, either in general (as a human being, as a man or woman, as a creature before God, or as one among many animals)—or in particular (as the person who can run the fastest mile, as an all-C student, or as the worst-dressed slob in your class). Self-identity of a person, in other words, is not merely the same as the identity of a "thing"—for example, the identity of a human body. It is a question of "who," not only "what," I am. [p. 188]

Sisyphus (myth of): In Greek mythology, a person whom the gods punished by making him spend all eternity pushing a rock up a mountain only to have it fall back down again. Albert Camus uses Sisyphus as a model for the **absurdity** of human life in general. [p. 57]

skepticism: The philosophical belief that knowledge is not possible, that doubt will not be overcome by any valid arguments. A philosopher who holds this belief is called a *skeptic*. Skepticism is not merely personal doubt but also requires systematic doubt, with reasons for that doubt. [p. 158]

social contract: An agreement, tacit or explicit, between all members of society, in which each citizen gives up certain rights and privileges in return for the protection and mutual advantage of society. [p. 305]

soft determinism: A thesis that accepts **determinism** but claims that certain kinds of causes—namely, a person's character—will allow us to call his or her actions free. The soft determinist is therefore a compatibilist, who believes in both freedom and **determinism**. See also **hard determinism**. [p. 242]

solipsism: The view that we can know only of the existence of our own minds: sometimes called the **egocentric predicament**. [p. 190]

soul: What is most essential to individual human existence; in some religions, including Christianity, that aspect of the person that survives death. More generally, we use the word *soul* to refer to whatever is basic and "deep down" in a person. [p. 187]

sound (argument): A good argument; a deductive argument that is valid and has true premises. [p. 17]

Spirit: In Hegel, the all-embracing idea that includes the entire universe and all of human-ity. More generally, *spirit* means enthusiasm (as in "team spirit" or "when the spirit moves me"); in religion, *spirit* usually refers to an intangible being, such as God or, sometimes, the human soul. [p. 79]

Stoicism: An ancient movement in philosophy that taught self-control and aimed to mini-mize passion, with a willingness to endure whatever fate has in store. [p. 59]

strong (argument): An inductive argument whose evidence makes the truth of the conclu-sion highly probable. [p. 17]

subjective idealism: The view that nothing exists except ideas and minds. The eighteenth-century idealist George Berkeley held the extreme position of subjective idealism, which, simply summarized, insisted that "to be is to be perceived" (*esse est percipi*). According to Berkeley, it makes no sense to believe in the existence of anything that we cannot experience. [p. 131]

subjective truth: An idea that might be said to be true for the person who believes it but possibly for no one else. In Kierkegaard, a subjective truth is an idea (for example, belief in God) that is believed passionately in the face of objective uncertainty but is not objectively true or false. [p. 177]

substance: The essential reality of a thing or things that underlies the various properties and changes of properties. Its most common definitions: "that which is indepen-dent and can exist by itself"; "the essence of a thing which does not and cannot change." In traditional **metaphysics**, substance is the same as "ultimate reality," and the study of substance is that branch of metaphysics that studies reality—namely, **ontology.** [p. 123]

syllogism: A kind of deductive reasoning. The best-known examples are those arguments of the form:

All P's are Q's. (Major premise)
S is a P. (Minor premise)
_____

Therefore, S is a Q. (Conclusion)

The major premise is a general claim; the minor premise is usually (but not always) a particular claim. [p. 16]

synthesis: Gathering together different ideas into a single, unified vision. For example, the Pythagorean notion of the "harmony of the spheres" synthesizes mathematics, music, physics, and astronomy. [p. 6]

tabula rasa: (Latin.) In Locke, the "blank tablet" metaphor of the mind, in opposition to the doctrine that there are innate ideas. In other words, the mind is a "blank" at birth, and everything we know must be "stamped in" through experience. [p. 153]

Tao: (Chinese.) See **Dao.** [p. 353]

Taoism (Taoists): See **Daoism.** [p. 357]

tautology: A trivially true statement, or a statement that is necessarily true by virtue of its form. [p. 21]

teleology: (From the Greek *telos,* meaning "purpose.") The belief that each phenomenon has a purpose, end, or goal. Aristotle's **metaphysics** is a teleology, which means that he believes that the universe itself—and consequently everything in it—operates for purposes and can be explained according to goals. A *teleological view* of the universe (or of any specific phenomenon) is a view that tries to explain in terms of purposes, rather than in terms of cause and effect or origins. [p. 136]

theist: A person who believes in God (no matter what particular conception of God). [p. 65]

theocracy: Rule by (i.e., leadership of the society accorded to) the most powerful religious people. (Literally, "rule by God.")

theodicy: An effort to explain how the existence of evil is compatible with the existence of God. [p. 86]

theology: The theoretical study and interpretation of religious doctrines, practices, and experiences. [p. 82]

theoretical language: Language scientists use to express concepts generated by theories(e.g., "atoms," "molecule," "element," "chemical bond," "oxidation"), as opposed to language directly reporting what is observed. The theories, however, were developed on the basis of observation, but they go beyond description. [p. 166]

thinking self: In Descartes, the real self, the self that discovers its own existence (beyond any doubt) by catching itself in the act of thinking (about itself). [p. 190]

tlamatinime: (Nahuatl, "knowers of things.") A thriving school of philosophers among the Aztecs of Mexico. All we have left are fragments of their teachings, largely because their Spanish conquerors deliberately burned most of their books. [p. 340]

tolerance: One of the central values of the multiracial, multiethnic, polydimensional society in the United States. Tolerance involves accepting differences within society without trying to eliminate or interfere with the views and practices of other groups that differ from one's own. [p. 282]

totalitarianism: Concept of political philosophy which considers the individual completely subordinate to the state. See also **fascism**.[p. 312]

transcendence: In the philosophy of existentialist Jean Paul Sartre, the concept that we can always transcend, or go beyond, the facts that are true of us, or what Sartre called our **facticity**. Transcendence means that the self is defined not by the facts about us but by what we make—and continue to make—of these facts. [p. 208]

transcendent: Independent of. In the philosophy of religion, a *transcendent God* is one who is distinct and separate from the universe he created. This is contrasted with the concept of an **immanent** God, for example, in pantheism, where God is identical with his creation, or, to take a different example, in certain forms of humanism, in which God is identical with humankind. (G. W. F. Hegel argued such a thesis.) [p. 73]

truth of reason: In traditional **rationalism**, a belief that can be justified solely by appeal to reason, through **intuition** or by **deduction** from **premises** based upon intuition. Arithmetic and geometry provided, for the rationalists as for the empiricists, paradigm cases of such truths. They disagreed mainly on the scope of such truths and on the restrictions to be placed on the problematic appeal to intuition. [p. 163]

tyranny: Rule by those who wield their power oppressively and abusively. [p. 294]

Übermensch: (German: "superhuman".) Friedrich Nietzsche's conception of a superior type of person, who might replace us in an ideal future society. [p. 285]

unextended: Not taking up space. Descartes defined mental substance, which is unextended, or not in space, as compared to physical things, which are **extended** in space. [p. 126]

universalism: The view that philosophy throughout the world has the same concerns and methods. [p. 339]

universalizability: The ability to be applied to everyone without exception. This is an essential feature of moral principles, according to Immanuel Kant and others. [p. 272]

unsound (argument): A bad **argument**; a deductive argument that is either **invalid** or has false **premises** (or both). [p. 17]

utilitarianism: The moral philosophy that says that we should act in such ways as to provide the greatest good (understood as happiness of pleasure) for the greatest number of people as we possibly can. [p. 273]

utopia, Utopia: A vision of the ideal society, usually without much indication about how one could possibly get there. [p. 46]

valid: Said of an **argument** that correctly follows agreed-upon rules of inference. Always applies to arguments, not statements. [p. 16]

virtue: An admirable personal quality; an aspect of good character. [pp. 276–277]

virtue ethics: The view that the central feature in the evaluation of people and their actions should be the character of the agent. Aristotle's ethics are often described as an form of virtue ethics. [p. 280]

weak (argument): An **inductive argument** whose evidence does not make the truth of the **conclusion** very probable. [p. 17]

Weltanschauung: (German.) **Worldview**; a way of looking at and understanding the world. [p. 10]

Will: The power of mind that allows us to choose our own actions or at least choose what we will try to do. In Kant, a good will is the only thing that is good "without qualification": in other words, acting for the right reasons and with good intentions. [p. 135]

wisdom: The ideal of human thinking—although it is by no means agreed what sorts of principles or personalities are most wise. Wisdom is essentially practical as well as abstract or theoretical knowledge, including "how to live (and live well)." [p. 60]

World of Becoming: In Plato's **metaphysics**, the world we live in, the world of change and objects perceived by the senses. [p. 121]

World of Being: In Plato's **metaphysics**, the world of ideal **Forms**, a world that is unchanging, a world we can know only through reason. [p. 121]

worldview: A way of seeing the world, a way of understanding the larger perspective. [p. 10]

wuwei: (Chinese.) Literally, nonaction. The ideal of nonassertion in one's actions. [p. 360]

yoga: spiritual discipline that aims to still the mind and thereby enable enlightenment. [p. 348]

Zen Buddhism: See **Buddhism.**

ziran: (Chinese.) Spontaneity, acting in attunement with the energies of (both internal and external) nature. [p. 360]

Zoroastrianism: Ancient Persian religion commonly recognized as a precursor of the other great Western religions and of many central conceptions of Western philosophy (for example, the basic opposition between good and evil). [p. 344]

Index